Rashi's Commentary on the Torah

Rashi's *Commentary on the Torah*

Canonization and Resistance in the Reception of a Jewish Classic

ERIC LAWEE

OXFORD
UNIVERSITY PRESS

OXFORD
UNIVERSITY PRESS

Oxford University Press is a department of the University of Oxford. It furthers the University's objective of excellence in research, scholarship, and education by publishing worldwide. Oxford is a registered trade mark of Oxford University Press in the UK and certain other countries.

Published in the United States of America by Oxford University Press
198 Madison Avenue, New York, NY 10016, United States of America.

First issued as an Oxford University Press paperback, 2021

CIP data is on file at the Library of Congress
ISBN 978–0–19–093783–6 (hardcover)
ISBN 978–0–19–758435–4 (paperback)

3 5 7 9 8 6 4

Printed by Integrated Books International, United States of America

For Mollie

With love and gratitude

Contents

Acknowledgments

IF, AS FRANCIS Bacon's authorial confession has it, "nothing is finished till all be finished," this book would not be complete without expressions of gratitude to the following institutions, funding bodies, and people.

Beyond all else, research and writing of the book was made possible by the Israel Science Foundation (grant no. 256/14). The project's earliest stages benefited from a grant from the Social Sciences and Humanities Research Council of Canada and sabbatical research sponsored by The Lady Davis Trust at The Hebrew University in Jerusalem. Most of the sabbatical was spent in the precincts of the Shalem Center, where I received an exceedingly warm welcome from the Center's leadership and fellows. York University provided sabbatical support and gave to me many fine colleagues, especially at The Israel and Golda Koschitzky Centre for Jewish Studies. I completed the book after joining the Department of Bible at Bar-Ilan University, where I have been the recipient of generous research funding from the Asher Weiser Chair for the Study of Medieval Jewish Biblical Interpretation and, on two occasions, Keren Beit Shalom (Kyoto, Japan).

The invitation to serve as Shoshana Shier Distinguished Visiting Professor of Jewish Studies at the Centre for Jewish Studies at the University of Toronto (U of T), and extremely warm reception that I was given there, provided an ideal milieu to apply the book's finishing touches. It also afforded the occasion to deliver lectures at the U of T, Columbia University, and Harvard University that yielded valuable responses leading to last-minute refinements. I owe special thanks to Ida Tugg for her extraordinary generosity during my stay in Toronto.

The book has benefited from vast stores of learning and increments of scarce time, as well as plain old encouragement, shared with me by colleagues and friends. They include Menachem Butler, Joseph Davis, Isaac Gottleib, Zeev Harvey, Menachem Kellner, Abraham Lieberman, and Moshe Rosman.

Danny Lasker remains an abiding source of academic inspiration, sound advice, and friendship.

A number of people made unique contributions. Beyond all call of duty, Gad Freudenthal helped me to gain access to the manuscript of Eleazar Ashkenazi's *Ṣafenat pa'neaḥ*. The immediate facilitator of that development was the wholly selfless good will of Ziva Galili. Marty Lockshin read most of the manuscript, saving me from blunders, routinely enhancing content and clarity, and providing infusions of enthusiasm when my owe store began to flag. Beyond continually urging the project's worthiness, Eddy Breuer supplied copious notes on several chapters that challenged me to rethink, clarify, and simplify. "Unstinting" only begins to describe the kindnesses that he and Shelley Sternberg have bestowed upon me and my family.

Two additional sources of aid deserve special mention. Angela Erisman suggested ways to turn bouts of chaos into models of clarity and stimulated countless improvements in structure and style. Doron Forte lent the book, and project of which it was born, his diverse skills as a fastidious scholar and vigilant writer. He also contributed a spirit of dedication that was ever palpable, in a way that cannot be repaid. Needless to say, no aforementioned individual or institution is responsible for deficiencies that remain.

As this study has been long in the making, I have had ample opportunity to conjure justifications for its frequent detours. Most significant was my family's "return to Zion," with the upheavals and challenges—but, more important, opportunities and blessings—that it conferred. Whatever angels (in the Maimonidean sense) brought about this life-changing move, its "proximate cause" (as Maimonides would say) was certainly Elie Assis, accomplished scholar and academic facilitator extraordinaire, who found a way to include me in the ranks of Bar-Ilan's esteemed Department of Tanakh. I offer him my deepest thanks. Many colleagues have helped to usher me into life in my new academic home. Some are owed special debts of gratitude for coming to my aid as I sought (read: struggled) to acclimate, including Michael Avioz, Josh Berman, Ed Greenstein, Jonathan Jacobs, David Malkiel, and Yosef Ofer. Josh made the match with the superb team at Oxford University Press headed by Cynthia Read that produced the book in its polished and precise final form, with special thanks to project manager Felshiya Samuel and copyeditor Brooke Smith. I also extend profound gratitude to two then anonymous readers, Zev Harvey and Haim Kreisel, admired senior scholars from whom I have learned a great deal. Their investment of time and thought yielded suggestions that led to significant reformulations and improvements.

It is in thinking about members of my family that words begin to fail me. The distance that separates me from my father, sister, brother, and their families does not diminish the sense of closeness, a feeling that sustained me as we experienced the loss of my mother just as the book's final lines were being written. I doubt my mother would have read the book; I know she would have been very proud of it, as she was of her children and grandchildren (and, late in life, new great-grandchild) and their accomplishments generally, such pride being one of her deepest pleasures. My parents' benevolence in support of my at times idiosyncratic life choices has never faltered. My father continues the tradition and continues to inspire. Different sorts of sustenance have been forthcoming from Aviezer, Noam and Adeena, Gavriella, Sarah, and Talia, who provide regular doses of joy, insight, and, as time goes on, ever more impressive models that keep me humble. My spirits are always raised in the presence of the next generation, Nehemiah and Yehoshua.

As always, the abiding source of meaning in my life is Mollie, to whom I owe many debts of gratitude, not least for persevering during a semester away from home that proved pivotal in completing the book but more difficult than anticipated (and regrettably consonant with the situation described by Rashi in his closing comment on Bereshit 24:67). Her support and sustaining stewardship of our family is the main "context" out of which I send forth the book to its own (presumably modest) reception history. May the Source of Blessings continue to grant her, and us, enduring achievements born of a sustained focus on ultimate goals, accompanied by inner peace.

Abbreviations

b.	Babylonian Talmud
EJ	*Encyclopaedia Judaica*
HBOT	*Hebrew Bible/Old Testament: The History of Its Interpretation*
HUCA	*Hebrew Union College Annual*
JQR	*Jewish Quarterly Review*
MGH	*Miqra'ot gedolot ha-keter* (= Mikra'ot Gedolot 'Haketer': A Revised and Augmented Scientific Edition of 'Mikra'ot Gedolot' Based on the Aleppo Codex and Early Medieval MSS, ed. Menachem Cohen. For individual volumes, see in the bibliography)
QI	Malachi Beit-Arié, *Qodiqologyah 'ivrit*, preprint internet version 9.0 (updated April 2018), edited by Zofia Lasman, available at http://web.nli.org.il/sites/NLI/Hebrew/collections/manuscripts/hebrewcodicology/Documents/Hebrew-Codicology-continuously-updated-online-version.pdf.
REJ	*Revue des études juives*
RRJ	*Review of Rabbinic Judaism*

Notes on Translations and Editions

1. Biblical translations follow *Tanakh: The Holy Scriptures* (Philadelphia: Jewish Publication Society, 1985), with alterations as required.
2. As discussed in chapter 1, Rashi's *Commentary* is likely the medieval Hebrew work that underwent more textual vicissitudes than any other. This being so, a study centered on Rashi's words exclusively must be consistently attentive to this basic problem and would, for instance, avoid reliance on printed editions. While I pay heed to this issue, I also relegate it to the margins in this study on the understanding that my focus on the *Commentary*'s reception acquits me of a routine need to engage in "lower criticism." What counts for this study is that a comment was received as a genuine part of Rash's reading of the Torah by a later reader or that it migrated to a particular locale as such, circulating as what "Rashi said." The issue of different versions can quickly overwhelm any study involving the *Commentary*, let alone one as broad-ranging as this book. Still, I do, in the notes, refer to textual issues of various sorts, especially when variants prove salient to the analysis. It is worth noting as well in the current context that the often slight differences in verbal formulation found in some variants, while always possibly significant for some purposes, often do little to affect the thrust of any given interpretation of Rashi, and thence the reception it was likely to receive on the part of a particular later reader.

Quotations from the *Commentary* follow the eclectic version in *Miqra'ot gedolot ha-keter*, edited by Menachem Cohen, as it appears in the volumes listed in the bibliography under "Main Editions of Rashi's *Commentary* Used." This edition lacks a critical apparatus (and thence transparency about its final holdings) and at points still accommodates, albeit with indications of likely accretions, the standard printed edition. Still, this version has many virtues. Most important, it reflects a handful of good manuscripts, including one that, as discussed in chapter 1, is seen by many scholars as the best (if by no means definitive) witness: Universitätsbibliothek Leipzig, B.H.1. For English translations, the edition of the *Commentary* by Rosenbaum and Silbermann (see bibliography) has often served as a point of reference. When a verse that Rashi explains is clearly identified in the body of the book , I omit a reference to it in a note.

Introduction

RASHI'S *Commentary on the Torah*: CANONICAL AND CLASSIC

THE *COMMENTARY ON THE TORAH* by Solomon ben Isaac (1040–1105)—also known as Shlomo Yitzhaki, or Rashi—stands out as the most widely studied and influential Hebrew Bible commentary of all time. It has shaped perceptions of the meaning of the Torah, Judaism's foundational document, for over nine centuries. Its students, direct and otherwise, have included all strata of Jewish society: young and old, scholars and lay persons, men and women. Even exacting and sober scholars reach for superlatives when discussing the *Commentary*, proposing that "with the exception of Scripture and the Talmud themselves, it is doubtful whether any other literary creation so greatly influenced the spiritual world of the Jew in the Jewish people's many dispersions in later medieval times and even beyond as did Rashi's *Commentary* on the Torah," or that "no other commentary on the Hebrew Scriptures in any language has ever attained comparable recognition, acceptance, and sustained popularity or similar wide geographic distribution, or ever equaled it in its profound impact on human lives." A vivid metaphor of a contemporary Torah commentator goes so far as to describe the *Commentary* as a work that was "absorbed into the bloodstream of Jewish culture."[1]

Rashi's enormous share in Jewish destiny owes to the fact that he astonishingly managed to write "the classic commentaries on the two classics of Judaism": the Bible, especially the Torah; and the Babylonian Talmud.[2] Perhaps Rashi regarded the commentaries on the Talmud, the staple of the advanced curriculum and heart of rabbinic Judaism, as his contribution of prime importance. These works supplied the talmudic text with "a connective tissue that wove its utterances into a comprehensible discourse."[3] With startling rapidity,

Rashi's commentaries consigned all competitors to the "dustbin of history," appearing in every printed edition of the Talmud from the first one in the 1480s.[4] Rashi's *Commentary on the Torah* (hereinafter: *Commentary*) also traveled a road leading to the highest distinction, but unlike the Talmud commentaries its pathway to preeminence involved, as we shall see, a large and diverse number of twists and turns. In another contrast with the Talmud commentaries, the *Commentary*'s eventual elevation to supreme stature never gained unanimous consent.

In the next chapter, we will describe in greater detail the *Commentary*'s textual vicissitudes, tackle the question of its elusive aims, and begin to see some of the sources of its appeal. For now, let it suffice to note that many factors must have commended it over the ages, even leaving aside its author's status as a devoted communal leader, a towering scholar, and, of course, his singular reputation as the foremost commentator on the Talmud. The *Commentary* explained the Torah in concise and digestible glosses where some later exegetes cultivated a more involved essayistic—or, alternatively, formidably recondite and laconic—style. The *Commentary* provided a more or less continuous running account of the Torah's narratives and laws where many later commentators glossed the Torah only intermittently. The *Commentary* offered an exposition of the "written Torah" basically in harmony with—and indeed heavily indebted to—the interpretations found in the authoritative corpora embodying the "oral Torah." By contrast, some of Rashi's medieval counterparts broke ranks with elements of ancient interpretation—nay, at times almost flaunted their stance of nonconformity.

But if such things all commended the *Commentary* as an instrument of education and insight, what may have endeared the work most to Jews over close to a millennium was Rashi's inclusion of classical rabbinic teachings, collectively called midrash, in his interpretation of the divine word. As we will see, his deployment of rabbinic interpretations was hardly a matter of cutting and pasting. Instead, working at his easel, Rashi carefully selected, refashioned, moved, and otherwise adapted these ancient dicta—according to principles that remain highly controverted, as we shall also see—in a way that quietly allowed him to hoist his own colors, often giving voice to the plurality of views present within and across the great tomes of rabbinic literature.

As he midrashically expanded on and filled in gaps in the biblical text, Rashi indelibly reconfigured the way the Torah became etched in the minds of Jews, as well as the manner in which the midrashic corpus was transmitted to them. As regards the former, many later readers would barely distinguish the words of scripture from Rashi's rabbinic readings of them. As regards the latter, those midrashim that Rashi excluded were left to bob in a vast sea of rabbinic lore that most Jews never laid eyes on, while those chosen for inclusion won an enduring place in Jewish consciousness, as Rashi's work became the most important vehicle of the transmission of classical rabbinic interpretation, theology, and lore to countless generations of Jews.

Although the *Commentary* has benefited from enormous scholarly attention, study of its reception outside the northern French school of biblical interpretation that Rashi essentially founded has been amazingly and inexplicably scant. The only book-length treatment, now more than a half century old, focuses on Rashi's reception among a segment of *Christian* scholars.[5] It is as if, even for critical scholars, the *Commentary*'s ubiquitous presence was ever thus—in the study hall and elementary classroom, on the bookshelf, in this sermon or that discussion at the Sabbath table, and yet more far-flung spheres of Jewish literature, including commentaries on liturgical poetry, iconography in medieval Haggadot, and traditionalist children's literature in the twentieth century.[6] As a result, basic questions posed with regard to other medieval classics, like Maimonides's legal code, have not been asked regarding the *Commentary*: When did it arrive in new centers? What responses did it receive, by whom, and why (bearing in mind that the history of Jewish learning is "the history of the sources scholars didn't know, as much as it is the history of what they did know")?[7] What larger intellectual, religious, and sociocultural contexts shaped those responses, whether adulatory, critical, or otherwise?[8] In the case of the *Commentary*, one could also wonder how a work so explicit about its "second-order status" left so outsized an imprint.[9] Whatever the answers, there is no doubt that the *Commentary* became, at the least, the closest thing Judaism knows to a canonical exposition of scripture.

If the *Commentary* was and remains the most important and influential of Jewish biblical commentaries, its designation as a canonical work invites scrutiny, and even some well-justified skepticism. True, some matter-of-factly assert the canonical status of the *Commentary*, and even assume that it "extends to this day."[10] Yet others, when presented with this notion, insist that canonization "has nothing to do with Rashi's *Commentary* to the Pentateuch" and find it "ridiculous" to adorn the work with research on the topic.[11] Though the hermeneutics of canonicity is increasingly invoked in many corners of Jewish studies scholarship, declamations of a work's canonicity are far more often propounded than defined. It seems well, then, before plunging into the complex story of the *Commentary*'s reception history seen at least partly through this lens, to ask what is meant when an assertion of a post-talmudic work's canonicity is dangled before our eyes. This is all the more vital when we recall that "canon" as a literary term is "quintessentially Christian" and hence "inevitably bound to be problematic if applied to Jewish tradition."[12]

On many definitions, the notion of the *Commentary* as a canonical work is easily dismissed. If such a work is one declared authoritative by political, ecclesiastical, institutional, or literary fiat, then the *Commentary* does not qualify. In Han China, an emperor could convene a conference of experts to decide on the delimitation and interpretation of the Confucian canon.[13] No rabbinic synod, let alone emperor, ever conferred canonicity in this way on the *Commentary* (or any other Jewish work, including the Talmud, which nevertheless is routinely described as canonical).[14] Likewise, if super-human inspiration is deemed "indispensable for canons," the *Commentary* also would not qualify.[15] Rashi certainly claimed no such quality for his writings nor did the vast majority of his devoted admirers (although we will meet a Spanish kabbalist who did so, presaging a trend among others, mainly the mystically inclined, in later centuries).

Textually, and typographically, the *Commentary* also lacks traits that might be considered common, if perhaps not essential, for a canonical text. Referring to the canonical work of Jewish mysticism, the *Zohar*, Boaz Huss remarks that the work's final format remained undefined until the mid-sixteenth century, when it was determined primarily by printers. He adds that the molding of the first printed collections "was a continuation and, to a great extent, the completion of the zoharic canonization and editing process."[16] To this day, the *Commentary* lacks an immutable version of its contents or standard *mise en page*.

Our effort to clarify the claim that the *Commentary* is, at the least, the closest thing Judaism knows to a canonical exposition of scripture must begin with different ways that the adjective "canonical" can be applied to texts. Helpful is a distinction between a "normative" canon, comprising texts meant to be "obeyed and followed," and a "formative" one, involving texts that are "taught, read, transmitted, and interpreted," thereby providing a society with a "shared vocabulary."[17] Such an approach fits snugly with a typology of texts based on their modes of reception, allowing for distinctions between "canonical," "holy," and "sacred" texts, with a canonical text regarded as one seen by a community as a "source of authority."[18] It also fits with a concept of canon formation understood in terms of "foundational texts" that embody the "essentials of a given community's collective self-consciousness."[19]

Compelling signs of the *Commentary*'s foundational status come from the sphere of Jewish education at all levels. The evidence awaits systematic study but largely supports the claim that the *Commentary* shaped the education of "every generation of Jews since its first appearance, at least until fairly recent times."[20] By the fifteenth century, a Sefardic scholar could speak of "the custom spread throughout all Jewry" to inaugurate beginners in Torah study in "the reading of Rashi."[21] The society of schoolteachers in sixteenth-century Cracow ruled that the Torah should be imparted with the Yiddish explanation, adding that more advanced students should not be taught "any other commentary than Rashi's, which is the correct interpretation according to the plain sense of scripture and according to the truth."[22]

Though canonicity cannot be inferred from statistics alone, the sheer numbers in which the *Commentary* was produced, in both the age of manuscript reproduction and the period of the early printed Hebrew book, certainly tell a tale. The *Commentary* survives in over two hundred manuscripts, with some one hundred and eighty preserving full versions.[23] That puts it almost entirely in a class apart, even if such quantitative measures must be supplemented by other types of data in order to measure impact and authority.[24] By comparison, leading works of medieval thought like Saadia Gaon's *Book of Doctrines and Beliefs* or Judah Halevi's *Kuzari* come down in dozens of manuscript copies or fewer.[25] Staying with Torah commentaries, that of Abraham Ibn Ezra, the most popular exegete to emerge from Muslim Spain, survives in around one hundred complete and partial manuscripts and that of Nahmanides, the most important exegete from Christian Spain, survives in some fifty complete and partial manuscripts.[26] The Torah commentary of Rashi's grandson, Samuel ben Meir (Rashbam), eventually survived in a single manuscript, now lost. We will see similar indicators of the unique status of the *Commentary* forthcoming from the age of early print.[27] For now, it is sufficient to note that by the early sixteenth century, Rashi's interpretation of the Torah became a "universal presence" in printed Jewish Bibles.[28]

Two other definitions of "canonical" are salient with respect to the *Commentary*, both incomparably so. One describes as canonical a work recognized as part of a tradition "that makes claims upon the participants" of that tradition.[29] Rashi's *Commentary* did just that time and again, among both admirers and detractors. According to another definition, a work's canonicity rests on its attraction of commentaries, as follows from the proposition that "the reception and use of a text as canonical implies the development of exegesis on it."[30] This argument has recently been made regarding the very first commentaries that have come down. Written in cuneiform script and the Akkadian language, they are deemed at once an indication of and a factor in the canonization of an ancient Mesopotamian library of texts.[31] In medieval and early modern Judaism, one can point to the role of commentaries in turning Nahmanides's Torah commentary into a canonical work of kabbalah and the *Shulḥan 'arukh* of Joseph Karo and Moses Isserles into modern Judaism's canonical code.[32] How commentators promote canon formation is a large question, but the first and most basic way is clear: they select a text as an object of exposition, thereby potentially initiating or confirming a process of canonization.[33] In light of such reflections, the *Commentary*, as a work that has attracted glosses numbering possibly in the hundreds, must be considered the most canonical Jewish work ever authored by a single hand.[34] More important than the numbers, however, is what the succession of glosses betokens—namely, the *Commentary*'s capacity for sustaining ongoing reading and interpretation in a way that has been cast as being of the essence in the "mechanics of canonization" in rabbinic Judaism.[35]

In taking up the theme of canon and commentary in the first part of this book, I stress the dynamic interaction between the *Commentary* and its wide range of readers, mainly scholars (since it is for them that we have a preponderance of evidence) but some ordinary Jews. We will see, for instance, how certain operations of interpretation performed on the *Commentary* could clarify it in ways that took Rashi's interpretive ideas in new and unexpected directions. Often, they were reflective of teachings and "protocols of reading"[36] that stood at a far remove from the Franco-German *paideia* out of which Rashi wrote (differences between its French and German constituents notwithstanding). Such readings rivet attention on the "power dynamics between source and commentary" and, in particular, the commentarial capacity to define the meaning of source texts, retroactively determining what Rashi "said."[37]

To speak in such terms is to see how study of the *Commentary*'s reception blends seamlessly with various trends in literary studies, most notably reception theory,[38] and with probing contemporary cultivation of book history (though as an exercise in fleeting defamiliarization, it is worth observing that the *Commentary* is a book only on a very broad definition of the term).[39] Such interest draws attention away from the author and the text and refocuses it on the text–reader relationship, attending all the while to ways that written compositions are disseminated, controlled, and received.[40] The new approaches tend to stress the importance of reading communities in determining meaning in ways that comport with the processes of canonization delineated here. To take an example, Miriam Fraenkel casts her definition of such a process as "an ongoing and dynamic interaction between the author, the audience, and the newly created work" and describes all who "unconsciously or intentionally publish, purchase, preserve, hold, present, quote, translate, mention, imitate or perform a literary creation" as agents who help to "establish a work's stature afresh."[41]

A major focus of commentaries on the *Commentary* were the midrashim of which Rashi frequently availed himself that endowed his exegesis with a rabbinic radiance. These midrashic expressions, authoritative though they might be perceived to be, were frequently pliable and even enigmatic, facilitating their later "appropriation," a conceptual category that moves away from the idea of one-way transmission and toward exploration of how intellectual, literary, and artifactual expressions come to represent something "different from their original purposes."[42] Rather than canon replacement, such appropriative readings redefined Rashi's meaning.[43] In the case of such readings, application to the *Commentary* of concepts drawn from the hermeneutics of canonicity proves itself by showing how processes familiar from diverse traditions, religious or otherwise, help us understand the *Commentary*'s reception.

The book's second part continues to view the *Commentary*'s path to preeminence through an array of religious, intellectual, and literary lens by exploring in depth a hitherto unexamined—and wholly unexpected—feature of its reception: critical, and at times astonishingly harsh, resistance to it. That the *Commentary* was subjected to criticism is hardly news. The best example, if not always sufficiently appreciated as such, is the critical scrutiny that it received from Nahmanides.[44] What unfolds in part II, however, is a record of unknown assaults on the *Commentary*—and, more startlingly, on its rabbinic sources—that is so rhetorically fierce it could only have made Nahmanides quake. The resistance to Rashi displayed in three late medieval works by Eleazar Ashkenazi, an unknown writer whom I call "Pseudo-Rabad," and Aaron Aboulrabi left next to no mark on the historical record, let alone on Jewish collective memory. Standing as the limit case of criticism of the *Commentary* in the annals of Jewish literature, I will argue that this corpus, too, attests in its own way to the *Commentary*'s growing canonical status.

A most startling element of the critiques studied in part II is their authors' use of various tropes of vituperation to frame their negative findings. We will come across expressions like "risibility," "ridiculousness," "absurdity," "senselessness," and "nonsense" used with regard to Rashi and his midrashic ideas. The provocation—and, as I propose, growing canonization—of the *Commentary* brought the critics to unheard-of levels of vitriol, requiring us to pay heed not only to their message but also to its medium.

A concern with critical vocabulary and rhetoric is part of a focus on different genres of exegetical expression, understanding that "what one believes is shaped by the means of communication by which the content is transmitted."[45] Commentaries on a commentary, what are often called supercommentaries, despite potential complexities, shape a discourse prone to canonizing reading. By contrast, the genre of "strictures" (*hassagot*), a Hebrew literary form first found in the Middle Ages but rarely used systematically in exegesis, provided a natural literary medium to channel acts of resisting reading. As a mode of Jewish expression, strictures have received little study, although the form was cultivated for centuries, sometimes by leading scholars, most notable among whom was the southern French talmudist Abraham ben David (Rabad). It is no accident that the most concentrated critique of the *Commentary* ever composed is a pseudonymous work written under his name.[46] The main aim of the genre was to expose errors in an earlier text, though the stricturalist at times went further by proposing what he took to be superior alternatives. The rhetorical and generic side of late medieval criticisms of the *Commentary* are therefore in no way incidental to their authors' substantive aim to reduce Rashi's exegesis to an inferior estate. Meanwhile, we note that another critic of the *Commentary*, who will stand at the center of our attention in the book's closing part, also wrote under a pseudonym: "Rabbi Palmon ben Pelet." In addition to strictures, then, pseudonymity comes into view as a literary vehicle at the heart of vehement *Commentary* criticism.

I designate the authors studied in part II "resisting readers," borrowing a coinage from feminist criticism as a heuristic shorthand to describe a stance that rejects interpretations and ideas in the *Commentary* and challenges the meanings they generate.[47] Feminist critics apply techniques of resistant reading to works of the literary canon perceived to embed and perpetuate biases against the feminine. Since critics lambasted not just the *Commentary* but the midrashic hermeneutic that largely informed it, this decidedly modern way of casting things seems to capture handsomely the stance adopted in whole or in part by the authors studied in part II.

Readings of the *Commentary* involving overt scorn turn out to have a specific geocultural locus, since all the writers studied in part II have clear or probable eastern Mediterranean ties. Study of their writings therefore takes us on a journey into a little-known domain of Jewish biblical scholarship in the cities of Byzantium and islands in the Aegean Sea. In general, scholarship tends to venture to this veritable Babel of discrepant Jewish intellectual and religious expression very little, while often working along a more familiar north–south geocultural axis (Ashkenaz versus Sefarad). Highlighting the axis running from west to east along the Mediterranean littoral, we encounter a zone of conflict and competition between "empires and caliphates, trading republics, and dynasties, cliques, and clans . . . who embodied a huge range of ethnic orientations and religious interpretations."[48] Resistance to Rashi took inspiration from a type of Western European rationalism that came east, riding the waves of the Latin ascendancy in Byzantine territories after the crusader sack of Constantinople in 1204. Yet the late medieval Byzantine redoubt of rationalism somehow provided especially salubrious soil for the flourishing of invective-laden *Commentary* criticism in a way that Western centers of philosophically minded exegesis and thought did not.

The discovery of harsh critics of the *Commentary*, even if obscure, may call into question proclamations of its canonical standing, or its status as a classic. The term "classic" has often been elided with "canonical," not least when the latter term came to be applied to secular literature in the eighteenth century. According to what is called "the usual definition" in his essay of 1850, Charles Augustin Sainte-Beuve, sometimes called the progenitor of modern criticism, defines a "classic" as "an old author canonised by admiration."[49] On this definition, our discovery of ferocious opposition to the *Commentary*, even if limited and obscure, presumably ought to give pause in conferring upon Rashi's work its status as a classic. Yet a more recent definition of "classic" pulls in the opposite direction. On this understanding, developed by writer J. M. Coetzee, "the classic defines itself by surviving." Interrogation of such a work, "no matter how hostile," is inevitable and "even to be welcomed." Rather than being a foe of the classic, "criticism, and indeed criticism of the most skeptical kind, may be what the classic uses to define itself and ensure its survival."[50] Seen thus, my focus on unknown examples of hostile criticism at once circumvents any neatly packaged picture of the *Commentary*'s rise to preeminent status and proves paradoxically revelatory for understanding its emergence as the classic Jewish biblical commentary.

For students of medieval Judaism, it will occasion no surprise that boundaries and crossing points on the intellectual maps of Ashkenaz (the term often used to encompass medieval Northern Europe's dominantly French and German Jewish communities) and Sefarad sound as a *basso continuo* throughout the book. In particular, the names of two Sefardic luminaries arise again and again because they served as rival claimants to the mantle of canonicity that some wished to bestow on Rashi. The first of these was Abraham ibn Ezra, a leading representative of the tradition of Andalusi-Jewish biblical commentary. The second was Moses Maimonides.

As the Torah commentaries of Rashi and Ibn Ezra jostled, each empowered by an increasingly large and dedicated phalanx of glossators and each inspiring diverse reading communities, Maimonides—he who bestrode the nexus of Jewish law, theology, and biblical interpretation like a colossus—shaped religious allegiances and literary productions of countless scholars in Mediterranean seats of Jewish learning and beyond. Maimonides wrote no running Torah commentary, though some will argue that his *Guide* is "best understood as a commentary on the Bible."[51] Many saw the exegetical methods that he pioneered, and the theological ideas that they legitimated, as salvific breakthroughs (or recoveries); others, as a foreign accretion fraught with mortal danger for the survival of authentic Judaism as revealed at Sinai. For exegetes of a philosophical outlook, Maimonides stood as a totem due to his powerful effort to demonstrate the basic congruence between the words of the Torah and finalities of scientific truth.

In light of such convictions, it is little wonder that a tendency arose to put Rashi and Maimonides into direct opposition in a variety of ways, though the two never met except in Jewish legend.[52] In one striking version, sixteenth-century writers report a "received tradition" (*qabbalah*) according to which Rashi's soul is a reincarnation of that of the Amora, Rav, and Maimonides's soul a reincarnation of the soul of Rav's disputant colleague, Samuel.[53] Over time, modern historiography also adopted a tendency to cast Rashi and Maimonides as foils, if not near-ontological antitheses, whose outlooks were said to shape Judaism over the *longue durée*. An extreme case speaks of two "utterly opposing tendencies in our spiritual history," one "romantic-conservative" fathered by Rashi and another "rational-progressive" by Maimonides. An "epic struggle" ensued, in which devotees of Rashi generated constrictive forces to counter the expansive ones of Maimonidean loyalists.[54] Needless to say, far more refined lenses are needed to discern the many possible and actual mediating positions of Jews who sought to chart a path through the rich but conflicting legacy of medieval model figures and classical works that they inherited. Yet there remains, for all that, something to commend this overarching perspective.

Thus does the third part of the book reconstruct, somewhat schematically to be sure, a battle for canonical supremacy involving the *Commentary*'s midrashic mentality on one side and the exegetical and theological teachings of Maimonides and Ibn Ezra on the other. Although in some ways highly disparate, these two Sefardic luminaries increasingly were seen as a pair of twelfth-century masters who made common cause.[55] The *Commentary*, Ibn Ezra's corpus, and Maimonides's writings (the latter two more than the first) can be seen as attempts to impose different forms of order on the vast and in many ways undefined canonical writings, with the author of each corpus generally attempting to give the most generous interpretations possible to classical texts.[56]

Whether some of Rashi's biblical commentaries carry a deliberate and substantive antirationalist message is a controverted point. His expositions of Proverbs, Ecclesiastes, and Job 28 are often held up for investigation on this score. In arguing nay, David Berger insists that the rationalist spirit of Sefardic philosophical thinkers was "alien to the most deeply embedded instincts of Ashkenazic Jews." Oblivious to the threat posed by philosophy, writers like Rashi did not try to repel it. This fits with a view that Rashi and his successors had only "a very vague and indistinct idea of philosophy."[57] Unlike the philosophers, such writers were disinclined to question the plain meaning of classical texts, both biblical and rabbinic, to valorize philosophical inquiry, to suspect miracles, or to pursue non-Jewish works.[58] Of course, a good deal turns on definition, such that one can accept the "well-known" view that "Rashi was not a philosopher" but still affirm that there are "bold philosophic elements" in his commentaries."[59] What we will also see is that the *Commentary* was sufficiently indeterminate in many places that it could be turned to philosophical purpose.

For rationalists, including Rashi's resisting readers, obliviousness of science, especially natural science (physics) and divine science (metaphysics), ensured a religiously disastrous combination of ignorance and credulity. It also necessarily resulted in many gross misreadings of scripture that brought the divine word, and thence Judaism *tout court*, into utter disrepute. Surprisingly, the resisting readers sometimes implicated Rashi's very rabbinic sources in this outcome. What proves crucial for current purposes is this: with Torah interpretation, especially in its midrashic variety, serving as a major battleground in ongoing disputes over rationalism, Rashi could be invoked by those suspicious of intellectualist ideas and aspirations as the one who spoke true about the Torah's meaning and message. In this way, his scriptural *magnum opus*, the foremost work of Franco-German biblical scholarship, served more self-conscious antiphilosophical traditionalists seeking to counter rationalist reconfigurations of Judaism that they thought left Jews prone to doubt and defection.

To speak in these terms is to emphasize a side of the *Commentary*'s legacy that has received relatively short shrift: its role not only as an exegetical work of the first rank but also as a rich source of ideas that, through Rashi's careful selection and at times decisive reformulation, shaped Jewish sensibilities and perceptions of the Torah's teachings. This dimension of Rashi's work points to a "new historical approach to Rashi as a medieval thinker." The implication is that Rashi's commentarial voice must be appreciated not only for its exegetical intentions and achievements but also in terms of the teachings that it set forth, allusively and elusively, by way of rewritten midrash.[60] The *Commentary* was, of course, a commentary, but it can also be seen as an important work of *thought*—one true to the texture of classical Jewish thinking "as an ongoing exegetical process" in which ideas "arise hermeneutically."[61] The clash between Rashi and the resisting readers often amounts to a fundamental dispute over the matter and modes of Torah, pitting a reading informed by quasimythical midrashic ideas involving frequent miracles and routine divine interventions in human affairs against a scientific understanding rooted in nature's intelligible workings as known from the everyday world.

The story of the *Commentary*'s reception, seen in terms of the idea that a literary work offers different views to different readers in each period,[62] summons a theme that recurs throughout: the meaning of the arrival of writings by a towering figure in new cultural environments.[63] In this way, this study dovetails with others of recent vintage that explore the receptions of other classic medieval and early modern writers and works (Judah Halevi, Maimonides, the Zohar, various popularizing works, the *Shulḥan 'arukh*). Such studies provide road maps to diverse intellectual traditions, the formation of different Jewish identities, and, at times, a window on what might be conceived of as "the rules of canonization" that shaped the ever evolving Jewish library.[64] Even as I have tried to evoke the rich and complex geocultural settings of various receptions of the *Commentary*, the emphasis remains—unabashedly—on ideas, literary creativity, intricacies of interpretation, and fundamental religious alternatives, with their many shadings. The situation of ideas, writers, and works in time and place is always close at hand, but I try to balance the provision of historical and cultural matrices with appreciation for "the individual talent" that does not reduce to contextual elements.[65] In the case of the reception of the *Commentary*, we deal not only with an author of untold genius but also with a work whose enduring resonance is, within Judaism, almost without equal. Although produced at a transformative moment in northern French (and more broadly Ashkenazic) learning and literary creativity, the *Commentary* was sufficiently free of the most ingrained signs of its origin, and sufficiently endowed with a rabbinic glow, to be able to transcend temporal and geographical limits to become the most widely studied and authoritative—that is, canonical and classic—Jewish biblical commentary of all time.

PART I

Toward Canonicity

I

Conundrums of the Commentary

CONTOURS OF A CLASSIC

BEFORE TRACING THE *Commentary*'s fate, it is obviously crucial to have a sense of what Rashi's readers were responding to. This chapter will delineate key features of Rashi's handiwork, seeking to identify why the *Commentary* became an authoritative and cherished classic while beginning to reveal how it could invite misgivings of various sorts. With the *Commentary*'s contours in hand, we may then enter the maze of its astonishingly multifarious receptions.

Textual Vicissitudes

To speak of Rashi's *Commentary* attaining a unique authority and popularity is to imply that its readers everywhere could and did peruse a single, uniform version. Yet nothing could be further from the truth. Indeed, granting that such things are hard to measure, it is nearly certain that no medieval Jewish work experienced as many textual fluctuations as Rashi's. The story of the reception of Rashi's *Commentary* should therefore begin with a probe of the varied exemplars of it that came into the hands of diverse readers and some of the causes of the proliferation of different versions of what Rashi said. Some scholars heap on the skepticism in describing the extent to which one who reads the *Commentary* reads Rashi's actual words. We may be told that as we say "Rashi says," we should think of a comment "compiled by Rashi as written down in disparate ways by students and variously altered by scribes."[1] One may even hear that while Rashi was not "the sole author" of the *Commentary*, still there ought to be ascribed to him a "pivotal role" in creating it![2] A question that looms large is how much the standard version that coalesced in the sixteenth century matches what left Rashi's pen. Following is an outline of this complex issue, studied with meticulous expertise elsewhere, focusing on aspects salient to Rashi's reception.[3]

The challenge of textual reconstruction begins with the fact that the earliest manuscripts of the *Commentary* are surprisingly late but it carries through to other factors. Even early exemplars date from a century or more after Rashi's death.[4] Yet the *Commentary*'s textual vagaries also reflect, in a rather extreme way, a general phenomenon of medieval Hebrew literature that Yisrael Ta-Shma called "the open book." The tendency of authors was to circulate different versions of their works in an interim state, at times on the basis of a concept of a text's collective ownership and understanding that scribes might alter or interpret a previously "published" work.[5] The author himself expected shifts in his state of knowledge for any number of reasons, the most obvious being the discovery of new insights over time, though other unexpected factors could play a role. Moses ben Nahman (Nahmanides) made hundreds of changes to his Torah commentary following his late-in-life arrival in the land of Israel, some of them born of fresh knowledge of realia in his new place of residence in the holy land or his exposure to previously unknown books there.[6] As for Rashi, he never authorized a definitive version of his *Commentary* and apparently continued to view his interpretation of the Torah as a work in progress.[7]

The textual hubbub created by Rashi's better second thoughts, the open book phenomenon, and other tendencies discussed anon that yielded multiple versions give rise to many methodological conundrums. Different ways of addressing them yield varied holdings regarding the status of any given version. Some advocate a purist approach: only a comment more or less universally attested in reliable manuscripts should be considered authentic to the original *Commentary*.[8] Yet others observe that comments more or less certainly attributable to Rashi can go missing in such manuscripts. Crediting the authenticity of around 90 percent of the standard version, Avraham Grossman readily grants that the notion of an *Urtext* is misplaced, not least because alternative versions existed already in Rashi's lifetime.[9]

One manuscript increasingly seen as the best witness (Universitätsbibliothek Leipzig, MS B.H.1) opens a window on the dynamism characteristic of Rashi's effort to understand the Torah. The manuscript's fame owes to an assertion of its scribe Makhir ben Karshavia that he worked from a model made by Rashi's close student and secretary, Shemaya. Some contend that "Leipzig 1," dating from the first half of the thirteenth century (early as such things go), "probably corresponds more closely than any other available version to what Rashi himself wrote,"[10] though others dissent.[11] Recent painstaking work has done a lot to bolster confidence in Leipzig 1 while indicating some of its limitations.[12]

Whatever the case, the manuscript certainly illustrates Rashi's openness to revisiting, refining, and if need be, altering ideas or their commentarial presentation to make his explications more user-friendly, a trait attested in Rashi's Talmud commentaries as well.[13] An example: Rashi initially omitted from his *Commentary* an account of the *'efod* garment worn by the high priest (including his notion that it was akin to the sort of apron worn by "women of rank" when they rode on horseback), but he eventually included an extended description at the end of his commentary on Exodus. He then relocated it into his running commentary, presumably for enhanced reader ease.[14] Leipzig 1 also reveals how Rashi's interactive pedagogy could generate modifications. When students queried Rashi, or even made bold to dispute him, this being a trait typical of Rashi's classroom, the results could find their way into the *Commentary*.[15]

If Rashi's exposition of the Torah took changing forms during its earliest stages of composition and diffusion, author-originated changes were hardly the main cause of the *Commentary*'s mutability. It owes more to interventions, conscious or otherwise, of those charged with transmitting the work. Already, Yekutiel ben Meshulam, an Italian who copied the *Commentary* in 1312, and the first Hebrew scribe on record announcing the technique of using more than one manuscript to achieve accuracy, confronted divergent texts.[16] Beyond standard scribal lapses, copyists could elide Rashi's glosses with jottings in the margins of an earlier model, producing admixtures of Rashi's ideas and those of students, like Joseph Kara and Samuel ben Meir.[17] Then, too, in the case of the *Commentary*, some versions came to reflect ideas of Rashi's loyal disciple, Shemaya. Though, in Leipzig 1, his interpolations were marked as such, later versions of the *Commentary* could present Shemaya's emendations, fresh interpretations, and citations of midrashim not traceable to Rashi (some based on traditions heard after Rashi's passing) as Rashi's own.[18] Conjectural textual emendation, a habit especially prevalent in French academies, also played a role. Though Rashi took the lead by proposing alternative readings of the Talmud on nearly 1500 occasions, Jacob Tam, his grandson, was at pains to note that Rashi placed these in the margins, never daring to alter the talmudic text.[19] Still, such emendations often entered versions of the Talmud in the course of time. In similar fashion, scribal interventions of various sorts increasingly played havoc with the *Commentary* as its transmitters acted on the widespread medieval view that fidelity to a work at times required its alteration.[20]

Beyond such common causes of textual divergence, the *Commentary*'s fluidity reflects features specific to it, not least its sheer popularity. With copyists churning out manuscripts in unprecedented numbers, and with many versions on the move, local variants were bound to emerge.[21] Most notable is an identifiably Ashkenazic version distinct from Sefardic counterparts in its omission of many midrashim. A version circulating in Italy may also have had its own distinctive tincturing, like others of Rashi's commentaries there.[22] The *Commentary* studied by Rashi's most influential Sefardic reader, Nahmanides, was not, in all particulars, the one that became standard.[23]

Perhaps the key point, though, is that idiosyncrasies of style, in addition to the *Commentary*'s midrashic contents, made it easy to alter the work, intentionally or otherwise, in ways that did not overtly disrupt a text's flow.[24] It suffices to peruse the version of the *Commentary* in *Miqra'ot gedolot ha-keter*, which retains some passages thought to be unoriginal but places them in square brackets, to see how smoothly accretions can blend with what is presented as some version of the base text. It took little effort, for example, to append a midrash as an "additional explanation" (*davar 'aḥer*) of just the sort that Rashi himself frequently supplied. An example is a well-known expression put in the mouth of Jacob at the time of a fraught encounter with older brother Esau: "I dwelled with the wicked Laban, yet I observed the 613 commandments and did not learn from his evil ways." The midrash appears as an "additional explanation" of Jacob's instructions to his messengers to inform Esau that "I stayed with Laban and remained until now" (Gen 32:5). It involves a classic anachronism of the sort adopted by Rashi elsewhere, according to which Israel's ancient ancestors observed most of the Torah's laws, imputing to Jacob observance of the full range of traditional commandments prior to their revelation.[25] It also displays the ancient midrashists' predilection for numerological interpretation (*gemaṭriya*) of the sort Rashi at times also indulged, using the numerical value of "stayed"/*garti* (g = 3 + r = 200 + t = 400 + i = 10) to buttress the notion that Jacob referred to the traditional count of 613 commandments. This was just the sort of midrash Rashi *could* have included in his *Commentary*. An "additional explanation" it indeed was—but one placed in the mouth of Rashi only a half-millennium after he ceased putting pen to paper, in printed versions of the *Commentary*.[26] Needless to say, its presence there ensured an enduring afterlife at the Sabbath table, in sermons, and in classes at all levels.

The *Commentary* fell prey to acts of omission as well as commission, though by their nature the former left fewer traces.[27] Some causes of disappearance are easily identified. Maps and diagrams in a number of Rashi's biblical commentaries presented special challenges to copyists. In the case of the *Commentary*, these included two maps relating to the wanderings of the Israelites in the wilderness and land of Israel, whose authenticity as issuing from Rashi's pen has been compellingly argued, and an illustration of the lampstand. However many of them were original, these visual commentaries all vanished (theories vary as to why) long before the advent of the first printed editions.[28]

Textual comments also disappeared, though a finding to this effect often involves surmise. In response to the famous question of why God tested Abraham, Nahmanides observed, among other things, that when God knew that a righteous person wished to fulfill the divine will, God tested the person "in order to bestow merit upon him." Encapsulating his point, Nahmanides adduces the verse, "The Lord seeks out the righteous man" (Ps 11:5).[29] Rashi's interpretation of the opening of the story of the Akedah as recorded in Leipzig 1 contains a comment to the same effect based on a midrash that adduces the same verse cited by Nahmanides. One might posit that Nahmanides would have referenced this precedent if he had this version of the *Commentary*, because he so often cites Rashi.[30] Assuming the exposition was one recorded by Rashi and then essentially lost, we are left to imagine the effect it would have had on readers, had it appeared in the standard version. For her part, Yedida Eisenstat draws a conclusion that is counterintuitive, not to mention difficult to substantiate: "citations were more likely to be lost from the text of Rashi's Torah commentary than added to it."[31]

Leaving aside techniques that have been developed to resolve textual doubts,[32] we consider implications of the history of textual fluidity fleetingly sketched here for investigation of the *Commentary*'s reception. An obvious finding is that reader responses to a comment in the work could very well be to an interpretation that Rashi never saw, or even one that he did but deliberately chose to omit, that was later added. A slightly less obvious conclusion is that great caution will always be in order when attempting to read silences regarding a comment that might be expected to elicit a response, elaboration, or rebuff, since any given reader's version of the *Commentary* may have lacked the gloss to begin with. All this said, for purposes of reception history, the question of whether a given comment left Rashi's pen is essentially moot as long as it was received as a genuine part of his exposition of the divine word. A response to such a gloss throws light on attitudes toward Rashi's legacy regardless.

The *Commentary*'s evolving textual history also highlights an unusual development in the history of canonical texts or, put otherwise, places a boundary on my casting of it as such a work. Whereas "textual fluidity is often arrested with canonization,"[33] the *Commentary* was not prevented from achieving its singular status even in the absence of a definitive *mise en texte*, let alone *mise en page*. In this it is partially akin to the Babylonian Talmud, which achieved canonicity before assuming completely fixed form, but which did eventually attain something bordering on that in a process that began with sixteenth-century printings and culminated in the 1880–1886 Vilna Shas of the Widow and the Brothers Romm.[34] Not so the *Commentary*, the contents of which can still appear in variant forms and which lacks a standardized presentational format to this day, even as the version produced by the Bomberg press in the third decade of the fifteenth century brought a high degree of standardization that proved lasting.[35] Put simply, establishment of it in a precise version was not required for the *Commentary* to become *the* Jewish commentary on the Torah.

Character, Aims, Authorial Voice

That the *Commentary* emerged in distinct registers—more plain sense in Northern Europe and more midrashic in Sefarad—implies different ideas about the work's character and aims and, possibly, disparate functions it was enlisted to fulfill in diverse places. Such an understanding fits with Micha Perry's ideas about changes in textual transmission that result less from error than from the needs or aspirations of later tradents and readers.[36] While there is nothing timid about his style, Rashi also made no effort to instruct readers on the proper way to approach his work. Even leading scholars seeking to navigate the thicket of subtopics that questions about the *Commentary*'s character bestir have no easy time of it.

True, parts of the road are well marked. The most striking feature of Rashi's exegesis generally, pronounced all the more in the *Commentary*, is its mixture of what Rashi calls *peshuṭo shel miqra'*, an elusive term often rendered as "plain sense" or "contextual" interpretation, and the classical midrashic expositions that he routinely drew on to explain scripture.[37] The problem lies in the relationship between the elements. As recently formulated by Mordechai Cohen, in a culture that studied the Bible exclusively through a midrashic lens, "Rashi sought to institute a philological, grammatical, and historically sensitive literary analysis, that is, *peshat*." Yet as Cohen quickly adds, Rashi mostly cites midrashic sources—"a conundrum that has plagued Rashi scholars for centuries."[38] In the *Commentary*, midrashic readings constitute an estimated three out of every four comments, with some affronting the canons of contextual interpretation Rashi ostensibly aims to uphold, and applies elsewhere.[39] Little wonder that the *Commentary*'s exegetical program can evoke puzzlement. Here Rashi supplements a plain-sense reading with a textually remote midrash; there, he does not. Here a single midrash is used to interpret a word or passage; there, a series. The *Commentary* may even cite a midrash relating to a topic in one place and contradict it elsewhere. The tack of the supercommentators and modern scholars is not generally to chalk up the phenomenon to textual accretions, leaving some to try to minimize or explain away the contradictions and others to conclude reluctantly that perfect consistency is simply not a trait of the work.[40]

Then, too, the *Commentary*'s style can be as shifting as its contents are inconsistent. Sometimes Rashi clarifies the stimulus for a given exposition. Most often, however, he leaves these prompts for his readers to discern. Occasionally, the *Commentary* declares the provenance of a midrash from among his vast range of sources, both rabbinic and medieval, but this is the atypical instance (clarifications of this sort may also be later additions). Rarely, Rashi names the rabbinic expositors of midrashim, but he usually omits such identifications in the manner that they routinely appear in his midrashic sources.[41]

A basic point of contention among the legion of scholars who have grappled with the nature of the interpretive endeavor in the *Commentary* stretches back to premodern times: Should it be seen as a work of exegesis pure and simple? Where Rashi treats matters of morphology, syntax, and so forth, his exegetical aim is obvious. Indeed, in such cases Rashi stands squarely in the category of practitioners of that new and in many ways daring post-classical enterprise subsumed under the heading *peshaṭ*. The interpretive sensibilities at play, however, become murkier when it comes to the *Commentary*'s midrashic side, since it is difficult, if not impossible, to sustain a view that every last midrash resolves an obvious or concealed textual difficulty, even as it may be anchorable in some attenuated way in an element of language or context.

Laboring intensely to uphold Rashi's exegetical purpose was the influential mid-twentieth-century Bible teacher Nehama Leibowitz, who taught generations of students to ask: "What is troubling Rashi?" (*mah qasheh le-rashi*). Presupposed was the existence of a difficulty spurring each of Rashi's comments, including exegetically strained midrashic ones. For Leibowitz, Rashi's reasons for adducing midrashim are "always textual, not arbitrary," deriving from "his understanding of the text alone."[42] Edward Greenstein also makes bold to proclaim that every use of nonlegal midrash by Rashi "can be understood as an effort to account for the specific language and rhetoric of the text."[43] Other scholars doubt blanket claims of a connection between every comment of Rashi and one or another nuance in the biblical text, or even the more modest assertion that Rashi invariably selects midrashim that appear to him nearest to the plain sense. To Avraham Grossman, Rashi may have aimed mainly to perform exegesis but he also felt obliged to "take advantage" of the Bible and its classical rabbinic expositions to teach Judaism.[44]

One reason, it is often argued, for Rashi to have diverged from a purely exegetical focus was the need to fortify the faith of embattled Jews facing at times daunting external challenges, not least Christian pressure. Toward the end of Rashi's life, the travails took the form of devastating massacres in the Rhineland Jewish communities at the time of the First Crusade. The question of Rashi's Latinity, relationship to his Christian surroundings (including what has been billed as a twelfth-century renaissance), detailed knowledge of specific Christian doctrines, awareness of prior and contemporary Christian exegesis, and role as an anti-Christian polemicist remain up for much-vexed debate. The discussion is hedged in by complex methodological issues and susceptible to various angles of approach. The question of how the *Commentary* in particular, in contradistinction to others of Rashi's commentaries, may have been shaped by such factors solicits much reflection.[45] Coming back to our current concern, suffice it to say that the pendulum has swung in the direction of a view of the *Commentary* as more than simply an assemblage of adroit resolutions to exegetical problems. On this view, Rashi sometimes summoned a midrash with weak or nonexistent textual moorings to further an educational, religious, polemical (however this may be defined), or inspirational goal.[46]

However much one may wish to herald Rashi's allegiance to the plain sense, there is no denying the work's heavily midrashic spirit, both in substance and in interpretive technique. True, in one place, after summoning a classic rabbinic idiom for the divine word's inherent polysemy (the Torah's words split into multiple interpretations "like a hammer that shatters rock" [Jer 23:29]), Rashi says that he comes only to uncover "*peshuṭo*"; yet his faith in the divine word's multiple significations, and keen desire to impart them, remains.[47] Indeed, it is this aspect of the *Commentary*'s interpretive fabric that sets it apart from more resolutely medieval peshatist traditions, whether they be direct offshoots of Rashi's own northern French school or the heralded focus on the plain sense in various strata of Sefardic exegesis. To illustrate, we have noted Rashi's interpretive assumption that the biblical patriarchs and matriarchs observed the Torah prior to its revelation at Sinai, a view denied by more insistent plain-sense commentators because it so obviously defied the biblical narrative. Adducing this example, and speaking more broadly, Uriel Simon observes that Rashi was in step with the ancient sages both in their "nonrealistic conception [of the biblical world] and the homiletical method that makes it possible to anchor this conception in the text."[48]

There is an obvious reason why Rashi's interpretive aims remain elusive: nowhere did he supply a full-blown statement of procedure. In the absence of one, scholars spend much energy parsing the closest thing, an observation prefaced to a gloss on Genesis 3:8:

> "And they heard [the sound of the Lord God moving about . . .]"—There are many aggadic midrashim [on this verse] and our rabbis have already arranged them in their proper place in Genesis Rabbah and other midrashic compilations. I, however, have come only for *peshuṭo shel miqra'* and such *'aggadah* as settles [or: conforms to] the scriptural word and its sense (*shemu'o*) in a fitting manner [or: as "a word fitly spoken" (Proverbs 25:11)].[49]

Its methodological timbre and appearance near the beginning of the *Commentary* notwithstanding, the remark does not occur in an introduction of the sort that Jewish writers in the Muslim East and Mediterranean seats of learning often used to announce goals and techniques.[50]

Some scholars, past and present, deny that these lines propound an overall approach, but even those who think otherwise are bound to admit that the statement is none too clear. Prominent is the resolute phrase "I, however, have come only," with its apparent emphasis on an exclusive quest for *peshuṭo shel miqra'*, though, here as elsewhere, Rashi fails to define it. Oft quoted is Sarah Kamin's delineation of exegesis according to "language, syntactical structure, thematic context, literary genre and literary structure, heeding the mutual relations between these elements."[51] Yet the apparent singled-minded fervor for contextual meaning is immediately complicated by an undefined linkage between the quest for the plain sense and a subset of midrashim that "settle" or at least "conform to" (how to render the verb *meyashevet* is disputed)[52] the "scriptural word and its sense." To this assertion Rashi appends a phrase from Proverbs, "a word fitly spoken," apparently reinforcing his plan to include only midrashim grounded in, or at least susceptible to integration into, the scriptural word.[53]

Such are the thin threads from which overarching theories are woven. Some urge that, although Rashi initiated a move toward *peshaṭ*-oriented commentary in the world of Franco-German Jewry, the *Commentary* is best understood as a midrashic anthology, with the statement at Genesis 3:8 establishing an "anthological selection principle" to determine the midrashim that merit inclusion.[54] Cautioning that it would be a great mistake to see Rashi's commentaries as "nothing more than anthologies," Grossman points to his careful selection of midrashim and typical reformulation of them prior to inclusion in his interpretation of holy writ. His metaphor for Rashi's handling of midrash is "dough to be kneaded."[55] Mordechai Cohen, by contrast, is more insistent on Rashi's bold advance, in this and in other ostensibly programmatic statements, of "his new standard of *peshuṭo shel miqra'*."[56] Such debates, it should be noted, often focus more (if also often implicitly) on the narrative rather than the legal side of Rashi's exegesis. As regards the latter, the standard finding is that Rashi usually reported one or another rabbinic view even as he "tried to follow the rules he had imposed upon himself throughout his work, both in the selection of midrashim and in their style and mode of presentation"[57] However this may be, whole chapters are written on Rashi's "methodological statements," with the gloss on Genesis 3:8 almost invariably featuring as the *locus classicus*.[58] These have their place, of course, but it remains well to heed Greenstein's wise caveat that "Rashi himself does not appear to have been quite so method-conscious as his critics."[59]

There may be more productive ways to characterize Rashi's manner of proceeding. One would be in terms of different "paradigms" to which his approach gave rise: instances where Rashi clearly states his adherence to the plain sense and exclusion of midrashim; others where a plain sense and alternative midrashic reading are both included (the so-called dual interpretations); and so forth. At any rate, there is no gainsaying that in the majority of cases, Rashi's commentaries "overstep the bounds of what would seem to be his own definition of *peshuto shel miqra*," even as such instances may in his mind fit with ("settle," in his common usage) the scriptural word.[60] Another way to describe Rashi's exegetical outlook in general and *Commentary* in particular is in terms of its continuity with classical rabbinic assumptions about the nature of scripture, especially what James Kugel calls the "omnisignificant" assumption of the ancient midrashists—namely, that every nuance of scripture is "comprehensible and significant" and hence must be accounted for.[61] Seen thus, Rashi's statement at Genesis 3:8 marks the moment when, for northern French exegetes, "the concept of 'Torah' begins to shift from an exclusively omnisignificant understanding to one that enabled the development of contextual exegesis."[62] As we will see, much of the *Commentary*'s reception over the ages turns on diverse responses to Rashi's handling of scriptural omnisignificance. Yet another helpful way to see the *Commentary* is in terms of contemporary cross-cultural parallels. Hanna Liss, for instance, proposes that Rashi's commentaries can be seen as a "Jewish Glossa Ordinaria" comparable to other Christian writings by Rashi's actual or near contemporaries, such as Gilbert of Poitiers.[63]

Where to go with all this? Needless to say, even if Rashi did not always live up to what we may decide were his official designs in the *Commentary*, he would hardly be the first writer in human history to fall short on this score, nor need we then say that he lacked methodical benchmarks. Staying with medieval Jewish biblical commentators, Abraham Ibn Ezra's strong critique of gaonic predecessors in the introduction to his Torah commentary for engaging in long excurses in their exegetical works hardly prepares his reader for his doing the same, with some frequency and enthusiasm, in this same commentary (though Ibn Ezra might have claimed that his digressions were salient and those of the Geonim not). Nahmanides's implication near the end of his introduction that he wrote for fairly average readers ("to put at ease the mind of students weary from the exile and adversities") meets with some incredulity when one turns to his often long, sometimes technical, and ocassionally rarified exegetical offerings.[64] Still, both commentators remain well within hailing distance of the sort of commentaries they promise. The elusive nature of Rashi's aims, by contrast, seems in a class all its own.

For current purposes, it may suffice to stipulate two points. The first is that there are good reasons to resist the temptation of closure when it comes to nailing down the meaning of key terms in Rashi's exegetical vocabulary, not least the issue of textual fluidity already discussed. A passage may be adduced as proof for one or another characterization of Rashi's mission without proper recognition that it appears four different ways in the hundreds of manuscripts and early printed editions. Consider the "fugitive" (Gen 14:13) who apprised Abraham of the capture of his nephew Lot, identified in midrashic sources with Og, king of Bashan, a figure not otherwise mentioned until Numbers. Either "Rashi" began his comment with the very strange phrase (otherwise absent from his *Commentary*) "its midrashic interpretation is its plain sense interpretation"; or he began with the more plausible "its plain sense is"; or he commented without using either the term *midrasho* or *peshuṭo*, or—what is most likely, although not attested in standard editions, including the best and most recent—the comment did indeed begin by referring to the plain sense (*peshuṭo*)—but omitted any reference to Og. The data one mines to clarify Rashi's critical vocabulary will, then, be subject to the vagaries of the version of the *Commentary* used. So, then, will any conclusions drawn from such data.[65] The second point may be stated more succinctly. It is that what matters in the current context is less how many possible ways there are to shade outstanding conceptual fine points of Rashi's commentarial enterprise and more the basic fact that it remains largely grounded in a conception of scripture and worldview deeply continuous with rabbinic perceptions of the divine word and its teachings. This awareness, explicit or otherwise, informs responses to the *Commentary*, pro and con, from the adulatory to the perturbed and, as we shall see, well beyond.

However one views the place of the midrashim in the *Commentary*, Rashi's creative, often subtle but in any event usually substantial role in transforming them in various ways is beyond doubt. Rashi typically leaves his stamp on a midrash in his verbal formulation, almost invariably compresses it, and at times recontextualizes it, bestowing new meaning simply by virtue of his placement of a midrashic idea at a certain juncture in his *Commentary*. For example, by inserting a midrash tied to a verse in Leviticus into his commentary on Genesis 17, Rashi cast circumcision in a whole new light as a rite related not only to the special connection between God and Israel but also to the nation's inheritance of the land.[66] Zooming out a bit more, we recall that the compendia on which Rashi drew, ancient and more recent, were just that: compendia. It was Rashi who drew dicta strewn across these often prolix, digressive, contradictory writings into the continuous narrative "fused with a careful selection of passages from rabbinic literature"[67] that turned compendia into a commentary.

The interpreter who emerges from this picture is a complex composite of conservatism and creativity. Even as he retains great deference before the rabbinic sages and their inheritance, he routinely displays elements (often astonishingly subtle) of "the individual talent." To put things in the terms of the Latin commentary tradition, Rashi was no mere *compilator* of dicta of earlier *auctoritates*. Rather, his discriminating selection from a vast store of lore, coupled with the license that he took to compress, reword, amalgamate, juxtapose, or relocate midrashic ideas, shifts him decisively to the category of an *auctor* with *intentio*.[68] This process, studied carefully in light of the range of midrashim at Rashi's disposal, provides insight into yet another dimension of his handicraft: midrashim that he rejected or, in an alternative scenario, included but altered, owing to his reservations regarding them.[69] Similar evidence of the deliberativeness lying behind the *Commentary* may emerge from what Ephraim Kanarfogel casts as Rashi's decision to omit esoteric teachings (of which, it is argued, he was aware) from his exposition.[70]

Once we conclude that some of Rashi's midrashim are so remote from the plain sense "that they could not possibly be intended to resolve some interpretive difficulty,"[71] it is a small step to contemplate the *Commentary* as a source not only of exegetical insight but also of theological edification, spiritual inspiration, and pastoral reassurance. The midrashic side of the *Commentary* reflects, that is, Rashi's role as an educator, communal leader, and defender of the faith looking to teach and encourage a flock in the face of difficult or even—after the First Crusade of 1096—catastrophic historical circumstances.[72] Later writers, not least a phalanx of supercommentators who came to surround Rashi, would ignore his historical context but often relate to his ideas.

210 Years of Egyptian Exile: A Midrash of Rashi and Its Afterlife

Challenges born of Rashi's midrashic bearing and the problem of textually tenuous interpretations are writ large in the vast supercommentary tradition that the *Commentary* solicited. How Rashi nourished an unceasing quest to bridge what could seem a troubling gap between the scriptural word and its midrashic exposition is best seen in the presence of a concrete example.

Faced with a famine in Canaan, Jacob tells his sons: "there are rations to be had in Egypt. Go down and procure rations for us there, that we may live and not die" (Gen 42:2). According to Rashi, the statement of the patriarch not only spoke to dire present circumstance and the need to buy grain in his sons' first visit in Egypt. It also peered into the distant future, alluding to his and his sons' descendants' sojourn in Egypt to come. Already some two dozen chapters earlier, at what rabbinic literature called "the covenant of the pieces," God tells Jacob's grandfather, Abra(ha)m, that his offspring will be "strangers in a land not theirs" for 400 years (Gen 15:13), presumably foreshadowing the Egyptian sojourn. Yet elsewhere the length of that sojourn is given as 430 years (Exod 12:40–41). Neither figure squares with genealogical data suggesting that Jacob's descendants remained in Egypt for only a few generations, like the partial genealogy of those descendants through the time of Moses in Exodus 6.[73] In the face of such data, Jewish interpreters developed a very different picture of the sojourn in Egypt involving a greatly foreshortened interval between the arrival of Jacob's family and the miraculous departure of the Israelites, with the most cited midrashic tradition being 210 years.[74] The years mentioned in the Torah, by contrast, were said to reach back to the time when Abraham first received his prophecy about this sojourn in Egypt (430) or to the slightly later date when he began to see the "offspring" mentioned in the divine promise whose descendants would dwell there, in the form of Isaac.

Yet the 210-year period of Egyptian exile had not even the slightest textual basis, or so it seemed. Enter a midrash that found this period of time alluded to in Jacob's instruction to his sons to "go down and procure rations." As Rashi reports, following rabbinic sources: "He did not say 'go' (*lekhu*) [but 'go down' (*redu*)], an allusion (*remez*) to the 210 years that they were [going to be] subjugated in Egypt, corresponding to the numerical value of *redu*."[75] In this comment—for which, somewhat uncharacteristically, he noted a textual spur—the artful weightiness of Rashi's midrashic approach comes into view. In addition to focusing on a single word in isolation from its context in the manner of the ancient rabbinic homilists, Rashi follows them in assuming a biblical figure's knowledge (or perhaps, quasiprophetic glimmering) of the future in a manner that adds untold historical meaning to Jacob's words.[76] Rashi also deploys a familiar rabbinic interpretive modality, the parasemantic technique of *gemaṭriya*, or calculation of the numerical value of letters making up a word. *Gemaṭriya* allowed Rashi to squeeze additional meaning from *redu* to clinch the rabbinically vouchsafed notion of an Israelite sojourn in Egypt considerably shorter than the figures reported in the Torah. Of course, Rashi also explains the numbers that appear explicitly in the Torah, indicating that they are pegged to the "covenant of the pieces" and birth of Isaac. In this way does Rashi seek to resolve, in a thoroughly midrashic manner, a real chronological problem in the text while justifying an element of rabbinic historiography that was by no means readily apparent. Beyond unpacking the hidden meaning of an alleged "surface irregularity" in the Torah of the sort that typically fired (or justified the fruits of) the midrashic imagination, the midrash implied a profound religious message made explicit in other versions of it: God was willing to contradict his own declaration to Abraham and remove the children of Israel from Egypt after only 210 years out of love and compassion for them.[77] This was the sort of message that could fill Jews with hope as they contemplated the seemingly interminable exile.

Just as the numerological gloss on "go down" that asserts a 210-year Egyptian sojourn illustrates how far removed midrashim in the *Commentary* could stand from the plain sense, so its reception over centuries tells a tale, showing how a comment made by Rashi with laconic insouciance could puzzle later readers. In particular, supercommentators mount ongoing efforts to explain it. The midrash proved insuperably baffling to the most influential of these, Elijah Mizrahi of Constantinople (ca. 1450–1526). The problem is that in biblical Hebrew, "descent" was standard as a way to describe departures from the land of Israel, as was the language of "ascent" to describe an arrival there, the land being deemed above all others spiritually, if not topographically. This being so, the wording of Jacob's order is wholly unexceptional. Indeed, the very next verse states that the sons of Jacob "descended" into Egypt, using the same verb that Rashi deemed so pregnant with meaning a verse earlier, yet he made no comment, suggesting that he suddenly found use of the verb devoid of significance.[78] Adopting the common assumption that a midrash in the *Commentary* must have a compelling textual spur, Mizrahi was left in a quandary when at a loss to find one.

The problem identified by Mizrahi had already been tackled by the Austrian rabbi Israel Isserlein (1390–1460), who thought he had a solution. If Jacob merely intended to instruct his sons to procure rations, he would have told them to "go down and procure rations for us there." Yet Jacob's statement in a word-for-word rendering read: "go down *to there* and procure rations for us *there.*" Owing to the seemingly superfluous initial "there," which drew attention to the preceding *redu*, Rashi and his midrashic source "perforce" understood that the statement of the patriarch encoded added meaning, such as Rashi deciphered by way of *redu*'s numerical value. Yet such deliverance for the seemingly baseless midrash came with, as it were, a price, since Isserlein supplied an explanation for the interpretation of a 210-year-long sojourn that Rashi's account, grounded in plain numerology, lacked. Yet, as Isserlein made clear, the *gemaṭriya*-based reading of "go down" as the only rationale for Rashi's midrash was not one he could accept. Anticipating and sharpening the point later made by Mizrahi, he rhymed off a litany of verses in the immediate vicinity that proved that "from the language of 'going down' [alone] we are able to draw no inferences," since this phrase appeared "throughout the pericope" to describe departures from the land: "So ten of Joseph's brothers went down" (Gen 42:3), "they made their way down to Egypt" (43:15), and "we came down once before" (43:20). In none of these cases did Rashi draw added meaning from the language of "descent." Another basis for his choice to do so in the case of Jacob's pronouncement had to be found.[79]

Isserlein's solution to the problem of Rashi's midrash on *redu* shows how those who sought to shore up the legitimacy of the *Commentary* at times had to be inventive in ways that departed from Rashi locally, even if they were very much true to the spirit of Rashi's larger midrashic hermeneutic. In this case, Isserlein's justification offered a novel rationale for the midrash different from the one supplied by Rashi himself. At the same time, this act of buttressing was attuned to Rashi's outlook, as Isserlein put his finger on what he called a "linguistic superfluity" (*yittur lashon*) that, for this very reason, demanded explanation. Here, he put himself in step with one of the most common justifications for midrashic exposition seen in light of the "omnisignificant" assumption mentioned prior. In Isserlein's run-of-the-mill gloss, then, lies something of a dramatic story that exemplifies the issues of loyalty and dissent that could arise almost imperceptibly as a supportive and even submissive reader of the *Commentary* quietly improved on Rashi's work in order to uphold it. Tensions of this sort would prove all the more challenging as the *Commentary* was read beyond the largely continuous intellectual milieu shared by Rashi and Isserlein, despite the centuries that separated them.

Writing in the sixteenth century, Judah Loew (Maharal) of Prague, one of many participants in what would prove to be the early modern golden age of Rashi supercommentary, proposed another justification for Rashi's midrash, this one grounded in a subtle literary approach.[80] In his *Gur 'aryeh* (*Lion's Whelp*), Loew concurred both in the premise that there must be a textual basis for Rashi's midrash and in the objection that the phrase "go down" alone provided no such spur, representing a conventional usage to describe departure from the land, since "the land of Israel is more elevated than all other lands." Still, Rashi's midrashic derivation of information regarding the Egyptian exile from Jacob's "go down" was sound. In fact, it reflected a finely honed literary sensibility that distinguished between the valence of a phrase in scriptural narrative and its use by a biblical speaker in direct discourse. In the context of his directive to his sons, Jacob could have been expected to speak in positive terms, whereas the phrase "go *down*" was neither "decent nor good" and even bore overtones of a "curse." This was the anomaly spurring a reading in terms of the dark exile to come. By contrast, when "descent" appeared outside of direct discourse, the term bore no freighted meaning, explaining why Rashi ignored it in the phrase "So ten of Joseph's brothers went down" (Gen 42:3).[81]

The supercommentators sampled thus far navigated the tension between plain sense and Rashi's midrash in one way, insisting that Jacob's "go down" must have a spur and engaging in a restless (if not necessarily successful) effort to find it. A minority voice belonging to the nineteenth-century Galician supercommentator Isaac Horowitz urged otherwise. After noting Mizrahi's unanswered questions, Horowitz insisted that Rashi's midrashic notion of a 210-year sojourn presented "no difficulty whatsoever by my reckoning." True, nothing in the text compelled the midrash, but this need not occasion perturbation. As he had explained elsewhere, some midrashim simply uncovered "hints" in the text, like the midrash on the numerical value of *redu*. These rabbinic ideas were perfectly valid but could hardly be said to respond to full-blown interpretive difficulties in need of resolution.[82] Yet Horowitz was one with the likes of Isserlein, Mizrahi, and Loew in valorizing midrash even as he, unlike them, did not see each midrash cited in the *Commentary* as evidence of Rashi's boundless sensitivity to some nuance in the divine word. In this stance, such supercommentators were light years away from the resisting readers we will meet, who, looking at Rashi's midrashic readings through much more disenchanted eyes, saw many of them as nothing less than interpretive malpractice.

Bloodstream of Jewish Culture

Seeking to identify the secret of the *Commentary*'s popularity, Eran Viezel goes so far as to say that Rashi created an expanded Torah "loved by its readers far more than the Torah itself," with the midrashim that he used to "thicken" the Torah as its key ingredient.[83] However this may be, Rashi's choice of midrashim proved fateful since, consciously or not, the *Commentary* would become a document after which Jews would pattern their lives, seeking to live as Rashi said Abraham and Sarah had, and observing the Torah's precepts in the spirit in which Rashi presented them. Rashi's interpretations, the midrashic ones in particular, left an indelible imprint. So, in its own way, did his decision to exclude a particular midrash. When Rashi included a midrash in his *Commentary*, it was assured of "meaningful survival"; if not, a midrash could mostly hope to eke out an afterlife in scholarly circles.[84]

A nearly endless array of concrete examples buttress such assessments. In some, the *Commentary* left a stamp that was by no means required by the aggregate of rabbinic dicta upon which Rashi drew. An example is his depiction of Esau/Edom, a key symbol of the Christian "other" in Jewish literature, where Rashi invoked a range of midrashic appraisals in a highly selective way to paint an unremittingly adverse picture of a biblical personage not dictated by the sum total of his rabbinic sources.[85] As noted, many midrashic interpretations and teachings that Rashi brought to the fore would have been consigned to oblivion, as least among the vast majority of Jews, had he not assigned them a place in his *Commentary*. One had the first model of humanity, Adam, committing serial acts of bestiality in paradise. Cited by Rashi, the midrash became the source of a protracted history of at times contentious wrangles that would never have arisen without Rashi's commentarial endorsement of this startling idea.[86] In other cases, an idiosyncratic verbal reformulation of a rabbinic idea created puzzlement that did not arise in the original, generating ample discussion as a result. A gloss implying that observance of the personal commandments of *tefillin* and *mezuzah* applied only in the land of Israel is a case in point.[87] So was it with a midrashic gloss on a verse taken to be the main locus of rabbinic authority: "You must not deviate from the verdict that they announce to you either to the right or to the left" (Deut 17:11). Rashi's version—"even if they say to you right is left and left is right"—riveted the attention of Nahmanides and still figures in disputes over the nature and scope of rabbinic authority.[88] The list of "classic Rashis" is long and impressive.[89]

That midrashim included in the *Commentary* won enduring prominence had another consequence: some of Rashi's midrashic ideas could, as least as he presented them, trouble readers so much that they sought to alter or omit them, knowing they would otherwise reach a wide audience. We speak, in effect, of the distinction drawn by Malachi Beit-Arié between "unconscious" and "critical" interference in a text's transmission.[90] An example is Rashi's version of the rabbinic idea of so-called corrections of the scribes (*tiqqunei soferim*) to some eighteen biblical passages (made to preclude their being misunderstood or giving offense). In the list was a correction that aimed to preserve divine honor by changing what originally read "the Lord was waiting for

Abraham" into the more palatable "Abraham remained standing before the Lord" (Gen 18:22). But when did the change occur, and did classical tradition really consider it an actual emendation? In this case, Rashi's gloss added a phrase that suggested a late date and thence the seemingly heretical idea of an actual change in the original formulation: "the rabbis reversed the phrase to write it this way." Despite reason to think these words are Rashi's and the existence of scandalized reactions to them attesting to their authenticity, the claim goes missing in many manuscripts and printed editions.[91]

In consequence of its heavily midrashic ambience, Rashi's reading of the Torah bore an implicit claim to rabbinically assured truth. Yet if Rashi's midrashim slowly became a kind of "second nature" in the traditional reading of the Torah, it is pertinent to recall that Rashi rarely explained—indeed, according to Grossman, rarely even grappled with (although such things are hard to know)—the message of these often aphoristic rabbinic sayings.[92] Taken together, the midrashim that Rashi cited hardly lacked for a trajectory of ideas on an almost boundless number of topics. Yet Rashi's midrashic modes were also by no means finely chiseled scholastic formulations. The element of midrash meant that the ever more classic *Commentary* imparted a Jewish vision whose overall thrust was often clear, but using an elusive, allusive medium whose constituents remained pliably open to interpretation. That left a gap, or opportunity, later interpreters were willing—or forced—to fill as the *Commentary* made claims on readers and elicited a nearly endless variety of responses.

2

Rashi's Commentary

RECEPTIONS, 1105–1527

THE *COMMENTARY'S* RECEPTION unfolded in diverse centers of Jewish life, across a large number of spheres: exegetical, educational, polemical, and more. The variety of manners and modes in which the *Commentary* entered Jewish life reflects the divergent cultural domains that it came to inhabit. In this chapter, we consider the work's fortunes from its beginnings through the period of the transition from manual to mechanical reproduction of Hebrew texts. The focus falls on the three most important centers of its reception: the Northern European Franco-German or Ashkenazic sphere, Spain, and southern France.[1] More marginal centers in the story, like Italy and Yemen, are left for future separate treatment.[2] One mode of response to the *Commentary* that played a decisive role in its canonization is the supercommentary tradition that the work called forth, and this merits the separate discussion it receives in the next chapter.

Medieval Ashkenaz

Rashi's reputation in the Northern European milieu that shaped him waxed throughout his lifetime, all the more upon his death. Eliezer ben Nathan of Mainz (Raban), the foremost German Tosafist in the half century after Rashi's death, extolled this "pillar of the world" from whose "waters we drink and by whose mouth we live."[3] This perception, of which Rashi was apparently unaware when he passed away, was due in the first instance to the Talmud commentaries.[4] While Eliezer's honorifics deploy classical tropes, they were anything but conventional. Rather, they attest to a growing awareness of a peerless sage. Coming from an authority in the Rhineland rabbinic academies where Rashi had studied, this was quite the compliment for one who had single-handedly turned France into the new capital of Ashkenazic learning.

Interactions between Rashi's *Commentary* and its Northern European readers through the end of the Middle Ages unfolded in a relatively cohesive Ashkenazic religious tradition continuous in many ways with the one in which Rashi thought, taught, and wrote. Yet there were changes in the sphere of Franco-German biblical learning, with fluctuating but generally increasing Ashkenazic ambivalence toward Bible study. There were also changes in sociocultural setting as Northern Europe's Jewries were beset by intense and at times fatal assaults. Anti-Jewish agitation culminated in the expulsion of Jews from the French crown lands in 1306 and horrific persecutions of Germany's Jewish communities during and after the Black Death (1348–1350). Gazing from afar, Sefardic grammarian Profayt Duran (Isaac ben Moses, also known by his *nom de plume*, "Efod") spoke at the turn of the fifteenth century of lassitude with regard to scripture that was "very potent in France and Germany in our generation." Scholars debate when Duran thought that Ashkenazic abandonment of Bible study commenced. One of them observes that he fails to mention a northern French exegete after Rashi.[5]

Despite the fact that Ashkenazic biblical studies continued to lag, there was ever-intensifying engagement with the *Commentary*. Here I trace selected developments in the centuries after Rashi's death, paying special attention as always to attitudes toward the *Commentary*'s midrashic voice as a key to understanding its varied receptions. I also note developments beyond the exegetical sphere that riveted novel attention on the *Commentary*, most notably the legal status conferred on it in conjunction with the talmudically mandated review of the weekly lectionary (*parashah*).

Study of the *Commentary* in the century after Rashi's death coincided with the great Tosafist revolution in Talmud study effected mostly by his descendants. Born of a new dialectical approach to talmudic interpretation, Tosafist insights were recorded in analytical "supplements" (*tosafot*) such that, in a memorable formulation, "the land of the Talmud was occupied, reorganized, and administered by Tosafist thought."[6] Most Tosafists eschewed scriptural study as a distinct intellectual endeavor; informal study was largely restricted to the Torah and parts of the Bible present in the liturgy. Still, it was common to pay heed to Rashi, and the parallel with rabbinic studies is clear: just as Tosafist talmudic supplements focused heavily on Rashi's talmudic commentaries, so it was with Tosafist insights on biblical texts.

Tosafist study houses nurtured a glossarial culture par excellence, and study of Rashi's exegesis was unquestionably going on in them. Some results of these interactions appear in the marginal scribbling in some manuscripts of the *Commentary* as these have begun to be studied systematically. Such manuscripts can put on display a complex process in which Rashi's commentaries are at once authorized by virtue of the heavy glossing they receive, in some cases by multiple hands, but also undermined, as various later readers offered alternative interpretations to his readings, very much not in the manner of a supercommentator, or even exposing Rashi's perceived errors. Such marginal notes are sometimes rendered graphically on the page in a way designed to call attention to themselves. These processes are on display in marginal notes attached to an undated version of the *Commentary* made in Vienna in the thirteenth or fourteenth century.[7]

Of the Tosafists who did cultivate scriptural study intensely, the most striking pattern was to admire Rashi's innovative plain sense (*peshaṭ*) approach but to enhance it, in effect dissenting from Rashi's still dominant reliance on midrash. The result was the appearance of a "variety of *peshaṭ* meanings" arising in northern France between 1050 and 1200, united in one degree or another by rejection of rabbinic interpretation as the main mode of exegesis.[8] Most heralded on this score is Rashi's grandson, Samuel ben Meir, who lauds his grandfather as one who "illumined the eyes of the exile."[9] Between the lines, however, and in rarer moments fairly explicitly, Samuel routinely, and roundly, criticizes Rashi's overly midrashic approach, presumably at a stage when the *Commentary* remained very close to a version that had left Rashi's pen. Whether opposition to Rashi was the main raison d'être of Samuel's exegetical enterprise is a controverted point, but nobody would deny its centrality in his commentarial legacy.[10]

The generation after Samuel saw a partial retreat from his intensive peshatist pursuits in the direction of a return to Rashi's midrashim that "settled the scriptural word." It was effected by a half dozen French and German exegetes, including students of Samuel ben Meir's younger brother Jacob Tam. Most famous is Joseph of Orléans (Bekhor Shor), who cites Rashi by name or by the title "our teacher" some fifty times in his Torah commentary, but relates to him much more. Like another of Tam's students from Orléans whose focus on Rashi was greater, this one named Jacob, Bekhor Shor's interaction with the *Commentary* takes in a range of responses.[11]

The twelfth century also saw the *Commentary* leave its mark on the other main center of Northern European learning, Germany. It was a region with a reasonably strong record of Bible study prior to the First Crusade, one where Rashi had first learned the craft of Bible commentary; yet, it was also a center with its own exegetical habits and aspirations.[12] Now the commentaries composed by the most illustrious student of the German rabbinic academies returned to the venerable centers of Mainz, Worms, and Speyer as they recovered from the First Crusade. The *Commentary* also reached newer southern and eastern locales like Regensburg.

Judah ben Samuel, a leading German Pietist (*ḥasid*) who died in Regensburg in 1217, was an early respondent to the *Commentary*.[13] His exegesis, recorded by his son Moshe Zaltman, resembles that of other works of the same period in being based on the *Commentary*, even as it offers explanatory remarks on other commentaries and independent comments.[14] The explicit references to Rashi do not do justice to the frequency with which Judah questioned and amplified the *Commentary*.[15] At the same time, Judah deploys popular techniques of German exegesis, many of a parasemantic sort, used by Rashi sparingly, if at all, like *gemaṭriya* in a variety of convoluted forms (e.g., parallel elements in the words of a verse, like first or last letters) and *noṭariqon* (interpretation of each letter in a word as an abbreviation for a whole word). He also take up themes that Rashi omitted, including various types of esoterica (*torat ha-sod*) focusing on divine names, as well as magical and angelogical interpretation.[16] It was in Germany that an Ashkenazic supercommentary tradition around the *Commentary* flourished in late medieval times.[17]

Though the authority enjoyed by the *Commentary* generally had nothing to do with legal fiat, a normative dimension did arise in the thirteenth century by way of the French Tosafist, Moses of Coucy, who completed his major legal work, *Sefer ha-miṣvot* (Book of Commandments; *Semag*), around 1250. Moses addressed a problem that had arisen over time with the review of the weekly lectionary in the talmudically enjoined format of "twice scripture [in the original Hebrew] and once in [Aramaic] translation (*targum*)" (שנים מקרא ואחד תרגום).[18] Reading of the once highly functional translation had become increasingly hollow as Aramaic ceased to be a Jewish lingua franca.[19] One response, allowed by some rabbis and discouraged by others, was to substitute for the Aramaic Targum a vernacular translation.[20] Perhaps to counter this trend, which was largely free of rabbinic oversight, Moses, whose own exegesis displays profound interaction with Rashi, proposed a fresh approach: "I argued before my masters that the commentary is more effectual than the Targum, and my masters agreed with me."[21] He did not have to explain that *the* commentary in question was Rashi's.

One can speculate about reasons the *Commentary* recommended itself for its new elevated status as an accompaniment to or replacement for the Targum, apart from the fact that in France at that time there were no obvious alternatives. One was its frequent generally appreciative citation of the Targum—more frequent, in fact, than any other work adduced by Rashi.[22] Hence, awareness of Targum would not lapse were the *Commentary* to replace it. Rashi's recourse to *le'azim*, or vernacular translations, though he presented them in Hebrew transliteration, was a clearly French dimension in his work.[23] In function, however, it matched the role of the now ever more inaccessible Targum. Indeed, in its own way, the *Commentary* functioned more than other commentaries as a sort of translation of the Torah, expanded in size and scope beyond the Targum, to be sure. Finally, Rashi's reliance on midrash bestowed an air of authority that comported with that of the Targum, seen as of a piece with the rabbinic inheritance.

Moses's idea was greeted variously, but the notion that the *Commentary* enjoyed halakhic standing had been launched, began to travel, and became a topic of debate. It arrived in Germany no later than the time of Asher ben Yehiel (known as Rosh), who brought it to Spain when he fled there in 1304. It is unclear whether Asher agreed with the view that the *Commentary* surpassed the Targum as a supplement to "twice scripture."[24] Beginning with his son, Jacob (d. 1343), the *Commentary*'s role in the weekly review was promulgated in authoritative legal codes, inviting discussion that transcended its Ashkenazic roots as the notion entered the mainstream. Jacob himself was a transitional figure "between Ashkenaz and Sefarad"[25] whose *'Arba'ah ṭurim* (Four Columns) became the most influential legal code of late medieval times. His formulation regarding the *Commentary* provided the template for its parallel in the most enduring of modern codes, the *Shulḥan 'arukh* of the greatest sixteenth-century Sefardic legist, Joseph Karo. The latter ruled that one could fulfill the weekly review with either the Targum or the *Commentary*, but added that a "God-fearing person" should do both.[26] Naturally, later halakhists chimed in with refinements of and deliberations on this stipulation. The towering sixteenth-century Polish talmudist Solomon Luria, who claimed descent from Rashi, contemplated a situation in which restrictions of time forced a choice between the Targum and the *Commentary*. His holding: better to read the latter, which was "sifted as fine flour" and at any rate drew on the best of the Targum while claiming authority owing to its grounding in the rabbinic legacy. To these merits he added an interesting historical perception: "most [other] commentators" bestowed on the *Commentary* "the crown of kingship."[27] For the seventeenth-century Ashkenazic halakhist Abraham Gumbiner, the *Commentary*'s claim to speak on rabbinic authority was decisive. As he put it, the *Commentary* was "fundamental" (*'iqqar*) in fulfilling the weekly obligation since it was "built on the foundation of the Talmud."[28] Thus did the idea of a thirteenth-century French rabbi become the patrimony of most of world Jewry, yielding a convergence of two types of canonization of the *Commentary*—the formative and the normative.[29]

Returning to medieval Ashkenaz, we may ask how much the *Commentary* did in practice become a companion of weekly *parashah* study. Such things are hard to measure, but circumstantial evidence can be mustered. Consider, for example, the format of texts of the Torah found in hundreds of French and German manuscripts produced in the centuries after Rashi. On the one hand, they suggest that the Targum had staying power.[30] On the other, there are hints that Moses's idea may increasingly have had practical effect in Pentateuchs, in some of which the *Commentary* replaces an omitted Targum or at least appears alongside it, at times in patterns that would facilitate the devotional practice of "twice scripture, once Targum, and once Rashi." An example of the latter is the "De Castro Pentateuch" hailing from Germany in 1344.[31] It correlates with other near-contemporary evidence pointing in the same direction, like the ethical will of Eleazar of Mainz (d. 1357), who enjoins the fixture of daily study of Torah, whether "of long or short duration," or at the least of "study of the *parashah* with Rashi's *Commentary*." This evidence is especially precious, since Eleazar was an "ordinary Jew" whose words presumably reflect trends beyond the scholarly elite.[32]

One might speculate that the idea of the *Commentary* as substitute for the Targum may have been more readily accepted on the formal level in France than in Germany, although, as the "De Castro Pentateuch" shows, evidence of its informal German presence in the weekly private reading of the lectionary is not lacking. It was in France that Rashi's work first appeared, that leading sages counted themselves among his descendants, and that the idea of using Rashi in place of the Targum first arose. Even by late medieval times, German authorities of the top rank insisted on the Targum as the cardinal supplement in reviewing the lectionary; so maintained Israel Isserlein and Jacob Weil, the two leading German rabbis of the fifteenth century. Yet here is a telling detail, as reported by Joseph ben Moses, a student who lovingly recorded Isserlein's practices. Despite Isserlein's resistance to the *Commentary* as a halakhic substitute for the Targum, it was his habit, and Joseph notes, Weil's as well, to keep the *Commentary* at hand when conducting their weekly review.[33] The *Commentary*, then, made its claim—or had its appeal—even where conferral on it of a normative legal status was rejected. What is more, that appeal would only be enhanced by being relayed in a work like Joseph's *Leqet yosher*, one of many books that flourished in late medieval Ashkenaz that recorded customs of prominent rabbis as models to be emulated and that reached a circle of educated readers beyond the elite.[34]

One result of interest in and study of the *Commentary* by the likes of Isserlein was supercommentarial expression, whether by the sages or by students eager to ensure that a teacher's orally reported insights were relayed. The origins of what has come down as Isserlein's *Be'urim le-rashi* (*Explications of Rashi*), the most important work of later medieval Ashkenazic biblical exegesis, may lie in such a development. At all events, his assemblage of glosses on Rashi betokens a shift in attention in Ashkenazic biblical exegesis that would only intensify. Fewer and fewer were the Ashkenazic sages who wrote commentaries on the Torah. More and more were those who substituted for that activity the production of glosses on the Torah's greatest Ashkenazic expositor.

Arrival in Spain

Beginning in the later tenth century, scholars and writers in Muslim Spain, or al-Andalus, began to articulate the dazzlingly diverse and sophisticated culture that has come to be called the Jewish golden age in medieval Iberia. Forged out of an intense dialogue and disputation with trends abroad in larger Islamic culture, this century and a half of intellectual achievement boasted new heights in religious poetry, the advent of secular Hebrew poetry, and trailblazing feats in linguistics, biblical scholarship, and theology.[35] This phase of Hispano-Jewish creativity ended abruptly when, in 1148, Almohad Berbers invaded Iberia from North Africa to foil a growing Christian threat to Islam's Andalusian citadels. Almohad rule may have produced the "golden age of Maghribi civilization,"[36] but it ensured the demise of Jewish life and learning in Muslim Spain, as Jews faced a cruel choice between martyrdom, apostasy, or flight. Soon after, as the chronicler Abraham ibn Daud put it, the "nation" completed its escape from the Muslim south, "passing over" to Christian Spain and centers farther north.[37]

At the time of the Almohad advent, less than a half century after his passing, Rashi's writings were just beginning to land in Muslim Spain. The last great Andalusian halakhist, Joseph ibn Migash, had died in 1141 barely acquainted with but seeking copies of Rashi's Talmud commentaries.[38] Now the Almohads saw to it that Rashi's Sefardic reception would unfold in the expanding domain of Spanish Christendom. Yet even this development took time, not least because the frenzied mass exodus from Muslim Spain created a lapse in learning as Jews struggled to establish new domiciles in the Christian north. Ibn Daud (ca. 1110–1180) spoke for the Andalusi-Jewish intelligentsia as he mourned a "world" made "desolate of academies of [Jewish] learning."[39]

An early Jewish Aristotelian thinker who lived under crescent and cross, Ibn Daud apparently attests to ongoing ignorance of Rashi even after efforts had taken root to put Andalusian Jewish life on a solid footing in new centers situated along the ever-shifting *reconquista* frontier. It was in Christian Toledo that Ibn Daud wrote, in the 1160s, his *Sefer ha-qabbalah* (Book of the Tradition). In it, he traced the chain of rabbinic tradition down through his day, taking the opportunity to stress the superiority of Jewish learning in Spain. Concluding his work, more than a full half century after Rashi's death, Ibn Daud fleetingly departed from his Sefardic focus to register a few rabbinic "eminences" (*ge'onim*) hailing from France, of whom he had "heard." All but one were from southern regions closer to Spain. The exception was Jacob ben Meir (Tam), then the presiding rabbinic presence in northern France.[40] Glaringly absent was Tam's grandfather, Rashi. Two explanations for the omission are possible. Either Ibn Daud was only referencing contemporaries like Tam or he had simply never heard of Rashi.[41] Although Toledo fell to Christian forces in 1085, the Arabized capital of the newly puissant kingdom of Castile remained politically and culturally distant from northern France. Ibn Daud's awareness of learning in Christendom, Jewish and general, seems to have been confined mostly to the trireligious reality of Toledo, where he participated in a program of Arabic-to-Latin translations.[42] Thus his obliviousness to Rashi is not out of the question.

The same goes for Jewish refugee scholars who fled al-Andalus but remained in the *dār al-islām*, including the most famous of them all, Moses ben Maimon (Maimonides). Ten years old at the time of the Almohad invasion and around twenty when his family left Spain for Fez and then Egypt, Maimonides evinces no hard evidence of having heard of Rashi as he wrote, in Fustat (old Cairo), his most famous works more than a half century after Rashi's death. (His late-in-life use of Rashi's talmudic commentaries is possible.)[43] Only at the turn of the thirteenth century were there glimmerings of a new awareness. Maimonides's son, Abraham, used Rashi's talmudic commentaries and, in a couple of instances, cited the *Commentary* in his own unfinished commentary on the Torah.[44] He may have come into possession of the work by way of French rabbis who immigrated to the land of Israel around 1211, some of whom passed through Egypt, raising awareness of French scholarship.[45] From that point forward, "Rabbi Solomon the Frenchman," or simply "the Frenchman, of blessed memory," began to be cited alongside gaonic and Andalusian figures long recognized as authorities in the East.[46]

Back in Spain, the thirteenth century saw a second renaissance of Ibero-Jewish learning that combined the brilliant achievements of Andalusian scholarship with novel forms of erudition, traditional and otherwise, born of new connections between Christian Spain and Jewish centers in European Christendom to the north.[47] Beyond major reconfigurations in such spheres as rabbinic learning, kabbalistic teachings that had entered the light of history at the end of the twelfth century in southern France now moved to Catalonia, then Castile. They eventually found their most vital and authoritative expression in the later thirteenth and early fourteenth centuries in writings that came together as *Sefer ha-zohar* (Book of Splendor). In the core branches of traditional learning, the Bible and Talmud, no Ashkenazic sage left so deep an impression on Sefardic scholarship as Rashi. At the same time, as other seminal branches of Sefardic religious pursuit developed independently of him, most notably philosophy and kabbalah, they came to shape decisively the environment in which Rashi's philosophically and kabbalistically innocent *Commentary* was read.

If it is possible that Abraham ibn Daud did not know Rashi in the Toledo of the 1160s, there is, at the dawn of the thirteenth century, suddenly evidence of Rashi's status as a towering figure in Spain. It comes from Barcelona, the major Jewish center in northeastern Iberia; and its source is unexpected and more than a little murky: partial correspondence from a wrenching intracommunal conflict that pitted Barcelona's Jewish aristocracy against an obscure group of rebels. Dating from between 1206 and 1213, this correspondence includes a letter by the city's leading Jewish aristocrat ("prince"), Makhir ben Shehshet, to leaders of the southern French Jewish community in Lunel. In it, Makhir lays a bizarre charge against the rebels' "lawless" leader, Samuel ben Benvenist, accusing him of speaking against "the holy one of God . . . our master, teacher, and eminence, light of the exile, the holy Rabbi Solomon (may the memory of the righteous and holy be for a blessing) . . . the righteous teacher for the whole Jewish diaspora, may he be remembered for good, since without him Torah would have been forgotten from Israel."[48] Makhir declined to detail Samuel's calumny: "Heaven forfend that we . . . utter outright what was heard from his mouth." He does report that those who did hear it (and the even stranger claim he imputes to Samuel that the prophet Samuel was greater than Moses) rent their garments as one would do when hearing blasphemy. Meanwhile, we learn that Samuel urged anyone who heard him speak "blasphemously" of Rashi to so testify "under pain of excommunication."[49]

Rashi's entry into an essentially economic and sociopolitical dispute in a rising Hispano-Jewish community in the emergent Catalan capital is a cipher.[50] Bernard Septimus surmises that Samuel may have directed a disparaging remark at an idea in Rashi's Talmud commentary, which Makhir then used to justify the strong measure of excommunication he had taken against him.[51] However this may be, the oblique testimony shows how far things had come since Ibn Daud, residing in Castilian Toledo several decades earlier, failed even to mention Rashi in his account of French rabbinic greats. At the beginning of the thirteenth century, it was apparently clear to many that Rashi was the teacher for the "whole Jewish diaspora," without whom "Torah would have been forgotten from Israel." At bitter odds in all else, both sides in the fierce dispute deemed any casting of aspersions on the "holy Rabbi Solomon" an unpardonable sin.

By the time of the Barcelona wrangle, mindfulness of Rashi, including his style of biblical interpretation, had made its way to Castile. Such is evident from the writings of Meir Halevi Abulafia (ca. 1165–1244), a Toledan scholar with Barcelonan ties, in whose day Spanish talmudists began to use Rashi's Talmud commentaries systematically.[52] In a rare surviving letter, Abulafia exhorts a fellow Toledan traveling in Aragon to purchase Rashi's commentaries to a few talmudic tractates. The context for this urging is ambiguous. Perhaps some commentaries had yet to make it to Toledo, or perhaps Abulafia wanted fresh copies against which to check versions already in hand.[53] What is certain is that the Talmud commentaries would quickly achieve a lasting place in Spain.[54]

Abulafia nowhere mentions the *Commentary*, but it is not entirely farfetched to surmise that it came into his hands. His senior colleague on the Toledo rabbinic court was Abraham ben Nathan (Raban; ca. 1155–1215), whose moniker "Ha-Yarhi" (Hebrew "lunar," reflecting French lune) signaled his close association with Lunel. Before arriving in Spain, Abraham pursued advanced studies in northern France with Jacob Tam's nephew, Isaac of Dampierre.[55] Given his training among leading offshoots of Rashi's family, Abraham's familiarity with Rashi's exegesis seems assured. As he crossed the Pyrenees one may speculate that his belongings included a copy of the *Commentary*, which he then showed to Abulafia, although one might then expect some reference to this discovery in Abulafia's works.

In any case, Abulafia was certainly acquainted with interpretations of verses or explanations of midrashic readings of them in Rashi's talmudic commentaries. Not always did Abulafia find them satisfying—or even intelligible. Indeed, as Septimus has shown, Abulafia could dissent forcefully, not least when Rashi's talmudic commentaries assumed a literal approach to midrash that the Sefardic sage deemed unsettling, or worse.

Consider Abulafia's response to Rashi's interpretation of a talmudic exposition of the last verse in Ezekiel (48:35), which reads: "Its [the city of Jerusalem's] circumference shall be 18,000 cubits; and the name of the city from that day on shall be 'The Lord is There.' " Expounding the verse, the Talmud tells of a row of righteous men standing before God in eschatological times, stretching eighteen thousand cubits. After adducing Rashi's idea "that this verse refers to the celestial Jerusalem," Abulafia expresses bafflement: "But we—in the poverty of our understanding—do not know where this celestial Jerusalem . . . is nor where it will be. If it be in the heavens—is there really building in the heavens?" It was the sort of query a Sefardic scholar, even one of a conservative bent like Abulafia, whose traditionalist protest ignited the first controversy over Maimonidean rationalism, would naturally raise. Abulafia left the matter unresolved, believing he had discharged his obligation to truth "by clarifying our doubts and the perplexity in which we find ourselves."[56] Elsewhere, Abulafia found Rashi's midrashic literalism impossible to ignore—nay, in the words of Septimus, "nothing short of scandalous."[57] In this way did Abulafia inaugurate a reckoning with Rashi's exegesis at the earliest stage of Jewish scholarship in Christian Spain that had not ceased when the last openly professing Jew left Spain in 1492.

Sefardic Biblical Scholarship I: Al-Andalus Comes to the Commentary

As the case of Abulafia begins to show, basic aspects of Rashi's scriptural hermeneutic could perturb Spanish scholars. Sefardic sensibilities could clash with it on a purely exegetical plane when Rashi seemed out of step with the plain sense he had alleged to uncover and relay. Many comments in the *Commentary*, often of a midrashic nature, ran afoul of the longstanding Sefardic yen for biblical exegesis grounded in philology, grammar, and syntax. Andalusian scholarship had achieved breakthroughs in these areas that reached their apex around a century prior to Rashi's *floruit*. Recorded in Judeo-Arabic, however, the most up-to-date of these remained inaccessible to Rashi, leaving his commentaries woefully deficient in this area.[58]

Beyond grammatical disabilities, Sefardic sages could wonder at or even recoil from Rashi's midrashic comments, understood literally. Rashi never showed any sign of being "taken aback" by a midrash, no matter how supernatural or seemingly bizarre it seemed. On the contrary, he gave every sign of accepting all such midrashim in their plain verbal meaning.[59] By contrast, in a tradition stretching back through al-Andalus to the later Geonim of the Muslim East, where a midrash defied nature or perhaps a basic precept of decency, it was assumed that the sage who uttered it had not intended it literally. Nor, in Spain, was it rationalists alone who cultivated nonliteral interpretations of midrash. Consider the Catalonian talmudist and kabbalist Solomon ben Adret, the leading Spanish rabbinic authority of the late thirteenth and early fourteenth centuries. He deemed philosophical allegorical interpretations of classical texts a betrayal of their true meaning, suggested they were more destructive to Judaism than Christian exegesis, issued a ban on the study of philosophy before age twenty-five, and excommunicated southern French philosophical allegorists. Yet he wrote an early entry in the genre of systematic midrashic interpretation that often took a nonliteralist approach.[60]

Another factor that impinged heavily on Sefardic thinking about midrash and thence, it stands to reason, on study of the *Commentary* was Christian attacks on the rabbinic legacy. These mounted in volume and intensity as the Middle Ages wore on, Spain being the epicenter of the polemical assault. True, some Sefardic savants might have appreciated elements in the *Commentary* designed to provide readers with ideas that reinforced rabbinic Judaism and undermined Christian interpretation, although how much anti-Christian animus animates the *Commentary* is, as we have noted, a much debated point.[61] At the same time, some passages in the *Commentary* could incite Christian obloquy while others made it easy for Christians to hold Judaism up to ridicule. It was Christians like Petrus Alphonsi, an Aragonese Jew whose conversion to Christianity occurred around the time of Rashi's death, who first engaged in criticisms of the (alleged) irrationalities in rabbinic dicta. In so doing, he foreshadowed features of the medieval Christian–Jewish debate, included the prominent role played by apostates in executing the assault on midrash. In a later development, apostates sought to put rabbinic dicta in the service of Christian missionizing.[62] Mindful of Christian disdain, figures like Shem Tov ibn Shaprut, a fourteenth-century Navarrese scholar, admitted in his commentary on rabbinic sayings that he aimed to interpret them "in a form that allows us to speak of them before the nations."[63] Yet the *Commentary* was replete with midrashim that scandalized Christians owing to their apparent blasphemy, absurdity, or anti-Christian animus or implications. An example, reviled by Hispano-Christian polemicists especially, was the enjoinder to "kill the best among the gentiles."[64]

As noted, the Almohads insured that an encounter between the *Commentary* and Andalusian exegesis in Muslim Spain was not to be, but such a meeting did take place when a product of the Andalusian school fled the "wrath of tormentors" to begin decades of itinerant scholarship in Christian Europe. Exegete, poet, theologian, mathematician, astronomer, astrologer, and more, Abraham Ibn Ezra arrived in Rome in 1140 and, after stopping at various places in Italy, he spent time in southern France, northern France, and England.[65] As far as we know, all the while he resided in Muslim Spain he wrote only poetry. Now he sought to transplant the "wisdom of Muslim Spain to Christian lands," with his most lasting contribution in the sphere of biblical exegesis.[66]

Ibn Ezra's exegesis was full of novelties, but its basic method was thoroughly Andalusian. The aim: discover the plain sense, or what Ibn Ezra called "the straight path." The way: attend to the two main axes of sound interpretation—linguistic accuracy (what Ibn Ezra called "the bonds of grammar" in a poetic introduction to one of his commentaries on the Torah) and reasonability (cast by him as the "eyes of knowledge").[67] This easily led to rejection of midrash.

Yet, as one allegiant to rabbinic tradition and critical of Karaites who denied it, Ibn Ezra insisted on the unimpeachable veracity of midrashic interpretations of biblical law.[68] His quest for the plain sense was akin to that of some of Rashi's French successors, but was more philological and, in large part due to the Karaite challenge, far less inclined to offer anti-midrashic readings in the legal sphere.[69]

Ibn Ezra's aims and techniques were commonplace in Muslim Spain but were anything but that in Christian Europe, where he often found himself "a man against the tide" even as he did win some admirers.[70] To accommodate to new and, in his view, regrettable intellectual conditions, if only to make ends meet, he would write in Hebrew for non-Arabophone audiences and shape his literary endeavors to fit changed circumstances in the form of different readers. While continuing to address an audience of "sagacious ones" (*maskilim*)—what he meant, in effect, were readers *au fait* with Andalusian scholarship—he would have to be mindful of Christendom's Jews. On the one hand, they sorely needed the tutelage of one such as himself; on the other, they were ill-equipped, and even less disposed, to receive it. In the sphere of exegesis, his efforts in remedial education involved penning Hebrew translations of works in the Judeo-Arabic tradition, like three of Judah Hayyuj's grammatical tomes, and original biblical commentaries on the Andalusian model. Yet such works could impugn local values.[71] One such value, Ibn Ezra quickly learned, was love for a French commentator of whom he might never have heard while in Spain, reverently called "Rabbi Solomon."

Ibn Ezra directly and generally assessed Rashi's exegesis once, and his evaluation was harsh. The venue was an out-of-the-way work on grammar, *Safah berurah* (Purified Language), probably composed in Verona around a half decade after his arrival in Christian Europe.[72] In it, Ibn Ezra urged that although the classical rabbinic sages had interpreted "sections, verses, words and even letters by way of *derash*," they certainly knew the "straight path [i.e., way of *peshaṭ*-interpretation] as it is." To clinch his point, which was aimed at putting rabbinic authority behind his own exegetical aspirations, he cited what he cast as the rabbinic "rule" requiring plain-sense interpretation: "A biblical verse is never divested of its *peshaṭ*." Midrash, he contended, at least in non-halakhic contexts, merely imparted additional (or "superimposed") meaning. It did not pretend to relay an actual interpretation of the text. In this (implausible) telling, the rabbinic legacy involved not only a consistent awareness of the *peshaṭ/derash* distinction but also insistence on the former's primacy. The avid peshatist lamented what he took to be a falling away from this alleged rabbinic ideal in "later generations" that had made midrashic interpretation "essential and fundamental." To illustrate the point, he drew on an example known to him since his advent among the Jewries of Christendom: "R. Solomon (of blessed memory), who interpreted Torah, Prophets, and Writings by way of *derash*." True, Rashi had aspired to uncover the plain sense, but—and here came the unkindest cut—he thought his exegesis was by way of *peshaṭ* when in outcome it actually attained that result "less than one in a thousand." Yet "the sages of our generation celebrate these books."[73]

On the heels of so incisive a rebuke one might expect Ibn Ezra to refute Rashi's midrashic faux pas at every turn, especially as he did not hesitate to pour opprobrium on those whom he thought wrongheaded.[74] While this expectation is not entirely disappointed, it takes a peculiar form in Ibn Ezra's Torah commentary. He does accord ample attention to midrash but rarely mentions Rashi, with little more than a dozen such references across the work.[75] Initially, one might think to chalk up this dearth to condescension—that is, a view that Rashi failed to rise to the level of an adversary worthy of refutation because he lacked what Ibn Ezra considered elementary tools of sound exegesis, most notably up-to-date knowledge of grammar on Arabic models. In a rare explicit rebuke, Ibn Ezra concludes that Rashi missed the mark in a way that would never have happened to an exegete "who understands the language of Ishmael."[76]

Yet Ibn Ezra's decision to ignore Rashi seems improbable in light of his animus toward the *derash* addiction that Rashi promoted and Ibn Ezra's eagerness to win converts to his own exegetical cause. Indeed, a careful forensic audit performed by Aaron Mondschein shows that Ibn Ezra remonstrated against the *Commentary* routinely but, except in rare cases, obliquely. The middle term here is likely prudence. Writing in Christian Europe, and depending on such writing for his livelihood, Ibn Ezra was mindful of the acclaim accorded to Rashi and the degree to which it made any direct confrontation with "R. Solomon" unwise.[77] Better to highlight defects quietly, thereby enlightening the midrashically oriented Jews who populated both "the lands of the Greeks"—that is, Byzantium—and the lands of the "Edomites," or the Latinate West of Christian Europe. In time, even the benighted Jews of these climes could be weaned from midrashim and come to appreciate the plain sense that Rashi so rarely uncovered.[78]

To see how such concealed assaults play out it will be helpful to summon two examples. On midrashic authority, Rashi interprets the description of Nimrod as a "mighty hunter by the grace of [literally: before] the Lord" (Gen 10:9) metaphorically. It means that this otherwise obscure figure "ensnared the minds of people by his words, misleading them to rebel against the Omnipresent." This finding was buttressed (if not precipitated) by the apparent etymology of his name: *nimrod*, from *m-r-d*, "to rebel."[79] Here is Rashi following the midrashic propensity to seek meaning and even moral evaluation in a moniker according to the principle (this much Latin Rashi probably knew) *nomen est omen*.[80] By contrast, Ibn Ezra stipulates in his first word on Nimrod that one should "not seek a meaning for every name, if one is not given [in scripture itself]." He therefore took the description of him as a hunter at face value. As for the appellation "mighty hunter," it means that Nimrod was the "first to display man's mastery over the animals." The attestation, using the Tetragrammaton no less, that Nimrod acted "before the Lord" implies piety, not effrontery. On its basis, Ibn Ezra infers Nimrod's habit of building altars "upon which he would offer the [hunted] animals as sacrifices to God." He concludes his account by observing that it is grounded in "the way of *peshaṭ*" while allowing that "the *derash* took a different way." Here, as so often elsewhere it would seem, Ibn Ezra overturns a midrashic reading that he might otherwise have ignored in apparent response to its broadcast by Rashi.[81] Such implicit rejection of the *Commentary* helps to explain the otherwise peculiar (and surely overstated) claim of the fourteenth-century Ibn Ezra supercommentator Judah ibn Moskoni that Ibn Ezra opposes Rashi "in the majority of his explanations."[82]

In some of Ibn Ezra's peshatist divergences from Rashi, as in the case of the story of the binding of Isaac (Akedah), the stakes are raised very high. Basing himself on what he presents as a *peshaṭ*-based chronological calculation drawn from midrashic sources, Rashi determines that Isaac was thirty-seven when his father came within a hair's breadth of killing him. In addition, he finds a hint in the text that Isaac knew of his impending fate. Nonetheless, father and son proceeded "with the same [ready] heart" to fulfill the terrifying divine command. In short, on Rashi's interpretation, Isaac was a willing and even active participant in his imminent sacrifice.[83] Here was one way to read the relationships between sacrifice, paternity, and filial consent in a narrative that remains, in the minds of many, a "touchstone of religious morality."[84]

Ibn Ezra's Akedah was a different story. He indicates a willingness to accede to the notion of Isaac's mature age at the time of his binding if it represents a true rabbinic tradition, but he proceeds to interpret the story on the basis of "independent ratiocination" (*sevara'*) in case it does not. Minimally, he does not scruple to show that the midrashic approach fits poorly with the biblical text. Were it correct, it would have been "fitting for Isaac's righteousness to have been revealed [in the text] and his reward would have been double his father's reward since he willingly handed himself over to be slaughtered. Yet there is nothing in scripture about Isaac [on these counts]." Surmising that Isaac at the Akedah was a lad of around thirteen, Ibn Ezra draws a chilling conclusion: "Abraham coerced Isaac and bound him without his consent." In so doing, Ibn Ezra denies the heroic conduct that Rashi imputes to Isaac. It was a model that inspired Jews to make the ultimate sacrifice throughout the ages, including those in the Rhineland of Rashi's day who endured the First Crusade; to emulate Isaac in submitting willingly to death rather than giving in to violent conversionary pressure.[85]

In short, as a Spanish exegete in Christian Europe Ibn Ezra could not ignore Rashi's *Commentary*, which was being taught and transmitted everywhere he turned. Like his contemporary, Rashi's grandson Samuel ben Meir, Ibn Ezra was eager to highlight failings of Ashkenazic Jewry's leading exegete, yet he was also alert to the imprudence of openly doing so. The solution was to undermine errors and excesses tacitly, a dimension of Ibn Ezra's literary expression that should be added to what Moshe Halbertal calls his "stratification of the learning public."[86]

Ibn Ezra's success in many of his sundry projects was mixed, subversion of the *Commentary* included. Among later French and German exegetes his sway was feeble.[87] His legacy did, however, live on mightily, if at times behind the scenes, in Christian Spain, not least in Nahmanides. Where he became most popular, however, was in eastern Mediterranean centers. As we will eventually see in detail, the adulation reserved for Ibn Ezra was a major reason the *Commentary* never made great headway there.[88]

Sefardic Biblical Scholarship II: Valorization and Ambivalence in Christian Spain

Having seen a foremost Andalusi exegete meet the *Commentary* on, as it were, its home territory, it remains to trace its fate in Spain itself. The story begins in the generation after Abulafia, with Moses ben Nahman (Nahmanides), an astonishingly multifaceted communal leader and sage whose biblical scholarship, like his talmudic studies, engaged in a critical dialogue with northern and southern French works while adding an array of innovative elements all its own. In routinely engaging Rashi and Ibn Ezra, Nahmanides made them pivots of future exegesis. With Nahmanides superadded, a classical triumvirate emerged that would cast a long shadow over interpretation of the Torah for centuries.[89] Other Torah commentaries from northern France, like that of Rashi's grandson Samuel ben Meir, did not even make it to Spain for Nahmanides and his successors to engage.[90]

Nahmanides expresses his intention to focus on Rashi and Ibn Ezra in a poetic preface to his commentary that grants to Rashi the status of commentarial primogeniture: "to him belongs the status of the first-born." He announces his intention to be "infatuated with the love of Rashi's words." As Septimus notes, the statement may hint at "critical distance as much as passionate commitment."[91] In any event, he promises to conduct a "negotiation" with Rashi's words—nay, subject them to "inquiry and examination."[92] Rashi's place in the work of Nahmanides is central, with the *Commentary* cited in an estimated 40 percent of Nahmanidean comments.[93] Some assert that Nahmanides is "for the most part favorably disposed to Rashi's commentary,"[94] but this judgment is a little facile, his generally respectful tone toward Rashi notwithstanding. Later writers were quite attuned to Nahmanides's trenchant criticisms of Rashi and sought to rebut them.[95] Meanwhile, although Nahmanides follows Ibn Ezra on dozens of occasions, his continuity with Andalusian exegesis can be missed because he almost always does so anonymously. He was often Ibn Ezra's disciple when it came to the disparity between *peshaṭ* and *derash*—a disparity of which he all too often found Rashi inexcusably unaware.[96]

There is another way in which Nahmanides aligned himself with a feature of Sefardic exegetical expression nowhere present in the *Commentary* that is represented definitively in the works of Ibn Ezra and in Maimonides's *Guide of the Perplexed*. Ibn Ezra was the first Jewish exegete (indeed, Jewish writer) to make extensive use of the concept of the "esoteric" as comprising a layer in a sacred work, in this case the Torah.[97] Although the "secrets of the Torah" thought to comprise the deepest meaning of the revealed divine word differed from one Sefardic scholar to another—for Ibn Ezra they related to astrology and astral magic; for Maimonides, to philosophy; and for Nahmanides, to kabbalah—Nahmanides nevertheless joined a novel and, in its inception, distinctly Sefardic movement that transformed Judaism and the study of classical texts that is without echo in the *Commentary*.[98]

For Nahmanides, as for Ibn Ezra, Rashi's use of midrash drew great attention on both the legal and the narrative planes. When it came to legal midrash, Nahmanides had a global criticism of Rashi: his failure to interpret the Torah according to final halakhic holdings forthcoming from the rabbinic record. The syntactically difficult divine dispensation for postdeluvian humankind to consume animal flesh (Gen 9:4) provides a case in point. Rashi extracts from it a twofold proscription: human beings were not to consume the limb of a living animal nor were they to eat the blood of an animal that was still alive. Nahmanides's rejection is likewise twofold. First, he complains that the interpretation is "incorrect" according to the plain sense, perhaps because Rashi's reading requires the addition of a conjunction not present in the verse to make the Torah refer to the animal's soul and the animal's blood as two separate items. But, second, the interpretation follows a minority opinion that gentiles ("Noahides") are prohibited from consuming both the limb and the blood of a living animal. Thus Rashi is wrong not only according to the plain sense but also on the plane of midrash because his gloss is out of step with the Talmud's conclusion that while all humankind must abstain from the limb of a living animal, consumption of blood is permitted.[99]

Interpretations of biblical narrative, even as they almost invariably differ from the *Commentary*, also provide support for the (still slightly overstated) claim that Nahmanides "stands close to the growing tendency to make Rashi's commentary the centerpiece of his biblical exegesis."[100] A case in point is Nahmanides's break with an interpretation of Rashi that brings to the fore his tendency to introduce psychological insight into his "portraiture" of scriptural figures.[101] A dramatic scene depicts the reunification of Jacob and Joseph after twenty-two years of separation: "Joseph ordered his chariot and went to Goshen to meet his father Israel; he presented himself to him and, embracing him around the neck, he wept on his neck *'od*" (Gen 46:29). Based on a midrash, Rashi explains that the Torah's ambiguous description of one of the two crying on the other's neck refers to Joseph, who wept even as his father's thoughts were elsewhere, because Jacob was reciting the *Shema* and could not interrupt to cry. Nahmanides, after citing Rashi, explains otherwise: "his father [Jacob] fell on his [Joseph's] neck and cried over him still, even as he had cried over him incessantly to this very day, when he had not seen him [after his disappearance]." The issues in the verse were semantic, grammatical, and, Nahmanides taught, ultimately psychological. Did the word *'od* here mean "more" or "much"? If "more," then the verse certainly refers to Jacob, who had been weeping constantly throughout Joseph's absence; if "much," it provides no indication who wept, leaving Joseph as a possibility. Who is the subject of the verbs "presented," "embracing," and "wept"—Joseph, who started as the subject of the verse, or Jacob, who perhaps turned into the unspecified subject of the verse midway through it? Nahmanides addresses all these questions in ways that make Jacob the agent of weeping. What moved him to do so was what he deemed an indisputable psychological point. He put it as a rhetorical question, asking who was more likely to weep, "the elderly father who finds his son alive after hopelessness and grief or the young son now ruling [all of Egypt]?"[102] Whether Nahmanides addressed the midrash because it had come to the awareness of many through Rashi or whether he used the *Commentary*'s invocation of it as an opportunity is not the main point. By interpreting compellingly in a manner at odds with Rashi, Nahmanides made it clear that the *Commentary* was not the final word; yet even such refutations enhanced Rashi's status as the basic point of reference.

Whether the *Commentary* made claims on Sefardic readers, or roiled them, prior to Nahmanides is hard to say, but after him the work's place in Sefardic awareness was assured. What remained up for debate was its place, and that of Rashi's other biblical commentaries, on the interpretive spectrum.[103] Bahya ben Asher of Barcelona, student of Solomon ben Adret and author of a widely influential Torah commentary, is frequently associated with the fourfold program of interpretation designated by the acronym PaRDeS: *peshaṭ, remez* (hint), *derash,* and *sod* (secret—namely, symbolic or esoteric interpretation, in his case almost always kabbalistic).[104] In the introduction to his Torah commentary, he proclaims Rashi a "great luminary" of "plain sense method" at its best.[105] Given the many instances where the head of the school from which Bahya hailed, Nahmanides, introduces his dissent from Rashi with the phrase "according to the method of the plain sense," one doubts Nahmanides would have agreed. Explaining such different perceptions is no easy task. An admittedly speculative possibility is that writers like Bahya became at least dimly aware of Christian perceptions of Rashi as a purveyor of the *sensus litteralis,* a claim made forcefully by the most important Latin biblical commentator of the Middle Ages, Bahya's exact contemporary, Nicholas of Lyre.[106]

Other kabbalists in the second half of the thirteenth and early fourteenth centuries were also giving the *Commentary* scrutiny, including those in Castile who produced the texts that would coalesce into the canonical work of kabbalah, the *Zohar*. Of course, the work's pseudepigraphic camouflage meant these writers could not acknowledge Rashi openly.[107] For all that, they included plain-sense interpretations indebted to Rashi in their expositions.[108] More notable, and surprising, is another trend: zoharic rejection of midrashim in Rashi's distinctive reformulation of them. Why the versions in the *Commentary* should be put at center stage is not entirely clear. It may be that the authors did not know the original sources, but this focus also may have been dictated by awareness that the specific versions in the *Commentary* were the ones familiar to all. As for the spur for rejection of midrashim in the *Zohar*, some ran afoul of basic theosophical principles. Then, too, rejection is not the whole story, and the zoharic authors could endorse one of two midrashic interpretations brought in the *Commentary* where they advanced the zoharic agenda.[109] In the case of the *Zohar*, then, interactions with the *Commentary* possess a unique character inasmuch as they are attributed to rabbinic sources, especially Rabbi Shimon ben Yohai and members of his circle. The *Zohar* is, however, not unique in criticizing the *Commentary* under cover of pseudepigraphy. As we shall see, the most concentrated attack on Rashi's interpretation of the Torah ever composed was written under such a guise, if in that case in a spirit of exegetical and philosophical rationalism.[110]

The *Commentary*'s growing centrality is attested in exegetical works written in fourteenth-century Spain. The arrival of Asher ben Yehiel in Toledo may have played a role. Here was a great German rabbinic authority who shaped key aspects of religious life in Castile and who, as we noted, brought to Spain the idea that Rashi's work could substitute for the Aramaic translation in fulfillment of "twice scripture and once Targum." His son Jacob, who made that idea a matter of a widely diffused Jewish law, also composed a Torah commentary. In it, his main influence was Nahmanides, but he also related to Rashi and Ibn Ezra, creating a dialogue between the great French commentator known to him from his youthful studies in Germany and the leading figures of Sefardic interpretation.[111]

Aragon also saw the production of new, if not well-known, biblical commentaries. Nissim ben Reuben Gerondi, the presiding rabbinic presence there in the third quarter of the fourteenth century, wrote an unfinished Torah commentary covering the opening sections of Genesis. It contains, among other things, a mostly hidden trialogue in which he sometimes takes up the cudgels on behalf of Rashi in the face of Nahmanidean criticism. *Midreshei ha-torah*, a Torah commentary composed by Anselm Astruc before anti-Jewish riots in 1391–1392 claimed his life, also attests to Rashi's sway, with Astruc "very often," but almost always tacitly, building on the *Commentary*.[112]

A century after the devastating riots that killed Astruc, Sefardic Jewry met its ignominious end as the Catholic monarchs issued a charter of expulsion, setting on an unpredictable new trajectory the life of the Iberian Jewish statesman and scholar Isaac Abarbanel (1437–1508). As a biblical commentator, Abarbanel was a man of many words. It remains challenging (and a matter for future research) to draw a full picture of his stance toward Rashi. A basic orientation emerges from the plainspoken comment that it was "bad and bitter" to Abarbanel that Rashi "contented himself in his commentaries on the Holy Scriptures in most matters with that which the rabbinic sages expounded." No better in his own way was Ibn Ezra, who explained "the grammar of the words and the superficial meaning of the text's simple sense." Both shared an overconcentration on one facet of the divine word at the cost of insufficient attentiveness to many others. Abarbanel depicts Rashi as spawning one of two interpretive schools (the other tracing to Ibn Ezra), each overly constricted in its view of the exegete's task and hence incapable of doing justice to scripture's multifaceted depths.[113]

Elsewhere, Abarbanel sounds a different note, acknowledging Rashi's willingness to deviate from midrash as a "good and upstanding exegete ought to do." The context is justificatory—that is, Abarbanel invokes Rashi (he finds it rhetorically congenial to speak of "his eminence") as a figure whose precedent paves the way for others, perhaps precisely because Rashi's allegiance to midrash is so sure: "Rashi wrote: 'I have seen many homiletical expositions concerning the verses . . . that do not fit the grammar of the words or the order of the verses.' Truly, the words of the rabbi are correct with respect to the method of midrashic homily. And his eminence emboldened himself to disagree with them [the sages] . . . and so a good and upstanding exegete ought to do."[114] When expressing his own interest in the plain sense, Abarbanel often echoes Rashi's formulation about coming only for *peshuṭo shel miqra'* and such midrashic dicta as settled the scriptural word. Tellingly, however, Abarbanel always omits the part of the declaration that mentions midrashim. Not that inclusion of them in his commentaries was against his principles; on the contrary, they had an honored place there. But in good Sefardic fashion, Abarbanel routinely indicates that the plain sense of a verse diverges from its midrashic elaboration, a distinction that he frequently found Rashi guilty of blurring.[115]

Beyond exegetical objections to Rashi's midrashic approach, his failure to use reasonability as a filter in deciding which rabbinic sayings to include and how to present them could rankle. In his first commentary on a complete biblical book, Abarbanel references a midrash imparted by Rashi that explains that the generation of Israelite males who engaged in a mass circumcision at Gilgal postponed the rite because the north wind required for healing them after such a procedure was absent. The midrash has it that this wind might have dispersed the "clouds of glory" that accompanied the Israelites in the wilderness; hence, no such wind blew in the forty years prior to the invasion of Canaan. Abarbanel protests that infants are circumcised all the time, "north wind or no."[116] Or, to take an example from the *Commentary*, Abarbanel undermines the alleged textual basis for a midrash of Rashi that has the primordial plants formulating an "a fortiori argument" in justification of their deviation from an aspect of God's command for their development. To Abarbanel, it is clear that plants possess no will of the sort that allows them to exercise discretion, let alone subvert the divine plan for creation.[117] Here Abarbanel displays characteristically Southern Mediterranean concerns with midrashim that fail to meet the test of empiricism or scientific tenability.

Abarbanel sometimes testifies to the degree to which midrashic ideas in the *Commentary* had become lodged in the minds of ordinary Jews. Consider how he initiates his account of Nimrod: "you already know what the rabbinic sages explained, that he would ensnare the minds of people."[118] Clearly, Abarbanel does not presuppose that his reader possesses encyclopedic knowledge of all midrashic literature. What he apparently does assume is awareness of Rashi's rabbinic reconstruction of a biblical figure. When dealing with a midrash requiring a response, he may not even bother to relay its contents, noting that it is "as Rashi recorded." Readers are assumed to be familiar with the canonical compendium of rabbinic lore. A midrash cited by Rashi can win endorsement once it is suitably explained in a way Rashi failed to do—more evidence of the claim made by the *Commentary* on exegetes four hundred years after its author disappeared from the scene.[119]

Similar testimonials to the *Commentary*'s pervasive influence are forthcoming in other commentaries from "the generation of the expulsion." One was composed by the great Aragonese preacher Isaac Arama (ca. 1420–1494) who, like Abarbanel, was a Sefardic traditionalist of broad learning. He cites a strange midrash used by Rashi to explain Adam's cry of "This one at last is bone of my bones" (Gen 2:23) that ascribed serial acts of bestiality to Adam. In Arama's case, he refers to the midrash as "their saying"—that is, as a dictum of the sages. When he cites it, however, he does so in a distinctive verbal reformulation given by Rashi. By contrast, Arama's younger contemporary, Isaac ben Joseph Caro of Toledo, mentions Rashi explicitly when adducing the same midrash.[120] It is plausible to surmise that these writers would have ignored the idea had Rashi not turned it into one for the ages, leading, or forcing, later exegetes to respond. And respond they did, with Abarbanel, Arama, and Caro all refusing to countenance the possibility of a sexual congress between Adam and animals. This refusal paved the way for an interpretation of the midrash that saw in the first model of humanity's mating with beasts a metaphor for an act of cognitive discernment, the better to ascertain each animal's nature as part of Adam's quest to find a fitting mate. In imbuing the midrashically conjured primordial act of mating with such a lofty intention, they trod a path marked out by a series of Sefardic supercommentators on Rashi that began a century before.[121]

Abroad in Hispano-Jewish Society

In high and late medieval times, the *Commentary*'s presence in Sefardic life extended to new spheres, attesting to its role as a foundational text so much so that there is even evidence of awareness of this truth among Spanish Christians. To see this side of the picture, we must move beyond the precincts of rabbinic academies and learned biblical commentaries to observe the *Commentary*'s growing role in such spheres as education, interreligious polemic, and Sefardic book culture.

Regarding education, evidence roughly from the days of Nahmanides lies in a curriculum presented by one Judah ibn Abbas (ca. 1250). In terms of traditional religious subjects, Ibn Abbas urged a program that included weekly study of "Torah commentaries," the "first" being that of Rashi. Although the nature of the primacy accorded to Rashi is unclear, it is striking coming from a Sefardic rationalist (of the moderate persuasion) who otherwise advocated scientific pursuits like medicine, mathematics, logic, astronomy, physics, and metaphysics and who considered excessive Talmud study with Tosafot a waste of valuable time.[122] Though this syllabus may suggest an ideal way of life more than an actual program of study, that does not detract from the significance of the central place accorded the *Commentary* at a relatively early stage of pedagogic development in Christian Spain.[123]

For the *Commentary*'s place in actual educational activities, other sorts of sources fill in gaps. At the turn of the fourteenth century, Solomon ben Adret received a legal query that mentioned a student who did not wish to attend study sessions with a hired mentor since the latter refused to teach him the *Commentary*. On this basis, the student sought the return of the collateral left with the teacher to cover his salary.[124] In terms of patterns of study, the impetus that Asher ben Yehiel gave to the inclusion of the *Commentary* in the mandated private review of the *parashah*, eventually codified by his youngest son Jacob, was reinforced for some of Asher's grandchildren in the "ethical will" of Asher's oldest son, Judah (1270–1349). He instructed his offspring to "fix times to read scripture with grammar and commentary" and, in particular, engage in weekly reading "with Rashi's commentary and other commentaries," clearly giving the *Commentary* pride of place. The same missive notes that Bible study was neglected in the German domain where Judah grew up. One can ponder the possibility that awareness of local cultivation of scripture among German immigrants to Spain helped to spur a return to such endeavors—but now with the classic work of Ashkenazic biblical commentary in hand.[125]

The *Commentary* was introduced at an early age, if a testimony composed on the eve of the 1492 expulsion by Rashi supercommentator Judah Khalatz is representative. Having moved under apparently unfortunate circumstances from Castile to Granada, Khalatz found himself teaching the *Commentary* to young charges. In the introduction to the supercommentary on it that he eventually wrote in North Africa, Khalatz offhandedly speaks of "the custom spread throughout all Jewry" to inaugurate beginners in Torah study in "the reading of Rashi."[126] Elsewhere he explains how, beyond guidance in understanding the Torah, the *Commentary* served an indispensable role as a platform for early learners developing the skills that would allow them to advance to "reading in the Talmud." As configured by Khalatz, then, the *Commentary*'s pedagogic function was twofold: first, as "foundation stone for all [biblical] commentaries" and "starting point for understanding of the written Torah *in toto*"; second, as steppingstone for "ascent" to the higher "wisdom of the Talmud."[127]

Another student of the Bible, Profayt Duran, whose condemnation of French and German neglect of scripture we noted at the chapter's outset, invoked Rashi as he sought to develop his teaching regarding what he called "the true wisdom of the Torah." A forcible convert to Christianity at the time of the 1391 riots, Duran sought ways to stem the "disease" of scriptural lassitude that he now saw infecting parts of Spain. To do so, he had to, among other things, refute scholars who deemed Talmud study the essential if not preferably almost exclusive element in the nation's curriculum. What better way than to appeal to the "great rabbi Rashi," the "crowning glory of talmudists," whom no one could accuse of slighting Talmud, yet who "delved deeply into scripture" as his "pleasing commentaries" on it showed. True, Duran judged Rashi too reliant on expositions "of the rabbinic sages [said] in the manner of *derash*," leaving little by way of *peshaṭ*. Still, this French talmudist par excellence stood as a rebuke to anyone who would call a Jew who would "fritter away time on scripture" a "dolt." Like Abarbanel's later appeal to Rashi to justify departures from midrash, Duran's invocation of the French master to buttress his case for biblicism assumes the purchase that Rashi's example had in a Sefardic environment.[128]

As Catalo-Aragonese Jewry's surviving remnant suffered further missionizing trials after 1391, spokesmen for Judaism and Christianity all made their case by laying claim to Rashi's authority. So it appears in partial Hebrew records and the full Latin protocol of the nearly two-year-long forced *Catechesis* held at Tortosa and San Mateo in 1413–1414. Operating under the auspices of the Avignonese Pope Benedict XIII, this last of the forced medieval public Jewish–Christian disputations was spearheaded by the apostate, Jerònim de Santa Fe, formerly Joshua Lorki. The *Commentary*, and Rashi's biblical commentaries more generally, had figured in thirteenth-century Talmud trials in France and earlier Hispano-Christian missionizing tracts, including the most injurious, *Pugio fidei*.[129] It now loomed large at Tortosa. As Judaism's defenders extolled Rashi's "high standing and importance," a Hebrew report tells how Jerònim also ranked Rashi "greatest" among the Jewish commentators, the better to bolster a christological reading of the classic crux "the scepter shall not depart from Judah" (Gen 49:10).[130] Such efforts to harness Rashi's prestige also appear in the disputation's Latin protocols.[131] Clearly, Christians thought they could strike a decisive blow if they showed they had Rashi on their side.[132]

A document resulting from an order of Benedict XIII following the disputation of Tortosa opens a window onto the general Jewish reading public in Spain, as well as the *Commentary*'s status within different layers of Sefardic society. Dated "the year of our Lord 1415," it lists holdings in twenty-six libraries of the Jews of Jaca comprising over six hundred volumes seized in the wake of Benedict's order to confiscate Hebrew books. The prevalence of "glosa de rabi Salamon de la Ley" (and other commentaries of Rashi) in the list is striking.

So is a tome called "declaraciones sobre rabi Salamon" in a library containing only one other volume, perhaps referring to a supercommentary of the sort then being composed by Aragonese rabbis in an increasing profusion.[133]

Study of Sefardic libraries and book culture is in its infancy.[134] While sources like book lists never fully expose the religious or intellectual world from which they hail,[135] they can provide precious glimpses of the way a work circulated—for instance, in the case of the *Commentary*, not always as a single unit but sometimes by individual books: Genesis, Exodus, and so forth.[136] More important, they can throw rare light on the place of a work among different circles of readers. A preliminary assessment of Spanish book lists suggests that the *Commentary*'s canonical materialization went beyond the intellectual elite to include ordinary Sefardic Jews.

Last Century in Spain: Between Embattlement and Diverse Forms of Enthronement

The closing century of Jewish life in Spain saw the *Commentary* achieve new forms of enthronement, yet we hear of groups who not only denounced the work but even subjected its author to mockery as Ibn Ezra and Nahmanides had never dared or, as best one can tell, wished to do. Reports of the latter come from Moses ibn Gabbai, an Aragonese rabbi of a traditionalist bent who authored a supercommentary on Rashi after fleeing anti-Jewish riots in Spain in 1391.[137] Ibn Gabbai moved in circles where Rashi was venerated, again, as in so many cases, first and foremost for his Talmud commentaries. Ibn Gabbai's teacher-colleague, Isaac ben Sheshet (1327–1408), went so far as to say that this "great luminary" from France had averted the Talmud's becoming "a sealed book."[138] For his part, Ibn Gabbai hailed Rashi as a "master, eminence, father of Israel" and "great luminary who enlightens the eyes of the blind with true precepts and just judgements."[139] Yet Ibn Gabbai knew of those who pilloried the *Commentary*, some with a zeal that, we might suspect, was proportional to its growing popularity. He reports their charges in the introduction to his supercommentary on the *Commentary* and responds in kind.[140]

The first group faulted the *Commentary* for being "utterly rife with *derashot* and *'aggadot*." Eschewing plain declarative sentences, they made it a point to "raise objections, cast doubt, and denigrate to satisfy their craving." For this, in ways Ibn Gabbai regrettably does not explain, they were rewarded with "public praise." Though some in Ibn Gabbai's day, like Profayt Duran, rued Rashi's overly midrashic approach, slashing criticism of this aspect of his exegesis as reported by Ibn Gabbai is clearly of a different order. Ibn Gabbai's retort is, if anything, more full throated. Reproving those "buried in their ignorance" who "pounced on the master's *Commentary*," Ibn Gabbai pronounces their "service" as "alien" (cf. Isa 28:21) and assails their temerity: "they say, 'By our tongues we shall prevail . . . who can be our master?' (Ps 12:5)." In biblically inflected prose, he goes so far as to demand their doom: "woe to them for they deserted him [Rashi]; destruction unto them for they make themselves distant from him." Allow such criticism of the *Commentary*, Ibn Gabbai seems to say, and all goes to ruin.

A second group of critics, "little foxes that ruin the vineyards" (Song 2:15), went so far as to "mock" Rashi himself, lambasting his ignorance of "scriptural plain sense meanings." What distinguishes them from the first group of detractors? It is hard to know for sure, but Ibn Gabbai seems to hint at an answer when he says that these naysayers "drank the seething waters (cf. Ps 124:5) that passed over the souls of those who study external disciplines" (*ḥokhmot ḥiṣoniyot*). By implication these critics saw Rashi's exegetical disabilities tied not so much to excessive use of midrash as to illiteracy in "external disciplines"—that is, science. Far from being extraneous, these detractors presumably saw the sciences as a key to unlocking the Torah's deepest meaning, either identifying the Torah's most profound esoteric layer with scientific truths or holding that certain sciences, like logic, were a prerequisite for sound exegesis. Minimally, the description of the second group summons a theme that hovered over reactions to the *Commentary* across Mediterranean lands: the conflict between rationalist understandings of Judaism and Rashi's philosophically innocent reading of the divine word. Again, Ibn Gabbai has no truck with the critics, nor does this occasion surprise. In the rabbinic circles in which he moved, science was not seen as the high road to Jewish enlightenment; indeed, it was viewed suspiciously, as a potentially injurious force. The point was acute in a post-1391 world where some blamed what they took to be insufficiently stalwart Sefardic resistance to Christian conversionary pressure on the corrosive effects of philosophy, facilitating the creation of the new subgroup in Spanish society called the *conversos*.[141] When Ibn Gabbai speaks of Rashi's critics drinking "seething waters" (*mayim ha-zedonim*), he uses a phrase largely reserved in post-1391 Sefardic discourse for those who immersed in the baptismal font, most under varying degrees of coercion.

As if responding to a blasphemy, Ibn Gabbai upbraids the critics for assailing "an angel of the Lord," but his rebuttal is not merely rhetorical. He knew that some rationalists invoked a talmudic tradition that "Greek wisdom" was studied in the patriarchal house of Rabban Gamliel of Yavne to justify their embrace of philosophy, even if cultivation of such learning might be prohibited more generally. The contents of the "wisdom" referenced in this rabbinic source is the subject of a responsum by Ibn Gabbai's colleague, Isaac ben Sheshet. In it, he indicates that the "famous books on physics" of the Greeks were excluded from the prohibition, but he still insists that study of this science all too easily leads to subversion of "the principles of our holy Torah," especially its two pillars, "creation ex nihilo and divine providence over individual members of the human race." The truth received at Sinai was "superior to everything," and certainly to Greek-based "investigations," which were "null and void compared to the Torah."[142] For his part, Ibn Gabbai stresses that the critics fail to note that the rabbinic license they invoke appertains, and even then only reluctantly, to leaders close to the government who need to refute "sectarians and heretics." Knowledge of "external disciplines," if perhaps a regrettable necessity, is not something to aspire to, especially given its potential to invite heresy. The conclusion was clear: "we have no need of, nor desire for, that wisdom to attain the truth of the true Torah." If the Judaism of Rashi's *Commentary* was devoid of "external sciences," this was a virtue, not a fatal flaw.

Yet Ibn Gabbai knew well that Maimonides had not only cultivated science but also ushered it into the holy of holies, making it central to theology and biblical interpretation. Having acquired a heroic image in segments of Sefardic scholarship, this great preceptor and his flagrantly intellectualist spirituality posed a challenge to Ibn Gabbai's conception of the *Commentary* as a supreme achievement. Already Isaac ben Sheshet had sought to weaken appeals to Maimonides's example in his responsum addressing "Greek wisdom." First, he explained, Maimonides had mastered the totality of Jewish law in a way that made him unique. This being so, his plunge into philosophy was a model for no one. Second, Maimonides wrote his *Guide of the Perplexed* to refute Aristotelianism, not consecrate it. Third, despite his good intentions, even Maimonides had been "drawn slightly" after Greek learning in detrimental ways. Ibn Gabbai confronts Maimonides's counterexample in a different way, pointing to a letter of Maimonides that cast the sciences as "maidservants, bakers, perfumers, and cooks" to the ultimate master, the Torah.[143] In other words, even Maimonides taught that the Torah was "a tree of life to all who hold fast to it" and science was but a subservient maidservant. Make no mistake about it, Ibn Gabbai as much as says. What is at stake in the battle over the *Commentary* is not just a proper reading of the Torah, as if this were a trifling thing, but irreconcilable visions of Judaism, with the *Commentary* embodying a traditionalist version of the faith untainted by distorting Greco-Arabic encumbrances.[144]

As if those who vilified Rashi for overuse of midrash or disregard of science were not enough, Ibn Gabbai upbraids another group, the "many" faultfinders of whom he has "heard" who trace what they deem Rashi's obliviousness to "the way of scripture" to his inadequate grammatical learning. That Rashi was not abreast of the great advances in Sefardic linguistic learning is undeniable, yet Ibn Gabbai is not ready to concede to those who took inspiration from "latter-day grammarians like David Kimhi and his successors" that this fact decisively compromises the *Commentary*. Indeed, he casts this blame as a "slander," apparently because he sees in it an indictment not just of Rashi but also of "the ancient [sages as] grammarians." To fault Rashi thus is in effect to say that the ancients upon whose linguistic insights he relied were innocent of the "truths of grammar" and "did not speak correctly." True, "the ancients trod a different path and spoke in a different parlance about the grammar of the holy tongue." Still, nomenclature should not be confused with insight. In outcome and depth, there is no divide between the "grammar of the ancients" upon whom Rashi relied and "moderns" like Kimhi. Not only are these defamers drowning in ignorance, but they will one day need to "face a reckoning."[145]

Ibn Gabbai's account of Rashi's fierce critics, without parallel in any other document by a Sefardic writer, prepares our study of the *Commentary*'s resisting readers in a wholly unexpected way. As we have seen, Ibn Gabbai was outraged by a composite of critics who disdained Rashi's grammatical learning, deplored his philosophical innocence, and scorned his overly midrashic exegesis. An exegetical work by a scholar from Aragonese Sicily that manifests all these dimensions appeared in the generation after Ibn Gabbai. What astonishes is that its author, Aaron Aboulrabi, was Moses ibn Gabbai's son-in-law!

In their own way, the vehement denunciations of the *Commentary* described by Ibn Gabbai attest to the work's outsized place in the minds of some in the opening decades of the fifteenth century. So does the assertion of an anonymous Spanish mystic nearer the end of the fifteenth century that Rashi's writings, including his "plain sense biblical commentaries," must be seen as a product of inspiration. The kabbalist, who presents himself as a personal recipient of revelatory experience, recorded his ideas in *Sefer ha-meshiv*, also known as *Sefer ha-mal'akh ha-meshiv* (Book of the Answering Angel). His vision of Rashi as literally inspired should be understood in the context of his teachings on canonical texts more generally, most notable among them that prophecy is a prerequisite for the composition of any authoritative work. Having noticed what he apparently considered an obvious fact, the authorization of Rashi's writings everywhere, he could only conclude that Rashi wrote under the aegis of what he calls the "secret of the garment," or "secret of Elijah."

After listing early figures whom he thought wrote through this revelatory medium—most long viewed as heroes of kabbalistic tradition, with the exception of Judah the Prince, redactor of the Mishnah—the kabbalist unexpectedly jumps to medieval times:

> Shimon bar Yohai and Jonathan ben Uzziel learned their wisdom, and they were deserving of the secret of the garment. . . . And Rabbi Hanina and Rabbi Nehunya ben ha-Kaneh and Rabbi Akiva and Rabbi Ishmael ben Elisha and our holy rabbi [Rabbi Judah the Prince] and Rashi and many others [learned] likewise. . . . The secret of the garment was given to those who fear God and meditate upon His Name; they have seen it, those men who are the men of God were worthy of this state. . . . Thus occurred in Rashi's time to his [Rashi's] master, and he taught him [Rashi] this secret, and by means of it [the secret] he composed whatever he composed, by means of his mentor and instructor.

In the continuation, the kabbalist insists that readers must "not ever believe" that Rashi composed either his talmudic glosses or "plain sense interpretations of scripture" (*peshaṭei ha-miqra'*) autonomously (*me-rosho*). These were revealed, explaining what the author presents as the surprising unanimity of approval Rashi commands: "This happened in the days of the Talmud and in the days of Rashi's master and in the days of Rashi too . . . and Rashi ended it . . . and this is the reason all the sages of Israel relied upon Rashi, as at that time they knew the secret."[146]

Interestingly, however much the author insists that the spirit filled Rashi, and however much the kabbalists generally (Nahmanides being an exception) are thought to devalue interpretation according to the plain sense, *Sefer ha-meshiv* does not impute a mystical meaning to Rashi's interpretations. On the contrary, it lauds Rashi's inspired transmission of scripture's plain sense.[147] Here is a vision of the superiority of Rashi's exegesis that rests neither on appreciation of its judicious mix of plain sense and midrashic interpretation nor its rootedness in rabbinic tradition but, rather, on its basis in revelation. Although Christian critics of Rashi in Paris in the 1240s had imputed a similar view to "the Jews," it remained idiosyncratic for the Middle Ages and only became more widespread in centuries to come, and is still sounded in various rhetorical registers.[148] On the eve of modern times, the *Commentary* had come to be viewed not only as the main commentary on the most important embodiment of revelation but, for one Sefardic kabbalist, also as a product of revelation itself.

Around the time a heavenly muse relayed Rashi's status as a quasi-prophet to the author of *Sefer ha-meshiv*, Rashi gained, in another apparently Spanish development, a new cognomen: "Parshan-data." The moniker played on the name of Haman's eldest son (Esth 9:6), dividing it into two words, one Hebrew (*parshan*) and one Aramaic (*data*), now taken to mean "explicator of the law." It appears first in a poem that to this day is almost always ascribed wrongly to Ibn Ezra. The poem speaks of a "star arising from France" (cf. Num 24:17), then offers a bit of advice in a rhymed couplet that would come to be sundered from the poem and cited separately as a ditty: "All French commentaries throw into the trash-heap (*'ashpata*) / Except for *Parshandata* and *Ben Porata.*" In the original, the referent of "Parshandata" was likely not Rashi.[149] Still, the figure in question was identified as Rashi by a student of Isaac Aboab, head of the foremost Castilian rabbinic academy on the eve of the expulsion. Another student of his spoke of "the great light who explained the Talmud and holy scriptures, Rashi the Frenchman—'Parshandata.'" Over the long term, it was in his role as explicator of scripture that the title endured.[150] As the last Jew left Spain, "Rashi the Frenchman" had come to be seen—in Spain, of all places—as "Parshandata," the Bible commentator par excellence.

Southern France: Initial Reception and Intercommunal Strife

When Rashi died in 1105, southern French Jewry was preparing to make its "literary debut."[151] The region, with its often-overlapping connections to northern Spain, encompassed Languedoc (Occitanea), Roussillon in northern Catalonia, and yet other geopolitical entities, most outside the county of Provence, although Jews often collectively called the region "Provence" (and so, following scholarly convention, shall I do at points as well).[152] Provençal scholars pursued traditional rabbinic studies in a network of rabbinic academies that produced a number of talmudic greats. As the twelfth century progressed, Rashi began to leave his mark, especially in writings of such rabbinic luminaries as Zerahyah Halevi of Lunel (b. ca. 1125) and Abraham ben David of Posquières (Rabad; d. ca. 1198). In Zerahyah's *Sefer ha-ma'or*, Rashi is extolled at Rabad's expense while Rabad chastises Zerahyah for what he deems uncritical reliance on northern French teachings that Rabad could find, even in the case of Rashi, "incorrect" or "insipid."[153] Yet when a disciple of Rabad, head of the prestigious school at Lunel Jonathan ben David Ha-Kohen, ranged glosses around the newly ascendant "mini-Talmud" of Isaac ben Jacob of Fez (Alfasi), he cited Rashi often.[154]

Details of the *Commentary*'s arrival in southern France are characteristically sparse. For reasons that remain obscure, Rabad accorded it more friendly treatment than Rashi's talmudic commentaries, even in disagreement with it.

In his largest work, a commentary on the halakhic midrash *Sifra'*, Rabad pronounces a gloss in the *Commentary* at odds with his opinion and the authoritative view in *Sifra'*, but forgoes explicit denigration, instead offering this cryptic remark: "the knowledgable will be radiant like the bright expanse of sky" (Dan 12:3). He presumably counted on his reader to recall the verse's interpretation in the Talmud ("this applies to a judge who gives a true verdict on true evidence") and thus get the point: "I'm right; Rashi is wrong."[155]

Rabad's rebuttals did not prevent others in southern France from depicting Rashi in the most grandiose terms. We recall that Abraham Ibn Daud offered a brief account of French rabbinic greats that omitted Rashi entirely. When it arrived in southern France, a flummoxed anonymous author, likely from Narbonne and writing no later than 1200, sought to make good the lacuna. In a heartfelt encomium that is still routinely ascribed in error to Ibn Daud, he told of

> a great light, unequaled in its brightness to the eye, he being the rabbi, great and pious, our teacher Solomon of Troyes . . . who received [his learning] from Rabbenu Gershom and his academy. He interpreted all of the Torah, Prophets, and Writings and the four orders of Gemara [in the Talmud]. . . . He left aside no matter, small or great, for which he did not offer a thorough explanation. Since the spread of his commentaries' character in the world . . . there has not appeared [such] in the whole world by any eminence [*ga'on*] or rabbi.[156]

Using a phrase that, in its original talmudic context, reinforced the idea of comprehensive learning ("no matter small or great"),[157] the Provençal glossator made it clear that Rashi's importance owed to his talmudic commentaries, but not to them alone. His achievements as a scriptural exegete also informed his unsurpassed status across the "whole world."

As Rashi's writings arrived in Provence, so did learning of a very different sort by way of scholars fleeing the Almohad invasion of Muslim Spain. While most settled in Christian Spain and some moved elsewhere in the "abode of Islam," a few headed for trans-Pyrenean Provence. There was the physician, linguist, and bibliophile Judah ibn Tibbon, "father of the translators." He settled in Lunel, where generations of "Tibbonids" produced original writings and continued the family tradition of translating Judeo-Arabic works, and eventually works by Aristotle and his Muslim expositor Ibn Rushd, into Hebrew.[158] There was also the grammarian and exegete, Joseph Kimhi (Kamhi), who resided in Narbonne, where sons Moses and David took up his exegetical metier.[159] Sponsored by influential rabbis and communal leaders,

Ibn Tibbon and Kimhi set out to apprise Provence of the scholarly feats of Jewish al-Andalus. Thus did "a Torah-centered community" respected for its "wide-ranging rabbinic scholarship and deep-rooted piety" turn with "remarkable zest and gusto to the cultivation of philosophy and other extra-talmudic disciplines."[160]

Among traditional fields already cultivated in the communities of southern France was biblical exegesis. It was nourished at its earliest stage by the eleventh-century native of Narbonne, Moses Hadarshan. A redactor and creator of midrashic collections, Moses also left a legacy of plain sense interpretation that, like his homilies, Rashi drew on, and thence preserved for eternity, in his *Commentary*.[161] At some point, Rashi's version of the combined plain-sense and midrashic approach, conceived in northern France, moved south, where it was bound to run up against the explosion of philological and rationalist interpretation advanced by the newly arrived Andalusians. The exegetical scene was further complicated by the legacy of another Andalusian pulling in a largely but not entirely similar direction, Abraham ibn Ezra. Having fled al-Andalus before the Almohad invasion, he had passed through southern French centers such as Béziers and Narbonne, engaging in oral exchanges and leaving behind exegetical works. A later rationalist from the region would hail his role in bringing rational "enlightenment" to it.[162]

With the permanent presence of Andalusian savants, prevailing southern French curricular emphases were swiftly overturned and biblical exegesis now developed along new lines. Standing at the head of the philological school was Joseph Kimhi, who decried commentators whose "*peshaṭ* is not *peshaṭ*" and imparted modes of interpretation grounded in grammar, philology, and reason.[163] Though rarely if ever mentioning Rashi in his commentaries, Kimhi did refer to him in a grammatical treatise in the course of seeking to justify his willingness to dispute earlier scholars of renown like Rashi's grandson Jacob Tam. To buttress his right to do so, he heralded Tam's own willingness to oppose an earlier great, his grandfather, despite Rashi's status as "the acme of scholars, chief enlightener, and crown of wise men."[164] Here was an expression of deep respect, but one that was also self-serving in a context where Kimhi sought to prove the right to contend even with those who bore wisdom's crown.

While Kimhi injected a heavy dose of Andalusian philology into Provençal exegesis, others inaugurated a philosophical approach shaped by Maimonides. The key figure was Judah ibn Tibbon's son Samuel, born in Lunel around 1165, who produced in 1204 the translation of Maimonides's *Guide of the Perplexed* that allowed local scholars to digest in Hebrew what would become the classic of medieval Jewish rationalism.[165] By that date, Maimonides's great legal tome, *Mishneh torah*, had been circulating for a decade, inviting Provençal accolades and critiques. In particular, its opening book, *Sefer ha-madda‘*, bestirred intense discussion and, in some quarters, serious misgivings owing to the intellectualist theology it promulgated as a matter of law. Samuel's original works included a commentary on Ecclesiastes and *Ma'amar yiqqavu ha-mayyim* (Treatise of the Gathering of the Waters), an involved exegesis of the creation story. In them, he theologized by way of biblical interpretation, often using allegory to make scripture speak in a philosophic key.[166] The goal was to mediate between science and tradition or, rather, reveal how scripture's inner meaning was partially philosophical.

Together, Maimonides's *magna opera*, Ibn Ezra's legacy, and inspiration provided by the Kimhi and Ibn Tibbon clans set the parameters within which subsequent receptions of Rashi's *Commentary* would unfold. If many Provençal scholars might once have welcomed a midrashic interpretation of the Torah full of tales involving supernatural events, they now viewed the *Commentary* through Andalusian-tinted glasses of one sort or another and, perhaps, a newly developing southern French stereotype of the northern French scholar as unenlightened, superstitious, graceless, and impulsive.[167]

Yet if southern France became Maimonindes's first and most stable European foothold where his philosophical, scientific, and legal heritage was revered for generations,[168] this abrupt new turn was hardly a matter of unanimous consent. On the contrary, in the 1230s it generated a bitter battle in which Rashi was destined to play a key role. As antirationalist factions sought to ban philosophical learning and its cherished Maimonidean textbooks, their opposite numbers argued that pursuit of philosophy enhanced religious understanding and enlivened the quest for spirituality. The storm quickly went intercommunal, drawing in Spain, northern France, and Maimonides's son in far-off Cairo. It also evoked harsh rhetoric. For example, southern French rationalists minced no words in casting northern French counterparts as "fools and lunatics with clogged minds" devoted to "superstitious nonsense and immersed in the fetid waters of unilluminated caves."[169] The gulf separating Andalusia and Ashkenaz became glaringly visible as the two traditions now mingled among various figures and factions in southern France. That gulf (and, for those who wished to draw them, any commonalities) could be cast in terms of the two cultures' emerging icons, Rashi and Maimonides.[170]

A basic issue concerned the way to interpret classical texts. The positions of both the rationalists and the antirationalists were complex. On the one hand, the latter condemned rationalist deviations from the plain sense of the words of scripture and the rabbinic sages in favor of nonliteral (often allegorical) interpretation. On the other hand, they could also object to rationalist commentaries that cultivated plain-sense exegesis of scripture in ways that sharply diverged from midrash.[171] For their part, rationalist exegetes inclined to philological plain-sense interpretation that typically undermined midrashic readings, but they recoiled at plain-sense understandings of scripture or rabbinic dicta that yielded "strangeness" (*zarut*, based on Arabic *gharib*, used to indicate apparent remoteness from rationality).[172] They had no trouble justifying rejection of midrash in certain circumstances, adducing gaonic and Andalusian precedents, but they could also see in rabbinic sayings a treasure trove of insight allusively expressed.[173]

As the assault on rationalism escalated, Rashi was brought into the fray as an authority of unsurpassed rank, or so some of the rationalists report. Two southern French Maimonideans even speak of a remarkable fiat, apparently accompanied by a curse for violators, in which the traditionalists proclaimed acceptance of Rashi's interpretations of biblical and talmudic texts a binding precept of Judaism. Here was a degree of canonical status accorded to Rashi nowhere attested in Ashkenazic literature itself. Indeed, we must, of necessity, interpret the sentiments imputed to the northern French traditionalists "not quite literally," for never do their writings "give the slightest hint of abdicating interpretive independence in favor of Rashi." [174]

At any rate, the rationalists rebuff the demand for unswerving fealty to Rashi with varying degrees of ire. As he admonishes anti-Maimonideans for, among other things, failing to examine Maimonides's writings properly, Samuel ben Abraham Saporta rejects what he casts as their call for all aggadic dicta to be interpreted according to Rashi. It, and the concomitant curse for transgressors, was "most extraordinary, a true wonder of wonders." If accepted, it would implicate not only contemporaries but also, retroactively, the Babylonian Geonim, whose interpretations often differed from Rashi's.[175] A more riled Asher ben Gershom thunders against "your decree to read the Torah, Prophets, Writings, and Talmud exclusively with our Rabbi Solomon's commentaries." If some wish to declare Rashi their sole "beloved," so be it, just as long as these self-appointed "princes and judges" do not foist this choice on others "without our consent."[176]

But Asher had another card to play, harnessing "Rabbi Solomon" to his own cause. Repulsing a condemnation of Maimonides for giving "reasons for the commandments," Asher points to Sefardic precedents, then deftly quotes the antirationalists' own highest authority. After all, had not Rabbi Solomon done the same—and regarding the ostensibly most incomprehensible precept, the red heifer, no less? While denying the interpretive veto his opponents wish to confer on Rashi, Asher nevertheless extols his intrepidity in interpreting certain verses in the Torah according to the plain sense, even if it means deviating from the Aramaic Targum or supplying an understanding without basis in the Talmud. Asher also gleefully highlights "many instances" (supposedly) where Rashi insists that scripture be read nonliterally on the understanding that it speaks with deliberate imprecision in order to "appease the ear"—that is, accommodate foibles of human understanding. In particular, he presents Rashi as holding, in accord with Maimonides but against the purported general outlook of northern French rabbis, that anthropomorphisms regarding the Deity are a product of the prophetic imagination rather than reality.[177] This is no small thing when we recall that no less an authority than Nahmanides relates that Maimonides's teaching on anthropomorphism played a major role in Ashkenazic condemnations of him.[178] So Asher found reason to praise "Rabbi Solomon," but it was for his own tactical gain and his praise was, in effect, that Rashi sometimes managed to glean what Maimonides so well knew. In this way he makes clear the conviction held by many rationalists, for whom Maimonides was the exalted standard against which all things, Rashi and his biblical scholarship included, ought to be measured.

Southern French Exegesis: Integration, Indifference, Indirect Criticism

As attempts to expel philosophically inspired teachings from southern French Jewry failed, biblical commentary became the genre of choice for articulating them.[179] A southern French school arose grounded in Maimonidean ideas and interpretive techniques as well as a library of non-Jewish philosophic literature translated from Arabic into Hebrew that allowed students to grasp the *Guide*.[180] Exegetes also walked in the footsteps of Abraham Ibn Ezra in his role as a pursuer of the plain sense and an exegete attentive to sometimes abstruse theological conundrums.[181] We have seen how these developments could generate attention to Rashi amid the heat of intra- and intercommunal strife. Away from the strife, the *Commentary* could be marginalized in later medieval southern French exegesis, but it was not invariably so. The general picture combines, among more subtle shadings, integration, indifference, and indirect criticism but no sustained frontal assaults. This picture began to be painted in earnest by the most influential of Provençal exegetes, Joseph Kimhi's younger son David.

A late-in-life participant in the rationalism controversy of the 1230s, David Kimhi took his interpretive cue from Rashi in some ways, but he developed, overall, an exegetical approach much more indebted to Andalusian biblical interpretation. Though generally allegiant to his Spanish predecessors' quest for the plain sense (and selectively open to allegory, writing a commentary in this vein on the early chapters of Genesis), Kimhi dealt with the gulf between plain-sense and rabbinic interpretation differently from the likes of Ibn Ezra. At the same time, he did not imitate Rashi's tendency to blur the lines between the two. Unlike Ibn Ezra, Kimhi incorporated large amounts of midrashim in his works, but unlike Rashi, he was very careful to distinguish them from grammatically and philologically informed interpretation of the plain sense. In juxtaposing *peshaṭ* and *derash*, Kimhi quoted midrashim cited by Rashi especially.[182] More than earlier scholars appreciated, he may also have learned the importance of "midrashic-type interpretations as an integral component in his commentary" from Rashi.[183] At the same time, Kimhi spells out some objections to rabbinic teachings in part as "a limited polemic" against Rashi.[184] Kimhi's dialogue with the *Commentary* was itself limited, since his Torah commentary was confined to Genesis. Still, like others, Kimhi testifies to Rashi's role as both a positive and a negative standard against which commentators defined themselves—or perhaps more to the point, felt compelled to define themselves.

Far more intense in its engagement with the *Commentary* is another work possibly emanating from southern France in the second half of the thirteenth century bearing the name "Ḥizzequni." (This work should not be confused with the better known work of this name penned by the northern French Hezekiah ben Manoah.) Composed by one Jacob ben Shabbetai, the work has affinities to the northern French Tosafist style, not least in relating to Rashi in some 70 percent of its comments.[185] The dominant concern is halakhic, with Rashi's Talmud commentaries also figuring.

Some early copyists bill Jacob's volume as a supercommentary on Rashi, as does its modern editor, but the work displays greater literary hybridity. Jacob does perform tasks associated with supercommentaries, as we shall see them in the next chapter, with some consistency: he establishes correct texts of the *Commentary*, indicates Rashi's sources, and of course, in a straightforward manner, explains Rashi. For all that, he interprets verses, or parts of them, that Rashi ignored, and cites over forty other authors and books.[186] His tract comprises a selected commentary on Maimonides's legal code, which, after the *Commentary*, attracts the lion's share of his attention. Jacob also has a good deal to say about Ibn Ezra, at times borrowing from him without attribution and even turning, momentarily, into an Ibn Ezra supercommentator.[187] Jacob's work is, then, hardly a pure supercommentary. If of southern French origin, it is not at all representative of exegesis from this sphere and easily stands as the closest thing to a supercommentary on Rashi ever written in that milieu—for lack of competition.

The closing phase of southern French exegesis increasingly operated within a philosophical framework, diminishing the likelihood the *Commentary* would impress, let alone inspire. At the same time, there is evidence that rationalist interpreters felt compelled to address Rashi, if only obliquely, aware that he had a popular audience. The greatest Jewish thinker of the fourteenth century, also the most important southern French Bible commentator of the period, Levi ben Gershom (Gersonides; 1288–1344) of Orange, had in his library two copies of the *Commentary*, in addition to a volume of Rashi's commentary on some of the Prophets.[188] Gersonides rarely cites the *Commentary*. Placing his work alongside Rashi's, one sometimes sees how the two commentators' vastly divergent religious presuppositions condition their differing interpretations of the same verse, as where, say, Gersonides's philosophically driven naturalism and praise for activist diligence clashes with the lessons taught by the *Commentary*, with its greater tendency toward quietism and reliance on God's providential hand. In Moses' declamation, "The Lord will battle for you; you hold your peace!" (Exod 14:14), Rashi finds a promise of supernatural victory because "the Lord will battle for you." Gersonides ventures that what may be intended is a military tactic: "it is possible that he [Moses] ordered them to be silent, neither to call out nor speak, so the Egyptians should not sense that they were very close to them and begin to shoot."[189]

Surface indifference to Rashi does not always tell the full story. Consider David Kimhi's contemporary and Samuel ibn Tibbon's relative and student, Jacob Anatoli, whose sermons, under the title *Malmad ha-talmidim* (Students' Goad), did much to expose Provençal Jews to philosophical ideas.[190] Rashi is barely mentioned in the work—but thrice by name, always in passing and regarding a minor point. On a few other occasions, Anatoli cites the *Commentary* without so stating.[191] As in Kimhi's case, however, it is possible that Anatoli addressed midrashim that he deemed problematic and might otherwise have ignored owing to the fame Rashi bestowed on them.

An example is the midrashic idea broached by Rashi that the reference to "all flesh" in the assertion that "all flesh (*kol basar*) had corrupted its ways on earth" (Gen 6:12) included the subhuman creatures. According to Rashi, the form that this corruption took was that "even domestic animals, beasts, and birds cohabited with those not of their own kind." By implication, then, the fauna shared responsibility with humankind for the depravity that had evoked the divinely wrought flood. For the likes of Anatoli, however, this line of interpretation violated a basic precept of science affirmed by Maimonides, after Aristotle: subhuman creations lack a capacity for choice, and hence for moral agency. If animals do not participate in the moral order, their requital due to good or bad conduct is ruled out from the start. Though Rashi goes unmentioned in Anatoli's discussion, a good reason to believe that Rashi's comment on the sins of the fauna in his *Commentary* loomed emerges from Anatoli's attempt to explain the scriptural attestation regarding "all flesh" that seemed so much at variance with finalities of science and theology. The expression "all flesh," he opined, refers to "humankind's conduct" alone. As for why scripture did not say so, Anatoli suggested that the anomaly rested on a broad-ranging interpretive principle that scripture at times uses a general term to refer to a single constituent encompassed by it where that constituent comprises the majority in the category or its "choice element." An example is Eve as "mother of all the living" (Gen 3:20), which obviously indicates her motherhood of terrestrial creation's choice element, people, and not of all living things despite what the Torah literally says. So it is with "all flesh," which refers to the select component in the category, humankind. Having devised an interpretation that reaffirms humankind's exclusive culpability for the flood, Anatoli might have left it there, but he instead pointedly contrasts "things" said according to "the method of *derash*" with what arose from analysis according to his "method of truth."[192] Why stress the point? Although silences are hard to read, Rashi's broadcast of the midrash, where it appeared as the embodiment of the plain sense, may have forced the issue or at least provided the irritant that spurred Anatoli to think about it.

Rationalist exegetes had another option when dealing with midrashim cited in the *Commentary*: to interpret them in keeping with philosophical precepts on a model exemplified in the first philosophical commentary on rabbinic dicta ever composed, by Samuel ibn Tibbon's son Moses.[193] A parade example of this phenomenon appears in the fourteenth-century Torah commentary of Nissim of Marseilles. It concerns the midrash adduced by Rashi about a miraculous fusing of the stones around Jacob's head at the time of his dream-revelation after these stones quarreled for the privilege of serving as the patriarch's pillow. For Nissim, the event described by the midrash occurred in a dream rather than in reality, although Rashi certainly provided no such indication. Still, even granting the point, a question remained as to the meaning of the midrash. Nissim dutifully explains how it contains a teaching about the need of the philosopher to delve into the ultimate origin of matter in order to arrive at a proof of the eternal creator who brought the physical world into existence. Thus was a midrash complete with quarreling stones turned into an instrument of discovery for those seeking guidance along the path of a philosophical life.[194] One cannot say for certain that Nissim never would have latched on to the midrash had Rashi not cited it, but it is undeniable that the *Commentary*'s increasing prominence gained for certain midrashim a familiarity that made them ripe for interpretation, especially if they contained elements inimical to the strict rationalist sensibilities Nissim and his ilk possessed in such abundance.

Another exegete hailing from the radically philosophical culture of late medieval southern France, Joseph ibn Kaspi, had little truck with midrashic fancies of the sort Rashi favored. As a commentator, he aimed to understand the Torah and other biblical books "by means of theoretical and logical speculation."[195] Yet this fervent Maimonidean found reasons to consult the *Commentary*. For instance, he referred readers to it for rabbinically authoritative explanations of the legal parts of the Torah that his own method, grounded in logic and normal linguistic usage, undermined. One who wished to know interpretations "faithful to the custom of our ancestors" in matters of normative practice should rely on "the *Commentary* of Rashi."[196] On a less complimentary note, in a youthful Ibn Ezra supercommentary, Ibn Kaspi invokes the principle of logic that a "thing cannot be known except by its contrariety" to explain how the *Commentary* can be revelatory. What he meant was this: to reveal the correctness of an interpretation of Ibn Ezra, one first needed to know its opposite, the wrongheaded reading of Rashi.[197]

And yet, because Rashi enjoyed a sterling reputation among traditionalists, Ibn Kaspi could find it convenient to trade on his name to defend Ibn Ezra against those who accused the Andalusian of harboring hidden hatred for the rabbinic sages and closet Karaite leanings. Critics of Ibn Ezra went so far as to allege concealment of his true view through false pledges of faithfulness to rabbinic tradition. To clear Ibn Ezra of the calumnies, Ibn Kaspi invokes "our Rabbi Solomon" who "always says, 'according to the method of *peshaṭ* this is the meaning.'" The idea was that Rashi provided an unimpeachably trustworthy precedent for deviation from midrash, thereby justifying Ibn Ezra.[198] Of course, Ibn Kaspi neglected to mention that Rashi had departed from midrashim of a legal sort in the name of plain-sense interpretation only on very rare occasion. Here, as in so many places elsewhere, the relationships between Rashi, the *Commentary*, and southern French readers prove complicated, with a rationalist devotee of the plain sense appealing to "our Rabbi Solomon" to clear a Sefardic hero of charges of heresy even as his own exegesis leaves little doubt that his invocation of Rashi is born mainly, if not wholly, of expediency.

Southern French Jewry shows as no other what happened to medieval Jewish communities after biblical exegesis and other branches of learning were transformed by the gradual injection and integration of philosophic notions into Jewish life.[199] With theological rationalism and a quest for the plain sense, sometimes in tandem, having come to figure centrally in exegesis in the Midi, it is little wonder that Rashi's heavily midrashic, philosophically innocent *Commentary* should have been seen as exemplifying a way of reading and thinking suitable, at best, for the multitude whom philosophically adept exegetes often disdained. And yet, this much Ibn Kaspi makes clear: the *Commentary* could not be shunted aside entirely.

While southern French Jewry breathed its last around 1500, literary achievement had seen a precipitous decline beginning as much as a century and a half before.[200] With the transfer of knowledge from Muslim Spain, Provençal savants commented on Maimonides's *Guide* and on Ibn Ezra's commentary on the Torah in profusion. By contrast, none ("Hizkuni" being a possible wholly aberrant exception) saw fit to write a commentary on the *Commentary*.

Augmented Impress in the Age of Print

By 1500, the invention that some Jews referred to as "the work of heaven" was around half a century old. By then, printing in Hebrew characters went back some three decades. While the new technology did not displace manual reproduction of Jewish books, it swiftly became the main way in which works like those of Rashi were broadcast. Like all books, the *Commentary*'s fate would henceforth be decided in the printing shop.[201]

Rashi's status as the paramount Torah commentator is brightly underscored in data from the first half century of Hebrew printing, during which time the books initially singled out for mechanical reproduction were those in demand in the manuscript age, whether for liturgical use, education, or moral instruction.[202] Since the *Commentary* served all three purposes (if we count as liturgical its use in "twice scripture and once Targum"), it is no wonder that it enjoyed prime status in early printing.

The *Commentary*'s history as a printed work is a story of firsts. In between 1469 and 1472/73, some two decades after the Gutenberg revolution and shortly after two Christian clerics from Germany issued the first publication ever to appear in Rome, eight Hebrew printed volumes, the first to be reproduced mechanically, saw the light of day in (or near) the same city. These included the *Commentary* which, typographical and paper analyses suggest, was one of the earlier volumes printed in the lot.[203] A new edition appeared in the southern Italian town of Reggio di Calabria on February 17, 1475, at the press of the Spaniard, Abraham ben Garton. It has the distinction of being the first dated Hebrew book ever printed. A year later, Solomon ben Moses Halevi Alkabetz printed the *Commentary* in Guadalajara, in an edition believed to be the first Hebrew book printed in Iberia, the other main center of early Hebrew printing after Italy.[204] An edition that appeared in Bologna in 1482, produced by Abraham ben Hayyim, was also pioneering. Not only did it contain printed vowels and cantillation signs for the first time but it also combined the text of the Torah with a commentary. This mixed-page format would become standard in the era of print, a layout that had been difficult to effect in manually reproduced works.[205]

When we recall that the advent of movable type made issues of canon more important,[206] it is certainly noteworthy that all but one of the Hebrew printing houses operating in the incunabular period issued an edition of the *Commentary*. (The lone exception, at Istanbul/Constantinople, issued only a single work during this time.) On a common estimate, 140 to 150 Hebrew books were printed in total circa 1470–1501. That nine were the *Commentary* speaks volumes for its centrality and, one assumes, its presumed marketability.[207] To the known incunabular editions others could possibly be added that left no trace. Following the three first printed editions (Rome, Reggio di Calabria, Guadalajara) the *Commentary* appeared in Bologna (1482); in the most famous Hebrew press in the incunabular period at Soncino (1483); in Naples and Lisbon (1491); and in Hijar (1490). The last incunabular edition appeared at Zamora in Castile in 1491–1492, as Spanish Jewry's demise loomed. One practically pictures traumatized Jews boarding leaky ships clutching copies of the newly printed *Commentary* to give them succor.

Beyond being printed frequently, the *Commentary* appeared in various configurations, some novel. There were lone editions, editions that included the text of the Torah, and editions that had both the Torah and the Targum. The most famous formal innovation was the so-called Rashi script, one of many ways Spanish script left its mark on Hebrew typefaces in Italy. The font, a semicursive Sefardic type embellished with an Italian roundness, would forever bear Rashi's name, even as it lacked any connection with the way Rashi wrote. The Soncino edition marked its first use for the *Commentary*, although it had by then appeared in Rashi's Talmud commentary.[208]

In the four centuries prior to print, the *Commentary* had circulated in hundreds of copies, an enormous number for a Hebrew work in the chirographic age. With printing, the number of copies exploded, reaching some three thousand in three decades.[209] Drawing on the formulation cited at the outset, we may say that the record of early printings points to the *Commentary*'s status as a foundational text transcending time and place and embodying a collective Jewish identity.

To the numbers that already testify eloquently to the *Commentary*'s popularity one can add "liminal devices"—those paratextual elements that mediated the *Commentary* to its readers—which further illustrate the work's growing reach.[210]Acclaiming his 1475 Reggio di Calabria edition, Abraham ben Garton cast the *Commentary* as "a light unto all the children of Abraham." Alkabetz included a similar flourish in his 1476 Guadalajara edition ("a light unto the Jews").[211] Coming from publishers, such lavish praises must obviously be taken with a grain of salt. Still, even if they were the stuff of marketing, such claims could only be made if they were believed to ring true with potential buyers. In this way they provide an oblique window on broader perceptions of Rashi's work.

Printing also facilitated the *Commentary*'s arrival in new regions. As the catastrophe of expulsion saw Spanish centers of Hebrew printing perish, the brothers Nahmias, Sefardic printers newly arrived in Istanbul (whether before or after 1492 is unknown), immediately printed Jacob ben Asher's *'Arba'ah turim*, the first known work produced with movable type in any language in the Ottoman Empire. Their next production, a dozen years later, was a Pentateuch with Rashi's *Commentary*, *haftarot*, and *megilot*, the latter two accompanied by the commentaries of David Kimhi and Ibn Ezra, respectively. In a colophon, the editor, Abraham ben Joseph ibn Yaish, described the plight of the exiles in *larmoyant* terms. In consequence of "tribulations," Bible study was in decline, owing partly to a dearth of copies of the Torah or, where such texts were available, to a lack of versions of it accompanied by the Targum or "the commentary." Though writing principally for Sefardic refugees, Abraham had no need to explain that the commentary in question was not one by a bygone Sefardic great but, rather, that of Rashi, viewed as an important element in Hispano-Jewish efforts at reconstitution after 1492.[212]

Print was the key to the creation of a standard version of the *Commentary* that would be relayed to posterity, slowing if not halting entirely the process of textual alteration to which Rashi's work had long been subject. Initially, early printed editions reflected fairly wide variations in the diverse manuscript traditions upon which they relied.[213] Accretions were possible even in the age of print, an example being, as we saw, the statement of Jacob to Esau at the time of their fraught encounter after years of separation: "I dwelled with the wicked Lavan, yet I observed the six hundred and thirteen commandments and did not learn from his evil ways."[214] In the main, however, the new technology curbed divergent readings. True, even centuries later issues of textual instability could bedevil, in part owing to heightened expectations of standardized texts that print created.[215] Still, as with other classics (e.g., the *Zohar*), a version of the *Commentary* determined mainly by printers that became the *textus receptus* was fixed.[216]

The emergence of a standard version is associated with the famous printing house in Venice of the Antwerp Christian, Daniel Bomberg (as he is referred to in Jewish sources), and, in particular, the rabbinic Bibles produced there. The latter provided a template for the format of Hebrew books for centuries—indeed, in many ways down to the present.[217] The first of these, produced by the Jewish apostate Felix Pratensis, appeared in Venice in 1517. Its format followed the pattern of codices intended for use in the synagogue; in David Stern's schematization of different Bibles, it was a "liturgical Pentateuch," a type of Bible in which the *Commentary* invariably appeared. The fact that Rashi's work appeared as the lone Torah commentary in this edition speaks for itself, indicating that the *Commentary* had become a "kind of universal presence in a Jewish Bible," despite its Ashkenazic origins.[218] In discussions of printing, emphasis is often placed on its revolutionary impact among Ashkenazic readers, now "exposed to the classics of the Sephardic library."[219] The point is certainly valid, but printing's role in disseminating the classic of Ashkenazic biblical scholarship to ever wider audiences is also worth remembering.

The *Commentary* reappeared in the far more influential second rabbinic Bible of 1525, though this edition added the Torah commentary of the most important model of Andalusian exegesis, Ibn Ezra. In so doing, Ashkenazic and Sefardic readers were symbolically joined into a single audience, as at least one manuscript had done almost exactly two hundred years earlier.[220] It was also this edition that largely determined what "Rashi said" forever, fixing the standard text.[221] As for rabbinic Bibles, they would appear in a plethora with an often shifting cast of commentarial characters, but Rashi's inclusion was always a given.[222]

That the 1517 rabbinic Bible came out in a slightly altered "Christian" version with a Latin dedication to the pope reminds us that the printed *Commentary* was also available to a Christian readership as never before. Already in the Middle Ages it had emerged as the "canonical" Jewish commentary in Christians eyes. Indeed, Christians often called it "the Hebrew gloss" (*Glossa Hebraica*), as if there were no other.[223] Now a much wider array of Christians, especially ones with Hebraist interests like Conrad Pellican and Paul Fagius, enjoyed access to this Jewish classic that had so decisively influenced greats of medieval Christian commentary like Nicholas of Lyre.[224] By the second half of the sixteenth century, with counter-Reformation militancy abroad, printing of the ever more famous *Commentary* became fraught. Where its inclusion in Bomberg's rabbinic Bibles once enhanced its dissemination and invited no remonstrance, a Venetian Christian incurred fines a half century later for printing the *Commentary* in too large a run.[225]

With heightened Christian awareness of the *Commentary* came a new type of reader who would influence its fate: church censors. Given its midrashic tilt, the *Commentary* was especially susceptible to censorial initiatives as virulent attacks on the Talmud and rabbinic literature intensified. Tomes in Latin,

German, Italian, and other languages—often appearing under menacing titles that spoke of "errors," "impieties," "perfidies," and "superstitions"—charged the rabbinic sages with immorality, blasphemy, and perversity. In 1553, anti-rabbinic words turned into anti-talmudic deeds against the backdrop of inflamed counter-Reformation antagonisms. Cardinal Giampietro Caraffa, soon to become Pope Paul IV but at the time head of the Inquisition in Rome, ordered the Talmud's burning, and other Italian cities followed suit.[226]

Already in the Middle Ages, church authorities had at times put the *Commentary* under the ban.[227] Now some sought its alteration, if not outright proscription. The *Index Lisbon* of 1581 interdicted Rashi's commentaries not only in Hebrew but also in the Latin translations of the Protestant "heretics," Pellican and Fagius.[228] In other *indices expurgatorii*, the policy was erasure of offensive passages and in some cases their replacement by more benign substitutes, rather than interdiction of the work as a whole. In 1584, the Franciscan monk Hipploitus Ferrariensis designated sixteen passages from the *Expositio Litteralis Magistri Schelohmó supra Pentateucum* for censorship.[229] An undated work by the architect of counter-Reformation theology, Robert Bellarmine (1542–1621), titled "Errors of Rabbi Solomon in the Five Books of Moses," singled out over fifty passages as blasphemous, offensive, obscene, or incriminating.[230] It is unclear how rigorously guidelines issuing from such works were applied and to what degree editions produced outside of Italy suffered suppression.[231]

Some of the Christians requiring a kosher version of the *Commentary* were Jewish apostates who, having studied Rashi in their youth, now exerted themselves to shape, or alter or delete, what Rashi taught his readers—that is, to suppress or "refine" the *Commentary*, as the term that came to be used for censorship, *ziqquq*, meant originally. In 1596, *Sefer ha-ziqquq* (*Index Expurgatorius* or *Book of Purification*), a work mainly of the apostate Domenico Gerosolomitano, required "thorough expurgation in all editions." Domenico introduced further erasures and changes to an already censored version of 1591.[232] Ciro da Correggio was another Jewish convert to Christianity who served as a corrector of Hebrew books. Viewing a copy of the *Commento di Rabbi Salomone sopra le leggi* that had already undergone censorship three times, he determined that it remained "partly still in need of expurgation" in three places, all involving midrashic interpretations, while noting that earlier erasures had become readable "because of the faded ink."[233]

Apart from objections deriving from traditional Christian anti-Jewish polemic, there was an additional reason that the *Commentary* bestirred censorial obsessions: a sense that it somehow lent credence to Protestant doctrine or abetted Protestant attacks on the Catholic Church. Seeing Christians as descendants of Esau/Edom, Rashi routinely blamed Esau/Edom (that is, Catholic Christendom) in his *Commentary*, not least for depredations committed against Jews. In what some censors saw as a parallel too close for comfort, reformers invoked the antichrist and his minions to condemn the enthralling church. On these grounds, certain of Rashi's glosses were deemed deserving of eradication "not only for their own merits" but also because they lent support to heretics.[234]

Censorial efforts remind us that the printed word became a medium in which authority was not only represented and communicated but also "denigrated and contested."[235] Witnessing this dialectic is an anthology of Rashi supercommentaries printed around 1525 in Istanbul (or, as the city's name appears on title pages of Hebrew books produced there, *Qushta / Qushtandina*—that is, Constantinople). The volume's name itself tells a tale: *[Super-]Commentaries on Rashi* (*Perushim le-rashi*). It stands as the first anthology of Hebrew exegetical supercommentaries ever printed. In this sense, its very format is instructive of the status of the *Commentary* in the main Jewish center in early modern Islamdom at the time Bomberg was helping to canonize it in Christendom. This is so, in the first instance, because an anthology requires sufficient commentaries to fill it; and in the second, because the decision of a publisher to gather expositions on a work suggests a reading public eager for such fare. The entries in *Commentaries on Rashi* are notable for their Sefardic origins, betokening the attention commanded by the main work of Ashkenazic exegesis at the dawn of early modernity.[236]

Yet a less harmonious story unfolds between the covers. Three of the anthology's four constituents—the glosses of Samuel Almosnino, Jacob Kenizal, and Moses Albelda—perform as expected, explicating the *Commentary*, addressing apparent contradictions, and otherwise fulfilling their supercommentarial calling. By contrast, the fourth, by Aaron Aboulrabi, often adopts an adversarial stance toward Rashi's handiwork that at times turned downright derisive. As no manuscript of his work survives, we have an anonymous printer to thank for keeping Aboulrabi's complex response to Rashi available for our consideration.

The decade that saw Bomberg produce what would become the standard version of the *Commentary* in Europe's leading center of printing and the appearance in the Ottoman capital of *Commentaries on Rashi* also marks what would prove to be the great divide in the history of Rashi supercommentary. It was in Istanbul that the leading Ottoman rabbi, Elijah Mizrahi (ca. 1450–1526), completed (as much as he ever would) what would become the classic entry in the field. Upon his death, Mizrahi's son, Israel, took his father's prodigious tome to Venice, where work on it was completed at the house of Bomberg in

August 1527. Before the century was out, it would be printed three more times. Interest in "the Re'em," as Mizrahi's work was called after his rabbinic acronym (**R**abbi **E**lijah **M**izrahi), increasingly took the form of glosses on it and a typically Jewish subgenre was born: the super-supercommentary.[237]

The role played by commentaries in turning Mizrahi's work into the classic supercommentary reenacts a process that saw supercommentators help to transform the *Commentary* into a classic. By the seventeenth century, we find the offshoot of a prominent Ashkenazic rabbinic family, Shabbetai Sheftil Horowitz (d. 1660), instructing his offspring in a sort of spiritual last will and testament to find each year a new *supercommentary* to supplement their weekly review of the pericope with Rashi.[238] By then, the choices were many. It is to this body of literature, and the way this particular exegetical form enhanced the *Commentary*'s authorization and naturalization in new environments, that we now turn.

3

Interpreting the Interpreter

SUPERCOMMENTARIAL RECEPTIONS IN ASHKENAZ AND SEFARAD

TO BOLSTER HIS claim that the *Commentary* acquired an "absolute indispensability quite apart from the function it was originally intended to fulfill," Nahum Sarna rightly points to the vast supercommentary tradition that came to surround it.[1] Those who chose to probe and enlarge on the *Commentary* number in the scores at least, and possibly in the hundreds, depending on how capacious a definition of "supercommentary" one uses.[2] (The degree to which the work has occupied attention orally over nine hundred years may border on the infinite.) Some supercommentaries have appeared time and again. In one extraordinary case, an anthology of four such works published in Warsaw in 1862 under the title *'Oṣar ha-perushim* may have reappeared in facsimile editions, on average, almost annually for over a century.[3] The genre has seen a recent surge in multiple languages, both in terms of printings of older supercommentaries appearing yet again or for the very first time, and in terms of new offerings, many pitched at popular audiences.[4] If a canonical work is one that attracts commentaries, then, as I noted at the outset, the *Commentary* may be the most canonical singled-authored Jewish work of all time.

Supercommentaries played a significant role in the *Commentary*'s authorization and valorization. Simply by selecting Rashi's interpretation of the Torah as their object of exposition, supercommentators accorded it a special status and stamp of *auctoritas*. In the case of some Spanish supercommentators, the approach they brought to their study of the *Commentary* and the interpretive techniques they applied to it could even bespeak a stance toward Rashi's exegetical word commensurate with the one adopted toward other sacred texts, up to and including scripture. By the end of the Middle Ages, most Sefardic supercommentators were reading the *Commentary* according to a principle of omnisignificance. This principle, most familiar from midrashic interpretations of scripture but also from amoraic readings of the Mishnah, posited that each nuance of the text under scrutiny bore a meaning "both comprehensible and significant."[5] Then, too, where Rashi presented ideas that troubled some of the supercommentators, they almost never sought to delegitimize or attack the *Commentary*, let alone Rashi's rabbinic sources. Rather, in keeping with propensities and strategies of commentators on canonical works across traditions, they found ways to read difficult ideas in a manner that naturalized them. Here we have an instance where Judaism, like the other "Abrahamic faiths," functions as much as a "religion of the commentary" as it does a "religion of the book," with supercommentators imbuing Rashi's text with a profusion of meanings as biblical commentators did the same with scripture.[6]

This astonishing "productivity" of the *Commentary*—what one can call its ability to "take on a new life in changing social and literary circumstances"[7]—is brought into sharp relief when compared with two medieval Latin counterparts from the spheres of exegesis and theology, Nicholas of Lyre's *Postills on the Entire Bible (Postilla super totam bibliam)* and the *Four Books of the Sentences* by Peter Lombard. Beginning in the fourteenth century, Nicholas's work became the most widely read Latin biblical commentary after the *Glossa ordinaria.* Circulating in an astoundingly large number of manuscripts, over eight hundred of which survive, it was the first Christian biblical commentary to be printed.[8] A recent student of the *Postills* observes that the work's "popularity withstood the test of time," but also notes that "the final print edition of the text appeared in 1634"![9] While most impressive by conventional standards, how fleeting such eminence seems alongside the timeless *Commentary* that, written more than two centuries before the *Postills*, is boundlessly reprinted and sets the curriculum of traditional Torah study nigh a millennium on. The only commentaries that Nicholas attracts nowadays are from scholars. Consider also Lombard's volume, the most commented-upon Christian text ever composed, save for scripture itself.[10] Although it served as the standard textbook for advanced theology in the Christian West from the twelfth through the sixteenth centuries, scholia on the *Sentences* petered out around the time of one of its last glossators, a friar named Martin Luther. By contrast, the *Commentary* attracted commentaries through modern times and yet does so.

In what follows, I trace the supercommentarial fortunes of the *Commentary* in France and, to a lesser extent, Germany, as well as in Hispano-Jewish domains, "Ashkenaz" and "Sefarad" being the two main medieval centers where works of Rashi supercommentary arose. The emphasis falls slightly more on Spain, first, because only there were supercommentaries in the strict sense produced. For their part, as we shall see, medieval French and German exegetes often poured their biblical scholarship into more pliable literary molds than the dichotomous categories of "commentary" and "supercommentary" are able to capture. The other reason for our focus on the Sefardic supercommentary tradition is that the sorts of canonizing processes mentioned in earlier discussions are most on display here. It was in Spain that the issue of the arrival of Rashi's work in a new religious environment played out most intensely.

Before plunging into the *Commentary*'s fate in works of supercommentary, some reconstruction of this largely neglected mode of exegetical expression is in order. I start with its generic contours, bearing in mind Jacques Derrida's observation that to say "genre" is to draw a limit, with "norms and interdictions not far behind";[11] I then touch on aspects of the genre's literary and intellectual dynamics, especially as they bear on processes of canonization. Some of these dynamics apply in the case of supercommentaries written in the other very different sphere in which medieval Jews cultivated the genre—namely, academic philosophy.[12]

Although glosses on an earlier biblical commentary took multiple forms and filled multiple offices, supercommentators took it as their main task to clarify the commentary with regard to its meaning, sources, and at times methods. Some supercommentators were aware of variant readings, some born of textual corruption, and they devoted energy to establishing the correct base text of a commentary. Regarding broader generic features, we may fruitfully consult a few highly insightful pages devoted to the topic by Uriel Simon in a study of Abraham ibn Ezra's supercommentators bearing the winning title "Interpreting the Interpreter."[13]

Simon's first observation is that a supercommentary "does not refer directly to the primary text being glossed and explained, that is, to scripture." Simon adds that a supercommentator's choice to gloss a commentary rather than scripture should elicit surprise in light of the latter's "double advantage." Scripture, as the product of revelation for traditional exegetes, bears the stamp of incontrovertible truth, whereas the veracity of the commentator's words is not assured and depends on "powers of persuasion." Scripture is also assumed by traditional readers to be immune from processes of textual corruption, whereas supercommentators grant the possibility of corruption in the commentaries. Simon further observes that the supercommentary's primary focus on a commentary is reflected in a conspicuous formal sign, its cueing device: the lemmas (Hebrew *dibbur* or *divrei ha-matḥil*) in a supercommentary come from the commentary rather than (or at least in addition to) scripture.[14] To illustrate graphically what this transformation in the supercommentarial lemma declares, Simon summons a manuscript in which Ibn Ezra's commentary stands as the visual focus at the center of the codex surrounded by five supercommentarial attendants.[15] Perhaps this format was not typical, but it certainly is symbolic. If we recall that the platform of the page itself sends a message, this layout illustrates the reality of supercommentary's creation of a new textual hierarchy.[16] In the presence of supercommentaries, commentators ascended to a higher pedestal, drawing admiration and study as never before. In this way, supercommentary by its nature speaks to issues of authority as cast in the distinction between "antiqui and moderni" (*rishonim* and *'aḥaronim*) and some of the classic tropes used to configure it, such as "decline of the generations" and "dwarfs on the shoulders of giants."[17]

Yet for all that the genre of supercommentary seems to epitomize "textual deference" even more than commentary,[18] writers in the field inhabited a complex discursive universe. As the modern coinage "supercommentary" implies, the genre involves a high degree of authorial self-positioning with respect to an earlier writer and a "deep consciousness of forming part of a tradition, whatever their authors' views on their relation to that tradition."[19] But there, in some measure, was the rub. While a biblical commentator directly engaged inerrant scripture, supercommentators engendered a trialogue among scripture, commentator, and themselves in which scripture presumably stood at the apex of authority, even as it was the commentator who remained at the center of the supercommentator's attention and even claimed his loyalty. The literary secondariness built into supercommentary was further complicated by an element of self-interest because, like commentators of all sorts, supercommentators connected their reputations to a "big name," reinforcing their authority by way of the text on which they commented.[20] Thus it was that observations attached to Rashi's "normative" exegesis could provide a way for a later writer to propagate his own ideas.[21]

So, we must not be beguiled by the often obsequious stance and tone of supercommentators, genuine though they may be. While insisting on the superior worth of their source texts, supercommentators, like commentators of all sorts, could write with impressive acumen, and minds of their own. Thus did they direct their readers to particular understandings of classic works.[22] In this way does supercommentary, like so much other glossatorial activity, summon the dialectical interplay between canonical limitation, on one hand, and commentarial expansion and revision, on the other.

The field in which Jewish scholars have most cultivated supercommentary is biblical interpretation, although the three main works that attracted such glosses—the Torah commentaries of Rashi, Ibn Ezra, and Nahmanides—did so, especially in Rashi's case, for different reasons. In the first instance, Ibn

Ezra called forth a supercommentarial response owing to his laconic style (or what one modern scholar calls a "hit-and-run approach") that left readers to flesh out the full import of his typically terse remarks, even where they lacked any esoteric content and addressed straightforward interpretive difficulties.[23] Also evoking a need for clarification were Ibn Ezra's excurses on arcane theological topics, like names of the deity, or his allusions to astrological and astromagical "secrets" that constituted, in his view, the deepest layer of the Torah's narratives and laws. He called attention to other topics that he wrapped in a layer of studied concealment ("the prudent one will stay silent"), like daring hints to post-Mosaisms in the Torah. Supercommentators could not resist the temptation to crack the code.[24] Similarly, Nahmanides's typically expansive and pellucid Torah commentary might have attracted little or no supercommentary absent its mystical allusions. Although the heavily veiled kabbalistic secrets make up less than a tenth of the work, they evoked a torrent of supercommentarial expansion.[25] Perhaps the key point in all this is that while, like Rashi's glossators, supercommentators on Ibn Ezra stemmed from a range of geocultural environments, they generally shared his exegetical approach and the main theological underpinnings of his commentary, as Nahmanides's glossators were fellow mystics who focused their attention on this commentator's kabbalistic ideas out of their shared conviction that these made up Judaism's deepest level of meaning. Supercommentators on Rashi, by contrast, came (and come) from a far wider range of backgrounds, and they have written over a far more sustained period of time. Little wonder that their works show more elaborate acts of mediation of the *Commentary* to new readerships, as well as a range of strategies to naturalize the work in diverse "foreign" environments, in the manner of other glosses on canonical works.

The *Commentary* had no "secrets," but it did have an often enigmatic component that bestirred supercommentarial impulses as no other: its midrashim. On the most basic level, glossators often sought to identify the source of a given midrash in one or another rabbinic compendium, which Rashi almost always left unstated, or to explain Rashi's preference for one version of a midrash over those found in other rabbinic sources. Even more energy was invested in what became perhaps the most ubiquitous of supercommentarial activities surrounding the *Commentary*: attempts to identify a textual trigger for the expositions that Rashi used in his quest to supply rabbinic interpretations that "settled the scriptural word and its sense in a fitting manner." On yet a different plane, since Rashi never explained the meaning of midrashim that he adduced, supercommentators, especially those outside the Ashkenazic world, often felt a need to unravel the significance of these dicta, especially if they seemed empirically, morally, or theologically questionable.

At times, this required an explanation that bridged the gap between a certain fantastical reading grounded in midrashim understood literally and presented without further discussion in the *Commentary*, at one end, and a different set of presuppositions and ideas that obtained widely in Mediterranean centers of Jewish learning, at the other end.

The impact of exegetical supercommentaries has barely been researched, but it stands to reason that it was considerable if supercommentaries on Quran commentaries are any indication. Walid Saleh observes that it was through supercommentarial works that the quranic commentary tradition was "assessed and developed."[26] In some cases, the difference made by the Jewish supercommentaries is striking and clear. Those who glossed Nahmanides's Torah commentary not only helped to turn it into a canonical work of kabbalah but also amplified Nahmanides's already mighty voice in an increasingly tense battle between mysticism and philosophy in later medieval times.[27] Although hard to measure, one effect of the growing body of supercommentary on Nahmanides was that Nahmanideanism became perhaps the most potent speculative alternative to Maimonideanism.[28] With such observations in mind, we seek to discern the significance of the supercommentary tradition on the *Commentary*, as it at once reflected and contributed to growing regard for the work in high and late medieval times.

Incipient Supercommentary in France and Germany

In the previous chapter, I surveyed high points of the *Commentary*'s fortune in France and Germany. It remains to look at its supercommentarial component in its mostly incipient forms. The story unfolds, as the Spanish scholar Profayt Duran observed, against generally increasing Ashkenazic abandonment of Bible study in high and later medieval times.[29] Despite this neglect, or perhaps in compensation for it, there swept through Ashkenaz something of a Great Awakening in terms of the *Commentary*, setting the stage for the supercommentaries on Rashi that proliferated in the central and eastern centers in early modern times. Prior to their advent, French and German writers often adopted literary forms that combined commentary and supercommentary in fluid ways.

On the whole, Rashi's northern French successors spared no time for distinct sessions devoted to the Bible within their academic curriculum.[30] While Jacob Tam, the mightiest name in the Tosafist pantheon, did not neglect the Bible entirely, he did tell a correspondent that study of it was for children.[31] He also coolly writes off an apparently categorical talmudic imperative to devote a third of one's study to scripture by insisting that, for those who study the Babylonian (*bavli*) Talmud, the obligations to devote a third of one's time to study of the Bible and another third to study of Mishnah is fulfilled since, as another rabbinic dictum had it, the Talmud was "suffused with scripture, Mishnah, and Talmud."[32] Tosafists who did cultivate the Bible saw scripture, not Rashi, as their primary object of study. Still, by the twelfth century's end, some in northern France devoted "intense, if not always consistent, scrutiny and analysis" to Rashi, asking why he chose to make a particular comment, what his sources were, and so forth.[33]

Over time, a large number of French and German collectanea, consonant with the style of the *Commentary* in varying degrees, took augmented account of Rashi. A list of such works, hardly exhaustive, includes *Da'at zeqenim, Hadar zeqenim, Moshav zeqenim, Pa'aneaḥ raza* of Isaac ben Judah Halevi, and Hayyim ben Paltiel.[34] Some Tosafists pursued midrashic exegesis; others, finding it impossible to return to the unaffected way that Rashi traversed the border between *peshaṭ*-oriented and rabbinic interpretation, pursued advances in peshatist analysis while declining to push independent interpretation shorn of midrashic accretion to its apogee, as had Rashi's grandson, Samuel ben Meir. At all events, the norms and interdictions of generic consistency weighed little. No pure supercommentaries emerged in the twelfth- and thirteenth-century writings designated collectively as "Tosafist Torah commentaries," which make up a midrash-oriented branch of French exegesis somewhat at odds with Rashi's more *peshaṭ*-oriented approach. Still, treatment of the *Commentary* as an increasingly central focal point is palpable, at times in ways that find expression in the layout of the manuscript page.[35]

Coming closest to an early supercommentator is the Tosafist Isaiah ben Mali di Trani (Rid; died ca. 1250). Although a product of Byzantine Italy, Isaiah spent his formative years in the Rhineland such that his learning can seem more Ashkenazic than Italian. His exegesis has points of contact with the early stratum of medieval Byzantine interpretation that may have influenced Rashi, but it is aberrant as a product of the Byzantine sphere in so strongly reflecting Ashkenazic trends. It is possible that Isaiah wrote his *Nimmuqei ḥumash* (*Explications of the Pentateuch*) while young, soon after departing Germany.[36] Of the work's roughly one hundred and fifty comments, around forty constitute independent plain sense readings, and a similar number address law, custom, numerology (*gemaṭriya*), theology, and esoterica. The rest, just under half, deal with Rashi, leading Ephraim Kanarfogel to call this work the closest thing to a supercommentary on Rashi produced through Isaiah's day, even if it is distant from this designation compared to entries to come.[37]

In the same century, Northern Europe produced a work sometimes billed as the first Rashi supercommentary, although this characterization does not really pass muster: Hezekiah ben Manoah's *Sefer Ḥizzequni* (*Ḥazzequni*).[38] Hezekiah culled from a wide range of sources including, in a rare departure for Northern European exegetes of his day, such representatives of the Spanish–Provençal tradition as Ibn Ezra, David Kimhi, and possibly Nahmanides.[39] In his introduction, Hezekiah refers to some twenty works, although he apparently consulted many more, from which he "extracted the best part."[40] This fact alone excludes his work from the category of supercommentary, moving it emphatically toward what Sara Japhet calls a "compilatory" form.[41] Still, Hezekiah does accord to Rashi pride of place, mentioning his name alone in the introduction and promising never to "dispute" but only to "augment" him.[42] Described in the manner of a bibliographer, then, *Ḥizzequni* comprises an anthology containing some original ideas (perhaps 10 percent of the total)[43] with a significant supercommentarial increment, the latter attesting to the ever greater claims that Rashi was making on writers in northern France.

To see the mix in Hezekiah's work, let us consider his handling of Rashi's midrashic interpretation of the phrase *zot ha-pa'am*, "this one" or "this time," in Adam's *cri de coeur*: "This one at last / Is bone of my bones / And flesh of my flesh" (Gen 2:23). The first speech of a human being reported in the Torah, it raises many questions, not least about the referent of *zot*: Does it refer to the woman (in which case the phrase means "this one") or to the occasion ("this time"), or to something else? More broadly, what inspired Adam's outpouring of relief or gratitude? The key could seem to lie in Adam's allusion to a prior event or series of events: "this time," unlike foregoing ones, or "this one," unlike preceding ones. But was the referent some earlier "unsuccessful fashioning of a man and a woman"[44] or Adam's prolonged search for a helper? If the latter, the sequence of verses might suggest that earlier candidates had come from the ranks of the animal kingdom, since the immediately prior verses describe a divine determination to resolve the problem that it was "not good for man to be alone" by creating a "fitting helper" followed by subhuman creatures and Adam's naming of them.[45]

Rashi, with characteristic concision, allayed a number of quandaries by reformulating a midrash on *zot ha-pa'am* in condensed fashion and giving it as his sole (and thence, one might argue, plain sense) interpretation: "it teaches that Adam mated with every domesticated animal and wild animal but his appetite was not assuaged by them."[46] Here, much was made plain in a few words. Adam's cry is indeed linked to the immediately preceding verses, which relate the genesis of the animals. (It also dovetails with the testimony in the following verse that "a man leaves his father and mother and clings to his wife, so that they become one flesh," a verse that suggests the union between man and woman was the end goal of the story of the primordial pair.)[47] By opting for the midrash that he did, Rashi, as in countless places, effectively banished from the popular mainstream other midrashim he thought lexically or contextually wobbly.[48]

Hezekiah expresses no concern whatsoever in the face of Rashi's assertion that the first human exemplar engaged in serial acts of bestiality. Still, before addressing this midrash, he supplies a reading of the verse that echoes an interpretation popular among Tosafist interpreters, some of whom ascribe it to Ibn Ezra (it does not appear in his commentary), although it may in fact trace to Rashbam. Requiring no data beyond those reported in the Torah, thereby qualifying as a reading in consonance with the plain sense, it takes "this one" to refer to a unique inversion of the natural order: "On this occasion, a female issued from a male, whereas henceforth it will not be thus but rather the male will issue from the female."[49] Here is the sort of immanent reading popular among some in northern France that clearly departs from Rashi's infiltration into the narrative of unattested midrashic details such as serial interspecial mating in paradise. Having recorded this reading, Hezekiah, *qua* Torah commentator, could have moved on, but in a manner that shows how his work marks a transitional phase to the world of late medieval Ashkenazic supercommentary, he instead notes how he was struck by a problematic implication of Rashi's interpretation. Projecting onto the primordial subhuman creatures a lone first model (despite scripture's suggestion that they were created in collectivities), Hezekiah observes that if each species had an initial single exemplar who mated with Adam, all primordial animals should have become extinct while in the garden because the Talmud teaches that animals who have intercourse with human beings become sterile. To this conundrum Hezekiah found a typically Tosafist harmonizing solution: "one must say that they [the other creatures] conceived prior to Adam's having intercourse with them."[50] However one rates this solution, such ruminations illustrate how French exegetes increasingly felt inclined, or impelled, to explain issues arising specifically from rabbinic dicta cited in the *Commentary*, bringing to mind one definition of a canonical work— namely, a work that makes a claim on participants in a tradition.

Traveling down the supercommentarial path most in northern France was Judah ben Eleazar of Troyes, whose *Minḥat yehudah* (Offering of Judah) is traditionally dated to 1313. To judge by its over twenty surviving manuscripts written in a range of scribal hands (Byzantine, Ashkenazic, Sefardic, Italian, and Provençal), Judah helped to spread the *Commentary*'s vision far and wide.[51] He begins by explaining why Rashi's words are occluded "from the eyes of many."

Some comments of Rashi are "opaque" and some contradictory. Yet others seem superfluous because what they teach appears obvious, such that their purport and necessity requires explanation. Then there are glosses that appear to contradict scripture or the Talmud. These were the main issues calling out for Judah's supercommentarial intervention.

In light of this point of departure, it is no wonder that his leading modern student concludes that Judah saw himself "first and foremost" as a supercommentator, while others go so far as to acclaim him the initiator (or at least among the founding fathers) of the tradition of supercommentary on Rashi.[52] Yet, Judah's supercommentarial impulse is not total. Even in his introduction, Judah states his intention to engage sources other than Rashi, both classical (Talmud, midrashic compendia) and recent (Tosafot, Moses of Coucy). In fact, he sometimes interprets the Torah in ways that depart from the *Commentary* and explains verses that Rashi passed over in silence. Hazoniel Touitou estimates that a fifth of *Minḥat yehudah* is unrelated to Rashi.[53] Here is a reminder of what was stated at the outset: Ashkenazic exegetes often poured exegesis into protean literary forms that the binary categories "commentary" and "supercommentary" fail to capture.

Decline of the Generations: German Supercommentary After the Black Death

With French Jews expelled from the royal domain and neighboring principalities in 1306, and the end of French Jewish life decreed in a final edict of expulsion in 1394, it fell to scholars in Germany to preserve the lamp of Ashkenazic learning, but they were often forced to do so amid devastating crises. A months-long paroxysm of violence in 1298 that came to be known as the Rintfleisch massacres and another wave of killing a generation later called Armleder (1336–1338) portended a frenzy of mass anti-Jewish violence in the wake of the Black Death. The calumny that Jews brought on the catastrophic plague by poisoning wells, springs, and streams, in tandem with accusations of ritual murder and charges of host desecration, fueled anti-Jewish animosity and gave rise to the judicial murder of Jews and state policies of expulsion.[54] German-Jewish literary expression, already laid low in the first half of the fourteenth century, ceased almost entirely in the second half, as leading rabbis were killed and as the survivors of the pogroms were hit with expulsions beginning around 1390, sundering the chains of transmission from teacher to student that had sustained Ashkenazic tradition. An eastward shift ensued as many sought refuge in Austrian centers such as Vienna, Wiener-Neustadt, and

Krems, where the violence had been less fierce—although in Vienna, too, in 1420–21, Duke Albrecht V had hundreds of Jews taken prisoner, tortured, forcibly baptized, despoiled, and executed, and the survivors expelled (the Gezerah of Vienna).[55] It was in this distressed, unstable setting that Ashkenazic exegesis, especially in new lower Austrian centers, fitfully continued to unfurl.

Opening a window on biblical scholarship in the shadow of the pogroms was an outsider to Ashkenazic culture, Dosa "the Greek" of Vidin, who fled Bulgaria as it was overrun by the Ottomans.[56] This Byzantine refugee found learning in Austria, mainly in the person of Shalom ben Isaac of Neustadt (ca. 1350–ca. 1413), a key rehabilitator of Ashkenazic life after the Black Death. In his extensive (if essentially unstudied) work that comes down under the name "commentary and addenda," filled as it is mostly with Rashi supercommentary, Dosa cites some fifty interpretations of his teacher Shalom.[57] The voices of other German savants also sound in Dosa's pages, such as his second principal teacher, Avraham Klausner, along with queries and ideas that he renders in the collective name of "the Ashkenazim."[58]

As Dosa records interpretations that otherwise would have gone unregistered, he provides precious indications of the *Commentary*'s place in the consciousness of German scholars, whether members of the rabbinic elite or their nameless disciples. He tells, for example, of consternation among "the Ashkenazim" as Rashi addressed an issue of considerable salience to German Jews at a time when memories of recent massacres remained deeply etched: the relationship of divine punishment to the vicarious atonement effected by the death of the righteous. The context was the juxtaposition of the red heifer rite with the death of Miriam in the Torah. Rashi cited a midrash that took the sequence to be intentional, with the aim of imparting an important tenet: "Why is the section narrating the death of Miriam placed immediately after the section [treating] the red heifer? To suggest to you [a comparison]: just as sacrifices effect atonement, so, too, does the death of the righteous effect atonement."[59] Yet Dosa's interlocutors were puzzled because, soon after the account of Miriam's death, the Torah describes the severe punishment meted out to Moses and Aaron after their provision of water from the rock at Meribah—nothing less than a ban on their entry into Canaan and consignment to death in the wilderness. Dosa's comrades wondered: should not the expiation generated by the death of righteous Miriam have averted her brothers' doom? Although initially tongue-tied, Dosa eventually found an answer: the demise of the righteous achieved vicarious expiation only for those "lower in rank and righteousness" than the deceased. Miriam's death failed to forestall her brothers' fate since they were "much greater in every respect" than was she.[60] Here as elsewhere, Dosa's tome (running 277 folio pages in manuscript) preserves engagement with Rashi's interpretations, midrashic and otherwise, in a period of mainly oral exegetical creativity in which insights would otherwise have disappeared. Like some of his French and German forerunners, Dosa admixes commentary and supercommentary, but his reports suggest a swing of the pendulum toward a mediated encounter with the Torah by way of Rashi in the German centers he inhabited. Fully half the interpretations Dosa relays from Shalom of Neustadt,[61] for instance, pertain to Rashi, although many of the rest involve techniques typical of German exegesis, like the transposition of letters, that Rashi used little, if at all.

Affirming the supercommentarial shift in the next generation is a collectanea that imparts exegesis by leading rabbis and many unknown ones. Its author-compiler hailed from the circle of Shalom of Neustadt's student, Jacob ben Moses Halevi Molin (Maharil; ca. 1360–1427). The collection includes comments in Molin's name heard by the compiler's father prior to Molin's death in 1427, as well as citations of such other rabbinic notables from the period as Yekutiel Suskind of Cologne. It also includes a wholly unexpected voice, reminding us of the abundant reward of sifting through such seemingly unpromising dusty documents: the voice of one Mistress Kila. Possibly a contemporary of Molin, to her belongs the honor of being the only premodern woman whose supercommentaries on Rashi survive.[62]

Returning to "mainstream" (that is, male rabbinic) exegesis, what we have started to see is ample if still episodic supercommentary emanating from rabbinic figures. But this pattern is broken, at least in terms of literary remains, with Molin's foremost student, Israel ben Petahiah Isserlein (d. 1460), author of the most important work of German biblical interpretation composed in late medieval times.[63] What, if anything, Isserlein called his work is unclear, as is the manner in which it came into being. A colophon of the earliest surviving copy of this assemblage casts it as "interpretations (*peshaṭim*) on the Pentateuch (*ḥumash*)." As the manuscript in question was produced in his lifetime in Wiener-Neustadt, where Isserlein studied and eventually returned to found a yeshiva, this characterization might be thought to carry some weight.[64]

Yet Isserlein's work would be mostly transmitted to posterity under the title *Be'urim le-rashi* (*Explications of Rashi*),[65] and the work's supercommentarial features are easy to see. They begin with the formulae used to introduce expositions: "he [Rashi] meant to say," "the interpretation [of Rashi] is," and so forth. Another prefatory phrase Isserlein deploys is "some raise an objection." What follows is an effort to arbitrate some lingering dispute surrounding Rashi's words and defend his acuity.[66] As the *Commentary* occupied an ever more central place in Ashkenaz, figures like Isserlein availed themselves of a burgeoning tradition of reflection on Rashi; indeed, debates between French and German predecessors naturally imposed themselves. How he resolved them could have a trickle-down effect, as his supercommentarial reflections informed the way the Torah was taught in popular settings. A case in point is one of the most massively circulated books ever to appear in Ashkenaz, *Ṣe'enah u-re'enah* (Yiddish: *Tzenerene*) of Jacob ben Isaac Ashkenazi of Janów (1550–1621). The principal way Jewish women learned the Bible on Sabbaths and holidays, this work often incorporated Rashi, at times as understood by one of his supercommentators, including Isserlein.[67]

A feature of Isserlein's work born of earlier models was a determination to disencumber the *Commentary* of any whiff of gratuitous reading-in by locating a goad for interpretations in a nuance of the biblical text. We saw his rationalization of the gloss on Jacob's instruction to his sons to "go down" to Egypt, where Rashi deployed *gemaṭriya* to buttress the rabbinic view of the length of Israel's sojourn in Egypt as 210 years, despite longer periods recorded in the Torah. In that case, Isserlein ignored Rashi's numerological rationale and replaced it with one of his own devising, deriving the midrash from a subtle biblical pleonasm.[68] Thus did he safeguard Rashi's rabbinic finding while putting it on what seemed to him a more solid basis, all the while making no effort to highlight his innovative departure from his revered source.

That Isserlein's supercommentary contains acts of fine textual discrimination is not surprising in light of his students' association with *Tosafot Gornish*, a turning point in the rise of the interpretive mode typically called *pilpul*.[69] As Isserlein lavished attention on subtle mechanics of Rashi's midrashic exegesis, both narrative and legal,[70] he presumed supreme nuance in Rashi's own commentarial expression. Where Rashi cites a verse to justify his translation of a word in one place, but omits such lexical buttressing elsewhere, Isserlein comes to explain.[71] Even the locus of a comment could bear import.[72] How methods of *pilpul* in Ashkenaz shaped study of the *Commentary* remains an open question, but certain features of the controversial method help to explain the ever more systematic study of Rashi there, as well as aspects of its character. Practitioners of *pilpul*, for instance, focused on the talmudic commentaries of Rashi and Tosafot, somewhat to the neglect of the talmudic text itself, and they read these commentaries with the same degree of precision as the Talmud.[73] Habituated to treating Rashi's Talmud commentaries in this way, it was natural to do the same with the *Commentary*.

Not all approved, however. As one sixteenth-century rabbinic great implied, *pilpul* on the *Commentary* could easily lapse into falsifying overinterpretation. Ruing a sorry process, Hayyim ben Bezalel of Friedberg described how a commentator concocted some notion born of thoughts flitting through his head and pinned his "erroneous conjecture" on Rashi ("the great luminary"), certain he had captured "Rashi's intention" when in fact nothing of the sort had crossed Rashi's mind. The result was readings of the *Commentary* "sundry and strange."[74]

Far more significant in the rise of supercommentary as a major and eventually dominant mode of Ashkenazic exegesis was the *Commentary*'s role in meeting the requirement of "twice scripture, once Targum." Even those like Isserlein who retained a view of Targum as the "cardinal" supplement in fulfillment of the requirement performed it with Rashi in hand.[75] From here it was a short step to compiling ideas accrued over years into a compendium of "explications of Rashi." In a variation on this theme, following patterns of knowledge transmission in Ashkenaz, students recorded oral expositions of Rashi by their teachers, perhaps in classes devoted to the weekly lectionary. This process explains why what came down from a single rabbinic figure as his supercommentary on Rashi can exist in multiple versions.[76] It is also possible that with the spread of "twice scripture, once Rashi" there may have arisen a heightened call by a growing base of readers for explications of the *Commentary*.[77]

Though *Be'urim le-rashi* is the closest thing to a supercommentary ever produced in Germany, it retains some of the generic flexibility of some of the writings sampled here. A rough calculation is that 85 percent of its comments explicate Rashi directly, while an added number of independent interpretations by Isserlein incorporate snippets of ideas from the *Commentary*. Few glosses ignore Rashi entirely, but Isserlein did feel free to interpret the Torah directly or to engage other figures like his illustrious martyred uncle, Aaron Blumlein, and such earlier Ashkenazic exegetes as Joseph Bekhor Shor, Moses of Coucy, and (a surprise in the context of biblical exegesis) Meir of Rothenberg.[78] Isserlein even arrogated to himself freedom to criticize the *Commentary*, including its interpretations made "in the aggadic manner."[79]

Although willing to dissent from Rashi, Isserlein sometimes conveys a sense that such criticism amounts to temerity requiring apology, at once attesting to the *Commentary*'s growing status as a foundational text and a pervasive substratum of pessimism among Ashkenazic rabbis as they mulled the question of intergenerational acumen after the Black Death. In one case, Isserlein rationalizes a divergence from Rashi by referring to scripture's polysemous character as captured in the image (used by Rashi himself) of the hammer blow that shatters the rock into many pieces.[80] His implication is that he is not actually dissenting from his great predecessor so much as bringing to light another of the Torah's multifaceted meanings. A dissent prefaced by "it seems to me"[81] may also reflect diffidence attesting to a sense of Rashi's ineluctable superiority. If so, it fits with the gloomy sense of Ashkenazic rabbis after 1348 that theirs was an era marked by steep religious and intellectual decline.

Looking back, such rabbis perhaps recalled Isaiah di Trani's insistence that, for all the superiority of the earlier authorities, later rabbis could, *qua* legists, surpass them.[82] He buttressed the claim by citing, for the first time in Jewish literature, the aphorism of a "dwarf standing on the shoulders of a giant" who sees farther despite his diminutive status ("we are dwarfs riding on the necks of giants, because, having digested their knowledge, we can transcend it").[83] By contrast, expressions in responsa of Isserlein's teacher, Jacob Molin, and his successors are replete with profound expressions of inferiority that go beyond conventional tropes. Molin lamented an "orphaned generation, in which no one knows between his right and his left."[84]

This sense of scholarship hobbled by decline and chronological belatedness suggests the possibility that the move to supercommentary, with its consecration of the *Commentary*, was born in part of the late medieval Ashkenazic sense of intellectual inadequacy. Replacing the "cultural chauvinism" long regnant among the Franco-German rabbinic elite was a crisis of confidence, the origins of which are contested.[85] Creativity did not cease, nor should what was produced be seen as a tale of "submissive dedication to the chains of tradition."[86] Still, leading rabbis discarded the basic premise on which earlier justifications of independent insight rested: that for all their limitations, latter-day scholars still inhabited the same universe of discourse as their earlier medieval predecessors.[87]

The belief that the wisdom of even their immediate predecessors, let alone such forerunners as Rashi, greatly outstripped their learning led rabbis in late medieval Ashkenaz to redefine a talmudic distinction between *rishonim* (early scholars, or *antiqui*) and *'aḥaronim* (latter-day scholars, or *moderni*). At the beginning of the fourteenth century, Asher ben Yehiel thought it clear that the "earlier scholars" were the rabbinic sages while latter-day ones, in aggregate, were their post-talmudic successors. But Yisrael Yuval suggests that a new view took hold in the wake of the dire events following the Black Death. This outlook cast the *rishonim* as the earliest stratum among *medieval* sages and applied the designation "later scholars" to either the last stratum of the early sages—still seen as titans, if of a lesser order—or the post-1348 rabbis themselves.[88] Molin and others invoked a rabbinic aphorism that cast the "fingernails" of earlier scholars as wider than the "bellies" of their successors.[89]

With such currents of thought (or drifts of feeling) abroad, Ashkenazic savants may have regarded the composition of a Torah commentary as presumptuous. Whatever its cause, the profound sense of inferiority informed the widespread notion that contemporary insight must surely falter before the great preceptors of yore. Add to this sentiment a deepening relegation of the Bible to the curricular margins, and it was natural for late medieval Ashkenazic rabbis to dare to understand the Torah only through the approved filter of the *Commentary*.

Among self-perceived dwarfs in the generation after Isserlein (though quite capable of acting boldly when required) was Joseph Colon (Mahariq; ca. 1420–ca. 1480), a late vestige of French rabbinic learning at a time when the collective identity of expelled French Jewry was beginning to wane.[90] His exegetical insights were born in part of his class on the weekly Torah portion, in which, it is now almost needless to say, he studied the lectionary as refracted through the *Commentary*.[91] One easily links this focus with Colon's deep sense of the "decline of the generations" and his veneration for predecessors—so much so that he demanded latter-day authorities accord halakhic weight even to these forerunners' marginalia.[92]

By 1500, then, a tradition in Ashkenaz of commentaries on Rashi was coming of age, having traveled from episodic beginnings, even as it did not yet produce pure supercommentary, and having found expression first in the margins of manuscripts and then having become more systematized. Isaiah di Trani, an Italian shaped by the German school, Hezekiah ben Manoah and, even more, Judah ben Eleazar augured patterns as the center of gravity of Ashkenazic exegesis shifted to German-speaking lands and, in embryo, more easterly centers like Poland. Their exertions and those of Isserlein point toward sixteenth- and seventeenth-century developments that played out from Friedberg to Cracow, Prague to Lublin. More and more, exegesis of the Torah receded. More and more, supercommentary on the canonical work of Ashkenazic exegesis replaced it.

Sefardic "Servants of Solomon": Exegesis and Appropriation

As in Northern Europe, any number of greater and lesser Sefardic minds invested energy in exposition of Rashi, with the crucial difference that in Spain, some produced works that bear all the features of supercommentary. Since the focus in what follows is on dissimilarities, it is important to stress that there are many points of contact between Rashi's Franco-German and Sefardic expositors. Students of the *Commentary* in both spheres discussed its grammatical insights, sought to identify Rashi's sources, pinpointed the textual spurs for his expositions, and so forth. These more quotidian activities of the supercommentators possess an integrity and importance all their own, but must perforce be left for separate study, as we focus on the varied and complex process that saw supercommentaries help to transform the *Commentary* into a classic in Spain. For example, we have noted the unexpected way in which Spanish supercommentaries composed in the half century prior to 1492 apply to the *Commentary* assumptions that fit with the time-honored principle of omnisignificance. Adumbrations of this approach are visible in the "first wave" of Sefardic supercommentaries written in the Catalo-Aragonese sphere, though the "second-wave" supercommentaries written in Castile are where it comes to full flower.[93]

The story of Rashi supercommentary in Christian Spain begins in embryo with the commentary of Nahmanides who, as we have seen, routinely engaged the *Commentary*, ushering it into Sefardic consciousness forever more.[94] Yet though a thoroughly independent and highly original exegete, he engaged in his fair share of Rashi supercommentary. The Sefardic supercommentator on the eve of the expulsion, Judah Khalatz, went so far as to call him one of Rashi's "prime" explicators.[95]

To see Nahmanides perform his expositional function, let us consider part of his comment on the laws prescribed for marriage to a captive woman set down in Deuteronomy 21, which begins with Rashi and his sources, including one side of a rabbinic dispute over an ambiguous word:

> "And [the woman captured in war whom an Israelite soldier wishes to wed shall] *'asetah* her nails"—"She should grow them in order to become repulsive" [becoming unattractive thereby to the Israelite soldier]. [This is] the language of our rabbi Solomon in accordance with the words of R. Akiva, and so Onkelos explained. Now according to their opinion [the word] "*ve-'asetah*" [is in keeping with Lev 25:21] "and [the earth] will do [grow] a crop."[96]

Were he a supercommentator, Nahmanides could (and should) have stopped there. As an autonomous exegete, he goes his own way, engaging in the very "inquiry and examination" of Rashi's words he promised in his commentary's introductory poem: "But in *Sifrei* there appears a proof for the view of R. Eliezer [that "to do" here means not "to grow" but "to cut"] . . . and it is a weighty proof. Therefore I say that all these are rites of mourning [rather than a way to make her unappealing]." The pattern of explanation followed by critique repeats itself frequently.

In addition to countless modest acts of supercommentary quietly undertaken, Nahmanides inaugurated a process that would figure routinely in Sefardic supercommentary, explaining Rashi's midrashim in ways congenial to what Sefardic scholars deemed scientific facts or fundaments of faith.[97] Consider his response to Rashi's interpretation of the reference to "all flesh" in the phrase, "all flesh (*kol basar*) corrupted its way on earth" (Gen 6:12). Taking it at face value, Rashi included subhuman creatures in the corruption that spurred God's decision to destroy the world, asserting that "even domestic animals, beasts, and birds cohabited with those not of their own kind." By implication, the fauna shared responsibility for the divinely wrought flood. The notion of fauna as moral agents resonated in any number of rabbinic texts where the physical world, inclusive of not only animals but even plants and inanimate objects, was depicted as feeling and thinking.[98] It was compatible with a view of animals prevalent in many Christian European settings where, for example, animal felons were tried in court. In a case not long after Rashi's death, caterpillars, flies, and field mice were arraigned on serious charges.[99]

After citing Rashi, Nahmanides clarifies a necessary supplement to his reading:

> If we interpret "all flesh" according to its literal denotation and say that even domestic animals, beasts, and birds corrupted their way by cohabiting with those not of their own kind, as Rashi explained, we would say that [God's subsequent statement explaining the reason for the flood] "for the earth is filled with lawlessness (*ḥamas*) because of them" [Gen 6:13] [means]: not because of all of them [fauna included, though the first half of the verse speaks of "all flesh"] but because of some of them, and what is related is humankind's punishment alone.[100]

Rashi, having implicated the fauna in the antediluvian corruption, presumably understood the condemnatory "because of them" to include the domestic animals, beasts, and birds. Not having made the point explicitly, however, he left room for Nahmanides to insist that the *ḥamas* mentioned prior to this phrase was, understood morally, only applicable to the people, on the view that only human beings possess moral agency. In this move, Nahmanides foreshadows a trend that, as we shall see, looms large in the Sefardic supercommentaries proper, whereby Rashi was read in ways that met conditions of understanding prevalent in the world in which the supercommentators thought, taught, and wrote.[101]

Nahmanides has another way to explain Rashi, building on what Ibn Ezra had described as a "fitting" view of "our [rabbinic] predecessors." Ibn Ezra understood that the fauna's "sins" consisted in the fact that "every living thing failed to preserve its natural way" and "warped the known path implanted [within it]." Dilating on this idea, Nahmanides observes that "we may say that they did not preserve their nature such that animals became predatory and the birds [became] raptors, in which case they too engaged in violence." On this view, the degeneracy of the animals expressed itself in a newfound predatory instinct, implicating them in the Torah's blame for antediluvian "violence." Artfully melding his main forerunners, Nahmanides rationalized a strange midrash in a way that made it compatible with what Sefardic scholars, including antirationalists like Nahmanides, regarded as finalities of science within which any acceptable exegesis of the flood narrative must fall.[102] His act of supercommentary complete, Nahmanides turns to his primary task of Torah commentary, offering a reading according to the "method of *peshaṭ*." In it, "all flesh" is taken as a reference to all of humankind. In this way did Nahmanides cut the ground out from under the midrash of Rashi that he had taken so much trouble to explain, at least as an embodiment of the plain sense.[103]

Nahmanides was the individual most responsible for making the *Commentary* something to test and probe in Spain, but other factors facilitated its ever more ineluctable presence as a spur to supercommentary. Some of these factors appear from an account of perhaps the earliest author of a sustained Sefardic supercommentary on Rashi, the later fourteenth-century Joseph ibn Shoshan of Aragon. The initial occasion for Ibn Shoshan's supercommentary was his annual perusal of the *Commentary*, presumably in conjunction with study in fulfillment of the weekly lectionary review. In passing the same locale in the *Commentary* year after year, Joseph wished to avoid continually having to start afresh. Better to "stop there to eat a meal and find a table [of accrued insight] spread before me."[104] Since insights grasped with difficulty were easily lost, prudence dictated their inscription both for one's own sake and for a larger readership including one's posterity. In the medieval world, writing largely functioned as a "servant to memory," with glosses being one form of "memorial cues and aids."[105] For Joseph—and many others, it turns out—a supercommentary served a mnemonic function.[106] With readers of Rashi savoring any twinkling of insight they managed to wrest from his deep and delectable words, they sought ways to ensure these would not be lost to oblivion.

Ibn Shoshan's urge to supercommentary was also born of his sense of a deep abyss separating ancients and moderns.[107] He uses classical imagery to emphasize the divide between the "early sages," who spoke with supreme concision, and latter-day readers, whose mental acuity fluctuates in ways that compromise their capacity to grasp such compressed speech. Invoking a rabbinic image, he compares the former to the twenty-cubit-wide entrance to the temple, the latter to an infinitesimally minute "eye of a fine needle."[108] Rashi's superiority, combined with his terseness, poses a formidable obstacle that in turn justifies clarificatory intervention. In sum, from Ibn Shoshan we glean a threefold prompt to supercommentary: "twice scripture and once Rashi"—which turned study of the *Commentary* into a quasi-normative practice; a sense of the work as a "classic" by one of the "ancients" that merits reverent study; and the universal hope of writers over the ages that hard-won insights would not be consigned to oblivion owing to forgetfulness.

Where Ibn Shoshan's supercommentary was short and episodic, another early supercommentator, Samuel Almosnino, produced a fuller work that ultimately proved resonant. Biographical details are scarce, but Almosnino's likely *floruit* is the later fourteenth century, meaning that his work is to be provisionally located in the Catalo-Aragonese sphere where the first wave of Sefardic glosses appeared. Although printed only in 1525 in the anthology published in Constantinople under the title *[Super-]Commentaries on Rashi* (*Perushim le-rashi*), Almosnino's work inspired others before its printing and left its mark on the dean of the supercommentators, whose exposition of Rashi would be printed in Venice two years later, Elijah Mizrahi.[109]

Almosnino fixes his eyes firmly on a number of duties that he feels it incumbent upon the supercommentator to discharge. He developed a specialty in "lower criticism," making prodigious efforts to locate manuscripts that could supply "precise" texts of the *Commentary* in place of the "confused" or "outlandish" ones upon which he too often stumbled.[110] Almosnino has a yen for grammatical comments, which he explains with a high degree of precision.[111] Like others, he strives to spot a basis for Rashi's seemingly groundless midrashim. On rabbinic authority, Rashi relays that the Canaanite king waged war on Israel only after learning of the departure of the protective clouds of glory following the death of Aaron. So much does Almosnino deem the midrash textually grounded that he casts it as being "according to the method of plain sense."[112]

If, across cultures, the idea that the canon is deep is associated with the assumption that the classics "are profound throughout, not just in certain key passages,"[113] Almosnino can take this notion to an extreme. For instance, he attends to what he deems Rashi's pregnant and precise *termini technici.* Each "that is to say" (*kelomar*) or "language of" (*leshon . . .*) or "according to its plain sense" is, he posits, there for a reason. Even Rashi's ordering of comments catches his critical eye, an aspect of textual analysis that would gain ever greater centrality in Sefardic hermeneutical technique, including applications to the *Commentary.*[114]

Further emblematic of the Sefardic character of his supercommentary is Almosnino's ability to make an initially opaque or perplexing comment of Rashi instructive—and even inspiring—to a rationalist community of readers.

His interpretation of a midrash on a verse that describes the return to Egypt of Moses's family illustrates the sort of interpretive modulations that paved the way for the *Commentary*'s appropriation, as well as perceptions of its religious depth, in Spain. In addressing the pedigree of the donkey mentioned in the verse that tells how "Moses took his wife and sons, mounted them on the donkey" (Exod 4:20) before going back to Egypt, Rashi indicates that, far from being an ordinary beast, this donkey had and would again figure in turning points in history: "'Mounted them on the donkey': the exceptional donkey, it being the donkey that Abraham saddled [to travel to Mount Moriah] for the binding of Isaac, and it being the one upon which in the future the King Messiah will be revealed, as it says: 'humble, riding on a donkey'" (Zech 9:9).[115] Here, as in countless other cases where Rashi finds occasion to cite a midrash, good reasons, textual and otherwise, could be found. As Avraham Grossman explains, the midrashist, and Rashi after him, seeks to clarify, first, why the Torah should at all bother to recount that Moses, on the cusp of his redemptive role, mounted his wife and family on the donkey. Second, Rashi responds to the Torah's reference to "*the* donkey," as if a specific or previously mentioned "exceptional" beast were meant.[116] Indeed, Nehama Leibowitz, who holds that Rashi cites midrashim only where a textual crux demands it, offers this instance to substantiate her claim, noting Rashi's failure to use the midrash in the other loci to which he referred for lack of such a warrant.[117]

Beyond a basis in a "surface irregularity" of the sort that routinely fired the midrashic imagination,[118] Rashi's exposition displays typically midrashic features in its substance. Most notable is the penchant of midrashists to concentrate the action of biblical narratives by identifying otherwise nameless or seemingly incidental figures, objects, or details and to conflate unrelated historical events. Isaac Heinemann speaks of a midrashic propensity to bridge "expanses of time" in ways that create a compressed historical picture easily seen. The result, in the case of the donkey, is "to envision and make visible the spiritual dimension embedded within the physical one."[119] More broadly, Rashi alerts readers to the beast's role as a bearer of Jewish and, ultimately, universal history: the donkey associated with the deliverer of the Israelites from bondage—that same beast that delivered Abraham to his supreme spiritual achievement—would convey the Messiah on his mission of final deliverance in the eschatological future.[120]

Yet, where some nowadays might see in this flight of midrashic imagination a charming product of the rabbinic mind, Sefardic sages of a more empirical and scientific bent, and not even the most rationalist among them, wondered how possibly to explain the idea. The foremost among them at the time of the 1492 expulsion, Isaac Abarbanel, although hardly a die-hard rationalist, insists that a literal reading of the midrash is clearly misdirected, since it is "impossible" that a donkey should live over three thousand years.[121] Now, this is precisely the sort of obvious objection Rashi never would have raised, although it is hard to say just how he thought about such midrashim that hovered over the faint line dividing the symbolic from the actual. Extraordinary longevity aside, one could wonder what commended a particular donkey for a repeated role in history's redemptive high points, including its messianic culmination, as did the foremost early modern Ashkenazic theologian, Judah Loew of Prague, when he asked: "What distinguishes this donkey from all other donkeys?"[122] Sefardic scholars might have escaped the need to reflect on the interpretation, which appeared in the possibly ninth-century medieval midrash *Pirkei de-rabbi 'Eliezer*. Once endorsed by Rashi, such obliviousness, actual or feigned, was less of an option.[123]

Enter Almosnino, who takes a midrash that could easily have led some Spanish readers to roll their eyes, or worse, and provides commentary to make it intelligible to a Sefardic audience by applying exegetical tools and a theological template familiar from the Sefardic philosophical tradition. The idea was to translate the imagery of the midrash into rational terms; that is, Almosnino appeals to the time-honored device of nonliteral interpretation of rabbinic sayings where these seem implausible or impossible when taken literally. It was an approach that received its authoritative rationale from Maimonides and came to be widely applied by later rationalists in works devoted to systematic midrashic interpretation. Indeed, if one can rely on the tentative dating of Almosnino to the later fourteenth century, one can point to contemporary works of aggadic interpretation that adopt just this strategy. The author of one, the Navarrese scholar Shem Tov ibn Shaprut, insisted that the sages spoke in "riddles and metaphors." It followed that "the more bizarre the riddle, the more impossible [that it should be understood according to] its plain sense." Samuel ibn Zarza, another possible contemporary of Almosnino, agreed that those who read rabbinic dicta "on the esoteric plane" would find "great and wondrous things."[124] In the context of his supercommentary, Joseph ibn Shoshan pronounced a strange midrash in the *Commentary* that had the height of Adam reaching from earth to heaven "all allegory without any plain sense [meaning] whatsoever."[125]

Almosnino's unearthing of wondrous things in Rashi's midrash began with his invocation of a stock metaphor attested in the sort of exegesis of midrash practiced by Ibn Shaprut and Ibn Zarza—in this case, a wordplay that parlayed appearances of a donkey (*ḥamor*) in biblical and rabbinic texts into references to a basic category of Hebrew Aristotelianism: matter (*ḥomer*). Several southern French writers had posited the interchange prior to Almosnino. Depending on

Almosnino's dates, Ibn Zarza may have anticipated him in Spain. At any rate, Almosnino turns Rashi into a mouthpiece for the idea:

> "On the donkey (Exod 4:20)." [Rashi says,] "the exceptional donkey, it being the donkey that Abraham saddled, etc." Now the principal engagement of the wise is to understand and apprehend intellectually, for which purpose it is necessary that the powers of the intellect prevail over the corporeal powers. Something that prevails may, figuratively speaking, be said to ride on that over which it prevails, while that which is prevailed upon is [represented figuratively] as a donkey [*ḥamor*] [being ridden upon] with respect to it [i.e., the prevailing force]. By contrast, among those who err, their matter prevails over their form [i.e., the intellect]. This being so, he [Rashi] said that it [Moses's donkey] was the very same donkey that Abraham saddled, subdued, and rode on. And so it is with the Messiah, because their form prevailed over the matter in them.[126]

Almosnino's interpretation of Rashi exudes a Maimonidean spirit, starting with its assertion that the principal occupation of the wise is intellectual apprehension, a notion of human flourishing that Maimonides argued with singular force. Next comes the idea that the goal of intellectual apprehension can be attained only by freeing the intellect from bodily appetites, or "corporeal powers." It is these that dominate in "those who err," obstructing higher pursuits. As Maimonides lamented, the human being's "very noble form" is inextricably bound up with the "earthly, turbid, and dark matter" that calls down "every imperfection and corruption." Yet that form also had within it the potential for "power, dominion, rule and control over matter," the better to quell matter's impulses.[127] Matter stands, then, in permanent tension with the material intellect's ability to attain its higher form—the "acquired intellect"—the "form" that was the divine image to which human beings ought to aspire.[128]

In the rest of his gloss, Almosnino continues his act of supercommentarial ventriloquism that has Rashi speak in a Maimonidean tongue. A prominent chapter in the *Guide* expounds the verbal root "to ride" with reference to the Deity as rider of the heavens, indicating that the verb is equivocal. It refers, in the first instance, to a person "riding in the usual manner on beasts," but can be used figuratively "to designate domination over a thing, for a rider dominates over and rules that which he rides."[129] Melding the two notions, Almosnino explains that to overcome *ḥomer*, the matter that generates bodily desire and impedes cognition, one must ensure that intellect dominates ("rides on") matter. With this understanding, what "he [Rashi] said" proves wholly luminous: Abraham and Moses overrode "the matter in them," as would the Messiah when fulfilling his redemptive role. By their attainment of human form in superlative measure, these figures offered a model for "the wise" in all times and places.

By having the *Commentary* impart an intellectualist view of human perfection, Almosnino made Rashi an advocate for a rationalist spiritual vision. A midrash in the *Commentary* that told of a donkey's improbable participation in great spiritual moments, past and future, became, in the right supercommentarial hands, a philosophically informed exemplum on human flourishing. Here was a recasting of the "matter" of Rashi's comment on the donkey in Maimonidean "form" in a way that, like Maimonidean interpretation of scripture and rabbinic lore generally, could only have left Rashi bewildered. Not only would he have been unfamiliar with its key terms of reference but also he would have been confounded by an interpretation that turned a midrash about a donkey into a taut, symbolically rich homily on the final human end. Yet as far as Almosnino's reader was concerned. Rashi taught that the achievement of the highest human models was just as Maimonides said: "to understand and apprehend intellectually."

What reception would this reading of Rashi have received in late medieval Spain? The answer depends on various factors, foremost being a reader's view on the legitimacy of philosophically informed nonliteral interpretations of rabbinic sayings, as well their place within a rather chaotic variety of Sefardic reactions to the notion that intellectual apprehension marked human perfection's apex. Philosophical stalwarts could have found in Almosnino's gloss a perfect realization of Maimonides's habit of uncovering philosophical truths within the nonlegal component of rabbinic discourse. They may have nodded in approval at the truths that Rashi taught by using the imagery of the "exceptional" donkey. But traditionalists might have found Almosnino's reading more problematic. While agreeing on the need to control physical temptations, many would have taken umbrage at what they would have seen as a superimposition on Judaism's spiritual luminaries of a vision of human flourishing they thought alien—nay, a transparent import from the world of Greco-Arabic philosophy. There was, as we will see in a later chapter, a third approach representing the road not taken: fierce criticism of Rashi's midrashic interpretation of the donkey as "futility and a grave evil." While this is not the response we would ever expect to find in a Sefardic supercommentary, it is the verdict on the midrash issued by the *Commentary*'s most sustained critic of all time, a writer eager not to canonize the *Commentary* but to highlight its exegetical and religious missteps.[130]

Almosnino does not mention the 1391 riots that left tens of thousands of Spanish Jews dead or forcibly converted to Christianity, and that laid Sefardic scholarship low for decades. A sign of recovery, in terms of supercommentary, is the appearance of an anonymous work by a contemporary of the grammarian and anti-Christian polemicist, Profayt Duran. The supercommentary runs, in the largely complete version that survives, 170 folio pages, putting it in a league with Almosnino's work for scale and reinforcing the devotion to the *Commentary* abroad in Aragon. Frequent references to what "some" interpret and "others" counter suggest a growing intensity and cross-pollination in study of the *Commentary*, orally and in writing.[131] Like Almosnino, "Anonymous" could interpret an opaque midrash in ways that turned it to theological purpose. When Rashi interprets Jacob's dream revelation at Bethel, with its angels said to be ascending and descending a ladder "set on the ground . . . [whose] top reached to the sky" (Gen 28:12), he describes two cohorts of angels—one accompanying Jacob "in the land [of Israel]" and ascending as Jacob prepares to depart the land and another coming down to replace it. "Anonymous" turns this idea into a vehicle for teaching about providence and the land of Israel, assimilating Rashi's midrashic imagery to more philosophical modes of discourse.[132]

"Anonymous" also shows how Sefardic study of the *Commentary* unfolded in a later medieval world where the boundaries between Sefarad and Ashkenaz were increasingly porous. More than Almosnino, he conducts a symposium among earlier classics: Rashi and Ibn Ezra disagree with Nahmanides; Rashi and Ibn Ezra disagree in a way that begs for elucidation of Rashi; Nahmanides explains Rashi. Most notably, Nahmanides is a recurrent presence as both explicator and critic of Rashi.[133] Yet Ashkenazic writers also figure among interlocutors of "Anonymous," creating a sort of ecumenical effort to understand Rashi. The author also applies formulae typical of Tosafist discourse such as "if you contend . . . one might reply" (*'im tomar . . . yesh lomar*) to signal an objection or resolution. The upshot is that Rashi appears as an authority who holds his own against Sefardic Jewry's best and brightest—after, that is, receiving interpretive ministrations from "Anonymous."

Another Aragon-born supercommentator was Moses ibn Gabbai who, put to flight by the 1391 anti-Jewish riots, passed his closing decades in North Africa, where he wrote *'Eved shelomo* (Servant [or even Slave] of Solomon). Throughout this work, Ibn Gabbai remained true to his stated aim—"explication of the book of Solomon"—in a tone that is respectful and often reverential. Yet from an intellectual, literary, and even psychological point of view, Ibn Gabbai's servitude (freely chosen, of course) proves compatible with his exercise of an inquiring mind. Though "Moses Gabbai the Sefardi," as he calls himself, is loyal in his way to "Solomon the Frenchman," as he calls Rashi, he is not straightforwardly servile nor, one is tempted to add, could he have been, given the differences in outlook between this son of Spain, traditionalist though he was, and his French "master."[134] To be sure, frontal confrontations, let alone broadsides, were out. What does occur is a range of interactions from the highly appreciative to the subtly (or, in the very rare case, openly) critical, as Ibn Gabbai seeks to ensure that the Torah is understood aright while also making sure that Rashi's explanations retain credibility for readers who might balk at some interpretations and ideas that Rashi presents.

One unique form that Ibn Gabbai's supercommentarial criticism takes is classification of Rashi's comments into two basic categories. His efforts on this score appear in what would normally be a supercommentary's most innocuous feature: lemmas that break up the commentary into atomized units of analysis. By prefacing certain lemmas with *peresh ha-rav*, "the master explained," a usage that on the surface appears wholly banal and certainly lacking in evaluative weight, Ibn Gabbai indicates a gloss thought to impart the "plain sense" (*peshaṭ*) or, at the least, an interpretation grounded in some textual implication (*diyyuq*). By introducing a lemma with "the master wrote" (*katav*), Ibn Gabbai signals that a comment comprises a "midrash or aggadah," or rabbinic interpretation given after a plain sense one, that is apparently not to be taken as exegesis, strictly speaking.[135] Even before he explains Rashi, then, Ibn Gabbai appraises his work based on benchmarks of his own devising.[136] Here was a "servant" of Rashi with a mind of his own.

As his classificatory scheme shows, it was Rashi's midrashim that riveted a good deal of Ibn Gabbai's attention. A discussion of eight modes of midrashic discourse in his introduction heralds this side of the supercommentary while showing how inextricably linked in Ibn Gabbai's mind were the rabbinic inheritance and Rashi's exegetical enterprise. Notable in this account are the ways this traditional talmudist draws on Maimonidean categories and prooftexts as he sets forth his vision of the midrash genre. For example, Ibn Gabbai speaks of midrashim that involve a willful misreading of the biblical text with the aim of inculcating "moral instruction," in this way following Maimonides on "poetic" figures deployed by the ancient midrashists.[137] Even before taking in the supercommentary proper, one can, on the basis of this discussion, sense that the master–servant relationship in Ibn Gabbai's work is going to be more intricate and, at times conflicted, than its title suggests.

For all that, Ibn Gabbai could explain how Rashi's rabbinically based "poetry" made good sense. Rashi midrashically expounds Moses's charge to the scouts to determine whether Canaan had trees—"are there in it trees, or not?" (Num 13:20). It was an instruction not about actual trees but whether an "upstanding person" (*'adam kasher*) resided in Canaan who might shield its inhabitants from the forthcoming Israelite assault "by virtue of his merit." This reading set the forthcoming battle on the plane of moral probity rather than military prowess. It was the only interpretation Rashi supplied and, in his usual way, he did not refer to its rabbinic provenance. In other words, readers of the *Commentary* could be forgiven for believing that Rashi thought the midrash an embodiment of the plain sense or at least a midrash that "settled" scripture in accordance with its language. But could this really be so?

When citing Rashi's interpretation, Ibn Gabbai uses the formula "the master wrote." In so doing, he telegraphs that the comment lacks a real textual spur. He goes further, stating that it reflects "the way of *derash*." Yet, Ibn Gabbai also insists that the sages were nevertheless "in the right" (*ha-din 'imahem*). Since there could be no doubting the existence of trees in Canaan, the directive could not have been meant precisely as stated (*'al peshuṭo*), leading the sages to expound it (*dareshu*) with reference to an upright person. Nor was the analogy between a righteous person and a tree adventitious: "just as a tree shields by its shade those strolling along pathways who lack vigor, so an upright person shields his generation [from the requital they otherwise might merit]." Seen thus, Rashi's gloss stands as "a most fitting homiletical exposition." Its ground, the implausibility of a literal reading of the Mosaic charge, was clear; its imagery was not only understandable but also artful.[138] There was, in short, a solid justification for his comment, which Rashi relays with his accustomed insouciance, but which Sefardic readers might find farfetched—until Ibn Gabbai came along to show otherwise.

Glimpses of the *Commentary*'s exalted status as a maximally meaningful text are forthcoming from Ibn Gabbai in a way that points back to Almosnino and anticipates the omnisignificant approach that became the rule in Sefardic supercommentary in the half century before 1492. This stance emerges, somewhat counterintuitively, from a remark in which Ibn Gabbai *denies* that each verbal element in a comment of Rashi must be substantively significant. Rather, he states, the comment reflects the principle of "the same idea repeated in different words" (*kefel 'inyan be-milim shonot*).[139] This was David Kimhi's formulation of an interpretive approach that was a hallmark of the Andalusian *peshaṭ* tradition, which refused to impute meaning to all repetitions in scripture. Instead, these could be chalked up to a stylistic convention.[140] Ibn Gabbai's application of the formula to the *Commentary* tacitly embeds an amazing premise: one ought to reflect on apparent redundancies in Rashi's expressions in the manner that those in scripture demand attention—even if, as here, a repetition of Rashi might be understood as a matter of style rather than substance.

Rashi's claim that "Adam mated with every [species of] beast and animal" allows us to see the transformations effected by practitioners of subordinate supercommentarial discourse that could turn problematic, if not potentially offensive, classical dicta made famous by Rashi into sources of supreme edification. Thus do they call into high relief the process of appropriation that the *Commentary* frequently underwent in Spain in ways that allowed it to achieve and maintain its standing as a classic. As so often, Rashi ushered into the mainstream a peculiar rabbinic teaching that, by virtue of its inclusion in his evermore omnipresent *Commentary*, had to be reckoned with. That reckoning takes the form of a successive unfolding of meaning in which the Torah is read by way of a midrash by Rashi, which in turn is refracted through Sefardic-tinted lenses in a manner that meets conditions of understanding in the world of philosophically inflected Mediterranean Judaism.[141]

Almosnino sets the pattern, insisting that Adam's "mating" with animals was cerebral, not physical. This statement assumes that Rashi intended his comment as "a figurative expression for his [Adam's] examining of the temperaments of the females among all the species."[142] Almosnino does not deny Adam's biological concern as he explored the fauna, but he does affirm the first man's purely procreative rather than erotic interests in so doing. In a not exactly romantic formulation, he had Adam pondering the nature of the female beasts to find "a receptacle for his seed so that he might procreate through them." Upon finding none suitable and then discovering Eve, Adam "had intercourse with her," understanding that "from her he would obtain fruit of the womb." Almosnino ends sermonically, imparting a lesson to his postlapsarian (male) readers: "this cautions us not to have intercourse with a woman merely in order to relieve our animalistic lust but rather with the intention of producing noble progeny."[143]

That Rashi's comment referred to noetic intercourse was also clear to "Anonymous," who spoke less of a search for a biologically suitable partner and more of Adam's quest for an intellectual soulmate. Adam engaged in "intense and ongoing investigation and careful study into each and every species" to discern its nature (*tiv'o*) and temperament. Failing to find a nature fitting and disposed (*mukhan*) to his own, Adam, upon discerning Eve's complementary nature, cried out: "this one."[144] When he speaks of Adam's "investigation" (*ḥaqirah*) into the nature of each species, the supercommentator uses a term that had come to be associated with the philosophical enterprise. The result is to (re)orient the teaching of the *Commentary* to a way of life in which Sefardic ideals like metaphysical discovery and introspection shine forth.

Not all Sefardic sages embraced the intellectualist ideal, yet even traditionalists suspicious of it as Ibn Gabbai was could align themselves with the standard Sefardic reading of Rashi's midrash on "this time." He introduces his citation with "the master wrote," in this way firing a shot at the comment's status as embodiment of the plain sense or even as a reading with some more subtle textual basis. Yet, Rashi's Talmud commentary provides an indication to the contrary: "[The Torah says] 'this time'—whence it may be inferred that he [Adam] had coitus on other occasions but they [the beasts] did not meet with his approval."[145] Ibn Gabbai's son-in-law, Aaron Aboulrabi, made this point in his own exegetical work, using the term reserved by Ibn Gabbai for a textually grounded comment: "[Rashi wrote:] 'it teaches that he had intercourse with every domesticated animal, and so forth.' He inferred it (*diyyeq*) from its saying 'this time.' "[146] So familiar was this passage that Jerònim de Santa Fe could cite it when invoking the midrash on "this time" at the disputation of Tortosa to disparage the Talmud's odious contents. Jerònim decried the midrash on "this time" as a blasphemous ascription of iniquity to prelapsarian Adam that flagrantly contradicted the attestation: "And God saw all that he made and found it very good" (Gen 1:31). Ultimately, in this view, the midrash cast aspersions on the Deity's own perfection. If a Jewish apostate knew to cite Rashi on "this time" in his Talmud commentary,[147] a superior talmudist like Ibn Gabbai surely had it engraved in mind. Yet in analyzing the midrash as it appears in the *Commentary*, Ibn Gabbai averts his eyes from this evidence from the Talmud commentary.

However excluded the midrash as embodiment of the plain sense, there it stood, with Rashi's imprimatur, crying out for a response. Ibn Gabbai follows earlier leads (Almosnino, "Anonymous") but with a difference: he raises the possibility of actual intercourse between Adam and the animals—that is, of a reading of the midrash according to what he calls its prima facie meaning (*kifeshutah*). Perhaps he does so because, more than most Sefardic supercommentators, he appears to have been in touch with Tosafist glosses where a literal reading in the standard Ashkenazic manner was a near invariable matter of course. His dismissal of literalism in this case is, of course, no surprise, but his halakhic grounds for doing so are novel. It is premised on a vision of Adam midrashically privy to laws of the sort that would eventually bind all humankind. To prove that Adam was subject to a proscription on bestiality, Ibn Gabbai cites a midrash on "And the Lord God commanded the man, saying" (Gen 2:16) that made it a basis for the Noahide laws.[148] On this view, Adam could not have embraced beasts carnally since such an act was proscribed under laws that Adam received. Ibn Gabbai reinforces this position by citing another verse: "hence a man leaves his father and mother and clings to his wife" (Gen 2:24). This verse was midrashically expounded to mean that a man should cling only to his wife "and not to another being [including animals]."

For Ibn Gabbai, these midrashically derived interdicts preempt a literal reading of Rashi's midrash: "Were the *'aggadah* cited by Rashi according to its prima facie meaning, there would be cause to marvel since, behold, he [Adam] had already been enjoined concerning illicit sexual relations."[149]

Before turning to Ibn Gabbai's predictable interpretation of what the midrash does mean, it is worth observing that later supercommentators with impeccable halakhic credentials faulted a rejection of Rashi's interpretation based on an appeal to such legal prescripts.[150] Ibn Gabbai could not point to explicit passages in the *Commentary* to clinch his reading since, although Rashi did (at Gen 2:24) assert a general prohibition on Noahide sexual immorality, he failed to register a specific prohibition on bestiality (or the existence of Noahide laws) in his commentary on Genesis. Still, the legal claim provided grounds for denying any actual intimacy between Adam and animals, as Ibn Gabbai was clearly at pains to do.

Having put to rest a literal interpretation of Rashi, Ibn Gabbai places himself in step with the Sefardic readings of his predecessors, but he interweaves into his verbal formulation the language of scripture and Rashi more than they did. The outcome is that three layers of tradition—his being the latest—read continuously. Thus does Ibn Gabbai illustrate how supercommentarial prose can appear simply to carry forward the exegetical process while masking its denial of "substantial parts or aspects of the received legacy."[151] To expose the layering, Ibn Gabbai appears in plain script, Rashi in italics, and scripture in bold, but the key is to appreciate how a reader of his gloss experiences it as a seamless whole, lulled into thinking that each layer naturally unfolds from the chronologically prior and authoritatively superior one: "It is to be explained by saying that *he came with* his intellect and investigated the nature (*toledet*) and temperament *of every domesticated animal and wild animal and did not* find one of them fitting for his temperament until God **brought** Eve (Gen 2:22), who was **bone of his bone and flesh of his flesh** (Gen 2:23)." Expanding in one last way, Ibn Gabbai, like Almosnino, affirms that the motive in this quest was not carnal desire but a search for one "through whom to beget children."[152]

Ibn Gabbai's interweaving of scripture, commentary, and supercommentary illustrates the humble literary medium through which one layer of tradition could adroitly be grafted onto another, even as substantial revision to the earlier tradition was being effected. In general, the supercommentarial format of lemma from commentary followed by gloss suggests subservience, or at least deference, to an earlier human mediator of the divine word. In the case of the Spanish supercommentators, however, this format can call attention to their estrangement from Rashi's interpretations and infiltration into the *Commentary* of ideas and frames of reference at a far remove from their pretext. All this raises the question: How aware were such supercommentators of innovating as they refashioned Rashi? Minimally, one can point to rare instances where they reread midrashim cited by Rashi in a manner that removed what they saw as a highly problematic element while granting that Rashi understood it differently.[153]

If the question of consciousness requires further inquiry, the kernel for the transformative Sefardic reading of Rashi's gloss on "this time" does not. That the re-presentations of Rashi just surveyed have much in common owes a great deal to Nahmanides, although he did not relate to Rashi on "this time" directly. Nahmanides gave a rather rare compliment to Rashi when speaking of his midrashic observation a couple of verses earlier that Adam was awakened to his loneliness owing to his encounter with the animals ("he explained well"). At the same time, Nahmanides taught that Adam's naming of the animals reflected his intellectual recognition of their "natures" and consequent unsuitability as the "helper" sought.[154] Here, as elsewhere, supercommentators infiltrated a Nahmanidean spirit into the *Commentary*, creating an overlay on Rashi's exegesis that responded keenly to a Sefardic sensibility.

Some of the Sefardic supercommentaries might have felt an added urgency to address Rashi's midrashic comment on Adam owing to the opprobrium heaped on it by Christians. As we have seen, the midrash was invoked to denigrate the Talmud in the anti-Jewish disputation of Tortosa and San Mateo held in 1413–14, in which Rashi's exegesis was often wielded as a polemical cudgel by those representing Christianity. The critique was reprised in an anti-Jewish work composed around 1460 by the Spanish Franciscan Alonso de Espina.[155] By explaining the midrash as they did, the supercommentators blunted such criticism, refashioning an apparently bizarre rabbinic idea on the assumption that its original speaker had never intended it (and Rashi had not understood it) literally. To interpret Rashi's comment on Adam's intercourse with animals cerebrally was, then, not only to allow Rashi to speak to Spanish Jews in ways they could admire but also to rebuff Christian attacks on the rabbinic inheritance at a time when stakes were high owing to an especially intense missionizing assault.

But there was a rub. In the *Commentary*, Rashi told of Adam "mating with" (*ba' 'al*) the animals. This formulation contained just enough semantic elasticity to allow the supercommentators to infuse it with a cognitive understanding of the act of conjunction that Rashi imputed to the first human being. By contrast, Rashi interpreted the saying in his Talmud commentary in a way that left no doubt Adam copulated with the animals—a clear countertestimony to their interpretation of the *Commentary* that all of Rashi's Sefardic supercommentators ignored. Little can be said about the talmudism of Almosnino or

"Anonymous," but there can be no doubt that Ibn Gabbai knew Rashi's talmudic gloss well. Leading supercommentators, most notably Elijah Mizrahi, eventually adduced it as clear evidence for the truth of a literal reading of the gloss in the *Commentary*.[156] The Sefardic supercommentators, to a one, ignored Rashi's talmudic gloss and deprived his comment in the *Commentary* of its literal purport, leaving the way open to an alternate reading they found exegetically tenable, religiously acceptable, and spiritually edifying. The one they created said, in Rashi's name, something profound about the character of the prototypical human couple's union in the garden at a time when masculinity and femininity were first being defined. The result was to take what could have been an embarrassment and turn it into a reason why the *Commentary* could be enshrined as a work worthy of study and, indeed, reverence.

"Rashi Is the Word of God": Supercommentary and the Omnisignificant Imperative

The context for the second wave of Sefardic supercommentaries, produced in the decades before and after the 1492 expulsion of Spanish Jewry, was the rise of an approach to textual study associated with Castile's presiding rabbinic presence for most of the fifteenth century, Isaac Canpanton. Before passing away in 1463, Canpanton authored a compact work of interpretive theory entitled *Darkhei ha-talmud* (*Ways of the Talmud*; in the 1593 Mantua edition, *Darkhei ha-gemara*), in which he detailed a set of interpretive principles called *'iyyun*. Most often rendered as "speculation" or "investigation," this term from the lexicon of medieval scientific Hebrew was associated with philosophical speculation by both friends and foes of this activity. In terms of hermeneutical application, its Ashkenazic cognate was the casuistic methods subsumed under the label *pilpul*.[157] The method's mainstays apparently derived from medieval traditions of Aristotelian logic and linguistic philosophy as mediated by Muslim (and in some measure Christian) tradents. The result was that a significant segment of Hispano-Jewish rabbis saw logic as the key to attaining truth, including that of the Torah.[158] Spanish supercommentators, while not in the vanguard of Jewish adaptations of logic to exegesis, reflect an intensity of engagement with this branch of philosophy seldom seen in the field.[159]

The methods honed by Canpanton comprised more than a set of precisely calibrated tools of textual analysis. They also bridged between teachings on human perfection propounded by medieval Judaism's philosophical wing and the pervasive focus on Talmud characteristic of higher Jewish education. So conceived, immersion in the thrust and parry of talmudic discourse could attract young minds drawn to philosophy. Indeed, by wedding traditional rabbinic study to a rationalist soteriology, Canpanton allowed practitioners of "speculation" to see such study as the route to human perfection and thence the intellect's eternal union with God. Those who studied the Talmud in the proper way actualized their rational potential and attained the sort of perfection that many in Spain saw as a *sine qua non* for salvation.[160]

Placed in a broader history of Jewish hermeneutics, Sefardic *'iyyun* stands as a particular application of the principle of omnisignificance. Canpanton's disciples used this approach not only to decode statements on the talmudic page but also, as their mentor urged, to unpack the talmudic commentaries investigated in Castilian rabbinic academies, those of Rashi and Nahmanides. The assumption was that speech—or at least superior speech—should be analyzed logically, on the view that "each and every word and part thereof signifies something new."[161] Canpanton even made bold to declare that "it was the habit of Rashi . . . not to utter a thing or let a word exit his mouth without need." What followed from this claim was the application of the "omnisignificant imperative" to the *Commentary*—in whatever version supercommentators had it—as a virtually flawless literary artifact.[162]

Given the apparent Aragonese roots of the *'iyyun* method, it is not surprising that the earlier stratum of glosses on the *Commentary* written in Aragon anticipate the critical vocabulary and exegetical applications of logic that flourished in the later Castilian supercommentaries.[163] Almosnino, for instance, could turn hortatory when extolling Rashi's verbal exactitude, urging readers to "marvel" at—and, of course, be "meticulous" in inspecting—Rashi's formulations "in every place." He was sure that Rashi "weighed" all in the "balance of his pure intellect" and communicated ideas with supreme care.[164] As noted, similar notions appear in Ibn Gabbai.

Habituated to omnisignificant study of Rashi's talmudic discourse, those who cultivated *'iyyun* found it natural to apply it in order to decipher what they took to be the supremely dense and economical discourse of the *Commentary*. More specifically, their doctrine of linguistic nonsuperfluity underwrote a threefold task: preemption, elucidation, and what they called "ineluctability."[165] Preemption grew out of Canpanton's understanding that a commentator came not only to interpret a text aright but also to preempt error. Even in the most precise linguistic formulations, multiple interpretations lay dormant, taxing the expositor to discern the fallacious readings Rashi forestalled or, in Canpantonian terminology, "preempted" (*nishmar*) or "heedfully eschewed" (*nizhar*). So central was this task that Canpanton's method came to be called the "method of preemptions" (*derekh ha-shemirot*). With forestalled readings identified, the supercommentator turned to elucidation (*perush*) of the interpretation that Rashi did supply and to a demonstration of not only its plausibility but also its "ineluctability" (*hekhreaḥ*). Elucidation focused on discernment of the textual naunce (*diyyuq*) that triggered Rashi's gloss, while the erroneous readings identified at the outset helped to clinch its ineluctability.

Though *ʻiyyun*, so described, may sound like a dry, even an overly clever exercise in exegetical technique, profound religious lessons could emerge from such an undertaking, as may be seen in a small sample from an anonymous Sefardic supercommentary on Rashi's account of the theophany in which the divine name YHVH is revealed to Moses: It begins: "God spoke (*vayedabber 'elohim*) to Moses and said to him, 'I am the Lord [YHVH]. I appeared to Abraham, Isaac, and Jacob as El Shaddai, but I did not make myself known to them by My name YHVH'" (Exod 6:2–3). Rashi clarifies the phrase "God spoke" as meaning that the Deity harshly reproved Moses (*dibber 'ito mishpaṭ*).[166] This rebuke marks a response to Moses's censorious query: "Why did You bring harm upon this people? Why did You send me?" (Exod 5:22). As for the statement "I am the Lord," it does not impart the revelation of an appellation theretofore unknown, but surreptitiously continues the reprimand by invoking a name that refers to God's attribute of faithfulness, whether in punishment or reward, as the name had been "midrashically exposited" (*nidrash*) in "a number of places":

> "I am the Lord"—[it means] faithful to requite, when said in the context of punishment. Example: "profaning the name of your God: I am the Lord" (Lev 19:12). When said in the context of fulfillment of commandments—example: "You shall faithfully observe My commandments: I am the Lord" (Leviticus 22:31)—[it means] faithful to reward.

YHVH was, then, a name known to the patriarchs (resolving the difficulty generated by the fact that the appellation appears in a number of interchanges between them and God), but not one by which the Deity had made Himself known to them in the sense that it reflected a divine attribute they had not experienced. In the words Rashi daringly imputed to God: "I made promises to them but did not fulfill them."[167]

At this point, we turn to the supercommentator, who offers a crowded half page of analysis (what follows is only a very partial rendering of the intricacies), full of *ʻiyyun*-laden terminology: *diqdeq, nizhar, hekhreaḥ, lashon, ʻinyan, leʻayyen*. (Elsewhere, our supercommentator uses a verb that supplied the coinage for the Canpantonian method's Ashkenazic analogue, *pilpul*.)[168] Addressing the apparent lack of grounding for the claim that God spoke to

Moses reprovingly, the supercommentator tries to show not only that it is plausible but also what "ineluctably caused the master" to make it. He furnishes a threefold rationale. First, there was a common rabbinic understanding of the divine name *'Elohim* that appeared at the beginning of the verse but otherwise went unmentioned in the larger passage, making its significance all the more apparent. In and of itself, it reflected "the attribute of [divine] judgment." Next was another midrashic commonplace, this one with a biblical prooftext: "[the usage] 'and He spoke' [using the root *dibber*] is a language of harshness, as we find [in the verse] 'the man who is lord of the land spoke,' etc. (Gen 42:30)." A third "element of ineluctability" for what could easily seem a comment of Rashi that lacks textual ground was an apparent pleonasm in the text. If God relayed to Moses no more than what is "related explicitly in the pericope," the verse ought to have said "God spoke to Moses and said, 'I am God.'" Instead, it begins "God spoke to Moses," then "repeats and says 'and He said to him,'" alluding to the unrecorded communication inferred by Rashi that occurred between the formulae introducing what were in fact two distinct speeches.[169]

The glossator, like other Sefardic supercommentators, finds meaning not only in Rashi's words but also in the manner in which he presents them. In exposition of Exodus 6, Rashi's observation that the name YHVH signifies faithfulness in fulfillment of promises was pitched toward a message of hope that Moses was to impart: despite the perilous pass in which the people found themselves, their deliverance was assured. Yet when illustrating this understanding of the divine name, Rashi chose first to exemplify its usage "in the context of punishment." To the supercommentator, it is obvious that Rashi "ought to have adduced initially a proof for the fact that He is faithful to give a good reward, in keeping with the immediate context." He therefore posits that Rashi wished to stress that YHVH referred to the attribute of honoring promises of all sorts including punitive ones, even though, unlike the divine name *'Elohim*, the name YHVH was also associated with the attribute of divine mercy. Interpreting the sequence of the exposition, the supercommentator finds an attempt to drive home the point that the divine pledge to be "true" to promises encompasses punishment, as well as reward.[170]

Read thus, Rashi's comment brimmed with easily missed theological depth. The stress on YHVH as a name indicative of faithfulness to execute promises fit the context of Exodus 6, which began the tale of divinely wrought scourges that eventually brought about the rescue of Abraham's descendants that God had promised, but did the act of deliverance result from justice or mercy? If Rashi seemingly eschewed such reflections in his glosses on Exodus 6, the Canpantonian knew better. God's use of YHVH, a name often taken to connote mercy, might suggest that the impending deliverance was an act of grace.

Rashi therefore took care—according to the supercommentator—to have God speak of faithfulness to fulfill promises, meaning "that God's intention was not to remove them [the Israelites] on the basis of mercy but, as it were, on the basis of an obligation since He is obliged to keep His good word."[171]

In the Canpantonian dispensation, Sefardic exegesis—which initially saw a flight from midrashic interpretation in a quest for scripture's "contextual sense"—came full circle and then some, addressing, if only obliquely, a question that challenged medieval commentators, Jewish and otherwise. To what extent was the divine speech in scripture to be seen as radically other than the sort of discourse that comprised texts created by human industry? To what degree could an aesthetic appreciation of scripture be used to account for such aspects of it as repetitions, seeming superfluities, and so forth? Ancient Christian interpreters found no contradiction between appreciating what they saw as scripture's aesthetic features and appreciating its revealed origins, although not all of them made strong claims for the revealed word's literary superiority.[172] By contrast, owing to the doctrine of *iʿjāz*, or "miraculous inimitability," commentators on the Quran tended to analyze its formal features in ways that justified the claim that no human production could match the Quran in substance or in formal excellence.[173] In Jewish exegesis, commentators associated with the Andalusian school and its offshoots treated questions of scriptural omnisignificance in terms of what would later come to be called "biblical poetics." The result was a blurring of any total disjunction between scriptural and human discourse, such that textual elements that were grist for the midrashic mill were now understood under a range of literary conventions and stylistic rules. In denying the significance of such things as repetitions or seemingly superfluous letters, these exegetes undercut the search for meaning in each detail.[174] In northern France, it was Rashi who oversaw a shift away from a totally omnisignificant approach—or "thinking outside the midrashic box," as Robert Harris puts it—in ways that created space for plain sense interpretation and paved the way for more consistent exegesis along these lines among some northern French successors.[175]

Yet in Rashi supercommentary on the eve of the expulsion, tools from the midrashic box were now returned to service, the better to understand the *Commentary*, viewed as an omnisignificant text on a par, at least functionally, with scripture. If the fate of the superfluous *vav* in rabbinic hermeneutics is "representative of the entire midrashic enterprise,"[176] Sefardic glossators now invested the one-letter conjunction with meaning in the *Commentary*. Where Rashi could have said "why is this pericope adjoined" but instead wrote "*And* why," a Canpantonian was there not just to explain what it meant but also to demonstrate how a single "and" of Rashi thwarted *in advance* an objection later to be raised by Nahmanides![177] Such claims of maximal meaning were bound to invite a reaction, and sure enough, debates broke out as *'iyyun*-based study of the *Commentary* threatened to create overinterpretation without restraint.[178]

In principle, Canpantonians were willing to apply to Nahmanides the same assumptions they brought to their study of the *Commentary*, but in practice only Rashi and his work attracted a raft of supercommentaries and the accolades to match. Judah Khalatz declared Rashi the "light of the exile." He also accorded him a laurel initially used for Maimonides and largely reserved for him after: Rashi was "last of the Geonim [chronologically] but first in importance."[179] The *Commentary* was nothing less than the "paradigm" (*binyan 'av*) for all works in the field. It had won renown "throughout all constituencies of Israel." Without it, "Heaven forefend, we would be as sheep gone astray, neither knowing nor understanding, going about in darkness—especially in this generation of ours." Khalatz held that Rashi, had he lived in the "period of the ancient authorities, the early Geonim," would not just have surpassed them, but "guided them on the path to an understanding in scripture and Talmud."[180]

For Khalatz, none like Rashi arose after Rashi, "all the more in this generation," a description that evoked the Torah's account of Moses *qua* prophet (Deut 34:10). As for the *Commentary*, it bore "multitudinous things" in its exposition of "every single verse." Reversing the letters of the first word in "Right (*yashar*) is the word of the Lord" (Ps 33:4) to equate it with *rashi*, Khalatz had the Psalmist declare: "Rashi is the word of the Lord."[181]

The Supercommentarial Difference: A Great Voice That Does Not Cease

Supercommentators, long ignored as contributors to the rich embroidery that is the Jewish exegetical tradition, exemplify the observation that what is commentary in one generation can become the prime matter of a later generation's own commentary.[182] As applied to the *Commentary*, supercommentators helped to turn Rashi's explanation of the Torah into a work that, practically without parallel among Jewish writings, exemplifies the trope that casts rabbinic canon formation as a tale of a "great voice that does not cease" (cf. Deut 5:19).[183]

In northern France, Rashi was a native son and founder of a school, whose reputation required no burnishing. No process of naturalization was needed for the *Commentary* to be ushered into the heart of Franco-German biblical scholarship, although supercommentaries in the strict sense arose only in early modern times. By then, Ashkenazic commentaries on the Torah were few and far between. Building on the developments we saw, Rashi supercommentary became, amazingly enough, the dominant form of exegetical expression in early modern Central and Eastern European seats of learning.[184]

In Spain, the *Commentary*'s reception often entailed negotiation as its words were made to appeal to a readership shaped by Sefardic intellectual trends and spiritual currents. Expositors now wrote full-blown supercommentaries that aimed to clarify the *Commentary*'s textual cruxes or deeper meanings. Following citations of a lemma, they typically used a formula like "he said" or "he meant that" to introduce their clarification of Rashi. Yet, modern-day readers can justifiably feel that the elaborations following such formulae sometimes depart decisively from what Rashi intended—indeed, at times, as we have seen, from what he *could* have intended.

By ascribing to the *Commentary* untold depth, and even, in the Canpantonian understanding, an omnisignificance bordering on perfection, Sefardic supercommentators enhanced the authority of all that they read out of, or into, this text. They sometimes—it is important to stress that this is hardly the whole story—illustrate the form that innovation usually takes in traditions that look to canonical texts for guidance. In these, breaks with tradition present themselves in terms of continuity with it. The question of appropriation in the reception of the *Commentary* becomes especially complicated when one considers the issue of the consciousness (or, as Bernard Levinson would have it, "false consciousness") of the hermeneut.[185] Put simply, while some of the Sefardic supercommentators at times engage in what seem like extravagant refashionings of Rashi's words, they provide no indication of doing so consciously. Instead, they display the sort of "exegetical ingenuity" that Jonathan Z. Smith calls "the most characteristic, persistent and obsessive religious activity."[186] These receptions of the *Commentary* underscore the observation that "the canonization of a book is not tantamount to an acceptance of its meanings as authoritative."[187] They help to explain how the *Commentary* attained its premier status among Torah commentaries when the last Jew left Spanish soil.

Having looked at processes of canonization in the Ashkenazic and Sefardic domains, broadly and then in the supercommentaries, we turn to some little-known counterparts of the supercommentators—writers who saw in Rashi's biblical scholarship deficiencies and, in some cases, scandalous and even dangerous distortions of the Torah's meaning and message. In what might be billed as their supercommentaries-in-reverse lies an unknown chapter of the *Commentary*'s reception as it mainly unfolded far from Ashkenaz and Sefarad, in eastern Mediterranean lands.

PART II

Resisting Readers

4

"Ridiculousness and Risibility"

RATIONALIST CRITICISM IN AN EASTERN MEDITERRANEAN KEY

THE RELIGIOCULTURAL SPHERE that seems to loom largest in tracing critical receptions of the *Commentary* is the veritable Babel of Jewish intellectual and literary expression in the late medieval eastern Mediterranean. In addition to parts of the "abode of Islam," the Jewries of the region comprised cities in Byzantium, outposts of Asia Minor, and islands in the Aegean Sea. The "Byzantine world"—shorthand for a cultural domain independent of the countless fluctuations in political dominance and frequent exchanges of territory in the region from the tenth century on[1]—counted among its important Jewish communities those in Constantinople and Crete. Delineation of the *Commentary*'s reception in such locales presents a challenge, not least due to scholarly neglect of Byzantine Jewish literature. The "ignorance and even contempt" with which Byzantine Jewish culture has too often been treated is only beginning to recede.[2]

When it comes to Hebrew Byzantine biblical scholarship in the late Middle Ages, there is a near total blank. Indeed, recognition of the very existence of the field is typically absent even from specialized literature.[3] By contrast, earlier strata of Byzantine exegesis have received attention, including a recently discovered phase comprising early medieval fragments from the Cairo Geniza that bring to light Rabbanite and Karaite commentaries with Judeo-Greek glosses. A later midrashic layer of Byzantine exegesis, whose most famous representative is *Midrash leqaḥ ṭov* by Rashi's contemporary Tobias ben Eliezer of Castoria, has received attention.[4] Neither of these phases of Byzantine exegesis, however, forms a part of the *Commentary*'s reception, being at best contemporary with the composition and earliest local dissemination of Rashi's work. More to the point, neither of these earlier strata of the Byzantine tradition reflects its rationalist turn following the Fourth Crusade (1204) as facilitated by the arrival of new interpretive methods, ideas, aims, and sources from Spain and southern France. In particular, Abraham Ibn Ezra and Maimonides pointed biblical commentary in new directions. The exegesis of their Byzantine disciples constitutes a little known closing chapter in the history of medieval Jewish rationalist biblical interpretation, with all the implications this fact has for Rashi's reception in the region.

In late medieval biblical scholarship, something unprecedented occurs in the writings of several scholars with certain or highly probable eastern Mediterranean affiliations: the *Commentary* is subjected to intense and at times systematic criticism from a position of frank superiority. The disapprobation is variously expressed as reservations between the lines, head-on assault, and occasionally, withering derision. The critics focus on two things: misguided exegesis, especially as expressed in the *Commentary*'s surfeit of midrash; and the scandalously unscientific understanding of the Torah that Rashi is charged with promoting.

As we begin to explore this little-known side of the *Commentary*'s reception, I first describe distinctive features of the eastern Mediterranean milieu and the rocky fate of Rashi's exegesis in the region broadly. I then zoom in on *Ṣafenat pa'neaḥ* (*Revealer of Secrets*), a Torah commentary by the ardent Maimonidean Eleazar Ashkenazi ben Natan ha-Bavli, the earliest datable figure known to me to adopt a stance of arrant scorn toward Rashi. Study of his work provides a window onto a world of rhetorically intense resistance to Rashi expressed more consistently by other scholars who deemed the *Commentary* in varying degrees inimical to, if not wholly subversive of, a true understanding of the Torah's meaning and thence of Judaism's main message.

Byzantine Jewry: Cultural Confluences and Conflicts

The eastern Mediterranean stands out as a late medieval Jewish multicultural mecca where the arrival of new ideas from abroad and intrareligious heterogeneity generated confluences and conflicts with implications for biblical scholarship generally, and the *Commentary*'s reception in particular. At the region's heart was the slowly ebbing Byzantine world that had succeeded the eastern Roman Empire. A decisive upheaval was the advent of Italian maritime powers following the Venetian-led Fourth Crusade of 1204, which yielded new ties to the European West. Subsequent centuries saw Ottoman conquests in the Balkans and Asia Minor reduce areas of Christian control, culminating in the greatest shock of all: the fall of Constantinople, the capital of eastern Christendom, in 1453. Carrying on and at times prospering in the increasingly wartorn, politically fractured environment were Jewish communities, home to an alien minority situated within the multicultural tableau of eastern Christianity.

Byzantine communities had long served as *entrepôts* for travelers and refugees, including scholars from the four corners of the Jewish world. Early medieval boundaries between Byzantium and the world of Islam were permeable, with Byzantine Jewish communities staying in close communication with the great rabbinic academies in Iraq and Palestine. Jews on pilgrimage to the Muslim East, including to the holy land, often stopped, temporarily or permanently, in Byzantine centers along the way.[5] After 1204, Greek-speaking Jews remained demographically dominant in both Byzantine- and Latin-controlled areas, but immigration from communities in Italy and Northern Europe increased. The eastward march of Ashkenazim intensified following the horrific persecutions associated with the Black Death and its aftermath. A half century later, the anti-Jewish riots of 1391–92 that devastated many of Spain's Jewish communities (Catalo-Aragonese ones in particular) propelled Spanish Jews eastward.[6] At this point, Spanish intellectual influence begins to leave, for instance, "an overwhelming mark on the Hebrew literary manuscripts written on Venetian Crete."[7]

Micha Perry describes Jewish Byzantium as a "junction of traditions" that, far from being a merely static channel for transmission, saw new types of religious observance and knowledge arrive from East and West that was then transformed according to the unique traits of Byzantine Jewry.[8] The shift toward a westward orientation over the course of the late Middle Ages was pronounced. After 1204, even the paper upon which Byzantine Jews wrote was affected, as Eastern types gave way to European ones.[9] Immigration could work to reconfigure the sociocultural and spiritual ethos of Byzantine communities, with some newcomers successfully imposing their religious practices or intellectual traditions on the native Romaniotes, as Judeo-Greek Jews called themselves (from "Romania," the Greek term for the Byzantine Empire). By the eve of its 1453 Ottoman conquest, the Constantinople Jewish community had, in Israel Ta-Shma's assessment, succumbed to Ashkenazic "spiritual hegemony."[10] After 1492, a mass influx of Spanish Jews set the stage for a battle for religiocultural supremacy ultimately decided in favor of the Hispanizing immigrants over the native Romaniotes.[11] The battle was the capstone of a long interval during which religious diversity undermined communal cohesion and created often strident forms of intrareligious dissent.[12]

In terms of scholarship, Romaniotes could lag. The names of dozens of Byzantine rabbis survive, but none counts as a towering figure. As late as Constantinople's fall, Byzantine scholars lacked elements of a "basic library," at least when it came to Jewish thought.[13] Talmud study was apparently scanted. Yohanan of Ochrida (in Macedonia), writing around the second quarter of the fifteenth century, related that Byzantine Jews were unable to study the "books of the Talmud" owing to their travails, preferring the eighth-century *She'iltot* of Aha of Shabha; hence, Yohanan's commentary on this gaonic tract.[14]

Jewish Byzantium stood at a junction between the Greco-Latin and Muslim spheres, creating multidirectional processes of exchange, including among native Judeo-Greek scholars, Rabbanite and Karaite. If not necessarily pioneering, Romaniote scholars did excel in the sort of intrareligious exchange enabled by the presence of Rabbanite communities alongside more recently organized Karaite ones.[15] Though a wall had to be built at one point to separate the groups in Constantinople,[16] Karaite scholars increasingly adopted and adapted Rabbanite models, whether by way of books or through personal contacts, as evidenced by Karaite students of the fifteenth-century Romaniote Rabbanites Mordechai Khomatiano (Komtino) and Shabbetai ben Malkiel.[17]

In terms of thought and biblical interpretation, 1204 (the year of Maimonides's passing, as it happens) marked a turning point. The violent occupation of Constantinople by Latin Crusaders heralded the arrival from the West of philosophical and scientific literature in Hebrew, a process of westernization also attested in the arrival of Latin literature on the Christian side.[18] An example of the expanded repertoire of available sources is *Ruaḥ ḥen*, an anonymous philosophical-scientific treatise of likely southern French origin that became a Byzantine favorite, cutting across denominational—that is, Rabbanite and Karaite—lines.[19] Most important for current purposes, a body of rationalist biblical commentary inspired by Abraham ibn Ezra and Maimonides arose as, like their Western counterparts, a segment of Byzantine scholars embraced what they deemed an enlightened Judaism grounded in reason-based exegesis. Their works represent the closing phase of rationalist Jewish biblical commentary in the Middle Ages.

A key center is Crete (Candia). Even before its conquest by Venice (rights acquired in 1204; actually ruled 1211–1669), this flagship Venetian colony in the eastern Mediterranean had a cross-cultural complexion born of a multiethnic and religiously plural environment comprising Latin Catholics and their Orthodox Greek, Armenian, and Jewish subjects.[20] Situated at the crossroads of three continents, and the first Byzantine holding to come under durable European rule, Crete stood at a nexus between the classical Greek heritage and Latin (eventually including incipient Renaissance) trends.[21] Its Jewish community came to be the largest of its sort in the Italian republic's Hellenic dominions. Following the Venetian advent, Jews hailing from France, Germany, Iberia, and elsewhere crowded into the Jewish quarter, all the more after Jews on Crete were forced to live there beginning around 1325.[22] Some were scholars with exegetical interests. The first surviving supercommentary on Abraham ibn Ezra, likely dating from the 1260s, was written by Eleazar ben Mattathias, a French scholar who came east and passed through (and may even have penned his work in) Crete. Judah ben Shemayah, after spending time in Germany and Venice, became the first German scholar to immigrate to Crete. At some point around the 1360s, he wrote a partially preserved Torah commentary. After arriving in Crete from Castile, Joseph ben Eliezer copied a supercommentary on Abraham ibn Ezra in 1375.[23]

The contribution to learning of Candiot Jewish scholars has much to do with the Hebrew book culture that flourished on the island. Scribes in Crete produced the vast majority of Hebrew manuscripts copied in medieval Byzantium.[24] Knowledge exchange to and from works in Greek was common.[25] An example is the Hebrew translation of Euclid's *Book of Elements* completed by Abraham ben Judah before he left Crete to study in Spain.[26] The work of translation was performed mostly by native sons, but also by copyists from abroad. Newly arrived scribes used the scripts (Italian, Spanish, etc.) to which they were accustomed, only later adopting the local Byzantine hand.[27] We have already noted the presence in Crete of the Sefardic Joseph ben Eliezer, copying an Ibn Ezra supercommentary. Around the same time, Moses ben Isaac ibn Tibbon, offshoot of the famous southern French clan, reproduced kabbalistic works on the island.[28] As it turns out, kabbalistic works constitute a higher percentage of writings copied in Byzantium than in any other medieval center.[29] Shabbetai ben Isaiah Hakohen Balbo, a descendant of one of Crete's venerable families, copied one of the earliest collections of zoharic writings to survive. (It eventually came to be the version of the *Zohar* used by Shabbetai Zvi.)[30]

Rashi's *Commentary* had a presence in Crete, as attested in the large fifteenth-century library of Levi ben Elijah Nomico,[31] but the island also proved to be the singular node of transmission of two rationalist works containing scathing attacks on the work. In 1399, Ephraim ben Shabbetai Ha-Melammed, describing Crete as his "place of exile," copied Eleazar Ashkenazi's *Ṣafenat pa'neaḥ* in the only version that survived. Around a decade later, the aforementioned Shabbetai Balbo preserved the sole surviving copy of the most concentrated assault on the *Commentary* of all times, *Sefer hassagot* (Book of Strictures).[32]

By the end of the fourteenth and into the fifteenth centuries, Crete stands out as something of a rationalist redoubt when centers of philosophic learning were contracting in the West. Elijah ben Eliezer wrote there a paraphrase of the book of Job in the spirit of that book's interpretation by Maimonides. In 1385, he wrote an anti-kabbalistic philosophic commentary on the classic work of early kabbalah, *Sefer ha-bahir* (The Book of Brilliance).[33] Another anti-kabbalistic blast filled with Aristotelian zeal stood at the center of a wrangle involving Shabbetai Balbo's son, Michael, *contestabile* (constable) or head of the Candiot community in the third quarter of the fifteenth century.

The clash occurred on Crete in the 1460s. It was instigated by a newcomer of, as his name implies, Franco-German pedigree, Moses Ashkenazi. Ashkenazi's Aristotelian ideas were presumably acquired in consequence of his family's sojourn in "the exile of Jerusalem residing in Spain."[34] He was, then, an immigrant, son of an immigrant, who aggressively challenged the support of the Cretan rabbinate for metempsychosis, the notion of posthumous migration of an individual soul into a new body. The idea was widespread in kabbalah and prominent in strands of then-emergent Renaissance thought. Ashkenazi, launching the most extensive statement of opposition to kabbalah since that body of learning had entered the light of Jewish history a few centuries earlier, insisted that reason denied this doctrine.[35] The immediate object of his campaign was local halakhic authorization for levirate marriage, a practice upheld by the mystical idea that the soul of a man who died childless would migrate into the son born of a union between his brother and former wife.[36] In sum, Ashkenazi's assault handsomely illustrates how ideas born of divergent traditions, some imported, could roil scholarship in the Byzantine East.

Ashkenazi's opponent, Michael Balbo, at once strikes a complex religious and intellectual profile while standing out as a representative of a certain Byzantine rabbinic type.[37] Though he engaged with philosophic ideas more than kabbalistic ones, Balbo sought to harmonize the two, an approach to the relationship between philosophy and kabbalah attested among other Byzantine thinkers.[38] In countering Ashkenazi, Balbo used exegetical and philosophical arguments to defend metempsychosis. At the same time, in this particular instance he also argued for kabbalah's superiority over philosophy and even engaged in some disparagement of the latter. The sharp tone of his attack on Ashkenazi is matched by the fiery rhetoric attested in Balbo's interchanges with a local Byzantine authority, Yedidyah Rakh of Rhodes.[39] As it turns out, attacks on the *Commentary* emanating from the East also feature high-pitched invective. Though Byzantine scholars mostly spared Rashi's work blunt disparagement, many, both Rabbanite and Karaite, had no hesitation in ignoring it while others were happy to lay bare some of its exegetical and theological shortcomings.

Eastern Mediterranean Exegetical Reception

One who seeks to track the reception of the *Commentary* in the East can only be chastened by the awareness that we lack a comprehensive study of the history and unique character of Jewish biblical interpretation in late medieval Byzantine climes.[40] The names even of some of the more salient figures remain unknown, and their often substantial codices, most still in manuscript, languish, so the first thing to say about any attempt at present to recover Rashi's fate in the East is that it is highly provisional.

While some facts might suggest prospects for the *Commentary*'s ready acceptance in the East, this was, over the long run, hardly what happened. Whether the early stratum of Byzantine exegesis recently uncovered in the Cairo Geniza supplied formative precursors for Rashi's approach is contested, but strong evidence has recently been adduced to support this claim.[41] Scholars have also noted affinities between Rashi's exegesis and that attested in works of Byzantine contemporaries, like *Leqaḥ ṭov* of Tobias ben Eliezer. Indeed, Ta-Shma went so far as to argue that Rashi himself added passages from *Leqaḥ ṭov* that appear in some manuscripts and printed versions of the *Commentary*, a view stoutly rejected by other scholars, past and present.[42] Yet in later medieval times, new spiritual winds blew. Now a number of forces began not only to pull away from potential approval of the *Commentary* but toward criticism of it. Thus, when the *Commentary* reached eastern Mediterranean centers, it was read, sifted, contemplated, and assessed as it was elsewhere, but beginning in the thirteenth century, such engagement increasingly unfolded against the backdrop of growing appreciation for Ibn Ezra's exegetical rationalism and teachings of a Maimonides-inspired Spanish-Provençal tradition of exegetical and theological discourse that militated heavily against the *Commentary*'s success. It was all part of a process that saw Byzantine writers adapt, compare, combine, and at times assail writings of now classic earlier medieval scholars.

The onset of the *Commentary*'s Byzantine reception predates the seismic transformation brought about by the sack of 1204, but earlier awareness of Rashi was apparently quite circumscribed. *Sefer rossina*, a work whose name reflects the southern Italian city of Rossano (Rusciana, Ruscianu), was composed soon after the Byzantine holding was conquered by Normans. It was, it would seem, intended as a sourcebook for study of the weekly pericope rather than a commentary proper. Apparently completed by Samuel of Rossano in 1124, and written in Hebrew, the work contains many more words in Byzantine

Greek than in Latin or the southern Italian vernacular. It combines a small amount of philological plain sense interpretation with a massive compendium of midrash.[43] Two references near its end suggest that the *Commentary* came into Samuel's hands as he put finishing touches on his own work.[44] Israel Ta-Shma proposed that Samuel also composed a gloss on Rashi, now lost. He does so based on two marginal notes found in a late manuscript containing a Torah commentary with a strong concentration on Rashi (Ta-Shma calls it a "quasi-supercommentary"). If true, Samuel would claim the mantle of Rashi's first supercommentator. As it is, the evidence is hardly sufficient to bear the weight Ta-Shma tries to give it.[45]

After Samuel's fleeting references to Rashi, the trail of the *Commentary*'s Byzantine reception goes cold for some time, a fact that is surprising only if we forget the general dearth of information regarding later twelfth- and early thirteenth-century Greek-Jewish intellectual life. We have already noted evidence of flagging Talmud study. What this may mean is that the canonical aura that Rashi enjoyed owing to his status as the prime talmudic expositor may have appertained less in the East. Still, in his commentary on the *She'iltot*, Yohanan of Ochrida privileges Rashi's talmudic commentaries, singling them out by name in contrast to works that he ascribes generically to "the rest of the commentators."[46]

In terms of thirteenth-century encounters with the *Commentary*, we have already mentioned Isaiah ben Mali di Trani (d. ca. 1250), whose *Nimmuqei ḥumash* frequently references Rashi, though we also saw that it is a special case. Though its author was indeed a product of Byzantine southern Italy, Isaiah studied in Germany such that no real inferences can be drawn about the *Commentary*'s presence in Byzantium on the basis of his work. His combination of earlier Byzantine sources along with Rashi and other European ones is, at this early stage, unique.[47] Another prospect for awareness of Rashi in the high Middle Ages is Meyuhas ben Elijah, whose exegesis includes citations of Rashi as part of its admixture of *peshaṭ* and *derash*, with a strong preference for the former. Gershon Brin dates Meyuhas to the thirteenth century, though Ta-Shma argued for a fourteenth-century setting and a twelfth century date is possible.[48] It is worth noting that by the late thirteenth century, others of Rashi's biblical commentaries were circulating in the region. His exposition of the Prophets appears in one of the earliest dated manuscripts from Byzantium, from 1298.[49]

If not a heyday of eastern Mediterranean Rabbanite learning, the twelfth and thirteenth centuries did see the emergence of Byzantine Karaite scholarship. Even after Constantinople's reclamation by the Byzantines in 1261 and onset of Palaiologan rule, all in the region had to adjust to the permanent presence of European outposts. The establishment of Italian Black Sea colonies created new trade routes that opened lines of communication between the Crimea and Mediterranean hubs.[50] Aaron ben Joseph "the Elder" (ca. 1250–ca. 1320), the earliest Byzantine Karaite exegete, was born in Sulkhat in the Crimea, but was active mainly in Constantinople. He does not mention Rashi, but cites midrashim apparently known to him from the *Commentary*.[51]

Aaron ben Joseph's seeming knowledge of the *Commentary* suggests that Rashi's exegesis must have been prevalent, but there are few consistent echoes (abstracting from Isaiah di Trani as a special case) prior to Shemaryah ben Elijah (1275–1355). Even absent its many missing parts, the corpus of this fourteenth-century polymath stands as the largest surviving one by a Byzantine Jew. Born in Rome or Crete, and associated with the city of Negroponte (modern-day Khalkís) but bearing the byname "the Cretan," Shemaryah displays traits that increasingly characterized Byzantine writers. These include absorption of philosophical learning and Christian scholasticism as well as engagement with Karaites. His *'Elef ha-magen* was a first attempt in the East to systematically expound talmudic midrashim, seemingly in the hope of furthering rationalist interpretation of rabbinic dicta in the manner of Maimonides. In the volume on *Megillah*, dating from 1309 and the only one to survive, Shemaryah departs from Rashi's literal understandings of midrash, as he sometimes is keen to stress. He also does not hesitate to brand some of Rashi's talmudic interpretations "foolishness."[52]

In an introduction to an intended commentary on the Bible that he later reproduced in a letter to the Jews of Rome, Shemaryah proudly characterizes his exegesis as devoid of *derash ve-'aggadah*.[53] Surviving specimens of his corpus, which include commentaries on Song of Songs, Esther, parts of Proverbs, and scattered citations of commentaries on Genesis and Exodus, indicate that he remained largely true to this claim. This is so in the Esther and Song of Songs commentaries, where Shemaryah departs from Rashi accordingly.[54] In the surviving excerpts from his Genesis and Exodus commentaries, preserved by the Torah commentator of the next generation, Abraham Kirimi, the *Commentary* is variously endorsed or rejected. An example of the latter involves Rashi's critical view of Joseph's brothers as grounded in a midrash on dots ("extraordinary points" in the Masorah) placed over a word in the verse that described their pasturing of their father's flock at Shechem (Gen 37:12). Shemaryah offers a long rebuttal prefaced by the incisive comment that he who so expounds (*doresh*) has "plunged into the sea of *derash*, whence he ought to have retrieved a pearl but instead retrieved a shard." [55] The implication is that, although midrashim properly understood (or, perhaps, judiciously selected) constitute a treasure trove, Rashi lacks the skills to select or present them in ways that make them worthy of the admiration they deserve.

Though the surviving fragments from his Torah commentaries do not allow us to piece together a full picture of Shemaryah's attitude toward Maimonides or Rashi's great exegetical competitor, Abraham ibn Ezra, they suffice to show that his deference to Maimonides was great and his allegiance to Ibn Ezra not thoroughgoing. Various traits of his biblical scholarship are owed directly to Maimonides, like his understanding that certain events described in the Bible occurred in a prophetic vision and not in reality, and his interpretation of a rabbinic statement regarding Esther's investiture with "the holy spirit" in terms of prophetological ideas in the *Guide*.[56] From Judah ibn Moskoni of Ochrida, we hear of an Ibn Ezra supercommentary composed by Shemaryah that Ibn Moskoni describes as "the life of my spirit in [understanding] the words of the scholar [Ibn Ezra]." Difficulties attend Ibn Moskoni's testimony, but do not wholly undermine its validity.[57] Minimally, the testimony accurately signals rising interest in Ibn Ezra in the Byzantium of Shemaryah's day.

Abraham Kirimi's Torah commentary bore the title *Sefat ha-'emet* (Language of Truth). That it cites Shemaryah evidences newly developed points of contact between Byzantine seats of learning and ones located along the shores of the Black Sea region. It may also suggest Kirimi's migration from his native town of Eski-Krym (Sulkhat in the Crimea) to destinations farther west.[58] Dating from around 1358, *Sefat ha-'emet* was written at the behest of the son of the head of the Karaite community in Sulkhat and was copied by Karaites in all three surviving manuscripts. Thus does it exemplify the Rabbanite–Karaite rapprochement that at times unfolded in late medieval eastern centers of Jewish life.[59]

True to its plain sense sensibilities and rationalist mien, Kirimi's approach to the *Commentary* leans to the critical. At the same time, regarding Rashi's assertion of Adam's intercourse with subhuman creatures, he states that "R. Solomon wrote nicely." The reason Kirimi can welcome so strange a midrash is that he imbues it with a version of its cognitive reconfiguration that, as we saw, became *de rigueur* among Sefardic supercommentators, though we have no datable example from Spain as early as the 1350s when Kirimi wrote.[60] Other midrashim cited by Rashi also win his approval.[61] Yet Kirimi can also instruct his reader to "pay no heed to Rashi's words" owing to a lack of grounding in "the method of *peshaṭ*"[62] and put himself in step with Ibn Ezra's stance on typical midrashic techniques. To explain Lamech's polygamy (Gen 4:19–24), Rashi cited a midrash that had Lamech opt for a division of labor, with one wife for breeding and the other for nonprocreative sexual gratification. The name of the second, Zillah, was said to allude to her role as an object of his self-indulgence: "she would always sit in his shadow (*ṣilo*)." In a manner reminiscent of Ibn Ezra's objection to Rashi's morally laden reading of Nimrod's name ("one should not seek a meaning for every name"), Kirimi asks: "[W]ho can fathom the meaning of every name?"[63]

Kirimi's routine promotion of ideas and techniques known to him from Maimonides and Ibn Ezra put a wide distance not just between him and Rashi's exegesis but between him and the Judaism of the *Commentary*. His teaching that love of God is consequent upon knowledge of the Deity is pristine testimony to his Maimonidean frame of mind.[64] He also invokes Maimonides when interpreting key passages, as when, citing the *Guide of the Perplexed*, II:42, he argues that Abraham's interaction with the angels occurred in a prophetic dream. Adducing *Guide*, I:15, Kirimi insists that Jacob's dream-revelation of angels ascending and descending on a ladder toward heaven is a parable with cosmological purport.[65] Elsewhere, he reads famous stories, like that concerning the golden calf, in the manner of Ibn Ezra, astromagically, going so far as to cast the calf as a praiseworthy talismanic device made "for the honor of God." [66] With such admiration for Ibn Ezra and Maimonides, Kirimi was sure to find in Rashi's midrashim many a sore point.

Kirimi's Byzantine Karaite contemporary, Torah commentator Aaron ben Elijah "the Younger" (ca. 1328–1369), also knew Rashi, although he predictably took a dim view of his exegesis for many of the same reasons as Kirimi. Struggling to preserve their heritage in a sea of Rabbanism, Aaron was among the Karaite authors who increasingly produced works on Rabbanite models, favoring Maimonides and Ibn Ezra.[67] Unlike his older namesake, Aaron ben Joseph "the Elder," Aaron "the Younger" cited Rashi by name but left no doubt of his far greater respect for Ibn Ezra.[68] When it came to grading Ibn Ezra and Rashi in a hierarchy, the Karaite exegetes were in accord with many of their rationalist Rabbanite counterparts.

As we will eventually see in detail, esteem for Ibn Ezra was perhaps the decisive factor relegating Rashi's *Commentary* to the Byzantine margins.[69] The peripatetic peshatist never set foot in Byzantium, yet he cast darts from afar at exegetes whom he called "the scholars of Greece," like Tobias ben Eliezer and Meir of Constantinople, for overreliance on midrash.[70] As Byzantine Jews absorbed previously unknown writings from the West, Ibn Ezra gained a heroic image.[71] Some Byzantine Karaites were so admiring that they sought to enlist Ibn Ezra for their cause, suggesting he was a closet Karaite despite his repeated harsh censure of Karaism.[72]

Ibn Ezra's dominance in the region is variously attested. More Byzantine manuscripts survive of his works than the writings of Rashi or Maimonides, with his Torah commentary coming down in many Byzantine exemplars.[73] Ibn Ezra supercommentaries written by Byzantine authors abound. Indeed, as we noted, the very first surviving Ibn Ezra supercommentary, by the thirteenth-century Eleazar ben Mattathias, was possibly produced in Crete but at any rate likely in Byzantium.[74] The reverence in which Ibn Ezra was held, and the rise of often (although not always) moderate rationalist strains, make eastern Mediterranean opposition to Rashi's exegesis unsurprising. Still, this fact does nothing to prepare us for the blasts of criticism leveled against the *Commentary* by writers with possible, probable, or certain ties to this religio-cultural sphere, the earliest datable one being Eleazar Ashkenazi ben Natan ha-Bavli.

"All Who Hear Will Laugh": Rashi Criticism in a Maimonidean Key

Eleazar wrote his *Ṣafenat pa'neaḥ* during an interval beginning no later than the mid-1360s and ending no earlier than 1371.[75] Although Rashi's exegesis figures in the work only sporadically, Eleazar's stance toward it, once brought to the surface, proves important both in itself and as an entrée into the more thoroughgoing critiques of other late medieval rationalists who skewered what they took to be the *Commentary*'s exegetically questionable and scandalously unscientific ideas.

Before delving into Eleazar's engagement with Rashi, a quick *tour d'horizon* is in order to capture his bio-bibliographic coordinates and something of his intellectual spirit. The data, though thin, converge to suggest that *Ṣafenat pa'neaḥ* was composed in an eastern Mediterranean locale, although some evidence can point in a different direction.[76] Minimally, onomastics, in tandem with other somewhat incidental bits of evidence, paint a complex picture of *Ṣafenat pa'neaḥ*'s geocultural background and possible place of origin. Eleazar's appellative "Ashkenazi" implies descent from Northern European stock, although the immediacy of his Franco-German heritage is impossible to judge. Assuming it was earlier generations of his family that immigrated, they followed a path trod by others of Ashkenazic provenance who ended up in Jewish communities in the Mediterranean East. The toponymic surname "ha-Bavli" (Babylonian) attached to his father in the manuscript of *Ṣafenat pa'neaḥ* suggests ties to the Islamic East, although other interpretations of it are possible.[77] Eleazar also shows unusually detailed knowledge of aspects of life in Egypt and its history.[78] A highly conjectural reconstruction is that he had ancestors from France or Germany who possibly sojourned in Babylonia, but at any rate passed time in Egypt, with Eleazar likely spending time there and in Byzantine lands, perhaps even Crete, where the only surviving copy of his work was made, in which case he could have been part of a longstanding flow of Jews from the Islamic East to the nearby territories of eastern Christendom.[79]

Languages reflected in *Ṣafenat pa'neaḥ* both support such a reconstruction and deepen the mystery of the work's origins and its author's possible boundary crossings. Given Eleazar's apparent Egyptian connections, one would assume acquaintance with Arabic, and in fact he does make passing allusions to reading in the Judeo-Arabic Torah commentary of Maimonides's son. He also registers common interchanges of letters between Hebrew and "the language of Ishmael." Remarkably, Eleazar relates to the post-Islamic transition from use of ancient Egyptian (Coptic) in the region to Arabic. Indeed, he may have been in touch with pockets of Coptic speakers, as his allusion to the definite article *pi* shows. Though such familiarity could comport with a life spent on islands like Cyprus, it is more readily associated with Egypt.[80] Complicating the picture, however, is the presence in *Ṣafenat pa'neaḥ* of several Hispanisms. Eleazar also observes that "the uncircumcised [Christians] pronounce [Hebrew] '*yehoshua*' [Joshua] '*ai zuah*' and [Hebrew] '*ḥavah*' [Eve] '*eva.*'"[81] One cannot, then, discount a Spanish sojourn like those attested for contemporary eastern Mediterranean savants such as Abraham ben Judah and Judah ibn Moskoni.[82]

Here is a key point: Eleazar makes it clear his own part of the world is far removed from the leading Western European rationalist centers. He observes that it was once engulfed in intellectual darkness and explicitly lauds thinkers of Western European origin who rescued "our [part of the] exile" from its tenebrous state. It seems likely that Eleazar refers to his situation somewhere in the East.

Discussing concealed parables embedded in the creation story that King Solomon had helped to decipher in some measure, but that remained full of perplexities, Eleazar credits the "sages of Spain" with decisive achievements in this area. Singled out are Maimonides and "his book, the *Guide*" and "R. Abraham ibn Ezra, the perfect, eminent scholar" who also explained "concealed" biblical passages by way of "hints that illumined our hearts in his commentary on the Torah and the rest of his books." Later offshoots of this foundational stratum of enlightenment are hailed in the continuation. The main figures mentioned are the thirteenth-century Toledan scientific encyclopedist Judah ben Solomon ha-Kohen, as well as Samuel ibn Tibbon and Jacob Anatoli, who "broadcast wisdom and taught students in Provence." Also mentioned is southern French biblical interpreter David Kimhi. This "wisdom spread to our [part of the] exile, whence we saw a great light." Eleazar invokes a verse (Ps 36:10) used by Maimonides to identify the intellect as a conduit between God and humankind that Kimhi applied to Maimonides himself, speaking of one who "taught us and illuminated our eyes about [many things] concerning which we walked in darkness before he came."[83] In so doing, Eleazar indicates that newly arrived Spanish and Provençal writings heralded the advent of Judaism rightly understood in a region that, as he describes it, otherwise would have remained mired in the Dark Ages.[84]

Since its completion in Crete in 1399, the copy of *Ṣafenat pa'neaḥ* produced by Ephraim ben Shabbetai has seen ups and downs, textually and otherwise. Already Ephraim did not work from a full version, although he made his copy only a few decades after Eleazar completed *Ṣafenat pa'neaḥ*, as is evident from his indication that a passage containing an esoteric interpretation of Eleazar was omitted by the scribe from whose copy he worked. (How he knows, he does not say.)[85] Ephraim's version of *Ṣafenat pa'neaḥ* was yet more maculate, reflecting expurgation of at least one passage that he (or perhaps his teacher) found "unable to abide." It relayed a reading of the miracle of the splitting of the Sea of Reeds that Ephraim says "split the sea of my heart." He expunged the offending account "so as not to be among those drowning in it," absolving this procedure by way of a biblicism: "I resolved to watch my words lest I offend by my speech (cf. Ps 39:2)."[86]

To finish out the story, Ephraim's version of *Ṣafenat pa'neaḥ* made its way at some point to Constantinople, and eventually Vienna, reaching the hands of the Russo-Austrian scholar and book collector Avraham Epstein, then moving to the Jewish Religious Community (Israelitische Kultusgemeinde), before joining the many artifacts and literary treasures looted by the Nazis.[87] As the Nazis sought to conceal plunder from a fast-approaching Soviet army, a train carrying documents and booty was intercepted by the Red Army and diverted to Moscow. Eleazar's work became part of a secret "Special Archive" eventually absorbed into the Russian State Military Archive. The full work, only recently recovered, remains to be integrated into the trajectory of rationalist Judaism in the East, which while largely derivative from Western models, had traits all its own.[88]

One way to approach Eleazar's aims and frame of mind is to consider his work's title, drawn as it is from the obscure name bestowed on Joseph by Pharaoh: *ṣafenat pa'neaḥ* (Gen 41:45). Although the folio where Eleazar expounds the name is sundered, the gist of his reading can be recovered. He took the first term to allude to "hidden and concealed secrets" and apparently thought the second component to be a word of Egyptian origin,[89] although like other medievals he may have taken it to mean something like "revealer." So understood, the title's summoning of the Torah's quintessential decipherer of hidden things proves apt, since Eleazar was largely preoccupied with disclosing "secrets of the Torah" to the discerning reader. At the same time, as was the wont of the medieval philosophers, he excludes from such revelations the multitude for whom, in typical Maimonidean fashion, he shows a profound elitist disdain.

In a passage that forthrightly discloses an elitist outlook, not to mention his Maimonidean aims and pretensions, Eleazar makes the point that the multitude often rest the delusions that they harbor on midrash. Furthermore, he contrasts an audience for whom rabbinic dicta "agreeable to hear among women and children" are appropriate with his own intended readership, adding that he cares not a whit whether the dolts who appreciate such midrashim despise his words, since "all my efforts are pitched toward edifying the perplexed individual (*ha-navokh*) [to disencumber him] from his perplexities." Eleazar obviously had in mind Maimonides's comment that it was better to satisfy a single virtuous (i.e., wise) person, even if to do so kindled displeasure among "ten thousand ignoramuses."[90] Clinching the Maimonidean character of the passage is the peroration, "Incline your ear and listen to the words of the sages" (Prov 22:17). Eleazar invokes the last of the three verses cited by Maimonides to introduce the *Guide*, thereby calling attention to the inestimable primacy of those who are wise in the manner that philosophical rationalists understood this term.

Eleazar learned well from Maimonides and his other rationalist models, applying their methods of scriptural decipherment with stark consistency. The cardinal rule, developed already in late gaonic literature, was that when literal interpretation contradicted a demonstrated truth, the latter must prevail. Maimonides applied this principle most famously to anthropomorphic descriptions of the Deity, but resolved other conflicts between scripture and reason on the basis of his view that "the gates of figurative interpretation" remain open.[91] Expressing the idea pointedly, Eleazar states that when plain sense readings contravene demonstrated truth, "we take them out of their plain sense so as to make them comply with the truth, for our Torah is truth and does not contradict the truth."[92] When stumbling on a classical text he found "strange," Maimonides often insisted on its allegorical purport. Little wonder, as Colette Sirat observes, that *Ṣafenat pa'neaḥ* follows Maimonidean leads in being replete with "decidedly intellectualist allegories."[93]

Similar rules applied to a proper understanding of midrash. As Maimonides lamented, the "multitude of Rabbanites," being rash fools "devoid of knowledge of the nature of being," merrily accepted the "impossibilities" that a literal understanding of rabbinic dicta often entailed.[94] Needless to say, Eleazar, who took his bearings from the nature of being at every turn, has no truck with this approach. He may have felt impelled, perhaps reluctantly at times, to assume that a hidden meaning was at hand wherever a biblical text taxed credulity, but midrashim were another matter. Departing from Maimonidean precedents, where the dignity of the sages was always maintained, he instructs his reader: "Do not let your brain be stuffed with midrashim positing impossibilities (*ha-derashot ha-nimna'ot*) about Nahum Ish Gam-Zu. . . . It is enough that we must believe what is stated explicitly in [the Torah of] the master of the prophets regarding the rod turning into a serpent and the serpent [back into] a rod, the secret of which (*sodo*) I shall explain."[95] Fabulous midrashim do not require charitable reading in the manner of their biblical counterparts. If they fail the test of rationality and prove impervious to nonliteral rehabilitation, they can be ignored, even rejected. Speaking with a directness that some rationalists committed to the substance of his position would eschew, Eleazar states flatly: "we shall not believe them."[96] Needless to say, such sentiments do not augur well for a warm embrace of Rashi's heavily midrashic *Commentary* and, indeed, Eleazar's complaints against the work, sporadic though they are, bear a disdain almost unique in the annals of Jewish literature. At the same time, his engagement with Rashi proves more variegated than one expects. Before turning to some undeniably eye-catching negative assessments, we should survey other types of interaction with the fruits of Rashi's interpretive enterprise.

Eleazar could reject some interpretations set forth by Rashi while adopting others. His reading of the verses introducing Noah is a case in point. In two interpretations, Rashi understood *toledot* in Genesis 6:9 ("This is the line [*toledot*] of Noah, Noah was a righteous man") as referring to offspring. In one, Rashi read the word to refer to biological offspring and in the other to metaphorical offspring, suggesting that the "real progeny" of the righteous were "their good deeds." In a straightforward disagreement about the plain sense—in which he characteristically sides with Ibn Ezra—Eleazar translates *toledot* differently, as "events."[97] According to Rashi, if *toledot* meant biological progeny, then the phrase "Noah was a righteous man" had to be understood as an apposition interpolated between "these are the *toledot* of Noah" and the actual listing of Noah's three sons in the following verse. Having mentioned Noah, scripture mentioned his righteousness (*sipper be-shivḥo*) as an aside. Eleazar uses almost the same phrase (*maggid be-shivḥo*) while placing himself in step with another plain sense reading of Rashi a few verses later.[98]

Even when Eleazar shares a bit of contextual interpretation with Rashi, he may turn it to a purpose far removed from the thrust of Rashi's explanation. Such is the case with the combination of imperative and preposition in Genesis 12:1, *lekh lekha*, in the divine command to Abram to separate himself from his home and his past. Paraphrasing a rabbinic idea, Rashi glossed "go forth from your native land" as being "for your own benefit" (*lehana'atekha*). He also defined the divinely promised benefactions: "I will make of you a great nation . . . moreover, I will make your character known in the world." Eleazar adopts Rashi's reading—"for your benefit"—but conceives the boon in a startlingly different manner: the benefit for departing Mesopotamia is "so [he] will not be killed."[99] While accepting Rashi's lexical-syntactic point, Eleazar focuses not on blessings to be accrued in Canaan but on the urgent need for Abram to flee a violent death owing to the intolerant polytheism that reigns in his native land. This political understanding of "for your benefit" bears more than a Maimonidean hue. Maimonides, basing himself on non-Jewish sources, told of the patriarch's persistent public refutation of pagan beliefs in response to which a king imprisoned him, confiscated his property, and expelled him.[100] Yet Maimonides stopped short of positing designs on Abram's life of the sort that Eleazar thought motivated the undeniably prudential command: "go forth." One might speculate about additional differences between Eleazar and Rashi in their interpretation of Genesis 12:1 if one assumes that Eleazar understood the command not as a direct divine communication but as a moment of prophetic self-enlightenment that allowed Abraham to perceive his desperate situation and escape it.[101] This understanding would fit with Eleazar's tendency to explain divine "particular providence" as self-providence—that is, as God providing human beings with the powers to preserve themselves through prudent action. Although this was a sort of providence that only a few intellectually perfect people enjoyed fully, Eleazar surely considered Abraham a person in this class.[102]

Eleazar's disinclination to name sources can leave Rashi's role in his exegesis open. Eleazar renders *ṣal'otav* (Gen 2:21) as "his sides." This reading may seem telling of Rashi's influence, especially as Eleazar cites the same prooftext as Rashi: "side of the tabernacle" (*ṣela' ha-mishkan*) in Exodus 26:20. Yet Ibn Ezra is just as likely to be the source, or even Maimonides.[103] Rashi invokes a threefold assonant wordplay to explicate the verbal root of the elusive word *mabbul: b-l-h* because the flood "ruined everything," *b-l-l* because the flood "confused everything," and *y-b-l* because the flood brought (*hovil*) everything from high to low. Eleazar derives the etymology from *n-b-l*, a verb of falling, decay, or destruction, understanding the root to denote general devastation by way of a natural cause.[104] Whether or not Eleazar aimed to bolster a more grammatically sound approach to counter Rashi's fanciful one, an example like this one highlights their differing approaches.

Though generally cool to midrashic interpretations, one can find Eleazar strikingly reconfiguring a midrash that Rashi brought to the fore, a pattern we have seen in other exegetes with strong philosophic convictions. Why did the snake approach the woman in particular as part of his plot to ensnare humanity's first models? Rashi thought that God revealed the motive in the snake's chastisement—"I will put enmity between you and the woman" (Gen 3:15); that is, the snake wished to kill Adam in order to take Eve. Rashi further noted: "you came to speak to Eve first only because women are easily seduced and know how to seduce their husbands." Eleazar's formulation seemingly has Rashi add that "women's minds are feeble," a rabbinic idea that appears in some versions of the *Commentary*, including Leipzig 1 and the first Spanish printed edition.[105] At all events, Eleazar deploys this idea when explicating the story allegorically: the "snake" (that is, imagination) sought to entice the woman (that is, matter) since the "initiation of incitement of the evil inclination" is to address the "woman" (or matter), since "she" heeds the serpentine imagination: "the woman's mind is feeble and readily seduced," whereas the man's is "settled and challenges the snake." Thus deployed, the midrash in Eleazar's version of Rashi helped him tell a story of how the imagination stimulates bodily desire in order to draw a person from cerebral pursuits, a cornerstone of Maimonides's reading of the narrative.[106] In such cases, Rashi served as an intermediary between rabbinic tradition and Eleazar, providing building blocks for interpretations that are incongruous with both Rashi's interpretive approach and his religious thought world.[107]

When not conjuring allegorical interpretations and instead reverting to his quest for *peshaṭ*, Eleazar generally campaigns against midrashic accretions and crudeness. I start with an overview of more oblique examples, in which Rashi's status as the main object of criticism is ambiguous. I then turn to Eleazar's openly withering critiques of midrashic ideas set forth in the *Commentary*.

A feature that undoubtedly enhanced the popularity of the *Commentary* was Rashi's propensity to offer midrashic "narrative expansions"[108] that supplied details nowhere stated in the Torah, filling in gaps in ways that usually provided a moral or doctrinal dividend. While not dismissing these out of hand, Eleazar is generally single-minded in his goal to debar such accretions, even at the cost of insisting on the most prosaic peshatist alternatives.

As God's call to Abraham to sacrifice his beloved son was, in Erich Auerbach's famous phrase, "fraught with background,"[109] Rashi finds license to clarify the background ("after these *devarim*") given at the outset of God's putting "Abraham to the test" (Gen 22:1). His assumption in two midrashic expansions is that the polyvalent word *devarim* refers not to prior "events" but to unrecorded "words" that set the trial in motion. In one scenario, the precipitating words were between Satan and God. When the former accused Abraham of lack of gratitude for Isaac as revealed in a failure to bring even a single sacrifice at any of his banquets, God created a trial to prove Abraham's absolute fidelity. Rashi has no qualms about introducing Satan into the story's *dramatis personae*, although he goes unmentioned there or, for that matter, anywhere else in the Torah. According to an alternate midrashic backstory, the "words" in question were exchanged between Ishmael and Isaac. When the former boasted of his voluntary submission to the trial of circumcision at the age of majority, Isaac responded that Ishmael's willingness to sacrifice one small part of his body could not compare to Isaac's own willingness to sacrifice his entire being, proving him the worthy heir of Abraham.[110] Rashi cites this midrash as well. Alongside such freighted ideas, Eleazar's reading is pure banality, reflecting a sequential approach and rejection of any extratextual infiltration. "After these things" simply meant after Abraham's planting of a tamarisk, as narrated two verses earlier.[111] How much this interpretation aims to undermine the *Commentary* is hard to say, but it certainly reveals Eleazar's effort to purge readers of the sort of extratextual midrashic fancies that make up so much of Rashi's retelling of the Torah. To achieve this, he is more than willing to say that *devarim* refers to events (or, in fact, a lone event) with no connection whatsoever to the great test.

Eleazar's peshatist minimalism also puts him at odds with Rashi's yen to identify obscure figures and places with known ones, a commonplace of rabbinic "creative historiography."[112] Rashi twice identifies Melchizedek, king of Salem who blesses Abraham and gives him gifts, as Noah's son Shem, in one case noting the aggadic origins of this identification. Rashi equates Salem with Jerusalem on the same basis. Rashi further observes that the gifts of bread and wine conferred on Abraham prefigure the "meal-offerings and libations" that his descendants would offer at the temple to be built in Salem/Jerusalem in the distant future.[113] Taken together, the midrashim assembled in the *Commentary* confer multiple benefits. They identify Melchizedek, a figure who otherwise suddenly emerges from the shadows and just as suddenly retreats into oblivion.[114] They explain the peculiarity that a king-priest living in otherwise idolatrous Canaan should share Abraham's monotheistic outlook and bless him in the name of "God Most High, creator of heaven and earth" (Gen 14:19). They turn the city that is to be Israel's future center of worship into a cradle of monotheism from early times. On their basis, the idea that Melchizedek's gifts intimate future priestly service makes sense, since it is now not some unknown Canaanite potentate who bestows them but Shem, to whom "all the descendants of Eber" (Gen 10:21), including Abraham, trace their roots.

Rather than simply ignore these identifications, Eleazar arraigns them. He grants that the equation of Salem and Jerusalem is "possible," perhaps because it can claim scriptural evidence in the form of a parallelism in Psalms (76:3).[115] By contrast, it is "unlikely" that Melchizedek is Shem, not only because "we do not find that he was a king" but also because of an unanswered question: Why should Shem have changed his name? Eleazar thinks that it makes more sense to see Mechizedek as a gentile king with a "composite" name—*melekh* + *zedeq* = king + justice—who retains his status as an otherwise unknown figure, but one perfect "in wisdom and all virtues."[116] Perhaps Eleazar saw Mechizedek as a prototype of the sort of wise gentile philosopher (philosopher king?) he admired. However this may be, in such instances he upends midrashim that became staples of Jewish understanding of the Torah under the influence of the *Commentary*.

Eleazar skirts the sort of moralizing midrashim with which the *Commentary* is replete in search of other explanations like those Ibn Ezra was likely to provision. Rashi explains that the flood's forty-day span (Gen 7:4) corresponds to the period of the formation of a fetus, since "by their [the antediluvians'] sinning [by illicit sexual relations] they troubled their Creator to fashion the form of illegitimate children." Eleazar cites Ibn Ezra as part of a disquisition on geographical and astronomical factors governing the need for a forty-day interval to execute the inhabited world's inundation.[117] Where Rashi sermonizes on the sin of sexual immorality to explain a key detail of the flood, Eleazar plumbs the duration of the cataclysm by drawing on insights into nature and astral decrees.

Taking "in his generations," a clause that followed the description of Noah as "a righteous man," as a qualifier (Gen 6:9), Rashi airs a rabbinic dispute that imbued the phrase with moral valence. Some sages read the phrase unsympathetically, viewing Noah as at best middling in his righteousness and exceptional only "in his generations" of surpassing wickedness. Others saw tacit praise: if Noah was a model of righteousness in the depraved generation of the flood, he surely would have attained greater heights of virtue in a more morally elevated era like Abraham's. Apart from his distaste for moralizing midrash, Eleazar considers Noah "perfect" in both "bodily constitution" and "wisdom," so he could hardly have sided with the naysayers. Naturally, he finds a way to interpret the qualifier in a manner having nothing to do with Noah's moral status. Focusing on the plural ("generations"), he builds on Ibn Ezra's view that the clause adds temporal stress. Its purport is that Noah's righteousness endured over his prolonged life span, even as generations of ordinary people expired.[118] This interpretation is in keeping with Eleazar's Maimonidean view that only antediluvians explicitly identified as enjoying uncommon longevity lived extraordinarily long life spans.[119]

In the case of the seven pairs of "pure" animals to be brought onto the ark in greater numbers than the "impure" ones (Gen 7:2–3), Rashi's characteristically carefree indulgence in midrashic anachronism stands in stark contrast to Eleazar's peshatist naturalism and the defiantly provocative interpretation it yields. The distinction between pure and impure animals in Genesis raises a raft of questions: Does it mark some essential characteristic in some animals as opposed to others? How does it relate to the dietary laws born of the same distinction in Leviticus? There is another question as well: Why was Noah told to take seven pairs of the pure and only two pairs of the impure animals?[120] Rashi, following midrashic precedent, does not find the matter especially puzzling. Pure and impure animals in Noah's time corresponded to the species classified as such in later Mosaic law: " 'pure'—in the future they would be permitted [for consumption] to Israel." From this fact follows another: Noah "learned Torah" long before its revelation at Sinai. As for the greater number of pure animals that Noah was commanded to take, it had to do with their fitness as sacrifices of the sort Noah would bring following the flood's cessation (Gen 8:20–21).[121]

Almost defiantly flaunting his departure from midrash, Eleazar claims that at this stage of history animals designated as "pure" were those that provided "good nutriment"; that is, they rendered the blood of those who consumed them "healthy and pure." On this definition, Eleazar thinks it "highly probable" that pigs, camels, hares, and other species later proscribed in the dietary laws were among the pure animals rescued in seven pairs. Impure species—that is, ones deleterious to health when consumed—were "horses, donkeys, dogs, wolves, and their like." Eleazar finds confirmation for this reading in the description of the latter as "not pure" (*lo ṭehorah;* Gen 7:2) rather than "impure" (*ṭeme'ah*). If the Torah had meant to refer to the ritual status of these animals, it would have called them "impure." Rounding out his account, Eleazar explains why seven pairs of the pure/healthy animals (like the pigs, on his understanding) were needed. It was to ensure a sufficient supply of wholesome victuals for the ark's human cargo, whereas a single pair of the others sufficed, since the aim in their rescue was simply to ensure the preservation of each species. In a fairly clear counterblast to Rashi, Eleazar observes that the dietary laws that classed, say, pigs as prohibited arose only "when Moses was commanded."[122] In his exegesis, time is linear, and in his legal theory, promulgation matters—in contrast to the midrashic anachronisms peddled by Rashi that could only swell his readers' credulity.

Where Eleazar challenges "one who implausibly interpreted" and the reading appears in Rashi, it is no rush to judgment to assume that he has the *Commentary* in mind. Take his dissatisfaction with the midrashic calculation of how old Isaac and Rebecca were at the time of their marriage; he is said to be a mature man of forty, she a wife but three years old. Undergirding these findings is the view that the binding of Isaac and the death of Sarah occurred proximately. Since Sarah was ninety years old at the time of Isaac's birth and

127 at the time of her death, it followed that Isaac was thirty-seven at the time of his binding, assuming the events occurred in chronological proximity, as their adjacency in the narrative might be taken to imply. This midrashic calculation has momentous consequences, even beyond, as Rashi has it, transforming Isaac's terrifying near-death experience into the cause of his mother's demise. It depicts Isaac as a man who was old enough to resist Abraham, but who instead embraced his sacrifice, as Rashi stressed, and went with a finding that Rebecca was born around the time of the binding, meaning that Isaac was forty years old at his betrothal three years on. As we saw, Ibn Ezra expressed willingness to accept the notion of Isaac as a mature agent at the time of his near-sacrifice if it were a true tradition—while suggesting it was not.[123]

Rashi infers the time of Rebecca's birth from a seemingly extraneous genealogy of Abraham's brother imparted to Abraham after Isaac's aborted sacrifice. It enumerated eight children born to Nahor and his wife Milcah. These included Bethuel, whose daughter, Rebecca, is the only member of the next generation mentioned in the family tree (Gen 22:20–24). Flagging this aberration, Rashi explains that the genealogy appeared "entirely for the sake of the verse" mentioning Rebecca, the point being to introduce her in order to intimate her impending marriage to Isaac.[124] Because the genealogy appeared between the binding of Isaac and the death of Sarah, it suggested synchronicity between Rebecca's birth as told to Abraham and the recently averted sacrifice of Isaac. The upshot is that Isaac, although cast in the story of the binding as a "boy" (Gen 22:12), was then thirty-seven, and forty when he married his bride of three years, this being the minimum halakhic age for females for the purpose of marital relations.

Arguing from the verse's denotation (*mashma'ut ha-katuv*), Eleazar indicates that the midrash infringes canons of plain sense realism. He also upbraids "he who implausibly interpreted that Rebecca's birth was imparted to Abraham at that time." On the contrary, Abraham was not informed of this fact. To make this claim convincing, Eleazar highlights an apparent pleonasm. The genealogy begins that "Abraham was told, Milcah too has borne children to your brother Nahor" (Gen 22:20) and ends "these eight Milcah bore to Nahor" (Gen 22:23). The seemingly unnecessary repetition delimits what Abraham was told—namely, only about the eight nephews and nieces—not about the later development that Bethuel fathered Rebecca. That phrase was not imparted to Abraham, but added at the time of the Torah's composition for the reader's benefit. Precisely because it was not part of the message to Abraham, the Torah went out of its way to indicate just what he did learn. On this reading, nothing could be inferred about the time of Rebecca's birth in relation to the binding of Isaac or, consequently, about their ages at the time of their nuptials. Like Ibn Ezra (in his independent reading), Eleazar insists that

Isaac was a lad of twelve at the time of his binding and denies that Rebecca was three. Meanwhile, his condemnation in the singular of "he who implausibly interpreted" just barely leaves his recoil from Rashi's interpretation at the level of insinuation.[125]

Where Rashi offers a miraculous midrash of the sort that many of his readers no doubt relished, Eleazar finds nothing to savor. He tells readers "not to listen to the words of the dreamer who said that the [plague of] darkness affected the Egyptians alone while there was light for the children of Israel, who entered the Egyptians' homes and saw their belongings." Readers could easily identify Rashi as the dreamer in question.[126] The critique displays Eleazar's inveterate naturalism, which sharply distinguishes the possible from the impossible. That light should be blotted out for one group and not for another in the same location is "impossible."[127]

Beyond barely oblique rebuke, *Ṣafenat pa'neaḥ* contains contemptuous attacks of which Rashi is the clear object. One concerns the parlay between Pharaoh and Jacob upon the latter's arrival in Egypt, which begins and ends with the indication that Jacob *b-r-kh* (Gen 47:7, 10) the Egyptian ruler. Yet it hardly seems plausible that a new arrival from famine-devastated Canaan should issue benedictions to a potentate deemed by himself and his subjects to be the source of all blessing.[128] Rashi, as plain sense interpreter, resolves the problem by reading the verbal root not in terms of its usual meaning ("blessing") but, rather, in reference to greetings that Jacob bestowed at the commencement and conclusion of his interview. With respect to the parting salutation, Rashi writes: "in the habitual manner for all those who take leave of an eminent figure: they bid them farewell and take permission [to withdraw]." In this case, however, he supplies a midrashic addendum that returns the verbal root to its usual signification and has Jacob serving as a conduit for a fruitful inundation of the Nile to fend off famine: "What was the blessing with which he blessed him [Pharaoh]? That the [waters of the] Nile might rise at his approach, [this being significant] since Egypt is not irrigated by rain water; rather the Nile rises and irrigates. Thenceforth from [the time of] Jacob's blessing Pharaoh would come to the Nile and it would rise to greet him and irrigate the land."[129] Here is a case where Rashi's inclusion of a midrash regarding the patriarchal powers of blessing left its mark in varied ways, including, it seems likely, iconography in a famous medieval Haggadah.[130] This is also a fine example of the sort of quasimythical product of the midrashic mind that Rashi reported with complete nonchalance in ways that could make rationalist tempers flare.

And so it is with Eleazar. He parses *b-r-kh* in both verses as Rashi initially does, in reference to a greeting. Jacob "saluted" Pharaoh in the "manner that is usual for all those who take leave of or enter before a king." Clearly agitated, however, Eleazar then denounces the "one who says that he [Jacob] blessed him [Pharaoh] that the [waters of the] Nile might rise before him." "Enlightened" ones (*maskilim*), understanding nature to operate with lawlike necessity, could only "laugh (*yishaqu*)." Eleazar summons Rashi's patronymic (Isaac/Yiṣḥaq), evoking the laughter associated with biblical Isaac (Gen 17:17, 18:12, 21:6) to sharpen his jeer. He further notes that "the time of the Nile's rising is known and is not dependent on Pharaoh nor any other person."[131] Eleazar takes as a given that Jacob knew this. Hence, he would not have conferred a blessing where a natural event not subject to benedictory manipulation was involved. Such ideas arose only in risible midrashim propounded by an unnamed but easily identifiable commentator whose interpretation anyone who wishes to be considered enlightened must reject, nay ridicule.

Eleazar sardonically puns on Rashi's patronymic in the case of another midrash, this one on the Egyptian plea to Joseph to "provide the seed, that we may live and not die" (Gen 47:19). Rashi explains that the request is for seed "to sow the ground." This request seems strange, as it comes before the end of the predicted seven-year interval of famine. Rashi explains that although Joseph said "And there are still five years to come in which there shall be no yield from tilling" (Gen 45:6), when Jacob came to Egypt so did "a blessing," and the Egyptians began to sow since "the famine ended."[132] This idea elicits Eleazar's scorn:

> Said Ha-Yitzhaki . . . . All who hear this will laugh at him (*kol ha-shomea' yiṣaḥaq lo*; cf. Gen 21:6): if it was within his [Jacob's] power to banish the famine that was decreed, how did he fail to banish famine from his own household and why, then, did he instruct [his sons] to go "procure rations for us there" (Gen 42:2), seeing as it was within his power [through his blessing] to cause death or bestow life.[133]

Striking here is that Eleazar directs ridicule not so much at the *Commentary* as at its author. In so doing, he may have fittingly borrowed from a gibe by one of his predecessors whose exegetical prowess he appreciated much more—namely, Ibn Ezra—who in one place hurls the following epithet at a commentator he deems wrongheaded: "rightly is his name called Isaac (*yiṣḥaq*) since all who hear will laugh at him."[134]

Eleazar's mockery differs slightly in the cases just discussed. In the first he says that the "enlightened" will scorn Rashi, in the second that "all" will. He may deem the second midrashic idea—the cessation of the famine upon Jacob's arrival in Egypt—to be outlandish even to ordinary readers, while feeling that the absurdity of the midrash regarding Jacob's blessing of the Nile might be evident only to those with a scientific understanding of rainfall, a phenomenon that, he elsewhere stresses, eludes the vulgar, who can understand precipitation only in terms of direct divine intervention.[135]

Eleazar's impulse to jeer using Rashi's patronymic allows us to identify Rashi as the likely object of his criticism where it otherwise is ambiguous. Rashi reads Jacob's blessing of Naphtali as relating to the victory hymn sung by Naphtali's descendants, Deborah and Barak. On this interpretation, the "blessing" entailed the patriarch's prophetic forecast of military exploits to be performed in a very distant future.[136] Pronouncing this interpretation "an error," Eleazar discounts it, first, because "we do not find that Deborah was an offshoot of Naphtali but rather dwelled in the hill country of Ephraim" (see Judg 4:5); and, second, because "a prophet does not foresee specific future events like these."[137] Who is the target of this refutation? On the merits, the answer is elusive since Eleazar's reproduction does not match Rashi's and bears affinity to an anonymous interpretation mentioned by Ibn Ezra that David Kimhi adopted.[138] But Eleazar introduces the discussion by saying that "one can only laugh at the commentator [who says] that '[Naphtali is] a hind [let loose]' alludes to Deborah and 'he gives beautiful words' alludes to Barak." In light of other passages where he invokes the same formula to assert an idea's risibility, it seems probable that here, as well, the commentator worthy of derision is "Ha-Yitzhaki."

Another case where Eleazar finds a midrash risible has to do with the notion that the corrupt conduct described as the prelude to the flood included the "sins of the fauna." We have seen how the archrationalist Jacob Anatoli—whom Eleazar greatly admires—likely addresses this rabbinic idea owing to its appearance in the *Commentary* and that even the antirationalist Nahmanides nevertheless feels compelled to find ways to ensure that Rashi's idea would not be taken at face value.[139] Like Anatoli, Eleazar does not mention Rashi when discussing the midrash, but he clearly responds to it as a consequence of Rashi's invocation. Let us look closely at his procedure as an example of his conviction that scripture must be read according to the findings of discursive reason, with the corollary that the *Commentary* must be dismissed, at times with dollops of derision.

Eleazar objects to the midrash on the fauna's sins for multiple reasons. First, interspecial breeding is an act no more unnatural for animals than the more frequently attested behavior of conspecific mating or promiscuity. The idea of animals perpetrating moral perversions while acting on the basis of natural instinct is "null." Second, it is untenable that the destruction of the fauna reflected a "sin residing in them," since as Eleazar elsewhere observes, animals lack a capacity for "choice," hence they are devoid of a capacity for moral (or immoral) action.[140] To these scientific claims Eleazar adds the theological one that animals are not subject to particular providence and therefore not to reward and punishment, either. This follows from his holding, after Maimonides, that the scientifically tenable view is that providence is commensurate with intellectual perfection. Because, among terrestrial beings, only humans possess reason, it follows that there is no "particular" providence over subhuman creatures. As Aristotle taught, their fate is left to chance, with providence ensuring only preservation of the species.[141] Rashi's exposition, opposed as it is to such demonstrated truths, had to be rejected.

Yet what to make of the biblical account, which did, after all, relate the destruction of the animals and not just the human beings? To explain the fate of the animals, Eleazar espouses a view in harmony with another midrash cited by Rashi in his interpretation of the divine promise to blot out "men together with beasts" (Gen 6:7). This midrash has God saying, "Now that humankind sins, what need have I for animals and beasts?" Eleazar expresses this anthropocentric teaching more clinically: the animals were "erased with humankind since they were only created for man, who is the ultimate purpose (*takhlit*) [of terrestrial creation]." As for scripture's "all flesh," it must refer to "all humankind." As we saw earlier, Nahmanides said the same. As prooftexts, Eleazar cites "Be silent, all flesh, before the Lord!" (Zech 2:17) and "All flesh shall come to worship Me" (Isa 66:23) as places where "flesh" clearly refers to human beings alone. Perhaps following Nahmanides, he also summons the broader phraseology later in the flood story, "And of all that lives, of all flesh" (Gen 6:19), to show how the Torah speaks when referring to animate life generally.[142]

Yet in the manner of Anatoli, Eleazar addresses a question that Nahmanides left untouched: Granting that the plain sense of "all flesh" might mean humankind alone, why should the Torah employ this ambiguous usage rather than speaking clearly? His explication is novel. The Torah used this phrase in order to allude to the *cause* of the calamity—namely, humanity's surrender to "flesh" or, as Eleazar broadens the term, "the evil impulse." In so saying, he relies on his reader to unpack what amounts to a highly compressed Maimonidean code such as commonly appears in *Ṣafenat pa'neaḥ*. Eleazar agrees with Maimonides that humankind's original failure amounted to detachment from rational knowledge and lapse into an existence overly determined by imagination and thus aimed mainly at physical pleasure. Identifying the evil impulse with imagination, Maimonides explains that "every deficiency of reason or character is due to the action of the imagination." The "act of imagination," which people share with beasts, was not "the act of the intellect" but its opposite, and it was tied to the evil impulse and to matter. Intellect, not imagination, separates man from beast.[143] One who studies *Ṣafenat pa'neaḥ* would, from Eleazar's exposition of the opening chapters of Genesis, already know that "flesh" was a code word. Eleazar understands God's closing of Adam's "flesh" after taking one of his sides in order to create Eve in light of the fact that "the flesh is what sins and what savors the sin." He explains Adam's becoming "one flesh" with Eve as a lamentable transition from the intellect's exclusive focus on theoretical truth to an existence ineluctably admixed with "the corporeal like her [Eve], since they were [now] one thing."[144] This reading of "flesh" carried over into later sections of *Ṣafenat pa'neaḥ*.[145] Returning to Genesis 6:12, although the word "flesh" referred to humankind, Eleazar explains that the term was used advisedly to highlight the cause of antediluvian humankind's ruin: immersion in fleshly things such as the imagination (or evil inclination, as it was also called) invariably entailed. Prior to the flood, people abandoned intellection, thereby furthering—or reenacting—the lapse of the first human beings who "perceived that they were naked" (Gen 3:7)—that is, "naked of all sciences." Seen in this way, Eleazar's compressed interpretation of "all flesh" amounts to a broad statement about the failure of the generation of the flood to actualize their intellect.[146] With the seduction of the first man by "his wife" (matter), man ate from the tree of knowledge of good and bad and became "like the beasts."[147] The generation of the flood marks a deepened human rejection of a concern for truth in favor of imagined desires and fleshly pleasures. Alluding to this in its infinitely economical way was the Torah's statement that "all flesh" corrupted its way.

Here as elsewhere, Eleazar's account integrates philosophical anthropology with theological Aristotelianism and allegorizing exegesis. As such, it stands at a very great distance from the midrashic idea of the fauna's sins as espoused by Rashi. Taking a parting shot at this idea in his concluding remark on Genesis 6:12, Eleazar notes that scripture could not possibly have meant that the fauna "corrupted its ways" morally, since to do so was to impute to subhuman creatures a moral agency that they lack. Rather, it was human sin that doomed the animals to perdition, since animals existed for the sake of people. One could therefore only "laugh (*lisḥoq*) at the *derash* that every species paired with a species not of its kind." This remark is anticipated when Eleazar states that what "they said" amounts to "ridiculousness and risibility" (*hittul u-seḥoq*).[148] For those attuned to the significance of Eleazar's deployment of the language of laughter, the meaning is clear. Rashi is the agent who brings rabbinic absurdity to the forefront of Jewish consciousness. Eleazar determines to laugh it out of the mainstream owing to its scientific and religious deviance and, of course, to explain the Torah aright.

Another bit of midrashic exegesis that Eleazar casts as a joke involves the time-honored parasemantic technique of *gemaṭriya*, or interpretation of words on the basis of their numerical value. Rashi, as we have seen, could derive, or at least buttress, crucial findings like the length of the Israelite sojourn in Egypt by way of this technique.[149] Wedding numerology to the aforementioned midrashic propensity to identify otherwise unnamed actors in the narrative, Rashi reports a startling finding regarding the 318 servants armed by Abraham (Gen 14:14): "our sages said that it was Eliezer" of Damascus. As Rashi notes, the sages based themselves on "the numerical value of his name," which totaled 318.[150] The midrash attests Rashi's tendency to turn biblical figures into prototypes for one or another virtue or vice. By having Eliezer join in Abraham's battle, the servant exemplifies the virtue of selflessness even when it stands in conflict with self-interest. In answering Abraham's call to arms and helping to save Lot, his master's natural heir, Eliezer jeopardized his own chances of inheriting from Abraham.[151] Needless to say, the midrash making Eliezer a lone ally of the patriarch sent a powerful message about the necessity for divine aid in military success.[152] Yet Ibn Ezra, here as elsewhere, strongly demurs: "the calculation of the [numerical values of] letters of [the name] Eliezer is by way of *derash*," a superimposition on scripture that invites interpretive anarchy since "anybody who wished could elicit [unverified information] from any name, for better or worse. Rather, the sum is as explicitly stated."[153] Numerological interpretation was one of a very few midrashic methods that evoked Ibn Ezra's open disparagement. That he stresses its whimsicality just here means he likely has Rashi in mind.[154]

Following Ibn Ezra, Eleazar states: "Know that there is no numerical value of letters in the Torah; it is only in *derash* [that letters are so construed]." Yet *gemaṭriya* could not be put down as some post-rabbinic confabulation. Even if he does not accept Nahmanides's claim that *gemaṭriyot* formed a part of the Sinaitic revelation along with other textual features like the crowns on the letters,[155] Eleazar has to deal with a mishnah's description of *gemaṭriya* as an "appetizer for wisdom." His response is to distinguish between the *gemaṭriya* about which the ancient sages spoke and the sort of exegesis called by this name. The latter was "tantamount to confusion and imaginary diversions," whereas what the sages stated about the calculation of cycles (*tequfot*) and *gemaṭriyot* being "appetizers for wisdom" was true, understanding that the former was the science of mathematical astronomy (*ḥokhmat ha-tekhunah*) and the latter geometry (*ḥokhmat ha-tishboret*): "Such [astronomical or geometric study] hones the mind for [study of] metaphysics and is an excellent propaedeutic, stimulating the human intellect just as victuals eaten without bread prior to a feast are called appetizers for the main feast, since they stimulate the appetite for eating."[156] In this passage, evocative of a metaphorical equation by Maimonides between eating and acquisition of knowledge,[157] Eleazar recaptures *gemaṭriya,* defined as geometry, as an "appetizer for wisdom" that leads to the highest intellectual pursuit. In this sense, *gemaṭriya* possesses worth, constituting a station on the way to ultimate perfection where students sharpen their minds in ways that set them on a path to metaphysical insight. None of this is to be confused with the numerological follies used to identify Abraham's armed followers with Eliezer of Damascus. Illustrating his conflicted approach to rabbinic dicta, Eleazar puts these down as a "joke" that can only yield "confusion" while lacking any textual grounding.[158] For the reader attuned to his use elsewhere of locutions involving the language of joking and familiar with Ibn Ezra's earlier attack on the midrash cited in the *Commentary,* the tacit targeting of Rashi here will be clear.

Another of Rashi's midrashim, this one regarding the reward extended to the midwives, Shifrah and Puah, for defying Pharaoh's order to kill the newborn Israelite males, leads Eleazar to a broad assault on the midrashic legacy, at least in its deleterious effects. Rashi uses midrash to identify the two otherwise unknown figures as Moses's mother and sister, Jochebed and Miriam. He glosses the highly ambiguous testimony that God "established households for them" (Exod 1:21) because of their fear of the Deity by eliding two talmudic views. The "houses" in question were taken to refer to two dynasties, one comprising Israel's future priests and Levites and the other Israel's future royalty. Rashi's exegesis is anchored in his indication that a verse in 1 Kgs designated these two dynasties by the appellation "houses": "When [Solomon] had finished building the House of the Lord [in which priests and Levites served] and the house of the king" (1 Kgs 9:1). At the same time, Rashi had to indicate how the houses did in fact descend from the midwives. In the case of priests and Levites, the matter was clear. This house clearly arose from Shifrah/Jochebed through Aaron and Moses. The dynasty of royalty was harder to explain, but Rashi managed by invoking a talmudic text that traced King David's lineage to Miriam.[159]

Eleazar's rejection of this reconstruction on technical grounds turns into an elegy for a Judaism perverted by midrashic distortions that conceal "the meaning of our God's Torah." Rashi's exegesis does not technically pass muster, since eligibility for offices like priest, Levite, or king depended on paternal rather than maternal pedigree. Pushing further, Eleazar boldly declaims the truth about the rabbinic legacy embodied in the *Commentary* despite the opprobrium likely to be poured on him in response:

> What should I say? These *derashot* are potent causes of the concealment of the Torah's true meaning from our people. Even as they were said in a distinct manner, the multitude understand them in this [straightforward] manner; nay, they believe in them and find them congenial more than the Torah's plain sense. Any discerning person ought to bewail the fact that they have drowned in a sea of *derashot*. Bottom line: I am that sort of person who refuses to pervert the meaning of our God's Torah, nor will I shrink before the multitude's revilement by withholding my opinion or kowtowing to another's opinions.[160]

Echoing Maimonides in the introduction to the *Guide* ("I am he who prefers to address that single person . . . I do not heed the blame of those many creatures"), [161] Eleazar conveys rage and despair at the effects of midrash on naive believers, at the absurdities that result when ordinary Jews (mis)read rabbinic dicta and midrashim displace the plain sense. The result of a community engulfed in a "sea of *derashot*" is nothing less than perversion of "the meaning of our God's Torah." He is diplomatic enough to suggest that the main culprit in this debacle is popular doltishness—a failure to appreciate that rabbinic dicta were set forth "in a distinct manner." Yet given his sharp jibes at Rashi, one can justifiably feel that his indictment is not limited to popular misconceptions. What is most salient for our purposes is that he leaves little doubt that the midrashim that falsify the meaning of God's Torah among "the multitude" are the ones made famous by "Ha-Yitzhaqi."

Unlike prior chastisers of Rashi such as his grandson Samuel ben Meir or Nahmanides, Eleazar deploys a weapon against the *Commentary* that wants for precedents (depending on how we date the work studied in the next chapter): ridicule. In wielding it, he may vaguely be seen to anticipate later advocates of Enlightenment as they set out to criticize orthodoxy. Invoking Gotthold Lessing, Leo Strauss says that these advocates "had to laugh orthodoxy out of the position from which it could not be driven by any other means. . . . The critique has a prospect of success, not by direct argumentation, but only by virtue of the mockery that lends spice to the arguments, and lodges them firmly in the hearer's mind."[162] Of course, Eleazar by no means forgoes direct argumentation, exegetical and theological. Yet he does take the added and seemingly gratuitous step of urging what Ralph Lerner has called "subversive laughter" with respect to the *Commentary*, knowing (or intuiting) that those who laugh "either join a community or invite others to create one because laughter excludes and includes." His harnessing of laughter's potentially rebellious force serves as a means for expanding the community of Rashi's derisive naysayers.[163]

Moving from rhetorical tactics to historical setting, we return to the eastern Mediterranean with its confluence of variegated Jewish intellectual and religious traditions in order to see how *Ṣafenat pa'neaḥ* might have emerged from them. The region provided an environment in which battles between various versions of the rationalist dispensation and a Judaism more continuous with the midrashic mentality apparently took an especially fierce and forthright turn. In this combat, Eleazar Ashkenazi aimed to arbitrate in favor of the former, taking inspiration from Ibn Ezra and Maimonides. Philosophers the multitude could not be, but their ignorance was not entirely invincible and Rashi stood culpable for nourishing it by way of his provision of a steady diet of midrashic homilies and legends.

To advance his cause, Eleazar did not scruple to denigrate Rashi as one who ensnarled Jews in midrashic distortions, of both the exegetical and the fabulist variety. Yet the fact that he raises his pitch so high might suggest a fear that Rashi was winning the day. Before settling on so weighty a conclusion, we obviously need to seek additional evidence beyond the episodic, if bracing confrontation with the *Commentary* in *Ṣafenat pa'neaḥ*. It comes in a tome titled the *Book of Strictures*, the lone work in the annals of Jewish literature written with the exclusive aim of reducing the *Commentary*'s reputation to an inferior state.

5

Rationalism versus the Rashi/ Rabbinic Axis

PSEUDO-RABAD'S *BOOK OF STRICTURES*

ELEAZAR ASHKENAZI DENOUNCED Rashi ("Ha-Yitzhaqi") sporadically. Not so a tract whose stance toward the *Commentary* is adversarial from start to finish: *The Book of Strictures in which Rabbi Abraham ben David Censured Our Rabbi Solomon the Frenchman (May His Memory Be a Blessing) Regarding the Commentary on the Torah* (in the original: *Sefer hassagot she-hissig ha-rav 'Avraham ben David zal 'al rabbenu Shelomo ha-ṣarfati zal be-ferush ha-torah*). In devoting himself to an often scornful assault on Rashi's exegesis and ideas, focusing almost exclusively on those of midrashic provenance, the author of *Sefer hassagot* put himself at odds with powerful intellectual, halakhic, and educational currents pulling in the opposite direction, each buttressing the work's growing reach and authority.[1]

Sefer hassagot is an undeniably obscure work that did nothing to seal the *Commentary*'s fate, yet it occupies a significant place in the reception history of Rashi's work, especially when viewed in terms of the hermeneutics of canonicity. The author's literary vehicle is the stricture (*hassagah*), to which he often appends a corrective to Rashi's interpretation. In so doing, he insistently contrasts an understanding of scripture grounded in canons of plain sense interpretation with Rashi's more fanciful midrashic methods. He also routinely contrasts the fantastical mentality attested in Rashi's midrashim with his own understanding of the world, steeped in scientifically informed criteria of credibility. The strictures medium, rare in the field of Jewish biblical interpretation, had its limitations. It could leave opaque the precise nature of an objection to Rashi and the preferred alternative unclear. Still, the result of the sustained critique is not in doubt. *Sefer hassagot* is the *ne plus ultra* of concentrated criticism of the *Commentary* in Jewish history, a work that raises basic questions not only about Rashi but also about the interpretive assumptions upon which rabbinic expositions of scripture stand. It also dismisses, often with a jeer, fundaments of the rabbinic worldview that, perhaps more than any other writer, Rashi, by way of his *Commentary*, etched into collective Jewish consciousness.

A Pseudepigraphic Stricturalist and His Aims

Sefer hassagot survives as a tiny entry in a vast, variegated manuscript copied in 1410 by Shabbetai ben Isaiah Balbo, a member of one of medieval Crete's most venerable Jewish families and one in a group of prolific copyists who inhabited the Venice-controlled island in late medieval times.[2] A scholar-copyist rather than a paid scribe, Balbo reproduced texts for personal use.[3] Indeed, he indicates in its colophon that he copied *Sefer hassagot* for himself.[4] There is no whisper of *Sefer hassagot*'s existence prior to Balbo's copy, nor did it leave much of an imprint on later writers with, as we shall see, the exception of a mid-fifteenth-century commentator, Aaron Aboulrabi.[5]

Sefer hassagot presents itself as a "book of *hassagot*" by "R. Abra(ha)m ben David."[6] The term "book" *(sefer)* could seem misleading for this lean volume of eleven leaves, but it was applied to medieval Hebrew texts of all lengths.[7] As for the work's status as compendium of strictures, it shines through at every turn. An invention of medieval Judaism, *hassagot* joined other post-talmudic forms of supplementary writing, like the famous additions to the Talmud by the Tosafists. Although the stricture was cultivated as a genre for centuries in a number of fields, including grammar and rabbinic study, strictures have received little study.[8] Beyond its most obvious element, exposing errors in a text under review, the genre could also involve defending an earlier work from critique and proposing (allegedly) superior alternatives. A classic case that came down under the rubric is Nahmanides's glosses on the methodological principles developed by Maimonides to enumerate the 613 commandments; among other things, these glosses at times defended an earlier list that Maimonides subjected to criticism.[9] As a term figuring in a work's title, *hassagot* first appears in a twelfth-century Hebrew version of *Kitāb al-mustalḥaq* (1012), a work of the eleventh-century Andalusian grammarian Jonah ibn Janah. Translated into Hebrew by Judah ibn Tibbon under the title *Sefer hahassagah*, it contains revisions, supplementations, and criticisms of the linguistic teachings of Ibn Janah's predecessor Judah ibn Hayyuj.[10]

Over time, the initially capacious semantic range of the term *hassagah* became increasingly constricted, referring more exclusively to a critical comment, often pungently formulated. This development may have had much to do with the deployment of such comments by a scholar who became permanently associated with the genre, the twelfth-century southern French talmudist, Abraham ben David of Posquières (Rabad). Rabad wrote strictures on earlier and contemporary greats of rabbinic literature: the Andalusi legist Isaac Alfasi; Rabad's Provençal contemporary Zerahyah Halevi; and a figure who, at the time of Rabad's death, was poised to become the greatest halakhist of all time, Moses ben Maimon. Regarding Rabad's animadversions on the latter, Isadore Twersky showed that the term *hassagah* encompassed "criticism and commentary, dissent and elaboration, stricture and supplement" or, more generally, that it was "not exclusively polemical."[11] Yet it is the critical aspect that gained Rabad his sobriquet as *ba'al ha-hassagot*, the "master stricturalist."

Given Rabad's strong association with strictures, it is safe to assume that the "Abraham ben David" in *Sefer hassagot*'s title is intended to refer to him. Yet Ephraim Urbach, the only twentieth-century scholar to devote an article to *Sefer hassagot*, has shown that Rabad did not actually author the work. His fully sufficient proofs have recently been reinforced and supplemented.[12] In fact, the author did not try his hardest to hide his act of pseudepigraphy. For example, Pseudo-Rabad, as we refer to him, calls Maimonides's *Guide of the Perplexed* a "precious" work, an unexpected characterization to have come from Rabad, particularly since he likely never saw the work, which appeared in Hebrew translation a number of years after the 1198 date usually given for his death.[13] More broadly, Pseudo-Rabad valorizes science in a way far removed from Rabad's single-minded talmudism, even on a rosy reading of Rabad's openness to secular learning.[14] Assuming the "Abraham ben David" in its title refers to Rabad of Posquières, *Sefer hassagot* becomes an assemblage of strictures written under a false name whose author's identity may never be known, although we can rule out that it is Balbo, as some have proposed.[15]

It is impossible to know how Pseudo-Rabad thought about his act of false attribution. Talya Fishman notes that moral evaluations of pseudonymity are highly variable and culturally specific.[16] Perhaps Pseudo-Rabad assuaged whatever pangs of conscience he experienced by telling himself that his work contained sufficient clues for a discerning reader to see through its literary disguise. Perhaps he felt that deflecting attention onto another writer would gain a fair hearing for his daring and at times vituperative arguments. Of course, ascribing his strictures to a consummate rabbinic authority could do much more—namely, give his delegitimization of Rashi an air of authority it would otherwise be hard pressed to claim and/or obscure his own identity so that no retribution could be taken against him. We also may note that not all signs of the work's status as a pseudepigraph would be evident to premodern readers.

Pseudo-Rabad bursts onto the scene in his work's prologue, proclaiming his cause:

> Since I saw, in the commentary on the Torah bearing the name "[that of] Rashi the Frenchman (his memory be for a blessing)," rabbinic homilies (*haggadot*) and interpretations (*perushim*) that stray from the intention of the Torah in many places—some being the very opposite of the correct intention and correct *peshaṭ* as well as the grammar as the matter appears to the eye of reason (*sekhel*)—I saw fit to note a number of the erroneous instances (*qeṣat meqomot ha-meshubbashim*) as regards the *haggadot* and plain sense interpretations (*peshaṭim*), in accordance with the apprehension of my limited understanding.[17]

The initial blame of Rashi is exegetical. His *Commentary* contains many interpretations that diverge from scripture's intention and a smaller number that totally oppose the "correct *peshaṭ*." The errors apparently pertain primarily to elements of the rabbinic legacy (*haggadot*), a fact fully borne out by the strictures themselves, but Pseudo-Rabad leaves open the possibility that Rashi's independent plain sense interpretations also stray. Other charges involve deviation from principles of grammar and what proves to be his gravamen against the *Commentary*, Rashi's tendency to be insensible to the demands of the intellect. Pseudo-Rabad states his intention to disclose "a number" of Rashi's blunders,[18] leaving the impression that this litany of lapses is but a sample, with many other permeable chinks in the *Commentary* left alone. Elsewhere, he suggests a more exhaustive approach, as when he justifies the lack of comments (but for one) on the opening sixteen chapters of Leviticus, stating, unexpectedly, that Rashi's explanations of them contain "nothing requiring refutation." In any case, Pseudo-Rabad leaves the vast majority of the *Commentary* untouched, even in his higher concentration on Genesis and Exodus.[19] After asserting that Rashi fails to comprehend the philosophical equation of the form of the human being with the intellect, and indicating Rashi's general obliviousness of fundaments such as this one, Pseudo-Rabad states: "it is not incumbent upon me to state each instance."[20] He thereby implies that the flaws he does expose make up only a portion *inter multa alia*.

The prologue only becomes more condescending as it shifts to a sphere beyond the purely exegetical, although Pseudo-Rabad does not fail to provide a formulaic expression of humility: "I did not embark on this endeavor because I fancy myself more proficient in Torah than others." The continuation of the sentence adds an element of self-aggrandizement: "but because I discerned the nature of the aforementioned commentator"—more than others,

Pseudo-Rabad implies. As described by Pseudo-Rabad, Rashi's "nature" is that he was "devoid of any sort of wisdom save for [facility in] navigation of the talmudic pericope alone."[21]

Having granted Rashi's talmudic expertise, Pseudo-Rabad immediately highlights a defect in Rashi's relationship to a segment of—indeed, the loftiest element of—rabbinic tradition:

> It seems from his words that he did not understand any other thing save for this [art of talmudic] navigation alone, without his understanding any *haggadah* as alluding to an esoteric matter, neither pertaining to wisdom nor anything else. He rather spoke about *haggadot* as a blind man [groping] at the opening of an attic [whose exit by way of it is purely adventitious].[22] In a few places, it seems from his words that he was, to put it by way of a parable, as a man in whose mouth were placed a few words from some foreign language. He utters them but does not understand it [the language]. When another person who does understand those words hears them coming out of his mouth, that person [mistakenly] thinks that he [the speaker of the words] understands what he says since they commonly trip off his tongue, but it is not so.

Here the author expresses the idea, little attested in the body of his work, that many midrashim, including even ones in the *Commentary*, are profound. His complaint at this point is that Rashi did not grasp them, although Rashi's frequency in citing such dicta misleads readers into thinking otherwise.[23]

Continuing the theme of midrashim "pertaining to wisdom," Pseudo-Rabad notes that they address "the matter of the 'work of creation' and matters of 'divine science,' prophecy, and other branches of knowledge (*ḥokhmot 'aḥerot*)."[24] Samuel ibn Tibbon, who invented the Hebrew coinage "divine science" (*ḥokhmat ha-'elohut*), closely tracks Maimonides in his *Treatise on the Art of Logic* when he explains that this science dealt with "things that are intellectual and separate from matter, like the Lord, His angels, and other things that derive from the actions of the intellect and from the knowledge of the intellect."[25] Pseudo-Rabad follows those expressions of Maimonides and his disciples that saw some rabbinic sayings not as contradicting the conclusions of metaphysics but as articulating them by way of hints, parables, and riddles.[26] Here is a crucial feature of midrash of which midrashic Rashi is ignorant.

How to understand the expression "work of creation" is clear in light of the reference to metaphysics. Unlike *ḥokhmat ha-'elohut,* this term does appear in classical rabbinic literature, where it designates the account in the opening chapters of Genesis. Maimonides boldly identifies it with natural science (physics), the discipline that, in the Aristotelian curriculum, served as a steppingstone to metaphysics. So Pseudo-Rabad lays a further heavy charge against Rashi when he claims that a class of midrashim that impart scientific cosmology are beyond Rashi's ken.

Pseudo-Rabad also proclaims Rashi's ignorance of other *ḥokhmot* attested in the midrashic inheritance. Maimonides uses *ḥokhmah* in the singular as a pliable term that straddles the divide between Jewish and gentile (read: scientific) learning. By contrast, post-Maimonideans speak of *ḥokhmot* in the plural, generally referring not to classical Jewish erudition but to the various disciplines born of rational speculation.[27] By identifying elements of midrashic discourse with such learning, Pseudo-Rabad in effect claims that the ancient midrashists imparted philosophic truths. While this, too, was a rationalist commonplace, the idea proves highly discordant with the prevailing stance that Pseudo-Rabad adopts toward the rabbinic sages in the rest of his work. That stance routinely contravenes the claim made on the sages' behalf by Maimonides (in his *Commentary on the Mishnah*) that the speakers of midrash grasped "the impossibility of the impossible and necessity of that which must exist" such that any of their dicta whose meaning was absurd when taken literally should be understood to contain some (nonliteral) inner meaning.[28] Rather than treating the sages as Rashi's accomplices (or, rather, forerunners) in confusing possible and impossible, Pseudo-Rabad's prologue drives a wedge between Rashi and the midrashists, positing the former's illiteracy in what he presents as a fundamental element of rabbinic discourse. To drive home the point, he concludes the substantive presentation in the prologue by claiming that Rashi understood "not one iota" of the lofty matters addressed in the deepest midrashim.[29]

The prologue concludes with a bit of procedure and a quick prayer. Pseudo-Rabad states that he will "clarify according to the weekly lectionaries wherever I discerned that the rabbi blundered." In so doing, he entreats divine aid ("May God help me").[30] Yet it is his pugnacious tone in the prologue, not its closing note of piety, that sets the pitch as Pseudo-Rabad moves from a statement of aims to their execution.

Midrashic Falsehoods

Pseudo-Rabad's prologue leaves the impression that his is a battle over the true understanding of the midrashic inheritance, which he aims to clarify in light of Rashi's ignorance of it. The rest of the work, however, reflects a very different outlook as exegetical and philosophic rationalism collide with a reading of the Torah grounded in the midrashic hermeneutic and rabbinic teachings.

Beyond his preamble, Pseudo-Rabad invokes the term *peshaṭ* but thrice;[31] yet his insistence that Rashi imparts the opposite of the "correct *peshaṭ*" and his own quest to uncover the Torah's straightforward and commonsense meaning is constant. With the exception of the creation story, warranted by the sages as Torah at its most abstruse, Pseudo-Rabad assumes that the plain sense is limpid and self-contained. Where Rashi finds the Torah imparting meanings that only midrashic interpretive devices reveal, Pseudo-Rabad begs to differ.

A common refrain of Pseudo-Rabad is that the Torah "verifies" straightforward interpretations at odds with Rashi's spurious midrashic ones. Jethro rejoicing over "all the kindness that the Lord had shown Israel" has nothing to do with the manna or a biblically unattested miraculous well that traveled with the Israelites, as Rashi has it. Rather, as "the end of the verse verifies," Jethro celebrated Israel's deliverance from Egyptian bondage.[32] Rashi interprets the sound (*kol 'anot;* Exod 32:18) heard by Moses emanating from the camp of those worshiping the golden calf as "a voice of defamations and blasphemies." Pseudo-Rabad thinks this "absurd," since "the end [of the verse] verifies that it was different types of singing, the proof being [as the next verse states] 'As soon as Moses came near the camp and saw the calf and the dancing [accompanying the singing].' "[33] Who charged the scouts to reconnoiter Canaan? Rashi takes an ostensible pleonasm in the divine imperative—"send for yourself men to scout" (*shelaḥ* ***lekha;*** Num 13:2)—as evidence that it was left to Moses's discretion: "I am not commanding you but if you wish you may send." Pseudo-Rabad deems its refutation immediately at hand (*teshuvato be-ṣido*) since the next verse expressly records "by the Lord's command."[34] On midrashic authority, Rashi teaches that the Canaanite king heard that the clouds of glory departed after Aaron's death. Pseudo-Rabad counters: "about this scripture said nothing at all." Rashi has the Israelites turning back toward the sea at that time. Pseudo-Rabad declares this "incorrect" because "scripture says nothing at all about it."[35]

Even if he does not invoke scriptural testimony explicitly, Pseudo-Rabad still tries to curb what he sees as unjustified midrashic excess. According to Pseudo-Rabad, the wives of Esau caused "bitterness" to Isaac and Rebecca (Gen 26:35) by being "insubordinate." There are no grounds for imputing idolatry to them as Rashi does.[36] On Rashi's understanding, Pharaoh's chief cupbearer was a wicked ingrate who, even when he brought Joseph's plight to Pharaoh's attention as promised, furtively disparaged Joseph by calling him, among other things, a "youth" (Gen 41:12). In this he insinuated to the Egyptian ruler, according to Rashi, that Joseph was "unwise, and unfitted for a high position." Rashi prefaces this local interpretation with a general execration: "cursed be the wicked, for the favors they do are never complete."

Pseudo-Rabad's typically decisive verdict is that this is "incorrect." His characteristically terse follow-up seems to mean that the cupbearer had no other way to describe Joseph other than the way he did, so there is no reason to impute dark motives to him or to issue blame.[37]

Beyond Genesis, Pseudo-Rabad again finds Rashi propounding an exegetical will-o'-the-wisp rather than engaging in sound interpretation. Miriam is called a prophet early in Exodus despite no evidence of her status as such. Abhorring a narrative vacuum, Rashi midrashically contends that she had prophesied by that point, making the prediction—absent from the biblical text—that her mother was "destined to bear a son." Abhorring a baseless accretion, Pseudo-Rabad counters that the reference is anticipatory, alluding to Miriam's status as a prophet as later attested, on his understanding, in Numbers 12:5: "[The Lord . . .] called out, 'Aaron and Miriam!' The two of them came forward."[38] A Sefardic supercommentator identifies the several spurs that "ineluctably" forced Rashi to say that God spoke to Moses reprovingly at the theophany at Horeb. Pseudo-Rabad is curt (and exceedingly short on particulars) when he insists that "there is no [grounds for] *derash*."[39] Rashi infuses into the rebellion of Korah a midrash relaying Korah's demagogic challenge to Moses by having the Israelites ask him a question about the obligation to put fringes on a cloak that was entirely blue, thereby evoking ridicule: "They began laughing at him [saying], 'Is it possible that a cloak of another [colored] material, one string of blue wool exempts it, and this one which is made entirely of blue wool, should not exempt itself?' "[40] Pseudo-Rabad takes as the banner under which the rebellion was conducted the explicit statement in scripture ascribed to the rebels: "all the community are holy" (Num 16:3). At the same time, he posits a personal motive in the case of Korah: "truth be told he was jealous [of Moses] since he was from his family."[41]

While Pseudo-Rabad faults specific interpretations of Rashi, his argument is, at bottom, over the nature of the divine word and proper ways to decode it. Thus, Pseudo-Rabad ignores textual irregularities that served as the lifeblood of the rabbinic hermeneutic, with alleged pleonasm perhaps the most basic of all. Moses is said to have enumerated the Levites "at the command of the Lord [*'al-pi 'adonai*, lit. 'from the divine mouth'], as he was bidden" (Num 3:16). Since the verse states "as he was bidden," why also *'al-pi 'adonai*? Rashi dissolved the problem by taking the latter phrase hyperliterally, having it impart information about the manner in which the census was conducted, quite literally on the basis of reports from the divine "mouth":

> Moses said to the Holy One blessed be He: "How can I enter all of their homes and their tents to know the number of their sucklings?" The

> Holy One blessed be He replied to him: "You do yours and I will do Mine." Moses went and stood at the entrance to the tent and the divine presence preceded him. A heavenly voice emanated from the tent, saying, "There are this many babies in this tent." Thus it says "from the divine mouth."[42]

Pseudo-Rabad opts to retain the conventional meaning of this familiar expression even if it may leave a redundancy: "It seems to me that it says 'at the command of the Lord' in the habitual sense (*ke-minhago*), since it was God who commanded him to count them."[43]

Another premise of the ancient midrashists was that ordinary connections between the letters of a word and between the words of a sentence are "broken," leaving each verbal component to become "extra-ordinary."[44] Even semantically irrelevant orthographic variations bear meaning. A full (*plene*) spelling, for instance, is significant, often pointing to some sort of increase while a deficient spelling may signify diminishment.[45] It was all part of the "fascinated scrutiny" that the sages bestowed on the scripture, "whose every peculiarity was familiar to them."[46]

Rashi, of course, drank deeply from this midrashic well, seeing significance in subsemantic elements like full or defective spellings. It is therefore no surprise that he can draw a lesson in character from a spelling of this sort.[47] When Ephron's name is spelled deficiently once in the account of Abraham's purchase of a field from him (in a passage where it spelled six times "full," including three times before the defective orthography), Rashi assumes there is a subtle allusion, in this case to his character: "[His name] is spelled without a *vav* because he promised much but did not do even a little."[48] Pseudo-Rabad rejoins that the case of the tabernacle vessels proves the meaninglessness of the phenomenon, with some initially spelled full and then defectively in a way that clearly lacks significance.[49] Pseudo-Rabad sees the acceptance of the type of midrashic reading Rashi provides, then, as an all-or-nothing affair. Provide one instance where it fails (by the critic's lights) and all inferences from full or defective spellings are discredited. One wonders if he recalled Ibn Ezra's plaint that the Masoretes "fabricated explanations for full and defective spellings." However this may be, its application to the sages and Rashi was patent, and Ibn Ezra's deflation of such modes as "in the manner of *derash*" and commitment to eschew them certainly would have cheered Pseudo-Rabad.[50]

Against the midrashic premise that no linguistic element is too small to tell (or, rather, intimate) a story, Pseudo-Rabad pits conventions of "the holy tongue" to dismiss the extra-biblical tales. In the report that "Moses took his wife and sons, mounted them on the donkey" (Exod 4:20), Rashi finds a reference to "the exceptional donkey"—that is, *the* donkey saddled by Abraham prior to his harrowing trial involving Isaac's sacrifice and *the* donkey upon which the king-messiah would one day appear. Samuel Almosnino manages to turn the comment into a homily on the engagement of the wise in intellectual apprehension and necessary concomitant suppression of "corporeal powers."[51] Pseudo-Rabad must have been tested sorely by the donkey's longevity, let alone his appearance at key junctures in history over millennia, but he chooses to contest the midrash that he calls "futility and a grave evil" in terms of the validity of its textual spur rather than its substance. The supposition that a definite article invariably indicates determination is incorrect, as a description of Absalom riding on "the mule" shows (2 Sam 18:9).[52] Where Rashi finds anomalies that provide a basis for midrashic exposition, Pseudo-Rabad, like earlier peshatists, finds linguistic and literary conventions that allow him to beat back the midrashic fancies that resulted from such omnisignificant assumptions.

Other linguistic conventions explain (read: explain away) triggers used by Rashi as the bases for expansions and evaluations that he interweaves into the fabric of the narrative. The word "years" appears after every digit in the Torah's indication of Sarah's life span (Gen 23:1). Rashi, positing this as a redundancy, divides Sarah's life into distinct periods, each said to merit individual exposition. For example, during the closing period of her life beginning at a hundred years, Rashi claims that the matriarch remained "as a twenty-year-old [deemed guiltless] with respect to sin."[53] Commentators prior to Pseudo-Rabad, like David Kimhi and Nahmanides, cast the repetition as "in the manner of elegant expression in the sacred tongue" or "the habit of the language," respectively.[54] Yet Kimhi also cites the midrash while identifying it as such and without mentioning Rashi, presumably seeing in it an edifying supplement to his stylistic plain sense reading. Pseudo-Rabad stresses the argument from style by underscoring that repetitions such as these occur "in the manner of the holy tongue" in "many places." In so doing, he pulls the textual ground out from under Rashi's valorization of Sarah's life as one lived heroically free of sin.[55]

Pseudo-Rabad's plain sense readings can also involve an appreciation of aesthetics, the better to ward off midrashic distortion. Consider Rashi's lesson-laden midrashic reconstruction of events at the Sea of Reeds on the basis of two verses, one in the prose account and one in the immediately following poem: "Israel saw the Egyptians dead on the shore of the sea" (Exod 14:30) and "You [God] put out Your right hand, the earth swallowed them [the Egyptians]" (Exod 15:12). As for the first of these, Rashi understood it to be the Egyptians who suddenly appeared "on the shore of the sea" after initially entering the watery depths, with a personified sea spewing them up to suffer final death throes in view of the Israelites. One aim of this arrangement was to assure the Israelites that their enemies were well and truly dead, and hence could no longer pursue them. In a related interpretation, Rashi indicated that while the Egyptians' downfall was certainly just and, in fact, the work of God's "right hand," their death on the seashore was followed by the "earth swallowed them"—that is, by their receiving a decent burial. The reason was the need for God to provide recompense for the fact that Pharaoh acknowledged the justice of the divine chastisement, as relayed in his statement: "The Lord is in the right" (Exod 9:27). Even while seeing to the demise of the wicked, then, God ensured that they received any reward due to them.[56]

Pseudo-Rabad resists this reconstruction on all counts. Since the plain sense clearly has the Egyptians dying in the sea, those on the seashore can only refer to the Israelites. Ibn Ezra makes the point without explicit reference to Rashi and, indeed, so did Rashi's grandson Samuel ben Meir. By using his characteristic expression "profound plain sense" (*'omeq peshuṭo*), the latter presumably meant to underscore that Rashi's interpretation was not.[57] Of course, Pseudo-Rabad is perfectly happy to engage in a direct confrontation: "He [Rashi] said 'that the sea threw them out [on its shore]' but this is incorrect since the verse does not say so." Rather, "it was the Israelites who stood on the seashore, whence they saw the Egyptians dying in the sea." Pseudo-Rabad stresses that this is indubitably what "the verse verifies."[58] Rashi's inference from "the earth swallowed them" is also "incorrect," running afoul of interpretation according to "the habit of language when people speak in the manner of poetry." Consider, says Pseudo-Rabad, a similar case involving images of sky and earth: "The skies above your head shall be copper and the earth under you iron" (Deut 28:23). Surely nobody would take these literally. He likely had Ibn Ezra in mind, whose gloss subtly made the point by adding a key preposition: " 'copper'—as copper (*ke-neḥoshet*); so too 'iron' [= "like iron"]."[59] Hardly enslaved to the literal word, peshatists sought a contextual understanding of language that often took on board a deep appreciation of metaphor. The upshot is that the Egyptians died by drowning, falling into oblivion on the seabed, and certainly did not did not receive the divinely conferred reward of a decent burial that Rashi midrashically granted them.

Awareness of habits of language can be supplemented by insight into universal patterns in human affairs to undermine textually baseless midrashic fancies. We have seen that the *Commentary* had the Egyptians expiring on dry land so the Israelites could be assured of their enslavers' demise. Rashi adds another reason for this divine contrivance. Since the Egyptians had "adorned their steeds with ornaments of gold, silver, and precious stones," their reappearance on the shore would allow the Israelites to seize the spoils. This narrative expansion provides the basis for another one based on the seemingly innocuous report that "Moses caused Israel to set out from the Sea of Reeds" (Exod 15:22). Taken literally, the Torah stated that Moses "caused the Israelites to depart." So understood, the wording provides reason to think his efforts to get the people to depart met with resistance and, indeed, Rashi reports that they left "against their will" since they preferred to stay and augment their booty. Pseudo-Rabad also feels obliged to account for the semantic peculiarity, but does so without reference to the immediate circumstances. The correct understanding, in his view, has to do with the fact that Moses was their leader. Because one role of a leader is to conduct the people's comings and goings, the causative is a habit of the language that bespeaks a common pattern. Gone are tales of the people's greedy disposition or God arranging for their enemies to be decked in precious things for them to plunder.[60]

Where Pseudo-Rabad might be expected to dispute the substance of a scientifically dubious midrash, he may still choose to focus on its exegetical baselessness. In a gloss on "Those were the sons whom Leah bore to Jacob . . . in addition to his daughter Dinah" (Gen 46:15), Rashi imparts lessons drawn from the world of midrashic embryology. The Torah associated the sons mentioned in the verse with their mother, since "if the woman emits seed first she gives birth to a male." By contrast, Dinah was called "his" (that is, Jacob's) daughter since "if the male emits seed first she gives birth to a female." Rather than contest this theory of sex determination, one debated by medieval scholars,[61] Pseudo-Rabad retorts: "earlier it says 'Dinah, the daughter of Leah . . . went out' " (Gen 34:1).[62] Whatever his view of the science, Pseudo-Rabad treats the countervailing scriptural evidence as decisive.

An argument from silence—the claim that the Torah's silence about events of moment reported by Rashi shows that they must not have happened—serves as another way to debunk the *Commentary*'s many midrashic expansions. Rashi has Jacob passing fourteen years at a rabbinic academy (*bet midrash*) led by Shem and Eber, an idea in keeping with the propensity of the midrashists to depict the forefathers as forerunners of their own most prized activity.[63] Not bothering to contest the anachronism, Pseudo-Rabad retorts: "were it so, scripture would have mentioned it, as it mentions that Jacob rolled the stone off the mouth of the well (Gen 29:10)." Then, a startling addendum: "as it [the Torah] recounts other details not worthy of being recorded" (*peraṭim 'aḥerim she-'enan re'uyim likatev*).[64] As we will see, Pseudo-Rabad uses this line of argument with gusto to refute midrashic miracles that Rashi infiltrates into the biblical narrative.

In another set of midrashim to which Pseudo-Rabad objects, Rashi identifies anonymous figures with ones known from elsewhere in a manner that

Isaac Heinemann sees as yet another way the ancient midrashists brought "focus" to the narrative.[65] The "two Hebrews" (Exod 2:13) in whose quarrel Moses intervened were, according to Rashi's midrashic reading, the same Dathan and Abiram who later rebelled against him (Num 16). Were it so, Pseudo-Rabad, replies, scripture "would have called them by their names." God told Moses he could return to Egypt since "all the men" (Exod 4:19) seeking to kill him died. Rashi identifies those in question with Dathan and Abiram—not that they had died, mind you, as was patent from their appearance in Numbers, but they became poor and one so impoverished is "as if dead." Pseudo-Rabad responds: If so, the Torah would have named the infamous pair rather than referring to "the men." Pseudo-Rabad thinks the reference is to Pharaoh, whose wish to slay Moses is stated (Exod 2:15), although, unlike Ibn Ezra before him, he fails to account for the plural "men."[66]

Pseudo-Rabad also disdains lapses in empirical or realistic interpretation. Appealing to the "custom of the smiths," Rashi teaches that the tabernacle candelabrum was formed from a single block of gold beaten with a hammer. Pseudo-Rabad casts aspersions on Rashi's metallurgical credentials: "would that I knew whether this man was expert in the art of smiths. Is it fitting for an artisan to do as he says?"[67] When Judah urged clemency for Benjamin before the Egyptian potentate, he said: "Do not be impatient with your servant, you who are the equal of Pharaoh" (Gen 44:18). While his plain sense reading has Judah showing due deference, Rashi also offers a midrashic one according to which the appeal to quell wrath was not uttered subserviently but menacingly, with Judah going so far as to threaten the viceroy's life and even that of Pharaoh. Seeing this scenario as contextually outlandish, Pseudo-Rabad points out that all earlier indications are that the brothers dreaded Joseph and saw him as "the equivalent of the king."[68]

While Pseudo-Rabad's interpretive realism in opposition to Rashi often has points of contact with Ibn Ezra, his anti-midrashic formulations are openly dismissive where Ibn Ezra keeps his polemic in the shadows. Explaining the wood used in such abundance in the construction of the tabernacle and its accessories, Rashi tells a tale of patriarchal prescience: "our father Jacob foresaw through the holy spirit that Israel would eventually build a tabernacle in the wilderness, so he brought acacia trees to Egypt and planted them, and instructed his descendants to take them with them upon leaving Egypt."[69] Rashi imparts the midrash to account for the unexpected presence of large amounts of wood in the wilderness and connects the site for divine worship constructed there to the ancestral past. Ibn Ezra expresses skepticism in one of his commentaries on Exodus. Because Pharaoh allowed the Israelites to leave on the basis of a stated wish to celebrate a three-day festival (Exod 5:3), it is difficult to see how they could have hauled a large store of wooden planks, "each at least ten cubits in length, not to mention [even larger] crossbars," without giving away their plan to effect a permanent departure. Still, Ibn Ezra expresses willingness to submit "if it is a tradition in their [the sages'] hands," while arguing that "independent analysis" (*sevara'*) suggests another view better fitted to the scriptural data and a realistic approach—namely, that the Israelites felled a grove of trees adjacent to Mount Sinai.[70] Pseudo-Rabad's stricture differs little in substance but has a fury all its own: "The one who asks whence they had the acacia trees, then answers that Jacob planted them—the question is unformed (*tohu*) and the answer void (*bohu*), since acacia was [apparently] more abundant than other types [of trees]. Had they had other types of trees, they would have used them. So you find that Solomon built the temple from cedar trees, which were more available than other types [of trees]."[71] Pseudo-Rabad makes no mention of inerrant rabbinic tradition and tacitly maligns Rashi. As for his explanation, one can say of it what Moshe Sokolow says of Ibn Ezra's: what it supplies on rational grounds "it takes away on emotional ones."[72]

Pseudo-Rabad registers strong objections against unrealistic midrashic chronologies and anachronisms. As we have seen, Rashi has Rebecca marrying Isaac at the age of three, evidencing his unrealistic conception. Pseudo-Rabad rails: "Is it fitting that a girl of three years of age should sally forth to draw water or know how to respond so adroitly yea or nay?"[73] The computation of Jacob's life, which involves the notion that he left home at age sixty-three, entails the consequence that he was still shepherding at eighty-four, which is so much "absurdity and senselessness."[74] Also standing in flagrant violation of canons of realism are Rashi's interpretations based on the rabbinic penchant for "creative anachronism"[75] like the one that Lot served flatbreads (*maṣṣot*) (Gen 19:3) to guests since "it was Passover." The insight owes to another midrashic staple to which Rashi subscribed: that Israel's patriarchs and matriarchs (and, in this case, their relations) observed the Torah prior to its promulgation.[76] Pseudo-Rabad offers a resounding twofold rejection: "Would that I could fathom whence Lot knew of Passover," commemorating as it did a future event about which he could not have been apprised, as he was no prophet. Second, it contradicts Rashi's depiction of Lot as "a complete reprobate." Was Abraham's errant nephew who opted to call Sodom home really a candidate for pious observance upon his arrival there? Pseudo-Rabad understands the menu functionally, asserting that Lot sought the best way to serve guests expeditiously. Kimhi draws the same conclusion and derives a lesson in hospitality ("thus was the story written, to teach you proper conduct"), turning Lot into a model in his uncle's image. Not one for moralizing, Pseudo-Rabad remarks only on the need for alacrity as the criterion governing the choice of victuals, bolstering his explanation with a bit of realia: "mountain-dwellers even today consume all their bread in the form of flatbread."[77]

The problem of anachronism also arises when, in the version of the *Commentary* in possession of Pseudo-Rabad, Rashi proposes that Rebecca ordered Jacob to fetch two kids for his father, since in addition to one for "tasty foods," another was needed for the Passover sacrifice.[78] As with Lot, Pseudo-Rabad insists that Israel's earliest ancestors knew nothing of the future sacred calendar. Here, however, he anticipates a counterclaim: Isaac was a prophet who could have been apprised of such things in advance. His response is that this is not so of Rebecca. True, the Torah said that "the Lord answered her" (Gen 25:23), but Rashi adopts a midrash that saw this not as direct prophecy but as second-hand communication "through the intermediation of an angel or [by way of intermediaries in] the study house of Eber." Since, on Rashi's own reckoning, the verse provides no proof of her prophetic powers, he could not use it to defend the proposition that Rebecca was aware of Passover *avant la lettre*.[79]

In the course of suppressing midrashic caprice, Pseudo-Rabad can take his propensity for prosaic plain sense to extremes. Rashi elaborates midrashically on the gifts given by Abraham's servant to Rebecca. In keeping with the rabbinic disposition to see in events and things meaning regarding Israel's future history, Rashi teaches that the two gold bands for her arms, ten shekels in weight (Gen 24:22), allude to the two tables and ten utterances of the Decalogue. Beyond endowing details of the gifts with meaning, the midrash imparts important lessons. On one level, it implies that it was not gold that induced Rebecca to marry Isaac but, rather, the prospect of a relationship prefiguratively built on Torah. So understood, it justifies her forthcoming role as a matriarch of the nation despite her "foreign" extraction. As in other midrashim about Rebecca, she gains a "Jewish" aura.[80] In contrast is Pseudo-Rabad's staggeringly mundane alternative: "I say she had two arms, so he gave her two bands."[81]

A similar sort of divergence is present in Rashi's and Pseudo-Rabad's interpretations of a detail in the account of Isaac's blessing of Jacob: "He smelled the fragrance of his garments and blessed him and said, 'Ah, the smell of my son is like the smell of the fields that the Lord has blessed'" (Gen 27:27). Rashi, contending that no odor is so offensive as that of washed goat skins, imparts the midrash that it could not then have been the garments that the blind patriarch smelled but that as Jacob came to claim Esau's blessing "the fragrance of the garden of Eden" accompanied him. Pseudo-Rabad thinks it patent "that there was not but the smell of [ordinary] clothes."[82]

Inconsistencies in Rashi's midrashic logic prod Pseudo-Rabad to pounce. In a reunion after decades of separation, Joseph fell upon Benjamin's neck and wept. Benjamin reciprocated (Gen 45:14). Rashi reinscribes the encounter in a way that adopts the midrashic predilection to imbue biblical figures with prophecy while also viewing them as transhistorical types whose doings allude to the nation's future. Joseph wept because he foresaw the destruction of the two temples that one day would be situated in the tribal land of Benjamin. Benjamin wept over the tabernacle to be erected in Shiloh, part of the inheritance of Ephraim, Joseph's son, which would eventually be destroyed. The prompt for this exposition is the ostensible anomaly that the Torah reported Joseph's falling on Benjamin's "necks" in the plural, taken as an allusion to the first and second temples.[83] This is the sort of midrash that became firmly planted in the Jewish psyche and was rebroadcast in countless settings. It figures, for instance, in Jacob ben Isaac Ashkenazi of Janów's *Ṣe'enah u-re'enah* (Yiddish: *tzenerene*), one of the most popular books ever to appear in Yiddish, which served as a major vector for the diffusion of Rashi's reading of the Torah. It also appears in a discourse delivered by Kalonymus Kalman Shapira of Piaseczno amid the horror of the Warsaw Ghetto.[84] Many Jews must have found the midrash moving, but Pseudo-Rabad remains impervious. What is more, he discerns a (to him) fatal flaw in its logic, even leaving aside what Rashi himself knew to say in his Talmud commentary: that plural "necks" was simply "common scriptural usage."[85] Rashi, mentioning only the singular Shiloh tabernacle, failed to expound two referents for the plural *ṣavarav* as the object of Benjamin's weeping, although this same form appears. This being so, his whole wobbly interpretive edifice crumbles.[86]

Rather arbitrarily, Pseudo-Rabad chastises Rashi for ignoring a midrash by which, Pseudo-Rabad implies, he ought to have been bound. Rashi cites a talmudic claim that the covenant curses in Leviticus differ from those in Deuteronomy since the former came from God directly while the latter Moses said "on his own." Pseudo-Rabad notes that "this is the opposite" of another rabbinic dictum stating that Moses received even the most seemingly innocuous parts of the Torah ("Ataroth" and "Dibon"; Num 32:3) at Sinai.[87] Exercising the stricturalist's license, he forgoes explanation of how the midrash cited by Rashi ought to be understood. It apparently suffices to show an inconsistency between the *Commentary* and another (more authoritative?) part of the rabbinic record. As an aside, the example suggests that Pseudo-Rabad, exegetical iconoclast and philosophic free thinker though he was, could at times strike a more theologically conservative stance than Rashi.

Even when Pseudo-Rabad concurs with Rashi, he may dispute a convoluted midrashic technique used to derive what he deems an obvious conclusion.

Who prostrated and kissed whom when Moses met Jethro (Exod 18:7)? Rashi makes a point of asserting that the question would be open were it not for a verbal association from far afield: "I do not know who prostrated himself to whom. [But] when [in this verse in Exodus] it says 'man to his friend,' [we are led to ask:] who is called 'a man'? This is Moses, as it is said: 'But the man Moses' (Num 12:3)." Pseudo-Rabad lambastes the convolution, thinking it "obvious" that Moses was the one who went out and bowed, "as scripture verifies."[88]

Legal matters also occupy Pseudo-Rabad at points and his strictures in this sphere display the same format and tone as those concerning Rashi's interpretations of biblical narrative. The phrase "the two men in the dispute shall appear before the Lord" (Deut 19:17) sounded like it spoke of the appearance of litigants before a court, but Rashi, following rabbinic interpretation, bisects it: "in the dispute" refers to the litigants but "the two men" refers to witnesses. On this basis he reports a raft of consequential rules governing judicial procedure, not least that "women's testimony is invalid." Without reprising Rashi, Pseudo-Rabad tersely opines: "'the two men in the dispute': these are the litigants."[89] It is left to the reader to grasp how the comment constitutes a stricture. Open still is Pseudo-Rabad's own position on the norms whose textual foundation he undercuts. One assumes that, as a Rabbanite, he endorses them on the basis of tradition in the manner of Ibn Ezra.[90]

Where Ibn Ezra routinely swears fealty to the "transmitters" of halakhic tradition and even upbraids Karaites for denying the veracity of the "oral law," Pseudo-Rabad is on some occasions (although not all, as we will see) content to deny *midrash halakhah* and leave it at that. Rashi identifies the altar from which the high priest was commanded to take a "panful of glowing coals . . . before the Lord" (Lev 16:12) on Yom Kippur as the "outside altar" used for burnt offerings rather than the inside altar used for incense. Pseudo-Rabad objects: "it seems to me that were it so, it would not say 'before the Lord.'" Pressing the point, he invokes Rashi's comment a few verses later, where "the altar that is before the Lord" (Lev 16:18) is said to refer to the inside altar. The conclusion is clear: "there is no distinction between 'before the Lord' and 'that is before the Lord'; it is all the same, that is, [both refer to] the inner altar." Pseudo-Rabad is sure that "this is the truth."[91]

Pseudo-Rabad also finds that Rashi's midrash-based reading of "you shall set apart the clean beast from the unclean" (Lev 20:25) egregiously violates the plain sense. Rashi's starting premise is that "it is not necessary for scripture to say [that we must distinguish] between a cow and a donkey, since they are easily distinguishable and identifiable." Rabbinic interpretation assumed that the verse spoke to a case involving much finer powers of discrimination—to wit, a single inherently permissible animal that was either pure or impure, depending (here was an element nowhere mentioned) on how it was slaughtered. Rashi gave two scenarios. Where the majority of the animal's gullet and windpipe (esophagus and trachea) was severed, it was edible; where one of the two was no more than half cleaved, it was not. It turned on the smallest "hairbreadth," explaining the call to carefully distinguish ("set apart") the situations with utmost care. Not surprisingly, Pseudo-Rabad's point of attack is Rashi's initial argument about the need to dismiss the plain sense of the verse, thereby justifying the halakhic reading. Echoing the sages, Rashi argues that the Torah could not be speaking of so straightforward a distinction as the one between pure and impure animals. Pseudo-Rabad begs to differ: "It appears to me that scripture does not come to speak about this [midrashic] interpretation. Though it is true that the distinction between donkey and cow is apparent, there are other less familiar animals like various wilderness beasts, whose status as impure or pure not every person is so expert to grasp." Again, Pseudo-Rabad does not disavow the holding associated with the midrashic reading. He does, however, undermine Rashi's effort to buttress its interpretive necessity. His curt conclusion, "about this there is no doubt to one who is discerning,"[92] forces readers to choose whether to ally themselves with self-evident truth (thereby joining the ranks of the "discerning") or opt for ongoing allegiance to Rashi's rabbinic distortion.

Pseudo-Rabad is sure to disavow a *midrash halakhah* involving a mythical monster and violations of nearly every rule of plain sense interpretation. Mentioned in Deuteronomy's list of borderline land animals possessing one of the two characteristics used to establish their permissibility for consumption (Deut 14:7), as also in a parallel in Leviticus, were three ruminants that did not part the hoof, as well as the pig that did part the hoof but did not chew its cud. Elaborating the later list, Rashi identifies a fifth animal in this class called a "cloven" (*shesu'ah*). Its discovery rests on a midrashic interpretation free of nearly all syntactic, grammatical, and lexical restraint. The midrash takes a feminine passive participle describing the hoof of animals and turns it into an otherwise unattested noun, requiring the addition of a missing object marker (*et*) before the word *shesu'ah* and a conjunction before the reference to the camel, since on this reading the camel no longer appears as the first in a list of four proscribed animals, but as the second in a list of five. Thus does the word for "hoof" in the phrase "of them that divide the hoof that is cloven" become the name of an otherwise unattested creature "with two backs and two backbones," the *shesu'ah*. Skipping particulars in the rabbinic record, Rashi reprises that "the cloven" was "a creature which has two backs and two backbones," then clarifies that what prompts the reading is a need to find in

Deuteronomy information not stated in Leviticus, saving the passage under consideration from redundancy.[93] The reader awaits an explosion of indignation from Pseudo-Rabad. Instead, with complete composure, he simply insists on a reading of the verse "according to its plain sense" (*kifshaṭo*) and "not as referring to a creature unto itself (*biryah bifnei 'azmo*)."[94]

In a unique case in his work and in a manner highly unusual in the history of medieval Jewish exegesis, Pseudo-Rabad denies a legal midrash because it runs athwart the ethical thrust of the biblical precept it expounds. Concerning the obligation to assist the animal of an "enemy" struggling under its load (Exod 23:5), rabbinic tradition went so far as to rule that one who was faced with a choice between aiding the animal of a friend or the animal of an enemy should first aid the latter. (Among definitions of "enemy" in rabbinic tradition are gentile idolater, relapsed convert to Judaism, or Jewish apostate.) Yet that same tradition also curbs the obligation by reading a syntactically ambiguous clause to mean that there were circumstances in which one could or should "refrain" from offering aid.[95] Rashi communicates a complex picture with typical clarity, including what he notes is a midrashic reading that alludes to two scenarios in which potential interveners had license to desist: an elder who thought it beneath his dignity to unload a beast,[96] or anyone in the case where an animal belonged to a gentile. Pseudo-Rabad protests that the second exclusion "is not correct since the [way of the] Torah is the antithesis of this, such that one should not desist from helping even if it [the animal] were to belong to a gentile."[97] Being incompatible with the inclusive ethos of the Torah, which Pseudo-Rabad apparently sees as extending to nonmonotheists, Rashi's halakhic interpretation must be errant.[98]

In two passages involving punishment, Pseudo-Rabad highlights the gulf separating the at times extremely harsh *peshaṭ* of biblical law and Rashi's rabbinic elaborations, yielding anti-halakhic interpretations of Karaite proportions. One involves execution by stoning. According to rabbinic procedure, this form of the death penalty had stones cast only if a transgressor remained alive after receiving a fatal push from witnesses at a two-story-high "stoning house." By contrast, it "seems" to Pseudo-Rabad that the verse "does not refer to anything other than actual stoning, as it says, 'and let the whole community stone him'" (Lev 24:14). Though the precise point of contention is slightly unclear, he buttresses it by adding "just as the gentiles do nowadays," apparently referencing a form of collective spectacle about which he had heard.[99] Pseudo-Rabad also dissents from Rashi's rabbinic reading of the punishment stipulated by the Torah in the case of wifely intervention in a fight on behalf of a husband that involved her grabbing the assailant's genitals: "you shall cut off her hand; show no pity" (Deut 25:12). Rashi relays a midrashic analogy to another instance where the phrase "show no pity" appears. In both cases, rabbinic law concluded that monetary compensation was sanctioned, not mutilation. After reprising "the commentator," Pseudo-Rabad contends that "actual slicing off of the hand" is meant. Only so understood does the call to take no pity make sense as seeking to forestall hesitation to enact the cruel response. In step with Karaite commentators, Pseudo-Rabad thinks there is "no doubt" that this was "the Torah's intention."[100]

In sum, one finds Pseudo-Rabad routinely testing Rashi's midrashic hermeneutic and finding it wanting, galled especially by interpretations peddled in the deceptive garb of *peshaṭ* when they are clearly imposters. Pseudo-Rabad's positive program continues, and often radicalizes, the quest for grammatical, stylistically attuned, realistic interpretation familiar from the Spanish-Provençal school. At the same time, like earlier great practitioners in this tradition, *Sefer hassagot* moves not only along an axis labeled "plain sense" but also another labeled "rationality." Where the latter is the main axis, Pseudo-Rabad can raise his critical pitch even higher.

Midrashic Absurdities

Sefer hassagot's prologue places its author among votaries of rationalism who hold that the divine word could be understood only if read, as Maimonides explains, by way of "the true nature of the intellect" after attaining "perfection in the demonstrative sciences."[101] This proposition informs Pseudo-Rabad's *hassagot* on Rashi regarding the opening chapters of Genesis, but it hovers over other strictures as well. Pseudo-Rabad's counterinterpretations routinely construe the Torah in terms of intelligible workings of nature familiar from the everyday world.

The very first of Pseudo-Rabad's strictures establishes a tacit hierarchy: exegetically misguided interpretations of Rashi may "entail no damage," whereas interpretations that are oblivious to the findings of science yield a serious missed opportunity or even grievous distortion. In advance of his plain sense interpretations of the Torah's opening word, *bereshit*, Rashi midrashically expounded its apparently anomalous form—anomalous because the second noun that ought to have immediately succeeded this word in its bound form was lacking. Turning the anomaly into an occasion, Rashi provides midrashic uplift by taking the opening verse as an account of the "why" of creation rather than its "how." In his midrashic readings, the world was created "for the sake of the Torah," which was, much later in the Bible, called "the beginning of His course" (Prov 8:22) or for the "sake of Israel," elsewhere also referred to as a "beginning" (*reshit*), as in "the first fruits of His harvest" (Jer 2:3). This is just the sort of midrash that could recommend the *Commentary* to so many, furnishing a Judeocentric teleology of the world that Judah Loew of Prague would later exalt in his supercommentary on the passage as a proclamation of the Jewish people's status as the "pinnacle," "crowning perfection," and "end goal" of creation.[102] Pseudo-Rabad's stricture is mild. True, these interpretations defy "the intention in that word [*bereshit*]," but they also "entail no harm."[103]

More than merely nettlesome, by contrast, is Rashi's (mis)handling of scientific particulars in Genesis 1. For example, where Rashi infers a sequence of events in which some elements of creation preceded others, Pseudo-Rabad insists that the Torah could not have imparted such a cosmogony since "no [element] . . . preceded any other, not the heavens the earth . . . not the water the earth, nor the earth the water."[104] Pseudo-Rabad does credit Rashi's rabbinically based insight that "the heavens were created from fire and water" or, as formulated later in the *Commentary*, that God "mingled them [fire and water] with one another and from them made the heavens." His criticism in this case takes a different form, recalling the image in *Sefer hassagot*'s prologue of a person uttering words in a language he does not understand: "the rabbi did not understand" the "wondrous truth" articulated here, presumably owing to his ignorance of science. Pseudo-Rabad obliges the reader with a correct interpretation of the midrashic images that so elude Rashi. He assumes they speak to processes described in Aristotle's *Meteorology*, addressing, for example, the nature of the "firmament that is called 'heavens' [in the Torah]."[105] As one immersed in philosophy in at least some measure (how deeply is impossible to say on the basis of *Sefer hassagot*) and convinced that natural science provided the semantics for a proper understanding of Genesis 1, he could only scorn Rashi's incapacity to expound the "work of the beginning," even if Rashi does cite profound midrashim that, alas, he did not understand.[106]

The end of Pseudo-Rabad's critique of the midrash on fire and water reveals his most notable heroes: "as Maimonides mentioned, and Abraham Ibn Ezra."[107] Although rarely named, and although Pseudo-Rabad can chart his own way, apparently denying that Miriam died through a divine kiss as Maimonides affirmed,[108] these Sefardic luminaries shape a good deal of *Sefer hassagot*—certainly well beyond the few direct references to them. Pseudo-Rabad also summons unnamed "philosophers" early in *Sefer hassagot*. They initially appear with respect to a midrash adduced by Rashi regarding the need for a terrestrial being created in the divine image—one that also asserted humanity's likeness to angels: "Among the heavenly beings there are some in My likeness. If there are none . . . among the earthly beings there will be envy." Pseudo-Rabad reads the gloss, which he ascribes directly to the sages, in characteristically apocopated fashion: "it was therefore necessary to say 'let us make man.'" His meaning is none too clear but one suspects he had in mind some notion that God created the first human being by way of intermediaries, the plural form reflecting an address to the immaterial intellects.[109] Pseudo-Rabad continues in an Aristotelian vein: "this is true, since the form of the human being is the intellect, as the philosophers explained, and inasmuch as a person has that form he is similar (*domeh*) to the angels." In this he recapitulates, in highly compressed form, ideas that readers of Maimonides would easily recognize. The basic upshot is a Maimonidean association of the divine image in human beings with the (acquired) intellect.[110] This is a rare instance where rather than faulting Rashi, Pseudo-Rabad provides a rationalist overlay for his words. Still, he quickly reassumes his standard bearing with a concluding *ad hominem* barb: "of all this the commentator understood nothing." He also issues a more global finding that Rashi "in general understood nothing in such instances," adding "it is not incumbent on me to state each instance."[111]

The philosophers make a further appearance in a stricture on the midrashic interpretation of Adam's cry, "this one at last is bone of my bones and flesh of my flesh" (Gen 2:23), formulated by Rashi as follows: "Adam mated with every [species of] beast and animal but his appetite was not assuaged by them." We have seen how this gloss was imbued with meanings that reflect the sensibilities of Sefardic scholars in supercommentaries on it, but Pseudo-Rabad is out to defeat Rashi, not redeem him. He states that the midrash is "incorrect" and that scripture does not "verify" it. According to what "the philosophers have said," there is a "profundity (*sod*)," although Pseudo-Rabad neither deigns to say who these figures are nor in what their insight consists. Based on habits of other rationalists, one could ascribe to Pseudo-Rabad some philosophical-allegorical understanding of the verse and midrash on it, but caution is due since *Sefer hassagot* displays next to no allegorizing tendencies.

One place where such an allegorizing approach does peek through is in an elaboration—a supercommentary, one could even say—on Rashi's exposition of "male and female He created them" (Gen 1:27). Adopting a rabbinic trope, Rashi cast the first model of humanity as "two-faced," apparently referring to a state of androgyny. According to Avraham Grossman, Rashi takes this idea of the bisexual nature of primeval man literally, not allegorically.[112] In the Middle Ages, the notion gained special prominence in kabbalistic literature, but Pseudo-Rabad imbues it with an Aristotelian valence: "'two faced'—that is, [comprising] matter and form."[113] In this and a few other instances Pseudo-Rabad presents like other rationalist readers of Rashi who take his pliable midrashic formulations and pour them into sharply defined philosophical molds. Yet this approach, familiar from Sefardic supercommentary, is restricted to the beginning of Genesis. Instead, resistance to midrash is, as we have amply begun to see, the nearly unfailing rule.

Rashi and Maimonides have been depicted as near-contemporaneous masters who represent "two opposing trends within Judaism," the first particularist and the other universalist, their comments on the creation story bringing this distinction into sharp relief.[114] A Maimonidean universalism informs Pseudo-Rabad's rebuff of a string of particularist midrashim in the *Commentary* on Genesis 1. For example, Pseudo-Rabad snubs a midrash on the definite article in reference to "*the* sixth day," an article that is textually aberrant inasmuch as it does not appear with respect to any of the other days of creation. Rashi found in the word *ha-shishi* a reference to the sixth day par excellence, that day in the month of Sivan on which the Jewish people traditionally were understood to have received the Torah. The midrash has it that at the time of creation, God stipulated that the permanent existence of the works of creation had to await "the sixth of Sivan, which was prepared for the giving of the Torah." Only if the Israelites accepted the Torah, fulfilling the purpose of creation, would all the rest of the creations continue to exist. Thus did Rashi reinforce the idea of the creation of the world for "the sake of the Torah" and "for the sake of Israel" as set forth in the *Commentary*'s opening comment. Pseudo-Rabad denies the whole approach, chalking up the aberration to what he casts as a common phenomenon of the definite article appearing in a terminal member of a longer enumeration.[115] Pseudo-Rabad also recoils from a Judeocentric reading of God's blessing of the seventh day. According to Rashi, the blessing conferred on the seventh day at the time of creation refers to the manna that Israel would eventually enjoy in the wilderness, "for on all the days of the week it descended for them . . . [but] it did not descend at all on the Sabbath." The verse in Genesis was "written with reference to the future." Pseudo-Rabad considers the midrash erroneous. The meaning is clarified instead "in the immediate sequel," where the reason given for the blessing of the seventh day and declaration of its holiness is as the Torah states: "because on it God ceased from all the work of creation that He had done."[116]

If Rashi reads Genesis to the effect that God created the world for the sake of Torah and the Jewish people, Maimonides casts it as an account of universal physics.[117] These conflicting approaches are writ large in Pseudo-Rabad's stricture on Rashi's midrashic reading of the word *mo'adim* in the account of God's appointment of heavenly "lights" as "signs for the set times—the days and the years" (Gen 1:14). Since the word also means "festivals," Rashi interprets it as a reference to "the future, when the Israelites are destined to be commanded concerning the festivals," the connection being that these days on the sacred calendar were to be reckoned "from the first phase of the moon."

Pseudo-Rabad replies that "it is not so," that *mo'adim* means "times," and that the Torah imparts the idea that time is a function of the movement of heavenly orbs ("its measure being time").[118]

The more starkly the *Commentary* teaches delusion, the harsher Pseudo-Rabad's response. To explain the divine statement, made partially in the third person, that "I will proclaim before you the name Lord" (Exod 33:19), Rashi summons a bold midrash suggesting that God instructed Moses in "the procedure for begging compassion," in part by wrapping Himself in a prayer shawl and proclaiming the "thirteen attributes of mercy." Here, without qualm, Rashi availed himself of the anthropomorphic imagery that abounds in midrash, solving an exegetical problem in a way that encouraged faith in the salvific power of a familiar liturgical formula. Waxing eloquent beyond his source, Rashi insists that prayer involving the "thirteen attributes" is efficacious even when the store of "ancestral merit" (*zekhut 'avot*) is "depleted."[119]

Pseudo-Rabad's response to Rashi's florid midrash is searing as it is pitched back to the rabbinic sources: "all those *derashot* that he [Moses] saw Him wrapped in a prayer shawl and proclaiming [the thirteen attributes] are fit to be burned like the books of the heretics." By "all those *derashot*" he may have had in mind a gloss of Rashi a few verses later (Exod 33:23) stating that Moses saw the "knot" of the divine *tefilin*. What, if anything, incensed him, beyond the defiantly anthropomorphic character of such dicta, Pseudo-Rabad does not say. An anthropomorphic conception of the Deity such as had been propounded by some Ashkenazic scholars and debated by others was certain to rile a philosophically minded Jew such as Pseudo-Rabad, who undoubtedly did deem such an understanding heretical.[120] Perhaps he was also aware of how critics of rabbinic Judaism seized on such absurd sounding midrashim as a way to ridicule the sages to whom its adherents looked as guiding lights.[121] One of Pseudo-Rabad's heroes, Ibn Ezra, does affirm the veracity of the midrash on the divine *tefilin*, naturally taking it figuratively. Maimonides may also have interpreted the midrash as a bearer of deep ideas.[122] For his part, the stricturalist excoriates Rashi for unthinkingly purveying teachings hostile to the fastidious conception of divine transcendence Pseudo-Rabad was sure Judaism upheld.

Where Rashi time and again conjures midrashic miracles nowhere reported in scripture, Pseudo-Rabad is driven to reassert "nature," the axial philosophical category.[123] Telescoping the journey of Abraham's servant from the land of Israel to Haran into a single day, the *Commentary* tells of a miraculous acceleration owing to the earth's "springing toward him." Among other things, this geological wonder bears the message that the servant's search for Isaac's wife was divinely steered.[124] Pseudo-Rabad tersely insists that "the verse verifies nothing of this."[125] In Pseudo-Rabad's version of the *Commentary*, one attested elsewhere, Rashi has Abraham's servant flying ("floating") through the air. As Pseudo-Rabad understood it, this flight of fancy was born of a midrashic elaboration on the ostensibly anomalous appearance of *'al* in the servant's statement: "As I stand by [lit. "on"] the spring of water."[126] He insists that the preposition provides "no rationale" for this interpretation, clinching the point by appealing to a verse that describes Balaam finding Balak "standing beside (*'al*) his offerings" (Num 23:17), from which, following the same pattern, one would have to infer "that he [Balak] was floating in the air." He finds no more support for the notion that the sun miraculously set for Jacob as he fled his parents' home or to bolster Rashi's claim that Jacob experienced a supernatural journey at that time. In Pseudo-Rabad's world, the sun sets according to the natural course of affairs (*me-'aṣmo*), not on account of interventions having to do with God's elect. As for Rashi's saying "that the earth sprang forward to him [Jacob]," it is "incorrect."[127]

Rashi's reconstruction of the children of Israel's journey from Raamses to Succoth (Exod 12:37) elicits a similar response. Rashi fixes it at a distance of one hundred and twenty miles, asserting that six hundred thousand men and their families arrived in Succoth in a single group more or less instantaneously. Thus was the divine promise to bear the Israelites "on eagles' wings" (Exod 19:4) (retrospectively) fulfilled. To Pseudo-Rabad, this latter description is patently a "poetic figure" (*meliṣat ha-shir*). What most likely happened is that the Israelites did not arrive in aggregate, but that each, after being informed of the day of departure and given instructions about the route, "went individually from his own locality to Succoth." Pseudo-Rabad punctuates his counterinterpretation with one of many self-assured concluding expressions: "this is the truth."[128]

Where Rashi posits midrashic miracles involving water, Pseudo-Rabad seeks to quench them. Having been commissioned to find a wife for Isaac, Abraham's servant spies Rebecca going down to the spring and filling her jar. Rashi taught that Rebecca's virtue was so great that a miracle occurred and the water rose to meet her. (Because Rashi had her as a girl of three at the time, there was a good logistical reason for him to commend this midrash.) Seeing this, the servant ran toward her, taking this miracle as a sure sign that she was the right woman for Isaac. Without citing Rashi, Pseudo-Rabad offers a more plain sense rebuttal that cuts out the miracle: the servant ran toward Rebecca on the basis of his prior plan to approach the first girl whom he saw drawing water.[129] Rashi finds a similar miracle embedded in the account of Jethro's daughters that "an Egyptian rescued us from the shepherds; he even drew water for us and watered our flock" (Exod 2:18–19). Jethro chastised the daughters for forsaking Moses. The father recognized in their deliverer an offshoot of Jacob on the basis of a midrashically supplied miracle: that well water rose toward him. Pseudo-Rabad's explanation that a father would naturally invite the rescuer of his daughters eliminates the wonder.[130]

Pseudo-Rabad advances an overarching argument of Ibn Ezra to confute midrashic miracles that Rashi asserts: had they happened, the Torah would have reported them. Rashi, as we have seen, reduces the 318 trained men who fought alongside Abram to his lone patriarchal "steward," Eliezer, using *gemaṭriya* to buttress this finding, since 318 was the numerical value of Eliezer's name. Abraham ibn Ezra, almost certainly in response to Rashi, seizes on this midrash to assert the irrelevance of *gemaṭriya* for plain sense interpretation. Eleazar Ashkenazi agrees that "only in *derash*" do such parasemantic exercises have any purchase.[131] Pseudo-Rabad first seeks to upend the midrash by way of countervailing textual evidence. A few verses later, Abraham spoke of "my servants" and the share of the "men" (plural) with whom he had waged the war, even naming "Aner, Eshkol, and Mamre" (Gen 14:24). The Torah itself told of "servants deployed against them [the kings]" (Gen 14:15). To this Pseudo-Rabad adds that had Eliezer been a lone ally invested with the strength of hundreds, this would constitute a miracle that surely ought to have been recorded. Eleazar Ashkenazi casts the *gemaṭriya*-based midrash of Rashi as "a joke." Pseudo-Rabad, not one even for captious jocularity, brands it an "absurdity."[132]

Another occasion for a clash between Rashi's supernatural approach and Pseudo-Rabad's naturalist one is the deliverance of Abraham from Nimrod's fiery furnace, Pseudo-Rabad again appealing to the idea that the wonder would have been recorded in the Torah had it occurred. As reported by Rashi, the story teaches an invaluable lesson about Abraham's unshakable trust in God and God's supernatural protection of people who bear such faith while providing a rationale for the selection of Abraham as patriarch, a choice unjustified in the Torah's account. Noting the Torah's failure to relay the story, Ibn Ezra affects a willingness to accept it as staunchly as "the words of the Torah" if based in a reliable tradition, but here as elsewhere, his conditional wording leaves the issue open. Nahmanides, who directs some of his harshest rhetoric against Ibn Ezra where the latter calls midrashic miracles into question, apparently found Ibn Ezra's pious representations to ring false. Urging readers to resist Ibn Ezra's "seducing" ways, he insists that a miracle occurred, be it openly, as in the midrash, or in the manner of a divinely engineered stratagem occluded from view—namely, Abraham's sudden release from captivity following a divinely effected change of heart on the part of Ur's king, a part of the patriarch's biography attested in pagan sources cited in the *Guide*.[133] Though eventually more expansive, Pseudo-Rabad begins his stricture with a customarily curt denial: "He [Rashi] . . . said that Abraham was cast into the fiery furnace, and so the mistaken ones among the nations affirm, but it is false." To buttress this assessment, he begins with a question: "Had the event actually occurred, would not Moses have recorded it as he wrote the matters of the wells he [Abraham] dug, his going down to Egypt, that his wife was snatched . . . all the more would it have been fitting to write this immense wonder were it true!" In a clinching point of a most non-Maimonidean sort, Pseudo-Rabad pronounces the absence of any reference to the miracle especially inexplicable since the raison d'être of the patriarchal narratives is to "publicize the miracles and good things the Creator did for those righteous ones." Here, he insists, is an objection to Rashi "ratified by the intellect."[134]

Pseudo-Rabad also deploys the argument from silence to mute some of Rashi's more fantastical midrashim. In one place, the *Commentary* has the Amalekites calculate a propitious time for victory over their Israelite enemies using astrology, to which Rashi has Moses respond by staying the setting of the sun, bringing "the hours into confusion." Pseudo-Rabad retorts: "were it so, it would have been written as it is written in Joshua's case" (see Josh 10).[135] Rashi has a miraculous well provide the Israelites with sustenance during their forty-year sojourn in the wilderness. Pseudo-Rabad invokes Moses's reminder to the nation that God "brought forth water for you from the flinty rock" (Deut 8:15). Had a miraculous well existed, Moses ought to have spoken otherwise and lauded God's provision of it, as this would have been "a miracle greater than the extraction of water from the flinty rock."[136] In Rashi's telling, Moses urged Aaron to deploy incense with alacrity to stem a divinely instigated plague that threatened the people with annihilation after the rebellion of Korah, Dathan, and Abiram (Num 17:11). But how did Moses know of the secret power of the incense to arrest plagues? Rashi answered by way of a talmudic midrash: the secret had been transmitted to Moses by the angel of death when he ascended to heaven. Pseudo-Rabad does not understand this *derash* "in the least." The matter would be entirely "supernatural" (*mufla'*) such that it would have been recorded, as were other such things.[137]

The more fantastic a midrashic miracle, the sharper Pseudo-Rabad's rejection of it. A case in point is Rashi's elaboration of "When the sun grew hot, it [the manna] would melt" (Exod 16:21), which has it that leftover manna "became streams from which deer and gazelles drank and the nations of the world would hunt some of them and taste in them the flavor of manna." It was another way for the nations to appreciate the greatness of the Jewish people. Pseudo-Rabad thinks processes of evaporation were at play. Minimally, it had nothing to do with "streams and all those absurdities that he wrote."[138]

Pseudo-Rabad is especially disparaging of midrashic miracles where language-based magic is afoot. In this, he follows Maimonides, who affirms an Aristotelian understanding of the nature of language and its human source, and denies the power of language to influence the natural, cosmic, or divine worlds.[139] It was clear to Maimonides that even divine names, oral or written, including the "ineffable" one reflecting the divine essence, lacked metaphysical potency. In adopting this stance, he set himself against powerful currents in rabbinic literature and medieval Judaism, including ideas that abounded in mystical tomes and a more speculative stream of religious thought associated with Ibn Ezra.[140] By contrast, as Ephraim Kanarfogel has shown, Rashi had fairly broad awareness of and openness to matters mystical and magical, including traditions regarding divine names.[141] Showing his antimagical spirit, Pseudo-Rabad negates a midrash adduced by Rashi that has Moses killing the Egyptian who struck a Hebrew slave by pronouncing the Tetragrammaton. Implied by the midrash was divine authorization for the slaying in a manner that subdued all halakhic or moral qualms.[142] Though presumably based in theological opposition, the point of attack is, in the first instance, exegetical. Pseudo-Rabad denies any prompt for this reading, although midrashists find such a hint in a strange response to Moses by the Hebrew maltreating his brother: "Do you *say* to kill me?" (Exod 2:14). The implication is that he anticipated an end similar to that experienced by the taskmaster, not through physical force but through deployment of the divine name. To bolster his view that the Egyptian's demise was effected naturally, Pseudo-Rabad notes Moses's effort to hide the crime by burying the victim. Such an expedient born of fear would, he implies, have been unnecessary if the killing was achieved through supernatural means.[143]

Pseudo-Rabad's anti-midrashic fury reaches a boil in a stricture on Rashi's interpretation of the incident with the golden calf. The spur is Rashi's suggestion that the calf came about through a plate inscribed with the ineffable divine name. This theory was based on another midrash that has Moses using this same plate to effect the lifting of Joseph's bones from the depths of the Nile. The stricture starts in a matter-of-fact manner, disputing Rashi's midrashic reconstruction of circumstances leading to the golden calf. Pseudo-Rabad denies that the Israelites were confused about the time of Moses's return as Rashi asserts, since the Torah does not indicate the length of Moses's anticipated absence and, indeed, it was unknown to Moses himself when he ascended Mount Sinai. Hence, contra Rashi, the calf could not have been made in the wake of a miscalculation regarding the time of Moses's expected return. Having contested one false midrash in the *Commentary*, Pseudo-Rabad's temperature rises as he turns to another that imbues the story of the calf with a demonic element. According to this midrash, Satan conjured a vision of Moses lying dead on a bier floating between heaven and earth, and deluded the Israelites into seeking his replacement, with the calf designed to fill the void. Pseudo-Rabad seethes at the idea of satanically evoked confusion and "all the other absurdities that he wrote."[144]

His recoil from midrashic folly in full swing, Pseudo-Rabad ponders the idea of a plate bearing the Tetragrammaton that served to bring the calf into existence based on the midrashic account of Moses's recovering Joseph's bones. His initial objection is familiar: "would the Torah publicize minor things and not publicize such a great miracle?" His concluding remark, perhaps hearkening to a passage in Maimonides's *Letter on Astrology*, invokes an image of arboreal destruction that connotes heresy. Yet, where Maimonides opposes what he takes to be a heretical fatalism rooted in judicial astrology foreign to Judaism, Pseudo-Rabad, in what surely marks a high-water mark of medieval Jewish anti-midrashic discourse, finds misbelief closer to home: "The truth is that "they hewed down the tree and cut it branches" (Dan 4:11) since this is all falsity concocted from the hearts of worthless men. They enthrall Israel in error and transpose the words of the living God, this being the written Torah, into words of absurdities and preposterousness invented from their heart."[145] Though stopping short of any accusation of willful distortion, Pseudo-Rabad condemns "worthless men" whose midrashim falsify the Torah and transform "the words of the living God" into fabrications at odds with nature and reason. It was such "absurdities" that Rashi frequently relayed.

Rabbinic Received Traditions, Peshatist Achievements

Having reached the limit case of Pseudo-Rabad's charges against Rashi and his rabbinic teachers, our investigation now moves in some unexpected directions. First, even while flaying the *Commentary*, Pseudo-Rabad can become mysteriously susceptible to deference before midrashim adduced in it. Second, he can herald Rashi, whether (most unexpectedly) for a midrashic interpretation or (less surprisingly) for a plain sense interpretation that departs from midrash. To behold these sides of *Sefer hassagot* is to encounter its author's almost Jekyll-and-Hyde relationship to rabbinic Judaism.

Long before *Sefer hassagot*, many Rabbanites distinguished between midrashim born of purely exegetical processes on the part of the rabbis and midrashim rooted in immaculate traditions handed down from biblical antiquity (*qabbalah*).[146] We might expect Pseudo-Rabad to eschew the latter notion entirely, but he does not. On the contrary, he proves open to it. This is so in the legal sphere ("I say [despite my disputing the salient midrashim] that perhaps nevertheless they possessed a tradition with regard to what they said about the day's [Yom Kippur's] service")[147] and even in the narrative sphere ("he [Rashi] said [that the assembly occurred] 'the day after Yom Kippur'. Perhaps they [the sages] possessed a received tradition").[148] In light of its author's frequent expressions of fury at the rabbinic inheritance, the reader of *Sefer hassagot* can suffer whiplash at seeing the sages suddenly invested with the prospect of inerrancy.

In the case of his assessment of Nimrod, the possibility that indubitably accurate historical information may have arrived in rabbinic hands bestirs second thoughts as Pseudo-Rabad weighs the disparate claims of Rashi and Ibn Ezra regarding Nimrod's standing and legacy. Suspended on the description of Nimrod as a "mighty hunter before God" (Gen 10:9) is a midrash endorsed by Rashi that has Nimrod ensnare people's minds in a rebellion "against the Omnipresent." Ibn Ezra, stressing the positive connotations of the phrase "before God," insists that a straightforward reading has Nimrod offering the animals he captured as sacrifices to God, not seeking to incite a rebellion against the Deity.[149] Pseudo-Rabad initially treads in Ibn Ezra's footsteps, invoking the same prooftext. If "mighty hunter" bears adverse meaning, why say "before the Lord"? But then, as a bolt from the blue appears a newly deferent Pseudo-Rabad, apparently of a mind to recant: "perhaps they [the sages] knew that he was an idolater from elsewhere, or possessed a received tradition; it is not far-fetched."[150] Here, in addition to received rabbinic tradition, Pseudo-Rabad apparently raises the prospect that extrabiblical knowledge could sway his assessment of Nimrod if it could be proven reliable—which, however, there is no way of doing.

Midrashic identifications of one biblical figure with another were a more "rigorously definable" area where an assertion of "received tradition" might win traction.[151] Here, too, Pseudo-Rabad can bewilder. As we have seen, he denies Rashi's identification of the men in whose quarrel Moses intervened with Dathan and Abiram, and insists that the perennial villains are not the ones intended by God's reference to "the men" who sought to kill Moses. When Rashi claims that the seditious men who left manna until morning and evoked God's stern judgement (Exod 16:19–21) were Dathan and Abiram, one expects the usual audible misgivings. Yet Pseudo-Rabad suddenly finds (Rabbanite) religion, granting: "perhaps they knew this by way of received tradition."[152]

But only "perhaps." Wherever he suggests a possible need to defer to Rashi's midrashim on the grounds of reliable tradition, Pseudo-Rabad invariably enters this qualifier: "perhaps" the sages knew about Nimrod; "perhaps" Dathan and Abiram transgressed with the manna; "perhaps" Moses gathered the people immediately after Yom Kippur; "perhaps" the sages possessed true information about the protocols of that day. Even such tepid assertions he can retract. Having disputed midrashim regarding the nature of the life-ending disaster that felled Korah and then turned to the question debated by midrashists about whether "the congregation of Korah are destined to rise up" in the future, Pseudo-Rabad says that the sages "perhaps" had a true tradition. Still, "a proof from scripture they do not have, and that is the truth for those who understand; do not think otherwise."[153]

To the reader's incredulity, Pseudo-Rabad on one occasion commends a midrash of Rashi. The *Commentary* reads "these are the rules that you shall set before them" (Exod 21:1) midrashically as an utterance addressed not to Moses but to every Jew. The pronominal suffix "before them" (*lifnehem*) is taken to refer to gentile judges. So understood, the verse instructs Jews to litigate only in a Jewish court. Rashi adds that the rule applies even if the principles of adjudication to be used differed not at all. Nor was this a little thing. To take the case to a gentile court was, Rashi warns sternly, tantamount to desecration of the divine name.[154] *Mirabile dictu*, Pseudo-Rabad finds that Rashi "explained well" (though he does not deign to explain why). Perhaps he shares a possible aim with Rashi in citing the midrash, to guard against Jews bringing cases to Christian courts.[155]

On two occasions, Pseudo-Rabad praises Rashi for imparting the plain sense. In one, Rashi opines that the charge that a jug of manna should be deposited "before the Lord" (Exod 16:33) means "before the Ark." He also observes that the instruction, delivered soon after the departure from Egypt, must have been said with reference to the future since the Ark was erected only at the first anniversary of the exodus (Exod 40:1–8). Still, it was appropriately recorded in the "section dealing with the manna." Pseudo-Rabad assesses that Rashi "interpreted well" while still managing to end on a note of lamentation: had Rashi pursued this approach in "many places, he would have been spared many mistakes."[156]

Perhaps not surprisingly, Pseudo-Rabad's warmest plaudit for Rashi occurs where Rashi asserts a midrashic deviation from the plain sense. It involves the case of "You shall neither side with the multitude to do wrong" (Exod 23:2), a testimony from which midrashists derived many legal procedures far removed from the plain sense, including the one that a court should reach a verdict according to the majority of the judges—this, though the verse itself warned against following the "multitude" where doing so would pervert justice. Before adducing what he calls the "midrashim of the sages of Israel," Rashi allows that the "language of scripture is not settled by them." Ibn Ezra had insisted on a gulf between midrash and *peshaṭ* in this verse. Now Pseudo-Rabad enlists the *Commentary* to this end, observing that Rashi "explained well by his own lights and not [according to] the ingenious midrashim [*midreshei hokhmah*, playing on Rashi's *midreshei hakhmei yisra'el*] that it is a commandment to follow the majority."[157] The Torah clearly "said the opposite," stipulating that one should not follow the majority for evil.[158] As soon as Rashi came out from under his rabbinic thrall, Pseudo-Rabad happily lauded him.

"*Rashi Said . . . Their Mistake Was*"

Formally speaking, Pseudo-Rabad mostly targets Rashi the messenger, but he makes no attempt to spare the sages upon whom Rashi relies. Indeed, we have seen him go so far as to speak of them as "worthless men who enthrall Israel in error" and who transpose "the words of the living God into words of absurdities and preposterousness."[159] Little wonder, then, that some strictures begin with Rashi as perpetrator but quickly shift to plural pronouns.

An example concerns the scouts as they returned from their expedition to Canaan. Although a verse describes the scouts bearing a cluster of grapes, as well as figs and pomegranates, it does not say who carried the latter, nor how many of these were brought. A reference to "two" with respect to the grapes seemingly refers to the number of carriers, apparently to emphasize that the supernaturally large fruit required at least two to haul it. Rashi, however, takes "by two" to refer to the number of staves. In his midrashic reading, no less than eight of the scouts bore this enormous cluster. Meanwhile, Rashi midrashically posits that only a single fig and pomegranate were brought, each by a lone scout, presumably because the verse speaks of their taking "some pomegranates and figs," technically leaving open the possibility that they took only one from each type. Rounding out Rashi's rabbinically based reconstruction was the notion that Joshua and Caleb refused to carry any of the fruits on the suspicion that their colleagues intended to use them as props in a "slanderous report" designed to dissuade the people from attempting to conquer the land, a claim they could buttress by pointing to the extraordinary size of the produce and extrapolating to the ostensibly insuperable formidability of the land's inhabitants.

Pseudo-Rabad's rebuff starts with a recapitulation of Rashi ("he said . . .") but the object of obloquy quickly becomes plural: "I am incredulous: what brought them to this affliction, to invent on their own a thing so false and full of absurdities (*devar sheqer ve-havalim*)?" The "truth according to the *peshaṭ*" includes all manner of realia: considerations of spoilage, endurance, and logistics, on the assumption that hauling techniques over distances were similar then and "nowadays":

> They took a single [grape] cluster and pomegranates and figs, all suspended on a single stave, which [all] twelve helped to transport, and this was since they had to transport it over a long distance for some twenty days in a way that the fruits would not spoil and they could transport them without great exertion. This is what those who wish to transport something do nowadays if they are afraid of it being damaged, such as glass or the like.[160]

Pseudo-Rabad also rebuts Rashi's unremittingly negative evaluation of the main body of scouts:

> They did not intend to [use the produce as props for] slander but rather [to fulfill the charge] from Moses, "And take pains to bring back some of the fruit of the land" (Numbers 13:20). The proof in scripture is their saying ["We came to the land . . .] it does indeed flow with milk and honey, and this is its fruit" (Numbers 13:27). Thus far did they praise. Only thenceforth did they intend to slander. The proof is [their saying] "However, the people who inhabit the country are powerful." Since they had been relating its [the land's] praise and illustrating by way of the very good fruit, they were constrained [to begin the critical report with the word] "however," meaning: "with all the praise we recounted, [still] the people who inhabit the country are powerful."[161]

A stricture that begins with a head-on assault on a rabbinic interpretation "so false and full of absurdities" ends with a more moderate shift away from Rashi's evaluation of the scouts.

We saw that Pseudo-Rabad insists that Moses's killing of the Egyptian occurred by natural means. His initial rejection of Rashi's interpretation of that event begins with Rashi's gloss on "He turned this way and that" (Exod 2:12). Rashi knew the plain sense: what was meant was that Moses issued furtive glances in all directions to ensure "that no one had seen him slay the Egyptian." Yet Rashi commenced his reading with a midrash according to which each glance of Moses referred to a prior extrabiblical incident—the Egyptian's rape of the Hebrew man's wife and subsequent beating of her husband—leading up to the assault on the slave. Pseudo-Rabad begins his riposte by noting that the verse should be read "according to its plain sense." When, however, he turns to Rashi's subsequent insinuation of the notion that

Moses killed the Egyptian by deploying the divine name, Pseudo-Rabad points to the source of the troubles and insists that the fact that it states "Do you *say* to kill me?" provides "no proof for their claim," as Moses's effort to hide the crime indicates. It is Rashi who makes rejection of the midrash necessary, but Pseudo-Rabad well knew that it was "their claim" he rebuffed.[162]

The *hassagah* on the contention that Rebecca was three at the time of her marriage also begins with "he said," but again rivets attention on the originators of the folly, speaking of "what led *them*" to "*their* mistake." The critique rests on a claim like the one of Eleazar Ashkenazi regarding the matter:

> Would that I could fathom what led them to this affliction. . . . Their mistake was due to [the surmise] that [since] he [Abraham] heard that Rebecca was born after the binding [of Isaac, this meant that she was just born] whereas what is correct is that she was born before that interval, proof being that others who were born are mentioned [in the genealogy] and surely they were not all born at once [despite the births all being recorded in one place], and that is the truth.[163]

Pseudo-Rabad owes "affliction" as a designation for misguided midrash to Ibn Ezra. One place where Ibn Ezra uses it is the midrash that places Moses's mother at one hundred and thirty years old when she gave birth to Moses. Rashi adduces the midrash in his account of the migration of Jacob and his family to Egypt, prompted by a need to enumerate the seventy people said to have accompanied the patriarch. While the Torah was clear that the wives of Jacob's sons were excluded (as, presumably, were Judah's sons Er and Onan, having died in Canaan), it remained unclear how to arrive at seventy. Rashi followed a midrashic computation that included Jochebed, daughter of Levi, on the view that she was born "between the walls" as the family cavalcade entered Egypt. Jochebed, plus the sixty-six family members listed, plus Joseph and his two sons yields the desired number. Corroboration for her birth at the border was forthcoming from an alleged subtlety in a later testimony regarding "Jochebed daughter of Levi, who was born to Levi in Egypt" (Num 26:59), a wording that can be taken to indicate that Jochebed was *born* in Egypt (just at the time of Levi's arrival), but not conceived there.[164] Exegetically all is well and good, but the inclusion of Moses's mother in the count of seventy does entail a surprise: she would have been one hundred and thirty years old when she bore Moses eighty years before the exodus. In this, Rashi presumably found nothing amiss. It was a fact vouchsafed by the sages. At any rate, Rashi registers no incredulity at the remarkable longevity of biblical figures, even imbuing some talmudic sages with exceptionally long life spans.[165]

By contrast, *fabulae* that Rashi takes for granted can bring Sefardic exegetes to blows. To rebut Jochebed's pregnancy at an advanced age, Ibn Ezra uses the argument of which Pseudo-Rabad would eventually avail himself: if this miracle, which far outstripped Sarah's wondrous pregnancy at ninety years, occurred, the Torah would have recorded it. As if the midrashic "affliction" were not enough, Ibn Ezra complains that liturgical poets make even more exaggerated claims for Jochebed's motherhood at such advanced ages as two hundred and fifty. These assertions provoke Nahmanides to issue a rebuke lest Ibn Ezra seem "wise in his eyes" in refuting the sages. The Torah recorded only some miracles, those ones revealed to prophets in advance, since only then did they strengthen faith in God, maker of wonders. Then, too, there was no need to record every miracle since "all the foundations of the Torah lie in hidden miracles."[166]

Without mentioning Rashi, Pseudo-Rabad expresses wonder at the "great blunder" into which the sages entered "since they felt constrained to say that Jochebed was born at the border. . . . This blunder led them to fall into a deep pit [as they were then forced to say] that Moses was born in his mother's one hundred and thirtieth year." He focuses on Ibn Ezra without saying so: "Look how the Torah made a point of testifying to what was a great wonder, namely that Sarah gave birth at the age of ninety years." But he also sharpens Ibn Ezra's point with the following addendum: since life spans had declined since Sarah's day, Jochebed's birthing at an even older age was all the more miraculous and therefore all the more worthy of inclusion in the Torah—had it occurred. He also reprises his idea that failure to mention the miracle was inconceivable in light of the Torah's overall goal of "publicizing all miracles done to the righteous." Compiling the data, the "truth without doubt" was that Jochebed was born "many years" after Jacob's arrival in Egypt and that Moses was born to her at a perfectly ordinary age.[167]

Pseudo-Rabad returns to the crux of Jochebed's age in a tirade that brings down the curtain on *Sefer hassagot*. The prompt is Moses's proclamation, "I am now one hundred and twenty years old, I can no longer be active" (Deut 31:2). Pseudo-Rabad comments: "From here arises a refutation to those who say that Moses was born when his mother was one hundred and thirty years old. If the Torah already says [about him] 'I am no longer able to go out and come' when one hundred and twenty, would it not be true of one who is a hundred and thirty all the more?" Pseudo-Rabad takes up the longevity ascribed to Og who, according to a midrash of Rashi, survived the flood and then lived for centuries.[168] If such a gift were due anybody, surely it was one of the patriarchs or Moses, not an "entirely wicked" gentile king. In a hail-and-farewell that takes the form of a final jeremiad that perhaps outdoes all his others for venom,

Pseudo-Rabad drives the deepest wedge between the biblical legacy and its later perversion by the rabbinic sources that Rashi reproduces in exposition of the Torah: "the truth is that all those midrashim were concocted by ones who are confused (Isaiah 29:24). They were sinners (*ḥot'im*) who perverted (*heḥti'u*) the Torah of God which is 'perfect, renewing life' (Psalm 19:8)."

Rhetoric of Resistance

The provocation of the *Commentary* brought Pseudo-Rabad to anti-rabbinic vitriol rarely seen in premodern Jewish literature, leading us to pay heed not only to *Sefer hassagot*'s message but also to its medium—that is, the devices Pseudo-Rabad uses to clinch a claim, plant a question, or generally induce readers to recoil from Rashi. Premodern Jewish exegesis is not usually studied in terms of such devices, but in *Sefer hassagot*'s case this element is evidently crucial. The point was intuited by S. M. Schiller-Szinessy in his 1876 catalogue of Hebrew manuscripts held at Cambridge University Library. He described *Sefer hassagot* as being of "the greatest importance," the main reason being the freedom "bordering on disrespect" with which its author spoke of "the otherwise universally venerated Rashi." As we know, this characterization barely begins to capture the opprobrium that Pseudo-Rabad heaps on the *Commentary* and its author.[169]

To some extent, the work's tonality came naturally in light of Pseudo-Rabad's chosen literary vehicle, the *hassagah*, a form of expression that by its nature established rank. It is, suggests José Faur, this aspect that generates what he describes as the genre's "need for intimidation and incivility."[170] Although Pseudo-Rabad's assault on Rashi inevitably brought him into conflict with the great sage, the stark, hostile, often vituperative rhetoric in which he couches his denunciations of the *Commentary* was hardly foreordained. We have seen how even the most devoted supercommentators did not treat Rashi's word as an oracle and found ways laden with nuance to express doubts without compromising respect. By contrast, Pseudo-Rabad is ostentatiously denigrating, issuing *hassagot* that elevate him and demote Rashi for, at times, a doltish lack of understanding. Israel M. Ta-Shma observes that *hassagot* typically display an "astonishing brusqueness." Those in *Sefer hassagot* often meet the standard and then some. Yet *Sefer hassagot* defies Ta-Shma's further claim that this style was "merely external and, in practice, was not taken amiss."[171] Even a casual reading shows that *Sefer hassagot*'s antagonistic tenor is no act of ritualized adversity. Its critical thrust is captured in the abovementioned remark in which Pseudo-Rabad explains that his pen has fallen silent for a stretch because the *Commentary* contains "nothing requiring refutation." (We will also meet a reader of *Sefer hassagot* who certainly did take amiss its denigration of Rashi.)

The range and registers of criticism vary, from cool dissent to crackling assertions of falsity and on to hyperbolic claims of borderline heresy. Many expressions fall within bounds of the often turbulent rough-and-tumble of medieval scholarly debate. There are simple assertions of what is "correct" in contrast to what Rashi says (six times). There is the even more frequent observation that Rashi "is incorrect" (fourteen times). Often couched in the language of persuasion, Pseudo-Rabad's strictures can become demands or certitudes. The reader is told "do not think other than this" or "it is the truth." Characterizations like "this is transparent" implicitly command assent. Professions of incredulity, a familiar part of the rhetorical repertoire in medieval Hebrew writing, do discursive work: "would that I could fathom whence Lot knew of Passover!" In addition to heaping scorn on Rashi, the manner of expression impliedly dares the reader to disagree—and, if unable to do so, to join in the critique. Hyperbole figures most clearly in the (one-time) demand to put certain *derashot* to the pyre like "books of the heretics," a censure possibly drawn from rabbinic literature or a metaphorical call by Ibn Ezra for the burning of certain books.[172]

Pseudo-Rabad's "would that I could fathom" (*mi yiten yada'ti*; Job 23:3) is a reminder of the role of biblicisms in the rhetoric of critique. In the case of Rashi on the divine blessing accorded to Ishmael, Pseudo-Rabad reaches for a double metaphor from Ecclesiastes to enhance the derision. Rooted in the polysemic character of a key term, the comment enabled Rashi to forecast a quick eclipse for Ishmael's chieftains (*nesi'im*) in the manner of clouds (*nesi'im*). Pseudo-Rabad's stricture is cutting: "He said 'like clouds.' This, too, is absurdity and senselessness (*hevel u-re'ut ruaḥ*)."[173]

In another pattern, a stricture that starts tentatively ends on a highly declarative note. Arguing that Pharaoh is the one to whom God refers in speaking about those who wished to kill Moses, Pseudo-Rabad begins with "it appears to me" but concludes: "this is the truth."[174] The *hassagah* concerning the clean versus unclean animal commences with "It seems to me" but ends: "this verse does not aim to address this [case, as Rashi interpreted] **at all**." A tacit invitational "we" gives the reader a chance to join the cognoscenti: "there is no doubt **to one who is discerning**." The *hassagah* attains a cumulative rhetorical force that practically requires acquiescence.[175]

Pseudo-Rabad also resorts to apodictic rebuttals. Consider the example seen earlier of Rashi's claim that Isaac knew that whoever stood before him was the worthy recipient of his blessing, since as Jacob approached his blind father smelled "the fragrance of the garden of Eden," understanding that the son about to receive his benediction was destined for the hereafter. Pseudo-Rabad professes astonishment at this "affliction (*ṣa'ar*) and folly (*ṭipshut*)." It is "obvious, apparent, and in no need of proof that there was not but the smell of [ordinary] clothes."[176]

The assertion of Rashi's certain failure without elaboration extends to legal matters. The *Commentary* reprises a midrash on the injunction against making "gods of silver" and "gods of gold" (Exod 20:20). It refers the prohibitions not to representations of the Deity or to the making of idols but to illicit activities involving the tabernacle cherubs (e.g., "if you make four [cherubim] they are to Me as gods of gold"). Pseudo-Rabad deems the gloss tantamount to "chaos and weights of emptiness" (Isa 34:11). On top of the biblicism, he makes use of mockery suitable to the occasion, saying that the gloss lacks "all substance and form." The final blow is a claim that the error is so blatant as to require no "eradication," since "it is eradicated in and of itself and does not stand."[177]

Though he leans to the bitingly sober, Pseudo-Rabad sounds a jeering tone familiar from Eleazar Ashkenazi on occasions where he deploys the *reductio ad ridiculum*. Rashi discerned peculiarities in the report that "When Abram entered Egypt, the Egyptians saw how very beautiful the woman was" (Gen 12:14). One peculiarity he notes is scripture's failure to describe Sarai's arrival. Another he had in mind is the Torah's implication that her beauty somehow came to light only after her arrival. Rashi uses a midrash to explain all: Abram had hidden his wife in a chest, which explains why her arrival went unmentioned; when the Egyptians demanded the customs duty, they opened the chest and saw Sarai, only then appreciating her beauty. Pseudo-Rabad solves the problem with a typical recourse to linguistic convention, the conventional habit (*derekh 'eretz*) to mention only males rather than their whole retinue, including their wives. To undermine the midrash further, however, he mocks Rashi's interpretation by applying its logic elsewhere. When the Torah reports that "Jacob arrived safe in the city of Shechem" (Gen 33:18) without mentioning other members of his entourage, ought we to say that they were all concealed in chests?! Having delivered himself of his umbrage, Pseudo-Rabad concludes that scripture "speaks fittingly," implying that Rashi's absurd midrashic over-reading makes it seem otherwise.[178] Pseudo-Rabad rebuts a supposed support for the notion of Abraham's rescue from the fiery furnace by noting that it would apply to others in his family: must we then conclude that "all of them were thrown into the furnace?"[179]

A *hassagah* on Rashi's midrashically embellished account of the construction of the tabernacle continues the pattern. According to it, God prevented the Israelites from erecting the tabernacle, since Moses had done no work on it and God therefore wanted to leave it for him to set up. The problem was that the task surely could not be accomplished by one man alone, given the heaviness of the planks. Moses inquired, and God replied: if Moses did his share, God would do His. In any case, Moses appeared to set it up, but in fact it "arose by itself." The miracle was hinted at in the Torah's passive formulation: "the tabernacle was set up" (*huqam*; Exod 40:17).[180] Invoking the *reductio ad ridiculum*, Pseudo-Rabad asks: When it says of Jerusalem that "the city was breached" (Jer 39:2), did it mean "breached by itself?!" Pseudo-Rabad thought not: "It appears to me that it was breached by the Chaldeans." It followed that "the tabernacle was set up by people."[181]

Pseudo-Rabad's rage can be so deep as to leave its precise cause, and upshot, beclouded. Interpreting the list of animals enumerated in the opening verses of Leviticus that discuss the burnt offering sacrifice, Rashi, following Sifra, took a perfectly natural partitive preposition (*min*), and on the omnisignificant principle, viewed it as ostensibly superfluous and hence especially meaning laden: " 'of cattle'—but not all of them. [The phrase comes] to exclude the case of the male or female animal that has cohabited with a human. 'From the flock': to exclude an animal that has been worshipped as a god." In his accustomed way, Pseudo-Rabad responds with piercing ferocity: "he wrote words of absurdity." He objects a bit more expansively to a further midrashic twist through which Rashi derives an additional exclusion, this one for a fatally sick or wounded (*ṭerefah*, "torn") animal, said to be embedded in the repetition of the phrase "from the herd" a verse later: "since [scripture] states below [Lev 1:3] 'of the herd,' it need not have been used [in Lev 1:2] . . . therefore, it comes to exclude the *ṭerefah*." To this last midrashic operation of analysis Pseudo-Rabad responds with still greater fury, calling it "words of falsehood" (*divrei sheqer*) that summon the divine grievance about things "I never commanded, which never came to My mind" (Jer 7:31).[182] But wherein lies the objection and what is its upshot? Presumably Pseudo-Rabad disputes the exegetical derivation but concurs in the legal holdings that, say, a *ṭerefah* is ineligible for sacrifice. Yet he seems too riled to offer a fully articulated clarification.

Another point emerges from the example just seen. Rashi was unique among medieval commentators in holding that the verse conveyed the legal exclusions in question, although Abraham ibn Ezra did grant the partitive *min* did have exclusionary force. The midrashic interpretations adduced by Rashi seem to be born less of a need to establish the ineligibility of certain animals for sacrifice, a fact the prior rabbinic discussions established as self-understood, and more to uphold a conception of the nature of scripture in which every verbal particle counts.[183] Seen thus, Pseudo-Rabad's objections push back not only against specific glosses of Rashi but also against his rabbinically grounded omnisignificant approach to the divine word.

We lack a database that allows us to rank quantitatively the rhetorical extravagance of any particular entry in the history of Hebrew invective, let alone one that could take into account qualitative factors like larger literary context or level of daring based on intended target. Abraham ben David, the figure under whose name *Sefer hasaggot* was written, protested that his condemnations of Zerahyah Halevi carried not a smidgen of personal belittlement, adding (to the bewilderment of modern scholars) that they sometimes took the form of what their author assumed to be the "implacable style" cultivated by Spanish scholars in halakhic debate.[184] However this may be, the two scholars' controversy has been described as "the most vituperative" in the history of halakhic correspondence.[185] Among biblical exegetes, Ibn Ezra produced an impressive panoply of expressions of derision and insult ("intellectually deficient," "mindless," empty-headed"), although some of the epithets may trace more to Hispanic mannerism than to real denunciation.[186] Nahmanides, in turn, could rebuke Ibn Ezra harshly.[187] In an admittedly unique case, Moses Taku, a thirteenth-century Ashkenazic writer, compares Saadia Gaon to Jesus and casts him as the root of all evil in Judaism.[188] Samuel ben Meir wields an occasional castigation of "absurdity" (*hevel*) even against Rashi, albeit without naming his target.[189] Still, it is safe to say that with respect to Rashi, Pseudo-Rabad's formulae of condemnation stand in a class all their own, especially within the short span of eleven folios, forming a steady a drumbeat of disparagement in which Rashi is repeatedly said to have "erred" (*ṭa'ah*) or "blundered."

Rhetorically, modes of disparagement range and combine. As we saw, Pseudo-Rabad does not scruple to depict a clueless commentator, as in the prologue where Rashi is said to reproduce midrashim "as a man in whose mouth were placed a few words from some foreign language. He utters them but does not understand it [the language]." The charge recurs when Pseudo-Rabad commends midrashim in the *Commentary* relating to the revelation at Sinai that "exquisitely explained" that formative event in ways Pseudo-Rabad does not deign to elaborate. All he says is that of them "the commentator understood not a thing."[190] In calling Rashi "the commentator" (*ha-mefaresh*), Pseudo-Rabad recalls some of the "chillingly neutral" references to Maimonides made by Abraham ben David in strictures he appended to Maimonides's legal code.[191] This same way of referring to Rashi, and a renewed charge of ignorance, occurs when Pseudo-Rabad assesses Jacob's nocturnal struggle with a nameless assailant. Rashi says that "an angel does not state his appellation, since the appellation of each is in accordance with its mission." True, says

Pseudo-Rabad, but true no less that "the commentator" understood not what he said.[192]

One barb of Pseudo-Rabad goes so far as to cast doubt on the nation's collective decision to honor Rashi's scholarship. Rashi read Abraham's statement that if Lot would go left "then I will go to the right, and if [you] to the right, then I will go to the left" (Gen 13:9) as a promise to stand by Lot and aid him if necessary, but at all events *not* to distance himself. Pseudo-Rabad objects that scripture states the very opposite, with Abraham declaring: "separate yourself from me." In so doing, the critic not only calls Rashi "the commentator" but, seeking to rouse the requisite outrage, fulminates: "Look, just look, at this blunder by this scholar who is deemed a scholar from among the scholars of Israel."[193] Such an assault imposes a twofold question: whom did Pseudo-Rabad seek to address and how did readers react to such insults?

Pseudo-Rabad's Readers: Intended, Actual, Censorious

Appearing to forgo a broad intended audience, Pseudo-Rabad refers to "the truth for those who understand," although he presumably hoped to enlarge the ranks of such people by securing an opening for his own interpretive vision. Here his resort to pseudepigraphy may have played a role in the plan for his work's diffusion. Had he published it under his own name, Pseudo-Rabad might have had to restrict that diffusion for fear of reprisal. Having concealed his authorship, he was free to wish it wide distribution. But did he?

The answer depends in part on our understanding of an entreaty found beneath the work's title in the Balbo manuscript: "I implore whoever comes into possession of this book not to publicize it among the many" (*lo' yefarsemeno ba-rabim*). If Pseudo-Rabad wrote this line, one could infer his aim to speak to a close circle of elite readers while withholding his critique of Rashi's *Commentary* from "the many." Urbach, thinking it obvious that it was the copyist (i.e., Balbo) who wrote the line, did assume that Pseudo-Rabad's intended audience was broad.[194] There is a third possibility—namely, that the author himself wrote the line as part of a clever marketing strategy to expand his audience, understanding that nothing ensures the broadcast of a subversive tract better than a plea to ensure that access to it be restricted.

In many cases, Pseudo-Rabad's compressed briefs presuppose ample acumen on the part of his readers. Consider his treatment of Rashi's rabbinic rendering of the pericope on the Hebrew slave girl, where obligations of one who purchased such a slave were spelled out, including the provision that where a second wife was taken, the slave girl had to be maintained with respect to "three things" (Exod 21:11).[195] Pseudo-Rabad explains that the reference is to "the three [previously] mentioned: sustenance, clothing, and *'onah*" (the latter a *hapax legomenon* traditionally understood as conjugal rights). To understand so aphoristic a gloss and see how it constitutes a stricture, a reader has to know the midrashic interpretation supplied by Rashi, where the reference is taken to be to three previously mentioned *scenarios*. Thus the *Commentary*: "What are these three things? That he designates her as a wife for himself, or for his son, or deducts from the money of her redemption and allows her to go free." Committed peshatists on both sides of the Ashkenazic/Sefardic divide, like Samuel ben Meir and Ibn Ezra, subscribed to this view, the latter even reproving those "many" who urge a reading like Pseudo-Rabad's. Only one apprised of all this could appreciate Pseudo-Rabad's stricture, concluding with the rhetorical punctuation: "do not think otherwise."[196]

Turning from intended to actual readers, we meet a blank beyond two. The first was the fifteenth-century exegete Aaron Aboulrabi who, as we will see, was in sympathy with some, but not all, of Pseudo-Rabad's *Commentary* criticism. Where he chanced upon the work is impossible to say. He does not mention Crete, where Balbo copied it, among his many ports of call, but he did travel in eastern Mediterranean locales where he could have stumbled on another version or perhaps the one produced by Balbo.[197]

Another reader, far less appreciative of Pseudo-Rabad than Aboulrabi, expressed outrage at his disparaging treatment of Rashi by mutilating Balbo's manuscript through selected erasures.[198] Most are small in scale and the acts of defacement cease two folios in. The most extensive crossings-out occur in the prologue, as indicated in bold:

> Since I saw, in the commentary . . . , homilies and interpretations **that stray from the intention of the Torah in many places—some being the very opposite of the correct intention** . . . I saw fit to note a number of the **erroneous** instances. . . . I did not embark on this endeavor because I fancy myself more proficient . . . but because I discerned the nature of the . . . commentator, **that he was devoid of any sort of wisdom save for [facility in] navigation of the talmudic pericope alone. It seems from his words that he did not** understand any other thing **save for this [art of talmudic] navigation alone, without his understanding** any ***haggadah*** **as alluding to an esoteric matter, neither pertaining to wisdom nor anything else. He rather spoke about *haggadot* as a blind man [groping] at the opening of an attic. . . . So it happened to** the . . . **rabbi** in a number

of the *haggadot* . . . **since he did not understand them one iota.** So it is that I shall clarify . . . wherever I discerned that the rabbi **blundered.**

The effort to guard Rashi's honor is evident in other passages that are crossed out. Where Pseudo-Rabad wrote that Rashi "did not understand," for instance, a later hand deleted the expression. A possibly still later hand had the text read neutrally that Rashi "did not explain." It has been conjectured that the censor betook himself to amend Balbo's version for more than one reason, perhaps including personal animus against Balbo, but the theory is tenuous.[199] The deletions clearly converge on passages with an irreverent stance toward Rashi. Thus does the work's only surviving copy illustrate graphically an attitude of respect, if not veneration, for Rashi that, as we have seen, was widely shared by the close of the Middle Ages.

Fragments in the (Eastern Mediterranean?) Round

Although Pseudo-Rabad did not paint on a broad canvas and generally meets the self-imposed demand of writers of *hassagot* to stay close to the base text, his work provides clear indications of his intellectual agenda and a slender basis for speculation on the religiocultural milieu in which it was executed. A highly literate scholar (how broadly so is hard to say), Pseudo-Rabad was a spirited rationalist who relished decisiveness and had an unimpeded view of what counted as wisdom or folly. Only twice does he reveal incertitude, as when departing from excoriation of Rashi to ponder the angels who visited Abraham. They came as three, but only one was addressed by Abraham, that angel's voice seemingly not his own but God's. Of this "wondrous" conundrum Pseudo-Rabad admits: "I do not understand it nor have I ever seen anything sufficient when it comes to this matter."[200] Otherwise, Pseudo-Rabad treats biblical interpretation as a sphere where cut-and-dried proofs are available for the "discerning" and where the choice between the competing readings that he ponders is a zero-sum game.

In addition to deploying the *hassagot* genre, Pseudo-Rabad used pseudepigraphy, a type of writing that left an indelible mark on late medieval Jewish literature, but one mostly cultivated by kabbalists.[201] By contrast, *Sefer hassagot* joined a few other works by rationalists written under cover of pseudonimity.[202] Unlike their kabbalistic counterparts, who generally ascribed works to ancient rabbinic figures, Pseudo-Rabad's unusual tactic was to adopt the false identity of a medieval with no rationalist credentials to abet his attack on the

Commentary, allowing him to compose a work of radical self-assertion against a towering figure while reducing his risk and imbuing his assault with unassailable traditionalist credentials.

For the historian, Pseudo-Rabad's mask of pseudonimity has the disadvantage of making his setting hard to pin down. Urbach's proposal that *Sefer hassagot* originated in a circle of fourteenth-century Italian or southern French rationalists is not easily credited.[203] For one thing, there is a dearth of leading Western European centers in which the sort of severe and open anti-midrashic criticism that is the hallmark of *Sefer hassagot* can be found. To be sure, in Italy, southern France, and Spain the problem of what were sometimes called "strange" midrashim certainly did vex those of a philosophic bent. It also took on fresh urgency owing to polemical pressures emanating from Christian quarters. But rationalists in these centers responded with full-blown works of midrashic interpretation that tended to defend the rabbinic inheritance and certainly not to join in Christian disparagement of it. This practice is attested already in *Sefer ha-pe'ah* of Moses ibn Tibbon, likely the first sustained philosophical commentary on midrash to emerge in southern France. Ibn Tibbon allowed that midrashim relayed impossibilities, putting in doubt the wisdom of their authors. He insisted, however, that the remedy was to understand them according to the nonliteral intent with which they were originally uttered. Italian, southern French, and Spanish rationalists like Hillel of Verona, Isaac ben Yedayah, Samuel ibn Zarza, and Shem Tov ibn Shaprut made this a standard interpretive assumption when they unpacked rabbinic sayings.[204]

By contrast, some data converge on an eastern Mediterranean provenance for *Sefer hassagot*. While here is not the place to reprise most of them,[205] two points are worthy of note. A striking socioreligious feature of late medieval Byzantine Judaism is a lack of overt interreligious concern of the sort that greatly shaped rationalist discourse on midrash in southern France and Spain. This absence may explain the willingness of scholars working in the region to criticize Rashi's midrashim with no restraint. To this point we may add another circumstantial bit of evidence. While Jewish scholars cultivated the genre of *hassagot* in various fields, biblical commentary was rarely one of them, perhaps because it was not deemed to be a realm of "right or wrong" in a way that made strictures a natural form of expression. Yet it would seem that in the East, strictures left a deeper mark on exegetical literature. Shortly after *The Book of Strictures* was copied in Crete by Balbo, another native of the island who was Balbo's younger contemporary, Zechariah ben Moshe, produced a similar work that, although technically a response to strictures made by Nahmanides on Maimonides and especially on Ibn Ezra, often took the form of strictures on Nahmanides himself. In both the colophon of one manuscript of Zechariah's work and a note penned by its owner, this work is called an assemblage of strictures. The work also uses harsh critical expressions, now directed at Nahmanides, of just the sort found in *Sefer hassagot*: "this is absurdity and senselessness"; "its refutation is immediately at hand."[206] Another set of exegetical *hassagot* appeared in the fifteenth century by another author born in Crete, Shabbetai ben Malkiel Hakohen. He protested what he considered the deficient respect for Ibn Ezra shown by his archrival, Mordechai Komtino.[207] If it proves true that the writing of exegetical *hassagot* won a cachet in the eastern Mediterranean, with Crete as its epicenter, this fact would lend further credence to the possibility that *Sefer hassagot* originated in this region.

The prospect of an eastern Mediterranean setting for *Sefer hassagot* invites further speculation about its place in a part of the world far removed from Ashkenaz but nevertheless shaped by Franco-German scholars. The title of *Sefer hassagot* refers to Rashi as "Solomon the Frenchman." Even if this is a later superscription, the author himself uses this epithet in *Sefer hassagot*'s opening line. A suggestion, perhaps too clever by half, would be that in so doing, the author wished to enhance the verisimilitude of his false cover, knowing that his assumed identity, Rabad, habitually referred to Rashi as "the Frenchman" or "French rabbi." But there is another possibility. As many southern French scholars reoriented themselves to a philosophical understanding of the faith in the wake of their Andalusian turn, they ceased to call themselves "French," reserving this as a derisive designation for their northern French counterparts.[208] To be sure, one can hardly assume that every reference to Rashi's geographical point of origin constitutes a tacit putdown. Some such references were obviously intended as factual, and others occur in explicitly laudatory contexts.[209] To some, however, "French" was shorthand for exegetical simple-mindedness, theological backwardness, and scientific ignorance. Given what Pseudo-Rabad says about Rashi, he may have intended "the Frenchman" not as a geocultural marker but, rather, as a cutting slight.

Beyond, possibly, cross-cultural clashes unfolding in Byzantium, another possible context in which to place *Sefer hassagot* might be found in Pseudo-Rabad's claims that some halakhic midrash embodies the antithesis of the Torah's intention. Such comments summon questions about his relationship to Karaism, a living religious alternative in the Byzantine East. In particular, one wonders if Pseudo-Rabad's anti-midrashic crusade was at all nursed by Karaite writings or by personal exchanges with Karaites. Apart from his anti-halakhic interpretations, there are other points of contact between Pseudo-Rabad's sensibilities and those of Karaite exegetes. His impatience with Rashi's use of *gemaṭriya*, for instance, to buttress the identification of Abraham's 318 allies with his lone servant, may be easily associated with Ibn Ezra, but also found like expression in the Torah commentary of the turn-of-the-fourteenth-century Karaite exegete, Aaron ben Joseph.[210] Whatever claim Karaite sensibilities may have made on him, a Rabbanite Pseudo-Rabad certainly remained, as shown by his references to possibly true rabbinic traditions and his insistence that some midrashic dicta harbor profound insights. Yet he was clearly a conflicted Rabbanite who in one line of his work can suggest that some midrashim ought to be burned and then immediately turn around in the next line to posit that the midrash on the assembly of Exodus 31 might transmit rabbinically vouchsafed historical truth.[211]

Pseudo-Rabad's plan to clarify blunders according to "the weekly lectionaries" may imply that he thought of the *Commentary* as a common companion in the study of the *parashah*. In executing this plan, he sought to show that what many took to be careful interpretation was distortion and what many took to be religious inspiration was groundless fabulism. He focuses his fire in the first instance on the plain sense Rashi claims to have sought but did not uncover, in large part because his midrashic suppositions about the nature of the divine word were misdirected. He goes further, however, when he casts midrashim such as those in the *Commentary* as distortions of the Torah which is "perfect, renewing life," implying that the damage Rashi causes transcends the exegetical to encompass the Torah's essence as a path to human perfection. Pseudo-Rabad's *ad hominem* criticism goes so far as to discount Rashi's basic competence and place under a dark shadow his status as "a scholar from among the scholars of Israel." Pseudo-Rabad's vision of the Torah's splendor lay elsewhere, with a Judaism sculpted by Maimonides and Ibn Ezra. Apparently insensible to the charms that commended the *Commentary* to so many scholars and ordinary readers, he set out to expose its inadequacies, using a scornful directness commensurate to the dire consequences he would have seen in the work's spread: nothing less than a threat to enlightened Judaism, of which the *Commentary*'s popularity was at once a telling symptom and, increasingly, a major cause. A later author writing under a more mysterious pseudonym than Pseudo-Rabad made this point more sharply, stating what Pseudo-Rabad may have intuited and feared: Rashi's vision of the Torah and version of Judaism were conquering the Jewish world.[212]

6

Aaron Aboulrabi and "The Straight One"

BETWEEN "GIRLS' FANTASIES" AND "SWEET MIDRASH"

IN 1878, THE Galician Enlightenment scholar Joshua Heschel Schorr told an American rabbi of his great admiration for a "precious" work by the mid-fifteenth-century exegete Aaron Aboulrabi: his "commentary on Rashi's commentary on the Torah." Schorr recalled a study he had devoted to Aboulrabi four decades earlier that left scholars "stupefied," not least because of its report of Aboulrabi's claim that Moses translated the Torah into Hebrew from Arabic. In that study, Schorr highlighted Aboulrabi's status as a "lover of truth" who directed "harsh words" at the rabbinic sages. It was only natural, then, that Aboulrabi "should cast aspersions on Rashi's interpretations and reprimand him."[1] Aboulrabi won accolades from others for similar reasons. In an entry co-authored by leading American reformer Kaufmann Kohler that appeared in *The Jewish Encyclopedia* (1901), Aboulrabi was again said to be "guided solely by the love of truth"—proof being that he did "not spare such great Bible commentators as Rashi and Nahmanides."[2]

Schorr was right that Aboulrabi did not hesitate to "unleash his tongue against the talmudic sages."[3] But Aboulrabi's main focus was Rashi, so his work opens yet another window on late medieval criticism of the *Commentary*. It is unique in drawing on *Sefer hassagot*. The latter remains the *pièce de résistance* of focused adversarial reading of Rashi, but Aboulrabi's is at once a fuller and more even-handed critique. More than other resisting readers, Aboulrabi came not just to bury the *Commentary* but, as warranted, to praise it. As even Schorr noted, when not busy excoriating Rashi, Aboulrabi can be seen standing at Rashi's "right side to vindicate him."[4] The result is an often-bewildering admixture of startlingly disdainful criticism with a willingness to reflect on different constituents of the *Commentary* and present some of them in a flattering light. Historically, Aboulrabi stands as last in a breed of critics of Rashi's exegesis who arose and then vanished, leaving the *Commentary* to its early modern destiny as an ever more revered icon and object of study, especially in Ashkenazic centers of Jewish life.

"From Pillar to Post"

Although Cecil Roth cast Aboulrabi as "perhaps the most interesting figure in Sicilian Jewish intellectual life in the Middle Ages," Schorr stressed Aboulrabi's utter obscurity prior to his rediscovery of him: "I have not found a single mention of him in Jewish historical literature."[5] This being so, a few words about his life, spiritual complexion, and sole surviving work are warranted before turning to his engagement with Rashi.[6]

Aboulrabi's exegesis survives in the rare printed volume *Perushim le-rashi* (*[Super]commentaries on Rashi*), which, as we saw, appeared around 1525 in Istanbul.[7] Aboulrabi's work came to its editor late.[8] The printed version does not relay all of his work, as the editor knew.[9] The most glaring lacuna is for the book of Leviticus, where commentary on the opening nine chapters and chapter twenty-five is lacking.[10]

Aboulrabi describes himself as being from "the province of Catania on the island of Sicily," referring to a region on the island's eastern coast.[11] The provincial capital, bearing the same name, housed one of late medieval Sicily's more sizable Jewish communities.[12] The Aboulrabi family may have been Spanish in origin and certainly had an Iberian branch. Still, Catania is Aboulrabi's likely place of birth or, at the least, a place where he passed formative years.[13] His interval on the island coincided with the reign of Aragon's Alfonso V (Alfonso I of Naples and Sicily), who spent time in Sicily, including a month in Catania, in the 1430s.[14] Unlike Jews situated on the Italian peninsula, those in Sicily belonged, from the time of the 1282 Sicilian Vespers, to the Spanish (Catalo-Aragonese) political sphere.[15] They constituted late medieval Italy's largest Jewry.[16] In the wake of the Spanish anti-Jewish riots in 1391, Jews and *conversos* came to Sicily.[17] Aboulrabi wed a daughter of Moses ibn Gabbai, the Aragonese Rashi supercommentator who fled to North Africa owing to the riots.

Aboulrabi's basic temporal moorings can be defined in a number of ways. An obvious point of reference is his father-in-law, who died around 1443.[18] An archival document from six years prior has Aboulrabi appointing an agent to deal with interests in eastern Sicily.[19] He twice mentions an exegetical exchange with "the sage and prince Moses Hefetz," called Moses Bonavoglia in Latin sources. The latter, one of the first Jews ever to attend a university, served as royal physician to Alfonso V and as Jewish Sicily's "supreme judge" (*dienchelele = dayyan kelali*).[20] Aboulrabi attaches to his name the blessing for the dead, so 1446 emerges as his work's *terminus a quo* in its present form.[21]

More precise dates involve guesswork. Arguments from silence, like Aboulrabi's failure to mention Constantinople's fall to the Ottomans, must be used with caution, if at all, as even scholars very close to the scene of this event that rocked the Mediterranean world do not always mention it.[22] On the basis of references to Ibn Gabbai, some with the blessing for the dead and some not, one might argue for the evolution of Aboulrabi's work over a long interval. It was finalized only after Aboulrabi departed Sicily since it mentions a raft of places he visited. Aboulrabi's awareness of Bonavoglia's death may suggest his presence in Sicily through the mid-1440s. Allowing a decade to reach the many places where he landed, including the far-off Genoese colony of Kaffa on the Crimean coast, his work would have been completed no earlier than the 1450s, assuming he did not travel at a very young age or return to Sicily after years of wandering, there to complete his work, a fact for which the work presents no evidence. He had written at least five works by the time he completed his exegetical volume. Their contents we know only through bare profiles found in Aboulrabi's surviving work.[23]

Aboulrabi depicts himself as one "hurled from pillar to post."[24] Joseph Hacker posits a sort of spiritual-psychological crisis resulting in peregrinations as Aboulrabi and others lost a peace of mind "never to be regained either in the diaspora or the land of Israel."[25] Glossing a report of Jacob's travels—"he lifted up his feet" (Gen 29:1)—Aboulrabi proposes that the unusual expression indicates an "inner volition" born of "a great desire to travel," making it "easy to journey."[26] One wonders if this comment is autobiographical, presenting a more sanguine view of his voyages. Aboulrabi offers fascinating accounts of some of his scholarly and interreligious exchanges during the course of his journeys. The most intriguing by far is a colloquy that he claims to have conducted "in the metropolis of Rome in the palace of the pope, with the cardinals surrounding him." Other embroilments involved Karaites (as we will see) and, in a case regarding the interpretation of a staple of the Christian mission, a "cleric from among the gentile scholars," and "all the eminent personages surrounding him."[27] As for his decision to leave Sicily, one reason may have been the dim view he took of aspects of Jewish life there.[28] Late medieval Sicily's credentials as a seat of Jewish learning were slight. In terms of general learning, the island in his day has been called part of a southern Italian cultural desert "with hardly an oasis in sight."[29]

Among places where he alighted, Aboulrabi mentions a yeshiva in Treviso in northern Italy, where he heard Rashi interpreted by "one of the garlic eaters"—that is, Ashkenazim. (His contemporary, Elijah Bashyatchi, suggested Ashkenazic consumers of garlic struck fear in Jews in ways that stymied their conversion to Karaism.)[30] As noted, Aboulrabi made it as far as Kaffa, home to Rabbanite and Karaite communities and a colorful mix of Armenians, Greeks, Italians, Provençals, Catalans, Russians, Circassians, Cumans, and Tartars. Muslim-ruled territories that he visited included Egypt, Syria, and Jerusalem. From all that he "saw and heard," there were "no regions (*medinot*) more exalted than Egypt and Damascus."[31] There were presumably stopovers in eastern Mediterranean locales under the cross along the way.

While crafting exegesis, Aboulrabi brooded over Jewish impotence. His inquietude bubbles to the surface in a gloss on Rashi's comment about the divine blessing accorded to Ishmael. To Rashi's vision of the downfall of Ishmael's puissant "chieftains" (*nesi'im*; Gen 17:20) like the disappearance of evanescent clouds (*nesi'im*)—"as clouds they will be consumed"—Aboulrabi counterposes the stark reality: while Ishmael's offshoots, the potentates of Islam, flourish, "it is we who, in consequence of our many sins, are 'consumed in His anger, are terror-struck by His fury' (see Ps 90:7)." Meanwhile, the hegemons are "established in God's blessing and are given leave by Him to lord over us."[32] Similar is his gloss on the Mosaic promise that those fallen into idolatry in exile could "find" God should they seek to do so with "all . . . heart and soul" (Deut 4:29):

> Woe to the ear that hears [this]. Behold, we have sought Him though in our hands there is no idolatry but rather anguish and sufferings all our days simply to hold fast to our faith, and He is like a deaf one, unhearing, like a dumb one who cannot speak (see Ps 38:14). Nor can one allege [our failure to seek God] "with all heart and soul" since, in light of the many evil calamities we suffer, it is indisputable that we are seeking with our heart and our soul. Indeed, we have not forborne to elevate and exalt His holy Torah to the point "that we are slain all day long" (Ps 44:23). With great bitterness of spirit, an aching heart, and streaming tears have I written these [words] here.[33]

Before and after 1492, Sefardic scholars invoked Psalm 44, particularly the verse cited by Aboulrabi, in a struggle to explain the fate of Spanish Jewry at its times of testing, which included a massive depletion in ranks owing to large-scale conversion to Christianity.[34] Encountering this verse, Aboulrabi deviates from his penchant for crisp exegesis and ponders in a *cri de coeur* the "calamities" by which Jews are beset, up to and including martyrdom.

Aboulrabi often ventured beyond clarification of Rashi, as evident from the passage just seen, yet his work is invariably billed as a supercommentary, beginning with its Constantinople publisher and continuing through Schorr and the few others who mention it. What may have been decisive was the work's inclusion in a volume containing other supercommentaries, cast as such in the volume's title. Closer inspection reveals that Aboulrabi's work is something of a complicated generic hybrid. Formally, his lemmata come not from the *Commentary* but from scripture, although he often cites Rashi's comments as well. Rashi goes missing for whole columns, although such prolonged absences are rare. Aboulrabi regularly explains verses or parts thereof that Rashi ignores. He occasionally probes midrashim that Rashi does not cite.[35] How all this independent exegesis relates to his stated plan to write separate "commentaries on the Torah" is hard to say.[36] At any rate, while some of his comments constitute Torah commentary and others supercommentary, Aboulrabi often commits his pen to a different type of discourse: strictures on the *Commentary* in the manner of *Sefer hassagot*.

Aboulrabi calls Rashi "the Straight One" (*Ha-yashar*). As we saw, a generation on Judah Khalatz plays with this moniker by inverting the letters of Rashi's rabbinic acronym, suggesting that "Right (*yashar*) is the word of the Lord" (Ps 33:4) might be taken to say that "Rashi is the word of the Lord."[37] Amid the mixed signals Aboulrabi left regarding Rashi, awe of this sort is not one of them. If anything, one suspects that his resort to *Ha-yashar* as a cognomen is meant to arouse a sense of Rashi's naiveté.

Aboulrabi explains his focus on Rashi in his introduction: "Since the words of *Ha-yashar* are mainly hewn from the 'eminent oaks' [= rabbinic sages], I have cast my gaze upon them more than [those of] other scholars whose words comprise [their own] individual opinion."[38] In effect, Aboulrabi affirms that Rashi's recourse to midrash lends an aura of authority to his *Commentary* that commands attention—a statement that fits snugly with the definition of a canonical work as one that makes claims on participants in a tradition.

"Derash *of Barbarians*," "Derash *of a Dolt*"

Turning to Aboulrabi's reception of the dicta of the "eminent oaks" as Rashi selected, transmitted, and reworked them, what initially leaps off his pages are scorching assaults that leave the substance and methods of the *Commentary*, as well as the reliability of the "eminent" sages upon whom Rashi draws, in the severest doubt. Like Pseudo-Rabad, whom he studied closely, Aboulrabi does not hesitate to pour scorn on Rashi and his midrashic mentors. Based on a midrash, Rashi homiletically teaches that the two *yods* that appear in *vayyiṣer* (Gen 2:7)—describing God's formation of Adam—reflect the human being's "two formations," one for "this world" and one for "resurrection of the dead." Rashi noted the exegetical basis for the observation, a contrast with the spelling of the same verb in the later description of God's formation of animals and birds (Gen 2:19), where only one *yod* appeared. While practicing his unparalleled art of concision, he alluded to deep issues aired in the two midrashic sources that his gloss elided, one containing a debate between the schools of Shammai and Hillel about the character of the resurrected body (Would the formation of a human being in "the next world" be like that of "this world"?) and the other asserting the sundering of the moral universe into human beings destined to account for themselves on judgement day and animals without responsibility who were not. Aboulrabi's response starts with a calm grammatical disquisition explaining (away) the double *yod* in *vayyiṣer*, thereby doing away with the textual spur to the midrash. It ends with a philosophic interpretation of the verb as comprising a dual element in the human being's creation—abstract representation (*tavnit meṣuyyar*) and palpable form (*to'ar murgash*)—that invokes language and teachings of medieval rationalism utterly foreign to Rashi. In between appears an assessment of Rashi's gloss as "a *derash* of barbarians (*barbarim*)."[39]

Such insults are legion. Rashi's view of the ages of some of the matriarchs at the time of their marriages evokes from Aboulrabi a chastisement of his rabbinic sources: "it is not from wisdom that they derive such nonsense (*sheṭuyot*)."[40] Rashi claimed that the "Canaanite woman" that Simeon married (Gen 46:10) was actually Dinah, so called because "she was violated by a Canaanite." Aboulrabi: "patently spurious" (*mevo'ar ha-baṭel*).[41] Rashi identifies the Amorite from whom Jacob wrested land as Esau. Aboulrabi: "a *derash* without purchase" (*derash 'en lo damim*).[42] Why did Pharaoh go down to the Nile in the morning (Exod 7:15)? Rashi: because he claimed divinity and tried to hide his need to relieve himself. Aboulrabi: "the *derash* of a dolt (*hedyoṭ*): had he no way to relieve himself in a concealed place such that he had to go down to the river?"[43] The Torah reported Miriam's and Aaron's criticism of Moses for marrying a "Cushite woman" (Num 12:1). Some sages, and Rashi in their wake, thought that the Cushite woman and Moses' wife, the Midianite Zipporah, were one and the same. She was called "Cushite" to indicate that she was especially beautiful. Aboulrabi: Although the sages are "exerting themselves mightily" to turn the term "Cushite" into a "beautiful woman" (*yefat to'ar*), "falsehood has no legs upon which to stand."[44] Such assertions of error and ignorance traduce by leaps and bounds the standard restraints of scholarly etiquette; yet there is more learning, depth, texture, and supple language to Aboulrabi's enterprise than is suggested by an easily produced litany of sardonic barbs. More samplings illustrate angles of collision that underlie the fiery formulations or, in the more common case, less charged if still often conflictual stance toward Rashi.

Aboulrabi occasionally addresses other layers of the Torah, among them a plane of interpretation that he calls "hint" (*remez*), as well as mystical signification, but his cardinal quest is the plain sense.[45] As it was bound to be for anyone taking Rashi as a focus in this quest, navigation of the *peshaṭ–derash* divide becomes a major preoccupation. After a compressed excursus on the kabbalistic meaning of God's pronouncement to Moses that "you cannot see My face, for man may not see Me and live" (Exod 33:20), Aboulrabi asserts that "this is not the place to explain the secrets of the divine kabbalah so I shall return to explication of the *peshaṭ*."[46] Dealing with one of the many problems with which the "Song of Heshbon" (Num 21:27–30) bristles, he offers a long grammatical disquisition that concludes, against Rashi, that the challenging word *niram* comprises a verb and accusative suffix meaning "and we shot them."[47] In so doing, he notes that this is "what is most plausible according to the word's grammar and context," paying homage to the peshatist credo, where coordinates of language and context anchor interpretation. Although he focuses mostly on Rashi's midrashim, Aboulrabi can stop to fault original plain sense explanations in the *Commentary*. As an offshoot of the Sefardic tradition, it is no surprise that he chalks up some of Rashi's exegetical missteps to imperfect powers of linguistic analysis.[48]

In dealing with *peshaṭ* and *derash*, Aboulrabi does not necessarily reject the latter, although he may be keen to identify a midrash as such—something Rashi usually failed to do. In such cases, he also relays what he views as the plain sense reading. Seeing three strangers (who turn out to be angels), Abraham ran to offer them a meal while urging them to "bathe your feet" (Gen 18:4). Following a midrash, Rashi sees in the request a concern diplomatically withheld from the guests by the patriarch: "He thought they were Arabs who prostrate [themselves] to the dust of their feet, and he was strict not to allow any idolatry into his house."[49] Aboulrabi lodges no objection but does call it, as Rashi does not, a *derash*. He then explains Abraham's proposal in a manner applicable to travelers in all times and places whose "habit" is to wish to refresh themselves by "washing up immediately upon arriving, due to fatigue." Rashi imparts a lesson in fastidious monotheism and good manners, displaying Abraham's concern, courteously left unstated, that the potential idolaters could contaminate his home. Aboulrabi tells of a patriarch performing a universal gesture of welcome devoid of religious intent. Yet he leaves Rashi's midrash intact alongside this plain sense interpretation.[50]

At other midrashim Aboulrabi shakes his head. An example is Rashi's frequent identification of obscure figures and places with more familiar ones. Rashi's interpretation of "The Canaanites were then in the land" (Gen 12:6) brings two issues into play: identification of biblical figures and places and geographical evidence arising from the plain sense. Accounting for the temporal particle ("then"), Rashi states that at the time of Abraham's arrival, the Canaanites were just then conquering the land from Shem's descendants, "for it had fallen to the portion of Shem . . . as it is said, 'And King Melchizedek of Salem'" (Gen 14:18). Unpacking this latter verse, Rashi wrote: "a *midrash 'aggadah*—he [Melchizedek] is Shem, son of Noah." This equation, and the cognate one of Salem and Jerusalem, was part of a rabbinic reflex to bring "focus" to narratives by identifying obscure figures or place names mentioned with known ones.[51] Beyond this aspect, however, the interpretation bore consequences for the issue of claims to the land of Israel as an everlasting Jewish possession at a time when Crusaders, most from Rashi's native France, were poised to conquer parts of the land (or possibly had already done so). Rashi's identification produced an aboriginal Jewish connection to "the land" since Shem was the one to whom all descendants of Eber (Gen 10:21), including Abraham, traced their origins.

Like Eleazar Ashkenazi, Aboulrabi rejects the identification of Melchizedek with Shem.[52] What warrants such an approach, or the identification of Salem with Jerusalem (which Ashkenazi thought possible), "but for much derash"? Nahmanides had observed that Jerusalem formed part of Canaanite territory "always." Agreeing, Aboulrabi wonders "whence the rabbis saw fit to say that the land fell to Shem's portion. It is surely more correct to say that it fell within Canaan's lot." He cites "The [original] Canaanite territory extended from Sidon, as far as Gerar, near Gaza" (Gen 10:19) to clinch the point, since they are all lands "close to Jerusalem." More generally, "we always find that the land is associated with the name of Canaan and his progeny."[53]

Further undermining Rashi's claim about Shem's inheritance of "the land" is his own inconsistency (by inference) on this score. Rashi raises the question in the opening lines of the *Commentary* why the Torah, understood as legal instruction, did not begin with Exodus 12:2 and what was taken to be the first communal commandment given to Israel concerning the ritual calendar. Rashi replies, following midrashic sources, that the Torah sought to emphasize the option of the Creator of the universe to give the land of Canaan to whomever He deemed worthy, in this way offering a counterclaim to prospective gentile charges that the Israelites were "robbers" whose conquest of the land was theft. Given Rashi's interpretation of "The Canaanite was then in the land," however, this account of the need for Genesis 1 proves extraneous, since a more "fitting riposte against the Canaanites" would be that "the land is ours since we are the progeny of Shem and the land fell into the possession of our ancestor and you conquered it illicitly." Even Rashi's most harmonistic interpreters found it impossible to resolve this inconsistency.[54] Apparently not worried that he has done anything to jeopardize claims to "the land," Aboulrabi takes the added step of using the inconsistency as another cudgel to attack the midrashic reconstruction that he has already dismissed on other grounds.

Aboulrabi spotlights a lack of interpretive congruence in Rashi's reading of Jacob's dramatic reunification with Joseph, which clarified an ambiguous description of one of the two crying on the other's neck (Gen 46:29). Rashi thinks that Joseph cried. Meanwhile, Jacob "neither fell on Joseph's neck nor kissed him. Our Sages said that he was reciting the *Shema*." Finding this view psychologically improbable, Nahmanides stakes the counterclaim that Jacob was the one who wept.[55] Rashi's later readers, meanwhile, find in the midrash much to ponder, including its possibly troubling depiction of Jacob as a patriarch so pious that he was impervious to basic human emotions and failed to react upon seeing the son whom he so long mourned. At the same time, the midrash inspired reflection on any number of theological issues, giving rise to, for example, a Hasidic mystical reading that saw in Jacob's *Shema* recitation an act directing his overwhelming love for Joseph back to its divine source.[56] But if for some the midrash could invite reflection on the right ordering of human loves, in Aboulrabi it evokes a verdict of "spuriousness." Explaining, he pits the ancient rabbis against themselves and Rashi against Rashi. He airs an idea found later in the *Commentary* that, according to what "the sages said," the main components of the prayer ("Hear, O Israel . . . "; "Blessed be the Name . . .") originated with Jacob on his deathbed. How, then, could Jacob have recited the *Shema* at this earlier stage? Thus is one midrash of Rashi subverted by recourse to another midrash of Rashi.[57]

Aboulrabi's handling of *midreshei halakhah* invites scrutiny in light of his apparent aptitude as a talmudist and his travels in locales where Karaism thrived.[58] Aboulrabi does not entirely suppress his doubting instincts in this sphere but after airing dubieties, he tends to submit, if at times grudgingly, to the rabbinic interpretations that Rashi faithfully relayed. Regarding the prohibition on a priest coming into contact with a dead body (except for seven relatives), Rashi reports the *halakhah* that priestly daughters are not bound by this law, basing himself on a midrashic exposition that reads the reference to "the sons (*benei*) of Aaron" (Lev 21:1) to exclude his daughters. Aboulrabi alerts his reader to a verse that uses the same expression but does not yield the same rabbinic exclusion: "that is why the children of Israel (*benei yisra'el*) to this day do not eat the thigh muscle" (Gen 32:33). Were the midrashic reading in the case of the priests applied consistently, women should be exempted from the prohibition against consuming the thigh muscle. The argument seems settled, but Aboulrabi concludes that "we cannot determine against the rabbinic sages who are stronger (*taqifin*) than us."[59]

Slightly more conciliatory is Aboulrabi's disquisition on Rashi's midrashic understanding of the point at which false witnesses became liable to punishment. Where the Torah states, "you shall do to him as he schemed to do to his fellow" (Deut 19:19), Rashi interprets: "'as he schemed'—and not as he [the false witness] did, whence they [the rabbinic sages] said: if they have already killed [the accused on the basis of the false testimony], they [the false witnesses] are not put to death." This reading produced the paradoxical outcome that the false witnesses were liable to sanction as long as their intention remained unfulfilled. Once, however, the accused was executed on the basis of the false testimony, the witnesses were no longer liable to punishment.

Aboulrabi pronounces himself "astonished at this law," insisting that "on the contrary" the *halakhah* "should be the reverse"—namely, only if an accused is executed owing to false testimony should the witness be killed. Aboulrabi's dissection of exegetical possibilities is meticulous:

> And if you were to object [in justification of Rashi]: why did scripture not say "as he did" [rather than "as they schemed to do," this phrase implying, as the midrash infers and Rashi reports, that it is the act of scheming that incurs punishment such that only if the witnesses do *not* realize their goal should they be killed, the answer is that] it was formulated [with the phrase "they schemed to do" not to trigger the midrashic understanding but] to tell you that even *before* he [the defendant] is killed, as long as they [the false witnesses] schemed, they deserve to be put to death since, by their scheming, they have already committed the iniquity they desired. What is more, it is clear from a precise textual inference (*diyyuqa*) in the verse—which states "as he schemed *to do*"—that the [punishable] scheming is [the one] completed by implementation of the [wrongful] death. And if you object that "to do" had to be said of necessity along with "as he schemed" since without it we would be unable to understand the [scheming's] ultimate goal, let your ears hear what your mouth is saying, for if this be so then [the phrase is devoid of any irregularity justifying a special inference, so] how can we derive from it the *halakhah* [of] "if he [the defendant] was put to death, they [the witnesses] are not put to death."

Having attended to interpretive nuances, Aboulrabi shifts the discussion from casuistry to common sense (*sevara'*), which dictates that the punishment should fit the crime. On this understanding, "schemed to do" would mean that only when the intention to bring about undeserved punishment was realized should there be punishment in kind. Yet, in an abrupt about-face, Aboulrabi pronounces just this sort of ratiocination irrelevant, swearing fealty to the midrashic reading and refusing to "put the Torah to shame [by treating its teachers irreverently]."[60] A clever *double entendre* justifies the subservience: the sages speak truly "and I am nullified in my smallness" (*baṭel be-mi'uṭi*)—meaning that Aboulrabi is both of lesser stature and in an outvoted minority.[61] The gesture of obeisance, while impressive, does nothing to alleviate his forcefully articulated objections.

Aboulrabi's strictures can cross the boundary separating the legal and the narrative, with a halakhic midrash used to subvert a nonlegal one. The Torah mandated an ear-piercing ceremony to mark the decision of a Hebrew who had fallen into servitude owing to an act of theft for which he was unable to make reparations to remain a slave, a ceremony to take place at the appointed time for the termination of his slavery after six years (Exod 21:6). Rashi, following a midrash, gives this ceremony a moral valance, explaining that "that ear which heard on Mount Sinai 'You shall not steal' (Exod 20:13) and yet he went and stole" ought to be pierced. Aboulrabi rejoins that the homily is "untrue" in light of the rabbinic understanding of the Decalogue which stipulated that the prohibition on stealing articulated there referred not to theft of property punishable (absent reparation) by servitude but to theft of people—that is, kidnapping. Violation of that prohibition incurred the death penalty, not servitude.[62] The *midrash 'aggadah* precedes on a premise invalidated by the *midrash halakhah*.

Aboulrabi's conception of the relationship between biblical law and *midrash halakhah* requires investigation, but his approach hardly reassures us of the unassailability of midrashically derived laws as transmitted in the *Commentary*. Aboulrabi often draws attention to divergences between rabbinic teaching and what he considers the findings of plain sense interpretation. In so doing, he does not speak, as had others, of a view of scripture as a polysemous text that accommodates both his understanding and that of the sages, nor does he claim, in the manner of such predecessors as Abraham ibn Ezra, that *midreshei halakhah* amount mainly to *post facto* linkages between laws known by tradition and the verses to which they were yoked.[63] As a Rabbanite, Aboulrabi does often accede to rabbinic legal interpretation even where it defies plain exegesis or common sense. Yet he at times openly breaks with Rashi's legal interpretations, which perhaps explains why Isaac Hirsch Weiss describes some of his pronouncements as a source of "embitterment to . . . talmudists wholesome in their opinions"[64] and why Joseph Perles declares that the one who deems Aboulrabi "tainted by Karaism" cannot be said to speak unjustly.[65] How much his approach to legal midrash reflects interchanges with Karaites or their writings is up for debate. Minimally, it suggests an occasional frustration at the binding but often problematic readings upon which Rabbanite life was based—ones all too blithely relayed in the *Commentary*.

Exculpating the Righteous, Anathematizing the Wicked

Aboulrabi's disdain for some midrashim enlisted by Rashi reaches a crescendo in disputes over the sensitive issue of sins or moral failings of the patriarchs and matriarchs. To be sure, the Bible itself often contained negative evaluations of such figures, yet many of these were voiced by other characters rather than the omniscient narrator, leaving their finality in doubt.[66] As for the midrashic heritage, the nineteenth-century Galician rabbi Zvi Hirsch Hayot does admit to a sort of manipulative tendency, if one born of wise and noble aims. He says that the midrashists tend to "amplify praise of the deeds of the righteous, represent them favorably, and tip scales of judgment in their favor" while "heaping all possible abominable acts" on biblical wrongdoers.[67] In truth, the picture was more complicated, as some midrashim imputed serious sins to biblical heroes with not the slightest basis in scripture, leaving later authorities to struggle to make sense of it all.[68] Rashi's legacy was similarly complex, but his commentaries were, on the whole, pitched toward justification of heroes and amplication of the flaws of evildoers, especially those who were gentiles.[69]

In dealing with conduct unbecoming of biblical greats, medieval exegetes juggle various factors including the plain meaning of the text, the educational value of defending the Jewish people's ancestors, and findings in the rabbinic record.[70] As the Middle Ages wore on, new factors arose, including a surprising tendency of some Christian polemicists to paint unflattering images of Israel's ancestors in order to excoriate their Jewish posterity.[71]

Another shaping force that plays a role in reckonings of conduct is the portrayals imprinted on Jewish memory by Rashi. As Jews read or heard the weekly portion, they knew (and still know) that the rabbis were divided on the extent of Noah's righteousness, that Nimrod rebelled against God, that Esau was a murderer (to speak of only one of his many midrashically imbued defects), that the heroic midwives who refused to comply with the murderous scheme of the Egyptian Pharaoh were Moses's mother, Jochebed, and sister, Miriam, and so forth. Whatever the variations, the theme in the *Commentary* is, indeed, to tip the scales of judgment in favor of scripture's heroes and heap abominable acts on wrongdoers. Aboulrabi is occasionally in step with the general thrust of the rabbinic program: "our sages stated that where there was room to confer merit upon the righteous, confer it one should. I therefore stipulate that what Jacob did with the staffs [to obtain the better portion of Laban's livestock] was a fitting stratagem [and not an act of cheating]."[72] Yet Sossnitz and Kohler were right in observing that Aboulrabi readily points out "blemishes . . . in the character of the Patriarchs."[73] He does so in the name of fidelity to the plain sense, to common sense, and to the demands of religious and moral probity—though his motivations in any given case, especially in their relative weightings, can be difficult to clarify.

Consider Abraham's concealment of his marital relationship with Sarah and the seemingly incestuous character of the relationship itself. Owing to a famine in Canaan, Abraham (then Abram) traveled to Egypt where, fearing for his life on account of his wife's beauty, he enjoined Sarah (then Sarai) to declare herself his sister "that it may go well with me because of you, and that I may remain alive thanks to you" (Gen 12:13). Faced with a similar situation in Gerar, Abraham directly informed Abimelech that Sarah was "my father's daughter though not my mother's" (Gen 20:12). In both cases, Sarah was abducted and taken to the ruler's house, and divine chastisements ensued. Each king proclaimed ignorance of Sarah's married status and objected to the deceit that brought unwarranted punishment. It is to Abimelech's complaint along these lines that Abraham rejoined, among other things, that Sarah is indeed his sister, on his father's side. These accounts could leave commentators perplexed. If Sarah was not Abraham's sister, his speech was deceptive; if she was, he practiced incest. After reproving Abraham's initial descent to Egypt, Nahmanides condemns his conduct in claiming Sarah as his sister, going so far as to draw a causal connection between this failure and the Jewish people's persecution in Egypt. These ideas of Nahmanides elicited declamations of protest from a string of successors, illustrating their sensitivity.[74]

For his part, Rashi assumes that Abraham's statement about his relationship with Sarah was technically true. He also dispatches the problem of brother–sister marriage later proscribed in the Torah (Lev 18:9 and 11; Lev 20:17; Deut 27:22) by asserting that the patriarchs were exempt from this prohibition because they lived prior to the promulgation of the Torah. In addition, a midrash identified Sarah as the daughter of Abraham's brother Haran (Gen 11:29), named Iscah, meaning that Sarah was Abraham's niece and was therefore permitted to him according to the list of proscribed and permitted unions later spelled out in the Torah. That she was called "sister," adds Rashi, accorded with a notion of kinship that viewed children's children as children—that is, that saw the two as siblings by dint of a shared grandfather.[75]

Aboulrabi addresses both the apparent duplicity and the apparent violation of incest prohibitions. Regarding the former, he cannot fathom how the patriarch could "utter a falsity before two great kings, saying 'she is my sister.'" If only for prudential reasons, the tactic seems so clearly ill-advised, as Abraham ought to have anticipated that people might wonder how an intelligent person (*piqeaḥ*) such as him could drag an alluring sister hither and yon instead of marrying her off to a gentleman in her home locality. As for the effort to justify the statement about Sarah's sisterhood as technically correct, it foundered on the point that Abraham was evidently still obliged to announce the truly salient aspect of the relationship, "that she was his wife." The excuse proffered to Abimelech, that withholding the truth was necessary since "there is no fear of God in this place" (Gen 20:11), does not appertain to Pharaoh, whose denizens displayed their "nobility" (just how Aboulrabi does not quite explain) by praising Sarah (Gen 12:15). Aboulrabi also levies judgment against Rashi on the issue of Abraham's pre-Sinaitic exemption from Mosaic legislation on the grounds that it is inconsistent with Rashi's own portrayal elsewhere according to which the patriarch observed the Torah in its totality, including later rabbinic "precautionary decrees." Indeed, although Aboulrabi does not mention the point, an example Rashi cites was "secondary forbidden sexual relations" in rabbinic law. Summoning a well-known midrash, Aboulrabi notes that the sages extend Abraham's scrupulosity to *'eruv tavshilin* ("mingling of dishes"), a rabbinic enactment. Without adducing that example (in most versions of the *Commentary*), Rashi expounds "Abraham obeyed Me and kept My charge" (Gen 26:5) to the same effect. Given Rashi's portrayal of Abraham as one who observed every jot and tittle of Jewish law, biblical and rabbinic, Aboulrabi wonders how Rashi can teach that the patriarch violated "a [biblically] prohibited sexual union by marrying his sister"?[76]

Among instances where Aboulrabi impugns Rashi's moral evaluations, Jacob's conduct in procuring his father's blessing stands out. As one of a number of stories about the sons of Isaac and Rebecca to which church and synagogue appealed as they carved out elements of identity over and against the religious "other," this event was no little thing. For medieval Christians, the rivalry of Esau and Jacob foretold the story of Christianity, the "true Israel" represented by the younger Jacob, superseding the old Israel, represented by Esau. For Jews, Jacob was the prototype of the Jewish people and Esau the progenitor of Rome, destroyer of the temple and perpetrator of cruel oppression against the Jewish people, whose mantle of anti-Jewish enmity was inherited by medieval Christendom.[77] Exercising the license of the controversialist to flip the symbolism as needed, Christians could cast Jacob as a Jewish prototype whose thievery and duplicity, as attested in his purloining of Esau's birthright and blessings, perdured in contemporary Jews.[78] Little wonder Rashi strove to depict Jacob favorably while going even beyond the midrashists in mustering one interpretation after another to blacken Esau.[79]

In the *Commentary*, the stereotyping began with the brothers yet *in utero*, and Aboulrabi's resistance to it follows in train. Regarding the testimony that "the children struggled" in Rebecca's womb (Gen 25:22), Rashi cites a midrash that had Jacob moving spasmodically and seeking to exit whenever Rebecca passed by an "academy of Torah" and Esau doing the same whenever she happened on a house of idolatry. Here was Jacob as a prefigurement of "rabbinic Israel" alongside Esau, whose idolatrous leanings *ab ovo* fit with Jewish conceptions of the medieval church.[80] Aboulrabi, who also authored an anti-Christian tract, presumably found it welcome to sharply distinguish faithful Jews and disbelieving Christians. Yet he has no truck with Rashi's midrash, rebutting it on the basis of scriptural plain sense in a stricture that, even by his standards, does not mince words: " 'They struggled'—that which they [the rabbinic sages] expounded (*dareshu*), 'When she passed by [academies of Torah study . . .],' these are all yarns of menstruating women since the verse says [in the sequel] 'When the boys grew up [Esau became a skillful hunter . . . but Jacob was a mild man] (Gen 25:27),' " meaning that their [the boys'] natures were discernible only after they matured."[81] That the midrash might reflect on Jews, gentiles, and the gulf separating their worldviews either escapes Aboulrabi (thus Nehama Leibowitz) or is a reading of Rashi from which he consciously prescinds.[82]

Rashi works assiduously to acquit Jacob of deceit in the matter of his father's blessing, although some find his efforts futile. Where Jacob told Isaac "I am Esau, your firstborn" (Gen 27:19), Rashi configures his meaning by dividing this utterance into two and having Jacob add mental reservations as needed: "*I am* the one who brings [food] to you and *Esau* he is *your first-born*." Rashi also fashions Jacob's claim to have done as asked by his father, although it was Esau who received the request to "prepare a dish for me to eat that I may bless you." "I have done as you have told me" means that *on other occasions* Jacob had indeed fulfilled his father's requests. Rashi found merit even in Jacob's bald pretense to be Esau. By saying "it is I" Jacob avoided the patently false claim to be Esau. As for Isaac's proclamation, "your brother came with *mirmah* and took away your blessing" (Gen 27:35), Rashi refuses to translate the word as "guile," instead following the Aramaic translation's "wisdom." In short, Rashi debars any midrashim that chastised Jacob or that cast Esau sympathetically, although such rabbinic assessments were not lacking.[83] Ibn Ezra clears a different way through the verses by casting Rashi's reading of "I am Esau" as "words of wind" and taking Isaac's claim of Jacob's "guile" as evidence that Jacob "did not speak the truth," opening a larger discussion of whether prophets could lie.[84]

Aboulrabi is in no way willing to accede to the "many commentators" bent on attaining "Jacob's vindication" (*haṣdaqat ya'aqov*) in advance. The fact is that Jacob's reply "was a lie" and the artifice of twisting words to preserve their technical veracity "full of wind." It violates the main principle of human communication—that the aim of speech is to convey truth *to another*. It is the auditor's understanding that is determinative in assessing truthful speech in such cases, not some sly equivocation or mental reservation on the part of the speaker. It all put Aboulrabi in mind of the prophetic rebuke of one who "speaks peace to his neighbor but inwardly sets an ambush for him" (Jer 9:7). Playing on a prophetic portrayal of Jacob, "In the womb he tried to supplant his brother; grown to manhood he strove with a divine being" (Hos 12:3–4), Aboulrabi concludes: "in the womb he supplanted his brother, grown to manhood he deceived his father."[85]

Just as startling is the sympathy for Esau Aboulrabi expresses in an encomium to he who had became the symbol of Israel's perennial enemy. By the time Rashi expounds the story of the blessings, he has cut through all ambiguities left behind by the biblical text to portray Esau as a doer of evil. When the Torah tells of Esau's skills as a hunter (Gen 25:27), Rashi interprets it to mean that he knew "how to entrap and deceive his father with his mouth." When the Torah pronounces Esau "weary" after returning from the field and before selling his birthright (Gen 25:29), Rashi reports that the fatigue owed to exhaustion from a killing spree. Aboulrabi conjures, at least initially, a different vision:

> Truly Esau was deserving of the blessing. He had his reward coming to him and his [meritorious] activity behind him, having honored his father in his time of distress, feeding him and giving him to drink [both ways to fulfill the obligation to honor parents in the rabbinic understanding]. He would put himself in mortal danger to trap game to bring [to Isaac]. With delectables of the sort he [Isaac] loved, he [Esau] kept his aging and blind father who was trapped at home alive. Alacritous and noble, he had every good intention to receive his father's blessings with great desire, proof being the alacrity with which he hunted game to bring to his father. His greatly embittered cry rose on high at

the usurpation of his blessing and [in connection with] other [similarly unjust] things.

Having concluded his paean to Esau, Aboulrabi again departs from Rashi in offering up a most unflattering depiction of his brother: "About Jacob what does it say? 'A mild man who stayed in camp' (Gen 25:27), [meaning he was] lazy and lacked initiative. Absent his mother's entreaty, he neither would have sought nor appreciated his father's blessing."[86] To be sure, Aboulrabi's fuller picture proves somewhat characteristically puzzling, speaking of Esau's wickedness and impure motives in pursuing a wholly this-worldly blessing and doing much to redeem Jacob.[87] For all that, his portrait remains at odds with Rashi's zeal to expose Esau's perfidies.

Aboulrabi also draws back from Rashi's exculpatory reading of the report that "Reuben went and lay with Bilhah, his father's concubine." (Gen 35:22). Already the Mishnah insisted that this incident should not be translated into Aramaic when recited in the Torah reading.[88] Yet if the Mishnah presupposed some failure (or at least inevitable popular perception of such) on Reuben's part, presumably a type of incest of the sort later forbidden in the Torah (where this sin incurred capital punishment for both parties),[89] a later rabbinic tradition proposed that "whoever says that Reuben sinned is naught but in error." To support the claim, the end of the verse was brought to bear: "since it states 'Now the sons of Jacob are twelve,' teaching that they were equal."[90] A full understanding of the story and talmudic prooftext involved decipherment of the scriptural non sequitur marked by the appearance of a rare "break in the middle of the verse" (*pisqa' be-'emṣa' pasuq*)—that is, blank space separating the statement about the progeny of Jacob being "twelve" from the prior account of Reuben's offense.[91]

Rashi dilutes Reuben's sin by recounting a midrash that explained his motive sympathetically. After Rachel's death, Jacob cohabited with Rachel's handmaiden, Bilhah. Reuben, Leah's oldest, was affronted at this slight to his mother now that the preferred Rachel was dead and he now sought to restore her honor. To do so, he transferred his father's bed from Bilhah's tent to Leah's: "if," Rashi has Reuben say, "mother's sister [Rachel] was her rival, is that any reason why the handmaid of mother's sister should become mother's rival?"[92] In terms of moral and legal calculus, then, Rashi wishes readers to know that Reuben acted out of a noble intention. He certainly had no sexual involvement with Bilhah. On this reading, it was granted that Reuben did commit an infraction "as if he had actually sinned [sexually]" with Bilhah. Yet, as the Talmud confirmed, his actual sin was sufficiently mild as to ensure no fissure in Jacob's family, hence the non sequitur after the space in the verse: "Now the sons of Jacob were twelve." The seemingly disconnected continuation taught that Jacob's sons remained "equally righteous" despite Reuben's regrettable deed. Rashi imparted a plain sense reading of the phrase but added the midrashic one, stressing it was one that "the rabbinic sages expounded."[93] Though Ibn Ezra baulked at this exculpatory interpretation, he was a bit cagey in his Torah commentary. In one version, he lauds the sages' concealment of Reuben's misconduct. In, however, a *reportatio* that transmits an oral explanation that he relayed to a student, and elsewhere in the Torah commentary, Ibn Ezra does not hesitate to speak openly of Reuben's sexual "defilement" of Bilhah.[94]

For his part, Aboulrabi accommodates Rashi's notion that Reuben harbored a noble intention but still manages to take the story to dark places where even Ibn Ezra might have feared to tread. Like Ibn Ezra's final holding on the misconduct, Aboulrabi takes Reuben's actual sexual congress with Bilhah as a given. He supplies a motive for it in step with Rashi, depicting an insulted Reuben trying to annul his mother's indignity by violating Bilhah so she would become prohibited to Jacob (as Aboulrabi apparently assumes was the practice). The end was that "all of Jacob's desire should be for his mother [Leah] exclusively." On the level of intention, then, Rashi's exposition stands, teaching that "all of them were righteous and equal, and that Reuben did not sin."

Still, Rashi's presentation is "absurd" (*hevel*) in its ensemble, regarding both its evaluation of the tactics used by Reuben and its discounting of the depths of Reuben's depravity. If the aim was to eradicate his mother's competitor, surely there was a better way, be it fatal drugs or surreptitious murder. Whatever the lofty motive, there is no greater ignominy than sexual depravity, especially involving a father's wife.[95] Ibn Ezra had praised the "ancients" for "handsomely interpreting" the story in the spirit of the enjoinder that "a prudent man conceals shame" (Prov 12:16), and Aboulrabi invokes the same slogan but to a different end. Ibn Ezra uses the formula to commend the rabbinic sages for making efforts to camouflage Reuben's sin. Aboulrabi uses it in a full-throated condemnation of Reuben, suggesting that he ought to have found a "prudent" (that is, secretive) way to achieve his goal that concealed his shame rather than being caught *in flagrante delicto*.[96]

Fatal substances and homicide figure in another of Aboulrabi's clashes with the *Commentary* where the issue is Moses's instruction to Korah and his company of 250 followers to take censers and "lay incense on them before the Lord" (Num 16:6). Why choose an incense offering to test the fitness of Korah and his party to serve as high priest in response to their efforts to usurp the position of Moses's brother, Aaron? In the version of the *Commentary* in the hands of Aboulrabi, Rashi explained that the cultic incense was "the most precious of sacrifices," yet it also possessed a "fatal substance" (*sam ha-mavet*) that had killed Aaron's sons Nadab and Abihu when they brought incense offerings that were unsolicited. In this reading, the choice of incense served as a warning, hinting to the rebels that only one could be chosen as high priest while the rest would pay with their lives.[97] Aboulrabi's brother, Shalom, sees Moses's strategy differently—namely, as a "subterfuge" worthy of the Moses depicted in the pages of Machiavelli; that is, aimed at enticing the mutineers to their doom. Aboulrabi reports that, so understood, this act of cunning left his brother Shalom "greatly appalled," as it seemed to put Moses in breach of the prohibition on premeditated murder. If members of Korah's faction were innocent, Moses clearly "did not do well" to ensure their demise. If not, God would have requited them without Mosaic intervention. Aboulrabi also reports the response of "my master, my father" who proposed that Moses, having sought the cause of Nadab's and Abihu's death after they were consumed, determined that it was a "substance that God prepared to avenge all who would offer incense God did not command." Sure in his conviction that the rebellion involved no "estimable intention toward God," only "jealousy and rivalry" against him and Aaron, Moses was entirely justified in acting as he did. Thus did the sages assert that Moses put the fatal substance in his rivals' incense. (Keen to forfend misunderstanding, Aboulrabi wishes to stress that Moses played no role in the demise of Nadab and Abihu!) In this and other cases, Aboulrabi puts notions in his readers' heads (if at times only to deny them) that might make even the most realist commentator recoil, ones that cast Moses in a far harsher light than any image of him that Rashi would entertain.[98]

Aboulrabi's place in the ongoing debates over the sins of biblical greats, with their complex amalgams of exegesis and ethics, remains to be delineated. Rashi's impulse was largely to vindicate such figures, Aboulrabi's to view them more "at eye level," as a contemporary usage has it, often filling in gaps in unexpected, not to speak of provocative ways.[99] Clearly he does not think that Rashi's black-and-white calculus conduced to finely drawn insight into the morally ambiguous figures Aboulrabi found depicted in the Torah. He can even leave the impression that he is eager to knock sanctified figures down a notch or two. The results are some of the most unvarnished criticisms of biblical greats in Jewish literature—ones very much inimical to midrashic efforts to "conceal their shame."

Sweet Midrash, True Midrash, Supercommentary

Criticism is certainly the most conspicuous feature of Aboulrabi's reception of the *Commentary*, but other dimensions signal open-mindedness on a case-by-case basis. Sometimes, Aboulrabi justifies the exegetical legitimacy of midrashim cited by Rashi. On other occasions, he goes much further, leaving no doubt that Rashi has left behind a legacy to cherish, even where the plain sense and midrashic interpretation diverge. In these ways, of course, Aboulrabi sounds a note very different from that of Pseudo-Rabad.

Regarding the report that "A new king arose over Egypt who did not know Joseph" (Exod 1:8), Rashi adduces a talmudic dispute: "Rav and Samuel. One said [the king was] really new; the other said [that it was same king and] he made new edicts." Rashi apparently follows the second view in his comment on the verse's conclusion, "who knew not Joseph," where he explains that the king, previously favorable to Joseph, now "comported himself as if he did not know him."[100] Aboulrabi hews to the denotation: the word "new" is used of the king in its plain sense. As for the difficulty that this reading made the phrase "he knew not Joseph" redundant, Aboulrabi has a solution—namely, to read it in pluperfect: the king "*had* not known Joseph" even prior to ascension. Still, Aboulrabi ascribes the other midrash to the drawing of a precise inference (*diyyequ*) on the part of the sages.[101] In so doing, he employs the critical vocabulary of Sefardic "speculation" (*'iyyun*) as it was being applied to the *Commentary* in his day in Spain.[102]

'Iyyun-based supercommentary analyzes the *Commentary* according to the same omnisignificant principle that midrashists applied to scripture. Perhaps the mainstay of the approach is the conviction that apparent redundancies are never real ones and that they invariably impart meaning. Aboulrabi does not read Rashi this way, but he does issue supercommentarial justifications for midrashim cited by Rashi that view scripture in this light. On midrashic authority, Rashi imbues Judah's urging his father to "send the boy in my care . . . that we may live and not die" (Gen 43:8) with a glimmer of prophecy: "The Holy Spirit flickered within him [Judah]. Through this trip your spirit will be revived, as it is said: 'the spirit of their father Jacob revived' (Gen 45:27)."[103] As Jacob anticipates the loss of Benjamin, having already lost Joseph, the firstborn of his beloved Rachel, Judah presages that the journey involving Benjamin's descent to Egypt will not just relieve the physical threat to the family but also restore to Jacob the living "spirit" long lost since Joseph's disappearance. Aboulrabi might be expected to spurn a midrashic conjuring of semiprophetic allusion such as this, but he endorses it on omnisignificant grounds. Judah's assertion "live and not die" would otherwise be redundant: if the journey resulted in relief from famine such that the family would live, then the family clearly would not die. "For this reason he [Rashi] explained well [by saying] 'The Holy Spirit flickered, etc'. since it says 'and live.' " Since "and not die" refers to biological survival, it proves necessary to find another referent

for "we may live," which Rashi does by seeing in it allusion to the approaching psycho-spiritual remedy to Jacob's despair owing to the loss of Joseph.[104]

Aboulrabi can also make an independent case for a finding grounded in midrashic techniques that he must have thought altogether flimsy. Take the idea that Haran's daughter Iscah was actually Sarah. To justify the twin designations, Rashi explains, in a typical midrashic manner, that one name was descriptive and one appellative. Sarah was her real name, whereas Iscah, which derives from a root meaning "to see," had to do with Sarah's status as a prophetess (she "could see the future by holy inspiration") or, alternatively, her attractiveness in the eyes of others ("everyone gazed at her beauty").[105] Ibn Ezra was cool to such exegetical fancies, although, using a favorite formula, he does pronounce himself willing to assent to the identification if it is a "received tradition."[106] By contrast, Aboulrabi finds that the scriptural data impel such an assent. The verse speaks of "Milkah, the daughter of Haran, the father of Milkah and the father of Iscah." Strictly speaking, the Torah imparted inert information, since the phrase "father of Iscah" would add nothing if the Iscah in question were unknown and the Haran in question were someone other than Abram's brother. The only way to make the Torah's statement informative was through the midrash: "Hence, our rabbis interpreted that she was [identical with] Sarai."[107] Still, this justification of the midrash on immanent grounds of lexical semantics stands at a far remove from the whimsical etymologies invoked by Rashi from the rabbinic record.

Jacob's sending of Joseph "from the valley of Hebron" to Shechem to find his brothers (Gen 37:14) is another instance where Aboulrabi finds a basis for Rashi's reading, just not the fanciful one Rashi himself supplies. Rashi highlights a problem, then provides a solution that puts the seemingly quotidian sending of Joseph in a very broad providential frame of reference: " 'From the valley (*'emeq*) of Hebron'—But Hebron is on a mountain. . . . However [the phrase alludes to] the deep [mysterious] counsel (*'eṣah 'amuqah*) [playing on *'emeq*, from the same root] of the righteous one [Abraham] buried in Hebron, to fulfill that which was told to Abraham . . . 'your offspring shall be strangers in a land not theirs' (Gen 15:13)."[108] Here was an understanding of Hebron not in merely locative-geographic terms but also in a deeper sense of "spiritual causation."[109] It meant that Jacob's otherwise peculiar consignment of his beloved Joseph to brothers who hated him was part of an unwitting inauguration of events in fulfillment of the "counsel" imparted to Abraham regarding the fate of his descendants. Aboulrabi accepts the idea, but places it on what he considers a surer footing. Omitting appeals to tenuous wordplay and topography (*'emeq* = *'amoq* = deep counsel; Hebron = the righteous one buried there), he directs attention to the sort of textual pleonasm to which he was so attuned, then imputes to Rashi an interpretive motive different from the one supplied in the *Commentary* itself: "he explained what he explained since the verse ought to have said that he [Jacob] sent him [Joseph] and he came to Shechem. What purpose is served by [saying] 'from the valley of Hebron,' and so forth."[110] Thus does Aboulrabi concur that whatever his personal motive, Jacob's sending of Joseph also complied with a divine master plan for the creation of the Jewish people in Egypt.

If, in the case just seen, Aboulrabi straddles the border between commentarial creativity and supercommentarial explanation, at other times he fulfills the role of supercommentator proper. Regarding God urging Abram to leave his native land, Rashi glosses the imperative + prepositional *lamed* in *lekh lekha* to mean "for your benefit." Aboulrabi comments: "the Straight One explained 'for your benefit.' Since *lekha* is superfluous as regards [the charge to] travel, he explained 'for your benefit.'"[111] He can explain both *peshaṭ* and *derash*, as with Rashi's dual interpretation of *kol ha-miṣvah* (Deut 8:1). After first suggesting that the phrase be read contextually (*kifeshuṭo*), meaning "all the instruction," Rashi adds what he identifies as a *midrash 'aggadah* that takes the term to refer to all elements of a single commandment. The lesson then is: "If you have started a commandment, complete it, because it is attributed only to the one who completes it." Aboulrabi explains both possibilities, commending the acuity of the midrash: "He meant [that according to the plain sense *kol ha-miṣvah* means] each one of the commandments. Yet the *derash* nicely drew a precise inference from the definite article of the word *ha-miṣvah*, since it did not say simply *miṣvah*, so it drew the precise inference [of reading] 'the whole of the commandment': 'he who starts [a commandment should finish it].'"[112]

In the case of "Jacob left Beersheba" (Gen 28:10), Aboulrabi's appreciation of the *Commentary*'s exactitude reaches new heights, but not before he lodges possible objections. Rashi observed that the description of Jacob's departure from home to find a wife (and flee his brother's murderous revenge) could have been written more economically: why mention the patriarch's departure from Beersheba when it sufficed to say, as in the sequel, that he "set out for Haran"? From the ostensible superfluity, Rashi draws an important moral-sociological truth: "it conveys that a righteous person's departure from a place leaves an impression." Since he supplies no other gloss, Rashi implies that the midrash comprises the plain sense, whereas Aboulrabi immediately brands the interpretation *derash*. Initially, he affects to reject the reading on the view that Rashi's isolation of the first half of the verse as a pleonasm is unjustified. His involved reasoning is that, according to the plain sense, there was no need for scripture to mention that Jacob set out for Haran since it stated earlier that he "went to Paddan-aram" (Gen 28:5, 7), "so let it state [straightaway] 'And he came upon a certain place' (Gen 28:11), and so forth, resuming the [account of the] occurrence of what happened on his way to Haran." But this proves only an interim analysis that underscores his appreciative final holding that "if you scrutinize well, you will find it [a justification for the midrash], and sweet it is." In the original instruction that Jacob received from his father, he was told, "Up, go to Paddan-aram" (Gen 28:2) with nothing said about a departure from Beersheba. The Torah therefore had reason to omit mention of Beersheba now. That the Torah refers to it creates an ineluctable necessity (*hekhreaḥ*) to "supply a rationale for mentioning the departure"—which is what Rashi does.[113] Apparently spurious, the midrash is not only justifiable but also imperative—nay, sweet.

Sometimes arrayed alongside considerations of exegesis and theology in Aboulrabi's supercommentarial cogitations are extratextual exigencies. Before him and in his day, Christian polemicists, in Spain especially, railed against the apparent hatred of Christians embodied in the midrashic enjoinder to "kill the best among the gentiles."[114] That the midrash appeared in the *Commentary*, a work increasingly familiar to a segment of Christian literati, must have pressed the drive to devise palliative interpretations. Aboulrabi insists that the sentiment applies only to "wicked" gentiles who "despise Israel." As proof that it does not encompass all non-Jews, Aboulrabi summons another rabbinic dictum that righteous gentiles (another way of saying "the best of the gentiles") have a portion in the world to come.[115]

When he is not countering Christian calumnies, Aboulrabi can put a perplexing midrash to theological purpose. Commenting on the promise that the Tent of Meeting shall be sanctified by God's "glory" (*bikhevodi;* Exod 29:43), he relates to the midrash that Rashi provides after giving a plain sense reading. According to the latter, "My Glory" refers to the divine indwelling (*shekhinah*) that will grace the shrine but a midrash, building on one of the seemingly more radical forms of rabbinic homily, *'al tiqrei*, revocalized the consonantal text to read, in this case, "not *bikhevodi* but *bikhevudai* [by my glorified ones]." In this way does Rashi relate this verse to a later anguished story in Leviticus, finding in the midrashically reread statement an allusion to the death of Aaron's sons that would mar the glad tidings of the day the desert tabernacle would be inaugurated. For his part, Aboulrabi sticks to a local analysis, but nevertheless remarks that "the sages did well to speak as they did"—otherwise what is the connection between divine sanctification and "My glory"? He explains Rashi's midrashic answer in light of the divine pronouncement that the tabernacle is to be a place of encounter ("for there I will meet with you") where God will speak to Moses and "meet with the Israelites" (Exod 29:42–43). This notion sets the stage for the powerful idea that the Jewish people are the agents to whom divine sanctification is entrusted: it comes "through them, since they are ones that honor Me."[116]

Legal midrashim also draw Aboulrabi's attention. He describes as "fitting" the analogy that Rashi makes between the two halves of Leviticus 19:32. As the "rising" required by "You shall rise before the aged" entails no material loss, so the "deference" mandated in "show deference to the old" contains no obligation to incur a loss. Rather, the "deference" that the Torah mandates is expressed in other ways, "as the rabbinic sages explained."[117]

As with some nonlegal midrashim, an inspection of a legal midrash may begin skeptically but end affirmatively. Rashi explains that the passive "they shall not be eaten" said of "all the things that swarm upon the earth" (Lev 11:41) not only implies a prohibition on consumers of the prohibited item but also renders guilty "one who causes another to eat." Aboulrabi initially states that he has "already clarified the refutation of this, since nowhere does the Torah make liable one who causes another to sin." He adds that the midrash is a postulate of rabbinic deduction (*sevarat ḥakhamim*). All this bestirs an expectation of stout rejection, but Aboulrabi pronounces the idea "appropriate," noting that it has a complement in rabbinic thinking, which teaches that a person who "catalyzes [another to action] is greater than the one who acts." What is more, there is logic here because one who draws others into transgression can lead many astray, whereas personal transgression is limited to one.[118]

Aboulrabi's handling of the law of talion, interpreted midrashically by Rashi as monetary compensation, progresses from ambivalence to acquiescence to reasonably sturdy affirmation. It begins with characteristic combativeness, calling Rashi's reading "twisted" (*me'uqqal*). Unexpectedly, the objection centers not on its divergence from the divine word's seemingly unequivocal proscription "an eye for an eye" but on deficiencies in the punitive scheme that arises from it. Financial compensation falls more lightly on the rich than the poor: a wealthy offender could indemnify a victim at inconsequential cost. Then, too, if wealthy, the victim gains nothing from such compensation. By all rights, measure for measure ought to apply, with each judged according to his deeds as per the "unadorned plain sense" (*peshaṭ ha-pashuṭ*). Yet Aboulrabi quickly pivots, insisting that "we have only the interpretation of our sages," and what is more, "it is true." Addressing the level of substance, he notes that the midrashic reading has the virtue of accounting for the injured party's stature in respect to two categories of compensation, "suffering" and "humiliation." One can also object to "eye for an eye" understood in its prima facie sense (*kifeshuṭo*), since the victim gains nothing from the perpetrator's mutilation. What is more, such a punishment smacks of revenge and cruelty, while the Torah forbids revenge. When the focus is shifted to substance, the rabbinic approach remains the most just.[119]

Aboulrabi is perhaps more inclined to be stalwart in defending the oral law reported by Rashi when he has in mind the presence of external foes. He describes himself as stepping forth as a great defender of rabbinic tradition in a showdown in Jerusalem in which "the point of contention between me and the Karaites" was whether to analogize the prohibition on muzzling an ox "in its threshing" (Deut 25:4) and the proscription on kindling a fire "on [lit. 'in'] the Sabbath day" (Exod 35:3). Rashi notes that one seeking to evade the ban on muzzling an ox might do so by inferring that one could not muzzle the ox while threshing but could do so while it was still "outside," that is before beginning to thresh, adding that this technicality is precluded by rabbinic interpretation: " 'You may not muzzle'—[meaning] anywhere." Seizing on this point, Karaites argue that just as the prohibition on muzzling applied before the onset of threshing, so, too, it ought to be with fire on the Sabbath. Here was support for their view that even a fire kindled before the Sabbath must not be used on the holy day.[120] Aboulrabi parries, first, by invoking an argument from the sphere of "reasons for the commandments." He posits that the prohibition against muzzling is "due to compassion." It therefore makes perfect sense that it should apply both before and at the time of threshing. No parallel rationale applies in the case of a fire kindled prior to the onset of the Sabbath. Second, Aboulrabi presses the exegetical argument that the Torah specifies proscribed kindling "on the Sabbath day"—that is, that day alone, and not beginning from the day before.[121] Where specific *midreshei halakhah* are targeted by Rabbanism's opponents, Aboulrabi stands in resolute defense, with the *Commentary*'s propensity to report interpretations in conformity with *halakhah* as his point of departure.

Aboulrabi's response to the *Commentary*, then, represents a strange hybrid, at times bearing points of contact with *Sefer hassagot* and at times fitting neatly into the world of late medieval Sefardic supercommentary. Aboulrabi explains the rationale for Rashi's interpretations and justifies them in the face of doubts, including his own. In the case of both aggadic and legal midrash, where Rashi's exegetical footing proves problematic in his eyes, Aboulrabi can shift focus, justifying midrashic readings on substantive rather than exegetical grounds. Like supercommentators before and after him, Aboulrabi is willing to defend Rashi from Nahmanides's strictures.[122] In a different vein, as we will see, he provides expositions of midrashim in ways that recalibrate them to meet the expectations of rationalist readers. In a more complicated response, Aboulrabi may sustain an idea in the *Commentary*, but in ways discordant with

Rashi's midrashic thought processes, straddling the border between super-commentator and independent expositor. In all of this, Aboulrabi remains his own man, but he does engage in a searching dialogue with Rashi's most searing and thoroughgoing critic, Pseudo-Rabad.

In Dialogue and Disputation with Pseudo-Rabad

Aboulrabi's engagement with Pseudo-Rabad is mostly sympathetic, even as he never mentions his work. Yet, as with many things Aboulrabian, there can be unpredictable twists and turns. In particular, where Pseudo-Rabad saw in Rashi's midrashim a stream of often outlandish contrivances, Aboulrabi did not share his predecessor's unremittingly profound misgivings when it came to Rashi's hermeneutic based in the omnisignificance principle.[123]

Nowhere is Aboulrabi's kinship with Pseudo-Rabad more evident than when he eviscerates fantastical chronologies propounded by Rashi. Speaking to the notion of Isaac as forty and Rebecca as a three-year-old at the time of their nuptials, Aboulrabi pronounces the "many far-fetched computations" deployed in support of this reconstruction "yarns of girls and their fantasies."[124] With regard to Rebecca, Pseudo-Rabad asks: "Is it fitting that a girl of three years of age should sally forth to draw water or know how to respond [to questions] so adroitly yea or nay?" Aboulrabi raises these exact objections in sequence: "How could it be that a small girl of three should possess such strength to bear a pitcher on her shoulders or such presence of mind to reply with such pleasant answers to Eliezer?" While the first point is made by other exegetes, the second, regarding Rebecca's practiced demeanor and perspicacity of speech, makes the dependence on Pseudo-Rabad clear, especially in light of the fairly close verbal formulations.[125] Aboulrabi adds an objection of his own that grows out of what he presents as a midrash on the description of Rebecca's fall from her camel at the time of her conferral to Isaac (Gen 24:64). On this view, she fell because she was experiencing menstrual flow, which allows Aboulrabi to clinch his case for her older age, since "a minor does not have a menstrual flow."[126] He relates a cognate point earlier in his work, where he dismisses an element tacitly present in Rashi's interpretation (even though Aboulrabi ascribes it to "a number of commentators")—namely, that three was the age at which *halakhah* allowed for the betrothal of a girl by intercourse because any breach of virginal membranes prior to that age left no lasting trace, since signs of virginity were restored in such a case. Aboulrabi excoriates this idea as "such inanities" (*ka-'eleh ha-sheṭuyot*).[127]

Another of Rashi's midrashic chronologies that irked Aboulrabi was the one that yielded Jochebed as a mother at the age of one hundred and thirty, and here, again, a detail in his account marks it as distinctively influenced by *Sefer hassagot.* To recall, Ibn Ezra urges that since the Torah reports the wonder of Sarah bearing a child at ninety, it surely ought to have recorded the greater wonder of Jochebed's motherhood at an even more advanced age, had it occurred. To this Pseudo-Rabad adds the point that this criticism was all the more cogent in light of the decline in life span between Sarah's day and Jochebed's day. Aboulrabi weaves this added nuance into his objection: "The one who says Jochebed was born "between the walls" is [stating] a nullity since it would come out that she gave birth to Moses at one hundred and thirty. That lies outside the natural order (*ḥuṣ me-ha-ṭeva'*) [all the more] since the matter of Sarah [giving birth] at ninety was in an earlier era and [even then] the whole world marveled."[128]

Like Pseudo-Rabad, Aboulrabi negates another miracle that Rashi affirms, this one in his account of the tabernacle's construction. Though no man was able to raise the structure owing to the weight of the planks, teaches Rashi, God told Moses to busy himself with the task while aiding him to erect it miraculously, a fact to which the Torah alluded by stating in the passive that "the tabernacle was set up" (*huqam*; Exod 40:17). Pseudo-Rabad undermines this inference by invoking the description of Jerusalem at the time of its destruction, that the city "was breached" (Jer 39:2). Just as, despite the passive construction, Jerusalem was obviously assaulted by people, "so, too, the tabernacle was set up by people" rather than erecting itself. Aboulrabi also indicts the sages who "chase" the notion reported by Rashi for imparting "hot air" (*divrei ruaḥ*). Bringing together his yens for grammar and naturalist theology, he insists that *huqam* "invariably implies [an act performed through] the agency of another, being from the verb pattern in which the agent goes unmentioned. Thus, this is *derash*. Indeed, the boards and posts were not so very heavy that they [the people] were unable to erect them. They [the planks] were the burden of the children of Merari [who proved able to transport them, showing they were not beyond lifting]."[129] Rashi takes the testimony that Moses "finished setting up the tabernacle" (Num 7:1) to mean that he performed the task alone. Aboulrabi, in the spirit of Pseudo-Rabad, relates the statement to the report that Solomon "completed" the temple's construction (1 Kgs 6:14), which obviously refers to his oversight, not execution, of the task.[130]

Aboulrabi could also concur with Pseudo-Rabad's anti-halakhic interpretations. Treating the pericope spelling out the obligations of one who purchased a Hebrew slave girl, Pseudo-Rabad, as we saw, takes the "three ways" (Exod 21:11) mentioned to refer to sustenance, clothing, and *'onah*. He tacitly denies

Rashi's rabbinic reading in reference to three scenarios: "He should designate her for himself [as a wife], or for his son [as a wife], or he should deduct from the money of her redemption and allow her to go free." Aboulrabi interprets like Pseudo-Rabad, but mentions the contending rabbinic view. Pseudo-Rabad ends his anti-halakhic interpretation with a curt instruction: "do not think otherwise." Aboulrabi uses his clever double entendre, "nullified in my smallness," to defer, but he also effectively demurs: "the rabbinic sages explained it in a different manner. I am nullified in my smallness, but this is how it seems to me on the basis of independent ratiocination."[131]

Standing in some ways as Pseudo-Rabad *redivivus*, Aboulrabi can yet display points of congruence with Rashi's midrashic tendencies. Consider Rashi's midrash on—as distinguished from his plain sense interpretation of—Judah's "do not be impatient with your servant" (Gen 44:18), which took Judah to address the Egyptian viceroy menacingly. Pseudo-Rabad dismisses the idea with a scoff, sure that the brothers not only feared the potentate but also treated him as "the equivalent of the king."[132] In a terse gloss, Aboulrabi subscribes to the notion that Judah uttered "words of ire," just as Rashi midrashically contended.[133] Rashi clarifies that the phrase "God spoke" means that the Deity took Moses to task (*dibber 'ito mishpaṭ*). Pseudo-Rabad insists that "there is no [grounds for] *derash*." Aboulrabi sides with Rashi's reading, advancing two of the three reasons adduced by a later Sefardic supercommentator to prove its "ineluctability," both based in rabbinic literature: " 'And God spoke.' He [Rashi] interpreted that 'he spoke reprovingly, etc.' [He did so] since the language 'He spoke' [*dibber*] is a language of harshness and [the name] *'Elohim* signifies the attribute of [divine] judgment."[134]

As we have seen, Aboulrabi takes seriously Rashi's propensity to invest apparent superfluities with omnisignificant meaning, a major cause of his parting of the ways with Pseudo-Rabad. From the fact that Moses was said to record the census of the Levites both "at the command of the Lord" (*'al-pi 'adonai*) and "as he was bidden" (Num 3:16), a midrash invoked by Rashi derived that the divine presence preceded Moses, who stood at the entrance to the tents, and "a heavenly voice (*bat qol*) emanated from the tent, saying, 'There are this many babies in this tent.' That is the reason it says 'from the divine mouth.' " Pseudo-Rabad rejoins that "it says 'at the command of the Lord' in the habitual sense, since it was God who commanded him to count them."[135] In theory, Aboulrabi might have written off the contents of the midrash, but he reveals its textual basis in a way that suggests sympathy for its interpretive principle: "it could have said 'as he was bidden' and that would have sufficed. It said [also] *'al-pi 'adonai* and our sages expounded 'a heavenly voice emanated from their house.' "[136] While he does not pass explicit judgment on the historicity of the midrash, he does imply its accuracy by clarifying the redundancy that it eliminates.

The exegetical gulf separating Aboulrabi and Pseudo-Rabad is especially gaping when their theological views are at odds, nowhere more than when it comes to magical elements in the *Commentary*. Pseudo-Rabad has no truck with midrashic accelerated journeys, such as the one Rashi ascribed to Jacob, owing to a miraculous "springing" forward of the earth. Aboulrabi affirms *qefiṣat ha-derekh* in this case, although he characteristically simplifies the basis for the midrash where Rashi supplies an especially circuitous one.[137] A more powerful witness to Aboulrabi's propensity for the magical and Pseudo-Rabad's recoil is the reaction of each to Rashi's deployment of the power of divine names in his interpretation of the golden calf. Pseudo-Rabad explodes at the idea the calf was fashioned using the plate inscribed with the ineffable divine name. Indeed, it is in that context that he casts the midrashists as ones who "hewed down the tree and cut its branches" by concocting ideas that enthralled Jews in error.[138] By contrast, Aboulrabi affirms that Aaron "intended to make a talisman in the form of a calf," then segues to Moses's use of "the power of holy names when he raised Joseph's casket."[139] Where Pseudo-Rabad contravenes Rashi's claim that Moses killed through enunciation of the tetragrammaton, Aboulrabi finds an abbreviated permutation of a name of God comprising seventy-two letters.[140]

Aboulrabi presents the peculiar spectacle of one who took inspiration from *Sefer hassagot* while at times displaying openness to Rashi's midrashic methods and the magical, miraculous world that his *Commentary* portrays. Yet Aboulrabi can also chafe at Rashi's philosophical innocence, as Eleazar Ashkenazi and Pseudo-Rabad certainly do, leading him to issue some of his most unsparing, condescending criticisms of the *Commentary*.

Confronting and Reconfiguring Rashi's Judaism: "I Shall Not Acquit the Wrongdoer"

Indicating what moved him to write, Aboulrabi begins at the beginning, describing the creation of the world by God, its hierarchical ordering, and the privileged place of humankind and Israel within it, all in the stately cadences of medieval rationalism. Sounding loudly is an intellectualist vision of true humanity: "May God be exalted . . . for the eminence of existence and its order and for the superiority with which God endowed the human species, hewn of matter and form, raising its station above all [other] constituents of existence." Being in the divine image and form, "it is incumbent upon a human being . . . to apprehend all of God's accomplishment, each person according to his intellect's apprehension."[141] Aboulrabi's rationalism often turned him in a direction very different from Rashi, drawing on a very different muse: Maimonides.

Many are the places where Aboulrabi's Maimonidean orientation is on display. For the meaning of "This shall be My name forever, This My appellation for all eternity" (Exod 3:15), he refers to the *Guide of the Perplexed*, I:63, and largely leaves it at that.[142] Elsewhere, he combines deprecation of the multitude and fear of persecution by them with the Maimonidean trope of divine accommodation:

> I have glanced a little at the books of wisdom that speak of such principles of knowledge but I fear to express myself in a way that would open the eyes of the blind out of dread of the ignorant (*'amei ha-'areṣ*) who walk in darkness. Still, as I already explained in *Nezer ha-qodesh* [one of Aboulrabi's lost works], it is not among the conditions of the divine to bear any relation to that which is physical. Rather, all that is said with respect to God is in accordance with our apprehension, since we do not grasp the abstract except by way of the physical inasmuch as we are physical. Thus, [strictly speaking] one must not ascribe to the deity judgment or mercy, descent or ascent, standing or sitting or speaking.[143]

Aware that the truth is not welcome in all (or even most) quarters, Aboulrabi refuses to feint, pressing forward with his analysis of biblical language relating to the Deity. As we will see, he deems Rashi's capacity to engage in this enterprise appallingly weak.

When it comes to a philosophical understanding of the Torah, Aboulrabi's dissent from Rashi begins at the outset. Rashi initially pronounces it necessary to adduce rabbinic ideas to understand the primordial light: "For this, too, we must have recourse to words of *'aggadah*: He [God] saw that the wicked were unworthy of using it [the light] and [therefore] He separated it for the righteous." Rashi then provides a "contextual" (*peshuṭo*) interpretation that is also of rabbinic origin: "He [God] saw that it 'was good,' and that it was not apt for it [the light] and the darkness to function in a confused manner."[144] Despite Rashi's reliance on rabbinic sources, Aboulrabi treats the final ensemble as Rashi's, issuing chastisement accordingly:

> "God saw that the light"—the Straight One interpreted that "the wicked were unworthy of using it," etc. I fail to grasp this utterance's rationale

> since if it [the light] is something sensate, how can it be concealed, and if something spiritual, how can the wicked use it? He [Rashi] also said: "He saw that it was good, and that it was not apt for it and the darkness to function in a confused manner." But this is an impossibility, so there is no need to state it [i.e., that the two need be segregated].

Going beyond the innate deficiency of each interpretation, Aboulrabi adds that a scrutiny of them in tandem reveals a further problem: "the second interpretation contradicts the first since how should it [the light] admix [with the darkness] inasmuch as He had already concealed it." Having impugned Rashi from a number of angles, he adds a broader charge: "even though these things were not intended to be understood literally, still he should have refrained from expressing them [openly], let alone writing them." Not all ideas are meant for public consumption, all the more if one's grasp is wanting. That said, his critique does point the way to redemption, as Aboulrabi indicates that the midrashim in question must be interpreted figuratively. This he does, offering a corrective to Rashi's failures. His exposition forms part of a syncretistic cosmogony that conflates kabbalistic and philosophical usages but leaves no doubt, if only by way of its reference to "books of the philosophers," of its rationalist thrust.[145]

As with Eleazar Ashkenazi and Pseudo-Rabad, what sometimes counts with Aboulrabi as much as the substance of his criticism of the *Commentary* is the rhetoric in which it is couched. In the passage just discussed, Aboulrabi lays stress on his right or, rather, obligation to dispute the *Commentary*. Invoking biblicisms, he is insistent that "I will show no regard for the elder" (see Deut 28:50). He also promises compliance with the biblical injunction to "not acquit the wrongdoer (*rasha'*, lit. 'evildoer')" (Exod 23:7).[146] Here, as with his critical forerunners, *ad hominem* animus fills out the substantive critique. Though the epithet "evildoer" may be more naughty than malign, one senses that Aboulrabi thinks the stakes very high in his dispute with this "elder" statesman of Torah interpretation so lacking in scientific erudition.

Contravening another of Rashi's expositions on Genesis 1, Aboulrabi again invokes a biblicism to decry Rashi's "wickedness." Rashi raises the question of why the first day of creation was not called on the pattern of the other days, using a cardinal number: "according to the accustomed language of this pericope it should have written 'the first day' as with the rest of the days: second, third, forth." His reply was that *yom 'eḥad* (Gen 1:5) made the point that "the Holy One blessed be He was one [i.e., alone] in His universe as the angels were only created on the second day," noting that it is thus explained in *Bereshit rabbah*.[147] The origin of the exposition notwithstanding, Aboulrabi makes Rashi bear the brunt of his emphatic (if elliptical, perhaps owing to textual corruption) critique. Minimally, Rashi is responsible both for ushering a hodgepodge of incompatible midrashim into his *Commentary* in a way that yields incoherence and for proffering misguided "surmises" of his own devising. Here, unlike elsewhere, Aboulrabi drives a wedge between the meritorious midrashic inheritance and its deployment by Rashi:

> He [Rashi] said: "Because the Holy One blessed be He was one in His universe." This *derash* has no purchase (*'en lo damim*] [since] He is always not alone (*tamid 'eno yaḥid*).[148] In addition, he stated the opposite of his words since he explained "Let there be an expanse" (Gen 1:6) [to mean that] "even though the heavens had already been created on the first day [they were still liquid]" and he explained [elsewhere] that the light was created before the heavens. If so, He was [never] alone in His world. [In fact] he [Rashi] said [that God was alone] in His world, whence it may be inferred that there was a world [and hence that God was not alone]. . . . The Straight One admixed the words of [*Bereshit*] *rabbah* with surmises (*sevarot*) that no prior sage ever conceived.[149]

Marred by inconsistency and faulty conjecture, the *Commentary*, or rather its author, faces a harsh (if, to be sure, rhetorically embellished) censure: "'How great is the wickedness of the person' (Gen 6:5) who says things devoid of insight."[150]

Aboulrabi concerns himself with issues of divine predication and anthropomorphic language, a preoccupation that comes into view as he finds Rashi (or thinks he does) perpetrating follies of a rank beginner. The issue is the word "hand" (*yad*) as related to God in the verse "I will lay My hand upon Egypt" (Exod 7:4), upon which Rashi comments: "an actual hand (*yad mamash*), with which to smite them." It was a case where he brought to bear his "meaning-minimalist" lexicographic approach that tried to identify in a range of meanings for any given word a basic signification.[151] Apparently understanding that Rashi posits the literal existence of a divine hand, Aboulrabi treats him (perhaps wrongly) as a corporealist in need of strong remedial measures: "he explained 'an actual hand.' This is false. [It means] rather, 'His power' [as in] 'the wondrous power' (literally 'hand'; Exod 14:31) [and] 'hand (*yad*) of the Lord will strike' (Exod 9:3)."[152]

Aboulrabi's philosophical purism regarding divine attributes leads him to assess Rashi as derelict in his interpretation of God's promise to Moses, "I will come down and speak with you" (Num 11:17). Rashi notes that "this is one of ten [divine] descents enumerated in the Torah." Aboulrabi chastises Rashi's failure to indicate "any reason for a single one of these." He makes good the lacuna by supplying a principle governing use of such locutions and applying it to the case at hand:

> It is known among the wise of heart that the human intellect's apprehension of a thing that is apprehended varies in accordance with that which is apprehended, meaning that . . . when the thing being apprehended is of lesser status than the status of the one doing the apprehending, "descent" is said with respect to the one apprehending. Thus it was with Moses . . . his apprehension ascended to the level of the divine indwelling [*shekhinah*] and he united with it through his apprehension . . . but where it was necessary for him to know some concept that was beneath his rank in order to inform Israel of God's will with respect to it, God would, as it were, cause the emanation of the divine indwelling to descend until it reached the rank of the thing to be apprehended. Thus the verse's locution regarding God: "I will come down and speak."[153]

In his application, Aboulrabi locates the element of descent in God's transfer of divine spirit from the higher Moses to his inferior recipients, the seventy elders. Informing this view of divine descent as an idiom for prophetic inspiration and the prophet's relationship to the divine indwelling is Maimonides who, in a chapter of his *Guide*, cites Numbers 11:17 as a prooftext for the signification of divine descent that Aboulrabi gives.[154] In effect, Rashi's incapacity to interpret the verse is brought into relief by Aboulrabi's Maimonidean dissection of it.

As we have seen, the *Commentary*'s rich load of allusive or elusive midrashim made it a springboard for fresh reflection and reinterpretation, ensuring its abiding contemporaneity. Aboulrabi does not lack for inventiveness on this score, prompting him to depart in one case from his more usual pattern of putting Maimonides in counterpart to Rashi and instead making an opaque midrash of Rashi a mouthpiece for rationalist precepts. The midrash was one Aboulrabi's father-in-law, Ibn Gabbai, had "heard" commentators struggling to explain "in this way and that," all, in his considered judgment, arriving at conclusions "full of hot air."[155]

The midrash centers on the oracle responding to Rebecca's distress in pregnancy that told her that "two nations (*goyim*) are in your womb" (Gen 25:23). On rabbinic authority, Rashi glosses it with regard to Rabbi, the sobriquet of

Judah the Prince, holder of the patriarchate, and a (supposed) Roman emperor named Antoninus. From their tables, Rashi stated, "neither radish nor cucumber were ever lacking, neither in the dry season or rainy season." The textual spur to the midrash is an aberrant spelling of the word for "nations" that yielded an allusion to "proud ones." In the rabbinic reckoning, Jacob and Esau spawned proud peoples, Jews and Romans, with Antoninus and Rabbi Judah emblematic of the two.[156] Reprising a question posed by his father-in-law, Aboulrabi asks why just these offshoots of the fraternal prototypes are mentioned. In addition, what was meant by their decidedly incongruous signs of grandeur, cucumbers and radishes? Aboulrabi clarifies:

> [Rashi wrote] that [*goyim* = nations] it is written *ge'im* [lords / proud ones] in reference to Antoninus and Rabbi, etc. . . . They [the rabbinic sages] fixed on these two as opposed to others like Solomon and Hiram or Mordechai and Haman or others also descended from Esau and Jacob since they lived in the time of the Tannaim [the earlier rabbinic sages] and hence [the sages] were familiar with their [Antoninus's and Judah's] achievements. The reason they did not mention all their achievements but the fact that their table lacked neither for radish (*ṣenon*) nor cucumber (*ḥazeret*) is that these two refer to two noble virtues, moral and intellectual. As regards the moral, they achieved the utmost of liberality as reflected in the fact that they fed cucumber to people who sat at their table, which whets the appetite and prevents [the vice of] drunkenness . . . and the radish aids digestion and makes it [the food] pass more quickly. As for the intellectual virtues, [the reference to radish and cucumber allude to] the abundance of their sagacity [which] meant that they knew the nature of different types of soils such that they could seed and cultivate at any given point in the year [hence these foods were never lacking].[157]

Its strange imagery clarified, the midrash that so many found opaque relays a vision of human flourishing in which ethical and intellectual virtue mark the acme of perfection. Maimonides himself could have happily endorsed Rashi's odd midrash after it had undergone Aboulrabi's supercommentarial elucidation.

Conclusion

The contexts for Aboulrabi's intense engagement with the *Commentary* are hard to pin down. As he grew up, his initiation into the world of the

Commentary seems to have been nursed at home. Casting himself as "the least in age and distinction in my father's whole house," Aboulrabi mentions a "notebook (*quntres*) of my master and father of blessed memory" and cites interpretations of the *Commentary* of his brothers.[158] One conjures the image of a precocious young Aaron keenly tracking debates around the dinner table and eventually joining in. More broadly, inventories of Judeo-Sicilian libraries and evidence from the Hebrew book trade in Sicily show that Rashi was, along with Maimonides, the most popular among individual authors.[159] How representative these testimonies are one cannot say. Most artifacts belonging to Sicilian Jews were lost amid the chaos of the community's dissolution by expulsion in 1493. Still, among printed volumes that had made it to the island at this early stage of the Hebrew press was an edition of the *Commentary*.[160]

As he traveled, if not before, Aboulrabi gained a sense that supercommentary involved participation in a ramified conversation long in progress. He reports what "many ask," "the difficulty many pose," what "confounds many commentators," and so forth.[161] Such statements recall a comment of his father-in-law, Moses ibn Gabbai, that "many more estimable than myself" had taken up the call to explicate Rashi's classic.[162] Aboulrabi was very aware of Ibn Gabbai's supercommentary[163] and, as we saw, he pondered what rang true and what did not in the critical shafts directed at Rashi in *Sefer hassagot*.

In his own work, Aboulrabi leaned to a manner of rhetorical expression cultivated before him by Pseudo-Rabad and Eleazar Ashkenazi. Although less inclined than them to discount Rashi's midrashim, he certainly agreed that unthinking reverence for Rashi was not the way. At each point Aboulrabi was willing to assess the *Commentary* in keeping with his view that "a wise person's failure to grasp a truth due to ignorance is less of a deficiency than substituting truth for falsehood."[164] Having brought an interpretation under scrutiny, Aboulrabi separated good from bad and sweet from foolish (or worse), not hesitating to tar Rashi, and even the sages, using choice epithets.

Aboulrabi's work marks something new, if entirely fleeting, in the *Commentary*'s reception: the emergence of a *tradition* of rhetorically biting resisting reading. His awareness of Eleazar Ashkenazi's Torah commentary is up for some debate, but more than one passage suggests he may have consulted it.[165] Like Ashkenazi and Pseudo-Rabad, Aboulrabi evaluates the *Commentary* in the first instance on the basis of consonance with the plain sense and frequently finds it wanting. Like them, he promotes an approach nourished by rationalist convictions. Nor does he scruple to hurl invective at "the Straight One" and the rabbinic "oaks of old" upon whom Rashi relied. In all of this, Aboulrabi, like his forerunners, carried on exegetical, theological, and rhetorical trends known to them from Ibn Ezra.[166] While sharing

Ashkenazi's and Pseudo-Rabad's incapacity for prevarication, Aboulrabi was more eclectic in his convictions and appreciated elements of Rashi's success, especially owing to his greater openness to the omnisignificance principle.

Aboulrabi's voice fell into oblivion until it was revived in the nineteenth century by a coterie of enlighteners and religious reformers. As part of their effort to remold time-honored practices and beliefs, advocates of Enlightenment took "special delight in pointing to historical antecedents which reflected unorthodox views."[167] Seen thus, Joshua Heschel Schorr's study of Aboulrabi in the pro-reform monthly, *Ṣiyyon*, fits with a tendency of Maskilim to venerate those whom they deemed (or could reframe as) precursors of Enlightenment.[168] Indeed, Schorr casts Aboulrabi as first in a continuum of writers displaying "religious radicalism."[169] For him, Aboulrabi's willingness to attack Rashi out of a "love of truth" ought to have been paradigmatic.

Of course, it was not. The era of openly derisive reading of Rashi was short-lived (how much so depends on a precise dating of *Sefer hassagot* that eludes us). If anything, Aboulrabi stands as the last Jew to devote such reserves of learning to correcting and lambasting what he took to be the *Commentary*'s variegated failings. In so doing, he joined, if only partially, an unsuccessful rearguard action to rouse resistance to a work whose artful and resonant deployment of the words of the "rabbinic oaks of old" was briskly striding toward its station as a sort of definitive word on the meaning of the divine word revealed at Sinai.

PART III

Commentary *Triumphant*

7

Competing Canons

RASHI'S *Commentary* IN A LATE MEDIEVAL BATTLE FOR JUDAISM'S SOUL

THE YEAR: NO LATER than 1468. The work: a tract bearing the bellicose title *Sefer 'alilot devarim* (Book of Accusations). The author: "Rabbi Palmon ben Pelet," described as "a son of 'Anonymous,' who married a daughter of 'So-and-So.'" Writing under the alias "Michael ben Reuben," the nineteenth-century editor who published this strange specimen of rationalist pseudepigraphy thought he knew whose hand lay behind it: Aaron Aboulrabi, whose exegetical tract had recently come to the notice of Jewish literati. Beyond chronological proximity, Michael pointed to Aboulrabi's "mockeries" of midrash as a point of contact with *'Alilot devarim.*[1]

In *'Alilot devarim,* satirical genius is deployed for an altogether serious purpose: exposure of the obscurantism that, in the view of the work's author, gradually had come to degrade Jewish life in post-talmudic times.[2] The corruption had infiltrated every sphere, from study and education to religious practice and popular piety. Sundry in manifestation, it was all ultimately traceable to a single cause: a falling away from rationality that left Jews spiritually bereft and politically powerless. A commentator on *'Alilot devarim* writing under yet another pseudonym ("Joseph ben Meshulam") explains that the work's main aim was to understand "the length of our exile despite the fact that we consider ourselves righteous."[3] Since the commentator is almost certainly identical with the author (despite his claim to have rescued *'Alilot devarim* from a half-rotted, mostly illegible manuscript), it is wise to take his prescience on this and all other scores seriously.[4]

Read broadly, *'Alilot devarim* reveals a struggle for the future of Judaism and the soul of the Jewish people; as the author paints it, Rashi's *Commentary* played a central role in this struggle. It was a battle in which scholars (the *moderni* of their day) often pointed to one of the "ancients" (that is, earlier medieval figures) as a teacher of boundless insight worthy of emulation. The question was: Who among these earlier greats could best show the nation a way forward? *'Alilot devarim* expresses awareness of the growing ubiquity of Rashi's writings, yet other preceptors presented themselves—not least two luminaries of Sefarad: Abraham ibn Ezra, champion of exegetical rationalism; and the figure whom *'Alilot devarim* celebrates as the supreme "master and guide," Maimonides. To be sure, other individuals and factors figured in the ongoing debate, not least theoretical and practical kabbalah, against which *'Alilot devarim* makes a furious assault, going so far as to depict elements of it as unwitting idolatry.[5] Still, amid a litany of gibes and blame, *'Alilot devarim* criticizes, if almost in passing, one work more frontally than any other as a symptom and cause of Judaism's catastrophic swerve away from its classical past rightly understood: Rashi's *Commentary*.[6]

Having studied three of Rashi's resisting readers in detail, now is the time to place their considerations of the *Commentary* and cognate ones on a broader canvas, at once consolidating and filling out our tracing of the various roads, whether smooth or rocky, that the *Commentary* traveled on its way to preeminence. We will first explore the place of Ibn Ezra's Torah commentary, already seen as an alternative to Rashi's *Commentary* in the battle for canonical supremacy, in two aspects. One is as the main competitor to Rashi's reading of the Torah, methodologically and substantively—that is, in terms of canon-*making*, as Ibn Ezra's work became a focus of canonizing processes similar to the ones undergone by Rashi's *Commentary*. Another aspect returns us to the resisting readers who took inspiration from Ibn Ezra's work in sometimes distinct ways and put it to use in their efforts at canon-*breaking*—that is, deploying ideas and techniques known to them from Ibn Ezra to undermine Rashi's interpretations.

Our second act takes up the treatment of the *Commentary* in *'Alilot devarim*, situating it within some of the work's larger concerns and, more speculatively, socioreligious contexts. Although fleeting, the sentences devoted to Rashi prove full of significance, and not only in terms of understanding the author's perceptions of Rashi's disabilities as an exegete. In addition, they throw light on what the author of *'Alilot devarim* surprisingly takes to be the dire spiritual implications of Rashi's exegetical writings, and the *Commentary* in particular. The author's comments also provide vital historical testimony, alluding as directly as any from the late Middle Ages to the *Commentary*'s creeping canonization.

To take a full measure of *'Alilot devarim*'s contribution to our understanding of the *Commentary*'s reception, it is not enough to focus on Rashi as anti-hero. Those figures whom the author presents as post-rabbinic Judaism's great preceptors must also be considered. One, though not the one situated at center stage, was Abraham ibn Ezra, as Reuven Bonfil has shown.[7] Far more important was another sage to whom our author assigns a unique and indeed divinely ordained mission in the life of the nation: Maimonides. The encomium to him in *'Alilot devarim* stands out even by the standards of the many adulatory ones that Maimonides won for himself.[8] Thus does *'Alilot devarim* summon to attention a pivot around which turned one of the decisive canonical battles of medieval Judaism, with Rashi serving as a counterweight to Ibn Ezra and Maimonides and furnishing one of the visions of the way forward from which Jews could choose—in *'Alilot devarim*'s estimation, a vision that, far from halting the decline that beset the people and its faith, threatened Judaism's very future.

The third act in our survey returns us to the eastern Mediterranean point of departure from which we began to learn about Rashi's resisting readers to see how and why its religiocultural terrain might have provided salubrious soil in which harsh critiques of the *Commentary* could flourish. A fourth and final act provides a later eastern matrix of comparison in the form of Elijah Mizrahi, the leading rabbi active in the period when Byzantine Jewish culture began to succumb to the influence of the mass influx of Iberian refugees after the 1492 Spanish expulsion and 1497 Portuguese forced conversions. It was Mizrahi's supercommentarial clarifications of Rashi that quickly became the most influential in the field. He is a suitable stopping point, then, betokening what can be cast, certainly with some qualifications, as the *Commentary*'s triumph in the battle for canonical supremacy.

"Like Any Prophet": Abraham ibn Ezra as Alternative and Rival

Though we lack a comprehensive and searching account of it, the reception of Ibn Ezra's exegesis intersects with the fate of Rashi's *Commentary* in many ways, historical and phenomenological. We have seen that Ibn Ezra was the first Sefardic exegete to encounter Rashi's work, from which he frequently dissented, if mostly indirectly. A key commonality is that the two works attracted more supercommentaries than any other expositions of the Torah. Uriel Simon lists supercommentaries on Ibn Ezra's Torah commentary, most medieval, in the dozens.[9] As the *Commentary* was being authorized by way of more or less formal glosses on it, so was Ibn Ezra's parallel work.

Supercommentators on Ibn Ezra could express the same rhetorically embellished reverence for their hero as expositors of Rashi's *Commentary* did for theirs. "We shall clarify the words of the scholar . . . and make them the main focus of this composition since they are to me like the words of any prophet and seer," intones an anonymous acolyte in his *'Avvat nefesh.*[10] The sentiment regarding Ibn Ezra's supremacy was widely shared, not only in southern France, where his supercommentary tradition had its inception, but also in Spain and Byzantium, where it flourished most copiously.

Appreciation for Ibn Ezra extended beyond his skillful zest to uncover the plain sense, his grammatical acumen, and his philological prowess to the insights he offered into the Torah's deepest esoteric layer, or "secrets." Indeed, his often cryptic exploration of these entailed a major transformation of Jewish tradition. Ibn Ezra was the first to view the concept of the "esoteric" as comprising not an independent body of wisdom but, rather, a "hidden layer of the meaning of a sacred work."[11] In his case, this layer was understood mainly to relate to astrology—a discipline long suspect because of its associations with pagan superstition and idolatry, but increasingly viewed in the central Middle Ages as a science. More boldly still, Ibn Ezra interpreted the subterranean message of the Torah in terms of astral magic, whether with respect to narratives or even laws, seeing the purpose of some of the latter in terms of a way to ward off pernicious astral influences.[12] It is easy to see why, from both the perspective of plain sense exegesis and esoterica, Ibn Ezra supercommentators would pay Rashi only the scantest, if any, heed. They found flagrant violations of the plain sense in his midrashim and could hardly respect Rashi's obliviousness of the Torah's deepest meaning, decipherment of which required astrological expertise of which Rashi was devoid.

Ibn Ezra's esotericism entailed a sharp distinction between an elite readership capable of deciphering and digesting his daring ideas and a multitude of noninitiates unable to understand them, and perhaps likely to suffer a lapse in faith if they did. To this end did one of his glossators, Ezra Gatigno, write two supercommentaries, one on Ibn Ezra's exoteric interpretations and one on his esoteric ones. Yet a problem clearly remained because insights placed in the latter work could fall into the wrong hands. To forestall this eventuality, Gatigno adjured qualified readers to relay his esoteric supercommentary only to "the elite few, the survivors whom the Lord calls (cf. Joel 3:5). For this reason I called it *The Lord's Secret Is With Them That Fear Him*. I wrote it only for the person accustomed to the commentary of the wise man, Ibn Ezra."[13] A recent study of esoteric writing casts doubt on the likely success of this tactic, arguing that over the long run it is "nearly impossible" to maintain the sort of sequestration of a reading audience that Gatigno sought.[14] Though the eyes of average readers may have glazed over at the tedious minutiae that they may have found embedded in some Rashi supercommentaries, the authors of these works certainly never sought any elitist stratification of those whom they addressed—a point to which we shall return when assessing why the *Commentary* did ultimately win the day over Ibn Ezra's alternative.

Ibn Ezra's writings supply no evidence that their author trained in philosophy or studied anything more than a small sampling of the relevant literature available in his day.[15] Still, his supercommentators usually assumed that a correct understanding of the Torah depended on scientific acumen of the sort Ibn Ezra was deemed to possess and Rashi, rightly, to lack. In so doing, they assimilated Ibn Ezra, tacitly or otherwise, to the far more philosophically attuned Maimonides. Eleazar ben Mattathias, author of the earliest Ibn Ezra supercommentary that survives, is a case in point.[16] Like Rashi, he hailed from northern France. At some point, however, he set his sights eastward and, after spending time in Crete, passed thirty-three years in Egypt. It was, however, apparently only after returning to Byzantium that he composed his supercommentary in the first half of the 1260s.[17] The work displays Eleazar's immersion in a body of Aristotelian texts that had become available in Hebrew translation not long before,[18] reflecting the post-1204 advent of Hispano-Provençal rationalism in the East. Had he not known of its impossibility on chronological grounds, Eleazar would have sworn that Ibn Ezra saw Maimonides's *Guide* and "imbibed its waters."[19] So disposed, he glossed over differences between Ibn Ezra and Maimonides, viewing them as a pair of masters who made common cause. In this way did he mirror both devotees of Ibn Ezra and opponents of rationalism, who tended to accept or reject Maimonides and Ibn Ezra in tandem.[20]

Eleazar's choice to write a commentary on Ibn Ezra sufficed to make his rejection of Rashi clear. Eleazar retained a solid rabbinic training quite possibly acquired in France, leaving him equipped to, say, supply Rashi's rabbinic source on a rare occasion when Ibn Ezra openly criticized "R. Solomon" by name.[21] Although he must have ingested a steady diet of the *Commentary* in earlier years, Eleazar's travels laid before him new intellectual horizons, leading to his embrace of a Judaism resting on a "ideational-philosophic foundation stone" supplied by Ibn Ezra and Maimonides.[22] For him and those of his ilk, *the* commentary on the Torah was Ibn Ezra's, read through a Maimonidean lens.

That Ibn Ezra never set foot in Byzantine centers did nothing to quell deep interest there in his literary legacy in general, and his Torah commentary in particular. Byzantine supercommentaries proliferated, although exactly how many were wrought is impossible to say. Some works did not survive. Others mentioned in a list compiled by the fourteenth-century supercommentator of Bulgarian origin, Judah ibn Moskoni, may not have existed. Beyond Eleazar (unknown to Ibn Moskoni), that list mentions a raft of obscure authors whose works disappeared, including Avishai of Bulgaria, Elijah of Serres (Macedonia), Caleb Korsinos of Constantinople, and David Pardeleon.[23] This plenitude is striking when seen alongside a dearth of medieval Rashi supercommentaries written in the region, although some such tracts were copied there or arrived from abroad, as attested by, for example, a record of purchase of such a work by one Ephraim of Romania in 1424.[24] Also striking is Ibn Moskoni's testimony that the teacher from whom most of his knowledge of Ibn Ezra stemmed was one "Obadiah the Egyptian," to whom Ibn Moskoni also ascribes a supercommentary, reminding us that veneration for Ibn Ezra in the eastern Mediterranean served as a bridge across the divide between scholars living under the cross and under the crescent.[25]

So great was the adulation for Ibn Ezra in Byzantium that scholarly disagreement sometimes came down to a difference of opinion as to whether the loyalty owing to him was total or something just shy of that. A fifteenth-century wrangle on this score involved the Constantinople rabbi, philosopher, astronomer, and mathematician Mordechai ben Eliezer Khomatiano (Hebrew Komtino; d. 1482) and Shabbetai ben Malkiel Hakohen from Crete. Komtino's allegiances appear from his decision to write commentaries on three works of Ibn Ezra—*Yesod mora', Sefer hashem, Sefer ha-'eḥad*—and on Maimonides's *Guide.*[26] Yet he did write an independent Torah commentary, completed just before Constantinople fell to the Ottomans in 1453, in which he treated Ibn Ezra as an indispensable resource. At the same time, he reserved the right—or, to speak more medievally, felt a duty—to confute "early scholars," including Ibn Ezra, when their words were not "true and correct."[27] For all that, Komtino remained, in the estimate of Jean-Christophe Attias, a "prisoner" to Ibn Ezra in terms of both his "rhetoric" and his "intellectual and referential universe."[28] Yet Shabbetai found that even this level of fidelity fell short, leading him to write strictures on Komtino and otherwise take it upon himself "to dispute anyone who disputed his [Ibn Ezra's] words."[29]

Shabbetai's rhetoric was extreme even by the standards of Ibn Ezra's most reverential devotees. Summoning the Psalmist's praise of God's lifegiving benevolence, Shabbetai hails Ibn Ezra as a "fountain of life" in whose light "we see light" (Ps 36:10). A prophetic proclamation of an utter incommensurability between divine and human thoughts (Isa 55:8–9) provides the basis for the chastisement that Komtino dared to consider Ibn Ezra's ideas comparable to his own patently inferior cogitations. In fact, Shabbetai insists, no less a figure than Maimonides had been Ibn Ezra's "faithful servant," again drawing on a biblical usage, echoing what was said about Moses with respect to God (Num 12:7).[30] With such veneration for Ibn Ezra as the gold standard of many in Byzantium, it is little wonder that Rashi never achieved there the prominence, let alone the preeminence, he so often won elsewhere.

Shabbetai's rebuke of Komtino is further nourished by an interesting source, an ethical will supposedly left by Maimonides to his son Abraham that casts Ibn Ezra as the only exegete worth studying. (In truth, Maimonides never mentions ibn Ezra and it is possible that he may never have read him.)[31] Indeed, Pseudo-Maimonides goes so far as to describe this twelfth-century Abraham as the like of the "[biblical] Abraham in his age." As Tamás Visi remarks, Ibn Ezra's commentary is canonized in this work. Had he cared to, Shabbetai might have noted that this missive of "Maimonides" also counseled avoidance of all works other than his own and Ibn Ezra's, urging in particular that "the words of most of the books by the people of *Ṣorfat*, that is, Francia," be shunned. Rashi goes unmentioned, but there is little doubt that the *Commẹntary* was one work the pseudepigraphist had in mind when having Maimonides pronounce these writings "useless and vain."[32] Apparently, Shabbetai and some of his Byzantine associates concurred in this assessment of "the books by the people of France."

The other great center of Ibn Ezra supercommentaries was Spain, to where Ibn Ezra's exegetical writings returned after their composition in Christian Europe following their author's flight from Muslim Iberia. There his works were engaged by Nahmanides and by a series of glossators, many riveted by the "secrets" concealed in Ibn Ezra's Torah commentary. The titles of Spanish Ibn Ezra supercommentaries make this fixation plain enough. There was Solomon Alconstantin's *Revealer of Depths*, Samuel ibn Matut's *Scroll of Secrets*, Gatigno's aforementioned *The Lord's Secret Is With Them That Fear Him*, Joseph ben Eliezer's *Revealer of Secrets*, and another gloss of the same name by Shem Tov ibn Shaprut. The larger dynamic in such works is what Moshe Idel describes as a twofold process of "arcanization." In the first stage, the Bible was said to contain secrets. In the second, some of the classic expositors who upheld this understanding, Ibn Ezra in the fore, themselves resorted to allusive literary strategies. The natural result was the composition of supercommentaries attempting to decode concealed ideas of these medieval classics.[33] Seen alongside the burgeoning commentary traditions on Maimonides's *Guide* and Nahmanides's Torah commentary, the latter devoted almost exclusively to kabbalistic secrets, the explosion of supercommentaries on Ibn Ezra reflects a development that saw the protective literary barriers erected by Ibn Ezra, Maimonides, and Nahmanides begin to be tested and eventually to crack.[34]

Yet Spain also highlights a supercommentarial trend that serves as a *pars pro toto* for the trajectory of exegetical supercommentary as the Middle Ages segued into early modern times. By the beginning of the fifteenth century, Sefardic glosses on Ibn Ezra began to wane while those on Rashi's *Commentary* multiplied through 1492 and beyond. One can only hazard guesses about the degree to which this retrenchment marks a response to the catastrophe that befell Spanish Jewry in 1391. The assault on Spanish Jewry led some to believe that the embrace of science and philosophy was a cause of religious enfeeblement that explained what they deemed Spanish Jewry's unjustified mass defection to Christianity.[35] True, the debate over faith and reason in Spain tended to focus on Maimonides more than Ibn Ezra but perhaps the sentiment helps to account for the sharp turn away from Ibn Ezra—though one must remember that it was precisely at this time that supercommentators in Spain began to read Rashi's *Commentary* in the manner of philosophically inspired techniques of Sefardic *'iyyun*.[36]

Ibn Ezra and Rashi's Resisting Readers

Ibn Ezra had conducted a critical audit of Rashi's *Commentary*, but mostly in concealed whispers.[37] Many of his methods and arguments resurface in the full-throated assault on Rashi carried out by the resisting readers. Consider Eleazar Ashkenazi. We have seen that he hailed Ibn Ezra as "the perfect, eminent scholar." He also joined Ibn Ezra in countless plain sense rejections of Rashi's midrashim. Unlike Ibn Ezra, though, Eleazar trumpeted his rejection of "Ha-Yitzhaki" with unabashed boldness. Recall Rashi's *gemaṭriya*-based midrash that reduced the 318 servants whom Abraham armed to a lone combatant, his servant Eliezer, in keeping with the numerical value of his name, which Ibn Ezra quietly dismissed—presumably in response to Rashi—as the "way of *derash*." Eleazar, by contrast, playing on Rashi's patronymic, rebuffed it as a ludicrous "joke."[38]

Ibn Ezra also presaged Eleazar's yen for naturalistic interpretation. Worried that the statement, "I have set my bow in the clouds, and it shall serve as a sign of the covenant between Me and the earth" (Gen 9:13) might lead some to think that rainbows were a post-diluvian novelty, Eleazar insists that they could have appeared "from the six days of creation since the rainbow is a natural thing." Still, as an exegete seeking to preserve not only laws of nature but also the scriptural letter, Eleazar follows Ibn Ezra's idea that after the flood God "intensified the power of the sun," causing processes inherent in creation to yield this "sign" as never before, just as the Torah intimated.[39] Rashi's lack of insistence on a permanent natural order made him oblivious to the issues Ibn Ezra and Eleazar felt compelled to address. One imagines Eleazar rolling his eyes at Rashi's further comment that God "pointed to the rainbow" and told Noah, "This is the sign of which I have spoken."[40]

Eleazar's quest for the esoteric, highlighted in the title of his work, *Revealer of Secrets*, furnishes another point of contact with Ibn Ezra that reminds us why he did not valorize the *Commentary*. His praise of Ibn Ezra as "the perfect, eminent scholar" is followed by the remark that he explained "concealed" passages by way of "hints that illumined our hearts." Eleazar even donned the garb of a supercommentator to decode Ibn Ezra's gnomic comments, like a famous one concerning divine providence ("the all knows every individual in a universal way and not through the particularity").[41]

Eleazar cites Ibn Ezra to buttress the necessity of a departure from the "prima facie meaning" (*mashma'am*) of some narratives, like the account of Abraham's encounter with the three angels. Maimonides denied this story's extramental reality, understanding it instead as a prophetic vision. This reading invited one of Nahmanides's harshest rebukes of him, as well as the counterclaim that Abraham's encounter with the angels was indeed historical, involving heavenly beings who appeared in visually accessible human form (*malbush*).[42] After offering an allegorical reading of its details, Eleazar presses the point that even those inclined to persist in the notion that "the matters are according to the prima facie meaning" must desist since this prospect was "remote, as Ibn Ezra explained."[43]

A different sort of secret to which Ibn Ezra cryptically alludes also rivets Eleazar's attention, as in due course it would that of Baruch Spinoza, who invoked Ibn Ezra when making his case for the post-Mosaic authorship of the Pentateuch.[44] This secret concerned the testimony that "the Canaanites were then in the land" (Gen 12:6) when Abraham arrived there. Ibn Ezra observes that possibly the Canaanites were at that time taking the land from others, but if this not be the case, "then I have a secret (*sod*), but the enlightened person will keep silent." At bar was the meaning of "then." According to the first explanation, it meant that Canaanites were "then" conquering the land from others. As for the secret, there were multiple interpretations, including a most daring one: that Ibn Ezra saw the verse as a post-Mosaic accretion since it implied authorship after the time the Canaanites had been expelled from the land, which happened only after Moses's death.[45] Presumably aware of Ibn Ezra, Eleazar is keen to refute this view: "'the Canaanite was then in the land'—the words of Moses." His interpretation reads the temporal particle according to Ibn Ezra's first opinion (and, in more general form, that of

Rashi): "then" meant that just as Abraham arrived in the land the Canaanites, until then based in southwesterly locales, were now diffusing throughout the whole of it.[46]

At this point, Eleazar could have moved on, but he instead becomes a supercommentator, citing Ibn Ezra and then readily divulging what his forerunner had cloaked: "that is to say, they are not the words of Moses."[47] Why explain this view of Ibn Ezra, with which Eleazar claims to disagree? A suspicious reader might say he wished to disclose the correctness of Ibn Ezra's view despite his words to the contrary and note his remark that it was "possible"—that is, not imperative—to interpret the words in their "plain sense," an unusual use of *kifeshuṭo* that means "in keeping with the doctrine of Mosaic authorship." Yet elsewhere Eleazar refuses to "assent" to post-Mosaisms and insists that "Moses composed all of the Torah through the holy spirit."[48] Even if he denied the Torah's composite authorship, he explains Ibn Ezra as affirming it in a manner that reinforces his place in a world of discourse shaped decisively by the Andalusian sage who stood at a far remove from Rashi—who, whatever nuances he entertained regarding the formation of the Torah, surely never contemplated later accretions to Genesis.[49]

Though shaped by Ibn Ezra, Eleazar can also reprimand him. In some cases, he finds straightforward errors.[50] His rebuke can even be stark, as in the case of the Akedah, where "the sage Ibn Ezra" successfully exposes the "nakedness" of "many views that proliferated among the commentators" but fails "to cover his own nakedness."[51] Ibn Ezra was, in the end, second to Maimonides in Eleazar's estimation, such that he minces no words in charging Ibn Ezra with the unpardonable sin of failing to anticipate Maimonides when it came to understanding the garden story as the tale of humankind's fall from a life of reason aimed at distinguishing "truth and falsehood" into a life "consumed by pleasure":

> "You will be like *'elohim*" (Genesis 3:5)—as the Targum [interprets]: "as rulers." So Maimonides interpreted in the *Guide* [I:2], meaning like people consumed by pleasure in the manner of deputies and kings who experience good and bad due to their predominant immersion in bodily pleasures but who know not truth and falsehood. It is false to say that " *'elohim*" alludes [here] to the separate intellects, as implied by the words of the sage Ibn Ezra.[52]

Still, whatever the local disagreements, Ibn Ezra's analysis is, Eleazar makes clear, the best place to turn for a running commentary. Even in sharp divergence, as here, he still foregoes the *ad hominem* disparagement to which he subjects "Ha-Yitzhaki" and some of his midrashic ideas.[53] Even in rejection, he treats Ibn Ezra with a seriousness that contrasts with the subversive laughter he was sometimes keen to induce with respect to Rashi's *Commentary*.

Pseudo-Rabad is another resisting reader of Rashi whose energetic receptivity to Ibn Ezra at times drives criticisms of the *Commentary*. His initial disparagement of Rashi as one who defies rules of language and canons of reasonability recalls Ibn Ezra's insistence on just these factors as the guiding principles of exegesis. Elsewhere, other aspects of Ibn Ezra's exegetical acuity, like deft attention to biblical chronology, inform a head-on clash with Rashi's faulty midrashic approach. For example, Pseudo-Rabad reprises and expands on Ibn Ezra to undermine the interpretive time frame for the story of Judah and Tamar. On its opening verse, "About that time Judah went down from his brothers" (Gen 38:1), Rashi, following a midrash, comments that the brothers "brought him down from his important position." In his otherwise textually baseless reconstruction, the brothers see their father's anguish at the loss of his beloved son, Joseph, they repent, and they rebuke Judah, to whom they had looked up, telling him: "You advised us to sell him [Joseph]. Had you advised us to return him we would have listened to you." The reconstruction seems to suffer from at least one glaring problem, since it presupposes that the narrative sequence reflected the actual chronology of events—that is, that the sale of Joseph occurred prior to Judah's descent. Ibn Ezra explains why he was "constrained" to reject the sequential reading—namely, that a careful calculation showed that it was not possible to squeeze Judah's story into the twenty-two-year period between the two stories on either side of it, the sale of Joseph and descent of Jacob and his family to Egypt. After all, Judah's biography encompassed his marriage to Shuah's daughter, the maturation of their three sons, the marriage of the eldest son to Tamar, Judah's unintentional impregnation of Tamar resulting in the birth of twins Perez and Zerah, and even the births of Perez's sons, Hezron and Hamul, confirmed by the genealogy of Jacob's entourage given as they entered Egypt.[54] Pseudo-Rabad pronounces the argument "known and evident to anyone who understands."[55] He does not say that it was made known *to him* by Ibn Ezra.

Other arguments traceable to Ibn Ezra appear in *Sefer hassagot* even if Pseudo-Rabad fails to identify their provenance. Consider two examples that have already been discussed. Rashi taught that the sea miraculously "spewed" Egyptians ashore where they engaged in a final death struggle and that the Israelites saw them there. Pseudo-Rabad offers as a counterreading that the Israelites stood on the shore as the Egyptians drowned in the sea, just as Ibn Ezra had before him. Similar is the case of Pseudo-Rabad's idea that the Israelites constructed the tabernacle from trees adjacent to Mount Sinai, not ones planted in Egypt by Jacob. Where Ibn Ezra left his duel with Rashi undeclared, Pseudo-Rabad scoffs at the midrashic interpretation, using locutions like "void" and "nothingness."[56]

Pseudo-Rabad also presses Ibn Ezra's *argumentum a silentio* against midrashic miracles that Rashi makes an integral part of the narrative. Abraham's deliverance from Nimrod's fiery furnace teaches an invaluable lesson about trust in God and God's supernatural protection of the bearers of faith. But did this event really happen? For readers of Rashi it certainly did. Readers of Ibn Ezra could not be as certain: While he pays obeisance to the possibility of a received and hence indubitably true tradition in rabbinic hands that Abraham was plucked from the fire, he also argues that the Torah would surely have reported the story had it occurred. Pseudo-Rabad follows Ibn Ezra's subversive argument while failing to mention the prospect of an inerrant tradition. He also cuts the textual ground out from under Rashi's reading. Where Rashi finds in the phrase *'ur kasdim* an allusion to the furnace, Pseudo-Rabad brusquely insists that it is "a toponym, as rabbi Abraham ibn Ezra explained."[57]

In Rashi's reading, the Torah was more miracle-studded even than it seemed. Taking inspiration from Ibn Ezra, Pseudo-Rabad often views Rashi's supernatural midrashic impositions on the text as nothing more than a distortion. Some examples already seen illustrate the Ibn Ezra connection. Rashi thinks that the 318 fighting men raised by Abraham (Gen 14:14) reduced to Eliezer. Pseudo-Rabad rejoins that had Abraham and his servant dealt a decisive defeat to multiple kings and their armies by themselves, it would have been a miracle that the Torah ought to have recorded. He sides with Ibn Ezra in arguing that the *gemaṭriya* adduced in support of the interpretation has no purchase. Pseudo-Rabad uses the same argument to discount other miracles that Rashi reports in the *Commentary*: Moses's alleged staying of the sun ("Were it so, it would have been written as it is written in the case of Joshua"), the miraculous well accompanying the Israelites in the wilderness, and, of course, the claim that Jochebed was 130 years old when she bore Moses. Here as elsewhere, Ibn Ezra goes unmentioned, but there is no gainsaying his role as Pseudo-Rabad's guiding spirit and, at times, the supplier of the pungent rhetoric ("affliction") used by Pseudo-Rabad in his rebuttal.

Pseudo-Rabad's exegetical minimalism can involve creative adaptation of an idea from Maimonides accompanied by the critique of *gemaṭriya* fashioned by Ibn Ezra. One stricture aims to refute Rashi's midrashic account of the offerings of the twelve "princes of Israel" at the time of the tabernacle's construction (Num 7:12–89), which explains the outwardly identical character of the offerings as recounted in the text (creating a massive repetition) by imbuing the same details of each prince's offerings with diverse historical-symbolic meanings relevant to each prince's tribe. At times, this involved a foray into numerology, while Rashi also draws on midrashic ideas known to him from Moses Hadarshan, a Narbonesse preacher of the previous generation. Where a prince brought a "silver bowl," Rashi might explain it in terms of its *gematriya*, which amounted to 930, corresponding to "the years of Adam, the first man."[58] To Pseudo-Rabad, all such interpretations are doomed, resting as they do on a false premise that there must be some meaning to the varying weights of the offerings. One who seeks such meaning "walks in darkness." After all, every object has to have "some weight or other."[59] Pseudo-Rabad's claim here apparently refits a daring Maimonidean motif concerning the lunacy of seeking meaning in each detail of the sacrificial cult. To Maimonides, it is clear that "no cause will ever be found for the fact that one particular sacrifice consists in a lamb and another in a ram. . . . The same holds for your asking why seven lambs and not eight have been prescribed, for a similar question would have been put if eight or ten or twenty had been prescribed."[60] Add a numerological element to Rashi's misguided view that all the details of the princes' offerings have meaning, says Pseudo-Rabad, and one can conjure "any words of absurdity" one wishes, as Rashi does "in many places." Here Pseudo-Rabad assails the interpretive anarchy that results from *gematriya*, exactly as Ibn Ezra does.[61] When Pseudo-Rabad asserts that Rashi's exegesis is "darkness and gloom" (*hoshekh va-'afelah*), he again may have in mind Ibn Ezra, who uses the phrase to criticize excessive allegory.[62] Pseudo-Rabad concludes with a parting shot: perhaps Rashi got his idea from Moses the Preacher "in a dream," a snicker that also may owe to Ibn Ezra's rich lexicon of put-downs.[63]

Turning to the third resisting reader, Aaron Aboulrabi, we find classic objections of Ibn Ezra appearing as distinctively inflected by Pseudo-Rabad. Aboulrabi's verdict on the "spurious" idea that Jochebed was one hundred and thirty at the time of Moses's birth is a case in point. Beyond lying "outside the natural order," it meets with the objection that, as a marvel that surpasses Sarah's conception of Isaac at ninety, the Torah surely would have recorded the greater wonder of Jochebed conceiving at an older age (Ibn Ezra's objection), made still more miraculous owing to the fact that life spans had diminished between Sarah's day and Jochebed's day (Pseudo-Rabad's supplement to Ibn Ezra). In the case of Judah and Tamar, Aboulrabi offers a more sanguine initial assessment of the approach in the *Commentary* before siding with Ibn Ezra's idea as Pseudo-Rabad refined it. Rashi's reading of "Judah went down from his brothers" (Gen 38:1) was, we recall, understood in terms of a demotion from his "important position" ("Had you advised us to return him, we would have listened"). Pseudo-Rabad thought it "evident to anyone who understands" that this reading was chronologically impossible. As a purely exegetical matter, Aboulrabi initially genuflects in Rashi's direction, locating a "precise textual inference" to support him. Had the Torah meant to relate to topography, there would have been no reason to mention brothers. For this reason, Rashi thinks the wording suggests a reference to a change in attitude towards Judah's status in the family. Yet Aboulrabi adds that there are those who wonder how Rashi's interpretation can be true given the chronology. Aboulrabi contents himself to present the difficulty raised by Ibn Ezra, doing so in a manner that tracks its formulation in *Sefer hassagot*.[64]

Aboulrabi can have sharp words for those who depart from Ibn Ezra's realistic approach. Consider his handling of the writing of "all the words of this Torah" on stones to be erected after the Israelites crossed the Jordan (Deut 27:8). Tannaitic sources divided on just what was recorded, some limiting the text "only" to Deuteronomy and others to "what the nations of the world would want." Rashi, on the authority of the Mishnah, contended that the Torah was engraved on the stones in "seventy languages."[65] Sensing a major logistical challenge, Nahmanides devises two solutions: either the Torah was squeezed onto very large stones or the command was executed by way of a miracle. Ibn Ezra solves the problem in a manner true to form by reducing it to naturalistic dimensions. A small writing surface sufficed if what was to be written was not too lengthy. He therefore commends Saadia Gaon who "handsomely explained" that not all the Torah's words were inscribed on the stones, only a sampling of commandments.[66] Aboulrabi likewise assesses that only "fundaments of the Torah," the commandments in a bare litany, appeared since "not even a thousand stones could encompass" the Torah in its entirety. The person who thought "all" the Torah's words appeared "by way of a miracle" was "a dunce who knows nothing" (see Prov 9:3).[67] Ibn Ezra escaped this critique, but Rashi, as well as Nahmanides in one of his interpretations, did not.

Aboulrabi's approach to Og's bedstead is in step with Ibn Ezra, although he might also have been thinking of Maimonides. The Torah stated that it was nine cubits long and four cubits broad "by a man's forearm (*be-'amat 'ish*)" (Deut 3:11). On the basis of a talmudic source, Rashi takes the "man" in proportion to whom the measurement was given to be Og, a remnant of a race of giants (*refa'im*), yielding the conclusion that the bedstead was immense. Disputing Rashi (without saying so) is Ibn Ezra, who issues the pithy rejoinder that the measurement was according to a forearm of "a normal person" of whom, at any rate, Ibn Ezra had Og as being only double the size. If it was as Rashi opined, then the Torah would have said nothing about what it purported to relay since on the midrashic reading, one could only know Og's size by knowing that of his enormous forearm, a datum absent in the text. Then, too, a moment's thought shows that Og lacks "any semblance of human form," according to Rashi, since if he was nine of his own cubits tall, his arms would proportionally be greatly undersized.[68] Maimonides also claims that "*be-'amat 'ish*" refers to "an average person" rather than some unique cubit of Og.[69]

Formally, Aboulrabi's remarks on Og gloss the *Commentary* but substantively they constitute a stricture on it informed by Ibn Ezra:

> "By a man's forearm"—The Straight one explained: "after the forearm of Og." But this contravenes common sense (*sevara'*). Were it so, the length of his bedstead would remain unknown since [to derive a measurement] we would first have to know his cubit relative to ours. . . . Thus the interpretation of "by a man's forearm" refers to an average person, in which case we are informed of his [Og's] length. Had he filled the full width of the bedstead . . . this would have deviated from human nature since any person four cubits in height will be one cubit in width, it [the ratio between the two] being a fourth.[70]

In effect, Aboulrabi transforms Ibn Ezra's surreptitious criticism of Rashi into an open rebuff, ending with a pun on a liturgical formula: "everything scripture says is 'true [*'emet*, playing on *'amat*] and enduring.'"[71] In context, the jest contains within it the assertion that the Torah speaks truly, that is reasonably, as Ibn Ezra and Maimonides interpret, not according to Rashi's confected midrashic fancies.

Nowhere is Aboulrabi's kinship with the distinctive religious outlook of Ibn Ezra more marked than in interpretations informed by astrology and astral magic, that part of Ibn Ezra's legacy where, on a Maimonidean reckoning, the requisite sharp lines between nature-based science and the irrational went hopelessly missing. In at least one case, Aboulrabi rereads to astrological effect a midrash in the *Commentary*. Rashi feels compelled to explain why there should be an equal number of cities of refuge on both the east and west sides of the Jordan River, given the imbalance of two and a half tribes residing in the east and nine and a half tribes residing in the west. His conclusion was that God "equalized the number of their refuge cities because Gilead [east of the Jordan] had many murderers."[72] Rashi leaves it at that, but Aboulrabi wonders why the inadvertent murder rate in these locales should differ so, suggesting that it has to do with "the nature of a place and its stellar aspect"—that is, astral-geographic features of the territories in question.[73] The argument is congruent with Ibn Ezra and his supercommentators who explain biblical laws and narratives having to do with the land of Israel in astral-geographic terms.[74] Aboulrabi presents it as if it were the view of Rashi and his midrashic source, although Rashi surely knew nothing of it.

Astral magic also figures in Aboulrabi's answer to the famous question raised in the *Commentary*'s opening line: Why did the Torah, understood primarily as divine law, commence not with the first commandment applicable to the nation in Exodus 12 but with narratives of the world's creation, stories of the nation's ancestors, and so forth? Rashi answers that all of the long prologue to the law was necessary to secure Israel's right to the land. Aboulrabi, reflecting a world of ideas familiar from Ibn Ezra, says that the creation story and subsequent narratives dispel the suspicions of "skeptics" (*meharherim*) that the Israelites' triumphs as described in Genesis and Exodus occurred owing to "service of the heavens performed through their wisdom [which is] akin to the craft of talismans." The accounts of creation through the miracle-studded reception of the Torah confute wrongheaded overemphasis on astral forces and stress that special divine providence shaped the chosen people's distinctive destiny.[75]

In thinking about how much Eleazar Ashkenazi, Pseudo-Rabad, and Aaron Aboulrabi make up an intellectual circle, one must seek criteria such as chronological and geographical proximity, shared terminology, and so forth. Beyond these, Dov Schwartz proposes as another criterion for the establishment of a circle scholars ranged around an authoritative figure who fructifies their ideas and modes of expression.[76] Seen thus, the resisting readers do constitute a circle, although one cannot speak fully to the issue of temporal and geographical proximity in the absence of confirmed data on Pseudo-Rabad's time and place. All of them certainly wrote within two and half centuries, though the likelihood of a much narrower temporal compass is strong. All have a clear or highly probable affiliation with eastern Mediterranean centers. All, as we have seen, were inspired by Ibn Ezra. Aboulrabi draws directly on Pseudo-Rabad. To these data points we can add what might be seen as one last criterion for a circle: a common foe. In excoriating Rashi's *Commentary*, the resisting readers were not alone. They were joined by another rock-hard rationalist of later medieval times: the author of *'Alilot devarim*.

The Book of Accusations: *"In Every Place Where His Name Is Invoked"*

The author of *'Alilot devarim* was not a resisting reader of Rashi in the same sense as those discussed thus far. He pondered Rashi's successes and failures only briefly, not in a work devoted to exegetical minutiae, as did the other resisting readers, but as part of his attempt to fathom the interminability of his people's exile and seek a remedy. In a historical retrospective, he cites as a main cause of the post-rabbinic "dark ages" the sundering of the integration of thought and deed that was the classical tradition's glory.[77] The cleavage is manifest in halakhic "abridgements" (*qiṣṣurim*) like Isaac Alfasi's code that reduced the Talmud to a "practical component pertinent [in post-temple times], omitting all else" and Rashi's Talmud commentaries that, while they otherwise "enlightened the nation's eyes," focused only on the "practical element [of the Talmud]."[78] As the commentary on *'Alilot devarim* clarifies, what this means is that these works do nothing to explain the part of the Talmud devoted to "the sciences" (*madda'ot*).[79]

Turning to Rashi as biblical exegete, *'Alilot devarim* finds that his partial success as an expositor of oral Torah has no parallel in his commentaries on scripture, despite his similar effort to "open the eyes of the blind." On the contrary, "the opposite occurred" (see Esth 9:1), and Rashi "blinded the eyes of God's righteous ones . . . and steered them to confusion." The key lapse involves a category error. Rashi conceived midrashim as interpretations when in fact they were uttered to "innovate things" rather than unfold "the verses' plain sense." The sages never for a moment thought that "these *derashot* should serve as explanations of those verses," as Rashi did. The result is that "most" of Rashi's commentaries constitute not interpretations (*perushim*) but "talmudic *derashot*."[80] Ibn Ezra had, in effect, also accused Rashi of misapprehending the genre of midrash. *'Alilot devarim* finds it pertinent to reinforce his point by adducing, like Ibn Ezra, the sages' dictum that scripture is "never divested of its plain sense."[81] Like Pseudo-Rabad and Aboulrabi, the author proposes another way in which Rashi falls short, noting that while some midrashim adduced by him were "profound," they require clarification by "enlightened ones" (*maskilim*) of the sort Rashi is incapable of supplying.[82]

Laying bare the source of all the missteps, *'Alilot devarim* pronounces Rashi "devoid of the science of logic, as is crystal-clear to anybody who has delved into this [branch of] wisdom even a little." In so stating, the author reverts to an earlier rebuke of the failure of Jews "to hark and to understand even a little of the science of logic, which is the root of all wisdom." In this respect, Rashi appears no better than the average Jew, barely half-competent to explain the divine word. The notion of logic's indispensability runs like a bright line through *'Alilot devarim*, not least in the author's account of his own liberation from superstition. Having been told that this discipline must be spurned as pernicious to faith, he discovered that it is actually the nurturing ground for all "good intelligence" and the source of any fear and knowledge of God as one can hope to attain.[83]

'Alilot devarim's indignation regarding the leading Franco-German Bible commentator is of a piece with his broader diagnosis of Jewish decline and fall. Although Ashkenazim go unmentioned in the work, an introduction possibly by the author or a close acquaintance (lacking in the printed edition but found in the earliest manuscript) refers to the "virgin of Israel in Ashkenaz" and her "defects in the eyes of those who love her."[84] Indeed, in a pioneering study, Yisrael Ta-Shma shows that the defects condemned in *'Alilot devarim* were habits of mind or religious practices associated dominantly or exclusively with Ashkenazic Jewry.[85] One example is what the author calls the "trespasses" that abound in the Ashkenazic prayer rite, replete as it is with problematic liturgical poetry of the sort that he says Maimonides inveighed against, and that Ibn Ezra famously lambasted in his celebrated critique of Kalirian *piyyuṭ*.[86] With slight hyperbole, one can say that *'Alilot devarim* proclaims the uninformed superstitions and deviant practices of Ashkenazic Jewry as the principle cause of Judaism's recent decay, although in his guise as commentator on his work he praises Rashi's student-colleague Joseph Kara as a sound practitioner of plain sense interpretation, fleetingly diluting his criticism of all things Ashkenazic.[87] The signs of a (limited) nascent late medieval philosophical culture in Ashkenaz, especially in Bohemia, which included adaptations of Maimonides, were clearly unknown to the author of *'Alilot devarim*, who may have predated these developments.[88]

Beyond the effects of the *Commentary*, *'Alilot devarim* is incensed by other Ashkenazic curricular distortions. First came the dialectical techniques of Talmud study honed by the Tosafists that, as he puts it, "your ancestors did not envision" (see Deut 32:17). Then, in his own day, came the casuistry classed under the rubric of *pilpul*. Of the latter, *'Alilot devarim* caustically says that while "some call this craft *pilpul*" others call it "*bilbul* [confusion], and so it is."[89] *'Alilot devarim*'s author, now in his role as glossator, explains how "the accusations" referenced in the title of the work can be seen to apply first and foremost to "the casuists" (*ba'alei ha-pilpul*). In so doing, he may revert to Ibn Ezra's interpretation of the biblical phrase from Deuteronomy 22 invoked in the work's title.[90] The author also draws an implicit connection between Rashi's exegesis and *pilpul*. As he calls the latter "*bilbul*" in the body of his work, so, in the commentary, he says that Rashi's biblical commentaries lead to "confusion" (*bilbul*), reminding his reader of his earlier characterization of *pilpul* as an illogical jumble of hair-splitting casuistry.[91]

In arguing logic's centrality to sound exegesis, the author of *'Alilot devarim* joined some rationalists who thought that this philosophic subdiscipline provided a royal road—perhaps the only one—to proper interpretation. Although Ibn Ezra had sung its praises—"How noble is the science of logic"—his use of it was rudimentary.[92] Maimonides, by contrast, wrote a treatise on the topic and fused logical principles born of Greco-Arabic philosophy with Andalusi-Jewish linguistic teachings to forestall fallacious scriptural interpretation, especially as it related to God.[93] Samuel ibn Tibbon may have been the first exegete to do the same in Hebrew biblical commentaries in ways that have been judged a signal contribution to the field.[94] Joseph ibn Kaspi cast logic as a *sine qua non* for reliable interpretation and chalked up the failures of his predecessors to deficiencies on this score. It was Ibn Kaspi who, invoking the logical proposition that "a thing is only known by its contrariety," urged study of the *Commentary* on the grounds that it revealed its "contrariety"—that is, true expositions propounded by Ibn Ezra.[95] Seen in this light, *'Alilot devarim*'s blame of Rashi for his ignorance of logic partakes of the work's stress on the inestimable cost of the Jewish failure to cultivate the sciences.

Foreseeing that some might try to exculpate the people and its leaders by attributing failures to inadvertence, the author of *'Alilot devarim* thunders prophetically that the nation's decline and attendant misery has been fully earned, having God intone: "Behold, I sent to you after the Talmud's closure a man in whom the divine spirit resided whose name was as that of his master." Piercing the vagueness is *'Alilot devarim*'s invariably keen commentary, which identifies the divine emissary as Moses Maimonides, whose namesake was the biblical Moses. His "noble, incomparable *Guide of the Perplexed*" explained of the sciences all that it was fitting to reveal "to the sort of addressee for whom it was composed." The work held out the prospect of a spiritual renaissance as did Maimonides's other writings, especially his *Mishneh torah*, which not only encompassed the "scientific disciplines" but also harmoniously integrated them. Ancient glories could have been restored had Jews heeded the call and, in fact, some did "repent from the sin of perplexity." However, the Jewish people's "evil shepherds" put the "divine" *Guide* to the pyre as if it were a work of soothsayers. They buried *Mishneh torah* in a sea of falsifying commentary that drowned out its aims. Lost was the unity of knowledge embracing all sciences and the integration of theory and practice that was Maimonides's supreme achievement. The people had repulsed its redeemer. Jews could now hardly claim inadvertence for a failure that was in fact a matter of "rebellion and iniquity."[96]

'Alilot devarim sought to mount a counterinsurgency and poise others to join. It was directed in the first instance at leaders and rabbis who lock "the gates of Torah and wisdom" before their congregations.[97] This aim seemingly helps to explain the work's authorial mask of "Palmon ben Pelet." The alias summons an insurrectionist movement by hearkening to On ben Pelet, a member of the desert rebellion against Moses and Aaron. *'Alilot devarim* also

seeks to foment a mutiny, now against leaders who have brought the people to spiritual wrack and ruin alongside untold depths of political enfeeblement. (As regards the latter, *'Alilot devarim* made an astonishing suggestion, hoping that those who had gone over to "the religion of the Trinity"—namely, the *conversos*—might in time return, the better to dethrone the religious establishment and bring political rationality and thence redemption to their erstwhile people.)[98]

Assessing the role of differing modes of biblical scholarship in creating the religious wreckage, the commentary on *'Alilot devarim* quietly contrasts the midrashic hermeneutic of Rashi with the approach of Maimonides. In the body, Rashi's interpretations are said to constitute not "explanations" (*perushim*) but midrashim whose original authors never intended their use for interpretive purposes. Explaining this idea as *'Alilot devarim*'s expositor, the author states that this truth is evident to anyone who knows "the definition of interpretation" (*geder ha-perush*), then describes midrashim as "poetical conceits." This definition is the one found for nonlegal midrashic dicta in the *Guide*. The author proceeds typically, leaving an idea at the level of insinuation in the body of the text for sharper clarification and elaboration in the commentary. In this case, the reader who troubles to consult the commentary learns, in effect, that the corrective for Rashi's failed exegesis is interpretive principles supplied by Maimonides. Naturally, the commentator also adds that a correct understanding of such midrashic "poetical conceits" requires an "explanation by enlightened ones."[99]

A subtle shift in rhetoric in *'Alilot devarim*'s treatment of Rashi's exegesis points to the outsized impact of one of his commentaries above all others. The author speaks initially of Rashi's explication of "scriptural things" (*devarim she-bi-khetav*) in the plural and of his glosses "in them"—that is, the commentaries in the plural. But then he goes on to rue the deleterious effect of "this commentary of his" in the singular. Parsing the reference to "every place where his [Rashi's] name is invoked," the commentary clarifies that what is meant is all places where Jews are "accustomed to his commentary" (*nohagim perusho*)—again, his *commentary*, in the singular. By the end of his discussion, that is, *'Alilot devarim* speaks not of the impact and defects of Rashi's commentaries but of his *Commentary*.

In a passage redolent of both Ibn Ezra and Maimonides, *'Alilot devarim* offers a startling assessment of the scope and nature of the *Commentary*'s injurious impact:

> It has arisen from this commentary of his in every place where his name is invoked that the children of Israel find themselves stripped of

> the Torah's and scripture's plain sense such that even if there were to be mentioned before them the explanations of one who explained the words of scripture according to their plain sense without any strangeness (*zarut*), they would ridicule him and insist that his words are estranged with respect to the scriptural plain sense. This is a cause of blindness and confusion with respect to the perfection of souls.[100]

If the goal of biblical interpretation is to uncover the plain sense in a way that avoids imputing irrational "strangeness" to the divine word, the reach of the *Commentary* had made this impossible to an untold degree.[101] Rashi's dominance meant that any attempt to promote the plain sense could only be subject to ridicule. This statement is almost as if taken from Eleazar Ashkenazi's plaint about the multitude of Jews engulfed in a sea of midrashic distortion that now prefer midrash, wrongly understood, to the plain sense ("they believe in them and find them congenial more than the Torah's plain sense. Any discerning person ought to bewail the fact that they have drowned in a sea of *derashot*.")[102]

There is more. By distancing Jews from rationality, the *Commentary* effects blindness and confusion not just with regard to scripture's true meaning but also "with respect to the perfection of souls." In writing those words, *'Alilot devarim* must have had in mind Maimonides's intellectualist vision of human perfection. So understood, the *Commentary*'s spread is more deleterious than meets the eye. Threatened is the very purpose of revelation, as Rashi abets the falling away from rationality that *'Alilot devarim* sees as the root of the people's spiritual malaise and sorry historical state.

Bonfil found *'Alilot devarim*'s assault on Jewish antirationalists lacking in "especially original ideas,"[103] but leaving aside a final global judgment on this claim, this assessment hardly applies to the work's critique of the *Commentary*. First, *'Alilot devarim* formulated in abstract terms what Ibn Ezra implied in arguing against Rashi— namely, that the *Commentary* missed the mark owing to a failure to grasp the genre of midrash, mistaking for interpretations what were intended, in Maimonides's terms, as "poetical conceits" bearing edification having nothing to do with exegesis. *'Alilot devarim* also innovates in urging in especially forthright terms the deleterious effects of the *Commentary* on understanding of not just the Torah but also the Jewish religious mentality, inculcating misconceptions that deflect Rashi's readers from the path to spiritual perfection. At the same time, *'Alilot devarim* surveys the terrain and proclaims the *Commentary*'s ever greater reach within the Jewish world.

For current purposes, this historical assessment marks a crucial point, even as it apparently spurs the author's response. Such deficiencies as *'Alilot devarim* found in Rashi's exegesis might have gone unremarked had it not been for a lamentable development that its author spotlights: the *Commentary*'s authorization across world Jewry. Rashi's reading of the Torah had become an ineluctable presence; Jews were increasingly becoming (in the words of the commentary on *'Alilot devarim* as seen earlier) "accustomed" to Rashi's interpretation of the Torah. The *Commentary* had become, in a word, canonical. In this fact, *'Alilot devarim*'s author, a man with a dire message, heard a death knell for the enlightened enterprise he took Judaism to be.

Resisting Reading in Religiocultural Context

In what socioreligious setting did *'Alilot devarim*'s author sound his alarm, and how might it explain the phenomenon of resisting reading of the *Commentary*? Dov Schwartz observes that "works sometimes thought canonical in the West were not conceived as such in the East."[104] Seen in the arc of its afterlife over its first half millennium, locales in the East would seem to be the main center of gravity for resistance to the *Commentary* (though this assessment in some measure depends on the accuracy of some of the historical reconstructions given here of the origins of works we have studied). Scholarly opinion divides on whether *'Alilot devarim* fits this pattern, in also belonging to an eastern Mediterranean setting.

'Alilot devarim's origins are murky, though a once-common view about origins in Spain can safely be dispatched.[105] Far more compelling is Ta-Shma's suggestion that *'Alilot devarim* is the work of a fifteenth-century scholar of Ashkenazic stock writing in Italy, although Ta-Shma remained open to the work's possible Sefardic authorship.[106] After the Black Death, large numbers of Ashkenazim immigrated to Italy. By the second half of the fifteenth century, they constituted a significant portion of the Jewish population there. On this view, *'Alilot devarim*'s vitriol was produced by an Ashkenazic renegade whose conversion to rationalism led him, among other things, to censure the biblical scholarship of the most important exegete of his native tradition. Perhaps the heretofore overlooked reference to Joseph Kara in *'Alilot devarim*'s commentary lends a bit of ballast to Ta-Shma's claim, as it seems reasonable to assume that so obscure an Ashkenazic exegete is more likely to have been known to an offshoot of that tradition than to a Sefardic sage. If the claim of its Ashkenazic filiation is correct, *'Alilot devarim* would prove an extreme example of the trend attested elsewhere of the veneration of Sefardic rationalism's leading figure by certain late medieval intellectuals with Ashkenazic roots. In *'Alilot devarim*, recoil from Rashi is the obverse of adoration of Maimonides.

Bonfil argues for *'Alilot devarim*'s fourteenth-century provenance and its composition by a Sefardic sage who came into contact with Ashkenazic mores in Crete or southern Italy. Bonfil even has a candidate for the author, the Castile-born Ibn Ezra supercommentator Joseph ben Eliezer, who traveled in the Christian and Muslim East, including Crete, where an Ashkenazic community did flourish. Joseph, who copied an Ibn Ezra supercommentary while in Crete in 1375, may even have met one of Rashi's resisting readers, Eleazar Ashkenazi, whose Torah commentary, completed no earlier than 1371 and copied in Crete in 1399, bore the very same name as Joseph's Ibn Ezra supercommentary, *Ṣafenat pa'neaḥ*.[107] Taking some historical license, we can imagine these two seekers of secrets exchanging their identically titled works. That said, one must square Bonfil's proposal that Joseph might be the author of *'Alilot devarim* with the absence of anti-Rashi animus in his supercommentary such as one could expect to find were the author of *'Alilot devarim* and the Ibn Ezra supercommentator identical. The impasse remains: *'Alilot devarim*'s author was either a Sefardic scholar repelled by Ashkenazic fideism and credulity or a thinker of Ashkenazic origin sworn to rationalism.

Whatever the way out from the impasse over its authorship, *'Alilot devarim* provides a clear sense of religious ferment in multicultural communities of the sort that flourished in parts of Italy and the eastern Mediterranean. We have visited places like Venice-ruled Crete and seen how conflict unfolded as scholars arrived in the East from intellectually and religiously divergent centers in Spain, France, Germany, North Africa, and Sicily, where they interacted with local (Romaniote) religious currents and intellectual streams. We have seen how waves of Ashkenazic immigrants shaped the *Commentary*'s fortunes in Byzantine and possibly even Arabophone communities that dotted the Jewish Mediterranean. Aboulrabi told of his sojourn in a yeshiva in northern Italy, where many Ashkenazic savants, like Judah Mintz, head of the Ashkenazi yeshivah in Padua, made their home. There he heard a comment of Rashi interpreted by "one of the garlic eaters"—that is, Ashkenazim.[108] He would have carried these experiences with him as he became more enmeshed in the ferment of the multicultural Jewish world in the East, an environment that, we surmise, bestirred the sorts of withering frontal assaults on Rashi found in *'Alilot devarim* and the resisting readers.

We have seen how in the East, those not indifferent to the *Commentary* generally took a dim view of it, possibly reacting to the influx of Ashkenazic culture into the region more generally but, in a surprising development, also potentially taking their lead from scholars of Ashkenazic origin who advocated types of rationalism inspired by Maimonides, Ibn Ezra, and their Western European disciples. The earliest example may be Eleazar ben Mattathias, whose years in France presumably saw him imbibe a traditional Ashkenazic education, but whose removal to places like Crete and Old Cairo bestirred his relish of philosophy. Eleazar Ashkenazi, whose origins in the Franco-German sphere, however attenuated, appear from his name, extolled Samuel ibn Tibbon and Jacob Anatoli for imparting the wisdom that "spread to our [part of the] exile, whence we saw a great light." In *'Alilot devarim*'s day, another immigrant with northern European roots, Moses Ashkenazi, inaugurated the debate in Crete over transmigration of souls, basing himself on an astringent Aristotelianism.[109] His son Saul followed in a similar path, learning from the Averroist Elijah Delmedigo. Descendant of the first scholarly Ashkenazic immigrant to Crete, Judah ben Shemaryah, Elijah studied Jewish philosophy in Crete before attaining fame in Padua.[110]

Of course, not all Ashkenazic Jews who came east swore fealty to philosophy or converted to rationalism. Elijah Delmedigo's ancestor Judah, a probable student of the prominent fourteenth-century German rabbi Meir Segal of Fulda, wrote a Torah commentary in which he denounced "the accused philosophy" and "accursed philosophers." Though not closed to science, this first Ashkenazic scholarly presence in Crete censured radical rationalist ideas like denial of the world's createdness, taking even Maimonides to task for "leaning to the words of the philosophers" on the matter.[111] Unfortunately, most of his Torah commentary is lost, leaving little basis for speculation about the place of Rashi's *Commentary* in it.

Other factors help to explain the phenomenon of strong critiques of the *Commentary* in the East besides those canvassed already in our study of its resisting readers—namely, eastern Mediterranean veneration of Ibn Ezra, cross-cultural ferment, and the absence of Christian anti-Jewish polemics focused on midrash of the sort that led rationalists in the West to circle the wagons and defend the rabbinic legacy.[112] One factor that remains to be investigated is the apparent lack of outstanding rabbinic authorities in the East who could suppress dissident expressions such as those found in the writings of the resisting readers. Another is the high degree of Jewish mobility in Byzantium by native scholars and those passing through, which certainly stimulated learning and may also have created a space for more unfettered expression.[113] More specifically, not rooted in any one place, certain scholars may have felt free to speak, and even write, without fear of reprisal—or in the knowledge that a safe haven on another Aegean island was not far away. Following a distinction drawn by Moshe Idel, one can associate the resisting readers with a "second order elite" who, not bearing the burden of communal leadership, were able to wander and speak as they wished, exercising a different conception of hermeneutic responsibility than Rashi.[114]

In any case, with Rashi's star on the rise, some late medieval writers concentrated, as best one can tell, in eastern Mediterranean centers of learning, were provoked to rebut the *Commentary* in response to its growing dominance. True, Rashi had largely walked in the tracks of the ancient sages. Still, as the leading ambassador of midrash, the canonization of whose *Commentary* promised to make regnant an exegetical and theological distortion of Judaism, he was now an important target.

Elijah Mizrahi: Rashi's "Trusted Servant"

A youth in 1468 when *'Alilot devarim* was copied in its earliest surviving version, Elijah Mizrahi, the last great Romaniote rabbi, breathed his last in 1526. At the time, he was still struggling to put final touches on a Rashi supercommentary that quickly became the classic in the field. His closing phase of life was, he explained to an inquirer,

> consumed by my great investigation which I undertake daily into the words of the great light [Rashi] in his monumental, distinguished Pentateuch commentary, each and every one of whose words demands profound analysis and utmost investigation . . . especially as regards the resolution of the doubts that descend [upon them] from the latter-day scholars who investigate his words and assail him, the great formidable lion Nahmanides most of all.

His powers were waning, but his focus was total: "I was unable to set aside this, my investigation; ever does it deter me from investigating other matters."[115]

Though he was not quite able to put it into final form or even give it a name, Mizrahi's supercommentary was seemingly close to complete when, as his son Israel reported, his father was summoned to the "rabbinic academy on high."[116] Bypassing the local Constantinople Hebrew press, presumably in the hope of securing the widest possible audience for the work, Israel headed for Venice, the great capital of printing and home to the famous Bomberg printing house. In August 1527, the 340 leaves making up what came to be called simply *Mizrahi*, or *Re'em*, after Mizrahi's rabbinic acronym (*R*abbi *E*lijah *M*izrahi), appeared.[117] Before the end of the sixteenth century, it was printed twice more in Venice (1544, 1574) and once in Cracow (1595). Abridgements also appeared, one by Jacob Marcaria in Riva di Trento (1561) and another in Prague about a half century later (1604–1607) by Isaac ben Naphtali Hakohen of Ostrog.[118] Eventually, Mizrahi's work spawned a vast literature of its own, most but not all of it generated in Ashkenazic centers where his tome joined a stream of foreign writings pouring into Central and Eastern European centers of learning from Italy.[119]

Among those who made Mizrahi their interlocutor of choice while studying the *Commentary* were the pillars of Polish learning. There was Moses Isserles, who appended marginal notes to his edition of Mizrahi (astonishingly, these glosses, which apparently never reached polished form, await study) and Solomon Luria (1510–1573), the second towering Polish rabbinic figure at midcentury, who claimed descent from Rashi and whose supercommentarial ideas found printed form in one of the several versions in which they were recorded by his students. As the disciple who brought the version he had in hand to press indicated, Luria's point of departure was "the great master, rabbi Elijah Mizrahi, the first to bring to light Rashi's secrets," from whose "waters" all who wished to fathom Rashi drank.[120] A comment by Mordechai Jaffe in *Levush 'orah,* his own Rashi supercommentary, likewise bespeaks Mizrahi's emerging semicanonical status. Alluding to God's warrant of the uniqueness of Moses—"My servant Moses, who is trusted throughout My household" (Num 12:7)—Jaffe cast Mizrahi as the uniquely reliable "servant in his [Rashi's] house."[121]

Over the course of the seventeenth and eighteenth centuries, Mizrahi continued to gain luster. When Isaac Hakohen published his Mizrahi abridgement *Mattenot 'ani* (also called *Kiṣṣur mizraḥi*), he explained that the supercommentator had clarified most every matter "great and small," leaving few ways for later writers to "distinguish" (*lehitgadder*) themselves, even as he mentioned later supercommentaries hailing from far-flung reaches of the Ashkenazic diaspora (*galut ha-'ashkenazim*).[122] Certainly, his own enterprise enhanced Mizrahi's status as *primus inter pares* among glossators, while dozens of studies focused on Mizrahi yielded that characteristically Jewish subgenre: the super-supercommentary.[123] In a clear sign of Mizrahi's own centrality, his rabbinic acronym even began to appear in titles of works, with no less than four seventeenth- and eighteenth-century tracts bearing the title *To'afot re'em* (playing on the obscure biblicism in Numbers 23:22 and 24:8, whose second word comprised the letters of Mizrahi's acronym).[124]

Yet here is something else to ponder: some who preoccupied themselves with Mizrahi became, at least in part, resisting readers. The title page of Judah Leib ben Ovadyah Eilenburg's *Minḥat yehudah* announced his plan to display "open rebuke and concealed love of our teacher, rabbi Elijah Mizrahi."[125] Especially comprehensive in his testing of Mizrahi's ideas, and often strident in criticism of them, was Jacob Slonik in his *Naḥalat ya'aqov* (1642). (Being diplomatic in some cases, he chalked up Mizrahi's oversights to a "magnitude of perspicacity," suggesting that Mizrahi had forgone points overly elementary to so great a mind.) Slonik found that some of Rashi's sources remained unidentified despite Mizrahi's massive effort. Aware of the fast-multiplying corpus of supercommentary, some composed in his lifetime by fellow Ashkenazim, Slonik resolved to ignore them and focus exclusively on Mizrahi, the singular "guide along the way." Slonik also opens a window on study of the *Commentary* as part of the rhythm of Jewish life when he notes that much of his work is based on ideas he heard on the Sabbath from his father Benjamin Slonik, student of both Isserles and Luria, as well as of Nathan Nata Spira, himself an author of a Rashi supercommentary.[126] Thus did study of the Torah with Rashi, and now with Mizrahi, become part of the warp and woof of daily (or at least weekly) life among the Ashkenazic elite, with teachers and students, fathers and sons, handing down, revising, debating, and if need be, rejecting ideas that they often found in Mizrahi, in a ceaseless plumbing of the *Commentary*'s boundless nuances and untold depths. Mizrahi was dictating much of the agenda, if sometimes only by inspiring dissent.

Mizrahi's splendor remained firmly in place and was explicitly proclaimed when, in 1680, Shabbetai Bass published *Siftei ḥakhamim*, a compilatory work that remains the most widely available example of Rashi supercommentary owing to its frequent appearance in an abbreviated version in traditional Pentateuchs. Bass lived in a world where a profusion of scholia on the *Commentary* was considered a boon, but that also created a problem that generated a rationale for his own work. He conjured a scene of young men appearing in the synagogue for Friday night prayers and brimming with questions about Rashi's exposition of the weekly lectionary, only to have their queries meet with a raft of disharmonious responses, "this one saying thus and this one thus." Bass took it upon himself to impose order for avid seekers of Rashi's wisdom by producing a supercommentary that culled from the best ideas in the extant literature. Amid the supercommentarial plenitude, one name stood out. Playing on a verse and on Elijah Mizrahi's last name (which evoked images of beaming), Bass enthused that Mizrahi's words were "as bright as the sun" and praised the classic supercommentator for "ministering to and serving his master [Rashi] all of his days, the nights included."[127]

At this point, circles begin to close as patterns seen earlier began to recur. For example, the second edition of Slonik's *Naḥalat ya'aqov* had a *mise en page* in which Mizrahi's supercommentary stood in the middle, with Slonik's glosses arranged around it. Here was graphic evidence of the primacy of Mizrahi in the hierarchy. In some works, lemmas from Mizrahi appeared in place of (or in addition to) ones from the Torah and the *Commentary*, as Mizrahi became a primary focus of attention among his own commentators. Still, nobody proclaimed Mizrahi's infallibility. Indeed, in the passage just mentioned where he described Mizrahi as Rashi's "trusted servant," Jaffe turned the compliment against him, expressing "the greatest astonishment" that so loyal an attendant had so badly failed to grasp Rashi's intention in the case at hand.

Returning to the late medieval eastern Mediterranean climes into which he was born, we may note that Mizrahi hardly constitutes a complete break with the rationalist tradition we have traced. He composed a mathematical work, the first ever printed in Hebrew, and notes on Euclid's geometry, as well as a commentary on Ptolemy's *Almagest*. He studied with the polymath, Mordechai Komtino. At the same time, he took tutelage from Ashkenazic greats like the legist Judah Mintz and sang the praises of the greatest of Ashkenazic exegetical works, Rashi's "monumental, distinguished Pentateuch commentary." In this and other ways, this son of Byzantium was cut from a very different cloth than Rashi's resisting readers shaped by the same geocultural sphere in centuries prior, who stridently declaimed rationalist religion.

Though a towering rabbinic authority in his own right, Mizrahi owes his enduring reputation in the Jewish public square to his paramount status among Rashi supercommentators. He could crown Ibn Ezra a "sage" and grant him his due as "foremost among the plain sense interpreters." Yet unlike his immediate Byzantine predecessors, including his teacher Komtino, his loyalty was not to this leading Andalusian commentator but rather, to his greatest Ashkenazic counterpart. He also explicitly directed a good deal of his work to a defense of Rashi from criticisms by Ibn Ezra's greatest Sefardic successor, "the awesome, fearful Nahmanides."[128] The appearance of Mizrahi's supercommentary on the *Commentary* and its spread to points far and wide, then, not only marks the great divide in the history of Rashi supercommentary but also can be said to betoken the paramount status that the *Commentary* achieved and retained over its Sefardic rivals, a paramountcy reinforced by the diverse and lively supercommentary tradition that Rashi's work inspires to the present day.

Commentary *Triumphant*

In assessing the *Commentary*, Rashi's harshest critics traduced habits of deference that many Jewish writers observed when relating to forerunners. Even when such writers attacked earlier greats, they often did so only after profuse apologies or presentation of some justifying plea. An example is those who renounced Maimonides's endorsement of philosophy on the grounds that Maimonides had undergone a late-in-life conversion to kabbalah. Because he himself recoiled from his earlier religious outlook, it was permissible for later generations to renounce it as well.[129] Rashi's resisting readers felt no need to apologize for their response to the *Commentary* with more than ordinary effrontery. They apparently felt that the high stakes involved required a head-on attack, especially when it came to midrashic fables that Rashi passed off as truth. At stake was wisdom versus folly, where wisdom so evidently lay with the "sage Ibn Ezra" and/or "master and guide, Maimonides."

Glossing Rashi critically and often bitingly, the resisting readers joined a battle in which some participants barely knew they were engaged as it spanned the Jewish Mediterranean. By early modern times, with Sefardic literature being churned out in new printed editions and arriving in Ashkenazic lands, new fronts in the battle opened in the Central and Eastern European heartland.[130] At stake was not only divergent paths in how to attain a proper understanding of the Torah but also how to realize the divine charge it communicated. Competing canons, with Rashi's *Commentary* standing in varying degrees of opposition to the exegetical and theological rationalism of Ibn Ezra and Maimonides, inspired those moving along the different paths. Neither Spanish sage disappeared from the scene, and the thought and religious model of Maimonides in particular continued to stir scholars and some members of the Jewish laity while engaging many more as a rich point of departure or, at the least, canonically compelling negative stimulus. Some of Maimonides's sweeping, utterly enduring achievements should not be gainsaid. For example, Alfred Ivry casts it as a sign of the "historic victory which the philosophical understanding of Scripture has achieved that many of the terms which Maimonides designates as anthropomorphisms are seen today, as for centuries past, as . . . non-literal expressions denoting various attributes of the deity."[131] Still, overall there can be no doubting the *Commentary*'s success over powerful rivals in shaping understandings of the Torah and sensibilities of world Jewry over the last five hundred years.

While this triumph can be viewed variously, it is, among other things, a victory of a certain type of exoteric Judaism over the blossoming of esoteric alternatives that informed the leading streams of primarily Sefardic exegesis and thought, whatever their contents (philosophy, kabbalah, or astrology). As we noted, in Ibn Ezra's Torah commentary, and then in the philosophical writings of Maimonides and the kabbalistic ones of Nahmanides, a new project took hold that separated biblical texts, and to some extent rabbinic ones, into exoteric and esoteric layers, creating a dual readership comprising a few adepts who could understand and the rest who, it was assumed, could not—nor even do themselves good by trying.[132] It was this side of the Torah commentaries of Ibn Ezra and Nahmanides that in large measure (and in the case of Nahmanides almost exclusively) impelled the creation over two or three centuries of the unceasing succession of supercommentaries that came to surround them.

Rashi's *Commentary* also worked with a dual plain sense and midrashic conception of scripture but these layers were not distinguished by the exoteric–esoteric dichotomy as were other forms of Ashkenazic exegetical expression.[133] This wholly exoteric exposition of the divine word left readers, however disparate in training and sagacity, as a single organic unit rather than as a sharply bifurcated audience of an elite and all the rest.[134] No Rashi supercommentator ever set out to reveal the *Commentary*'s esoteric meanings in the manner of glossators on Ibn Ezra's and Nahmanides's Torah commentaries or Maimonides's *Guide*. There were none. Not that the *Commentary* was a simple text. Scores of supercommentaries, many by leading rabbis, could hardly have come to grace it, were it so. But, as Raymond Aron said of Karl Marx, his teaching lent itself to "simplification for the simple and to subtlety for the subtle."[135] So it was with the *Commentary*, and that, plus its protean and self-replenishing character, was, and remains, a large part of its greatness.

In the end, the *Commentary* endured: in the schoolhouse and in the synagogue, in sermons and in the public square. Whether or not Rashi intended to write for the people as a whole or a more elite audience is, in terms of his rich and variegated reception history, not the point.[136] His work became, directly and through a nearly endless variety of intermediaries, the inheritance of those upon whom the resisting readers looked down, those whom philosophers and kabbalists alike viewed as the unsophisticated multitude. At the same time, the *Commentary* attracted boundless attention from some of medieval and modern Judaism's foremost rabbinic figures. As we have seen, there was nothing predetermined about this outcome.

The resisting readers' engagement with the *Commentary* brings to the fore competing Jewish visions going down to fundamentals: on issues of exegetical method, the status of midrash, scripture as a repository of esoteric teachings to be identified with, or at least read in accord with, science, and more. Some may feel that their effort to undo Rashi's interweaving of text and midrashic tradition merits commendation, that their puncturing of the fabulous midrashic version of the Torah brings readers much closer to biblical bedrock. Others may counter that their assault is a caricature. More to the point, they may charge the resisting readers with propagating a version of Judaism that is exegetically cramped and theologically deflating. One thing is certain: the resisting readers' insistence, delivered from the rarified heights, that the *Commentary* was largely an assemblage of errors, and at times even a betrayal of classical Judaism, did not prevail.

'Alilot devarim's nightmare came to pass. The *Commentary*'s Judaism emerged triumphant. It was a Judaism born, as *'Alilot devarim* thought, of a scholar devoid of rudimentary exegetical tools who also knew not—nay even

undermined—basic truths about Judaism's inspired vision of the "perfection of souls." The full-throated strictures of Pseudo-Rabad, the purposive and often derisive debunkings of Eleazar Ashkenazi, the incisive rebukes of Aaron Aboulrabi fell into oblivion. No doubt some will have it that divine providence ensured this deserved fate. In keeping with Eleazar Ashkenazi's and *'Alilot devarim*'s penchant for naturalistic causal explanation, however, one can suggest that the resisting readers' exegetically and theologically rationalist remodelings of scripture and Jewish faith could not have nourished Jews intellectually, spiritually, and educationally, as has the *Commentary*, going on nigh a millennium. The strident certainties of his critics regarding the inadequacies of his *Commentary* notwithstanding, it was Rashi's Torah that was handed down to and received—and, yes, creatively reread and reconfigured—by future generations. The *Commentary* weathered the interrogations and criticisms, and proved itself classic. By all indications, it promises to remain so in every place that Rashi's "name is invoked" for a long time to come.

Afterword

RASHI'S *Commentary on the Torah* IN MODERN TIMES

SO DEEPLY AND DIVERSELY EMBEDDED in Jewish life has the *Commentary* become—as an object of supercommentary, formal and informal; in the curriculum; in study of the *parashah*; in sermons; in discussions around the Sabbath table, and more—that its astonishing transformation into a foundational text of Judaism is easily missed. This mostly midrashic reading of the Torah traveled to points far and wide to shape Judaism, perhaps as no other work save the Bible and the Talmud. Moshe Idel calls the Zohar "the third most important work" of the Jewish religion after, one presumes, these two classic texts.[1] Yet it seems at least arguable (granting difficulties in adjudicating such claims) that it is Rashi's *Commentary* that merits this distinction.

Because the *Commentary* became a kind of "second nature" in the traditional reading of the Torah,[2] it could seem as if it were ever thus, yet we have seen that this has not universally been the case. Uneasiness or even disaffection with Rashi's reading of the Torah, sometimes considerable, was never entirely wanting, especially in the earlier stages of the work's dissemination, though at times it was prudently concealed. Even as the *Commentary* continued its rise to preeminence in early modern times, the canonical platform on which it increasingly came to rest showed fresh cracks, or at least the conditions for such fissures began to appear. With the advent of Jewish modernity, pockets of disaffection and alienation were bound to mount as the disintegrative fragmentation in Jewish life and learning increased. We are, then, not surprised to find signs in recent centuries of the *Commentary*'s decanonization. Yet, one can point to corresponding indicators of its abiding influence and almost preternatural contemporaneity. Without remotely attempting a full survey, a *tour d'horizon* focusing mostly on the *Commentary*'s abiding centrality, and new expressions of valorization of it, provides a few key reference points and thence a road map to an as yet unwritten history of the *Commentary*'s modern fate.

By incipient modern times, as Elijah Mizrahi engaged in minute scrutiny of the *Commentary* (drawing, as we saw, such scrutiny in turn), even those who took an unblinkered view of what they deemed Rashi's exegetical liabilities could provide testimony to the *Commentary*'s central place in the (Jewish equivalent of the) public square. Consider Joseph Solomon Delmedigo ("Yashar of Candia"; 1591–1655), who hailed from Crete, the island that figured so centrally in the transmission of writings critical of the *Commentary* in medieval times. Joseph's letter to the Lithuanian Karaite Zerah ben Nathan of Troki, called the "Aḥuz" letter, ranks biblical commentators. Most admired is Abraham ibn Ezra, followed by Karaite commentators. Then comes David Kimhi. Rashi ranks lowest. As Delmedigo informed his addressee, Rashi's interpretations were not likely to appeal to him (a Karaite) since they were "for the most part distant from the *peshaṭ* and logical inference, all of them [midrash from] *sifra'* and *gemara.*'"[3] Yet Zerah tells us that when Delmedigo taught the Torah portion on "the holy Sabbath," he did so with the *Commentary*, and with Mizrahi's supercommentary to boot.[4]

A younger contemporary of Delmedigo, born in Amsterdam a few years after he taught there, Barukh/Benedict de Spinoza, must have studied the *Commentary* fairly extensively in his younger years. Indeed, the work appears in his personal Bible.[5] Hero to some, heretic to others, Spinoza actually cites Rashi in the very first note of the opening chapter of his *Theologico-Political Treatise* (1670), endorsing his understanding of the word *navi* ("prophet") as "speaker or interpreter." He adds pointedly that the correct interpretation eluded Ibn Ezra, "who was not so good a Hebraist."[6] For all that, Spinoza's "biblical science" was far closer to Ibn Ezra's biblical hermeneutics than to Rashi's. Tamar Rudavsky goes so far as to speak of Spinoza's "abhorrence of *derash*"[7] and, indeed, Spinoza's advocacy of a type of critical approach grounded in a literal or "natural" understanding of the text stood very much at odds with Rashi's extratextual midrashic interpretations. For the latter, Spinoza had disdain, at times casting them in a sacrilegious, or even criminal, light.[8] Where Rashi took miraculous accounts in scripture at face value and did not hesitate to enhance biblical supernaturalism by heaping midrashic wonders onto scriptural accounts, Spinoza maintained that nothing happens contrary to nature and, hence, that the word "miracle" must be defined accordingly.[9] Views such as these, established by one who is sometimes billed (however dubiously) as "the first modern Jew,"[10] provided many basic parameters within which modern biblical scholarship unfolded. To those who accepted them, the *Commentary*'s naive readings could seem, exegetically and otherwise, the height of fancy and hardly meriting consideration.

Writing in the shadow of the new critical dispensation was Moses Mendelssohn (1729–1786), whose edition of the Torah with German translation and commentary displayed both traditional and modernizing tendencies. The work appeared at the dawn of the Jewish Enlightenment (Haskalah) under the title *Sefer netivot ha-shalom* (Book of the Paths of Peace). Resisting the most subversive consequences of the new biblical science, Mendelssohn and his associates—Naftali Wessely and Solomon Dubno, most notably—strove, as had Mendelssohn in earlier commentaries, to explicate the relationship of midrash to plain sense in a natural way that upheld as much as possible the perspicacity of rabbinic interpretation.[11] Rashi was frequently mentioned in the component of *Netivot ha-shalom* devoted to commentary (called *Be'ur*).[12] At the same time, the text of the *Commentary* was omitted from the work's traditional-looking page which otherwise approximated, in various ways, the look of the classic printed rabbinic Bible, including use of "Rashi script" for the commentary of Mendelssohn and his colleagues.[13] Yet here is a telling point: while a number of editions appeared as Mendelssohn first published his work in Berlin in the 1780s, variations began to emerge quickly, with some now adding Rashi's *Commentary*.[14] The process began in editions aimed at more traditional circles in southern Germany and continued in ones aimed at Central and Eastern European audiences. In a unique edition published in Vilna in the mid-nineteenth century, while the famous German translation of the Torah in Hebrew letters was omitted, the *Commentary* (and, of course, *Be'ur*) was not.[15] Such developments can be seen in terms of larger processes of canonization and decanonization that played out at the end of the eighteenth and beginning of the nineteenth century with, for example, some Maskilim decanonizing the Zohar even as others of a more Romantic persuasion attempted to restore its central status.[16]

Of Torah commentaries in modern times there is no end, and they range along the widest imaginable spectrum of methods and aims.[17] Seeking to uphold tradition where it was embattled was *Der Pentateuch, übersetzt und erläutert* (1867–1878) of Samson Raphael Hirsch, although it broke with traditional patterns to achieve its aims. Most notably, Hirsch wrote in German rather than Hebrew. He also did not include the *Commentary* alongside his gloss, as had often occurred in the past, perhaps justifying the omission on grounds that a work already sundered from longstanding habits by use of German need not include Rashi's Hebrew work. Substantively, Hirsch found little cause to refer to Rashi, although he was not averse to following him at points.[18]

In the first half of the next century and on into the second, the *Commentary* continued to figure in the curriculum, but also suffered neglect in light of altered audiences and the new languages in which they needed to be addressed. In an essay that laid the foundation for his renowned Freies Jüdisches Lehrhaus (Free Jewish House of Learning) inaugurated in 1920, Franz Rosenzweig proposed that in the fourth year of the curriculum the Torah be studied with Rashi. The reason given had to do not with Rashi's plain sense insights but his status as "that great and popular commentator who transmitted to the second millennium of the Exile the vast treasure of the first" while serving as a conduit to "the spiritual world of the Talmud and Midrash."[19] At the end of the same decade, Joseph Hertz, chief rabbi of Great Britain, published a Torah commentary that quickly became "the synagogue Bible of choice for Anglo-American readers."[20] It did not include the *Commentary*, in this way breaking "radically from custom"[21] like other English-language commentaries later in the century. Not at all surprising is the Commentary's omission in *The Torah: A Modern Commentary*, by W. Gunther Plaut (1981), the first non-Orthodox Torah produced for an Anglophone audience. Yet even in this work of an unabashedly liberal and critical outlook, Rashi was the most cited commentator.[22]

Another striking tendency appears in *Da'at miqra'* (1971–2003), a series produced by Israeli Orthodox scholars that has been said to lie, at least in some respects, between "tradition and criticism."[23] The policy in the volumes on Prophets and Writings broke with tradition by omitting Rashi's commentaries; not so the edition of the Torah, which included the *Commentary*. Barry Levy suggests that this change served a strategic purpose, affirming "a link with traditional interpretation that was less apparent in the earlier volumes."[24] In other words, the editors traded on, and thereby reinforced, the *Commentary*'s canonical status by ensuring its presence, perhaps not so much to be studied as to confer on their own work a greater "patent of Jewish authenticity."[25]

The *Commentary* found its way into many places beyond the world of exegetical cognoscenti. In his Yiddish poem of 1890, "Akhdes" ("Unity"), Morris Winchevsky, a student at the yeshiva in Vilna who became an atheist and socialist, expressed in passing the Torah's inseparability from Rashi's commentary in the collective *imaginaire* (that is, the manner in which the community imagines and portrays itself): "We're all brothers. . . . Religious and leftists are all united, like groom and bride . . . like Humash and Rashe [Rashi], like kugel and kashah."[26]

More *larmoyant* was the testimony of Israeli poet Samson Meltzer, whose life spanned the route traveled by many Eastern European Jews (*Ostjuden*) as they transformed themselves into "New Jews" in Palestine. In a 1940 ballad titled "Of Rashi I Sing," Meltzer nostalgically summoned the traditional *ḥeder* (elementary religious school) in which he himself was reared, where the *Commentary* was introduced to the young (male) charges at an early stage.[27]

Conjuring a vision of such boys seeing "the contents of the great Humash / Shut and closed as in a fortress," Meltzer had them discover the "luminescent stone" that peered out from this forbidding wall, then intoned: "That was your stone, dear old Rashi / Your stone, the most precious of stones!" His ballad ended with an expression of distress as Meltzer contemplated the alienation from a traditional heritage experienced by a new generation of socialist pioneers, with his own son of six years beginning to learn "Bible stories" in second grade. Here Meltzer adopts the cadences of ancient lament: "And my heart to me speaks / My heart, in me, is faint; can it be— / Alas and woe, it is actually possible! — that he will not study Humash with Rashi . . . "[28] Such testimonials to the *Commentary*'s centrality appear in other branches of Israeli literature, such as S. Y. Agnon's "In Search of a Rabbi or The Governor's Whim," which tells of a rabbi whose unsurpassed mastery of classic literature grew out of intense childhood instruction in "Humash and Rashi."[29]

While Agnon was transforming Hebrew literature, Nehama Leibowitz was reviving Bible study in Israel in fresh ways while continuing a lifelong engagement with the *Commentary* that was nothing less than a labor of love. Citing the *Commentary* hundreds if not thousands of times in her variously formatted studies of the weekly *parashah*, Leibowitz brought to her highly variegated readership an awareness of the loving attention lavished on Rashi's words by a long tradition of supercommentators. She seems to have been aware that not all shared her boundless esteem for the *Commentary*, hence her felt need to "eradicate the viewpoint that is so stupid and so prevalent—even amongst Torah scholars, to my astonishment—that Rashi is some light, popular commentary, a congenial grandmother figure who tells educational fables that elevate the soul."[30] In a recent study, Mordechai Cohen reads Leibowitz's engagement with Rashi (but primarily the *Commentary*) though the lens of what she learned about the New Criticism from her mentor, Ludwig Strauss. Comparing Rashi to commentators of a more rigorously peshatist persuasion, Leibowitz (in Cohen's reconstruction) devised a broader concept of *peshaṭ* based on the view that "literary interpretation does not aim to get at the author's intention, but rather to construct one of the potential meanings of the text, a 'reproduction' of the text." This conception created ample space for Rashi's extensive use of midrash in ways eschewed by his more stringently plain sense successors, both Ashkenazic and Sefardic.[31]

Some prominent recent admirers of the *Commentary* might come as a surprise. One, who was famous for philosophical ideas like "ethics precedes ontology" and, in the sphere of Jewish interpretation, creative readings of the Talmud, also conducted a lifelong love affair with the *Commentary*. Alas, the supercommentarial legacy of Emmanuel Levinas has left next to no written trace. In one place, he defines Judaism as "the Bible and Talmud . . . read by way of Rashi's commentaries" ("Le judaïsme, c'est la Bible et le Talmud francisés, je veux dire, lus à travers les commentaires de Rachi"). An oral report even has him calling Rashi "the greatest Jewish philosopher"![32] More specific to the *Commentary* were classes delivered on the weekly Torah portion by Levinas every Sabbath for some four decades. Those who attended observed traditional restrictions on writing, so little remains of these discourses but second-hand oral accounts. These and other indications suffice to show that for purposes of these classes Levinas read the Torah by way of Rashi ("toujours à travers le prisme du commentaire de Rachi").[33]

What of engagements with the *Commentary* in recent times, including ones reflecting certain post-modern sensibilities, popularizing trends, and use of new media and technologies? The *Commentary* is extremely prominent in the biblical interpretation of the turn of the twentieth-first century commentator, Avivah Zornberg, who, among other things, finds multiple types of meaning in it, including psychoanalytic significances, even in Rashi's "most—apparently—fantastic citations from the midrash."[34] In an entirely different vein, a recent book, *The JPS Rashi Discussion Torah Commentary*, takes insights from the *Commentary* as a point of departure for discussion of (to name but a few topics) "Conflict Resolution," "Sweat Equity," "WYSIWYG (What You See Is What You Get)," and "BFF (Best Friends Forever)."[35] This juxtaposition of such disparate types of contemporary interaction with the *Commentary* illustrates as starkly as anything the work's capacity for sustaining ongoing reading and interpretation in a way that, as noted at this study's outset, can be seen as being of the essence in processes of canonization in rabbinic Judaism. Meanwhile, engagement with the *Commentary* nowadays extends to many a digital platform, with the work itself produced on websites in editions based on manuscripts or analyzed though distribution lists that offer a daily or weekly "dose" of the work by way of "Rashi newsletters."[36]

In terms of reverence, two highly influential facilitators of *Commentary* study merit attention.[37] When his mother passed away in 1964, Menachem Mendel Schneerson, the last Rebbe of Lubavitch, initiated the process of giving, over two and half decades, "Rashi discourses" (*sichos*, in Lubavitch parlance) as part of his weekly public gatherings (*farbrengens*). At least half of these roughly eight hundred supercommentarial discourses were then developed into essays that have appeared in multiple languages beyond their original Yiddish. A defining feature of the in-depth treatments of the *Commentary*, reminiscent of the Canpantonian approach developed in Spain, is the premise that "every nuance of Rashi is calculated with great precision" and that every gesture in Rashi's format and language must be seen as significant.

An editor of a recent volume of Schneerson's supercommentarial endeavor speaks of a "stunning . . . linguistic precision" on Rashi's part that is said to reveal "layers of meaning buried deep within the text and between the lines" of his *Commentary*—layers Schneerson's minute analyses aim to bring out, premised on the view that every word was "chosen with the utmost precision and contributes to Rashi's explanation."[38] Schneerson's boundless esteem for the *Commentary*, and his followers' unbounded esteem for him, ensure that the *Commentary* and its loving exposition by "the Rebbe" are reflected in a broad array of publications produced by the movement. In some, the *Commentary* attains as canonical a status as can be imagined for a work of its kind, supplying the basis upon which God's words are relayed in English translation. Indeed, in one publication a sort of transitive property of canonicity makes the *Commentary* a part of the original revelation, with Rashi's interpretation said to be "on a par" with the Targum which, based on a talmudic text, is presented in turn as a product of the revelation at Mount Sinai.[39]

Similarly lofty in its assessment of Rashi is the encomium found in a five-volume edition of the *Commentary* produced under the "Artscroll" imprint of Mesorah Publications, whose creators sponsor a spectacularly successful line of Jewish classics produced in user-friendly and elegant but uncompromisingly (ultra-)Orthodox formats. The editor states that the "messages implied by the nuances of Rashi are infinite," such that readers of the *Commentary* should approach it with the same attitude that "Rashi himself adopted towards Scripture," namely that "not the slightest aspect is arbitrary."[40] At least functionally, the *Commentary* is elevated almost to the level of scripture itself.[41]

Needless to say, there were demurrers. One was an amateur Bible scholar often cast as the state of Israel's founding father. In an essay (originally a letter) published in 1953, David Ben-Gurion allowed that Rashi's interpretation of the Bible "is very important." He immediately added, however, that it was "only the commentary of Rashi." Besides making no claim on Jews generally, Ben-Gurion contended that Rashi suffered from a defect that afflicted all Bible commentators prior to the Jewish return to Zion. Through no fault of their own, such writers could not connect with the "spiritual and material climate of the Bible" in a way that was necessary to arrive at the Bible's "essence and truth—historical and geographic as well as religious and cultural."[42] Alan Levenson remarks that in such statements Ben-Gurion was drawing lines of battle: "On the one side, Zionist, Israelocentric, biblical; on the other, Orthodox, diasporic, and rabbinic."[43] For Ben-Gurion, Rashi's exegesis fell squarely in the latter category.

More than the attacks of its medieval resisting readers, radical shifts in modernity did sever the *Commentary*'s universal hold. So, in some measure,

Ben-Gurion's remark shows. Yet Rashi's interpretation of the Torah retained—and retains—its central, and beloved, status among significant segments of world Jewry. Indeed, we should note that it was Rashi alone whose exegesis Ben-Gurion felt compelled to contest; no other commentator is mentioned. In every act of decanonization lies tacit recognition that the work being dethroned has a hold on a community.

Notes

INTRODUCTION

1. Avivah Gottlieb Zornberg, *The Particulars of Rapture: Reflections on Exodus* (New York: Doubleday, 2001) , 1–2. For the other assessments, see, respectively, Avraham Grossman, "Ha-reqa' ha-histori," in Nehama Leibowitz and Moshe Arend, *Perush rashi la-torah: 'iyyunim be-shiṭato*, 2 vols. (Jerusalem: Open University of Israel, 1990), 2:252; and Nahum Sarna, "Rashi the Commentator," in *Studies in Biblical Interpretation* (Philadelphia: Jewish Publication Society, 2000), 128.
2. This brilliantly concise formulation was used by my teacher, Isadore Twersky, to impart to Harvard undergraduates a glimmer of Rashi's significance. For a possible source, see Jacob Mann, "A Commentary to the Pentateuch à la Rashi's," *HUCA* 15 (1940): 497. It is generally thought that Rashi commented on the whole of the Bible, but the question is moot; see Mayer I. Gruber, *Rashi's Commentary on Psalms* (Atlanta, GA: Scholars Press, 1998), 52–75; and Eran Viezel, "Ha-perush ha-meyuḥas le-rashi le-sefer 'ezra-neḥemyah," *Jewish Studies Internet Journal* 9 (2010): 1–58.
3. Talya Fishman, *Becoming the People of the Talmud: Oral Torah as Written Tradition in Medieval Jewish Cultures* (Philadelphia: University of Pennsylvania Press, 2011), 132.
4. For the cited formulation, see Haym Soloveitchik, "Catastrophe and Halakhic Creativity: Ashkenaz – 1096, 1242, 1306 and 1298," *Jewish History* 12 (1998): 80.
5. Herman Hailperin, *Rashi and the Christian Scholars* (Pittsburgh, PA: University of Pittsburgh Press, 1963). The interest in Christian receptions has only intensified. See, e.g., Michael T. Walton and Phyllis J. Walton, "In Defense of the Church Militant: The Censorship of the Rashi Commentary in the *Magna Biblia Rabbinica*," *Sixteenth Century Journal* 21 (1990): 385–400; Deeana Copeland

Klepper, *The Insight of Unbelievers: Nicholas of Lyra and Christian Reading of Jewish Text in the Later Middle Ages* (Philadelphia: University of Pennsylvania Press, 2007); Ari Geiger, "A Student and an Opponent: Nicholas of Lyre and His Jewish Sources," in *Nicolas de Lyre: franciscain du XIVe siècle, exégète et théologien*, ed. Gilbert Dahan (Paris: Institut d'Études Augustiniennes, 2011), 167–203; Piet van Boxel, "Robert Bellarmine Reads Rashi: Rabbinic Bible Commentaries and the Burning of the Talmud," in *The Hebrew Book in Early Modern Italy*, ed. Joseph R. Hacker and Adam Shear (Philadelphia: University of Pennsylvania Press, 2011), 121–32; Eva De Visscher, *Reading the Rabbis: Christian Hebraism in the Works of Herbert of Bosham* (Leiden: Brill, 2014), 81–105.

6. Elisabeth Hollender, *Piyyut Commentary in Medieval Ashkenaz* (Berlin: De Gruyter, 2008), 119–20. For iconography, see Marc M. Epstein, *The Medieval Haggadah: Art, Narrative, and Religious Imagination* (New Haven, CT: Yale University Press, 2010), 166; and Marc M. Epstein, "Another Flight into Egypt: Confluence, Coincidence, the Cross-cultural Dialectics of Messianism and Iconographic Appropriation in Medieval Jewish and Christian Culture," in *Imagining the Self, Imagining the Other: Visual Representation and Jewish-Christian Dynamics in the Middle Ages and Early Modern Period*, ed. Eva Frojmovic (Leiden: Brill, 2002), 39, 48–50. The *Commentary*'s impact on retellings of Bible stories in children's literature must be vast and is at times explicit. See, e.g., Miriam Chaikin, *Clouds of Glory: Legends and Stories about Bible Times* (New York: Clarion, 1998): "The stories in this book are largely based on Rashi's commentary on the book of Genesis." Consider the title in a popular traditionalist series still in circulation: *The Little Midrash Says: A Digest of the Weekly Torah-Portion based on Rashi, Rishonim and Midrashim Adapted for Junior Readers and to Read Aloud* (Brooklyn, NY: Benei Yakov, 1986).
7. Avriel Bar-Levav, "The Religious Order of Jewish Books: Structuring Hebrew Knowledge in Amsterdam," in *Mapping Jewish Amsterdam: The Early Modern Perspective* (= *Studia Rosenthaliana* 44), ed. Shlomo Berger, Emile G. L. Schrijver, and Irene Zwiep (Leuven: Peeters, 2012), 3n8.
8. For reception of Maimonides's code, see, e.g., Isadore Twersky, "The Beginnings of Mishneh Torah Criticism," in *Studies in Jewish Law and Philosophy* (New York: Ktav, 1982), 30–51; Israel M. Ta-Shma, "The Acceptance of Maimonides' *Mishneh Torah* in Italy," *Italia* 13–15 (2001): 79–90; Jeffrey R. Woolf, "Admiration and Apathy: Maimonides' *Mishneh Torah* in High and Late Medieval Ashkenaz," in *Be'erot Yitzhak: Studies in Memory of Isadore Twersky*, ed. Jay Harris (Cambridge, MA: Harvard University Center for Jewish Studies, 2005), 427–53.
9. For the cited usage, see Ineke Sluiter, "The Dialectics of Genre: Some Aspects of Secondary Literature and Genre in Antiquity," in *Matrices of Genre: Authors, Canons, and Society*, ed. Mary Depew and Dirk Obbink (Cambridge, MA: Harvard University Press, 2000), 183.

10. Barry Dov Walfish, in the sub-entry "Medieval Judaism," in the entry on "Commentaries (Genre)," in *Encyclopedia of the Bible and Its Reception*, ed. Christine Helmer et al. (Berlin: De Gruyter, 2012), 5:105. See also the title of Yitzhak S. Penkower, "Tahalikh ha-qanonizaṣiyah shel perush rashi la-torah," in *Limmud ve-da'at be-maḥashavah yehudit*, ed. Haim Kreisel (Beer-Sheva: Ben Gurion University Press of the Negev, 2006), 123–46.
11. I cite some of the tart remonstrance that I received some years back in a prepublication review of an article.
12. David Stern, "On Canonization in Rabbinic Judaism," in *Homer, the Bible, and Beyond: Literary and Religious Canons in the Ancient World*, ed. Margalit Finkelberg and Guy G. Stroumsa (Leiden: Brill, 2003), 229–30. On the Christian origin of the use of the term "canon" for a collection of religious writings, see Robert Brody, "Ha-musag ha-ḥamaqmaq shel ha-qanon," in *Ha-qanon ha-samui min ha-'ayin: ḥiqrei qanon u-genizah*, ed. Menahem Ben-Sasson et al. (Jerusalem: Magnes, 2010), 11; and Yaacov Shavit, "Introduction [special issue on 'Canon and Holy Scriptures']," *Teudah* 23 (2009): xiv.
13. John B. Henderson, *Scripture, Canon, and Commentary: A Comparison of Confucian and Western Exegesis* (Princeton, NJ: Princeton University Press, 1991), 38–39.
14. E.g., Tzvi Marx, "Judaic Doctrine of Scripture," in *Holy Scriptures in Judaism, Christianity and Islam: Hermeneutics, Values and Society*, ed. Hendrik M. Vroom and Jerald D. Gort (Amsterdam: Rodopi, 1997), 43 ("the Talmud is canonical, together with the Bible").
15. Hagith Sivan, "Canonizing Law in Late Antiquity: Legal Constructions of Judaism in the Theodosian Code," in *Homer, the Bible, and Beyond: Literary and Religious Canons in the Ancient World*, ed. Margalit Finkelberg and Guy G. Stroumsa (Leiden: Brill, 2003), 214.
16. Boaz Huss, *The Zohar: Reception and Impact*, trans. Yudith Nave (Oxford: Littman Library of Jewish Civilization, 2016), 99.
17. Moshe Halbertal, *People of the Book: Canon, Meaning, and Authority* (Cambridge, MA: Harvard University Press, 1997), 3.
18. Boaz Huss, "*Sefer Ha-Zohar* as a Canonical, Sacred and Holy Text: Changing Perspectives on the Book of Splendor between the Thirteenth and Eighteenth Centuries," *Journal of Jewish Thought and Philosophy* 7 (1998): 257–68 (257 for the cited passage).
19. Margalit Finkelberg and Guy G. Stroumsa, "Introduction: Before the Western Canon," in *Homer, the Bible, and Beyond: Literary and Religious Canons in the Ancient World*, ed. Margalit Finkelberg and Guy G. Stroumsa (Leiden: Brill, 2003), 5.
20. Sarna, "Rashi," 128.
21. Judah Khalatz, *Mesiaḥ 'illemim*, ed. Moshe Filip (Petah Tikvah: Filip, 2001), 28.

22. Jacob Elbaum, *Petiḥut ve-histagrut: ha-yeṣirah ha-ruḥanit-ha-sifrutit be-folin u-ve-'arṣot 'ashkenaz be-shilhei ha-me'ah ha-shesh-'esrei* (Jerusalem: Magnes, 1990), 84.
23. Jonathan Jacobs, *Bekhor shoro hadar lo: r[abbi] Yosef Bekhor Shor ben hemshekhiyut le-ḥiddush* (Jerusalem: Magnes, 2017), 288.
24. For recent reflection on this theme, see Sarah Stroumsa, "Between 'Canon' and Library in Medieval Jewish Philosophical Thought," *Intellectual History of the Islamicate World* 5 (2017): 28–54.
25. Adam Shear, *The Kuzari and the Shaping of Jewish Identity, 1167–1900* (Cambridge: Cambridge University Press, 2008), 22, who mentions the exception of Maimonides's *Guide of the Perplexed*, which survives in about one hundred manuscripts—still less than half the number of copies of the *Commentary* that come down in this form.
26. For manuscripts of Ibn Ezra's and Nahmanides's Torah commentaries, see Jacobs, *Bekhor shoro*, 291–92; and Yosef Ofer and Jonathan Jacobs, *Tosafot ramban le-ferusho la-torah she-nikhtevo be-'ereṣ yisra'el* (Jerusalem: Herzog Academic College and World Union of Jewish Studies, 2013), 647–50.
27. See chapter 2, this volume.
28. David Stern, *The Jewish Bible: A Material History* (Seattle: University of Washington Press, 2017), 153.
29. Th. L. Hettema, "The Canon: Authority and Fascination," in *Canonization and Decanonization*, ed. A. Van Der Kooij and K. Van Der Toorn (Leiden: Brill, 1998), 391.
30. Huss, "*Sefer Ha-Zohar*," 260.
31. Uri Gabbay, "Specification as a Hermeneutical Technique in Babylonian and Assyrian Commentaries," *Hebrew Bible and Ancient Israel* 4 (2015): 361; and Eckart Frahm, *Babylonian and Assyrian Text Commentaries: Origins of Interpretation* (Munich: Ugarit-Verlag, 2011), 317–38.
32. For the role of the commentary tradition in authorizing the *Shulḥan 'arukh*, see Yaacob Dweck, "What Is a Jewish Book?" *AJS Review* 34 (2010): 370–71, which, however, does not speak of canonization. For Nahmanides, see Moshe Idel, "On Maimonides in Nahmanides and His School," in *Between Rashi and Maimonides: Themes in Medieval Jewish Thought, Literature and Exegesis*, ed. Ephraim Kanarfogel and Moshe Sokolow (Jersey City, NJ: Ktav, 2010), 134.
33. For the basic formulation, see Ineke Sluiter, "The Violent Scholiast: Power Issues in Ancient Commentaries," in *Writing Science: Medical and Mathematical Authorship in Ancient Greece*, ed. Markus Asper (Berlin: De Gruyter, 2013), 195.
34. See chapter 3, this volume.
35. Stern, "On Canonization," 250–51.
36. Evelyn B. Tribble, *Margins and Marginality: The Printed Page in Early Modern England* (Charlottesville: University Press of Virginia, 1993), 58–59.
37. For the basic idea, see Sluiter, "Violent Scholiast," 191 (192 for the cited passage).

38. For an introduction, see Robert C. Holub, *Reception Theory: A Critical Introduction* (London: Methuen, 1984).
39. For such a definition, see the one of Immanuel Kant (in *The Metaphysics of Morals*): "a writing, which represents a discourse that someone delivers to the public by visible linguistic signs" (cited in Dweck, "What is a Jewish Book," 368).
40. Christine Pawley, "Seeking 'Significance': Actual Readers, Specific Reading Communities," *Book History* 5 (2002): 143–60. Exemplifying such interest in Jewish studies is a title like Scott Mandelbrote and Joanna Weinberg, eds., *Jewish Books and Their Readers: Aspects of the Intellectual Life of Christians and Jews in Early Modern Europe* (Leiden: Brill, 2016).
41. Miriam Fraenkel, "Qanon ve-ḥevrah: ha-qanon ha-sifruti ki-kheli le-gibbush ha-'ilit ha-ḥevratit be-ḥevrat ha-genizah," in *Ha-qanon ha-samui min ha-'ayin: ḥiqrei qanon u-genizah*, ed. Menahem Ben-Sasson et al. (Jerusalem: Magnes, 2010), 88.
42. Kathleen Ashley and Véronique Plesch, "The Cultural Processes of 'Appropriation,'" *Journal of Medieval and Early Modern Studies* 32 (2002): 6.
43. For the larger theme, see Margalit Finkelberg, "Canon-Replacement Versus Canon-Appropriation: The Case of Homer," in *Cultural Repertoires: Structure, Function, and Dynamics*, ed. Gillis J. Dorleijn and Herman L. J. Vanstiphout (Leuven: Peeters, 2003), 145–60.
44. See chapter 2, this volume.
45. Brian Stock, *Listening for the Text: On the Uses of the Past* (Baltimore, MD: Johns Hopkins University Press, 1990), 157. A collection that emphasizes "modes of transmission" is Yaakov Elman and Israel Gershoni, eds., *Transmitting Jewish Traditions: Orality, Textuality, and Cultural Diffusion* (New Haven, CT: Yale University Press, 2000).
46. See chapter 5, this volume.
47. For the coinage, see Judith Fetterley, *The Resisting Reader: A Feminist Approach to American Fiction* (Bloomington: Indiana University Press, 1978). For the definition of resisting reading interwoven here, see Anne Cranny-Francis et al., *Gender Studies: Terms and Debates* (New York: Palgrave Macmillan, 2003), 118.
48. See Brian A. Catlos, "Why the Mediterranean?," in *Can We Talk Mediterranean? Conversations on an Emerging Field in Medieval and Early Modern Studies*, ed. Brian A. Catlos and Sharon Kinoshita (Cham, Switzerland: Palgrave Macmillan, 2017), 5.
49. Charles Augustin Sainte-Beuve, "What Is a Classic?" in *Literary and Philosophical Essays: French, German and Italian* (= The Harvard Classics 32), ed. Charles W. Eliot (New York: P.F. Collier, 1910), 126.
50. J. M. Coetzee, "What Is a Classic: A Lecture," in *Stranger Shores: Literary Essays, 1986–1999* (New York: Viking, 2001), 16.

51. Arthur Hyman, "Maimonides as Biblical Exegete," in *Maimonides and His Heritage*, ed. Idit Dobbs-Weinstein, Lenn E. Goodman, and James Allen Grady (Albany: State University of New York Press, 2009), 1.
52. Isaiah Berger, "Rashi be-'aggadat ha-'am," in *Rashi: torato ve-'ishiyuto*, ed. Simon Federbush (New York: World Jewish Congress/Jewish Agency of New York, 1958), 165–66; Eli Yassif, "Rashi Legends and Medieval Popular Culture," in *Rashi 1040–1990: Hommage à Ephraïm E. Urbach*, ed. Gabrielle Sed-Rajna (Paris: Éditions du Cerf, 1993), 485.
53. Reported in the sixteenth century by Gedalyah ibn Yahya and Menachem Azariah da Fano, this metaphysical insight was said to have implications for Rashi's and Maimonides's legal authority. Both sources tell of a tradition dating back several generations. See Gedalyah ibn Yahya, *Shalshelet ha-qabbalah* (Warsaw: Abraham Kahana, 1902), 12–13; Menachem Azariah da Fano, *Gilgulei neshamot* (Jerusalem: Yerid Hasefarim, 1997), 81–82.
54. Judah Rozenthal, "Rashi ve-ha-rambam be-ha'arakhat ha-dorot," in *Meḥqarim u-meqorot*, 2 vols. (Jerusalem: Reuven Mas, 1967), 1:117–25. A milder version of this approach appears in Wilhelm Bacher, "Raschi und Maimuni," *Monatsschrift für Geschichte und Wissenschaft des Judentums* 49 (1905): 1–11.
55. Tamás Visi, "Ibn Ezra, A Maimonidean Authority: The Evidence of the Early Ibn Ezra Supercommentaries," in *The Cultures of Maimonideanism: New Approaches to the History of Jewish Thought*, ed. James T. Robinson (Leiden: Brill, 2009), 89–131.
56. The general formulation borrows from Moshe Idel's preface to *Black Fire on White Fire: An Essay on Jewish Hermeneutics, from Midrash to Kabbalah* by Betty Rojtman, trans. Steven Rendall (Berkeley: University of California Press, 1998), ix.
57. Tamás Visi, *On the Peripheries of Ashkenaz: Medieval Jewish Philosophers in Normandy and in the Czech Lands from the Twelfth to the Fifteenth Century* (Olomouc: Kurt and Ursula Schubert Center for Jewish Studies, 2011), 22. He documents this claim by way of Rashi's gloss (essentially followed by the Tosafists) on a talmudic appearance of the word *filosofa*, to which Rashi appends the comment: *min*. Visi translates the talmudic usage as "heretic," though in the context it could mean "Christian." See b. Shabbat 116a and, for the Christian dimension, Holger M. Zellentin, *Rabbinic Parodies of Jewish and Christian Literature* (Tübingen: Mohr Siebeck, 2011), 153–64. For Berger, see next note.
58. David Berger, "Polemic, Exegesis, Philosophy, and Science: On the Tenacity of Ashkenazic Modes of Thought," *Simon Dubnow Institute Yearbook* 8 (2009): 39. For the object of critique, see the article by Avraham Grossman, "Rashi's Rejection of Philosophy: Devine [*sic*] and Human Wisdoms Juxtaposed," *Simon Dubnow Institute Yearbook* 8 (2009): 95–118.
59. Warren Zev Harvey, "Rashi on Creation: Beyond Plato and Derrida," *Aleph* 18 (2018): 28. Note that Harvey focuses attention only on Rashi's account of the

creation of the world, leaving open the question of philosophic dimensions in the rest of the *Commentary*.

60. Ivan G. Marcus, "Rashi's Choice: The Humash Commentary as Rewritten Midrash," in *Studies in Medieval Jewish Intellectual and Social History: Festschrift in Honor of Robert Chazan*, ed. David Engel, Lawrence H. Schiffman, and Elliot R. Wolfson (Leiden: Brill, 2012), 31. Often overlooked is Dov Rapel, *Rashi: temunat 'olamo ha-yehudit* (Jerusalem: Misrad ha-ḥinukh ha-tarbut ve-ha-sporṭ, 1995). More comprehensive is Avraham Grossman, *'Emunot ve-de'ot be-'olamo shel rashi* (Alon Shevut: Tevunot, 2008).
61. Michael Fishbane, *The Exegetical Imagination: On Jewish Thought and Theology* (Cambridge, MA: Harvard University Press, 1998), ix.
62. Hans Robert Jauss, *Toward an Aesthetic of Reception*, trans. Timothy Bahti (Brighton: Harvester Press, 1982), 20.
63. Adapting Moshe Idel, "Italy in Safed, Safed in Italy: Toward an Interactive History of Sixteenth-Century Kabbalah," in *Cultural Intermediaries: Jewish Intellectuals in Early Modern Italy*, ed. David B. Ruderman and Giuseppe Veltri (Philadelphia: University of Pennsylvania Press, 2004), 241.
64. For the Kuzari, see Shear, *Kuzari*; for Maimonides, see James A. Diamond, *Maimonides and the Shaping of the Jewish Canon* (New York: Cambridge University Press, 2014); for the Zohar, see Huss, *Zohar*; for the reception of a popularizing work, see Ofer Elior, *Ruaḥ ḥen yaḥalof 'al panai* (Jerusalem: Mekhon Ben-Zvi, 2017); for *Shulḥan 'arukh*, see Joseph Davis, "The Reception of the *Shulḥan 'Arukh* and the Formation of Ashkenazic Jewish Identity," *AJS Review* 26 (2002): 251–76. For "rules of canonization" in relation to the Jewish library, see the introduction to *Ha-qanon ha-samui min ha-'ayin: ḥiqrei qanon u-genizah*, ed. Menahem Ben-Sasson et al. (Jerusalem: Magnes, 2010), 3.
65. John Patrick Diggins, "The Oyster and the Pearl: The Problem of Contextualism in Intellectual History," *History and Theory* 23 (1984): 151–69.

CHAPTER 1

1. Menahem Banitt, *Rashi: Interpreter of the Biblical Letter* (Tel Aviv: Chaim Rosenberg School of Jewish Studies, 1985), 4n14.
2. Deborah Schoenfeld, *Isaac on Jewish and Christian Altars: Polemic and Exegesis in Rashi and the Glossa Ordinaria* (New York: Fordham University Press, 2013), 3.
3. The fullest exploration is Yeshayahu Maori, "Nosaḥ perush rashi la-torah: maṣav ha-meḥqar," in *Rashi: demuto vi-yeṣirato*, ed. Avraham Grossman and Sara Japhet, 2 vols. (Jerusalem: Zalman Shazar, 2008), 1:63–98. A recent survey is Ariel Shaveh, "Ha-'ivrit shel rashi: 'al-pi kitvei yad nivḥarim shel ha-perush la-torah" (PhD diss., Hebrew University, 2017), 3–48.

4. Oxford, Bodleian 2440 (MS Corpus Christi Coll. 165) is thought to date from as early as 1200. See Peter E. Pormann, ed., *A Descriptive Catalogue of the Hebrew Manuscripts of Corpus Christi College, Oxford* (Cambridge: D.S. Brewer, 2015), 98–105. Munich, Bayerische Staatsbibliothek, MS Cod. Hebr. 5, is dated in its colophon to the Hebrew year 4993 (corresponding to 1232 or 1233). See Eva Frojmovic, "Jewish Scribes and Christian Illuminators: Interstitial Encounters and Cultural Negotiation," in *Between Judaism and Christianity: Art Historical Essays in Honor of Elisheva (Elisabeth) Revel-Neher*, ed. Katrin Kogman-Appel and Mati Meyer (Leiden: Brill, 2009), 301.
5. Malachi Beit-Arié, "Transmission of Texts by Scribes and Copyists: Unconscious and Critical Interferences," *Bulletin of the John Rylands University Library of Manchester* 75 (1993): 33–51; and Israel M. Ta-Shma, "The 'Open' Book in Medieval Hebrew Literature: The Problem of Authorized Editions," in *Creativity and Tradition: Studies in Medieval Rabbinic Scholarship, Literature and Thought* (Cambridge, MA: Harvard University Center for Jewish Studies, 2006), 193–200. For a different understanding of "open book," see Ivan G. Marcus, Sefer Hasidim *and the Ashkenazic Book in Medieval Europe* (Philadelphia: University of Pennsylvania Press, 2018), 13–30.
6. Yosef Ofer and Jonathan Jacobs, *Tosafot ramban le-ferusho la-torah she-nikhtevo be-'ereṣ yisra'el* (Jerusalem: Herzog Academic College and World Union of Jewish Studies, 2013), where all of the changes are catalogued and contributing factors for each, exegetical and contextual, expertly discussed.
7. Ta-Shma, "'Open' Book," 197, went so far as to claim "proof" that Rashi wrote an early version of the *Commentary*, then fashioned a heavily abridged one, but never evidenced this claim.
8. Eleazar Touitou, "'Al gilgulei ha-nosaḥ shel perush rashi la-torah," *Tarbiẓ* 56 (1986): 211–42.
9. Avraham Grossman, "The School of Literal Jewish Exegesis in Northern France," in *HBOT*, ed. Magne Sæbø, vol. I/2: *From the Beginnings to the Middle Ages*, part 2: *The Middle Ages* (Göttingen: Vanderhoeck & Ruprecht, 2000), 333–34; Grossman, *Ḥakhmei ṣorfat ha-rishonim: qorotehem, darkam be-hanhagat ha-ṣibbur, yeṣiratam ha-ruḥanit* (Jerusalem: Magnes, 1995), 184–93.
10. Grossman, "School," 334. For Shemaya as both a reverent student and an active transmitter of Rashi's exegesis as well as independent commentator, see Grossman, *Ḥakhmei ṣorfat*, 347–426. Grossman, "Hagahot r[abbi] Shema'yah ve-nosaḥ perush rashi la-torah," *Tarbiẓ* 60 (1990): 80, thinks Shemaya made the copy in question in Rashi's lifetime.
11. For earlier debate over Leipzig 1 and the current state of the question, see Shaveh, "Ha-'ivrit," 11–32.
12. Yitshak S. Penkower, "Hagahot rashi le-ferusho la-torah," *Jewish Studies Internet Journal* 6 (2007): 1–48; and Penkower, "Hagahot nosafot shel rashi le-ferusho 'al

ha-torah," in *'Or le-me'ir: meḥqarim be-miqra', ba-leshonot ha-shemiyot, be-sifrut ḥazal u-ve-tarbuyot 'atiqot mugashim le-Mayer Gruber*, ed. Shamir Yona (Beer-Sheva: Ben Gurion University Press, 2010), 363–409.

13. Shamma Friedman, "Perushei rashi la-talmud: hagahot u-mahadurot," in *Rashi: 'iyyunim bi-yeṣirato*, ed. Zevi Aryeh Steinfeld (Ramat-Gan: Bar-Ilan University Press, 1993), 147–75.
14. Penkower, "Hagahot nosafot," 363–73.
15. Avraham Grossman, *Rashi*, trans. Joel Linsider (Oxford: Littman Library of Jewish Civilization, 2012), 291. For an interchange between master and student (likely Judah ben Abraham) regarding the Torah's two apparently contrary instructions regarding the staves of the ark—in one place they must not be removed (Exod 25:15); in another the priests must put "the staves in place" (Num 4:14) prior to porterage—see Yitzhak S. Penkower, "Shnei ḥakhamim ha-nizkarim be-khitvei ha-yad shel perushei rashi la-miqra' – r[abbi] Yehudah ve-r[abbi] Yehudah ha-darshan," in *Shai le-Sarah Yafet: meḥqarim ba-miqra', be-farshanuto, u-vi-leshono*, ed. Moshe Bar-Asher et al. (Jerusalem: Bialik, 2007), 241–43.
16. Malachi Beit-Arié, *QI*, 505–506.
17. Eleazar Touitou, *"Ha-peshaṭot ha-mitḥaddeshim be-khol yom": 'iyyunim be-ferusho shel rashbam la-torah* (Ramat-Gan: Bar-Ilan University Press, 2003), 229–37.
18. Grossman, "Hagahot."
19. Mordechai Breuer, *'Ohalei torah: ha-yeshivah, tavnitah ve-toledoteha* (Jerusalem: Zalman Shazar, 2003), 175–76; Avraham (Rami) Reiner, "Mumar 'okhel nevelot le-te'avon – pasul? mashehu 'al nosaḥ u-ferusho bi-yedei rashi," in *Lo yasur shevet mi-yehudah: hanhagah, rabanut, u-qehilah be-toledot yisra'el—meḥqarim mugashim le-prof' Shimon Schwarzfuchs*, ed. Joseph R. Hacker and Yaron Harel (Jerusalem: Bialik, 2011), 219–28; and Yaakov Shmuel Spiegel, *'Amudim be-toledot ha-sefer ha-'ivri: hagahot u-megihim*, 2nd ed. (Ramat-Gan: Bar-Ilan University, 1996), 104, 127–56. For Tam's openness to "proper" emendation, see Talya Fishman, *Becoming the People of the Talmud: Oral Torah as Written Tradition in Medieval Jewish Cultures* (Philadelphia: University of Pennsylvania Press, 2011), 146–47.
20. Dino Buzzetti and Peter Denley, "Maestri e scolari bolognesi nel tardo Medioevo: Per l'edizione elettronica delle fonti," in *La storia delle università italiane*, ed. L. Sitran Rea (Bologna: Edizioni LINT, 1996), 206.
21. Rivka Zevulun, "Ha-nosaḥ shel perush rashi la-torah ba-defusim ha-rishonim: yaḥasam zeh le-zeh ve-hishtalshalut nosḥam 'ad le-mahadurot yamenu," 2 vols. (MA thesis, Hebrew University, 1997), 1:9. For the unprecedented number of manuscripts, see note 23 in the introduction.
22. Isaiah Sonne, "Le-viqoret ha-ṭeqsṭ shel perush rashi 'al ha-torah," *HUCA* 15 (1940): 37–56 (Hebrew section); Zevulun, "Ha-nosaḥ," 8; Yeshayahu

Maori, " 'Al nusaḥ perush rashi la-torah she-hayah lifnei ramban," in *Sha'arei lashon: meḥqarim bi-leshon ha-'ivrit, ba-'aramit u-vi-leshonot ha-yehudim mugashim le-Moshe bar 'Asher*, ed. Aharon Maman, Steven E. Fassberg, and Yohanan Breuer, 3 vols. (Jerusalem: Bialik, 2007), 1:215–17 (for Italy, 215n87); Shaveh, "Ha-'ivrit," 35.

23. Maori, " 'Al nusaḥ."
24. Zevulun, "Ha-nosaḥ," 9.
25. See at note 48, this chapter.
26. Hananel Mack, "' 'Im lavan garti ve-taryag miṣvot shamarti': darkah shel ha-derashah mi-sifro shel r[abbi] Moshe hadarshan 'el perush rashi la-torah," *Tarbiẓ* 65 (1996): 251–61.
27. Shlomo Zalman Havlin, "Haggahot," in *EJ*, 8:218.
28. The maps in the *Commentary* as they appear in Leipzig 1 can be viewed online: Leipzig, Universitätsbibliothek, MS B.H.1, at "AlHaTorah.org Rashi Project," edited by Aviva Novetsky. https://alhatorah.org/Commentators:Rashi_Leipzig_1/Bemidbar_34. The maps and other illustrative material have been amply studied. See, e.g., Mayer I. Gruber, "Light on Rashi's Diagrams from the Asher Library of Spertus College of Judaica," *Solomon Goldman Lectures* 6, ed. Mayer I. Gruber (Chicago: Spertus College of Judaica Press, 1993): 73–85; Gabrielle Sed-Rajna, "Some Further Data on Rashi's Diagrams to His Commentary on the Bible," *Jewish Studies Quarterly* 1 (1993/94): 149–57; and Rehav Rubin, *Portraying the Land: Hebrew Maps of the Land of Israel from Rashi to the Early 20th Century* (Berlin: De Gruyter, 2018), 1–22. A connection first drawn by Grossman between the maps and Leipzig 1 is further explored in Yosef Ofer, "Mapot 'ereṣ yisra'el be-ferush rashi la-torah – u-ma'amado shel k[etav] y[ad] leipzig 1," *Tarbiẓ* 76 (2007): 435–44. David Shneor, "Sugyat mapot rashi le-miqra': meḥqeran ve-he'edran mi-mahadurot ha-defus shel perusho," *Shenaton le-ḥeqer ha-miqra' ve-ha-mizraḥ ha-qadum* 24 (2016): 255–66 proposes (or rather, surmises) that the absence of maps and images in printed editions of the *Commentary* should be ascribed not to technical impediments but a "religious-mystical" discomfort with printed images.
29. *MGH: Sefer Bereshit*, ed. Menachem Cohen, 2 vols. (Ramat-Gan: Bar-Ilan University Press, 1993), 1:193.
30. Thus Yedida Chaya Eisenstat, "Rashi's Midrashic Anthology: The Torah Commentary Re-Examined" (PhD diss., Jewish Theological Seminary, 2014), 83. Whatever its point of contact with Rashi's interpretation in Leipzig 1, Nahmanides's reading moves in directions not reflected in Rashi or his midrashic source; see Bernard Septimus, "A Medieval Judeo-Spanish Poem on the Complementarity of Faith and Works and Its Intellectual Roots," in *New Perspectives on Jewish-Christian Relations: In Honor of David Berger*, ed. Elisheva Carlebach and Jacob J. Schacter (Leiden: Brill, 2012), 232–33.

31. Eisenstat, "Rashi's Midrashic Anthology," 82–84.
32. The most obvious one, beyond recourse to early manuscripts, is the cross-checking of citations in later works like Tosafist literature or the commentary of Nahmanides; see Deborah Abecassis, "Reconstructing Rashi's Commentary on Genesis from Citations in the Torah Commentaries of the Tosafot" (PhD diss., McGill University, 1999); and Yeshayahu Maori, "'Ha-yerushalmi ha-katuv be-ferushei rashi' (ramban la-bemidbar 4:16) ve-nosaḥ divrei rashi," *'Iyyunei miqra' u-farshanut* 7 (2005): 385–97. Some supercommentators, such as Abraham Bokhrat, invested considerable energy in study of variants with a view to supplying good readings; see the editor's introduction to Abraham Bokhrat, *Sefer zikaron*, ed. Moshe Filip, corrected ed. (Petah Tikvah: Filip, 1985), 13–28.
33. Moshe Halbertal, *People of the Book: Canon, Meaning, and Authority* (Cambridge, MA: Harvard University Press, 1997), 33.
34. For the history, see Shamma Friedman, "The Transmission of the Talmud and the Computer Age," in *Printing the Talmud: From Bomberg to Schottenstein*, ed. Sharon Liberman Mintz and Gabriel M. Goldstein (New York: Yeshiva University Museum, 2005), 143–54.
35. See at note 221 in chapter 2, this volume.
36. Micha Perry, *Masoret ve-shinui: mesirat yeda' be-qerev yehudei ma'arav 'eropah bi-yemei ha-benayim* (Tel-Aviv: Hakibbutz Hameuhad, 2010).
37. For *peshaṭ* and *peshuṭo shel miqra'* as terms that "elude translation," see Sara Japhet, "The Tension between Rabbinic Legal Midrash and the 'Plain Meaning' (*Peshat*) of the Biblical Text – An Unresolved Problem?: In the Wake of Rashbam's Commentary on the Pentateuch," in *Sefer Moshe: The Moshe Weinfeld Jubilee Volume: Studies in the Bible and the Ancient Near East, Qumran, and Post-Biblical Judaism*, ed. Chaim Cohen, Avi Hurvitz, and Shalom M. Paul (Winona Lake, IN: Eisenbrauns, 2004), 403n1. On the scope of Rashi's biblical commentaries, see Grossman, *Rashi*, 74; Mayer I. Gruber, *Rashi's Commentary on Psalms* (Atlanta, GA: Scholars Press, 1998), 52–75; and Eran Viezel, "Ha-perush ha-meyuḥas le-rashi le-sefer 'ezra-neḥemyah," *Jewish Studies Internet Journal* 9 (2010): 1–58.
38. Mordechai Z. Cohen, "Nahmanides' Four Senses of Scriptural Signification: Jewish and Christian Contexts," in *Entangled Histories: Knowledge, Authority, and Jewish Culture in the Thirteenth Century*, ed. Elisheva Baumgarten, Ruth Mazo Karras, and Katelyn Mesler (Philadelphia: University of Pennsylvania Press, 2017), 42.
39. The precise place of midrash in the nonpentateuchal commentaries is as yet up for discussion; see, e.g., Yosef Tabori, "Perush rashi le-'ester u-meqorotav," in *Rashi: demuto vi-yeṣirato*, ed. Avraham Grossman and Sara Japhet, 2 vols. (Jerusalem: Zalman Shazar, 2008), 2:295–309; and Gila Prebor, "Darko ha-parshanit shel rashi be-shimusho be-midrashei ḥazal be-ferusho le-qohelet," *Shenaton le-ḥeqer ha-miqra' ve-ha-mizraḥ ha-qadum* 19 (2009): 209–29.

40. Yeshayahu Maori, "'Aggadot ḥaluqot' be-ferush rashi la-miqra'," *Shenaton le-ḥeqer ha-miqra' ve-ha-mizraḥ ha-qadum* 19 (2009): 155–207. Not all examples of contradiction in the *Commentary* involve midrashim; see Hanokh Gamliel, *Rashi ke-farshan u-khe-valshan: tefisot taḥbiriyyot be-ferush rashi la-torah* (Jerusalem: Bialik, 2010), 19–20.
41. These and other aspects of the style of the *Commentary*, especially in its handling of rabbinic sources, are handsomely illustrated in Eleazar Touitou, "Darko shel rashi be-shimusho be-midrashei ḥazal: 'iyyun be-ferush rashi li-shemot 1:8–22," *Ṭalelei 'orot: shenaton mikhlelet 'orot yisra'el* 9 (2000): 51–78.
42. Nehama Leibowitz, *Limmud parshanei ha-torah u-derakhim lehora'atam: sefer bereshit* (Jerusalem: World Zionist Organization, 1975), 133 (and 154, for the same sentiment, prefaced by "It is known that . . ."). Leibowitz, "Darko shel rashi be-hava'at midrashim be-ferusho la-torah," in *'Iyunim be-sefer shemot*, 2nd ed. (Jerusalem: World Zionist Organization, 1970), 495–524, tried to document these claims.
43. Edward Greenstein, "Sensitivity to Language in Rashi's Commentary on the Torah," *Solomon Goldman Lectures* 6, ed. Mayer I. Gruber (Chicago: Spertus College of Judaica Press, 1993), 56.
44. Grossman, *Rashi*, 98–99.
45. Without attempting to address the issues or cite much of the abundant literature, I note that Eleazar Touitou, followed to a lesser degree by Avraham Grossman, was sure that the combination of the twelfth-century renaissance and engagement in Jewish-Christian controversy were the "fundamental factors" underlying Rashi's whole exegetical movement. See, e.g., Eleazar Touitou, "Rashi and His School: The Exegesis on the Halakhic Part of the Pentateuch in the Context of the Judeo-Christian Controversy," in *Medieval Studies in Honour of Avrom Saltman*, ed. Bat-Sheva Albert, Yvonne Friedman, and Simon Schwarzfuchs (Ramat-Gan: Bar-Ilan University Press, 1995), 234; and Touitou, *"Ha-peshaṭot,"* 1–33. Daniel Lasker, "Rashi and Maimonides on Christianity," in *Between Rashi and Maimonides: Themes in Medieval Jewish Thought, Literature and Exegesis*, ed. Ephraim Kanarfogel and Moshe Sokolow (Jersey City, NJ: Ktav, 2010), 3–21, cites Grossman at length, the better to dissent from this view. Inclined also toward a basically negative response to the question in its title is Shaye J. D. Cohen, "Does Rashi's Torah Commentary Respond to Christianity? A Comparison of Rashi with Rashbam and Bekhor Shor," in *The Idea of Biblical Interpretation: Essays in Honor of James L. Kugel*, ed. Hindy Najman and Judith H. Newman (Leiden: Brill, 2004), 449–72. A recent study that attempts to link Rashi's exegetical enterprise to developments in contemporary Christian biblical scholarship is Mordechai Z. Cohen, "A New Perspective on Rashi of Troyes in Light of Bruno the Carthusian: Exploring Jewish and Christian Bible Interpretation in Eleventh-Century Northern France," *Viator* 48 (2017): 39–86.

46. From a large literature, see Avraham Grossman, "Polmos dati u-megamah ḥinukhit be-ferush rashi la-torah," in *Pirqei Neḥamah: sefer zikaron le-Neḥamah Lebovits*, ed. Moshe Ahrend and Rut Ben-Meir (Jerusalem: Ha-Sokhnut Ha-Yehudit, 2001), 187–205; and Ivan G. Marcus, "Rashi's Choice: The Humash Commentary as Rewritten Midrash," in *Studies in Medieval Jewish Intellectual and Social History: Festschrift in Honor of Robert Chazan*, ed. David Engel, Lawrence H. Schiffman, and Elliot R. Wolfson (Leiden: Brill, 2012), 29–45.
47. Rashi on Gen 33:20. See Sarah Kamin, *Rashi: peshuṭo shel miqra' u-midrasho shel miqra'* (Jerusalem: Magnes, 1986), 181–82. For "inherent polysemy" as an arch principle of midrash, see Myrna Solotorevsky, "The Model of Midrash and Borges's Interpretative Tales and Essays," in *Midrash and Literature*, ed. Geoffrey H. Hartman and Sanford Budick (New Haven, CT: Yale University Press, 1986), 255.
48. Uriel Simon, *'Ozen milin tivḥan: meḥqarim be-darko ha-parshanit shel r[abbi] 'Avraham 'ibn 'Ezra* (Ramat-Gan: Bar-Ilan University Press, 2013), 319–37.
49. The term *shemu'o* does not appear in standard editions of the *Commentary* but is found in a number of good manuscripts. See Leipzig, Universitätsbibliothek, MS B.H.1, at "AlHaTorah.org Rashi Project," at Gen 3:8, n. 4 (the reading in "Leipzig 1" differs slightly: *shemu'ato*). Robert Harris, "What's In a Blessing? Rashi and the Priestly Benediction of Numbers 6:22–27," in *Birkat Kohanim: The Priestly Benediction in Jewish Tradition*, ed. Martin S. Cohen and David Birnbaum (New York: New Paradigm Matrix, 2016), 254n10 emends to *mashma'o*.
50. Jean-Christophe Attias, "L'Âme et la Clef: De l'introduction comme genre littéraire dans la production exégètique du judaïsme médiéval," in *Entrer en Matière*, ed. Jean-Daniel Dubois and Bernard Roussel (Paris: Cerf, 1998), 337–58.
51. Kamin, *Rashi*, 14 (23–56, for rabbinic expressions). For summary and criticism of Kamin's conclusions, see Mordechai Z. Cohen, "Hirhurim 'al ḥeqer ha-munaḥ 'peshuṭo shel miqra'' bi-teḥilat ha-me'ah ha-'esrim ve-'aḥat," in *'Leyashev peshuṭo shel miqra': 'asupat meḥqarim be-farshanut ha-miqra'*, ed. Eran Viezel and Sara Japhet (Jerusalem: Bialik and Mandel Institute of Jewish Studies, 2011), 5–58.
52. Yonah Fraenkel, "Ha-piyyuṭ ve-ha-perush: li-meqorot ha-'aggadah be-ferusho shel rashi la-torah," *'Iyyunei miqra' u-farshanut* 7 (2005): 475n1.
53. Grossman, *Rashi*, 85.
54. Eisenstat, "Rashi's Midrashic Anthology," 30–40. On this view, the main reason this feature of the work is easily missed is its form, with midrashim presented in *ad locum* glosses.
55. Grossman, *Rashi*, 88.
56. Mordechai Z. Cohen, "Emergence of the Rule of Peshat in Jewish Bible Exegesis," in *Interpreting Scriptures in Judaism, Christianity and Islam: Overlapping Inquiries*, ed. Mordechai Z. Cohen and Adele Berlin (Cambridge: Cambridge University Press, 2016), 213.

57. Grossman, "School," 336. Still, there are "rare occasions" of anti-halakhic interpretation (Grossman, *Rashi*, 96–97). For the interreligious context for Rashi's interpretation of biblical law (without addressing the hermeneutical issue), see Touitou, "Rashi and His School," 231–51.
58. See, especially, Kamin, *Rashi*, 57–110.
59. Edward L. Greenstein, "Medieval Bible Commentaries," in *Back to the Sources: Reading the Classic Jewish Texts*, ed. Barry W. Holtz (New York: Summit, 1984), 229.
60. Cohen, "A New Perspective," 47–57. A key claim of Sarah Kamin (*Rashi*, 57–110) was that Rashi's *peshuo shel miqra'* and the sort of midrashim that "settle" the language of scripture were distinct interpretive categories with disparate aims.
61. James L. Kugel, *The Idea of Biblical Poetry: Parallelism and Its History* (New Haven, CT, and London: Yale University Press, 1981), 104.
62. Robert A. Harris, "Concepts of Scripture in the School of Rashi," in *Jewish Concepts of Scripture: A Comparative Introduction*, ed. Benjamin D. Sommer (New York: New York University Press, 2012), 106.
63. Hanna Liss, *Creating Fictional Worlds: Peshat-Exegesis and Narrativity in Rashbam's Commentary on the Torah* (Leiden: Brill, 2011), 39–44.
64. *MGH: Sefer Bereshit*, 1:24 and 36, respectively, for Ibn Ezra and Nahmanides.
65. The example is dissected in Maori, "Nosaḥ," 91–93, where the version *midrash ki-feshuṭo* found in *MGH: Sefer Bereshit*, 1:134, is convincingly discounted.
66. Grossman, *Rashi*, 177–78.
67. Michael A. Signer, "Rashi's Reading of the Akedah," in *Memoria–Wege jüdischen Erinnerns: Festschrift für Michael Brocke zum 65. Geburtstag*, ed. Birgit E. Klein and Christiane E. Müller (Berlin: Metropol, 2005), 614.
68. For this critical vocabulary in medieval Latin literary activity, see A. J. Minnis, *Medieval Theory of Authorship: Scholastic Literary Attitudes in the Later Middle Ages*, 2nd ed. (Aldershot: Scolar, 1988), esp. 94–102; and Rita Copeland, *Rhetoric, Hermeneutics, and Translation in the Middle Ages: Academic Traditions and Vernacular Texts* (Cambridge: Cambridge University Press, 1991), 87–126.
69. Yosefah Rachaman, "'Ibbud midrashim be-ferusho shel rashi la-torah," *Teudah* 3 (1983): 261–68; and Yosef Ofer, "Histaigut semuyah mi-midrashim be-ferushei rashi la-torah," *'Iyyunei miqra' u-farshanut* 8 (2008): 279–92.
70. Ephraim Kanarfogel, "Rashi's Awareness of Jewish Mystical Traditions and Literature," in *Raschi und sein Erbe*, ed. Daniel Krochmalnik, Hanna Liss, and Ronen Reichman (Heidelberg: Universitätsverlag, 2007), 23–34.
71. Grossman, "School," 336.
72. Jeffrey Woolf, *The Fabric of Religious Life in Medieval Ashkenaz (1000–1300): Creating Sacred Communities* (Leiden: Brill, 2015), frequently lays stress on the *Commentary* as an embodiment of specifically Ashkenazic ideals, going so far as to say that Rashi's intention was to impart "religious, spiritual, and

moral values that stood at the center of Ashkenazic Jewish tradition" (8). Though Rashi hardly could have conceived things this way, the question of the degree to which, as Woolf puts it, his commentaries specifically mirror "the basic values of pre-Crusade Ashkenazic culture" (30) merits reflection.

73. It lists a couple of generations between Moses's grandfather, Kohath, who came to Egypt (Gen 46:11), and Moses himself, who brought the Israelites out—a span too short to bridge 400 or 430 years. For discussion, see David A. Glatt-Gilad, "How Many Years Were the Israelites in Egypt?," TheTorah.com, at http://thetorah.com/how-many-years-were-the-israelites-in-egypt/.
74. For the way this number was derived, and alternatives to it in some Jewish sources, see Joseph Heinemann, "210 Years of Egyptian Exile," *Journal of Jewish Studies* 22 (1971): 19–30. For the typological and eschatological element in this and related speculations, see Oded Irshai, "Dating the Eschaton: Jewish and Christian Apocalyptic Calculation in Late Antiquity," in *Apocalyptic Time*, ed. Albert Baumgarten (Leiden: Brill, 2000), 138.
75. On Gen 42:2. For rabbinic sources and parallels, see *Ḥamishah ḥumshei torah: rashi ha-shalem*, 7 vols. to date (Jerusalem: Ariel, 1986–), *Bereshit*, 3:46–47. See, more fully, Rashi at Exod 12:40: "because Keḥat [Moses's grandfather] was of those who came with Jacob [to Egypt]. Go and figure all his years [133 years], all the years of his son Amram [137 years], and Moses' 80 years [until the exodus]; you will not find them [to be] that many."
76. Isaac Heinemann, *Darkhei ha-'aggadah*, 3rd. ed. (Jerusalem: Magnes, 1974), 40–41, for this trait of midrashic discourse..
77. Eliezer Segal, *Reading Jewish Religious Texts* (Abingdon: Routledge, 2012), 44–46. For the coinage "surface irregularity," see James L. Kugel, "Two Introductions to Midrash," *Prooftexts* 3 (1983): 144.
78. Elijah Mizrahi, *Ḥumash ha-re'em*, ed. Moshe Filip, 6 vols. (Petah Tikvah: Filip, 1994), 2:577.
79. Israel Isserlein, *Be'urei maharai 'al ha-torah*, ed. Menachem Doitsh (Lakewood, NJ: Mekhon Be'er Ha-Torah, 1996), 20 at Gen 42:2. On Isserlein, see Shlomo Spitzer, *Bne chet: die österreichischen Juden im Mittelalter. Eine Sozial- und Kulturgeschichte* (Vienna: Böhlau, 1997), 181–86, 191–94.
80. This golden age remains to be brought into the light of historiography. For now, see Eric Lawee, "Biblical Scholarship in Late Medieval Ashkenaz: The Turn to Rashi Supercommentary," *HUCA* 86 (2015): 299–302. From a voluminous literature on Loew, see, recently, *Maharal: 'aqdamot – pirqei ḥayyim, mishnah, hashpa'ah*, ed. Elchanan Reiner (Jerusalem: Zalman Shazar, 2015).
81. Judah Loew, *Ḥumash gur 'aryeh ha-shalem*, ed. Joshua Hartman, 9 vols. (Jerusalem: Mekhon Yerushalayim, 1989), 2:297–98.
82. Isaac Horowitz, *Be'er yiṣḥaq*, [ed. Yehudah Cooperman], 2 vols. (Jerusalem: Kiryah Ne'emanah, 1967), 1:106. On Horowitz, see the editor's introduction (1:3–12). In

this instance, Horowitz may have taken his cue from the verbal formulation in the *Commentary*, with Rashi casting the 210 years foreshadowed in Jacob's pronouncement as a hint (*remez*).

83. Eran Viezel, "The Secret of the Popularity of Rashi's Commentary on the Torah," *RRJ* 17 (2014): 207. See further, Grossman, *Rashi*, 108–109.
84. Gerald J. Blidstein, "In the Shadow of the Mountain: Consent and Coercion at Sinai," *Jewish Political Studies Review* 4 (1992): 41.
85. See note 83 in chapter 6, this volume.
86. Eric Lawee, "From Sefarad to Ashkenaz: A Case Study in the Rashi Supercommentary Tradition," *AJS Review* 30 (2006): 393–425; Lawee, "The Reception of Rashi's *Commentary on the Torah* in Spain: The Case of Adam's Mating with the Animals," *JQR* 97 (2007): 33–66.
87. Aviezer Ravitzky, "'Haṣivi lakh ṣiyyunim' le-ṣiyyon: gilgulo shel ra'ayon," in *'Al da'at ha-maqom: meḥqarim ba-hagut ha-yehudit u-ve-toldoteha* (Jerusalem: Keter, 1991), 34–73; and Avraham Grossman, "'Ereṣ yisra'el be-mishnato shel rashi," *Shalem* 7 (2002): 18–22.
88. Lawrence Kaplan, "*Daas Torah:* A Modern Conception of Rabbinic Authority," in *Rabbinic Authority and Personal Autonomy*, ed. Moshe Sokol (Northvale, NJ: J. Aronson, 1992), 33–34, 43. Kaplan views the subsequent discussion of Nahmanides as, in effect, a supercommentary on Rashi. Indeed, Nahmanides starts out with a citation of Rashi but his account of the duty to defer to high court rulings pointedly concludes with a citation of the original rabbinic formula from which Rashi deviates that subtly undercuts Rashi's implication of the possibility of outright error on the part of rabbinic decisors. See Nahmanides on Deut 17:11 in *MGH: Sefer Devarim*, ed. Menachem Cohen (Ramat-Gan: Bar-Ilan University, 2011), 114.
89. For another instance, see Blidstein, "In the Shadow."
90. Beit-Arié, "Transmission of Texts."
91. Yeshayahu Maori, "'Tiqqun soferim' ve-'kinnah ha-katuv' be-ferush rashi la-miqra'," in *Neṭi'ot le-david: sefer yovel le-David Halivni*, ed. Yaakov Elman, Ephraim Bezalel Halivni, and Zvi Arie Steinfeld (Jerusalem: Orhot, 2004), 99–108; and Aharon Mondschein, "Rashi, rashbam ve-'ibn 'Ezra shonim mishnatam be-sugiyat 'tiqqun soferim,'" *'Iyyunei miqra' u-farshanut* 8 (2008): 409–50. For later supercommentarial reactions, see note 153 in chapter 3, this volume, and Marc B. Shapiro, *The Limits of Orthodox Theology: Maimonides' Thirteen Principles Reappraised* (Oxford: Littman Library of Jewish Civilization, 2004), 99n57. For a different sort of case involving a divergence between a verse in Exodus as quoted by Rashi and its appearance in some Torah scrolls, which led to emendation of the *Commentary* and, perforce, Rashi's explanation of a *vav* in the Torah whose existence later readers denied, see Yitshak S. Penkower, "Nosaḥ ha-miqra' she-'amad lifnei rashi ke-fi she-hu mishtaqqef be-ferushav la-miqra'," in *Rashi: demuto vi-yeṣirato*, ed. Avraham Grossman and Sara Japhet,

2 vols. (Jerusalem: Zalman Shazar, 2008), 1:103; Shnayer Z. Leiman, "Ve-'et kol 'asher 'aṣavveh 'otekha: Was Rashi's Torah Scroll Flawed?," *Judaic Studies* 2 (2003): 3–21.

92. Grossman, *Rashi*, 90. For "second nature," see Avivah Gottlieb Zornberg, *The Particulars of Rapture: Reflections on Exodus* (New York: Doubleday, 2001), 2.

CHAPTER 2

1. Northern Europe gets less attention here as the most familiar part of the story of the *Commentary*'s reception and as the center that least attests to the dynamic of the work's integration into a divergent religiocultural milieu. "Ashkenaz" is used as a designation for the north in contrast to Mediterranean counterparts, understanding that it elides its dominantly German and French constituent parts in ways that sometimes oversimplify. On the designation "Ashkenaz," including Rashi's possibly decisive influence on its use, see Ivan G. Marcus, "A Jewish-Christian Symbiosis: The Culture of Early Ashkenaz," in *Cultures of the Jews: A New History*, ed. David Biale (New York: Schocken, 2002), 449–50, 501n2. For an example of fluctuating regional interconnections between Germany and northern France, see Ephraim Kanarfogel, "From Germany to Northern France and Back Again: A Tale of Two Tosafist Centres," in *Regional Identities and Cultures of Medieval Jews*, ed. Javier Castaño, Talya Fishman, and Ephraim Kanarfogel (London: Littman Library of Jewish Civilization, 2018), 149–71.
2. For a manuscript of the *Commentary* from Yemen dating to around 1440, see Manfred R. Lehmann, *Perush rashi 'al ha-torah* (New York: Manfred and Anne Lehmann Foundation, 1981).
3. *Sefer 'even ha-'ezer*, 107; cited in Avraham Grossman, *Ḥakhmei ṣorfat ha-rishonim: qorotehem, darkam be-hanhagat ha-ṣibbur, yeṣiratam ha-ruḥanit* (Jerusalem: Magnes, 1995), 175.
4. Grossman, *Ḥakhmei ṣorfat*, 175; and Avraham Grossman, *Rashi*, trans. Joel Linsider (Oxford: Littman Library of Jewish Civilization, 2012), 44–45.
5. Profayt Duran, *Ma'aseh 'efod*, ed. John Friedländer and Jakob Kohn (Vienna, 1865), 10, 13. For Duran's failure to mention Ashkenazic exegetes after Rashi, see Mordechai Breuer, "Min'u benekhem min ha-higayon," in *Mikhtam le-david: sefer zikaron ha-rav David 'Oqs*, ed. Yitzhak D. Gilat and Eliezer Stern (Ramat-Gan: Bar-Ilan Univeristy Press, 1978), 250–51. Frank Talmage, "Keep Your Sons from Scripture: The Bible in Medieval Jewish Scholarship and Spirituality," in *Understanding Scripture: Explorations of Jewish and Christian Traditions of Interpretation*, ed. Clemens Thoma and Michael Wyschogrod (New York: Paulist, 1987), 86–87, thinks that Duran's critique was limited to the fourteenth century. Ephraim Kanarfogel, "On the Role of Bible Study in Medieval Ashkenaz," in *The Frank Talmage Memorial Volume*, ed. Barry Dov

Walfish, 2 vols. (Haifa: Haifa University Press, 1993), 1:164n 52, suggests Duran thought more in terms of a deterioration beginning closer to Rashi's day.

6. Haym Soloveitchik, "Three Themes in the *Sefer Ḥasidim*," *AJS Review* 1 (1976): 339.
7. I owe this paragraph to Hanna Liss, "Scepticism, Critique, and the Art of Writing: Preliminary Considerations on the Question of Textual Authority in Medieval Peshaṭ Exegesis," *Yearbook of the Maimonides Centre for Advanced Studies*, ed. Bill Rebiger (Berlin/Boston: De Gruyter, 2018), 15–46. With thanks to Professor Liss for putting this valuable study at my disposal prior to publication.
8. Hanna Liss, *Creating Fictional Worlds: Peshat-Exegesis and Narrativity in Rashbam's Commentary on the Torah* (Leiden: Brill, 2011), 12.
9. Gloss on Gen 37:2 (*MGH: Sefer Bereshit*, ed. Menachem Cohen, 2 vols. [Ramat-Gan: Bar-Ilan University Press, 1993], 2:94–95). For his exegesis, see the introduction to *Perush ha-rashbam 'al ha-torah*, ed. Meir Lockshin, 2 vols. (Jerusalem: Chorev, 2009), 1–35; and Jonathan Jacobs, "Rashbam's Major Principles of Interpretation as Deduced from a Manuscript Fragment Discovered in 1984," *REJ* 170 (2011): 443–63.
10. Martin I. Lockshin, *Rabbi Samuel Ben Meir's Commentary on Genesis* (Lewiston, NY: Edwin Mellen, 1989), 13–23. Cf. Jonathan Jacobs, "Tefuṣat perushei rashbam la-torah: mabaṭ meḥudash," *Beit Mikra* 62 (2017): 49.
11. Jonathan Jacobs, *Bekhor shoro hadar lo: r[abbi] Yosef Bekhor Shor ben hemshekhiyut le-ḥiddush* (Jerusalem: Magnes, 2017), 63–91; and Ephraim Kanarfogel, *The Intellectual History and Rabbinic Culture of Medieval Ashkenaz* (Detroit: Wayne State University Press, 2013), 111–288.
12. For pre-Crusade Germany and Rashi's start as an exegete there, see Avraham Grossman, *Ḥakhmei 'ashkenaz ha-rishonim: qorotehem, darkam be-hanhagat ha-ṣibbur, yeṣiratam ha-ruḥanit, me-reshit yishuvam ve-'ad li-gezerot 856 (1096)* (Jerusalem: Magnes, 1981), 64–66, 430–32.
13. The most recent study of his exegesis is Kanarfogel, *Intellectual History*, 207–38.
14. Eran Viezel, "R. Judah He-Hasid or R. Moshe Zaltman: Who Proposed that Torah Verses Were Written after the Time of Moses?," *Journal of Jewish Studies* 66 (2015): 102.
15. Kanarfogel, *Intellectual History*, 210 speaks of Judah referring to Rashi "with a degree of frequency."
16. See Ivan G. Marcus, "Exegesis for the Few and for the Many: Judah He-Hasid's Biblical Commentaries," *Meḥqerei yerushalayim be-maḥashevet yisra'el* 8 (1988): 1–24 (English section); and Moshe Idel, "On Angels and Biblical Exegesis in Thirteenth-Century Ashkenaz," in *Scriptural Exegesis: The Shapes of Culture and the Religious Imagination: Essays in Honour of Michael Fishbane*, ed. Deborah A. Green and Laura S. Lieber (Oxford: Oxford University Press, 2009), 211–44. Kanarfogel, *Intellectual History*, 233 notes that Judah at times applies to Rashi's

Commentary the parasemantic techniques used by the German Pietists to read scripture.

17. See chapter 3, this volume.
18. b. Berakhot 8a–b.
19. In a later twist on this development, when the *Commentary* became inaccessible to some due to variations in Hebrew literacy, it was deemed expedient (and potentially profitable) to supply it in Yiddish translation. See Edward Fram, "Some Preliminary Observations on the First Published Translation of Rashi's Commentary on the Pentateuch in Yiddish (Cremona, 1560)," *HUCA* 86 (2016): 305–42.
20. Chayim Talbi, "Le-hishtalshelutah shel qeri'at shnayim miqra' ve-'eḥad targum," *Kenishta* 4 (2010): 176–90, esp. 179–83 for vernacular translations. For Targum in the curriculum, see Alberdina Houtman, "The Role of the Targum in Jewish Education in Medieval Europe," in *A Jewish Targum in a Christian World*, ed. Alberdina Houtman, Eveline van Staalduine-Sulman, and Hans-Martin Kim (Leiden: Brill, 2014), 81–98.
21. Moses of Coucy, *Sefer miṣvot gadol* (*Semag*), end of *'aseh* 19. See *Sefer miṣvot gadol*, ed. Alter P. Farber, 2 vols. (Jerusalem: n.p., 2001), 2:28. For Moses and Rashi's exegesis, see Kanarfogel, *Intellectual History*, 290–328; and Judah ben Eleazar, *Minḥat yehudah: perush la-torah me-'et rabbi Yehudah ben 'Ele'azar mi-rabotenu ba'alei ha-tosafot*, ed. Hazoniel Touitou (Jerusalem: Mosad Harav Kuk, 2012), *Bereshit*, 1:90–98.
22. Rafael B. Posen, "Yaḥaso shel rashi le-targum 'onkelos," in *Rashi: demuto vi-yeṣirato*, ed. Avraham Grossman and Sara Japhet, 2 vols. (Jerusalem: Zalman Shazar, 2008), 2:275–93; and Eran Viezel, "Targum Onkelos in Rashi's Exegetical Consciousness," *RRJ* 15 (2012): 1–19.
23. Shael Herman, "Rashi's Glosses *Belaaz*: Navigating Hebrew Scripture under Feudal Lanterns," *RRJ* 18 (2015): 102–34.
24. Yitzhak S. Penkower, "Tahalikh ha-qanonizaṣiyah shel perush rashi la-torah," in *Limmud ve-da'at be-maḥashavah yehudit*, ed. Haim Kreisel, 2 vols. (Beer-Sheva: Ben Gurion University Press of the Negev, 2006), 2:143–44. For reservations, see Talbi, "Le-hishtalshelutah," 185–86n106.
25. Israel M. Ta-Shma, "Rabbenu 'Asher u-veno r[abbi] Ya'aqov ba'al ha-ṭurim: ben 'ashkenaz li-sefarad," *Pe'amim* 46–47 (1991): 75–91; Judah Galinsky, "Ashkenazim in Sefarad: The Rosh and the Tur on the Codification of Jewish Law," *Jewish Law Annual* 16 (2006): 3–23; Galinsky, "An Ashkenazic Rabbi Encounters Sephardic Culture: R. Asher Ben Jehiel's Attitude Towards Philosophy and Science," *Simon Dubnow Institute Yearbook* 8 (2009): 191–211.
26. *Shulḥan 'arukh, 'Oraḥ ḥayyim* 285:2. See Penkower, "Tahalikh," 137–44. For Jacob's influence, see Judah Galinsky, "'Ve-zakhah zeh ha-ḥakham yoter mikulam she-ha-kol lamedu mi-sefarav': 'al tefuṣat "Arba'ah ṭurim' le-rabbi Ya'aqov ben 'Asher mi-zeman ketivato ve'ad sof ha-me'ah ha-15," *Sidra* 19 (2004): 25–45.

27. Solomon Luria, *Yam shel shelomo* (Jerusalem: Mechon Mishnat David, 1996), 78n14 on b. Kiddushin 41a.
28. *Magen 'avraham* on *Shulḥan 'arukh, 'Oraḥ ḥayyim*, 285:2 (echoed in a ruling at the same place in *Mishnah berurah* of Israel Meir Ha-Kohen, s.v. "*ḥashuv kemo targum*," with the further observation that the *Commentary* is superior to the Targum in its emphasis on "the midrashim of the rabbinic sages").
29. Moshe Halbertal, *People of the Book: Canon, Meaning, and Authority* (Cambridge, MA: Harvard University Press, 1997), 3.
30. Yosi Peretz, "Shnayim miqra' ve-'eḥad targum: le-'or ha-mimṣa be-khitvei ha-yad ha-'ashkenaziyim shel ha-torah bi-yemei ha-benayim," *Ṭalelei 'Orot* 14 (2008): 53–61; and Talbi, "Le-hishtalshelutah," 186–87. For more on the Targum's status, see Élodie Attia, "Targum's Layout in Ashkenazic Manuscripts: Preliminary Methodological Observations," in *A Jewish Targum in a Christian World*, ed. Alberdina Houtman, Eveline van Staalduine-Sulman, and Hans-Martin Kim (Leiden: Brill, 2014), 99–122.
31. For an image, see David Stern, *The Jewish Bible: A Material History* (Seattle: University of Washington Press, 2017), 108, fig. 2.18.
32. Israel Abrahams, ed., *Hebrew Ethical Wills* (Philadelphia: Jewish Publication Society, 1976), 214.
33. Joseph ben Moses, *Sefer leqeṭ yosher: kolel minhagim pisqei halakhot u-teshuvot . . .*, ed. Jakob Freimann (Berlin: H. Itzkowski, 1902–1904; photo offset, 2 vols. in 1; Jerusalem: Mekizei Nirdamim, 1964), 1:54.
34. For part of the characterization given here, see Rachel Zohn Mincer, "The Increasing Reliance on Ritual Handbooks in Pre–Print Era Ashkenaz," *Jewish History* 31 (2017): 105 (n. 7 with regard to Joseph's work).
35. For an overview, see Raymond Scheindlin, "Merchants and Intellectuals, Rabbis and Poets: Judeo-Arabic Culture in the Golden Age of Islam," in *Cultures of the Jews: A New History*, ed. David Biale (New York: Schocken, 2002), 313–86.
36. Lamin Sanneh, *Beyond Jihad: The Pacifist Tradition in West African Islam* (Oxford: Oxford University Press, 2016), 41.
37. Abraham ibn Daud, *The Book of Tradition (Sefer Ha-Qabbalah)*, ed. Gerson D. Cohen (Philadelphia: Jewish Publication Society, 1967), 99. For Ibn Daud's oversimplification, not least in his abstracting from those like Maimonides who remained in the Muslim world, see Bernard Septimus, *Hispano-Jewish Culture in Transition: The Career and Controversies of Ramah* (Cambridge, MA: Harvard University Press, 1982), 117–18n10.
38. Grossman, *Ḥakhmei ṣorfat*, 178n198, 569–70.
39. Ibn Daud, *Sefer ha-qabbalah*, 65. For the period of transition, see Jonathan Ray, *The Sephardic Frontier: The Reconquista and the Jewish Community in Medieval Iberia* (Ithaca, NY: Cornell University Press, 2006).
40. Ibn Daud, *Sefer ha-qabbalah*, 58, 66.

41. The first explanation is deemed wanting in Avraham Gross, "Rashi u-masoret limmud ha-torah she-bi-khetav bi-sefarad," in *Rashi: 'iyyunim bi-yeṣirato*, ed. Zvi Aryeh Steinfeld (Ramat-Gan: Bar-Ilan University Press, 1993), 28n4. Within a few decades, a later glossator infiltrated an encomium to Rashi into Ibn Daud's text; see note 156, this chapter.
42. The long-conjectural identification of Ibn Daud with the Arabic-into-Latin translator "Avendauth" is clinched. See Krisztina Szilágyi, "A Fragment of a Book of Physics from the David Kaufmann *Genizah* Collection [Budapest] and the Identity of Ibn Daud with Avendauth," *Aleph* 16 (2016): 11–31; and Gad Freudenthal, "Abraham Ibn Daud, Avendauth Dominicus Gundissalinus and Practical Mathematics in Mid-Twelfth Century Toledo," *Aleph* 16 (2016): 61–106. For the larger translation movement, see Charles Burnett, "The Coherence of the Arabic-Latin Translation Programme in Toledo in the Twelfth Century," *Science in Context* 14 (2001): 249–88.
43. Shamma Friedman, "Klum lo niṣneṣ perush rashi be-vet midrasho shel ha-rambam?," in *Rashi: demuto vi-yeṣirato*, ed. Avraham Grossman and Sara Japhet, 2 vols. (Jerusalem: Zalman Shazar, 2008), 2:403–64.
44. Avraham ben ha-Rambam, *Perush rabbenu 'Avraham ben ha-rambam 'al bereshit u-shemot*, ed. Ephraim Wiesenberg (Letchworth: Rabbi S. D. Sassoon, 1959), 40–41, 435–37. In the first instance (on Gen 20:16), the ideas imputed to Rashi do not appear in current editions of the *Commentary*. In the second, Abraham refers to a French commentator, who may or may not be Rashi. Paul B. Fenton, "The Post-Maimonidean Schools of Exegesis in the East: Abraham Maimonides, the Pietists, Tanḥûm Ha-Yərušalmi and the Yemenite School," in *HBOT*, ed. Magne Sæbø , vol. I/2: *From the Beginnings to the Middle Ages*, part 2: *The Middle Ages* (Göttingen: Vanderhoeck & Ruprecht, 2000), 436, includes Rashi among Abraham's sources as if it were simply assured. A document from the Cairo Geniza probably datable to the thirteenth century registers the *Commentary* in a list of items included in an estate sale, slightly arabicizing its name (*per[ush] 'al-ta[w]ra le-rabbenu Shelomo*(; see Nehemiah Allony, *Ha-sifriyah ha-yehudit bi-yemei ha-benayim: reshimot sefarim mi-genizat qahir*, ed. Miriam Frenkel and Haggai Ben-Shammai (Jerusalem: Mechon Ben-Zvi, 2006), 216.
45. Elisha R. Russ-Fishbane, "Between Politics and Piety: Abraham Maimonides and His Times" (PhD diss., Harvard University, 2009), 70–95; and Friedman, "Klum," 411. For a French rabbi in contact with Abraham, see Ephraim Kanarfogel and Moshe Sokolow, "Rashi ve-rambam nifgashim be-genizah ha-qahirit: hafnayah 'el sefer 'mishneh torah' be-mikhtav me-'et 'ehad mi-ba'alei ha-tosafot," *Tarbiz* 67 (1998): 411–16. See further Ephraim Kanarfogel, "The 'Aliyah of 'Three Hundred Rabbis' in 1211: Tosafist Attitudes Toward Settling in the Land of Israel," *JQR* 76 (1986): 191–215.

46. Elisha Russ-Fishbane, "Maimonidean Controversies After Maimonides: The Egyptian Context," *HUCA* 88 (2017): 202. Note the scholar in the Near East who modeled his work after Rashi as discussed in Jacob Mann, "A Commentary to the Pentateuch à la Rashi's," *HUCA* 15 (1940): 497–527.
47. On northern connections, see Septimus, *Hispano-Jewish Culture*, 26–38. For overviews of some of the new learning, see Israel M. Ta-Shma, "Halakhah, qabbalah u-filosofyah bi-sefarad ha-noṣerit (le-viqoret ha-sefer 'Toledot ha-yehudim bi-sefarad ha-noṣerit')," in *Keneset meḥqarim: 'iyyunim ba-sifrut ha-rabbanit bi-yemei ha-benayim*, vol. 2: *Sefarad* (Jerusalem: Bialik, 2004–10), 279–98; and Eric Lawee, "Sephardic Intellectuals: Challenges and Creativity (1391–1492)," in *The Jew in Medieval Iberia*, ed. Jonathan Ray (Boston: Academic Studies, 2012), 350–91.
48. Ad. Neubauer, "Ergänzungen und Verbesserungen zu Abba Mari's מנחת קנאות aus Hanschriften," *Israelietische Letterbode* 4/5 (1878–1879): 4:162.
49. Neubauer, "Ergänzungen," 163. For the larger dispute, see Bernard Septimus, "Piety and Power in Thirteenth-Century Catalonia," in *Studies in Medieval Jewish History and Literature* [I], ed. Isadore Twersky (Cambridge, MA: Harvard University Press, 1979); and Elka Klein, *Jews, Christian Society, and Royal Power in Medieval Barcelona* (Ann Arbor: University of Michigan Press, 2006), 96–110.
50. For Barcelona as an emergent center at the time, see Stephen P. Bensch, *Barcelona and Its Rulers, 1096–1291* (Cambridge: Cambridge University Press, 1995), 2.
51. Septimus, "Piety and Power," 209, 222n18.
52. Ephraim Kanarfogel, "Between Ashkenaz and Sefarad: Tosafist Teachings in the Talmudic Commentaries of Ritva," in *Between Rashi and Maimonides: Themes in Medieval Jewish Thought, Literature and Exegesis*, ed. Ephraim Kanarfogel and Moshe Sokolow (Jersey City, NJ: Ktav, 2010), 239.
53. Septimus, *Hispano-Jewish Culture*, 12, 21, 130n155.
54. Israel M. Ta-Shma, *Ha-sifrut ha-parshanit la-talmud be-'eropah u-vi-ṣefon 'afriqah: qorot, 'ishim, ve-shiṭot*, 2 vols. (Jerusalem: Magnes, 2004), 2:22, 40–41, 49–50, 84, 90.
55. Isadore Twersky, *Rabad of Posquieres: A Twelfth-Century Talmudist* (Cambridge, MA: Harvard University Press, 1962), 240–44; Septimus, *Hispano-Jewish Culture*, 32–35.
56. *Ḥiddushei ha-ramah 'al masekhet sanhedrin* (New York: Hotsa'at H.Y.L, 1953), 169a, as in Septimus, *Hispano-Jewish Culture*, 76–77.
57. Septimus, *Hispano-Jewish Culture*, 78.
58. For scholarship on the topic, see Jonathan Kearney, *Rashi: Linguist Despite Himself: A Study of the Linguistic Dimension of Rabbi Solomon Yishaqi's Commentary on Deuteronomy* (New York: T&T Clark, 2010), 33–37, to which can be added

Hanokh Gamliel, *Rashi ke-farshan u-khe-valshan: tefisot taḥbiriyyot be-ferush rashi la-torah* (Jerusalem: Bialik, 2010).

59. For the cited expression, see Israel M. Ta-Shma, "The Study of Aggadah and Its Interpretation in Early Rabbinic Literature," in *Creativity and Tradition: Studies in Medieval Rabbinic Scholarship, Literature and Thought* (Cambridge, MA: Harvard University Center for Jewish Studies, 2006), 205.
60. Carmi Horowitz, "'Al perush ha-'aggadot shel ha-rashba: ben qabbalah le-filosofyah," *Daat* 18 (1987): 15–27. For Adret's antirationalist polemical activity, see Gregg Stern, *Philosophy and Rabbinic Culture: Jewish Interpretation and Controversy in Medieval Languedoc* (Abingdon: Routledge, 2009), 144–212.
61. See note 45 in chapter 1, this volume.
62. See, in general, Ch. Merchavia, *Ha-talmud bi-re'i ha-naṣrut* (Jerusalem: Bialik, 1970). For more recent bibliography, see Talya Fishman, *Becoming the People of the Talmud: Oral Torah as Written Tradition in Medieval Jewish Cultures* (Philadelphia: University of Pennsylvania Press, 2011), 171–74.
63. Shem Tov ben Shaprut, *Pardes rimmonim* (Sabbioneta, 1554), 1–2. See Lester A. Segal, "Late-Fourteenth Century Perception of Classical Jewish Lore: Shem Tob Ben Isaac Shaprut's Aggadic Exegesis," in *From Ancient Israel to Modern Judaism: Intellect in Quest of Understanding: Essays in Honor of Marvin Fox*, ed. Jacob Neusner, Ernest S. Frerichs, and Nahum M. Sarna, 4 vols. (Atlanta, GA.: Scholars Press, 1989), 2:206–28.
64. Rashi on Exodus 14:7. See, briefly, Jeremy Cohen, *A Historian in Exile: Solomon Ibn Verga, Shevet Yehudah, and the Jewish-Christian Encounter* (Philadelphia: University of Pennsylvania Press), 74, and note 114 in chapter 6, this volume.
65. For the description of the cause of his departure, see Ibn Ezra's introduction to his commentary on Lamentations (*MGH: Ḥamesh megillot*, ed. Menachem Cohen [Ramat-Gan: Bar-Ilan University, 2012], 29). On the identity of the "tormentors," see Uriel Simon, "Madua' 'azav r[abbi] 'Avraham 'ibn 'Ezra 'et sefarad 'be-nefesh nivhelet'?" in *Zer rimonim: meḥqarim ba-miqra' u-ve-farshanuto muqdashim le-prof' Rimon Kasher*, ed. Michael Avioz, Elie Assis, and Yael Shemesh (Atlanta, GA: Society of Biblical Literature, 2013), 489–502. For his itinerary, see Norman Golb, *The Jews in Medieval Normandy* (Cambridge: Cambridge University Press, 1998), 253–96. For his works correlated with provenance, see Shlomo Sela and Gad Freudenthal, "Abraham Ibn Ezra's Scholarly Writings: A Chronological Listing," *Aleph* 6 (2006): 13–55.
66. Uriel Simon, "Transplanting the Wisdom of Spain to Christian Lands: The Failed Efforts of R. Abraham Ibn Ezra," *Simon Dubnow Institute Yearbook* 8 (2009): 139–89. For his literary output in Muslim Spain, see Gad Freudenthal, "Abraham Ibn Ezra and Judah Ibn Tibbon as Cultural Intermediaries. Early Stages in the Introduction of Non-Rabbinic Learning into Provence in the Mid-Twelfth

Century," in *Exchange and Transmission Across Cultural Boundaries: Philosophy, Mysticism and Science in the Mediterranean World,* ed. Sarah Stroumsa and Haggai Ben-Shammai (Jerusalem: Israel Academy of Science and Humanities, 2013), 64.

67. *MGH: Sefer Bereshit,* 1:24. See Uriel Simon, *'Ozen milin tivḥan: meḥqarim be-darko ha-parshanit shel r[abbi] 'Avraham 'ibn 'Ezra* (Ramat-Gan: Bar-Ilan University Press, 2013), 13–30 and Mordechai Z. Cohen, "Emergence of the Rule of Peshat in Jewish Bible Exegesis," in *Interpreting Scriptures in Judaism, Christianity and Islam: Overlapping Inquiries,* ed. Mordechai Z. Cohen and Adele Berlin (Cambridge: Cambridge University Press, 2016), 216–19.
68. Jay M. Harris, *How Do We Know This? Midrash and the Fragmentation of Modern Judaism* (Albany: SUNY Press, 1995), 82–85.
69. Martin I. Lockshin, "Tradition or Context: Two Exegetes Struggle with Peshat," in *From Ancient Israel to Modern Judaism: Essays in Honor of Marvin Fox,* ed. Jacob Neusner, Ernest S. Frerichs, Nahum M. Sarna, 4 vols. (Atlanta, GA: Scholars Press, 1989), 2:173–86.
70. For his alienation, see Aharon Mondschein, "R[abbi] 'Avraham 'ibn 'Ezra – ha-'ish neged ha-zerem," *Beit Mikra* 49 (2004): 140–55. For often overlooked enthusiastic reaction, see Gad Freudenthal, "Abraham Ibn Ezra and Judah Ibn Tibbon," 59–66.
71. Simon, *'Ozen,* 31–67; and Joseph Yahalom, "Aesthetic Models in Conflict: Classicist versus Ornamental in Jewish Poetics," in *Renewing the Past, Reconfiguring Jewish Culture,* ed. Ross Brann and Adam Sutcliffe (Philadelphia: University of Pennsylvania Press, 2004), 22.
72. Sela and Freudenthal, "Abraham Ibn Ezra's Scholarly Writings," 19.
73. Abraham Ibn Ezra, *Safah berurah* (partial annotated edition), ed. M. Wilensky, *Devir* 2 (1924), 288. See Cohen, "Emergence," 217; and, for possible hyperbole in the statement regarding Rashi, Aharon Mondschein, "'Ve-'en bi-sefarav peshaṭ raq 'ehad mini 'elef': le-derekh ha-hityaḥasut shel ra'ba' le-ferush rashi la-torah," *'Iyyunei miqra' u-farshanut* 5 (2000): 226.
74. Simon, *'Ozen,* 249–98.
75. Abraham ibn Ezra, *Perushei ha-torah le-rabbenu 'Avraham 'ibn 'Ezra,* ed. Asher Weiser, 3 vols. (Jerusalem: Mosad Harav Kuk, 1976), 1:68 lists fourteen references to Rashi, to which can be added one from what remains of the long commentary on Genesis; see Mondschein, "Ve-'en," 226n16. For Ibn Ezra's diverse interactions with midrash, see Ezra Zion Melamed, *Mefareshei ha-miqra': darkhehem ve-shiṭotehem,* 2nd ed., 2 vols. (Jerusalem: Magnes, 1979), 1:678–94.
76. On Exod 15:2, see *MGH:* Sefer *Shemot,* ed. Menachem Cohen, 2 vols. (Ramat-Gan: Bar-Ilan University, 2007–2012), 1:119. The example is complicated, as his harsh assessment may in this case be inaccurate. If it is, one might conclude that his aim was to use expertise in Arabic as a way to assert superiority in a manner that Jews in Christian Europe could not contest. For this conclusion, see Miriam

Goldstein and Itamar Kislev, "Abraham b. Ezra's 'Spirantized *peh* in the Arabic Language': The Rules of Grammar versus the Requirements of Exegesis and Polemic," *Journal of Jewish Studies* 67 (2016): 152–56.

77. Mondschein, "Ve-'en," especially at 242–43; and Simon, *'Ozen*, 46n56.
78. For the habit of the sages "in the lands of the Greeks and Edomites" to "chase after" midrash, see in the introduction to Ibn Ezra's "Shorter Commentary on the Torah," the "fourth way" (*MGH: Sefer Bereshit*, 1:25 [Hebrew pagination]).
79. On Gen 10:8–9. Rabbinic sources: *Ḥamishah ḥumshei torah: Rashi ha-shalem*, 7 vols. to date (Jerusalem: Ariel, 1986-), *Bereshit*, 1:105–106. For precursors and parallels, see K. van der Toorn and P. W. van der Horst, "Nimrod Before and After the Bible," *Harvard Theological Review* 83 (1990): 17–29.
80. Further examples include Rashi on Gen 11:29 and Exod 1:15. For rabbinic background, see Isaac Heinemann, *Darkhei ha-'aggadah*, 3rd. ed. (Jerusalem: Magnes, 1974), 28–29, 110–12. For the likelihood that Rashi did not know Latin, see Daniel J. Lasker, "Jewish Knowledge of Christianity in the Twelfth and Thirteenth Centuries," in *Studies in Medieval Jewish Intellectual and Social History: Festschrift in Honor of Robert Chazan*, ed. David Engel, Lawrence H. Schiffman, and Elliot R. Wolfson (Leiden: Brill, 2012), 99.
81. On Gen 10:4 (*MGH: Sefer Bereshit*, 1:108). Mondschein, "Ve-'en," 231, mentions this example only with respect to Ibn Ezra's treatment of name etymologies, but the positive portrayal of Nimrod further supports his claim that Ibn Ezra tacitly responds to Rashi in this case.
82. Judah ibn Moskoni, "Introduction to *'Even ha-'ezer*," ed. Abraham Berliner, *'Oṣar ṭov* 2 (= Hebrew appendix to *Magazin für die Wissenschaft des Judenthums* 5) (1878): 9. On this as the correct version of Ibn Moskoni's name, see Steven Bowman, "The Jewish Experience in Byzantium," in *The Jewish-Greek Tradition in Antiquity and the Byzantine Empire*, ed. James K. Aitken and James Carleton Paget (New York: Cambridge University Press, 2014), 51–52; and Israel Moshe Sandman, "The MeSOBEB NeTIBOT of Samuel Ibn Matut ('Motot'): Introductory Excursus, Critical Edition, and Annotated Translation," 2 vols. (PhD diss., University of Chicago, 2006), 1:5n.20.
83. Rashi on Gen 22:8. For Isaac's age, see Rashi on Gen 25:20. For Isaac as an "active and willing participant" in his near sacrifice on Rashi's telling and its status as a test of son as much as father, see Devorah Schoenfeld, *Isaac on Jewish and Christian Altars: Polemic and Exegesis in Rashi and the Glossa Ordinaria* (New York: Fordham University Press, 2013), 117–18.
84. Emil L. Fackenheim, *Encounters Between Judaism and Modern Philosophy: A Preface to Future Jewish Thought* (New York: Basic Books, 1973), 54.
85. Rashi on Gen 22:6, 8; 25:20 (*MGH: Sefer Bereshit*, 1:194, 196; and 2:2), and Ibn Ezra on Gen 22:4–5 (*MGH: Sefer Bereshit*, 1:194). On active martyrdom in Ashkenaz, see Abraham Gross, *Struggling with Tradition: Reservations about Active Martyrdom in the Middle Ages* (Leiden: Brill, 2004).

86. Moshe Halbertal, *Concealment and Revelation: Esotericism in Jewish Thought and Its Philosophical Implications*, trans. Jackie Feldman (Princeton, NJ: Princeton University Press, 2007), 36.
87. Uriel Simon, "Transplanting," 181–89.
88. See chapter 7, this volume.
89. Isadore Twersky, "Introduction," in *Rabbi Moses Naḥmanides (Ramban): Explorations in His Religious and Literary Virtuosity*, ed. Isadore Twersky (Cambridge, MA: Harvard University Press, 1983), 4.
90. Jonathan Jacobs, "Ha-'im hikkir ramban 'et perush rashbam la-torah?" *Madda'ei ha-yahadut* 46 (2009): 85–108.
91. Bernard Septimus, "'Open Rebuke and Concealed Love': Naḥmanides and the Andalusian Tradition," in *Rabbi Moses Naḥmanides (Ramban): Explorations in His Religious and Literary Virtuosity*, ed. Isadore Twersky (Cambridge, MA: Harvard University Press, 1983), 16.
92. *MGH: Sefer Bereshit*, 1:34.
93. Yaakov Licht, "Le-darko shel ha-ramban," in *Meḥqarim be-sifrut ha-talmud bi-leshon ḥazal u-ve-farshanut ha-miqra'*, ed. Mordechai A. Friedman et al. (Tel Aviv: University Publishing Projects, 1983), 228.
94. Aaron W. Hughes, "Concepts of Scripture in Nahmanides," in *Jewish Concepts of Scripture: A Comparative Introduction*, ed. Benjamin D. Sommer (New York: New York University Press, 2012), 153. Septimus, "Open Rebuke," 16n21, concludes more justly: "Nahmanides' *Commentary* is, among other things, a sustained critique of Rashi's more midrashic interpretations of Scripture. Although this criticism never approaches the harsh language occasionally directed at Ibn Ezra, it seems to me, substantively, more fundamental and thoroughgoing than the critique of Ibn Ezra." For samplings of a range of interactions with Rashi, see Melamed, *Mefareshei*, 2:989–96.
95. Twersky, "Introduction," 4n10.
96. Miriam Sklarz, "Darko shel ramban be-'immuṣ divrei ra'ba' ve-hava'atam shelo' be-shem 'omram," *Shenaton le-ḥeqer ha-miqra' ve-ha-mizraḥ ha-qadum* 24 (2016): 285–302. On the surface, Nahmanides casts his relationship with Ibn Ezra in more restive terms than his stance toward Rashi, speaking of "open rebuke and concealed love." In the event, there are some two dozen places where Nahmanides flays Ibn Ezra for an unforgivable trespass; see Miriam (Hoffman) Sklarz, "Ha-leshonot 'shibbesh' u-'fittah' be-tokhaḥto shel ramban le-ra'ba'," *'Iyyunei miqra' u-farshanut* 8 (2008): 553–71. In these cases, however, the failing invariably involves a larger religious principle, as when Ibn Ezra casts doubt on the historicity of a miracle posited by the sages. A case in point is Abraham's miraculous escape from the fiery furnace, a reading Rashi had brought to the fore. See Miriam Sklarz, "Hashlakhat 'avram le-khivshan ha-'esh be-khitvehem shel ra'ba' ve-ramban: ben parshanut, shirah

u-derashah," *'Areshet* 3 (2012): 23–33. For Nahmanides on miracles, see David Berger, "Miracles and the Natural Order in Naḥmanides," in *Rabbi Moses Naḥmanides (Ramban): Explorations in His Religious and Literary Virtuosity*, ed. Isadore Twersky (Cambridge, MA: Harvard University Press, 1983), 107–28; and Miriam Sklarz, "''O she-hayah mi-ma'aseh nisim' – meqom ha-nes be-hakhra'otav ha-parshaniyot shel ramban," *Bet miqra'* 58 (2013): 100–16.

97. Halbertal, *Concealment and Revelation*, 35.

98. Rashi's interests were not restricted wholly to the exoteric, but he basically excluded esoterica from his *Commentary*; see Ephraim Kanarfogel, *"Peering Through the Lattices": Mystical, Magical, and Pietistic Dimensions in the Tosafist Period* (Detroit, MI: Wayne State University Press, 2000), 144–53. For Nahmanides's kabbalistic exegesis, see Elliot R. Wolfson, "By Way of Truth: Aspects of Nahmanides' Kabbalistic Hermeneutic," *AJS Review* 14 (1989): 153–76. For esotericism as a point of contact between Nahmanides and Ibn Ezra, see Miriam Sklarz, "Sodotav shel ra'ba' be-ferush ramban la-torah—ziqato shel minuaḥ ve-heqsher parshani," in *Zer rimonim: meḥqarim ba-miqra' u-ve-farshanuto muqdashim le-prof' Rimon Kasher*, ed. Michael Avioz, Elie Assis, and Yael Shemesh (Atlanta, GA: Society of Biblical Literature, 2013), 503–23.

99. On Gen 9:4 (*MGH: Sefer Bereshit*, 1:99). Cf. b. Sanhedrin 59a. On the larger issue, see Yossi Erel, "Parshanut peshaṭ la-miqra' ve-halakhah pesuqah ba-'avodato shel ramban," *Jewish Studies Internet Journal* 8 (2009): 1–36.

100. Yaakov Elman, "'It Is No Empty Thing': Nahmanides and the Search for Omnisignificance," *Torah U-Madda Journal* 4 (1993): 28.

101. For this aspect of Nahmanides's exegesis, see Michelle J. Levine, *Nahmanides on Genesis: The Art of Biblical Portraiture* (Providence, RI: Brown University, 2009).

102. On Gen 46:29 (*MGH: Sefer Bereshit*, 157–58). For discussion and the translation cited here, see Levine, *Nahmanides on Genesis*, 251–52. For analysis, see Nehama Leibowitz, *Limmud parshanei ha-torah u-derakhim lehora'atam: sefer bereshit* (Jerusalem: World Zionist Organization, 1975), 357–61; and Mordechai Cohen, "Gedolim ḥiqrei lev: regishut pesikhologit be-ferushei ramban la-torah u-le-'iyov," in *Teshurah le-'Amos: 'asupat meḥqarim be-farshanut ha-miqra' mugeshet le-'Amos Ḥakham*, ed. Moshe Bar-Asher, Noah Ḥakham, and Yosef Ofer (Alon Shevut: Tevunot, 2007), 215.

103. For relatively early evidence of the presence of other commentaries of Rashi in Sefardic awareness, see the findings regarding a fragmentary Proverbs commentary included in a thirteenth-century anonymous codex produced in the Iberian Peninsula, in Esperanza Alfonso, "In Between Cultures: An Anonymous Commentary on the Book of Proverbs from Iberia," *Journal of Jewish Studies* 64 (2013): 132–34.

104. See Moshe Idel, *Absorbing Perfections: Kabbalah and Interpretation* (New Haven, CT: Yale University Press, 2002), 429–37.
105. Bahya ben Asher, *Be'ur 'al ha-torah*, ed. Hayyim D. Chavel, 3 vols. (Jerusalem: Mosad Harav Kuk, 1966), 1:5.
106. "My intention is to cite the statements not only of Catholic but also of Jewish teachers, and especially Rabbi Solomon, who among all the Jewish exegetes has put forward the most reasonable arguments, in order to illuminate the literal meaning of the text." As in A. J. Minnis and A. B. Scott, eds., *Medieval Literary Theory and Criticism, c. 1100–c. 1375: The Commentary Tradition* (Oxford: Clarendon, 1988), 270.
107. For the Zohar's literary character, including stress on anonymity rather than pseudepigraphy, see Daniel Abrams, *Kabbalistic Manuscripts and Textual Theory: Methodologies of Textual Scholarship and Editorial Practice in the Study of Jewish Mysticism* (Jerusalem: Magnes, 2010), 224–428; and Elliot R. Wolfson, "Anonymity and the Kabbalistic Ethos: A Fourteenth-Century Supercommentary on the Commentary on the Sefirot," *Kabbalah* 35 (2016): 55–112.
108. Wilhelm Bacher, "L'exégèse biblique dans le Zohar," *REJ* 22 (1891): 41–42.
109. Oded Yisraeli, "Midrashic Disputations in the *Zohar*," *HUCA* 84–85 (2013–14): 127–46.
110. See chapter 5, this volume.
111. Aharon Mondschein, "'Ḥakhmei ha-masoret bade'u mi-libam ṭe'amim li-mele'im u-le-ḥaserim': 'al ma'avaqo shel r[abbi] 'Avraham 'ibn 'Ezra be-niṣṣul ha-ketiv ha-miqra'i ke-kheli parshani," *Shenaton le-ḥeqer ha-miqra' ve-ha-mizraḥ ha-qadum* 19 (2009): 311.
112. Aryeh Leib (Leon) Feldman, "Teshuvot ha-ran le-hassagot ha-ramban 'al divrei rashi be-ferusho la-torah," *Sinai* 137 (2006): 208–17; and the introduction to Anselm Astruc, *Midreshei ha-torah*, ed. Shimon Eppenstein (Berlin, 1899), xi.
113. Isaac Abarbanel, *Perush 'al nevi'im rishonim* (Jerusalem: Torah ve-Daat, 1955), 13. See Eric Lawee, "Isaac Abarbanel: From Medieval to Renaissance Jewish Biblical Scholarship," in *HBOT*, ed. Magne Sæbø, vol. II: *From the Renaissance to the Enlightenment* (Göttingen: Vanderhoeck & Ruprecht, 2008), 195–99; and Jair Haas, "Divine Perfection and Methodological Inconsistency: Towards an Understanding of Isaac Abarbanel's Exegetical Frame of Mind," *Jewish Studies Quarterly* 17 (2010): 302–57.
114. On Isa 26:7, in Isaac Abarbanel, *Perush 'al nevi'im 'aḥaronim* (Jerusalem: Benei Arabel, 1979), 141. Cp. Rashi on Isa 26:11, (*MGH: Sefer Yisha'yahu*, ed. Menachem Cohen [Ramat-Gan: Bar-Ilan University, 1996], 170).
115. Eric Lawee, *Isaac Abarbanel's Stance Toward Tradition: Defense, Dissent, and Dialogue* (Albany: SUNY Press, 2001), 93–125.
116. On Josh 5:4, in Abarbanel, *Perush 'al nevi'im rishonim*, 30–31.

117. Isaac Abarbanel, *Perush 'al ha-torah*, 3 vols. (Jerusalem: Benei Arabel, 1964), 1:51.
118. On Gen 10:8, in Abarbanel, *Perush 'al ha-torah*, 1:172.
119. Lawee, *Isaac Abarbanel's Stance*, 97–99, 125.
120. Eric Lawee, "From Sefarad to Ashkenaz: A Case Study in the Rashi Supercommentary Tradition," *AJS Review* 30 (2006): 401–402.
121. See chapter 3, this volume.
122. Simcha Assaf, *Meqorot le-toledot ha-ḥinukh be-yisra'el*, ed. Shmuel Glick, 6 vols. (New York: Jewish Theological Seminary of America, 2002), 2:67. On Ibn Abbas, see Dov Schwartz, "'Meharsim', 'talmudiyim' ve-'anshei ha-ḥokhmah: 'emdato ve-darshanuto shel r[abbi] Yehudah ben Shemu'el 'ibn 'Abbas," *Tarbiẓ* 62 (1993): 585–615.
123. For the curriculum as more ideal than real, see Gerrit Bos, "R. Moshe Narboni: Philosopher and Physician, a Critical Analysis of *Sefer Oraḥ Ḥayyim*," *Medieval Encounters* 1 (1995): 246.
124. Solomon ben Adret, *Teshuvot ha-rashba' ha-meyuḥasot le-ha-ramban* (Tel Aviv: Eshel, 1959), 3 (responsum 1).
125. Abrahams ed., *Hebrew Ethical Wills*, 174. Despite the urgings of Judah ben Asher in his ethical will, Judah's father, Asher, did much to ensure that Bible study was not a staple of the curriculum in Castile; see Yoel Marciano, "Ḥakhamim bi-sefarad ba-me'ah ha-ḥamesh-'esrei: ḥinukham, limmudam, yeṣiratam, ma'amadam, u-demutam" (PhD diss., Hebrew University, 2012), 25.
126. Judah Khalatz, *Mesiaḥ 'illemim*, ed. Moshe Filip (Petah Tikvah: Filip, 2001), 28.
127. Khalatz, *Mesiaḥ 'illemim*, 31. For "reading" in the Talmud in the Sefardic context, see Mordechai Breuer, *'Ohalei torah: ha-yeshivah, tavnitah ve-toledoteha* (Jerusalem: Zalman Shazar, 2003), 179.
128. Duran, *Ma'aseh 'efod*, 17, 41; Gross, "Rashi," 43–45; and Maud Kozodoy, *The Secret Faith of Maestre Honoratus: Profayt Duran and Jewish Identity in Late Medieval Iberia* (Philadelphia: University of Pennsylvania Press, 2015), 161–203. In Duran's day, the status of Rashi's exegesis even became a point of contention in internal Christian discourse, in this case owing to a willing convert. Pablo de Santa Maria, archbishop of Burgos (1351–1435), born Solomon Halevi, composed *Additiones ad postillam Nicolai de Lira*, a work of over a thousand comments, essentially strictures, on interpretations of his famous predecessor, Nicholas of Lyre. His main complaint was Nicholas's overreliance on "the glosses of Solomon" (*glossa Salomonis*) despite "the absurdity of Rashi's commentaries on the sacred scripture." Elsewhere he explained Rashi's indispensable role as an expositor of Talmud while insisting that the value of Rashi's work in that sphere was not matched by "his interpretation of the scripture." Pablo did not denounce recourse to Jewish sources, but true to his Sefardic heritage, he praised writers such as Ibn Ezra and Maimonides as being "greater

and more solemn" in their sagacity than Rashi. The main exegete among Pablo's Jewish sources was probably another Sefardic writer, Nahmanides. See Yosi Yisraeli, "A Christianized Sephardic Critique of Rashi's *Peshaṭ* in Pablo de Santa María's *Additiones ad Postillam Nicolai de Lyra*," in *Medieval Exegesis and Religious Difference: Commentary, Conflict, and Community in the Premodern Mediterranean*, ed. Ryan Szpiech (New York: Fordham University Press, 2015), 138, who goes so far as to speak of the "Nahmanides-Pablo critique of the Rashi-Lyre commentary" (132–33). For Nicholas and Rashi, see the studies of Deeana Copeland Klepper and Ari Geiger cited in note 5 in the introduction, this volume.

129. Görge K. Hasselhoff, "The Parisian Talmud Trials and the Translation of Rashi's Bible Commentaries," *Henoch* 37 (2015): 29–42; and Philippe Bobichon, "Quotations, Translations, and Uses of Jewish Texts in Ramon Martí's *Pugio fidei*," in *The Late Medieval Hebrew Book in the Western Mediterranean: Hebrew Manuscripts and Incunabula in Context*, ed. Javier del Barco (Leiden: Brill, 2015), 276–77.

130. Solomon ibn Verga, *Shevet yehudah*, ed. Azriel Shohat (Jerusalem: Bialik, 1946), 99, 107.

131. Moisés Orfali, "Alusiones polémicas a la exégesis de Rasi en la controversia de Tortosa," *Helmantica* 36 (1985): 107–17.

132. Meanwhile, the *Commentary* proved influential at a more cooperative end of the spectrum of Christian–Jewish interaction, figuring in the Castilian translation of the Hebrew Bible produced around 1430 by Moses Arragel and his Christian associates that came to be called the "Biblia de Alba," a work that also attests the impact of others of Rashi's biblical commentaries. See Ángel Sáenz-Badillos, "Jewish and Christian Interpretations in Arragel's Biblical Glosses," in *Medieval Exegesis and Religious Difference: Commentary, Conflict, and Community in the Premodern Mediterranean*, ed. Ryan Szpiech (New York: Fordham University Press, 2015), 142; and Eleazar Gutwirth, "Arragel on Ruth: Rashi in Fifteenth Century Castilian?," in *Rashi 1040–1990: Hommage à Ephraïm E. Urbach*, ed. Gabrielle Sed-Rajna (Paris: Cerf, 1993), 657–62.

133. Eleazar Gutwirth and Miguel Angel Motis Dolader, "Twenty-Six Jewish Libraries from Fifteenth-Century Spain," *Library* 18 (1996): 27–53. References to the *Commentary* appear on 35, 37, 40, 41 (twice), 42, 45, 46 (twice), 51, 52. There are also general references to Rashi's "glosses on the Bible" on 34, 39, 44, 45 (three times), 47 (twice), 48 (twice), 49 (twice). For "declaraciones," see 38.

134. For pioneering studies, see Joseph Hacker, "Ha-'midrash' ha-sefaradi: sifriyah ṣiburit yehudit," in *Rishonim ve-'aḥaronim: meḥqarim be-toledot yisra'el mugashim le-'Avraham Grossman*, ed. Joseph R. Hacker, B. Z. Kedar, and Yosef Kaplan (Jerusalem: Zalman Shazar, 2010), 263–92; and Hacker, "Jewish Book Owners and Their Libraries in the Iberian Peninsula, Fourteenth-Fifteenth Centuries,"

in *The Late Medieval Hebrew Book in the Western Mediterranean: Hebrew Manuscripts and Incunabula in Context*, ed. Javier del Barco (Leiden; Brill, 2015), 70–104. Spanish (Catalonian, Majorcan, and Aragonese-Sicilian) sources are included for discussion in Danièle Iancu-Agou, "L'importance des écrits de Rachi dans les bibliothèques juives médiévales de l'Europe du Sud," in *Héritages de Rachi*, ed. René-Samuel Sirat (Paris: Éditions de l'éclat, 2006), 151–65.

135. Miriam Frenkel, "Book Lists from the Cairo Genizah: A Window on the Production of Texts in the Middle Ages," *Bulletin of the School of Oriental and African Studies* 80 (2017): 238.

136. See, e.g., Josep Perarnau i Espelt, "Notícia de més de setanta inventaris de llibres de jueus gironins," in *Per a una història de la Girona jueva*, ed. David Romano, 2 vols. (Gerona: Ajuntament de Girona, 1988), 1:283–334 (nos. 128 [separate volumes on Genesis, Exodus, and Leviticus] and, for other references, 205, 200, 235, 344). For further evidence of this form of circulation, see Pierre Vidal, *Les juifs des anciens comtés de Rousillon et de Cerdagne* (Perpignan: Mare Nostrum, 1992), 87.

137. On Ibn Gabbai, see Isidore Epstein, *The Responsa of Rabbi Simon B. Zemah Duran: As a Source of the History of the Jews in North Africa* (London: Oxford University Press, 1930), 98–99; Yitzhak Baer, *A History of the Jews in Christian Spain*, translated by Louis Schoffman, 2 vols. (Philadelphia: Jewish Publication Society, 1961–1966), 2:121–22; and Israel M. Ta-Shma, "Gabbai, Moses Ben Shem-Tov," in *EJ*, ed. Michael Berenbaum and Fred Skolnik, 22 vols. (Detroit: Macmillan, 2007), 7:319.

138. Isaac bar Sheshet, *She'elot u-teshuvot le-rabenu Yiṣḥaq bar Sheshet*, ed. David Metzger, 2 vols. (Jerusalem: Mekhon Yerushalayim, 1993), 2:574 (responsum 394).

139. Moses ibn Gabbai, *'Eved shelomo*, ed. Moshe Filip (Petah Tikvah: Filip 2006), 41.

140. The following draws on Ibn Gabbai, *'Eved shelomo*, 43–44.

141. For philosophy as a cause of alleged weakness in Sefardic resistance to conversion, see Baer, *History of the Jews*, 2:234–37; and Lawee, "Sephardic Intellectuals," 355–58.

142. Bar Sheshet, *She'elot u-teshuvot*, 1:49–51 (responsum 45), translated in Menachem M. Kellner, "Rabbi Isaac Bar Sheshet's Responsum Concerning the Study of Greek Philosophy," *Tradition* 15 (1975): 110–18.

143. Moses Maimonides, *'Iggerot ha-rambam*, ed. Yitzhaq Shailat, 2 vols. (Jerusalem: Ma'aliyot, 1987–1988), 2:502 (based on 1 Sam 8:13).

144. As we will see in chapter 3, this volume, the *Commentary* conveyed the Jewish vision that Ibn Gabbai wished to have it impart in many cases only after his decidedly non-Ashkenazic ministrations.

145. For all that, Ibn Gabbai could himself object to Rashi's grammar based on ideas known from Kimhi. See *'Eved shelomo* on Lev 14:43 (299), where what Rashi regards as a "*niphal* infinitive" Ibn Gabbai regards as a "*hiphil* infinitive" with uncommon vocalization.
146. Cited in Moshe Idel, "'Iyyunim be-shiṭato shel ba'al 'sefer ha-meshiv': pereq be-toledot ha-qabbalah ha-sefaradit," *Sefunot* 17 (1983): 340–41. See further Idel, *Kabbalah: New Perspectives* (New Haven, CT: Yale University Press, 1988), 237–38; Idel, "Noctural Kabbalists," *ARCHÆVS: Études d'histoire des religions* 4 (2000): 63–67; and Lawrence Fine, *Physician of the Soul, Healer of the Cosmos: Isaac Luria and His Kabbalistic Fellowship* (Stanford, CA: Stanford University Press, 2003), 113–15. For bibliography on *Sefer ha-meshiv*, see Moshe Idel, "Revelation and the 'Crisis of Tradition' in Kabbalah: 1475–1575," in *Constructing Tradition: Means and Myths of Transmission in Western Esotericism*, ed. Andreas B. Kilcher (Leiden: Brill, 2010), 265n29; and Amos Goldreich, *Shem ha-kotev u-khetivah 'oṭomaṭit be-sifrut ha-zohar u-ve-modernizm* (Los Angeles: Cherub, 2010), 18n25. For the "secret of the garment," see Elliot R. Wolfson, "The Secret of the Garment in Naḥmanides," *Daat* 24 (1990): xxv–xlix.
147. The author of *Sefer ha-meshiv* was not the first Sefardic savant to ascribe elements of Rashi's corpus to a supernal source. Menahem ben Zerah, a fourteenth-century Castilian scholar from a French background, argued that the Talmud would have been "forgotten from Israel" had not the "holy spirit" rested on Rashi when his wrote his commentaries on it. Even if it says a great deal about Rashi's status as a Talmud scholar in Spain, however, this account should probably be seen as partially if not wholly figurative; see Menahem ben Zerah, *Ṣedah la-derekh* (Warsaw, 1880), 6. For his expression's likely nonliteral purport, see Twersky, *Rabad of Posquieres*, 297.
148. For the Christians, see Görge K. Hasselhoff, "Rashi's Glosses on Isaiah in Bibliothèque Nationale de France, Ms. Lat. 16558," in *Studies on the Latin Talmud*, ed. Ulisse Cecini and Eulàlia Vernet i Pons (Barcelona: Publicacions de la Universitat Autònoma de Barcelona, 2017), 111. For a modern-day resonance, see the editor's note on Rashi's comment on the opening verse of the Torah in *Perushei rashi 'al ha-torah*, ed. Hayyim D. Chavel (Jerusalem: Mosad Harav Kuk, 1990), 2.
149. It may be Rashi's grandson, Samuel ben Meir. See Abraham ibn Ezra, *Yesod mora' ve-sod torah*, ed. Joseph Cohen and Uriel Simon, 2nd rev. ed. (Ramat-Gan: Bar-Ilan University Press, 2007), 218–19.
150. Ephraim Urbach, "Ba-meh zakhah rashi la-to'ar 'parshandata'?" in *Meḥqarim be-madda'ei ha-yahadut*, ed. Moshe David Herr and Yonah Fraenkel, 2 vols. (Jerusalem: Magnes, 1998), 1:15–22, esp. 18 for the cited passage. Note the name that Isaac Maarsen gave to his editions of Rashi's commentaries on

Prophets and Writings: *Parshandata: the Commentary of Raschi on the Prophets and Hagiographs*, 3 vols (Amsterdam and Jerusalem, 1930-36).

151. Isadore Twersky, "Aspects of the Social and Cultural History of Provençal Jewry," in *Studies in Jewish Law and Philosophy* (New York: Ktav, 1982), 186.
152. See Pinchas Roth, "Regional Boundaries and Medieval Halakhah: Rabbinic Responsa from Catalonia to Southern France in the Thirteenth and Fourteenth Centuries," *JQR* 105 (2015): 72–73; and the map of the "self-conceived" territory in question in Stern, *Philosophy and Rabbinic Culture*, 8.
153. Twersky, *Rabad of Posquieres*, 233.
154. Israel M. Ta-Shma, *Rabbi Zeraḥyah ha-levi ba'al ha-ma'or u-venei ḥugo: le-toledot ha-sifrut ha-rabbanit be-provans* (Jerusalem: Mosad Harav Kuk, 1992), 104; Ta-Shma, *Ha-sifrut*, 1:211–12.
155. Abraham ben David, *Sifra devei rav hu sefer torat kohanim . . . 'im perush . . . rabenu 'Avraham ben David* (New York: Om, 1947), 62r. Cf. b. Bava Batra 8b.
156. Penkower, "Tahalikh," 124–25 (citing the gloss as it appears New York, Jewish Theological Seminary, MS R34 [Adler 2237]). Penkower clarifies the likely date and provenance of the gloss.
157. b. Sukkah 28a (there: "a great matter and a small matter").
158. See S. J. Pearce, *The Andalusi Literary & Intellectual Tradition: The Role of Arabic in Judah Ibn Tibbon's Ethical Will* (Bloomington, IN: Indiana University Press, 2017), and literature cited there. For later generations, see James T. Robinson, "The Ibn Tibbon Family: A Dynasty of Translators in Medieval 'Provence'," in *Be'erot Yitzhak: Studies in Memory of Isadore Twersky*, ed. Jay M. Harris (Cambridge, MA: Harvard University Center for Jewish Studies, 2005), 193–224.
159. For Kamhi as the correct vocalization, see Roth, "Regional Boundaries," 83n47. I retain the conventional pronunciation.
160. Twersky, "Aspects," 185–86. Freudenthal, "Abraham Ibn Ezra and Judah Ibn Tibbon," 66–72, posits a modicum of interest in nontraditional literature in Provence prior to the arrival of Andalusian émigré scholars.
161. Hananel Mack, "'Maṣati bi-yesodo shel rabbi Moshe ha-darshan': mah hevi' u-mah lo hevi' rashi be-ferushav mi-torato shel r[abbi] Moshe ha-darshan," in *Rashi: demuto vi-yeṣirato*, ed. Avraham Grossman and Sara Japhet, 2 vols. (Jerusalem: Zalman Shazar, 2008), 2:327–51; and Mack, "The Bifurcated Legacy of Rabbi Moses Hadarshan and the Rise of *Peshat* Exegesis in Medieval France," in *Regional Identities and Cultures of Medieval Jews*, ed. Javier Castaño, Talya Fishman, and Ephraim Kanarfogel (London: Littman Library of Jewish Civilization, 2018), 73–92.
162. Yedayah ben Avraham Ha-Penini (Bedersi), *Ketav ha-hitnaṣṣelut*, in Solomon ben Adret, *She'elot u-teshuvot r[abbi] Shlomo ben 'Adret*, ed. Aaron Zaleznik, 7 vols. (Jerusalem: Mekhon Or ha-Mizrah, 1996), 1:118. Ibn Ezra may have

alighted in other regional centers like Montpellier, Lunel, and Posquières; see Golb, *Jews in Medieval Normandy*, 258–61.

163. Mordechai Cohen, "The Qimhi Family," in *HBOT*, ed. Magne Sæbø, vol. I/2: *From the Beginnings to the Middle Ages*, part 2: *The Middle Ages* (Göttingen: Vandenhoeck & Ruprecht, 1996), 389; and Yehiel Tzeitkin, "Me'afyenei parshanut ha-miqra' bi-yeṣirotehem shel parshanei ha-peshaṭ benei ha-'askolah ha-maimonit shel provans ba-me'ot ha-13–ha-14" (PhD diss., Bar-Ilan University, 2011), 11–14.
164. Joseph Kimhi, *Sefer ha-galui*, ed. Henry J. Mathews (n.p., 1887) (photo offset Jerusalem, 1966), 2–3. See Ram Ben-Shalom, *Yehudei provans: renesans be-ṣel ha-kenesiyah* (Raanana: Open University of Israel, 2017), 420–23; and Abraham Melamed, *'Al kitfei 'anaqim: toledot ha-polmos ben 'aḥaronim le-rishonim ba-hagut ha-yehudit bi-yemei ha-benayim u-ve-reshit ha-'et ha-ḥadashah* (Ramat-Gan: Bar-Ilan University, 2003), 50–51.
165. On whom, see Carlos Fraenkel, *Min ha-rambam li-Shemu'el 'ibn Tibbon: darko shel dalalah al-ha'irin le-moreh ha-nevukhim* (Jerusalem: Magnes, 2007); Freudenthal, "Abraham Ibn Ezra," 66–77.
166. See, respectively, James T. Robinson, *Samuel Ibn Tibbon's Commentary on Ecclesiastes: The Book of the Soul of Man* (Tübingen: Mohr Siebeck, 2007); and Rivka Kneller, "Ma'amar yiqqavu ha-mayyim: ḥibbur parshani filosofi li-Shemu'el 'ibn Tibbon," 2 vols. (PhD diss., Tel Aviv University, 2011).
167. Joseph Shatzmiller, "Li-temunat ha-maḥaloqet ha-rishonah 'al kitvei ha-rambam," *Zion* 34 (1969): 143–44; and Septimus, *Hispano-Jewish Culture*, 64.
168. Pinchas Roth, "Rabbinic Politics, Royal Conquest, and the Creation of a Halakhic Tradition in Medieval Provence," in *Regional Identities and Cultures of Medieval Jews*, ed. Javier Castaño, Talya Fishman, and Ephraim Kanarfogel (London: Littman Library of Jewish Civilization, 2018), 174.
169. Cited from a Narbonesse circular in David Berger, "Judaism and General Culture in Medieval and Early Modern Times," in *Judaism's Encounter with Other Cultures: Rejection or Integration*, ed. Jacob J. Schacter (Northvale, NJ: Aronson, 1997), 118.
170. For an overview, see Ben-Shalom, *Yehudei provans*, 517–33.
171. For this twofold critique, see Tamás Visi, "Ibn Ezra, A Maimonidean Authority: The Evidence of the Early Ibn Ezra Supercommentaries," in *The Cultures of Maimonideanism: New Approaches to the History of Jewish Thought*, ed. James T. Robinson (Leiden: Brill, 2009), 91.
172. See Avraham Nuriel, "Ha-shimmush ba-milah 'gharib' be-'moreh nevukhim'," in *Galui ve-samui ba-filosofyah ha-yehudit bi-yemei ha-benayim* (Jerusalem: Magnes, 2000), 158–64. The definition "remoteness from rationality" appears in Isadore Twersky, *Introduction to the Code of Maimonides (*Mishneh Torah) (New Haven, CT: Yale University Press, 1980), 387.
173. Septimus, *Hispano-Jewish Culture*, 61–103.

174. Septimus, *Hispano-Jewish Culture*, 78.
175. Samuel ben Abraham Saporta, "Katav 'asher shalaḥ ha-rav r[abbi] Shemu'el be-r[abbi] 'Avraham'," in Shlomo Zalman Chaim Halberstam, ed. "Milḥemet ha-dat," *Yeshurun* 8 (1872–1875), 152.
176. Joseph Shatzmiller, "Les tossafistes et la première controverse maïmonidienne," in *Rashi et la culture juive en France du Nord au moyen âge*, ed. Gilbert Dahan et al. (Paris-Leuven: Peeters, 1997), 55–82, esp. 79–80 for the cited passages; and Visi, "Ibn Ezra," 93–94.
177. Shatzmiller, "Les tossafistes," 75–77, 79–80; and Visi, "Ibn Ezra," 93–94. Ephraim Kanarfogel, "Varieties of Belief in Medieval Ashkenaz: The Case of Anthropomorphism," in *Rabbinic Culture and Its Critics: Jewish Authority, Dissent, and Heresy in Medieval and Early Modern Times*, ed. Daniel Frank and Matt Goldish (Detroit, MI: Wayne State University Press, 2008), 136, argues that the impression created by Maimonideans during the controversy that many or most northern French rabbis believed in divine anthropomorphism was "rather exaggerated."
178. Septimus, *Hispano-Jewish Culture*, 79.
179. Stern, *Philosophy and Rabbinic Culture*, 26; Howard Kreisel, "Philosophical Interpretations of the Bible," in *The Cambridge History of Jewish Philosophy: From Antiquity Through the Seventeenth Century*, ed. Steven Nadler and T.M. Rudavsky (Cambridge: Cambridge University Press, 2009), 100.
180. James T. Robinson, "We Drink Only from the Master's Water: Maimonides and Maimonideanism in Southern France, 1200–1306," in *Epigonism and the Dynamics of Jewish Culture*, ed. Shlomo Berger and Irene E. Zwiep (Leuven: Peeters, 2008), 27–60.
181. Howard Kreisel, *Judaism as Philosophy: Studies in Maimonides and the Medieval Jewish Philosophers of Provence* (Boston, MA: Academic Studies Press, 2015), 83.
182. Naomi Grunhaus, "The Dependence of Rabbi David Kimhi (Radak) on Rashi in His Quotation of Midrashic Traditions," *JQR* 93 (2003): 415–30, esp. 417.
183. Naomi Grunhaus, *The Challenge of Received Tradition: Dilemmas of Interpretation in Radak's Biblical Commentaries* (Oxford: Oxford University Press, 2013), 57–58.
184. Grunhaus, *Challenge of Received Tradition*, 118.
185. Claude Brahami, "Le manuscrit hébreu 167 de la bibliothèque nationale de Paris contient-il une copie du Ḥīzqūnī?" *REJ* 127 (1968): 215–16; and Israel M. Ta-Shma, "Quntres 'Sodot ha-tefilah' le-rabbi Yehudah Ha-Ḥasid," in *Keneset meḥqarim: 'iyyunim ba-sifrut ha-rabbanit bi-yemei ha-benayim*, vol. 1: *'Ashkenaz* (Jerusalem: Bialik, 2004–2010), 219–20.
186. Jacob ben Shabbetai, *Ḥizquni 'al perush rashi*, ed. Moshe Filip (Petah Tikvah: Filip, 2009), 20, for the numerical estimate of 70 percent and 28n92 for other figures or works cited. This work remains basically unknown.
187. E.g., on Gen 2:15 (53); 27:29 (98).

188. See Gérard E. Weil, *La bibliothèque de Gersonide d'après son catalogue autographe* (Leuven: Peeters, 1991), 56, 57, 84.
189. *MGH: Sefer Shemot,* 1:113. For a rare citation by Gersonides of Rashi (in this case in order to refute Rashi), see the gloss on Exod 10:14 (*MGH: Sefer Shemot,* 1:71).
190. Yisrael Ben-Simon, "Mishnato ha-filosofit ve-ha-'alegorit shel R. Ya'aqov 'Anatoli ve-hashpa'atah 'al ha-hagut ve-ha-'alegoryah ha-yehudit be-me'ot ha-13 ve-ha-14" (PhD diss., Haifa University, 2010).
191. For the explicit mentions, see Jacob Anatoli, *Malmad ha-talmidim,* ed. L. Silbermann (Lyck, Prussia [now Ełk, Poland], 1866), 75r, 85v, 120r; for tacit ones 176r, 178r, 195r (with thanks to Yisrael ben-Simon for these references).
192. Anatoli, *Malmad,* 10r. See Eric Lawee, "The Sins of the Fauna in Midrash, Rashi, and Their Medieval Interlocutors," *Jewish Studies Quarterly* 17 (2010): 76–77.
193. Moses ibn Tibbon, *Sefer pe'ah* in *Kitvei R. Mosheh 'ibn Tibbon: Sefer pe'ah; Ma'amar ha-taninim; Perush ha-'azharot le-R. Shelomo 'ibn Gabirol,* ed. Haim Kreisel, Colette Sirat, and Avraham Yisra'el (Beer-Sheva: Ben Gurion University of the Negev Press, 2010).
194. Nissim of Marseille, *Ma'aseh nissim: perush la-torah le-r[abbi] Nissim ben r[abbi] Moshe mi-marseille,* ed. Haim (Howard) Kreisel (Jerusalem: Mekize Nirdamim, 2000), 293–94. In the same pericope, Nissim discusses other midrashim mentioned by Rashi without mentioning his name.
195. An up-to-date study is Adrian Sackson, *Joseph Ibn Kaspi: Portrait of a Hebrew Philosopher in Medieval Provence* (Leiden: Brill, 2017) (97 for the cited passage). For logic as a basic component of Ibn Kaspi's exegesis, see Shalom Rosenberg, "Higayon, safah u-farshanut ha-miqra' bi-khetavav shel r[abbi] Yosef 'ibn Kaspi," in *Dat ve-safah,* ed. Moshe Hallamish and Asa Kasher (Tel Aviv: University Publishing Projects, 1981), 105–14.
196. Joseph ibn Kaspi, *Maṣref la-kesef* in *Mishneh kesef,* ed. Isaac Last, 2 vols. (Cracow: Joseph Fischer, 1905), 2:210–11.
197. Visi, "Ibn Ezra," 111, where *Parashat ha-kesef,* Paris, MS BNF héb 184 is cited. For the principle of logic invoked by Ibn Kaspi, see Yoel Marciano, "Me-'aragon le-qasṭilyah—le-toledot shiṭat limmudam shel ḥakhmei sefarad ba-me'ah ha-ḥamesh 'esreh," *Tarbiẓ* 77 (2008): 598. In light of this comment by Ibn Kaspi, it is hard to endorse unqualifiedly the claim that his approach to Rashi is "very moderate" and done "with dignity" or that he refrains from attacking Rashi directly (Tzeitkin, "Me'afyenei," 152).
198. Visi, "Ibn Ezra," 110n47.
199. Stern, *Philosophy and Rabbinic Culture,* 4.
200. For the onset of the decline in writing, see Stern, *Philosophy and Rabbinic Culture,* 228. For political developments, see Robert Chazan, *The Jews of Medieval Western Christendom, 1000–1500* (Cambridge: Cambridge University Press, 2006), 88.

201. For the larger theme, see Roger Chartier, *Inscription and Erasure: Literature and Written Culture from the Eleventh to the Eighteenth Century*, trans. Arthur Goldhammer (Philadelphia: University of Pennsylvania Press, 2007), xi.

202. Zeev Gries, *The Book in the Jewish World: 1700–1900* (Oxford: Littman Library of Jewish Civilization, 2007), ix.

203. Moses Marx, "On the Date of Appearance of the First Printed Hebrew Books," in *Alexander Marx Jubilee Volume*, ed. Saul Lieberman, 2 vols. (New York: Jewish Theological Seminary of America, 1950), 1:481–502 (English section). A. K. Offenberg, ed., *Catalogue of Books Printed in the XVth Century Now in the British Library; BMC Part XIII: Hebraica* (The Netherlands: Hes & De Graaf, 2004), 13, thinks Rashi was printed third, after Kimhi's *Sefer ha-shorashim* and the responsa of Solomon ben Adret. For prior manual copying of the *Commentary* in Rome, see Giulio Busi, *Libri e scrittori nella roma ebraica del Medioevo* (Rimini: Luisè, 1990), 63. The Rome Hebrew press operated under the auspices of Obadayah, Menasheh, and Benjamin of Rome, about whom nothing is known. For the Rome publishing activities of the Christians Sweyheym and Pannartz, see Anna Modigliani, "Tipografi a Roma (1467–1477)," in *Gutenberg e Roma: le origini della stampa nella Città dei Papi (1467–1477)*, ed. Massimo Miglio and Orietta Rossini (Naples: Electa Napoli, 1997), 41–48.

204. Adri K. Offenberg, *A Choice of Corals: Facets of Fifteenth-Century Hebrew Printing* (Nieuwkoop: De Graaf, 1992), 133–37. For the *Commentary* as likely the first book printed in Iberia, see Adri K. Offenberg, "What Do We Know about Hebrew Printing in Guadalajara, Híjar, and Zamora?" in *The Late Medieval Hebrew Book in the Western Mediterranean: Hebrew Manuscripts and Incunabula in Context*, ed. Javier del Barco (Leiden: Brill, 2015), 318. There were reasons why exegetical works like the *Commentary* were printed even prior to the biblical text, even though explanation of the latter was the object of the commentaries. For example, as unpointed texts, printers were more inclined to begin with these easier texts and then progress to scripture, which presented greater technical challenges; see *Exceptional Printed Books, Sixty-Five Hebrew Incunabula* (New York: Kestenbaum, 2004), 83 (no. 55).

205. David Stern, "The Rabbinic Bible and Its Sixteenth-Century Context," in *The Hebrew Book in Early Modern Italy*, ed. Joseph R. Hacker and Adam Shear (Philadelphia: University of Pennsylvania Press, 2011), 98. For vowels and cantillation signs, see Offenberg, *Choice of Corals*, 141.

206. Christopher S. Celenza, "Creating Canons in Fifteenth-Century Ferrara: Angelo Decembrio's *De politia litterari*, 1.10," *Renaissance Quarterly* 57 (2004): 97.

207. Adam Shear and Joseph R. Hacker, "Introduction," in *The Hebrew Book in Early Modern Italy*, ed. Joseph R. Hacker and Adam Shear (Philadelphia: University of Pennsylvania Press, 2011), 2; and Offenberg, *Choice of Corals*, 140. For differing estimates of the number of Hebrew incunabula, see Menahem H. Schmelzer, "Hebrew Incunabula: An Agenda for Research," in Menahem Schmelzer,

Studies in Jewish Bibliography and Medieval Hebrew Poetry (New York: Jewish Theological Seminary of America, 2006), 30 (English section).

208. Colette Sirat, *Hebrew Manuscripts of the Middle Ages*, ed. and trans. Nicholas de Lange (Cambridge: Cambridge University Press, 2002), 186; and Malachi Beit-Arié, *QI*, 410–11n10. Inclusion of the Targum was another innovation in this edition, repeated in the one produced in the small Spanish village of Híjar in 1490. The influence of Sefardic scripts in southern Italy and Sicily owes to the political status of the area, ruled as it was by Aragon; see Malachi Beit-Arié, *The Makings of the Medieval Hebrew Book: Studies in Palaeography and Codicology* (Jerusalem: Magnes, 1993), 257, 259.
209. Offenberg, *Choice of Corals*, 147. For the persistence of manual copying after the rise of printing, see Pavel Sládek, "The Printed Book in 15th- and 16th-Century Jewish Culture," in *Hebrew Printing in Bohemia and Moravia*, ed. Olga Sixtová (Prague: Jewish Museum–Academia, 2012), 14, 17.
210. See Gérard Genette, *Paratexts: Thresholds of Interpretation*, trans. Jane E. Lewin (Cambridge: Cambridge University Press, 1997).
211. Ada Yardeni, *The Book of Hebrew Script: History, Palaeography, Script Styles, Calligraphy and Design* (London: Oak Knoll, 2002), 102; Isaia Sonne, "Le-reshito shel ha-defus ha-'ivri bi-sefarad," *Kiryat sefer* 14 (1937–1938): 374; and Peretz Tishbi, "Defusei-'eres ('inqunabulim) 'ivriyyim: sefarad u-fortugal," *Kiryat Sefer* 61 (1986–1987): 526–29.
212. Abraham Yaari, *Ha-defus ha-'ivri be-qushta* (Jerusalem: Magnes, 1967), 60.
213. This can be seen graphically from the first three editions (Rome, Reggio, Guadalajara) printed in *Rashi ha-shalem* (which, however, at present covers only Genesis and Exodus). Of these three, the one produced at Reggio most shaped modern editions. For a chart tracing patterns of influence from the early through modern printings, see Rivka Zevulun, "Ha-nosaḥ shel perush rashi la-torah ba-defusim ha-rishonim: yaḥasam zeh le-zeh ve-hishtalshalut nosḥam 'ad le-mahadurot yamenu," 2 vols. (Master's thesis, Hebrew University of Jerusalem, 1997), 1:128. As discussed in chapter 1, this volume, the diverse versions reflect distinctive Ashkenazic and Sefardic recensions of Rashi's work.
214. See note 26 in chapter 1, this volume.
215. Joseph ben Issachar Baer, an early seventeenth-century student of Judah Loew of Prague, devoted much energy to remedying the problem. Though born partly of longstanding Jewish editorial sensibilities, his effort toward this end in his supercommentary *Yosef da'at* took inspiration from the talmudic textual criticism of Loew and, possibly, text-critical Renaissance techniques that had just arrived in Northern Europe. Joseph's work was printed in Prague in 1609. Reflecting the traditional Jewish trope of the "decline of the generations," Joseph argued that publishers were no more immune to the rule of human devolution than others such that their products, literary artifacts, were necessarily subject to ever greater

increments of fallibility. Joseph, who had seen evidence of such decline in recent editions of exegetical classics, set to recovering Rashi's words in part by relying on a manuscript he had chanced upon in Lublin that, he believed, was some three centuries old. His "lower criticism" shaped the version of the *Commentary* passed down to modern times, although comments ascribed to "the old version of Rashi" (*rashi yashan*) that still appear in contemporary editions do not reflect his handiwork, as some (like Avraham Berliner) have thought; see Yeshayahu Maori, "Nosaḥ perush rashi la-torah–maṣav ha-meḥqar," in *Rashi: demuto vi-yeṣirato*, ed. Avraham Grossman and Sara Japhet, 2 vols. (Jerusalem: Mercaz Zalman Shazar, 2008), 1:78n55, who observes that their origin remains unknown. For renaissance techniques come north, see John F. D'Amico, *Theory and Practice in Renaissance Textual Criticism: Beatus Rhenanus Between Conjecture and History* (Berkeley: University of California Press, 1988), 8–38.

216. For the Zohar, see Boaz Huss, *The Zohar: Reception and Impact*, trans. Yudith Nave (Oxford: Littman Library of Jewish Civilization, 2016), 99.

217. Robert Bonfil, "Reading in the Jewish Communities of Western Europe in the Middle Ages," in *A History of Reading in the West*, ed. Guglielmo Cavallo and Roger Chartier, trans. Lydia G. Cochrane (Amherst: University of Massachusetts Press, 1999), 171.

218. Stern, "Rabbinic Bible," 95–96, 98–99.

219. David B. Ruderman, *Early Modern Jewry: A New Cultural History* (Princeton, NJ: Princeton University Press, 2010), 102.

220. See, e.g., a manuscript from 1322 mentioned in Beit-Arié, *QI*, 454–55. For the point about the second rabbinic Bible, see Stern, "Rabbinic Bible," 100.

221. Zevulun, "Ha-nosaḥ," 1:128, for a chart of lines of development leading to the 1525 version. That version still appears in contemporary editions such as *Rashi ha-shalem.*

222. To the degree they were available, Rashi's commentaries on other biblical books also appeared in rabbinic Bibles; see Elchanan Reiner, "'En ṣarikh shum yehudi lilmod davar raq ha-talmud levado': 'al limmud ve-tokhanei limmud be-'ashkenaz bi-yemei ha-sefer ha-rishonim," in *Ta shema: meḥqarim be-madda'ei ha-yahadut le-zikhro shel Yisra'el M. Ta-Shma*, ed. Avraham (Rami) Reiner et al., 2 vols. (Alon Shvut: Tevunot, 2012), 2:736.

223. Benjamin Williams, "*Glossa Ordinaria* and *Glossa Hebraica*: Midrash in Rashi and the *Gloss*," *Traditio* 71 (2016): 183.

224. For Lyre, see note 5 in the introduction, this volume. Evidence of early Christian Hebraist interest in the *Commentary* lies in the still unpublished Latin translation by Pellican of Rashi's commentaries on Genesis and Exodus; see Sophie Kessler Mesguich, "Early Christian Hebraists," in *HBOT*, ed. Magne Sæbø, vol. II: *From the Renaissance to the Enlightenment* (Göttingen: Vanderhoeck & Ruprecht, 2008), 267n59.

225. Paul F. Grendler, "The Destruction of Hebrew Books in Venice, 1568," *Proceedings of the American Academy for Jewish Research* 45 (1978): 115–16.
226. Kenneth R. Stow, "The Burning of the Talmud in 1553, in Light of Sixteenth-Century Catholic Attitudes Toward the Talmud," in *Essential Papers on Judaism and Christianity in Conflict: From Late Antiquity to the Reformation*, ed. Jeremy Cohen (New York: New York University Press, 1991), 401–28.
227. Nurit Pasternak, "Marchion in Hebrew Manuscripts: State Censorship in Florence, 1472," in *The Hebrew Book in Early Modern Italy*, ed. Joseph R. Hacker and Adam Shear (Philadelphia: University of Pennsylvania Press, 2011), 38.
228. Amnon Raz-Krakotzkin, *The Censor, the Editor, and the Text: The Catholic Church and the Shaping of the Jewish Canon in the Sixteenth Century*, trans. Jackie Feldman (Philadelphia: University of Pennsylvania Press, 2007), 75.
229. Federica Francesconi, "'The Passage Can Also Be Read Differently . . .:' How Jews And Christians Censored Hebrew Texts in Early Modern Modena," *Jewish History* 26 (2012): 146–47, 159n69.
230. Piet van Boxel, "Robert Bellarmine Reads Rashi: Rabbinic Bible Commentaries and the Burning of the Talmud," in *The Hebrew Book in Early Modern Italy*, ed. Joseph R. Hacker and Adam Shear (Philadelphia: University of Pennsylvania Press, 2011), 121–32, esp. 131 for the cited statistic.
231. Michael T. Walton and Phyllis J. Walton, "In Defense of the Church Militant: The Censorship of the Rashi Commentary in the *Magna Biblia Rabbinica*," *Sixteenth Century Journal* 21 (1990): 393; and Kenneth Stow, review of *The Censor, the Editor, and the Text* by Amnon Raz-Krakotzkin, *AJS Review* 33 (2009): 181.
232. Raz-Krakotzkin, *Censor*, 149 (for the citation), 113 and 251n74 for the edition of 1591. On Domenico, see Gila Prebor, "'Sefer ha-ziqquq' shel Domenico yerushalmi," *Italia* 18 (2008): 7–296.
233. Francesconi, "Passage," 150. See also Fracesconi, "Jews under Surveillance: Censorship and Reading in Early Modern Italy," Early Modern Workshop: Jewish History Resources, vol. 6, at https://fordham.bepress.com/cgi/viewcontent.cgi?article=1082&context=emw.
234. Walton and Walton, "In Defense," 397, for the cited passage.
235. Kevin Sharpe, *Reading Revolutions: The Politics of Reading in Early Modern England* (New Haven, CT: Yale University Press, 2000), 28.
236. For details, see Yaari, *Ha-defus*, 86; and Joseph Hacker, "Defusei qushta be-me'ah ha-shesh-'esrei," *'Areshet* 5 (1972): 480n 101. For awareness of it among earlier bibliographers, see Menachem Kasher, *Sarei ha-'elef* (New York: Torah Shelemah, 1959), 61. For the divergent forms in which it comes down, see Yitzhak Yudlov, "Kamah she'arim le-sefer *perushim le-rashi* defus qushta?" *'Alei sefer* 17 (1992): 137–38. Regarding its rarity, see Moritz Steinschneider, *Catalogus Librorum Hebraeorum in Bibliotheca Bodleiana* (Berlin, 1852–1860), col. 1196 ("liber ad rarissimos pertinet").

237. See the list in Elijah Mizrahi, *Ḥumash ha-re'em*, ed. Moshe Filip, 6 vols. (Petah Tikvah: Filip, 1994), 1:16–23.
238. For the passage from the ethical will of Horowitz, see Abraham ben Shabbetai Sheftel Horowitz, *Yesh noḥalin* (Jerusalem: Chai Waldman, 1993), 313. On this work, see Avriel Bar-Levav, "'When I Was Alive': Jewish Ethical Wills as Egodocuments," in *Egodocuments and History: Autobiographical Writing in its Social Context since the Middle Ages*, ed. Rudolf Dekker (Hilversum: Verloren, 2002), 56.

CHAPTER 3

1. Nahum Sarna, "Rashi the Commentator," in *Studies in Biblical Interpretation* (Philadelphia: Jewish Publication Society, 2000), 128.
2. For reasons why a precise calculation of the number is difficult, if not impossible, see Eran Viezel, "'Osim 'oznayim le-toratam shel parshanim, ke-'oznei kli she-'ohazin 'oto bam,'" *Shenaton le-ḥeqer ha-miqra' ve-ha-mizraḥ ha-qadum* 20 (2010): 271n 50. A search under "commentary on Rashi's Torah Commentary" (*perush 'al perush ha-torah le-rashi*) in the catalogue of the Institute of Microfilmed Hebrew Manuscripts in Jerusalem yields over one hundred entries, which means that, even allowing for overlap among works that have since been printed, many entries in the field have yet to enter the light of history. The fullest printed lists of supercommentaries in manuscript appeared long ago; see Israel Shapira, "Parshanei rashi 'al ha-torah," *Bizaron* 2 (1940): 426–37; and Aron Freimann, "Manuscript Supercommentaries on Rashi's Commentary on the Pentateuch," in *Rashi Anniversary Volume* (New York: Press of the Jewish Publication Society, 1941), 73–114. For printed supercommentaries, see Pinchus Krieger, *Parshan-data': reshimat ha-perushim le-ferush rashi 'al ha-torah*, 2 vols. (Monsey, NY: Pinchus Krieger, 2005–2018).
3. Elijah Mizrahi, *Ḥumash ha-re'em*, ed. Moshe Filip, 6 vols. (Petah Tikvah: Filip, 1994), 1:12. This estimate by the editor goes back a few decades. Even if it was only roughly accurate, it would remain utterly remarkable.
4. For works in the field since 1970, see the second volume of Krieger's catalogue (note 2, in this chapter). Samples in different languages are, in Hebrew, Shmuel Gelbard, *Lifeshuto shel rashi: be'ur le-ferush rashi 'al ha-torah*, 2nd ed., 5 vols. (Tel Aviv: Mif'al Rashi, 1990); in English, Avigdor Bonchek, *What's Bothering Rashi? A Guide to In-Depth Analysis of His Torah Commentary*, 5 vols. (Jerusalem: Feldheim, 1997–2002); and Menachem M. Schneerson, *Studies in Rashi: From the Teachings of the Lubavitcher Rebbe, Menachem M. Schneerson*, trans. Y. Eliezer Danzinger (Brooklyn, NY: Kehot, 2011); and in French, Shaoul David Botschko, *Les lumières de Rachi* (Jerusalem–Paris: A.J. Press / Bibliophane–Daniel Radford / Lichma Diffusion / Etz Hayim, 2004–2012), of which at least eight volumes have appeared. See Krieger, *Parshan-data'*, 2:28–29.

5. James L. Kugel, *The Idea of Biblical Poetry: Parallelism and Its History* (New Haven, CT and London: Yale University Press, 1981), 104. For the *Commentary* as in some degree marking a break from rabbinic omnisignificant principles of scriptural interpretation, see at note 62 in chapter 1, this volume.
6. See the editors' introduction in Bruno Chiesa, Meir Bar-Asher, and Sarah Stroumsa, eds., *Davar davur 'al 'ofanav: meḥqarim be-farshanut ha-miqra' ve-ha-qur'an bi-yemei ha-benayim mugashim le-Ḥaggai ben Shammai* (Jerusalem: Mekhon Ben-Zvi, 2007), 7.
7. Janusz Sławiński, "Reading and Reader in the Literary Historical Process," *New Literary History* 19 (1988): 528.
8. E. A. Gosselin, "A Listing of the Printed Editions of Nicolaus de Lyra," *Traditio* 26 (1970): 411; and Lesley Smith, "Nicholas of Lyra and Old Testament Interpretation," in *HBOT*, ed. Magne Sæbø, vol. II: *From the Renaissance to the Enlightenment* (Göttingen: Vanderhoeck & Ruprecht, 2008), 49–50.
9. Deeana Copeland Klepper, *The Insight of Unbelievers: Nicholas of Lyra and Christian Reading of Jewish Text in the Later Middle Ages* (Philadelphia: University of Pennsylvania Press, 2007), 118.
10. Philipp W. Rosemann, *The Story of a Great Medieval Book: Peter Lombard's Sentences* (Peterborough, Ontario: Broadview, 2007), 14.
11. Jacques Derrida, "The Law of Genre," trans. Avita Ronell, *Critical Inquiry* 7 (1980): 56. For a fuller account of the genre's origin, literary character, and intellectual dynamics, see Eric Lawee, "A Genre Is Born: The Genesis, Dynamics, and Role of Hebrew Exegetical Supercommentaries," *REJ* 176 (2017): 295–332. The coinage "supercommentary" (other names for this subgenre are "super-gloss" and "metacommentary") merits study. Clearly not born of Jewish tradition, it goes back in Latin at least as far as the seventeenth century; see, e.g., Thomas Hyde, ed., *Catalogus impressorum librorum Bibliothecae Bodlejanae in Academia Oxoniensi* (Oxford, 1674), 212.
12. See, e.g., Ruth Glasner, "The Evolution of the Genre of Philosophical-Scientific Commentary: Hebrew Supercommentaries on Aristotle's Physics," in *Science in Medieval Jewish Cultures*, ed. Gad Freudenthal (Cambridge: Cambridge University Press, 2011), 182–96; and Sara Klein-Braslavy, "Gersonides as Commentator on Averroes," in *Without any Doubt: Gersonides on Method and Knowledge*, trans. and ed. Lenn J. Schramm (Leiden: Brill, 2011), 181–219.
13. Uriel Simon, "Interpreting the Interpreter: Supercommentaries on Ibn Ezra's Commentaries," in *Rabbi Abraham Ibn Ezra: Studies in the Writings of a Twelfth-Century Polymath*, ed. Isadore Twersky and Jay M. Harris (Cambridge, MA: Harvard University Center for Jewish Studies, 1993), 86–87. An updated and expanded Hebrew version appears in Uriel Simon, *'Ozen milin tivḥan: meḥqarim be-darko ha-parshanit shel r[abbi] 'Avraham 'ibn 'Ezra* (Ramat-Gan: Bar-Ilan University Press, 2013), 370–406.

14. Simon, *'Ozen*, 370–74.
15. Simon, *'Ozen*, 375.
16. For "platform of the page," see Bonnie Mak, *How the Page Matters* (Toronto: University of Toronto Press, 2011), 9. For "textual hierarchy," see David Stern, "The Hebrew Bible in Europe in the Middle Ages: A Preliminary Typology," *Jewish Studies Internet Journal* 11 (2012): 76.
17. For "decline of the generations," see Yisrael Yaakov Yuval, "Rishonim ve-'aḥaronim, antiqui et moderni," *Zion* 57 (1992): 369–94; and Menachem Kellner, *Maimonides on the "Decline of the Generations" and the Nature of Rabbinic Authority* (Albany: SUNY Press, 1996). For "dwarfs on the shoulders of giants," see Abraham Melamed, *'Al kitfei 'anaqim: toledot ha-polmos ben 'aḥaronim le-rishonim ba-hagut ha-yehudit bi-yemei ha-benayim u-ve-reshit ha-'et ha-ḥadashah* (Ramat-Gan: Bar Ilan University, 2003).
18. I draw on Barry Smith, "Textual Deference," *American Philosophical Quarterly* 28 (1991): 1–12.
19. Ineke Sluiter, "The Dialectics of Genre: Some Aspects of Secondary Literature and Genre in Antiquity," in *Matrices of Genre: Authors, Canons, and Society*, ed. Mary Depew and Dirk Obbink (Cambridge, MA: Harvard University Press, 2000), 183.
20. Karel Enenkel and Henk Nellen, "Introduction," *Neo-Latin Commentaries and the Management of Knowledge in the Late Middle Ages and the Early Modern Period (1400–1700)*, ed. Karel Enenkel and Henk Nellen (Leuven: Leuven University Press, 2013), 16.
21. Arieh Graboïs, *Les sources hébraïques médiévales*, vol. 2: *Les commentaires exégétiques* (Turnhout, Belgium: Brepols, 1993), 45.
22. The formulation in Robert S. Sturges, "Medieval Authorship and the Polyphonic Text: From Manuscript Commentary to the Modern Novel," in *Bakhtin and Medieval Voices*, ed. Thomas J. Farrell (Gainesville: University Press of Florida, 1995), 125.
23. Y. Tzvi Langermann, "Review of R. Abraham Ibn Ezra, *Yesod Mora ve-Sod Torah*," *AJS Review* 30 (2006): 461.
24. From a considerable literature, see Simon, *'Ozen*, 370–406; and Dov Schwartz, "Le-darkhei ha-parshanut ha-filosofit 'al perushei r[abbi] 'Avraham 'ibn 'Ezra," *'Alei sefer* 18 (1996): 71–114. For supercommentarial investigation of Ibn Ezra's (apparent) claim of post-Mosaisms, see Simon, *'Ozen*, 407–64; and Warren Zev Harvey, "Spinoza on Ibn Ezra's 'Secret of the Twelve,'" in *Spinoza's 'Theological-Political Treatise': A Critical Guide*, ed. Yitzhak Y. Melamed and Michael A. Rosenthal (New York: Cambridge University Press, 2010), 41–55.
25. On the underdeveloped topic of Nahmanidean supercommentary, see Daniel Abrams, *Kabbalistic Manuscripts and Textual Theory: Methodologies of Textual Scholarship and Editorial Practice in the Study of Jewish Mysticism* (Jerusalem: Magnes,

2010), 198–223; and Haviva Pedaya, *Ha-ramban – hit'alut: zeman maḥzori ve-teqst qadosh* (Tel Aviv: Am Oved, 2003), 98–119. Yaakov Elman, "Moses ben Nahman/ Nahmanides (Ramban)," in *HBOT*, ed. Magne Sæbø , vol. I/2: *From the Beginnings to the Middle Ages*, part 2: *The Middle Ages* (Göttingen: Vanderhoeck & Ruprecht, 2000), 432, puts the kabbalistic component of the work at 8 percent. The urge to engage in supercommentary on kabbalistic ideas presented conundrums, not least since Nahmanides himself stipulated that a correct understanding of esoteric passages in his commentary must rest on authenticated oral traditions. Yet one who had such traditions in hand had to ask how much, if at all, he was permitted to reveal them in writing. The desire to preserve truths threatened by extinction pulled Nahmanidean supercommentators in one direction, the requirement to preserve secrecy in another; see Lawee, "Genre," 326.

26. Walid A. Saleh, "Preliminary Remarks on the Historiography of *Tafsīr* in Arabic: A History of the Book Approach," *Journal of Qur'anic Studies* 12 (2010): 21.
27. For a case study in supercommentarial amplification, see Dov Schwartz, "From Theurgy to Magic: The Evolution of the Magical-Talismanic Justification of Sacrifice in the Circle of Nahmanides and His Interpreters," *Aleph* 1 (2001): 165–213. For Nahmanides's "kabbalistic assault" on Maimonides, see James A. Diamond, *Maimonides and the Shaping of the Jewish Canon* (New York: Cambridge University Press, 2014), 69–86.
28. Moshe Idel, "On Maimonides in Nahmanides and His School," in *Between Rashi and Maimonides: Themes in Medieval Jewish Thought, Literature and Exegesis*, ed. Ephraim Kanarfogel and Moshe Sokolow (Jersey City, NJ: Ktav, 2010), 134.
29. See note 5 in chapter 2, this volume. In addition to the literature cited there, see Rivka Kneller, "Haznaḥat limmud ha-miqra' bi-yemei ha-benayim u-ve-shilhei ha-'et ha-ḥadashah," in *Mas'at moshe*, ed. Shaul Miezlisch (Tel Aviv: Kneller Family, 1989), 188–225.
30. Ephraim Kanarfogel, "On the Role of Bible Study in Medieval Ashkenaz," in *The Frank Talmage Memorial Volume*, ed. Barry Dov Walfish, 2 vols. (Haifa: Haifa University Press, 1993), 1:156.
31. Avraham (Rami) Reiner, "Bible and Politics: A Correspondence Between Rabbenu Tam and the Authorities of Champagne," in *Entangled Histories: Knowledge, Authority, and Jewish Culture in the Thirteenth Century*, ed. Elisheva Baumgarten, Ruth Mazo Karras, and Katelyn Mesler (Philadelphia: University of Pennsylvania Press, 2017), 63.
32. Tosafot to 'Avodah zara 19b, s.v. "*yeshallesh*" (cf. b. Sanhedrin 24a). For various possible interpretations of this statement, see Kanarfogel, "On the Role," 151.
33. Ephraim Kanarfogel, *The Intellectual History and Rabbinic Culture of Medieval Ashkenaz* (Detroit, MI: Wayne State University Press, 2013), 123.
34. Bibliography in *Tosafot ha-shalem*, ed. Jacob Gellis, 9 vols. (Jerusalem: Machon Harry Fischel, 1982), 1:11–42; Yosef Priel, "Darko ha-parshanit shel rabbi

Ḥizqiyah ben Manoaḥ (Ḥizzequni) be-ferusho la-torah" (PhD diss., Bar-Ilan University, 2010), 185–207.

35. See the article of Hanna Liss cited in note 7 of chapter 2, this volume.
36. Yisrael Ta-Shma, "Sefer 'nimmuqei ḥumash' le-rabbi Yisha'yah di-ṭrani," in *Keneset meḥqarim: 'iyyunim ba-sifrut ha-rabbanit bi-yemei ha-benayim*, vol. 3: *'Iṭalyah u-vizanṭyon* (Jerusalem: Bialik, 2004–2010), 259–94. For his awareness of earlier Byzantine exegesis, see Gershon Brin, "Ben r[abbi] Yesha'yah mi-ṭrani la-parshanim ha-bizanṭiyim ha-qedumin," *Beit Mikra* 59 (2014): 60–75. For his learning deemed more Ashkenazi than Italian, see Isadore Twersky, "The Contribution of Italian Sages to Rabbinic Literature," in *Italia Judaica: Atti del I Convegno Internazionale Bari* (Rome: Multigrafica, 1983), 390.
37. Kanarfogel, *Intellectual History*, 244.
38. For its classification as a supercommentary, see the sources cited in Priel, "Darko," 10–13, 101. This view also appears in popular literature, e.g., Yonatan Kolatch, *Masters of the Word: Traditional Jewish Bible Commentary from the First Through Tenth Centuries* (Jersey City, NJ: Ktav, 2006), 181.
39. Kanarfogel, *Intellectual History*, 121. For Ibn Ezra, see Priel, "Darko," 178–85.
40. Priel, "Darko," 153–56.
41. Sarah Japhet, *Dor dor u-farshanav: 'asupat meḥqarim be-farshanut ha-miqra'* (Jerusalem: Bialik, 2008), 364–82. For compilatory exegesis more generally, see 341–63.
42. Hezekiah ben Manoah, *Ḥizzequni, perushei ha-torah le-rabbenu Ḥizqiyah b"r Manoaḥ*, ed. Hayyim D. Chavel (Jerusalem: Mosad Harav Kuk, 1981), introduction. For Hezekiah's interaction with Rashi, see Priel, "Darko," 101–20. A thematic study is Roland Goetschel, "Rashi et le Ḥizzeqûni sur la 'aqedah et les sacrifices," in *Rashi et la culture juive en France du Nord au moyen âge*, ed. Gilbert Dahan et al. (Paris-Leuven: Peeters, 1997), 305–13.
43. Priel, "Darko," 211–15.
44. Cyrus H. Gordon, "'This Time' (Genesis 2:23)," in *"Sha'arei Talmon": Studies in the Bible, Qumran, and the Ancient Near East Presented to Shemaryahu Talmon*, ed. Michael Fishbane and Emanuel Tov (Winona Lake, IN: Eisenbrauns, 1992), 47.
45. James L. Kugel, *Traditions of the Bible: A Guide to the Bible as It Was at the Start of the Common Era* (Cambridge, MA: Harvard University Press, 1998), 114.
46. b. Yevamot 63a. For the midrash's afterlife, see Eric Lawee, "From Sefarad to Ashkenaz: A Case Study in the Rashi Supercommentary Tradition," *AJS Review* 30 (2006): 393–425; Lawee, "The Reception of Rashi's *Commentary on the Torah* in Spain: The Case of Adam's Mating with the Animals," *JQR* 97 (2007): 33–66; and Lawee, "Embarrassment and Re-Embracement of a Midrash on Genesis 2," in *Vixens Disturbing Vineyards: The Embarrassment and Embracement of Scriptures (A Festschrift Honoring Harry Fox Le'Veit Yoreh)*, ed. Aubrey Glazer et al. (Boston, MA: Academic Studies, 2010), 192–207.

47. Gary A. Anderson, *The Genesis of Perfection: Adam and Eve in Jewish and Christian Imagination* (Louisville, KY: Westminster John Knox, 2001), 43.
48. For these, see Lieve Teugels, "The Creation of the Human in Rabbinic Interpretation," in *The Creation of Man and Woman: Interpretations of the Biblical Narratives in Jewish and Christian Traditions*, ed. Gerard P. Luttikhuizen (Leiden: Brill, 2000), 114–15.
49. Hezikiah Ben Manoah, *Ḥizzequni*, 17. See also Samuel ben Meir, *Perush ha-rashbam 'al ha-torah*, ed. Meir (Martin) Lockshin, 2 vols. (Jerusalem: Chorev, 2009), 1:14–15n37; Aaron ben Yosi, *Sefer ha-gan*, ed. Yehiel M. Orlian (Jerusalem: Mosad Harav Kuk, 2009), 29; Judah ben Eleazar, *Minḥat yehudah: perush la-torah me-'et rabbi Yehudah ben 'Ele'azar mi-rabotenu ba'alei ha-tosafot*, ed. Hazoniel Touitou (Jerusalem: Mosad Harav Kuk, 2012–), 1:114, note to line 37. On Ibn Ezra in Tosafist commentaries, see Avraham Lipshitz, "Ha-ra'ba' be-ferushei ba'alei ha-tosafot 'al ha-torah," *Ha-Darom* 28 (1969): 202–21.
50. Hezikiah ben Manoah, *Ḥizzequni*, 17.
51. Touitou, introduction to Judah ben Eleazar, *Minḥat yehudah*, 148–52.
52. Touitou, introduction to Judah ben Eleazar, *Minḥat yehudah*, 85, 141. For claims that Judah was the (or at least a) pioneer in Rashi supercommentary, see Roland Goetschel, "L'exégèse de Rashi à la lumière du Maharal de Prague," in *Rashi 1040–1990: Hommage à Ephraïm E. Urbach*, ed. Gabrielle Sed-Rajna (Paris: Cerf, 1993), 466n1; and Tovia Preschel, "Supercommentaries on the Pentateuch," in *EJ*, 19:315.
53. Touitou, introduction to Judah ben Eleazar, *Minḥat yehudah*, 129.
54. An overview is Jörg R. Müller, "'*Ereẓ gezerah:* 'Land of Persecution': Pogroms against the Jews in the *regnum Teutonicum* from c. 1280 to 1350," in *The Jews of Europe in the Middle Ages (Tenth to Fifteenth Centuries)*, ed. Christoph Cluse (Turnhout, Belgium: Brepols, 2004), 245–58.
55. Alfred Haverkamp, *Jews in the Medieval German Kingdom*, trans. Christoph Cluse, Trier University Library, 2015, 53, ubt.opus.hbz-nrw.de/volltexte/2015/916/pdf/Jews_German_Kingdom.pdf.
56. Shlomo Spitzer, "Yedi'ot 'al rabbi Dosa ha-yevani me-ḥibburo 'al ha-torah," in *Sefer zikaron le-ha-rav Yiṣḥak Nissim*, ed. Meir Benayahu, 4 vols. (Jerusalem: Yad ha-rav Nissim, 1985), 4:177–84.
57. See, for these, Shlomo Spitzer, *Halakhot u-minhagei rabbi Shalom mi-neustadt* (Jerusalem: Mekhon Yerushalayim, 1977), 180–89.
58. For figures cited by Dosa, see Ad. Neubauer, "Commentar zu Rashi's Pentateuch-Commentar von Dossa aus Widdin," *Israelietische Letterbode* 8 (1882–83): 49–54. For discussion, see Eric Lawee, "Biblical Scholarship in Late Medieval Ashkenaz: The Turn to Rashi Supercommentary," *HUCA* 86 (2015): 278–83.
59. On Num 20:1. For rabbinic background, see Yaakov Elman, "The Suffering of the Righteous in Palestinian and Babylonian Sources," *JQR* 80 (1990): 315–39.

For Rashi on adjoining pericopae in the Torah, see Isaac B. Gottlieb, *Yesh seder la-miqra': ḥazal u-farshanei yemei ha-benayim 'al mukdam u-me'uhar ba-torah* (Jerusalem and Ramat-Gan: Magnes and Bar-Ilan University Press, 2009), 77–178.

60. Neubauer, "Commentar," 40; and Spitzer, "Yedi'ot," 178.
61. See note 57, this chapter.
62. Zurich, Zentralbibliothek MS Heid. 26. For her three feats of supercommentary reported in the manuscript and their context in terms of women's learning in late medieval Ashkenaz, see Shlomo Eidelberg, "Sefer 'be'ur 'al ha-torah,'" *Horev* 14–15 (1960): 248 in conjunction with Lawee, "Biblical Scholarship," 283–85. Mistress Kila and Jacob Molin are both mentioned with blessings for the departed, suggesting their possible contemporaneity, assuming these blessings are original to the 1434 manuscript, which is now lost (the Zurich manuscript being a copy made in Laibach, modern Ljubljana, in 1515).
63. On Isserlein, see Shlomo Eidelberg, *Jewish Life in Austria in the XVth Century* (Philadelphia: Dropsie College, 1962), 38–59; Shlomo Spitzer, *Bne chet: die österreichischen Juden im Mittelalter. Eine Sozial- und Kulturgeschichte* (Vienna: Böhlau, 1997), 181–86, 191–94; and David Tamar, "Demuto ha-ruḥanit shel r[abbi] Yisra'el 'Isserlein," *Sinai* 32 (1953): 175–85.
64. Parma, Biblioteca Palatina, MS 2382, 25v, which forms the basis of Israel Isserlein, *Be'urei maharai 'al ha-torah*, ed. Menachem Doitsh (Lakewood, NJ: Mekhon Be'er Ha-Torah, 1996), the edition cited here. The meaning and semantic range of the term *peshaṭim* merit study. Comments of Moses of Coucy and of Eleazar ben Judah's teacher, Elyakim, appear under this heading in earlier Ashkenazic exegesis; see Ephraim Kanarfogel, *Jewish Education and Society in the High Middle Ages* (Detroit, MI: Wayne State University Press, 1992), 290–91; and Touitou, introduction to Judah ben Eleazar, *Minḥat yehudah*, 83–85. Here as elsewhere, it does not appear to refer exclusively to plain sense readings, nor could it from the evidence of Isserlein's work. The word is used with a similarly broadened sense by Hayyim ben Bezalel of Friedberg (d. 1588) in his Rashi supercommentary; see *Be'er mayyim ḥayyim*, ed. S. F. Schneebalg, 3 vols. (London: Honig, 1964–71), vol. 1, author's introduction.
65. Krieger, *Parshan-data'*, 19–24.
66. For an example, see Lawee, "Biblical Scholarship," 280.
67. Jacob Elbaum and Chava Turniansky, "Tsene-Rene," *YIVO Encyclopedia of Jews in Eastern Europe*, http://www.yivoencyclopedia.org/article.aspx/Tsene-rene. For this work's stunningly wide diffusion, see Silke Muter Goldberg, "Language and Gender in Early Modern and 19th Century Jewish Devotional Literature," in *Gender, Tradition, and Renewal*, ed. Robert L. Platzner (Oxford: Peter Lang, 2005), 102–103.
68. See at note 79 in chapter 1, this volume.

69. Israel M. Ta-Shma, "Tosafot gornish: mahutan ve-yaḥasan 'el shitot ha-'pilpul' ve-ha-'ḥiluqim,'" in *Keneset meḥqarim: 'iyyunim ba-sifrut ha-rabbanit bi-yemei ha-benayim*, vol. 1: *Ashkenaz*. (Jerusalem: Bialik, 2004–10), 349; and Elchanan Reiner, "Temurot bi-yeshivot polin ve-'ashkenaz ba-me'ot ha-tet-zayin – ha-yod-zayin ve-ha-vikkuaḥ 'al ha-pilpul," in *Ke-minhag 'ashkenaz u-folin: sefer yovel le-Chone Shmeruk: qovets meḥkarim be-tarbut yehudit*, ed. Israel Bartal, Ezra Mendelsohn, and Chava Turniansky (Jerusalem: Zalman Shazar, 1993), 12–15.
70. E.g., on Gen 45:14 and Exod 31:13 (Isserlein, *Be'urei maharai*, 22, 40–41).
71. On Exod 32:6 (Isserlein, *Be'urei maharai*, 41).
72. On Exod 1:7 (Isserlein, *Be'urei maharai*, 27), regarding placement of Rashi's comment regarding the Israelite women's extraordinary fertility in Egypt that saw them bear sextuplets.
73. Jeffrey R. Woolf, "Between Diffidence and Initiative: Ashkenazic Legal Decision-Making in the Late Middle Ages (1350–1500)," *Journal of Jewish Studies* 52 (2001): 95–96; Yuval, "Rishonim," 385; and Aaron Ahrend, "'Al parshanut ha-'aḥaronim le-ferush rashi la-talmud," in *Rashi u-vet midrasho*, ed. Avinoam Kohen (Ramat-Gan: Bar-Ilan University Press, 2013), 23–24.
74. Hayyim ben Bezalel, *Be'er mayyim ḥayyim*, introduction. For Hayyim and casuistry, see Yitzhak (Eric) Zimmer, *Gaḥalatan shel ḥakhamim: peraqim be-toledot ha-rabanut be-germanyah ba-me'ah ha-shesh-'esreh u-va-me'ah ha-sheva'-'esreh* (Beer-Sheva: Ben-Gurion University of the Negev Press, 1999), 204.
75. See note 33 in chapter 2, this volume.
76. Elchanan Reiner, "''En ṣarikh shum yehudi lilmod davar raq ha-talmud levado': 'al limmud ve-tokhanei limmud be-'ashkenaz bi-yemei ha-sefer ha-rishonim," in *Ta shema: meḥqarim be-madda'ei ha-yahadut le-zikhro shel Yisra'el M. Ta-Shma*, ed. Avraham (Rami) Reiner et al., 2 vols. (Alon Shvut: Tevunot, 2012), 2:727n33.
77. Thus, Ahrend ("'Al parshanut," 13), though, to sustain this point one would need to know how widespread the habit of reading the *Commentary* became, by whom, and to what degree people actually studied the work as part of the exercise, as opposed to reciting it in more formal fashion.
78. On Gen 48:14 (*Be'urei maharai*, 24), Isserlein cites his paternal grandfather, Hayyim, and refers to his famous great-grandfather, Israel of Krems.
79. Jacob Elbaum, *Petiḥut ve-histagrut: ha-yeṣirah ha-ruḥanit-ha-sifrutit be-folin u-ve-'arṣot 'ashkenaz be-shilhei ha-me'ah ha-shesh-'esrei* (Jerusalem: Magnes, 1990), 86n11.
80. On Deut 4:19 (Isserlein, *Be'urei maharai*, 78–79). For Rashi's use of image, see note 47 in chapter 1, this volume.
81. On Exod 13:18 (Isserlein, *Be'urei maharai*, 32–33).
82. Twersky, "Contribution," 396–98; Ephraim Kanarfogel, "Progress and Tradition in Medieval Ashkenaz," *Jewish History* 14 (2000): 288–90; and Avi Sagi,

The Open Canon: On the Meaning of Halakhic Discourse, trans. Batya Stein (London: Continuum, 2007), 38–40.

83. Isaiah di Trani, *Teshuvot ha-ri"d,* ed. A. J. Wertheimer (Jerusalem: Mekhon ha-talmud ha-yisra'eli ha-shalem, 1967), no. 61. For discussion, see Melamed, *'Al kitfei,* 177–82.

84. Indeed, Yedidyah Dinari, *Ḥakhmei 'ashkenaz be-shilhei yemei ha-benayim: dark-hehem ve-khitvehem ba-halakhah* (Jerusalem: Bialik, 1984), 15, 17, invokes such observations in the opening lines of his book to justify treatment of the post-1348 period as a distinct one in Ashkenazic rabbinic history.

85. Dinari and Yuval, like Graetz and Güdemann before them, trace it to the Black Death, but others find this explanation insufficient; see Woolf, "Between Diffidence and Initiative," 94–95. For the phrase "cultural chauvinism," see Haym Soloveitchik, "The Halakhic Isolation of the Ashkenazic Community," in *Collected Essays* I (Oxford: Littman Library of Jewish Civilization, 2013), 37. A "doomed sense of continuous and accelerating decline" resounds also in a good number of late medieval Christian works; see Francis Oakley, *The Western Church in the Later Middle Ages* (Ithaca, NY: Cornell University Press, 1979), 314.

86. Israel M. Ta-Shma, "Rabbinic Literature in the Middle Ages," in *The Oxford Handbook of Jewish Studies,* ed. Martin Goodman (Oxford: Oxford University Press, 2002), 224.

87. Woolf, "Between Diffidence and Initiative," 93n50.

88. Yuval, "Rishonim"; and Israel M. Ta-Shma, "Rishonim," in *EJ,* 17:339–43.

89. Noting an earlier scholar who had spoken of a great diminution in learning even before "the decrees" of 1348–1349, Jacob Weil, *Responsa Mahari Weil,* no. 146, added that the problem could only be more acute in his day "since compared to them, we are nothing—their fingernails were wider than our bellies!" (as related in Hanina Ben-Menahem, "Doubt, Choice and Conviction: A Comparison of the Kim Li Doctrine and Probabilism," *Jewish Law Annual* 14 [2003]: 8).

90. Ivan G. Marcus, "Why Did Medieval Northern French Jewry (Ṣarfat) Disappear?" in *Jews, Christians and Muslims in Medieval and Early Modern Times: A Festschrift in Honor of Mark R. Cohen,* ed. Arnold E. Franklin et al. (Leiden: Brill, 2014), 99–117, and 103n15 for Colon's awareness of himself as an offshoot of France (*ṣarfati*).

91. Jeffrey R. Woolf, "The Life and Responsa of Rabbi Joseph Colon b. Solomon Trabotto" (PhD diss., Harvard University, 1991), 28, 36–40. Some of his interpretations of Rashi appear in a supercommentary titled *'Amar neqe'*, which is almost always erroneously ascribed to the Italian Mishnah commentator, Obadiah of Bertinoro. For the likely correct attribution, see Avraham Yosef Havazelet, "Be'ur 'amar neqe' 'al perush rashi la-torah," *Moriyah* 17 (1991): 117–22. In a fascinating development—how many other examples there are remains to be determined—Colon was willing to count the *Commentary* as a halakhic source deemed to record Rashi's ruling on talmudic disputes. See Woolf, "The Life," 94n104.

92. Woolf, "Between Diffidence and Initiative," 95, observes that Colon's sense runs parallel to that of his German colleagues, although Colon was of French extraction and training. For the probative weight to be accorded to the marginal notes of earlier greats in Colon's mind, see Yaakov Shmuel Spiegel, *'Amudim be-toledot ha-sefer ha-'ivri: hagahot u-megihim*, 2nd ed. (Ramat-Gan: Bar-Ilan University Press, 1996), 207.
93. For the two waves, see Yoel Marciano, "Ḥakhamim bi-sefarad ba-me'ah ha-ḥamesh-'esrei: ḥinukham, limmudam, yeṣiratam, ma'amadam, u-demutam" (PhD diss., Hebrew University, 2012), 227–40.
94. See chapter 2, this volume.
95. Judah Khalatz, *Mesiaḥ 'illemim*, ed. Moshe Filip (Petah Tikvah: Filip, 2001), 31.
96. On Deut 21:12 in *MGH: Sefer Devarim*, ed. Menachem Cohen (Ramat-Gan: Bar-Ilan University Press, 2011), 140.
97. For an example of quietly proffered "modest" supercommentary, see, e.g., Nahmanides on Exod 2:5 in *MGH: Sefer Shemot*, ed. Menachem Cohen, 2 vols. (Ramat-Gan: Bar-Ilan University Press, 2007–12), 1:11, where he notes that if Rashi is correct in understanding that Pharaoh's daughter went down to the river to bathe, this interpretation not only requires an adjustment of the word order, as Rashi notes, but also an understanding of the preposition *'al* to mean *'el*. After supplying support for this possibility as attested by other verses, Nahmanides proposes a possible alternative not subject to the deficiencies of Rashi's interpretation.
98. V. Aptowitzer, "The Rewarding and Punishing of Animals and Inanimate Objects: On the Aggadic View of the World," *HUCA* 3 (1926): 128.
99. Eric Lawee, "The Sins of the Fauna in Midrash, Rashi, and Their Medieval Interlocutors," *Jewish Studies Quarterly* 17 (2010): 56–98.
100. On Gen 6:12 in *MGH: Sefer Bereshit*, ed. Menachem Cohen, 2 vols. (Ramat-Gan: Bar-Ilan University, 1993), 1:81.
101. Adapting a formulation from Rita Copeland, *Rhetoric, Hermeneutics, and Translation in the Middle Ages: Academic Traditions and Vernacular Texts* (Cambridge: Cambridge University Press, 1991), 64.
102. This is one of many examples showing that Nahmanides possessed a greater inclination to work with midrash on its own terms rather than simply take recourse to mystical interpretation to solve the problem of difficult midrashim; see Moshe Halbertal, *'Al derekh ha-'emet: ha-ramban vi-yeṣiratah shel masoret* (Jerusalem: Shalom Hartman Institute, 2006), 184.
103. On Gen 6:12 in *MGH: Sefer Bereshit*, 1:80. To bolster his reading, Nahmanides notes the more capacious phrases "of all that lives, of all flesh" (Gen 6:19) and "all flesh in which there was breath of life" (Gen 7:15) later in the narrative, contending that they include the fauna, whereas "all flesh" without further adornment refers only to humanity. Other verses, like Isaiah's "All flesh shall

come to worship Me, said the Lord" (Isa 66:23), which surely did not include subhuman creatures, helped clinch the point. Verbal parallels between Ibn Ezra and Nahmanides suggest the former's influence here. For example, both use *toledet* as a way of expressing the idea of nature in their glosses; see, on this usage, Shlomo Sela, *Abraham ibn Ezra and the Rise of Medieval Hebrew Science* (Leiden: Brill, 2003), 130–37. At Lev 26:6, Nahmanides describes how universally pacific animals lost their nonpredatory character as a result of Adam's sin and how, in messianic times, the predators would cease to prey in keeping with their "first nature"; see *MGH: Sefer Vayyiqra'*, ed. Menachem Cohen (Ramat-Gan: Bar-Ilan University Press, 2013), 224. For discussion, see Dov Rapel, "Ha-ramban 'al ha-galut ve-'al ha-ge'ulah," in *Ge'ulah u-medinah* (Jerusalem: Misrad ha-hinukh veha-tarbut, 1979), 105–106; Dov Schwartz, *Ha-ra'ayon ha-meshiḥi ba-hagut ha-yehudit bi-yemei ha-benayim* (Ramat-Gan: Bar-Ilan University Press, 1997), 104; and Ephraim Kanarfogel, "Medieval Rabbinic Conceptions of the Messianic Age: The View of the Tosafists," in *Me'ah She'arim: Studies in Medieval Jewish Spiritual Life in Memory of Isadore Twersky*, ed. Ezra Fleischer et al. (Jerusalem: Magnes, 2001), 167–69 (English section). In his gloss on Gen 6:12, Nahmanides posits a further lapse, it would seem.

104. Joseph ibn Shoshan, *Ḥazur ve-shoshan*, Oxford, Bodleian Library, MS Opp. Add. fol. 38, 1r. For the work's name, see the copyist's introduction on the same folio.
105. Mary Carruthers, *The Book of Memory: A Study of Memory in Medieval Culture*, 2nd ed. (Cambridge: Cambridge University Press, 2008), 18 and 139, respectively.
106. For this motive for supercommentary, see Lawee, "Genre," 316.
107. For this motive for supercommentary, see Lawee, "Genre," 318–19.
108. Ibn Shoshan, *Ḥazur ve-shoshan*, 1r. Cf. b. 'Eruvin 53a.
109. Avraham Ovadyah, "Perush r[abbi] 'E[liyahu] Mizraḥi 'al rashi," in *Ketavim nivḥarim*, 2 vols. (Jerusalem: Mosad Harav Kuk, 1942), 1:158–64. Almosnino's name goes unmentioned by Mizrahi. For *Perushim le-rashi*, see at note 236 in chapter 2, this volume.
110. For textual criticism, see the examples gathered in Samuel Almosnino, *Perush le-perush rashi me-ha-rav ha-gadol rabbi Shemu'el 'Almosnino*, ed. Moshe Filip (Petah Tikvah: Filip, 1998), 11.
111. E.g., on Exod 10:1, 8 (Almosnino, *Perush*, 119).
112. On Num 21:1 (Almosnino, *Perush*, 260).
113. John B. Henderson, *Scripture, Canon, and Commentary: A Comparison of Confucian and Western Exegesis* (Princeton, NJ: Princeton University Press, 1991), 131.
114. For Almosnino, see on Exod 17:16 and Num 13:18 (Almosino, *Perush*, 138, 241). Concern with the "ordering" (*siddur*) of discourse was not cardinal in the

hermeneutic method of Isaac Canpanton that we will study later in this chapter, but it attained centrality in later iterations of his method, such as in *Kelalei shemu'el* (*Principles of Samuel*) of Samuel ibn Sid; see Daniel Boyarin, "Moslem, Christian, and Jewish Cultural Interaction in Sefardic Talmudic Interpretation," *Review of Rabbinic Judaism* 5 (2002): 13–16; and Aviram Ravitsky, *Logiqah 'arisṭoṭelit u-metodologyah talmudit: yissumah shel ha-logiqah ha-'arisṭoṭelit ba-perushim la-midot she-ha-torah nidreshet bahen* (Jerusalem: Magnes, 2009), 269–76. For a fleeting imputation of meaning to order with respect to the *Commentary* on Canpanton's part, see Isaac Canpanton, *Darkhei ha-talmud*, ed. Yitzhaq Lange (Jerusalem: "Shalem" sokhnut le-hafaṣat sefarim, 1980), 60.

115. For Rashi's source in *Pirkei de-rabbi Eliezer*, see Rashi, *Ḥamishah ḥumshei torah: rashi ha-shalem*, 7 vols. to date (Jerusalem: Ariel, 1986), 1:117–18.

116. Avraham Grossman, *Rashi*, trans. Joel Linsider (Oxford: Littman Library of Jewish Civilization, 2012), 89–90.

117. In describing Abraham's donkey at Gen 22:3, the Torah does not use a definite article, which is also lacking in the verse in Zechariah. Since the donkey appears in these verses without a definite article, Rashi refrains from adducing the midrash in his explanations of them. By contrast, he cites it at Exod 4, where the textual trigger is present; see Nehama Leibowitz, "Darko shel rashi be-hava'at midrashim be-ferusho la-torah," in *'Iyunim be-sefer shemot*, 2nd ed. (Jerusalem: World Zionist Organization, 1970), 513. Midrashists routinely made homiletical hay out of scriptural definite articles; see Isaac Heinemann, *Darkhei ha-'aggadah*, 3rd ed. (Jerusalem: Magnes, 1974), 117. Modern biblicists, by contrast, are likely to explain instances of the article such as the one in Exod 4:20 as the equivalent of a possessive pronoun, signifying that Moses mounted his family on *his* donkey; see Victor P. Hamilton, *Exodus: An Exegetical Commentary* (Grand Rapids, MI: Baker Academic, 2011), 177. For this meaning of the definite article, see Bill T. Arnold and John H. Choi, *A Guide to Biblical Hebrew Syntax* (New York: Cambridge University Press, 2003), 32. The definite article can indicate generic reference; see Peter Bekins, "Non-Prototypical Uses of the Definite Article in Biblical Hebrew," *Journal of Semitic Studies* 58 (2013): 225–40; and James Barr, "'Determination' and the Definite Article in Biblical Hebrew," *Journal of Semitic Studies* 34 (1989): 312–13.

118. James L. Kugel, "Two Introductions to Midrash," *Prooftexts* 3 (1983): 144.

119. Heinemann, *Darkhei*, 27, 30.

120. Burton L. Visotzky, *Reading the Book: Making the Bible a Timeless Text* (New York: Anchor, 1991), 96.

121. Isaac Abarbanel, *Yeshu'ot meshiḥo* (Königsberg, 1861), 48r. The same author elsewhere offered a slightly more muted rejection of the midrash's literal interpretation as "far-fetched and nigh impossible for it to be explained literally"; see Abarbanel, *Perush 'al ha-torah*, 3 vols. (Jerusalem: Benei Arabel, 1964), 1:263.

122. Judah Loew, *Gevurot 'adonai* (London: L. Honig, 1964), 114.
123. Referring to the fourteenth century, Marc M. Epstein, "Another Flight into Egypt: Confluence, Coincidence, the Cross-cultural Dialectics of Messianism and Iconographic Appropriation in Medieval Jewish and Christian Culture," in *Imagining the Self, Imagining the Other: Visual Representation and Jewish-Christian Dynamics in the Middle Ages and Early Modern Period*, ed. Eva Frojmovic (Leiden: Brill, 2002), 48n35, notes that the interpretation given by Rashi is not cited by Sefardic commentators. He also observes its origin in *Pirkei de-rabbi 'Eliezer* which, he adds, "would have been well-known to a contemporary Spanish Jewish audience." Epstein might have noted the obvious: by a certain juncture the midrash would have become very well known in Spain due to its appearance in the *Commentary*, where it was dealt with by Sefardic commentators—or rather, Rashi supercommentators. For *Pirkei de-rabbi 'Eliezer*, see most recently Katharina E. Keim, *Pirqei DeRabbi Eliezer: Structure, Coherence, Intertextuality* (Leiden: Brill, 2017).
124. Shem Tov ben Shaprut, *Pardes rimmonim* (Sabbioneta, 1554), 2r; and Gitit Holzman, "Haqdamat sefer 'Mikhlol yofi' le-r[abbi] Shemu'el Ṣarṣah: hahadarah u-mavo'," *Sinai* 109 (1992): 27.
125. Joseph ibn Shoshan, *Ḥazur ve-shoshan*, 20r, glossing Rashi's comment on Deut 4:32.
126. Almosnino, *Perush*, 108. For Samuel ibn Zarza, see, e.g., *Meqor ḥayyim* (Mantua, 1559), 32v. For the *ḥamor/ḥomer* interchange in earlier philosophical writers of southern French origin such as Isaac ben Yedayah and Levi ben Avraham, see Marc Saperstein, *Decoding the Rabbis: A Thirteenth-Century Commentary on the Aggadah* (Cambridge, MA: Harvard University Press, 1980), 113 and, for an example from the sphere of biblical interpretation, Levi ben Avraham, *Livyat ḥen*, in Munich, Bayerische Staatsbibliothek, Cod. hebr. 58, fol. 37r, where the prohibition on plowing with an ox and donkey together (Deut 22:10) is explained in terms of a proscription on the yoking of the intellectual faculty ("ox") to the "beastly, material" (*bahami, ḥomri*) parts of a person symbolized by the donkey. Jacob Anatoli, *Malmad ha-talmidim*, ed. L. Silbermann (Lyck, Prussia [now Ełk, Poland], 1866), 85v, fleetingly suggests a reading of the donkeys of Abraham, Moses, and the Messiah in the manner developed much more fully here by Almosnino. It is by no means certain that Almosnino would have known this apparently pioneering development of the idea.
127. Maimonides, *The Guide of the Perplexed*, trans. Shlomo Pines, 2 vols. (Chicago: University of Chicago Press, 1963), III:8 (2:432–33). See Josef Stern, *The Matter and Form of Maimonides' Guide* (Cambridge, MA: Harvard University Press, 2013), 97–131.
128. *Mishneh torah*, Hilkhot yesode ha-torah 4:8 as in Moses Maimonides, *Mishneh Torah: The Book of Knowledge by Maimonides*, ed. Moses Hyamson (Jerusalem and New York: Bloch, 1937), 39a; and Maimonides, *Guide* I:1–2 (Pines 1:21–26).

129. Maimonides, *Guide* I:70 (Pines 1:171). The metaphorical meaning of "riding" as domination figures in Maimonides's exposition of an obscure midrashic dictum elsewhere in the *Guide*; see Stern, *Matter*, 177–81.
130. See at note 52 in chapter 5, this volume.
131. Anonymous, "Supercommentary on Rashi," in New York, JTS MS Lutski 802 (with thanks to the librarian and faculty of the Jewish Theological Seminary for permitting me the use of a copy of this manuscript). The dating appears from references to Duran's work of 1403, *Ma'aseh 'efod*, on the one hand, and to Duran as yet being among the living, on the other. (For a comment combining both references, see 4r.) It seems Duran died in 1433; see Maud Kozodoy, *The Secret Faith of Maestre Honoratus: Profayt Duran and Jewish Identity in Late Medieval Iberia* (Philadelphia: University of Pennsylvania Press, 2015), 28. For an especially intense set of references to other commentators, see on Gen 32:4 (32r).
132. Eric Lawee, "Exegesis and Appropriation: Reading Rashi in Late Medieval Spain," *Harvard Theological Review* 110 (2017): 505–508.
133. E.g., Anonymous, "Supercommentary," MS Lutski 802, 69r (Exod 13:17); 36v (Gen 37:2); and 109v (Lev 9:22).
134. Moses ibn Gabbai, *'Eved shelomo*, ed. Moshe Filip (Petah Tikvah: Filip, 2006), 42. On the author, see note 137 in chapter 2, this volume. The work awaits systematic study. See Eric Lawee, "'Servant of Solomon': Sensitivity to Language and Context in Moses ibn Gabbai's Supercommentary on Rashi's Commentary on the Torah, in *Ve-'Ed Ya'aleh (Gen 2:6): Essays in Biblical and Ancient Near Eastern Studies Presented to Edward L. Greenstein*. Forthcoming.
135. I write "a gloss thought to impart the 'plain sense'" to point to the question: thought by whom, commentator or supercommentator? Here one ought to note a deviation between Filip's printed text and the manuscript, where the latter reads "*yira'eh lo*" (referring to Rashi, not to Ibn Gabbai) and, not as in printed version, "*yira'eh li*." See Moses ibn Gabbai, *'Eved shelomo*, Oxford, Bodleian Library, MS Hunt. Don. 25, 1r. The possible significance would be in a case where Ibn Gabbai introduces what he thinks *Rashi* held to be a reading embodying a textually grounded interpretation, making his use of the formula understandable, even though Ibn Gabbai dissents from Rashi's view. For such a case, see his comment on Gen 4:15 (*'Eved shelomo*, 65–66), which introduces Rashi's comment with "*peresh ha-rav*." Ibn Gabbai does not explain the distinction between midrash and aggadah in his formulation; he may have considered sayings in the class of aggadah of lesser weight, as Nahmanides's use of this term sometimes implies; see Bernard Septimus, "'Open Rebuke and Concealed Love': Naḥmanides and the Andalusian Tradition," in *Rabbi Moses Naḥmanides (Ramban): Explorations in His Religious and Literary Virtuosity*, ed. Isadore Twersky (Cambridge, MA: Harvard University Press, 1983), 21–22.

136. This interpretive operation requires separate study, but it is clear that the essential features of what are presented as two clearly defined categories in Rashi's expositions prove more elusive than the introduction to *'Eved shelomo* suggests. Thus, Ibn Gabbai can find a basis for midrashim introduced in a way (*katav ha-rav*) that suggests they have none (*'Eved shelomo*, 68, on Gen 6:2). The formula for a textually grounded reading (*peresh ha-rav*) can introduce an interpretation said to be arrived at midrashically (*derekh derash*) rather than by "the method of *peshaṭ*" (*'Eved shelomo*, 88, on Gen 16:11). In a few cases, an apparently neutral formula, *'amar ha-rav* (Ibn Gabbai, *'Eved shelomo*, 54, on Gen 1:12, 1:14), appears.
137. Ibn Gabbai, *'Eved shelomo*, 44. Cf. Maimonides, *Guide* III:43 (Pines 2:573); and see Eliezer Segal, "Midrash and Literature: Some Medieval Views," *Prooftexts* 11 (1991): 57–65. Ibn Gabbai's category of "riddle" (*'Eved shelomo*, 44) also carries strong Maimonidean resonances, although Ibn Gabbai has no desire to assimilate rabbinic use of this discursive form to the predilection for it among ancient philosophers, as did Maimonides. See *Guide*, I:17 (Pines 1:42–43), where Maimonides points to Plato and his predecessors as exemplars of this sort of discourse, stressing their representation of matter as female and form as male.
138. Num 13:20 (Ibn Gabbai, *'Eved shelomo*, 338). For some reason, Ibn Gabbai leaves unremarked a textual prompt for at least one element of midrash: the congruence between the Torah's use of a collective noun in the singular ("*'eṣ*" for trees) and the midrash's concern with the prospect that a single upstanding Canaanite will thrwart the entry of the Israelites into the land.
139. Ibn Gabbai, *'Eved shelomo*, 162 (on Gen 44:18).
140. For bibliography, see Naomi Grunhaus, *The Challenge of Received Tradition: Dilemmas of Interpretation in Radak's Biblical Commentaries* (Oxford: Oxford University Press, 2013), 215n68.
141. The presentation here draws heavily on my "Reception."
142. Among other things, Almosnino, in his quiet supercommentarial way, corrects for what could be seen as homosexual implications of the comment, an aspect of the original midrash that a later Christian critic, the Jewish apostate Sixtus of Siena, who oversaw the incineration of more than ten thousand Hebrew books in Cremona, would condemn in his *Bibliotheca Sancta* of 1566; see Ch. Merchavia, "Qunṭres neged ha-talmud mimei serefat ha-talmud be-'iṭalyah," *Tarbiẓ* 37 (1967): 198.
143. Almosnino, *Perush*, 23.
144. Anonymous. "Supercommentary," in New York, Jewish Theological Seminary, MS Lutski 802, 4r.
145. b. Yevamot 63a: "*'zot ha-pa'am'—mikhlal di-fe'amim 'aḥerim shimmesh ve-lo' 'alu be-da'ato.*"

146. Aaron Aboulrabi, [*Commentary on the Torah / Supercommentary on Rashi*], in *Perushim le-rashi* (Constantinople, [1525?]), 16v.
147. Antonio Pacios Lopez, *La Disputa de Tortosa*, 2 vols. (Madrid: Consejo superior de investigaciones cientificas, 1957), 2:564: *quia inquit textus "hoc nunc," ostenditur quod alias habuerat copulam.*
148. b. Sanhedrin 56b. See David Novak, *The Image of the Non-Jew in Judaism: An Historical and Constructive Study of the Noahide Laws* (New York: Mellen, 1983), 4–6.
149. Ibn Gabbai, *'Eved shelomo*, 59. For Gen 2:24 as warrant for the interdiction on bestiality, see b. Sanhedrin 58a. One might speculate that the reference to the midrash as an *'aggadah* indicates a further effort by Ibn Gabbai to distance it from the plain sense, a tactic in line with Nahmanides's occasional use of the term to describe a midrash that he found less than compelling; see note 135, this chapter. For other places where Ibn Gabbai casts a midrash he deems especially irrational as an *'aggadah*, see *'Eved shelomo*, 53, on Gen 1:11; *'Eved shelomo*, 54, on Gen 1:12.
150. See, e.g., the comment by Mordechai Jaffe, *Levush 'orah*, in *'Oṣar perushim 'al ha-torah*, 2 vols. (Jerusalem: Divrei Ḥakhamim, 1958), 1:14r.
151. Francesco del Punta, "The Genre of Commentaries in the Middle Ages and Its Relation to the Nature and Originality of Medieval Thought," in *Was ist Philosophie Im Mittelalter?* (= *Miscellanea Mediaevalia* 26), ed. Jan A. Aertsen and Andreas Speer (Berlin: De Gruyter, 1998), 151.
152. Ibn Gabbai, *'Eved shelomo*, 59, on Gen 2:22.
153. An example is the response of post-1492 supercommentator Abraham Bokhrat to Rashi's teaching on "corrections of the scribes" (*tiqqune soferim*) at Gen 18:22. Regarding the possibility that this rabbinic idea was meant to signal an actual change in the scriptural text effected by later scribes, Bokhrat responds with a pious shudder: "The mouth cannot utter such a thing!" On the basis of earlier Sefardic sources, Bokhrat is able to cite a perfectly valid explanation for the phenomenon mentioned by Rashi that, in his view, "handsomely" addresses the problem. Still, he throws up his hands when it comes to Rashi himself, admitting that his particular formulation of the midrashic motif (on which, see note 91 in chapter 1, this volume) is at odds with the theologically acceptable interpretation. Bokhrat even reports his attempt to locate a different base text of Rashi's gloss that might allow him to posit scribal error as the source of Rashi's idea of later alterations to the biblical text. With intellectual integrity, he admits that this effort came up empty: "All versions that we have seen, recent as well as ancient," contain the offending passage; see Abraham Bokhrat, *Sefer zikaron*, ed. Moshe Filip, corrected ed. (Petah Tikvah: Filip, 1985), 123.
154. On Gen 2:20 (*MGH: Sefer Bereshit*, 1:44).

155. For this midrash at Tortosa, see Lopez, *La Disputa*, 2:564. For criticism of it in Alonso's *Fortalitium fidei*, see Merchavia, "Quntres," 198n42.
156. Mizrahi, *Ḥumash ha-re'em*, 1:63. See also David ben Samuel Halevi, *Divrei David*, ed. Hayyim D. Chavel (Jerusalem: Mosad Harav Kuk, 1978), 16.
157. Indeed, Daniel Boyarin, *A Traveling Homeland: The Babylonian Talmud as Diaspora* (Philadelphia: University of Pennsylvania Press, 2015), 110–13, proposes that the Sefardic world was the source of the interpretive modes that eventually came to be called *pilpul* in Ashkenaz.
158. Classic is Daniel Boyarin, *Ha-'iyyun ha-sefaradi: le-farshanut ha-talmud shel megorashei sefarad* (Jerusalem: Mekhon Ben-Zvi, 1989). See also Boyarin, "Moslem, Christian, and Jewish," 1–33; Sergey Dolgopolski, *What Is Talmud? The Art of Disagreement* (New York: Fordham University Press, 2009); and Marciano, "Ḥakhamim," 89–161. For *'iyyun* and *pilpul* together, see Mordechai Breuer, *'Ohalei torah: ha-yeshivah, tavnitah ve-toledoteha* (Jerusalem: Zalman Shazar, 2003), 186–94. Not all Sefardic scholars joined the Canpantonian revolution; see Israel M. Ta-Shma, "Li-yedi'at maṣṣav limmud ha-torah bi-sefarad ba-me'ah ha-15," in *Dor gerush sefarad*, ed. Yom Tov Assis and Yosef Kaplan (Jerusalem: Zalman Shazar, 1999), 61.
159. That logic was ushered into the precincts of traditional late medieval Sefardic learning may owe to its status in the minds of some as a "neutral" discipline that could therefore not undermine faith or religious practice, but critics of this development saw things otherwise. See Marciano, "Ḥakhamim," 142–46; and Aviram Ravitsky, "Aristotelian Logic and Talmudic Methodology: The Commentaries on the 13 Hermeneutic Principles and Their Application to Logic," in *Judaic Logic*, ed. Andrew Schumann (Piscataway, NJ: Gorgias, 2010), 128–29.
160. Yoel Marciano, "Me-'aragon le-qasṭilyah: le-toledot shiṭat limmudam shel ḥakhmei sefarad ba-me'ah ha-ḥamesh 'esreh," *Tarbiẓ* 77 (2008): 592–99; and Hava Tirosh-Samuelson, "Jewish Philosophy on the Eve of Modernity," in *History of Jewish Philosophy*, ed. Daniel H. Frank and Oliver Leaman (London: Routledge, 1997), 503.
161. Canpanton, *Darkhei ha-talmud*, 22, reading *ve-khol* for *be-khol*; see apparatus, l. 8. In the formulation of Nahman S. Greenspan, *Melekhet maḥashevet* (London: M.L. Tsaylingold, 1955), 13, the basic premise of *'iyyun* is "subjugation to the linguistic formulation."
162. Canpanton, *Darkhei ha-talmud*, 57, 59. For the cited usage, see Yaakov Elman, "Classical Rabbinic Interpretation," in *The Jewish Study Bible*, ed. Adele Berlin and Marc Zvi Brettler (Oxford: Oxford University Press, 2004), 1849.
163. Marciano, "Me-'aragon."
164. See the examples in Almosnino, *Perush*, 11–12. For Almosnino's use of key terms associated with that revolution, including the most important of all,

"investigate" (*le'ayyen*), as well as "guard against" (*shamar/nizhar*), see, e.g., *Perush*, 116, 138, and 300. For logic as an "instrument" that all use, even "against their will," including some subhuman creatures, see *Perush*, 199, on Lev 18:4.

165. The threefold goal finds concise expression in Anonymous. "Supercommentary on Rashi," New York, Jewish Theological Seminary, MS Lutski 801, fol. 97b: "כל מי שירצה לעיין בפי' רש"י ז"ל צריך לשום נגד עיניו שלשה דברי[ם] ... הא' שמירה השנית פי' והשלישית הכרח, והסימן שפה ברורה".

166. Baruch J. Schwartz, "Perusho shel rashi li-shemot 6:1–9: beḥinah meḥudeshet," in *'Leyashev peshuṭo shel miqra': 'asupat meḥqarim be-farshanut ha-miqra'*, ed. Eran Viezel and Sara Japhet (Jerusalem: Bialik / Mandel Institute, 2011), 104n13, proposes that the correct translation of this somewhat elusive phrase is: "in the manner of a litigant."

167. In comments on Exod 6:2–3, Nahmanides, after citing Rashi, reads this gloss in a way that softens its stark formulation.

168. Anonymous, "Supercommentary on Rashi," in Warsaw, Jewish Historical Institute, MS 204, 87v: "*ve-rabbenu pilpel mah she-'amar rashi.*" In a passage such as this, as in late medieval Spain generally, the stem "*pilpel*" generally carried a positive or neutral valence, but some used it as a term of opprobrium. See Marciano, "Ḥakhamim," 58, 59n20, 70–71 (positive) and 145, 183 (negative).

169. Anonymous, "Supercommentary," in Warsaw, JHI, MS 204, 87v. The gloss made its way into a later compilatory supercommentary; see Jacob Kanisal, *Sefer rabbi Ya'aqov Qanisal 'al perush rashi*, ed. Moshe Filip (Petah Tikvah: Filip, 1998), 206 (for *beni u-veni* in the printed text read *beno u-veno* as in the manuscript).

170. Anonymous, "Supercommentary," Warsaw, JHI, MS 204, 87v–88r (Kanisal, *Sefer rabbi Ya'aqov Qanisal*, 206).

171. Anonymous, "Supercommentary," Warsaw, JHI, MS 204, 88r (*Qanizal*, 207). This reading may have taken inspiration from Nahmanides's gloss on Exod 3:13, where the question "What is His name?" was interpreted with reference to the divine attribute that was to underwrite the redemption.

172. James L. Kugel, "The 'Bible as Literature' in Late Antiquity and the Middle Ages," *Hebrew University Studies in Literature and the Arts* 11 (1983): 20–70.

173. William A. Graham and Navid Kermani, "Recitation and Aesthetic Reception," in *The Cambridge Companion to the Qur'an*, ed. Jane Dammen McAuliffe (Cambridge: Cambridge University Press, 2006), 115–44, esp. 130.

174. Mordechai Z. Cohen, "'The Best of Poetry . . . ': Literary Approaches to the Bible in the Spanish *Peshat* Tradition," *Torah U-Madda Journal* 6 (1995–96): 15–57; and Meira Polliack, "The Spanish Legacy in the Hebrew Bible Commentaries of Abraham Ibn Ezra and Profayt Duran," in *"Encuentros" and "Desencuentros": Spanish Jewish Cultural Interaction Throughout History*, ed. Carlos Carrete Parrondo et al. (Tel Aviv: University Publishing Projects, 2000),

87–89. In rare cases they denied any meaning to scriptural details; see Richard C. Steiner, "Meaninglessness, Meaningfulness, and Super-Meaningfulness in Scripture: An Analysis of the Controversy Surrounding Dan 2:12 in the Middle Ages," *JQR* 82 (1992): 431–49.

175. Robert A. Harris, "Concepts of Scripture in the School of Rashi," in *Jewish Concepts of Scripture: A Comparative Introduction*, ed. Benjamin D. Sommer (New York: New York University Press, 2012), 106.

176. Yaakov Elman, "'It Is No Empty Thing': Nahmanides and the Search for Omnisignificance," *Torah U-Madda Journal* 4 (1993): 5.

177. Kanisal, *Sefer rabbi Ya'aqov Qanisal*, 239, 281 (to Exod 13:17; 21:1).

178. Abraham Gross, "Polmos 'al shiṭat ha-'shemirah': le-toledot limmud perush rashi 'al ha-torah be-dor gerush sefarad," *AJS Review* 18 (1993): 1–20 (Hebrew section).

179. For this acclaim, see Shlomo Zalman Havlin, "'Al 'ha-ḥatimah ha-sifrutit' ki-yesod ha-ḥaluqah li-tequfot ha-halakhah," in *Meḥqarim be-sifrut ha-talmudit* (Jerusalem: Israel Academy of the Sciences, 1983), 153–54n53; and Bernard Septimus, "'Ide'ologyah leshonit ve-hegmonyah tarbutit: teshuvah le-r[abbi] Shemu'el de Medina, meqoroteha ve-hashlakhoteha," in *Rishonim ve-'aḥaronim: meḥkarim be-toledot yisra'el mugashim le-'Avraham Grossman*, ed. Joseph R. Hacker, B. Z. Kedar, and Yosef Kaplan (Jerusalem: Zalman Shazar, 2010), 296.

180. Khalatz, *Mesiaḥ 'illemim*, 28.

181. Khalatz, *Mesiaḥ 'illemim*, 28.

182. Aaron Hughes, "Presenting the Past: The Genre of Commentary in Theoretical Perspective," *Method and Theory in the Study of Religion* 15 (2003): 150.

183. In *Tanakh: The Holy Scriptures*, the reading is "The Lord spoke those words—those and no more," but see the Targum on the verse, which Rashi cites in his first gloss on it. For the larger theme, see Michael Chernick, *A Great Voice That Did Not Cease: The Growth of the Rabbinic Canon and Its Interpretation* (Cincinnati, OH: Hebrew Union College Press, 2009).

184. Lawee, "Biblical Scholarship," 299–302.

185. Bernard M. Levinson, "*You Must Not Add Anything to What I Command You*: Paradoxes of Canon and Authorship in Ancient Israel," *Numen* 50 (2003): 47; and Levinson, "The Human Voice in Divine Revelation: The Problem of Authority in Biblical Law," in *Innovation in Religious Traditions: Essays in the Interpretation of Religious Change*, ed. Michael A. Williams, Collett Cox, and Martin S. Jaffee (Berlin: De Gruyter, 1992), 37.

186. Jonathan Z. Smith, *Imagining Religion: From Babylon to Jonestown* (Chicago: University of Chicago Press, 1982), 48. How much such ingenuity is a source as opposed to a *post facto* legitimator of innovation is debatable; see Martin S. Jaffee, "*Halakhah* in Early Rabbinic Judaism: Innovation Beyond Exegesis, Tradition Before Oral Torah," in *Innovation in Religious Traditions: Essays in the

Interpretation of Religious Change, ed. Michael A. Williams, Collett Cox, and Martin S. Jaffee (Berlin: De Gruyter, 1992), 112.

187. Moshe Halbertal, *People of the Book: Canon, Meaning, and Authority* (Cambridge, MA: Harvard University Press, 1997), 26.

CHAPTER 4

1. See David Jacoby, "The Jewish Communities of the Byzantine World from the Tenth to the Mid-Fifteenth Century: Some Aspects of Their Evolution," in *Jewish Reception of Greek Bible Versions: Studies in Their Use in Late Antiquity and the Middle Ages*, ed. Nicholas de Lange, Julia G. Krivoruchko, and Cameron Boyd-Taylor (Tübingen: Mohr Siebeck, 2009), 157.
2. Nicholas de Lange, "Hebrew Scholarship in Byzantium," in *Hebrew Scholarship and the Medieval World*, ed. Nicholas de Lange (New York: Cambridge University Press, 2001), 23, for the cited characterization. The best overall survey remains Steven B. Bowman, *The Jews of Byzantium 1204–1453* (Tuscaloosa: University of Alabama Press, 1985). A recent leap forward for Jewish thought is Dov Schwartz, *Raḥaq ve-qeruv: hagut yehudit be-vizanṭyon be-shilhei yemei ha-benayim* (Jerusalem: Magnes, 2016), which contains an up-to-date bibliography. For Karaite thought, see Daniel J. Lasker, *From Judah Hadassi to Elijah Bashyatchi: Studies in Late Medieval Karaite Philosophy* (Leiden: Brill, 2008). For rabbinic literature, see Israel M. Ta-Shma, "Le-toledot ha-sifrut ha-rabbanit be-yavan ba-me'ah ha-14," *Tarbiẓ* 62 (1993): 101–14; and Ta-Shma, "Rabbinic Literature in the Late Byzantine and Early Ottoman Periods," in *Jews, Turks, Ottomans: A Shared History, Fifteenth Through the Twentieth Century*, ed. Avigdor Levy (Syracuse, NY: Syracuse University Press, 2002), 52–60.
3. Without documenting this claim, I note exceptions: Dov Schwartz, "Seridim mi-perusho shel r[abbi] Shemaryah ha-'iqriṭi la-torah," in *'Alei sefer* 26–27 (= *Bi-netivei ha-sefer ha-'ivri: mi-sefer yeṣirah ve-'ad le-khitvei ha-rav Yosef Dov Soloveitchiq*, ed. Dov Schwartz and Gila Prebor) (2017): 95–148; Schwartz, "Perush filosofi ve-qabali shel R. Micha'el ben Shabtai Balbo le-mizmor 29 be-tehilim," *Kobez Al Yad* 24 (34) 2016: 205–58; Saskia Dönitz, "Shemarya ha-Ikriti and the Karaite Exegetical Challenge," in *Exegesis and Poetry in Medieval Karaite and Rabbanite Texts*, ed. Joachim Yeshaya and Elisabeth Hollender (Leiden: Brill, 2017), 228–48. An important monograph is Jean-Christophe Attias, *Ha-perush ke-di'alog: Mordekhai ben 'Eli'ezer Komṭino 'al ha-torah*, trans. Yisrael Meir (Jerusalem: Magnes, 2007). (Appeared originally in French: *Le commentaire biblique: Mordekhai Komtino ou l'herméneutique du dialogue* [Paris: Éditions du Cerf, 1991.). See generally Nicholas de Lange, *Japheth in the Tents of Shem: Greek Bible Translations in Byzantine Judaism* (Tübingen: Mohr Siebeck, 2015).

4. For the earlier stratum, see Nicholas de Lange, *Greek Jewish Texts from the Cairo Geniza* (Tübingen: J. C. B. Mohr, 1996); and Gershon Brin, *Re'u'el va-ḥaverav: parshanim yehudiyim mi-bizanṭyon mi-sevivot ha-me'ah ha-'asirit la-sefirah* (Tel Aviv: Haim Rubin Tel Aviv University Press, 2012). For *Leqaḥ ṭov*, see Israel M. Ta-Shma, "Midrash 'leqaḥ ṭov' – riq'o ve-'ofyo," in *Keneset meḥqarim: 'iyyunim ba-sifrut ha-rabbanit bi-yemei ha-benayim*, vol. 3: *'Iṭalyah u-vizanṭyon* (Jerusalem: Bialik, 2004–2010), 259–94.
5. Joshua Holo, *Byzantine Jewry in the Mediterranean Economy* (Cambridge: Cambridge University Press, 2009), 86–89; and *Taqanot qandi'ah ve-zikhronoteha*, ed. Elias S. Hartom and M. D. A. Cassuto (Jerusalem: Mekizei Nirdamim, 1943), 10.
6. For eastward Ashkenazic migration generally, see, e.g., Alexandra Cuffel, "Call and Response: European Jewish Emigration to Egypt and Palestine in the Middle Ages," *JQR* 90 (1999): 61–102; Elchanan Reiner, "Ben 'ashkenaz li-rushalayim: ḥakhamim 'ashkenazim be-'ereṣ yisra'el le-'aḥar ha-mavet ha-shaḥor," *Shalem* 4 (1984): 27–62; Shlomo Spitzer, "Ha-'ashkenazim ba-ḥaṣi ha-'i ha-balqani be-me'ot ha-15 ve-ha-16," *Mi-mizraḥ u-ma'arav* 1 (1974): 59–79. For Sefardic migration, see Joseph Hacker, "Ziqatam ve-'aliyatam shel yehudei sefarad le-'ereṣ yisra'el, 1391–1492," *Qatedrah* 36 (1985): 3–34; and Rena Lauer, "Cretan Jews and the First Sephardic Encounter in the Fifteenth Century," *Mediterranean Historical Review* 27 (2012): 129–40.
7. Lauer, "Cretan Jews," 131.
8. Micha Perry, "Byzantium's Role in the Transmission of Jewish Knowledge in the Middle Ages: The Attitude Toward Circumcision," in *Jews in Byzantium: Dialectics of Minority and Majority Cultures*, ed. Robert Bonfil et al. (Leiden: Brill, 2012), 645.
9. Malachi Beit-Arié, *QI*, 193.
10. Ta-Shma, "Rabbinic Literature," 60.
11. Esther Benbassa and Aron Rodrigue, *Sephardi Jewry: A History of the Judeo-Spanish Community, 14th–20th Centuries* (Berkeley: University of California Press, 2000), 11–16. For a case study, see Bernard Septimus, "'Ide'ologyah leshonit ve-hegmonyah tarbutit: teshuvah le-r[abbi] Shemu'el de Medina, meqoroteha ve-hashlakhoteha," in *Rishonim ve-'aḥaronim: meḥkarim be-toledot yisra'el mugashim le-'Avraham Grossman*, ed. Joseph R. Hacker, B. Z. Kedar, and Yosef Kaplan (Jerusalem: Zalman Shazar, 2010), 293–308.
12. Martin Borýsek, "The Jews of Venetian Candia: The Challenges of External Influences and Internal Diversity as Reflected in *Takkanot Kandiyah*," *Al-Masāq: Journal of the Medieval Mediterranean* 26 (2014): 241–66.
13. Schwartz, *Raḥaq*, 17.
14. Ta-Shma, "Le-toledot ha-sifrut," 102.
15. For Byzantine Karaism's advent, see Golda Akhiezer, "Byzantine Karaism in the Eleventh to Fifteenth Centuries," in *Jews in Byzantium: Dialectics of Minority and Majority Cultures*, ed. Robert Bonfil et al. (Leiden: Brill, 2012), 724.

16. De Lange, *Japheth*, 29.
17. Jean-Christophe Attias, "Intellectual Leadership: Rabbanite-Karaite Relations in Constantinople as Seen Through the Works and Activity of Mordekhai Comtino in the Fifteenth Century," in *Ottoman and Turkish Jewry: Community and Leadership*, ed. Aron Rodrigue (Bloomington: Indiana University Press, 1992), 67–86. Generally, see, Schwartz, *Rahḥaq*, 253–91.
18. Schwartz, *Raḥaq*, 17–18; Y. Tzvi Langermann, "Science in the Jewish Communities of the Byzantine Cultural Orbit: New Perspectives," in *Science in Medieval Jewish Cultures*, ed. Gad Freudenthal (Cambridge: Cambridge University Press, 2011), 438–53; Ofer Elior, "Rabbi Yedidyah Rakh on Ezekiel's 'I Heard': A Case Study in Byzantine Jews' Reception of Spanish-Provencal Jewish Philosophical-Scientific Culture," in *Texts in Transit in the Medieval Mediterranean*, ed. Y. Tzvi Langermann and Robert G. Morrison (University Park: Penn State University Press, 2016), 29–30.
19. Ofer Elior, *Ruaḥ ḥen yaḥalof 'al panai* (Jerusalem: Mekhon Ben-Zvi, 2017), 112–14.
20. David Jacoby, "Jews and Christians in Venetian Crete: Segregation, Interaction, and Conflict," in *"Interstizi": Culture ebraico-cristane a Venezia e nei suoi domini dal Medioevo all'Età moderna*, ed. Uwe Israel, Robert Jütte, and Reinhold C. Mueller (Rome: Edizioni di Storia e Letteratura, 2010), 239–75; and Sally McKee, *Uncommon Dominion: Venetian Crete and the Myth of Ethnic Purity* (Philadelphia: University of Pennsylvania Press, 2000).
21. Freddy Thiriet, *La Romanie vénitienne au Moyen Age: le développement et l'exploitation du domaine colonial vénitien, XIIe–XVe siècles* (Paris: de Boccard, 1975); and David Holton, "The Cretan Renaissance," in *Literature and Society in Renaissance Crete*, ed. David Holton (Cambridge: Cambridge University Press, 1991), 1–16.
22. Benjamin Arbel, "Introduction" [to special issue on "Minorities in Colonial Settings: The Jews in Venice's Hellenic Territories (15th–18th Centuries)]," *Mediterranean Historical Review* 27:2 (2012): 117; Lauer, "Cretan Jews," 130; Giacomo Corazzol, "La vita culturale ebraica a Candia nei secoli XIV–XVI: l'impatto dell'immigrazione sulla cultura della comunità locale" (PhD diss., University of Bologna, 2015), 11–49.
23. Tamás Visi, "The Early Ibn Ezra Supercommentaries: A Chapter in Medieval Jewish Intellectual History" (PhD diss., Central European University, 2006), 109. For Judah's Torah commentary, see Leah Naomi Goldfeld, "Perush la-torah shel Yehudah ben Shemaryah bi-khetav yad she-ba-genizah," *Kobez Al Yad* 10 (1982): 125–60. On him, see Benjamin Arbel, "Notes on the Delmedigo of Candia," in *Non solo verso Oriente: Studi sull'ebraismo in onore di Piercesare Ioly Zorattini*, ed. Maddalena Del Bianco Cotrozzi, Riccardo Di Segni, and Marcello Massenzio (Florence: L. S. Olschki, 2014), 119–30; and Corazzol, "Vita,"

72–76. For Joseph ben Eliezer's copying of the Ibn Ezra supercommentary, see Eliezer Davidovitch, "Be'ur r[abbi] Yish'ayah ben Meir," in *Ḥamishah qadmonei mefareshei r[abbi] 'Avraham 'ibn 'Ezra*, ed. Haim Kreisel (Beer-Sheva: Ben-Gurion University of the Negev Press, 2017), 70–71 (Hebrew pagination).

24. Michael Rigler, "Ha-yehudim be-'iyei 'agan ha-yam ha-tikhon ha-mizraḥi ke-sappaqei sefarim," *'Alei sefer* 21 (2010): 76–80, esp. 77.
25. Langermann, "Science," 442.
26. Shalom Rosenberg, "'Arba'ah ṭurim' le-r[abbi] 'Avraham be-r[abbi] Yehudah talmido shel don Ḥasdai Qresqes," *Meḥqerei yerushalayim be-maḥashevet yisra'el* 3 (1984): 526.
27. Jacoby, "Jewish Communities," 180.
28. Rigler, "Ha-yehudim," 80; Ta-Shma, "Rabbinic Literature," 54–55; and Benjamin Richler, ed., *Hebrew Manuscripts in the Vatican Library: Catalogue* (Vatican City: Biblioteca apostolica Vaticana, 2008), 509.
29. Israel M. Ta-Shma, "Rabbi Yosef Qaro ben 'ashkenaz li-sefarad: le-ḥeqer hitpashṭut sefer ha-zohar," *Tarbiẓ* 59 (1990): 169; and Moshe Idel, "Ha-qabbalah ba-'ezor ha-bizanṭi: 'iyyunim rishonim," *Kabbalah* 18 (2008): 223.
30. Boaz Huss, *The Zohar: Reception and Impact*, trans. Yudith Nave (Oxford: Littman Library of Jewish Civilization, 2016), 80; and Avraham Elqayam, "Ha-zohar ha-qadosh shel Shabbetai Zvi," *Kabbalah* 3 (1998): 345–87.
31. Corazzol, "Vita," 166, 173.
32. See chapter 5, this volume.
33. On the anti-kabbalistic commentary, see Uri Gershowitz, "Perush filosofi le-sefer ha-bahir me-ha-me'ah ha-14," *Judaica Petropolitana* 1 (2013): 20–40 (Hebrew section). For the Job commentary, see Gershowitz, "Perush sefer 'iyov le-r[abbi] 'Eliyahu ben 'Eli'ezer ha-yerushalmi be-heqsher ha-parshanut ha-filosofit ha-yehudit bi-yemei ha-benayim" (PhD diss., Jerusalem: Hebrew University of Jerusalem, 2008) and, in summary, Robert Eisen, *The Book of Job in Medieval Jewish Philosophy* (New York: Oxford University Press, 2004), 107–108.
34. Saul Hakohen Ashkenazi, *She'elot u-teshuvot Shaul Hakohen* (Venice, 1574; photo offset, Jerusalem, 1966), 11r. See further Corazzol, "La vita," 78.
35. Idel, "Ha-qabbalah," 224.
36. The fullest account is Brian Ogren, *Renaissance and Rebirth: Reincarnation in Early Modern Italian Kabbalah* (Leiden: Brill, 2009), 41–101. See also Aviezer Ravitzky, "'Ma'amad raglei ha-mequbbalim be-rashei ha-filosofim?' 'Al vikkuaḥ qandi'ah ba-me'ah ha-ḥamesh-'esrei," in *'Al da'at ha-maqom: meḥqarim ba-hagut ha-yehudit u-ve-toldoteha* (Jerusalem: Keter, 1991), 182–211.
37. Schwartz, "Perush filosofi"; and Schwartz, "Filosofyah ki-kheli tiqshoret be-bizanṭyon be-shilhei yemei ha-benayim: r[abbi] Mikha'el ben Shabbetai Balbo ve-r[abbi] Shalom ben Yosef 'Anavi," *Sefunot* (n.s.) 10 (2017): 317–93.

38. Schwartz, *Raḥaq*, 25–27; Schwartz, "Perush filosofi," 208; Schwartz, *Qame'ot segulot u-sekhaltanut ba-hagut ha-yehudit bi-yemei ha-benayim* (Ramat-Gan: Bar-Ilan University Press, 2004), 151.
39. Dov Schwartz, "Sefer 'Mesharet Moshe' be-'en ha-se'arah: tikhtovet ben r[abbi] Yedidyah Rakh le-r[abbi] Micha'el Balbo be-sugiyot ha-nevu'ah u-nevu'at moshe," *'Alei Sefer* 24–25 (2015): 81–187; and Elior, "Rabbi Yedidyah Rakh."
40. Ofer Elior, "'Pri ha-gan' le-rabbi Shalom ben rabbi Yosef 'Anavi," *Kobez Al Yad* 21 (2012): 207n39.
41. Efraim Sand, "'Aqevot shel parshanut yehudit-bizanṭit be-ferushei rashi u-vet midrasho," *Madda'ei ha-yahadut* 50 (2015): 1–47. The argument of influence from the East on Rashi stretches back to Menahem Banitt, *Rashi: Interpreter of the Biblical Letter* (Tel Aviv: Chaim Rosenberg School of Jewish Studies, 1985). It was endorsed by Israel M. Ta-Shma in "Parshanut miqra' 'ivrit-bizanṭit qedumah, seviv shenat 1000, min ha-genizah," *Tarbiẓ* 69 (2000): 253–54 and in other publications.
42. Ta-Shma, "Midrash leqaḥ ṭov," 266; and Ta-Shma, "Le-toledot ha-qesharim ha-tarbutiyim ben yehudei bizanṭyon ve-'ashkenaz," in *Me'ah She'arim: Studies in Medieval Jewish Spiritual Life in Memory of Isadore Twersky*, ed. Ezra Fleischer et al. (Jerusalem: Magnes, 2001), 63. For dissent, see Avraham Grossman, "Rishumam shel r[abbi] Shemu'el 'he-ḥasid' ha-sefaradi u-Re'u'el ha-bizanṭi be-vet midrasho shel rashi," *Tarbiẓ* 82 (2014): 464–67.
43. Israel M. Ta-Shma, "'Sefer rossina': parshanut miqra' derom 'iṭalqit mi-sof ha-me'ah ha-'aḥat 'esrei," *Tarbiẓ* 72 (2003): 567–80; and Ta-Shma, "Le-toledot ha-qesharim," 65–66. For the toponym (and for Samuel and his three sons as part of a gift given by Sikelgaita, Robert Guiscard's second wife, to the bishop of Rossano), see Cesare Colafemmina, *The Jews in Calabria* (Leiden: Brill, 2012), 8–9.
44. Ta-Shma, "'Sefer rossina,'" 569.
45. Ta-Shma, "'Sefer rossina,'" 569, 580; and Ta-Shma, "Le-toledot ha-qesharim," 66n17. Only one of the notes was deemed truly supercommentarial by Ta-Shma himself, albeit on the basis of a distinction none too clear. For the larger work, see Anonymous, "Torah Commentary," in Moscow, Russian State Library, MS Guenzburg 265, 66r–168r. The notes appear on fols. 76v, 77v. The manuscript was copied in Bursa (Turkey) in 1559.
46. Ta-Shma, "Le-toledot ha-sifrut," 102.
47. His work is discussed in chapter 3, this volume. For its unusual combination of European and Byzantine sources, see Gershon Brin, "Ben r[abbi] Yesha'yah mi-ṭrani la-parshanim ha-bizanṭiyim ha-qedumin." *Beit Mikra* 59 (2014): 60–75.
48. Ta-Shma, "Le-toledot ha-sifrut," 112–13. On his exegesis, see Eliezer Schlossberg, "'Iyyunim be-darkhei parshanuto shel R. Meyuḥas ben 'Eliyahu," *Megadim* 23

(1995): 83–96, esp. 85–86 for citations of Rashi; Gershon Brin, "Shimushei r[abbi] Meyuḥas b[e]-r[abbi] 'Eliyahu bi-khelalei ha-parshanut she-nusḥu bi-leshon 'derekh ha-miqra'," *Beit Mikra* 58 (2013): 117–29 (117n4 for dating).

49. Beit-Arié, *QI*, 118.

50. Steven A. Epstein, *Genoa and the Genoese, 958–1528* (Chapel Hill: University of North Carolina Press, 1996), 142–43, 193–94.

51. Paul Fenton, "De quelques attitudes qaraïtes enver la Qabbale," *REJ* 142 (1983): 6–10; and Daniel Frank, "Karaite Exegesis," in *HBOT*, ed. Magne Sæbø, vol. I/2: *From the Beginnings to the Middle Ages*, part 2: *The Middle Ages* (Göttingen: Vanderhoeck & Ruprecht, 2000), 128.

52. Shemaryah ha-Ikriti, *'Elef ha-magen: perush 'al 'aggadot masekhet megillah le-R. Shemaryah ben 'Eliyahu ha-'iqriṭi*, ed. Aaron Ahrend (Jerusalem: Mekize Nirdamim, 2003), 53–54, 206.

53. Abraham Geiger, "Shemaryah ha-'iqriṭi," in *'Oṣar neḥmad* 2 (1856): 90–94 ,91 for the cited passage. For English excerpts, see Bowman, *Jews*, no. 53.

54. Some of his Esther commentary may have been influenced by Rashi, but Shemaryah also excises or tacitly opposes midrashim in this work; see Aaron Ahrend, "Perush megillat 'ester le-r[abbi] Shemaryah ben 'Eliyah ha-'iqriṭi," in *Meḥqarim be-miqra' u-ve-ḥinukh mugashim le-prof' Moshe 'Ahrend*, ed. Dov Rappel (Jerusalem: Touro College, 1996), 39. In the Song of Songs commentary, two versions of which survive, Rashi appears alongside Maimonides to the former's disfavor, as Shemaryah discounts Rashi's midrashic reading of the book as a historical allegory on the mutual love of God and Israel. First, if Song of Songs is an allusive recapitulation of events explicitly recounted elsewhere in the Bible, the book would be redundant. Second, Rashi fails to explain why the wholly exoteric historical events that he takes to be the book's substance should be communicated by "covert and concealed" expression. Third, Rashi's prosaic reading makes rabbinic praises heaped on Solomon's song incomprehensible. See Dov Schwartz, "He'arot 'al perushei shir ha-shirim le-R. Shemaryah ha-'iqriṭi," in *Sefer zikaron le-rav Yosef ben David Qapaḥ*, ed. Zohar Omer and Hananel Sari (Ramat-Gan: Lishkat rav ha-Kampus, Bar-Ilan University, 2001), 319–33. Like other rationalists such as Moses ibn Tibbon or Immanuel of Rome, Shemaryah reads the book as a philosophical-psychological allegory; see Levi Ben Gershom, *Commentary on Song of Songs [by] Levi Ben Gershom (Gersonides)*, trans. Menachem Kellner (New Haven, CT: Yale University Press, 1998), xvi–xvii.

55. Schwartz, "Seridim," 121.

56. Eric Lawee, "Maimonides in the Eastern Mediterranean: The Case of Rashi's Resisting Readers," in *Maimonides After 800 Years: Essays on Maimonides and His Influence*, ed. Jay M. Harris (Cambridge, MA: Harvard University Center for Jewish Studies, 2007), 186–87.

57. Uriel Simon, "Interpreting the Interpreter: Supercommentaries on Ibn Ezra's Commentaries," in *Rabbi Abraham Ibn Ezra: Studies in the Writings of a Twelfth-Century Polymath*, ed. Isadore Twersky and Jay M. Harris (Cambridge, MA: Harvard University Center for Jewish Studies, 1993), 99; and Visi, "Early Ibn Ezra Supercommentaries," 80.
58. Though its introduction was printed long ago as Abraham Kirimi, "Sefat ha-'emet," ed. Abraham Firkovich, *Ha-Karmel* 3 (1863): 53–54, the work has received next to no attention since the treatment in Israel Zinberg, *Toledot sifrut yisra'el*, 2nd ed., 7 vols. (Rehavia and Tel Aviv: Kibbutz Ha-Artzi / Y. Sherberk, 1959–1971), 3:157–61. See Schwartz, "Seridim," 97; and Akhiezer, "Byzantine Karaism," 753.
59. Attias, "Intellectual Leadership."
60. Abraham Kirimi, *Sefat 'emet*, in Bodleian Library, MS Opp. Add., fol. 45, 8r–v. For Sefardic exemplars, see chapter 3, this volume.
61. Kirimi, *Sefat 'emet*, MS Opp. Add., fol. 45, 13v, 27r.
62. Zinberg, *Toledot*, 3:157–61, 353n21.
63. Kirimi, *Sefat 'emet*, MS Opp. Add., fol. 45, 12v, on Gen 4:19. For Ibn Ezra, see at note 81 in chapter 2, this volume.
64. E.g., Kirimi, *Sefat 'emet*, MS Opp. Add., fol. 45, 2r, 7r, 7v. See also Zinberg, *Toledot*, 3:158; and Akhiezer, "Byzantine Karaism," 753.
65. Zinberg, *Toledot*, 3:158–60. Kirimi's comments on Abraham and the angels are cited in Dov Schwartz, *Ma'avaq ha-paradigmot: ben te'ologyah le-filosofyah ba-hagut ha-yehudit bi-yemei ha-benayim* (Jerusalem: Magnes, 2018), 222–23.
66. Dov Schwartz, *'Asṭrologyah u-magyah ba-hagut ha-yehudit bi-yemei ha-benayim* (Ramat-Gan: Bar-Ilan University, 1999), 203–204.
67. Lasker, *From Judah Hadassi to Elijah Bashyatchi*; and Daniel Frank, "Elijah Yerushalmi and Karaite Ambivalence Toward Rabbanite Literature," in *Rabbinic Culture and Its Critics: Jewish Authority, Dissent, and Heresy in Medieval and Early Modern Times*, ed. Daniel Frank and Matt Goldish (Detroit, MI: Wayne State University Press, 2008), 251–60.
68. E.g., in his treatment of Rashi versus Ibn Ezra on the first word of the Torah in Aaron ben Elijah "the Younger," *Sefer keter torah*, 5 vols. in 1 (Gözleve [Eupatoria], 1867), 1:6r.
69. See chapter 7, this volume.
70. *MGH: Sefer Bereshit*, ed. Menachem Cohen, 2 vols. (Ramat-Gan: Bar-Ilan University, 1993), 1:25; and Nicholas de Lange, "Abraham Ibn Ezra and Byzantium," in *Abraham ibn Ezra y su tiempo*, ed. Fernando Díaz Esteban (Madrid: Asociación Española de Orientalistas, 1990), 181–82.
71. For Ibn Ezra's image in Byzantium, see Mordechai Komtino, *Perush qadmon 'al sefer yesod mora': "be'ur yesod mora'" le-r[abbi] Mordekhai ben 'Eli'ezer Komṭino*, ed. Dov Schwartz (Ramat-Gan: Bar-Ilan University Press, 2010), 13–24; and chapter 7, this volume.

72. Daniel Frank, "Ibn Ezra and the Karaite Exegetes Aaron Ben Joseph and Aaron Ben Elijah," in *Abraham ibn Ezra y su tiempo*, ed. Fernando Díaz Esteban (Madrid: Asociación Española de Orientalistas, 1990), 99–107; and Daniel J. Lasker, "Maimonides and the Karaites: From Critic to Cultural Hero," in *Maimónides y su época*, ed. Carlos del Valle et al. (Madrid: Sociedad estatal de conmemoraciones culturales, 2007), 311–25.
73. De Lange, "Abraham Ibn Ezra," 188–92.
74. For the Ibn Ezra supercommentary tradition in the eastern Mediterranean, including the work of Eleazar ben Mattathias, see chapter 7, this volume.
75. The following discussion is based mainly on remains of Eleazar's work as available prior to my only recent access to the full manuscript: Eleazar Askenazi, *Ṣafenat pa'neaḥ*, MS Moscow, Russian State Military Archive, 707/3/6, shelfmark II, 8, on which see A. Z. Schwarz, *Die hebräischen Handschriften in Österreich* (Leipzig: K. W. Hiersemann, 1931), 30–31. The main basis is Eleazar Askenazi, *Ṣafenat pa'neaḥ*, ed. Shlomo Rappaport (Johannesburg: Kayor, 1965), which contains commentaries on the first four weekly Torah readings of Genesis (*Bereshit–Vayyera'*); and Abraham Epstein, "Ma'amar 'al ḥibbur *Ṣafenat pa'neaḥ*," in *Kitvei R. 'Avraham 'Epshṭein*, ed. A. M. Haberman, 2 vols. (Jerusalem: Mosad Harav Kuk, 1949), 116–29, a study first published in 1887. In all cases, citations have been checked against the manuscript, references to which are provided using the abbreviation RGVA (= Rossiiskii gosudarstvennyi voennyi arkhiv). The manuscript is doubly foliated, with older numbers not always visible and newer ones sometimes written over them. Folios cited are according to the newer version (Epstein's references are to the older set of numbers, which begin with Eleazar's introductory essays). For dating, see Epstein, "Ma'amar," 116; and RGVA, 107v, 77r for the first and last date, respectively. The grounds for ascribing to Eleazar a commentary on a few chapters of Maimonides's *Guide*, as Epstein did, are shaky, more even than is suggested in Eric Lawee, "'Epigon no'az: R. 'Ele'azar 'Ashkenazi ben R. Natan ha-bavli u-ferusho la-torah 'ṣafenat pa'neaḥ'," in *'Asupah le-yosef: qoveṣ meḥqarim shai le-Yosef Haqer*, ed. Yaron Ben Naeh et al. (Jerusalem: Zalman Shazar, 2014), 172n6. No longer extant, if they ever existed, are commentaries on Proverbs and Job; see Epstein, "Ma'amar," 118.
76. Lawee, "'Epigon," 171–73.
77. If the family had no Babylonian connection, the appellative of Eleazar's father could be taken to reflect slippage found in other cases resulting from the moniker attached to one of the second-century rabbinic sages named Natan. See Ezra Fleischer, *Piyyuṭei Shelomo ha-Bavli* (Jerusalem: Israel Academy of Sciences and Humanities, 1973), 16.
78. Lawee, "'Epigon," 172.
79. For the latter, see Jacoby, "Jewish Communities," 178–79.

80. Epstein, "Ma'amar," 117 (the passages are in RGVA, 56v, for Coptic; 119v for "pi"). For Cypriot Copts, see Chris Schabel, "Religion," in *Cyprus: Society and Culture 1191–1374*, ed. Angel Nicolaou-Konnari and Chris Schabel (Leiden: Brill, 2005), 163. For the transition to Arabic, see Jason R. Zaborowski, "From Coptic to Arabic in Medieval Egypt," *Medieval Encounters* 14 (2008): 15–40. Like a few earlier exegetes, Eleazar proposed Egyptian origins for words, including names like Pharaoh and Pinchas and the *hapax legomenon* "Avrekh" (Gen 41:43). He translates the latter as meaning either "herald" or "the text proclaimed before a newly appointed high official"; see Ashkenazi, *Ṣafenat pa'neaḥ*, RGVA, 56v (Epstein, "Ma'amar," 117–18). Modern scholars propose different etymologies, e.g., J. Severino Croatto, "'Abrek 'Intendant' dans Gén. XLI 41, 43," *Vetus Testamentum* 16 (1966): 113–15; and Gary A. Rendsburg, "The Joseph Story: Ancient Literary Art at Its Best," Torah.com, at http://thetorah.com/the-joseph-story-ancient-literary-art-at-its-best/.
81. Ashkenazi, *Ṣafenat pa'neaḥ*, RGVA, 69v (Epstein, "Ma'amar," 117, 119). For decoding of the Hispanisms, see Lawee, "'Epigon," 185 n. 56.
82. Abraham pursued studies in Spain with Hasdai Crescas. See Eric Lawee, "The Path to Felicity: Teachings and Tensions in *'Even Shetiyyah* of Abraham Ben Judah, Disciple of Hasdai Crescas," *Mediaeval Studies* 59 (1997): 183–223.
83. Ashkenazi, *Ṣafenat pa'neaḥ*, RGVA, 21v (Epstein, "Ma'amar," 118–19).
84. Ashkenazi, *Ṣafenat pa'neaḥ*, RGVA, 21r–v (Epstein, "Ma'amar," 118–19). For use of a part of the verse by Maimonides, see *The Guide of the Perplexed*, trans. Shlomo Pines, 2 vols. (Chicago: University of Chicago Press, 1963), III:52 (Pines, 2:629). For Kimhi, see Frank Ephraim Talmage, *Apples of Gold in Settings of Silver: Studies in Medieval Jewish Exegesis and Polemics*, ed. Barry Dov Walfish (Toronto: Pontifical Institute of Mediaeval Studies, 1999), 52. For the verse's possible significance in later appropriations, see James A. Diamond, *Maimonides and the Shaping of the Jewish Canon* (New York: Cambridge University Press, 2014), 90.
85. Ashkenazi, *Ṣafenat pa'neaḥ*, RGVA, 51r (Epstein, "Ma'amar," 116).
86. Ashkenazi, *Ṣafenat pa'neaḥ*, RGVA, 80r (Epstein, "Ma'amar," 128–29nn10–11). In the case of a naturalistic understanding of the ten plagues, Ephraim put aside reservations and included the repellent passages while reproaching Eleazar for "casting aspersions on the ten plagues without restraint," thereby revealing in a small way what Ephraim calls Eleazar's more general culpability for other sacrileges in his tome.
87. Konstantin Akinsha, *Manuscripts and Archival Documents of the Vienna Jewish Community held in Russian Collections: Catalogue* (Moscow: Rudomino, 2006), 99. On the contents of the collection from Vienna, see David E. Fishman, Mark Kupovetsky, and Vladimir Kuzelenkov, eds., *Nazi-Looted Jewish Archives in Moscow: A Guide to Jewish Historical and Cultural Collections in the Russian State Military Archive* (Scranton, PA: University of Scranton Press, 2010), 57–62.

88. Schwartz, *Raḥaq*, 25–40.
89. Ashkenazi, *Ṣafenat pa'neaḥ*, RGVA, 57v (Epstein, "Ma'amar," 117–18).
90. Ashkenazi, *Ṣafenat pa'neaḥ* on Gen 18:9 (Rappaport, 59), reading *ha-nashim* for *'anashim* and *ḥibbur* for *dibbur* on the basis of RGVA, 39v. For "a single virtuous man," see Maimonides, *Guide*, I: introduction (1:16).
91. Maimonides, *Guide*, II:25 (Pines, 2:327–28).
92. Ashkenazi, *Ṣafenat pa'neaḥ*, RGVA, 18v (Rappaport, 76).
93. Colette Sirat, *A History of Jewish Philosophy in the Middle Ages*, rev. ed. (Cambridge: Cambridge University Press, 1985), 343. For the term "strange," see note 172 in chapter 2, this volume.
94. Maimonides, *Guide*, I: introduction (Pines, 1:10).
95. Ashkenazi, *Ṣafenat pa'neaḥ* on Gen 14:1, RGVA, 37r (Rappaport, 49). The example of the rod may echo Maimonides, *Guide*, II:29 (Pines, 2:345).
96. Ashkenazi, *Ṣafenat pa'neaḥ*, RGVA, 18v (Rappaport, 76).
97. Ashkenazi, *Ṣafenat pa'neaḥ*, RGVA, 28v (Rappaport, 33). For Ibn Ezra, see *MGH: Sefer Bereshit*, 1:80.
98. Ashkenazi, *Ṣafenat pa'neaḥ*, RGVA, 28v–29r (Rappaport, 33). *Ṣafenat pa'neaḥ* on Gen 6:13, RGVA, 29r (Rappaport, 34) is another case, with Eleazar concurring in one of Rashi's two interpretations of God's pledge to destroy antediluvian life *'et ha-'areṣ*, where Rashi says *'et* has prepositional meaning rather than marking the direct object, meaning that humankind and the fauna would be destroyed "together *with* the earth."
99. Ashkenazi, *Ṣafenat pa'neaḥ* on Gen 12:1, RGVA, 35v (Rappaport, 44).
100. Maimonides, *Guide*, III:29 (Pines, 2:514–16). For Maimonides's so-called Sabian sources, see Paul Fenton, "Maïmonide et *L'Agriculture nabatéeanne*," in *Maimonide: Philosophe et Savant (1138–1204)*, ed. Tony Lévy and Roshdi Rashed (Leuven: Peeters, 2004), 303–27.
101. For Maimonides's understanding of *lekh lekha* as enlightenment attained naturalistically, see Howard Kreisel, *Maimonides' Political Thought: Studies in Ethics, Law, and the Human Ideal* (Albany: SUNY Press, 1999), 31.
102. Lawee, "'Epigon," 177–78.
103. Ashkenazi, *Ṣafenat pa'neaḥ* on Gen 2:21, RGVA, 23r (Rappaport, 15). See also Rashi and Ibn Ezra (*MGH: Sefer Bereshit*, 1:44) and Maimonides, *Guide*, II:30 (Pines, 2:355).
104. Ashkenazi, *Ṣafenat pa'neaḥ*, RGVA, 31v (Rappaport, 35). This view allowed Eleazar to explain the otherwise apparently pleonastic clarification in the Torah that the *mabbul* took the form of "waters upon the earth" (Gen 6:17): since a *mabbul* could encompass a range of destructive agents, the type of ruination needed to be explicit. Eleazar opts for one of two etymologies supplied by Ibn Ezra (*MGH: Sefer Bereshit*, 1:82). He may have been following David Kimhi on Gen 6:17 (*MGH: Sefer Bereshit*, 1:83, 85) who, however, has the term refer not

to earthly items falling or being destroyed but to the heavenly source of the destruction.

105. For the latter, see *Ḥamishah ḥumshei torah: rashi ha-shalem*, 7 vols. to date (Jerusalem: Ariel, 1986–), Bereshit 1:319. For the midrash, see b. Shabbat 33b.
106. Maimonides, *Guide*, II:30 (Pines, 2:356). Maimonides states that the serpent had no direct relations with Adam (the intellect) and that "extreme enmity only comes to be realized between the Serpent and Eve."
107. Ashkenazi, *Ṣafenat pa'neaḥ* on Gen 3:1, RGVA, 23v (Rappaport, 16). For another case where Eleazar refits a midrash adduced by Rashi for an allegorical use distant from Rashi, see *Ṣafenat pa'neaḥ* on Gen 19:2, RGVA, 41v (Rappaport, 63). Here, as elsewhere, Rappaport cites the midrash without reference to its appearance in the *Commentary*.
108. James L. Kugel, *In Potiphar's House* (San Francisco: HarperCollins, 1990), 4–5.
109. Erich Auerbach, *Mimesis; the Representation of Reality in Western Literature*, trans. Willard R. Trask (Princeton, NJ: Princeton University Press, 1953), 12.
110. Devorah Schoenfeld, *Isaac on Jewish and Christian Altars: Polemic and Exegesis in Rashi and the Glossa Ordinaria* (New York: Fordham University Press, 2013), 89–91.
111. Ashkenazi, *Ṣafenat pa'neaḥ* on Gen 22:1, RGVA, 43v (Rappaport, 69).
112. Isaac Heinemann, *Darkhei ha-'aggadah*, 3rd. ed. (Jerusalem: Magnes, 1974), 28–31.
113. Glosses to Gen 12:6 and 14:18 ("a *midrash 'aggadah* is that he is identical with Shem son of Noah"); see Eitan Sandorfi, "Le-mi nitenah 'ereṣ yisra'el 'aḥar ha-mabbul," *Shema'tin* 136 (1999): 137–44.
114. *The JPS Torah Commentary: Genesis*, commentary by Nahum Sarna (Philadelphia: Jewish Publication Society, 1989), 109.
115. Ibn Ezra asserted the identification of Salem and Jerusalem more than once on the basis of this verse, e.g., in his comments on Ps 76:3 and Eccl 1:1; see, respectively, *MGH: Sefer Tehilim*, ed. Menachem Cohen, 2 vols. (Ramat-Gan: Bar-Ilan University, 2003), 2:14; and *MGH: Ḥamesh megillot*, ed. Menachem Cohen (Ramat-Gan: Bar-Ilan University, 2012), 124.
116. Ashkenazi, *Ṣafenat pa'neaḥ* on Gen 14:18, RGVA, 37r (Rappaport, 49).
117. Ashkenazi, *Ṣafenat pa'neaḥ* on Gen 7:4, RGVA, 32r (Rappaport, 36).
118. Ashkenazi, *Ṣafenat pa'neaḥ* on Gen 6:9, RGVA, 29r (Rappaport, 33). Cf. Rashi (following b. Sanhedrin 108a). Ibn Ezra's approach was sustained by David Kimhi and Nahmanides; for all three, see *MGH: Sefer Bereshit*, 1:80–81.
119. Lawee, "'Epigon," 47–48; and Maimonides, *Guide*, II:47 (Pines, 2:408). See Daniel J. Lasker, "'Arikhut ha-yamim shel ha-qadmonim: dat u-madda' ba-hagut yehudit bi-yemei ha-benayim," *Dine Israel* 26–27 (2010): 53–54.
120. Moshe Blidstein, "How Many Pigs Were on Noah's Ark? An Exegetical Encounter on the Nature of Impurity," *Harvard Theological Review* 108 (2015): 448–70.

121. See Rashi on Gen 7:2 and 8:20 in *MGH: Sefer Bereshit*, 1:86, 96; and *Ḥamishah ḥumshei torah*, Bereshit 1:79 for rabbinic sources.
122. Askenazi, *Ṣafenat pa'neaḥ* on Gen 7:2, RGVA, 31v (Rappaport, 35). Eleazar leaves the impression that human beings were already carnivorous or were to become so on the ark, a fact which does not emerge from his gloss on the permission to consume animal flesh announced after the flood (Gen 9:2–3, 5); see *Ṣafenat pa'neaḥ* on Gen 9:5, RGVA, 34r (Rappaport, 40).
123. Rashi on Gen 22:8: "with the same [ready] heart." Rashi on Gen 25:20 for Isaac's age. For Ibn Ezra, see at note 85 in chapter 2, this volume.
124. Rashi on Gen 22:23. Ibn Ezra notes: "'Milcah too had borne children'—to mention Rebecca's ancestry" (*MGH: Sefer Bereshit*, 1:199).
125. *Ṣafenat pa'neaḥ* on Gen 22:20, RGVA, 44r (Rappaport, 72).
126. Rashi on Exod 10:23.
127. Ashkenazi, *Ṣafenat pa'neaḥ*, RGVA, 75v (Epstein, "Ma'amar," 128).
128. Even a biblicist who deems it plausible that an audience could have occurred between Jacob and Pharaoh after Jacob's arrival in Egypt doubts that Jacob would have conferred a blessing upon Pharaoh, but not all concur. Contrast Joseph Blenkinsopp, "Genesis 12–50," in *The Pentateuch*, ed. Laurence Bright (London: Sheed and Ward, 1971), 130; with Robert Alter, *The Five Books of Moses: A Translation with Commentary* (New York: W. W. Norton, 2004), 280: "it would be entirely in keeping with his own highly developed sense of his patriarchal role" that Jacob, though "a mere Semitic herdsman chief addressing the head of the mighty Egyptian empire," should pronounce a blessing.
129. Rashi on Gen 47:10. For midrashic traditions, see Rivka Ulmer, *Egyptian Cultural Icons in Midrash* (Berlin: De Gruyter, 2009), 63. For different understandings of the link between the two components of Rashi's comment, see *Ḥamishah ḥumshei torah*, Bereshit, 3:137–38.
130. Marc Michael Epstein, *The Medieval Haggadah: Art, Narrative, and Religious Imagination* (New Haven, CT: Yale University Press, 2010), 166.
131. Ashkenazi, *Ṣafenat pa'neaḥ*, RGVA, 60v (Epstein, "Ma'amar," 118). Eleazar's text has *kenegdo* in place of *liqerato*, conforming with a version of Rashi found in Tosafist literature (*Ḥamishah ḥumshei torah*, Bereshit 3:137–38).
132. Rashi on Gen 47:19.
133. Ashkenazi, *Ṣafenat pa'neaḥ*, RGVA, 60v (Epstein, "Ma'amar," 124).
134. Ibn Ezra on Gen 36:31 (*MGH: Sefer Bereshit*, 2:93); and Simon, *'Ozen*, 275–98, esp. 288–94, for the case in question.
135. When the Torah had God say, "I bring clouds over the earth" (Gen 9:14), what was meant was that God was the ultimate source of the series of natural causes that yielded rain. The biblical formulation reflected scripture's habit of ascribing "every natural thing to the Creator since he is the First [ultimate] Cause." See Ashkenazi, *Ṣafenat pa'neaḥ* on Gen 19:13, RGVA, 42r (Rappaport, 64) and

on Gen 9:14, RGVA, 34v (Rappaport, 40). Cf. Maimonides, *Guide*, II:48 (Pines, 2:409–12); and Aviezer Ravitzky, "Aristotle's *Meteorology* and the Maimonidean Modes of Interpreting the Account of Creation," *Aleph* 8 (2008): 373. In the generation after Eleazar, *Guide* commentator Asher Crescas connected the naturalist understanding of rain with subversion of the belief of ordinary Jews in providence, with this understanding entailing "alienation from [the idea of] God's providence among our people." See his commentary on Maimonides, *Guide*, II:30, in Moses Maimonides, *Moreh nevukhim le-ha-rav Moshe ben Maimon . . . be-ha'ataqat ha-rav Shemu'el 'ibn Tibbon 'im 'arba'ah perushim* (Warsaw, 1872; reprint, Jerusalem, 1961), 60r.

136. Rashi on Gen 49:21.

137. RGVA, 64v: *'al ha-mefaresh* (cf. Epstein, Ma'amar," 127: *'al ha-meforash*). The expression Eleazar uses is *'atidot peraṭiyot*. Elsewhere, accounting for specifics of place and time that do appear in many prophecies, Eleazar ventures the daring "secret" that these details were appended to the prophecies long after the original divine communication, which was received in more general terms; see RGVA, 62r (Epstein, "Ma'amar," 126). Eleazar puts his principle that prophecies lack pointers to specific distant future events to polemical use with respect to the charged passage in Genesis referring to the coming of Shiloh; see Adolf Posnanski, *Schiloh, ein beitrag zur geschichte der messiaslehre* (Leipzig: Hinrichs, 1904), xxviii.

138. After all, Rashi had taken the direct referent of Jacob's image of a "hind let loose" to refer not to Deborah and Barak but to "sons of Naphtali" who contributed to the victory that caused these two leaders to sing their song. See Ibn Ezra and Kimhi on Gen 49:21 (*MGH: Sefer Bereshit*, 2:182–83).

139. For Anatoli, see chapter 2, this volume. For Nahmanides, see chapter 3, this volume.

140. Ashkenazi, *Ṣafenat pa'neaḥ* on Gen 6:6–7, RGVA, 28v (Rappaport, 32) and on Gen 4:4, RGVA, 28v (Rappaport, 25). In the manuscript (RGVA, 26v), this passage does have an ascription of choice to animals, but it is apparent both from the context and assertions elsewhere that Rappaport's correction in the printed edition (reading *'en* for *yesh*) must be correct.

141. Maimonides, *Guide*, III:17 (Pines, 2:471–74). For discussion and additional sources, see Eric Lawee, "The Sins of the Fauna in Midrash, Rashi, and Their Medieval Interlocutors," *Jewish Studies Quarterly* 17 (2010): 56–98. The seeming wonder that not a single animal on the ark perished during its year-long voyage had nothing to do with individual providence. Rather, providence works to preserve the species. Since the exemplars were the remaining agents of the regeneration of their kind, providence preserved them "by way of nature, which governs"; see Ashkenazi, *Ṣafenat pa'neaḥ* on Gen 8:16, RGVA, 33r (Rappaport, 38–39).

142. Ashkenazi, *Ṣafenat pa'neaḥ* on Gen 6:12, RGVA, 29r (Rappaport, 33–34).
143. Maimonides, *Guide*, I:73 (Pines, 1:209). For identification of the evil impulse with imagination, see Maimonides, *Guide*, II:12 (Pines, 2:280). For discussion, see Sara Klein-Braslavy, *Perush ha-rambam le-sippurim 'al 'adam be-farashat bereshit: peraqim be-toledot ha-'adam shel ha-rambam* (Jerusalem: Reuven Mas, 1986), 212–15; and Sarah Pessin, "Matter, Metaphor, and Privative Pointing: Maimonides on the Complexity of Human Being," *American Catholic Philosophical Quarterly* 76 (2002): 75–88.
144. Ashkenazi, *Ṣafenat pa'neaḥ* on Gen 2:21, 24, RGVA, 23v (Rappaport, 15).
145. E.g., Eleazar's allegorical interpretation of Gen 18:7, which involves an understanding of the flesh of the calf given by Abraham to his "servant-boy" in terms of the "flesh of desire," "appetitive" part of his soul, and so forth.
146. Ashkenazi, *Ṣafenat pa'neaḥ*, RGVA, 24r, 28v–29r (Rappaport, 18).
147. Ashkenazi, *Ṣafenat pa'neaḥ*, RGVA, 24v (Rappaport, 19). To make the point, Eleazar cites a verse from Psalms (49:13) that struck the dark note on which Maimonides had concluded his account of the fall of humankind (*Guide* I:2; Pines, 1:23–26): "unable to dwell in dignity, it is like the beasts that speak not." (The latter phrase is often translated: "like the beasts that perish." On Pines's translation, see Marvin Fox, *Interpreting Maimonides: Studies in Methodology, Metaphysics, and Moral Philosophy* [Chicago: University of Chicago Press, 1990], 192).
148. Ashkenazi, *Ṣafenat pa'neaḥ* on Gen 6:12 and 6:6-7 respectively, RGVA, 28v, 29r (Rappaport, 32, 33–34).
149. See chapter 1, this volume. Or the origins of rabbinic numerological interpretation, see Aharon Mondschein, "'Ḥakhmei ha-masoret bade'u mi-libam ṭe'amim li-mele'im u-le-ḥaserim': 'al ma'avaqo shel r[abbi] 'Avraham 'ibn 'Ezra be-niṣṣul ha-ketiv ha-miqra'i ke-kheli parshani," *Shenaton le-ḥeqer ha-miqra' ve-ha-mizraḥ ha-qadum* 19 (2009): 314–16.
150. Rashi on Gen 14:14 (for rabbinic sources, see *Ḥamishah ḥumshei torah*, Bereshit 1:143–44).
151. L. I. Rabinowitz, "The Study of a Midrash," *JQR* 58 (1967): 149.
152. A prompt for the midrash could have been the otherwise biblically unattested number of 318 (see the commentary of Sarna in *JPS Torah Commentary: Genesis*, 108), which the midrash handsomely explained.
153. *MGH: Sefer Bereshit*, 1:34.
154. For his tendency to rebut Rashi without saying so, see chapter 2, this volume. For a textured treatment of Ibn Ezra's stance on numerological interpretation and factors that inform it, see Aharon Mondschein, "Le-yaḥaso shel ra'ba' 'el ha-shimmush ha-parshani be-middat ha-gemaṭriyah," *Teudah* 8 (1982): 131–61.
155. *MGH: Sefer Bereshit*, 1:35. In *Torat hashem temimah*, Nahmanides insists: "Let no one deride me because I rely on the calculation of the value of the letters called

gematria." See Moshe Idel, *Absorbing Perfections: Kabbalah and Interpretation* (New Haven, CT: Yale University Press, 2002), 258.

156. Ashkenazi, *Ṣafenat pa'neaḥ*, RGVA, 37r (Rappaport, 49). Cf. m. 'Avot 3:18. For *ḥokhmat ha-tishboret*, see Israel Efros, "Studies in Pre-Tibbonian Philosophical Terminology: I. Abraham Bar Hiyya, the Prince," *JQR* 17 (1927): 358.
157. Mordechai Z. Cohen, *Three Approaches to Biblical Metaphor: From Abraham Ibn Ezra and Maimonides to David Kimhi* (Leiden: Brill, 2003), 126–29.
158. Ashkenazi, *Ṣafenat pa'neaḥ*, RGVA, 37r (Rappaport, 49).
159. For complexity in Rashi's exposition, see Yonatan Cohen, "La-meyalledot ha-'ivriyot," *Lešonenu* 55 (1991): 295–97; *Pentateuch with Targum Onkelos, Haphtaroth and Rashi's Commentary*, ed. M. Rosenbaum and A. M. Silbermann, 5 vols. (Jerusalem: Silbermann Family, 1934), 2:228n3. For rabbinic sources and issues surrounding them, see Devorah Steinmetz, "A Portrait of Miriam in Rabbinic Midrash," *Prooftexts* 8 (1988): 40–42; and Barukh Halevi Epstein, *Torah temimah*, 5 vols. (Vilna, 1902; photo offset, Tel Aviv: M. & R. Grauer, 1981), 2:4v.
160. Ashkenazi, *Ṣafenat pa'neaḥ*, RGVA, 67r (Epstein, "Ma'amar," 124).
161. Maimonides, *Guide*, I: introduction (Pines, 1:10).
162. Leo Strauss, *Spinoza's Critique of Religion*, trans. E. M. Sinclair, 2nd ed. (New York: Schocken, 1962), 143, 145–46 (originally published 1930). For discussion, see David Janssens, *Between Athens and Jerusalem: Philosophy, Prophecy, and Politics in Leo Strauss's Early Thought* (Albany: SUNY Press, 2008), 70–71; and Laurence Lampert, *The Enduring Importance of Leo Strauss* (Chicago: University of Chicago Press, 2013), 201.
163. For the cited passage, see Anna Foka and Jonas Liliequist, "Introduction," *Laughter, Humor, and the (Un)Making of Gender: Historical and Cultural Perspectives*, ed. Anna Foka and Jonas Liliequist (London: Palgrave, 2015), 1. For subversive laughter, see Ralph Lerner, *Playing the Fool: Subversive Laughter in Troubled Times* (Chicago: University of Chicago Press, 2009).

CHAPTER 5

1. After its purchase by Cambridge University, the enormous manuscript in which the work appears was divided into eight tomes, with *Sefer hassagot* occupying the first eleven folios of volume 3. This manuscript (Cambridge, University Library, MS Add. 377.3, 1v–11r) is the only one in which *Sefer hassagot* survives. It has recently been published. See Eric Lawee and Doron Forte, "'Sefer hassagot' 'al perush rashi la-torah ha-meyuḥas le-rabad," *Kobez Al Yad* 26 (2018): 77–134. Citations from the work are according to this edition (hereafter in this chapter "Sefer hassagot"), followed by reference to manuscript folio.

2. The group included Ephraim ben Shabbetai, copyist of *Ṣafenat paneaḥ*; see chapter 4, this volume. For more on Balbo and *Sefer hassagot*'s bio-bibliographic parameters, see "Sefer hassagot," 81–103.
3. For the distinction, see Malachi Beit-Arié, "Publication and Reproduction of Literary Texts in Medieval Jewish Civilization: Jewish Scribality and Its Impact on the Texts Transmitted," in *Transmitting Jewish Traditions: Orality, Textuality, and Cultural Diffusion*, ed. Yaakov Elman and Israel Gershoni (New Haven, CT: Yale University Press, 2000), 230–37.
4. The phrase in the colophon that indicates copying for private use is *sheli katavti* ("Sefer hassagot," 134 [11r]).
5. See chapter 6, this volume.
6. The scribe wrote "Abram ben David" in the heading, which became "Abraham" owing to a later hand. "Abraham" also appears in the colophon.
7. Daniel Abrams, *Kabbalistic Manuscripts and Textual Theory: Methodologies of Textual Scholarship and Editorial Practice in the Study of Jewish Mysticism* (Jerusalem: Magnes, 2010), 228.
8. Israel M. Ta-Shma, "Hassagot," in *EJ*, 8:453–54; and "Sefer hassagot," 99–102.
9. Moshe Halbertal, *'Al derekh ha-'emet: ha-ramban vi-yeṣiratah shel masoret* (Jerusalem: Shalom Hartman Institute, 2006), 21–76.
10. Jonah ibn Janach, *Sefer ha-hassagah, hu' Kitāb al-mustalḥaq le-rabbi Yonaḥ 'ibn Janaḥ be-targumo ha-'ivri shel 'Ovadyah ha-sefaradi*, ed. David Téné, completed by Aharon Maman (Jerusalem: Bialik, 2006), 28. The earliest use of the new coinage in a verbal form (*lehassig*) may be that of Ibn Tibbon's southern French contemporary, Zerahyah Halevi. See Jonah ibn Janach, *Sefer ha-riqmah*, Hebrew trans. Judah Ibn Tibbon, ed. Michael Wilensky, 2nd ed., 2 vols. (Jerusalem: Akademyah la-Lashon ha-'Ivrit, 1964), 1:19n7.
11. Isadore Twersky, *Rabad of Posquieres: A Twelfth-Century Talmudist* (Cambridge, MA: Harvard University Press, 1962), 117.
12. Ephraim E. Urbach, "Hassagot ha-rabad 'al perush rashi la-torah?" *Qiryat sefer* 34 (1958): 102. See further "Sefer hassagot," 88–89.
13. "Sefer hassagot," 88.
14. Twersky, *Rabad*, 260–68.
15. "Sefer hassagot," 83–86.
16. Talya Fishman, *Shaking the Pillars of Exile: "Voice of a Fool," an Early Modern Critique of Rabbinic Culture* (Stanford, CA: Stanford University Press, 1997), 60.
17. "Sefer hassagot," 108 (1v).
18. For *qeṣat* in medieval Hebrew as "a number of" (reflecting Arabic *ba'ḍ*), see Frank Ephraim Talmage, *David Kimhi: The Man and the Commentaries* (Cambridge, MA: Harvard University Press, 1975), 74.
19. "Sefer hassagot," 100–101 (8r). Gaps in Genesis include 2:23–10:9 and in Exod 4:20–12:37.

20. On Gen 1:26 ("Sefer hassagot," 110 [2r]).
21. "Sefer hassagot," 108 (1v).
22. The key expression is *ke-suma' ba-'arubah* (see b. Baba Batra 12b; b. Niddah 20b).
23. "Sefer hassagot," 108 (1v). Pseudo-Rabad may have been thinking about an observation at the beginning of Moses Maimonides, The *Guide of the Perplexed*, trans. Shlomo Pines, 2 vols. (Chicago: University of Chicago Press, 1963), II:29 (2:336) that notes problematic outcomes that can arise from ignorance of a language, although Maimonides speaks of one who does not understand another's language, not of a speaker's incapacity to understand himself.
24. "Sefer hassagot," 108 (1v).
25. Samuel ibn Tibbon, "Perush ha-millot ha-zarot," in *Moreh nevukhim le-ha-rav Moshe ben Maimon . . . be-ha'ataqat ha-rav Shemu'el 'ibn Tibbon 'im 'arba'ah perushim* (Warsaw, 1872; photo offset, Jerusalem, 1961), 52. For an English translation, see James T. Robinson, "Samuel ibn Tibbon," in *Stanford Encyclopedia of Philosophy*, http://plato.stanford.edu/entries/tibbon/. For Maimonides in his work on logic (whose authenticity I assume), see Joel L. Kraemer, "Maimonides on the Philosophic Sciences in His Treatise on the Art of Logic," in *Perspectives on Maimonides: Philosophical and Historical Studies*, ed. Joel L. Kraemer (Oxford: Oxford University Press, 1991), 88–89.
26. Yair Lorberbaum, "Temurot be-yaḥaso shel ha-rambam le-midrashot ḥazal," *Tarbiẓ* 78 (2009): 81–122; and Lorberbaum, "'Haṭ 'oznekhah u-shema' le-divrei ḥakhamim': biqoret ha-'aggadah ba-'moreh nevukhim'," *Tarbiẓ* 78 (2009): 203–30, although these studies stress (a bit too totally in my view) Maimonides's evolution away from midrash as a bearer of philosophical ideas.
27. For Maimonides, see Isadore Twersky, "Some Non-Halakhic Aspects of the Mishneh Torah," in *Jewish Medieval and Renaissance Studies*, ed. Alexander Altmann (Cambridge, MA: Harvard University Press, 1967), 98–106. Maimonides does use the plural form; see Bernard Septimus, "What Did Maimonides Mean by *Madda'*?" in *Me'ah She'arim: Studies in Medieval Jewish Spiritual Life in Memory of Isadore Twersky*, ed. Ezra Fleischer et al. (Jerusalem: Magnes, 2001), 87–88. For post-Maimonidean usage, see Jean-Pierre Rothschild, "*Scientia bifrons*: Les ambivalences de la *'hokhmâh* (*sapientia/scientia*) dans la pensée juive du moyen âge occidental après Maïmonide," in *"Scientia" und "Ars" Im Hoch- und Spätmittelalter*, 2 vols. (= *Miscellanea Mediaevalia* 22), ed. Ingrid Craemer-Ruegenberg and Andreas Speer (Berlin: De Gruyter, 1994), 2:667–84.
28. Moses Maimonides, *Haqdamot ha-rambam la-mishnah*, ed. Yitzhak Shailat (Jerusalem: Hoza'at Shailat, 1996), 134.
29. "Sefer hassagot," 108 (1v).
30. "Sefer hassagot," 108 (1v).
31. On Exod 2:12 ("Sefer hassagot," 119 [5r]), on Deut 11:10 ("Sefer hassagot," 132 [10v]), and on Deut 14:7 ("Sefer hassagot," 133 [11r]).

32. Rashi on Exod 18:9 and "Sefer hassagot," 121 (6v).
33. Rashi on Exod 32:18 and "Sefer hassagot," 124 (7v).
34. Rashi on Num 13:2 and "Sefer hassagot," 127 (9r).
35. Rashi on Num 21:1, 4 and "Sefer hassagot," 131 (10r).
36. Rashi on Gen 26:35 and "Sefer hassagot," 115 (4r). Here, as occasionally elsewhere, Pseudo-Rabad does not cite Rashi before refuting him. *Sefer hassagot*'s "*sarvaniyot*" is close to Targum Onkelos's "insubordinate" (*mesarvan*). For another place where Pseudo-Rabad is in step with the targum while taking issue with Rashi, see the gloss on "a hundred kesitahs" (Gen 33:19). Against Rashi, who takes the medium of payment to be coins, Pseudo-Rabad thinks that Jacob purchased a parcel of land from the children of Hamor using his ample livestock (the targum reads "sheep").
37. Rashi on Gen 41:12 and "Sefer hassagot," 117 (5r).
38. Rashi on Exod 15:20 and "Sefer hassagot," 121 (6r).
39. Rashi on Exod 6:2 and "Sefer hassagot," 120 (6r). For the discussion of the Sefardic supercommentator, see note 169 in chapter 3, this volume.
40. Rashi on Num 16:1.
41. On Num 16:3 ("Sefer hassagot," 129 [9r]).
42. Rashi on Num 3:16.
43. On Num 3:16 ("Sefer hassagot," 127 [8v]). For a modern biblical scholar possibly sympathetic to the midrashic approach, see *The JPS Torah Commentary: Numbers*, commentary by Jacob Milgrom (Philadelphia: Jewish Publication Society, 1989), 19 (note to verse 16).
44. Michael Fishbane, *The Exegetical Imagination: On Jewish Thought and Theology* (Cambridge, MA: Harvard University Press, 1998), 12.
45. Arnold Goldberg, "The Rabbinic View of Scripture," in *A Tribute to Geza Vermes: Essays on Jewish and Christian Literature and History*, ed. Philip R. Davies and Richard T. White (Sheffield: JSOT Press, 1990), 159.
46. David Stern, "The First Jewish Books and the Early History of Jewish Reading," *JQR* 98 (2008): 171.
47. Aharon Mondschein, "'Ḥakhmei ha-masoret bade'u mi-libam ṭe'amim li-mele'im u-le-ḥaserim': 'al ma'avaqo shel r[abbi] 'Avraham 'ibn 'Ezra be-niṣṣul ha-ketiv ha-miqra'i ke-kheli parshani," *Shenaton le-ḥeqer ha-miqra' ve-ha-mizraḥ ha-qadum* 19 (2009): 282–86, esp. 283 for such expositions on topics of education and morals.
48. On Gen 23:16. The question of rabbinic sources in relation to Rashi's singling out of unusual orthography proves complicated. See *Ḥamishah ḥumshei torah: rashi ha-shalem*, 7 vols. to date (Jerusalem: Ariel, 1986–), *Bereshit*, 1:265–66, and nn.20 and 21 there. Some of the confusion is reflected in the diverse versions of Rashi's comment in the earliest printed editions (1:372).
49. Rashi on Gen 23:16 and "Sefer hassagot," 124 (3v).

50. For Ibn Ezra, see Mondschein, "Ḥakhmei."
51. See at note 126 in chapter 3, this volume.
52. Rashi on Exod 4:20 and "Sefer hassagot," 119–20 (5v). For the grammatical issue, see note 117 in chapter 3, this volume.
53. Rashi on Gen 23:1.
54. *MGH: Sefer Bereshit*, ed. Menachem Cohen, 2 vols. (Ramat-Gan: Bar-Ilan University, 1993), 1:199.
55. On Gen 23:1 ("Sefer hassagot," 114 [3v]).
56. Rashi on Exod 14:30.
57. *MGH: Sefer Shemot*, ed. Menachem Cohen, 2 vols. (Ramat-Gan: Bar-Ilan University, 2007–12), 1:117–18.
58. On Exod 14:30 ("Sefer hassagot," 120 [6r]). Cf. Ibn Ezra on Exod 14:30 (*MGH: Sefer Shemot*, 1:117).
59. On Exod 15:12 ("Sefer hassagot," 120 [6r]) and Ibn Ezra on Deut 28:23 (*MGH: Sefer Devarim*, ed. Menachem Cohen (Ramat-Gan: Bar-Ilan University, 2011), 191).
60. On Exod 15:22 ("Sefer hassagot," 121 [6r]).
61. E.g., Eric Lawee, "Aaron Aboulrabi: Maverick Exegete from Aragonese Sicily," *Hispania Judaica Bulletin* 9 (2013): 144–46. For rabbinic background, see Gwynn Kessler, *Conceiving Israel: The Fetus in Rabbinic Narratives* (Philadelphia: University of Pennsylvania Press, 2009), 77–79; and Yitzhak Roness and Aviad Y. Hollander, "Keṣad yihiyu ha-yeladim na'im: rabbi 'Eli'ezer ve-ha-'ugeniqah be-'enei ḥazal," *Jewish Studies Internet Journal* 10 (2012): 12–14, https://www.biu.ac.il/JS/JSIJ/jsij10.html.
62. Rashi on Gen 46:15 and "Sefer hassagot," 118 (5v).
63. Rashi on Gen 28:9.
64. "Sefer hassagot," 115 (4r).
65. Isaac Heinemann, *Darkhei ha-'aggadah*, 3rd ed. (Jerusalem: Magnes, 1974), 28.
66. Rashi on Exod 2:12 and 4:19; and "Sefer hassagot," 119 (5v). For Ibn Ezra, see *MGH: Sefer shemot*, 1:32 (Short Commentary).
67. Rashi on Exod 25:31 and "Sefer hassagot," 123 (7r).
68. Rashi on Gen 44:18 and "Sefer hassagot," 117 (5r).
69. Rashi on Exod 25:5.
70. *MGH: Sefer shemot*, 2:67, 69.
71. "Sefer hassagot," 123 (7r).
72. Moshe Sokolow, "T'rumah: Wood in the Wilderness," *Jewish Ideas Daily*, February 4, 2011, http://www.jewishideasdaily.com/4248/weekly-portion/trumah-wood-in-the-wilderness/?print.
73. "Sefer hassagot," 115 (4r).
74. Rashi on Gen 28:9 and "Sefer hassagot," 115–16 (4r).
75. Heinemann, *Darkhei*, 39–43.

76. Uriel Simon, *'Ozen milin tivḥan: meḥqarim be-darko ha-parshanit shel r[abbi] 'Avraham 'ibn 'Ezra* (Ramat-Gan: Bar-Ilan University Press, 2013), 319–37; and Menachem Kellner, "Rashi and Maimonides on the Relationship Between Torah and the Cosmos," in *Between Rashi and Maimonides: Themes in Medieval Jewish Thought, Literature and Exegesis*, ed. Ephraim Kanarfogel and Moshe Sokolow (Jersey City, NJ: Ktav, 2010), 35n33, for bibliography.
77. Rashi on Gen 19:3 and "Sefer hassagot," 114 (3v). For Kimhi, see *MGH: Sefer Bereshit*, 1:171.
78. Rashi on Gen 27:9. *MGH: Sefer Bereshit*, 2:16, places the gloss in square parentheses, suggesting it is a later accretion.
79. Rashi on Gen 27:9 and "Sefer hassagot," 115 (4r). Cf. Rashi on Gen 25:23.
80. Lieve M. Teugels, *Bible and Midrash: The Story of "The Wooing of Rebekah" (Gen. 24)* (Leuven: Peeters, 2004), 206.
81. Rashi on Gen 24:22 and "Sefer hassagot," 114 (3v).
82. Rashi on Gen 27:27 and "Sefer hassagot," 115 (4r). Pseudo-Rabad studiously ignores Isaac's cry that presumably gave the midrash its impetus, that the fragrance in question was that of a field "which the Lord blessed."
83. Heinemann, *Darkhei*, 118.
84. See, respectively, Morris M. Faierstein, *Ze'enah U-Re'enah: A Critical Translation into English* (Berlin: De Gruyter, 2017), 328; and Kalonymus Kalmish Shapira, *Sefer 'esh qodesh* (Jerusalem: Va'ad Hasidei Piaszenah, 1960), 16–17. For Rashi's *Commentary* in the former generally, see Jacob Elbaum and Chava Turniansky, "Tsene-Rene," trans. Deborah Weissman, *YIVO Encyclopedia of Jews in Eastern Europe*, http://www.yivoencyclopedia.org/article.aspx/Tsene-rene.
85. Rashi to b. Megillah 16b, s.v. "*[k]amah ṣavarin hayu lo le-vinyamin.*"
86. On Gen 45:14 ("Sefer hassagot," 119 [5v]). The problem was noticed by more sympathetic readers, evoking attempts at its resolution; see, e.g., Abraham Bokhrat, *Sefer zikaron*, ed. Moshe Filip, corrected edition (Petah Tikvah: Filip, 1985), 184; and Eliezer Segal, "The Exegetical Craft of the *Zohar*: Toward an Appreciation," *AJS Review* 17 (1992): 33–35.
87. Rashi on Deut 28:23 and "Sefer hassagot," 133 (11r). For Pseudo-Rabad's intention, see Urbach, "Hassagot," 107n 42.
88. Rashi on Exod 18:7 and "Sefer hassagot," 121 (6v). The prooftext in Rashi's gloss is placed in square parentheses in *MGH: Sefer Shemot*, 1:150, suggesting it is a later accretion.
89. Rashi on Deut 19:17 and "Sefer hassagot," 133 (11r).
90. For relevant texts and nuances in Ibn Ezra's approach, see Jay M. Harris, *How Do We Know This? Midrash and the Fragmentation of Modern Judaism* (Albany: SUNY Press, 1995), 83–85; and Mordechai Cohen, *Opening the Gates of Interpretation: Maimonides' Biblical Hermeneutics in Light of His Geonic-Andalusian Heritage and Muslim Milieu* (Leiden: Brill, 2011), 75–77, 80–82, 510–13.

91. Rashi on Lev 16:12, 18 and "Sefer hassagot," 125 (8r), on Lev 16:12.
92. Rashi on Lev 20:25 and "Sefer hassagot," 126 (8v).
93. Rashi on Deut 14:7. See Jonathan Kearney, *Rashi: Linguist Despite Himself: A Study of the Linguistic Dimension of Rabbi Solomon Yishaqi's Commentary on Deuteronomy* (New York: T&T Clark, 2010), 157. One sage (Rav) maintained that the *shesu'ah* enjoyed no existence outside its mother, another (Samuel) that it could exist independently. For rabbinic sources, see Jordan D. Rosenblum, *The Jewish Dietary Laws in the Ancient World* (New York: Cambridge University Press, 2016), 116n43. For imaginary creatures in rabbinic literature, see Meir Bar-Ilan, "Miflaṣot vi-yeṣurim dimyoniyim ba-'aggadah ha-yehudit ha-'atiqah," *Maḥanayim* 7 (1994): 104–13.
94. On Deut 14:17 ("Sefer hassagot," 133 [11r]).
95. For the plain sense as possibly instructing the person to leave the animal alone, see Alan Cooper, "The Plain Sense of Exodus 23:5," *HUCA* 59 (1988): 1–22.
96. On the exception, see *Ḥamishah ḥumshei torah, Shemot* 2:121.
97. Rashi on Exod 23:5 and "Sefer hassagot," 123 (7r).
98. Pseudo-Rabad's approach is more liberal, then, than the oft celebrated rejection of discriminatory legislation by Menahem Hameiri, on which see Yaakov Elman, "Meiri and the Non-Jew: A Comparative Investigation," in *New Perspectives on Jewish-Christian Relations: In Honor of David Berger*, ed. Elisheva Carlebach and Jacob J. Schacter (Leiden: Brill, 2012), 263–96.
99. Rashi on Lev 24:23 and "Sefer hassagot," 126 (8v), on Lev 24:14. (The "verse" cited by Pseudo-Rabad conflates the two verses mentioned in this note.)
100. Rashi on Deut 25:12 and "Sefer hassagot," 133 (11r). For the Karaites, see Bernard Revel, "Inquiry into the Sources of Karaite Halakah," *JQR* 3 (1913): 367.
101. Maimonides, *Guide*, II:29 (Pines, 2:347).
102. Judah Loew, *Ḥumash gur 'aryeh ha-shalem*, ed. Joshua Hartman, 9 vols. (Jerusalem: Mekhon Yerushalayim, 1989), 1:8–9.
103. "Sefer hassagot," 108 (1v). For another place where Pseudo-Rabad indicates that Rashi's midrashic interpretations "neither enhance nor detract," see on Num 15:39 ("Sefer hassagot," 129 [9r]).
104. Rashi on Gen 1:1 and "Sefer hassagot," 109 (2r).
105. "Sefer hassagot," 109n111.
106. Rashi on Gen 1:1, 8 and "Sefer hassagot," 109 (2r) (on Gen 1:1).
107. Most relevant is Maimonides, *Guide*, II:30 (Pines, 2:348–59); see Sara Klein-Braslavy, *Perush ha-rambam le-sippur beri'at ha-'olam*, 2nd ed. (Jerusalem: Reuven Mas, 1988), 165–68. Lineaments of Pseudo-Rabad's presentation are harder to find in Ibn Ezra. He may have meant to invoke his overall approach. See, however, Ibn Ezra on Gen 1:1: "David spoke initially of the work of creation. . . . 'He spreads out the heavens'—that is, the firmament, with the waters above it, and fire, snow and wind" (*MGH: Sefer Bereshit*, 1:2).

108. On Num 20:1 ("Sefer hassagot," 139n364); Maimonides, *Guide*, III:54 (Pines, 2:627–28). Rashi on Num 20:1 also taught the midrashic idea of Miriam's death by divine kiss, without elaboration.
109. Cf. Maimonides, *Guide*, II:6 (Pines, 2:261–65).
110. Regarding Pseudo-Rabad's *domeh*, see *Mishneh torah, H. Yesodei ha-torah*, 4:8 (reading *yeddammeh* as vocalized in the Huntington manuscript; see Moses Maimonides, *Mishneh Torah: The Book of Knowledge by Maimonides*, ed. Moses Hyamson (New York: Bloch,1937), 39a.
111. Rashi on Gen 1:26 and "Sefer hassagot," 110 (2r).
112. Avraham Grossman, *Ve-hu yimshol bakh?: ha-'ishah be-mishnatam shel ḥakhmei yisra'el bi-yemei ha-benayim* (Jerusalem: Zalman Shazar, 2011), 52.
113. Rashi on Gen 1:27 and "Sefer hassagot," 110 (2r). For kabbalistic sources, see Moshe Idel, *Kabbalah and Eros* (New Haven, CT: Yale University Press, 2005), 53–103.
114. Menachem Kellner, "Overcoming Chosenness," in *Covenant and Chosenness in Judaism and Mormonism*, ed. Raphael Jospe et al. (Madison, NJ: Fairleigh Dickinson University Press, 2001), 147, 149; and Kellner, "Rashi and Maimonides," 23–33.
115. Rashi on Gen 1:31 and "Sefer hassagot," 110 (2r).
116. Rashi on Gen 2:3 and "Sefer hassagot," 110 (2r).
117. Kellner, "Rashi and Maimonides," 31.
118. Rashi on Gen 1:14 and "Sefer hassagot," 109 (2r).
119. Avraham Grossman, *'Emunot ve-de'ot be-'olamo shel rashi* (Alon Shevut: Tevunot, 2008), 176.
120. For a conspectus of Ashkenazic views, see Ephraim Kanarfogel, "Varieties of Belief in Medieval Ashkenaz: The Case of Anthropomorphism," in *Rabbinic Culture and Its Critics: Jewish Authority, Dissent, and Heresy in Medieval and Early Modern Times*, ed. Daniel Frank and Matt Goldish (Detroit, MI: Wayne State University Press, 2008), 117–159.
121. Marc Saperstein, *Decoding the Rabbis: A Thirteenth-Century Commentary on the Aggadah* (Cambridge, MA: Harvard University Press, 1980), 83–92.
122. Warren Zev Harvey, "Maimonides' Critical Epistemology and *Guide* 2:24," *Aleph* 8 (2008): 216–18.
123. Leo Strauss, *Natural Right and History* (Chicago: University of Chicago Press, 1950), 82, who notes that "the first philosopher was the first man who discovered nature."
124. Teugels, *Bible and Midrash*, 42. On *kefiṣat ha-derekh* as a geological miracle according to Rashi, see Mark Verman and Shulamit Adler, "Path Jumping in the Jewish Magical Tradition," *Jewish Studies Quarterly* 1 (1993–94): 133.
125. Rashi on Gen 24:42 and "Sefer hassagot," 114 (3v–4r).
126. For the idea in other sources, see "Sefer hassagot," 114n200.

127. Rashi on Gen 28:11, 28:17; and "Sefer hassagot," 116 (4v).
128. Rashi on Exod 12:37 and "Sefer hassagot," 120 (6r). For *meliṣat ha-shir* as a coinage invented by Samuel ibn Tibbon for use in his *Guide* translation, see James T. Robinson, "Samuel Ibn Tibbon's *Commentary on Ecclesiastes* and the Philosopher's Prooemium," in *Studies in Medieval Jewish History and Literature III*, ed. Isadore Twersky and Jay M. Harris (Cambridge, MA: Harvard University Press, 2000), 139n197.
129. Rashi on Gen 24:17 and "Sefer hassagot," 114 (3v).
130. Rashi on Exod 2:20 and "Sefer hassagot," 119 (5v).
131. See chapter 4, this volume.
132. Rashi on Gen 14:14 and "Sefer hassagot," 112 (3r); cp. "Sefer hassagot," 127 (8v–9r), on Num 7:1.
133. *MGH: Sefer Bereshit*, 1:118–19. For discussion, see Miriam Sklarz, "Hashlakhat 'avram le-khivshan ha-'esh be-khitvehem shel ra'ba' ve-ramban: ben parshanut, shirah u-derashah," *'Areshet* 3 (2012): 23–33.
134. "Sefer hassagot," 111 (2v). The claim is highly dissonant with Maimonides's tendency to downplay the miraculous.
135. Rashi on Exod 17:12 and "Sefer hassagot," 124 (6v).
136. Rashi on Num 21:15 and "Sefer hassagot," 132 (10v).
137. Rashi on Num 17:11 and "Sefer hassagot," 131 (9v).
138. Rashi on Exod 16:21 and "Sefer hassagot," 121 (6v).
139. Maimonides, *Guide*, I:61–62 (Pines, 1:152); and Aviezer Ravitzky, "'The Ravings of Amulet Writers': Maimonides and Disciples on Language, Nature and Magic," in *Between Rashi and Maimonides: Themes in Medieval Jewish Thought, Literature and Exegesis*, ed. Ephraim Kanarfogel and Moshe Sokolow (Jersey City, NJ: Ktav, 2010), 93–130, esp. 103 for the formulations discussed here.
140. Menachem Kellner, *Maimonides' Confrontation with Mysticism* (Oxford: Littman Library of Jewish Civilization, 2006), 173–75, who cites kabbalistic sources. For rabbinic sources, see Hans-Jürgen Becker, "The Magic of the Name and Palestinian Rabbinic Literature," in *The Talmud Yerushalmi and Graeco-Roman Culture*, ed. Peter Schäfer (Tübingen: J. C. B. Mohr, 2002), 393–96. For Ibn Ezra, see his commentary on Exod 3:15 (*MGH: Sefer Shemot*, 1:22–23).
141. Ephraim Kanarfogel, *"Peering through the Lattices": Mystical, Magical, and Pietistic Dimensions in the Tosafist Period* (Detroit, MI: Wayne State University Press, 2000), 144–53.
142. Avi Sagi, "'He Slew the Egyptian and Hid Him in the Sand': Jewish Tradition and the Moral Element," *HUCA* 67 (1996): 55–76 for those qualms and efforts to allay them.
143. Rashi on Exod 2:14 and "Sefer hassagot," 119 (5v). Nahmanides had already aired issues of this sort regarding Rashi's reading, called by him a "midrash of our sages"; see *MGH: Sefer Shemot*, 1:13.

144. "Sefer hassagot," 124 (7v).
145. Rashi on Exod 32:1, 4; and "Sefer hassagot," 124 (7v). For Maimonides, see *'Iggerot ha-rambam*, ed. Yitzhaq Shailat, 2 vols. (Jerusalem: Ma'aliyot, 1987–88), 2:490.
146. See, e.g., Naomi Grunhaus, *The Challenge of Received Tradition: Dilemmas of Interpretation in Radak's Biblical Commentaries* (Oxford: Oxford University Press, 2013), 23–27, 29, 37–38, 112–13 and bibliography cited there.
147. On Lev 16:23 ("Sefer hassagot," 126 [8r]) (for *'ulam* read *'ulai*).
148. Rashi on Exod 35:1 and "Sefer hassagot," 125 (7v).
149. See at note 81 in chapter 2, this volume.
150. On Gen 10:9 ("Sefer hassagot," 111 [2v]).
151. Yitzhak Berger, "*Peshat* and the Authority of *Ḥazal* in the Commentaries of Radak," *AJS Review* 31 (2007): 44.
152. Rashi on Exod 16:20 and "Sefer hassagot," 121 (6v).
153. "Sefer hassagot," 139 (9v–10r).
154. Rashi on Exod 21:1.
155. "Sefer hassagot," 122 (6v). For this possible aim of Rashi, see Robert A. Harris, "Rashi's Introductions to His Biblical Commentaries," in *Shai le-Sarah Yafet: meḥqarim ba-miqra' be-farshanuto u-vi-leshono*, ed. Moshe Bar-Asher et al. (Jerusalem: Bialik, 2007), 241 (English section).
156. Rashi on Exod 16:33 and "Sefer hassagot," 121 (6v).
157. Thus reads the manuscript, although a different original (e.g., *midreshei ḥakhamim*) is possible.
158. On Exod 23:3 ("Sefer hassagot," 122–23 [7a]).
159. In a single instance, Pseudo-Rabad disputes a midrash not cited by Rashi that taught that, since Abraham was afraid to circumcise himself, God "stretched out His hand" and wielded the knife jointly with Abraham to perform the operation. The basis was the wording in Neh (9:6–8) that God "made"—more literarlly "cut"—a covenant with Abraham. The midrash appears in some versions of Genesis Rabbah, Midrash Tanhuma, and elsewhere. See J. Theodor and Ch. Albeck, eds., *Midrash Bereshit Rabbah*, 2nd ed., 3 vols. (Jerusalem: Shalem, 1996), 2:499. Pointing to "many places" where the same verbal formulation appears without bearing any pregnant implication, Pseudo-Rabad instructs his reader to "fathom this massive blunder"; see "Sefer hassagot," 112 (3r).
160. On Num 13:22 ("Sefer hassagot," 128 [9r]).
161. On Num 13:22 ("Sefer hassagot," 128 [9r]).
162. Rashi on Exod 2:14 and "Sefer hassagot," 119 (5v).
163. On Gen 25:19 ("Sefer hassagot," 115 [4r]). For Eleazar, see chapter 4, this volume.
164. Rashi on Gen 46:15 and Num 26:59.

165. Barak Shlomo Cohen, "'May You Live to One Hundred and Twenty': The Extraordinary Life-Span of Several Babylonian Amoraim According to Rashi," *RRJ* 10 (2007): 221–35.
166. *MGH: Sefer Bereshit,* 2:155–57. See further Miriam (Hoffman) Sklarz, "Ha-leshonot 'shibbesh' u-'fittah' be-tokhahto shel ramban le-ra'ba'," *'Iyyunei miqra' u-farshanut* 8 (2008): 562–66; and, for complexities in Nahmanides's doctrine of miracles, David Berger, "Miracles and the Natural Order in Naḥmanides," in *Rabbi Moses Naḥmanides (Ramban): Explorations in His Religious and Literary Virtuosity,* ed. Isadore Twersky (Cambridge, MA: Harvard University Press, 1983), 107–28..
167. "Sefer hassagot," 118 (5r–5v).
168. Rashi on Gen 14:13.
169. S. M. Schiller-Szinessy, *Catalogue of the Hebrew Manuscripts Preserved in the University Library, Cambridge* (Cambridge: University Library, 1876), 52.
170. José Faur, *The Horizontal Society: Understanding the Covenant and Alphabetic Judaism,* 2 vols. (Boston: Academic Studies, 2008), 1:415.
171. Ta-Shma, "Hassagot," 454.
172. Cf. b. Ḥullin 60b, which speaks of verses that, at first blush, are "worthy of being burnt," even as they turn out to contain scriptural essentials. For Ibn Ezra's metaphorical call for the burning of books, see Uriel Simon, "Ibn Ezra's Harsh Language and Biting Humor: Real Denunciation or Hispanic Mannerism," in *Abraham ibn Ezra y su tiempo,* ed. Fernando Díaz Esteban (Madrid: Asociación Española de Orientalistas, 1990), 326–27.
173. Rashi on Gen 17:20 and "Sefer hassagot," 112 (3r). Muslim controversialists saw an allusion to Muhammad in this verse; see Hava Lazarus-Yafeh, *Intertwined Worlds: Medieval Islam and Bible Criticism* (Princeton, NJ: Princeton University Press, 1992), 107–108. Whether Pseudo-Rabad read literature directly in Arabic is impossible to say, although he does use an Arabic cognate to explain *miqshah* at Exod 25:31, rendering it by *muṣmat,* the passive participle of a verb meaning "to render something solid" ("Sefer hassagot," 123 [7r]). Pseudo-Rabad could have known of the use to which the verse was put by Muslim controversialists by way of Maimonides's "Letter to the Jews of Yemen" (*'Iggerot ha-rambam,* 1:92 [Arabic]; 1:131 [Hebrew translation]).
174. On Exod 4:19 ("Sefer hassagot," 119 [5v]). These same terms bracket a *hassagah* disputing Rashi's interpretation of "those men's eyes" (on Num 16:14; "Sefer hassagot," 129 [9r]).
175. The insistence, "there is no doubt to one who is discerning," is reprised in a stricture on Rashi's reading of Exod 32:18. See "Sefer hassagot," 124 (7r).
176. Above, at note 82.
177. "Sefer hassagot," 122 (6v).
178. "Sefer hassagot," 112 (2v–3r).

179. On Gen 11:28 ("Sefer hassagot," 111 [2v]). Cf. Rashi on Gen 11:28. The focus of the stricture is such that Pseudo-Rabad may have had in mind the effort of Nahmanides to find a hint to the miracle in the text; see "Sefer hassagot," 112n159.
180. Rashi on Exod 39:33.
181. "Sefer hassagot," 125 (7v).
182. Rashi on Lev 1:2 and "Sefer hassagot," 125 (7v).
183. See Harris, *How Do We Know*, 12–15, for rabbinic and medieval discussion, including Rashi's uniqueness.
184. Israel M. Ta-Shma, *Rabbi Zeraḥyah ha-levi ba'al ha-ma'or u-venei ḥugo: le-toledot ha-sifrut ha-rabbanit be-provans* (Jerusalem: Mosad Harav Kuk, 1992), 138–41.
185. Haym Soloveitchik, "History of Halakhah – Methodological Issues: A Review Essay of I. Twersky's *Rabad of Posquières*," *Jewish History* 5 (1991): 78.
186. For a catalogue, see Ezra Zion Melamed, *Mefareshei ha-miqra': darkhehem ve-shiṭotehem*, 2nd ed., 2 vols. (Jerusalem: Magnes, 1979), 2:592–96. See Simon, "Ibn Ezra's Harsh Language," 325–34. On another surmise, occasionally overstated criticisms of others may have served to deflect hostility and charges of heresy directed at Ibn Ezra himself. See Nahum M. Sarna, "Abraham Ibn Ezra as an Exegete," in *Rabbi Abraham Ibn Ezra: Studies in the Writings of a Twelfth-Century Polymath*, ed. Isadore Twersky and Jay M. Harris (Cambridge, MA: Harvard University Center for Jewish Studies, 1993), 17 (16 for the cited examples).
187. Sklarz, "Ha-leshonot," 553–54. Bernard Septimus, "'Open Rebuke and Concealed Love': Naḥmanides and the Andalusian Tradition," in *Rabbi Moses Naḥmanides (Ramban): Explorations in His Religious and Literary Virtuosity*, ed. Isadore Twersky (Cambridge, MA: Harvard University Press, 1983), 16n21; and James A. Diamond, "Nahmanides and Rashi on the One Flesh of Conjugal Union: Lovemaking vs. Duty," *Harvard Theological Review* 102 (2009): 195n6.
188. Joseph Dan, "Ashkenazic Hasidism and the Maimonidean Controversy," *Maimonidean Studies* 3 (1992–93): 45.
189. Samuel ben Meir, *Perush ha-rashbam 'al ha-torah*, ed. Meir (Martin) Lockshin, 2 vols. (Jerusalem: Chorev, 2009), 1:106 (with editorial comment in nn24–25).
190. On Exod 18:9 ("Sefer hassagot," 122 [6v]).
191. Twersky, *Rabad*, 194.
192. On Gen 32:30 ("Sefer hassagot," 116 [4v]). Pseudo-Rabad may have been thinking of Maimonides's effort to depersonify angels and equate them with impersonal natural forces; see Kellner, *Maimonides' Confrontation*, 265–85, esp. 273. For "chillingly neutral" as a description of some of Abraham ben David's references to Maimonides, see Twersky, *Rabad*, 194.
193. On Gen 13:9 ("Sefer hassagot," 112 [3r]).

194. Urbach, "Hassagot," 101. The assumption becomes more questionable, but not entirely vitiated by Balbo's indication that he copied the work for private use; see note 4 above.

195. For intricacies of the passage, see Bernard S. Jackson, *Wisdom-Laws: A Study of the Mishpatim of Exodus 21:1–22:16* (Oxford: Oxford University Press, 2006), 79–101.

196. Rashi on Exod 21:11 and "Sefer hassagot," 122 (7r). For Ibn Ezra and Rashbam, see *MGH: Sefer Shemot*, 2:10. One exegete who advocated an approach like Pseudo-Rabad's was Hezekiah ben Manoah; see *Ḥizzequni, perushei ha-torah le-rabbenu ḥizqiyah b"r manoaḥ*, ed. Hayyim D. Chavel (Jerusalem: Mosad Harav Kuk, 1981), 267.

197. See chapter 6, this volume.

198. See the front cover of this book. There are two places in Balbo's manuscript where the person whom Schiller-Szinessy, *Catalogue*, 60, identifies as the censor, one Ibn Tarshish, gives his name. For mutilation of offensive manuscripts, see Michael Camille, "Obscenity under Erasure: Censorship in Medieval Illuminated Manuscripts," in *Obscenity: Social Control and Artistic Creation in the European Middle Ages*, ed. Jan M. Ziolkowski (Leiden: Brill, 1998), 139–54.

199. Zevi Malachi, *Be-no'am siaḥ: peraqim mi-toledot sifrutenu* (Lod: Habermann Institute for Literary Research, 1983), 256, has suggested that this assault may have been born of a private animus against Balbo. It is true that other erasures in the manuscript display the strange phenomenon of colophons in which Balbo's name is invariably scored through; see Cambridge University Library, Add. 377.3, 11r, 16r, 87r, 116r, 119r; and Schiller-Szinessy, *Catalogue*, 60–61. Still, nowhere else do erasures appear on the scale of those in *Sefer hassagot*.

200. On Gen 18:7–8 ("Sefer hassagot," 113 [3r]; also on Exod 12:40 [120]).

201. Reasons for their use of it included a wish to graft mystical teachings onto the oral Torah and a reluctance to reveal the nature of mystical experience; see Joseph Dan, *The 'Unique Cherub' Circle: A School of Mystics and Esoterics in Medieval Germany* (Tübingen: Mohr Siebeck, 1999), 14.

202. Another rationalist pseudepigraph likely written after *Sefer hassagot* voiced strong opposition to the creeping canonization of Rashi's *Commentary*; see chapter 7, this volume.

203. Urbach, "Hassagot," 103.

204. "Sefer hassagot," 93–97.

205. "Sefer hassagot," 89–103.

206. Eli Gurfinkel, "Minḥat qena'ot le-r[abbi] Zekharyah ben Moshe ha-kohen mi-qandi'ah," *Kobez Al Yad* 20 (2011): 125–280 (127–28 for Cretan origins; 264–65 for references to the work's character as *hassagot*; 244, 254 for the cited expressions, respectively)..

207. On Shabbetai's strictures on Komtino, see chapter 7, this volume.
208. Bernard Septimus, *Hispano-Jewish Culture in Transition: The Career and Controversies of Ramah* (Cambridge, MA: Harvard University Press, 1982), 64.
209. The author of a Spanish supercommentary on Rashi, for instance, speaks of his plan to "explicate the words of the great rabbi, R. Solomon the Frenchman"; see Anonymous, "Supercommentary on Rashi," Leeuwarden, Provinciale Bibliotheek van Friesland, MS B. A. Fr. 19, 50r.
210. Daniel Frank, "Karaite Exegetical and Halakhic Literature in Byzantium and Turkey," in *Karaite Judaism: A Guide to Its History and Literary Sources*, ed. Meira Polliack (Leiden: Brill, 2003), 539.
211. "Sefer hassagot," 124–25 (7v).
212. See chapter 7, this volume.

CHAPTER 6

1. Ezra Spicehandler, "Mikhtevei Yehoshua' Heschel Schorr le-Barukh Felsental," *HUCA* 28 (1957): 14. For the earlier article, including the claim regarding the Arabic original of the Torah, see Joshua Heschel Schorr, "Toledot ḥakhmei yisra'el: r[abbi] 'Aharon 'Al Rabi," *Ṣiyyon* 1 (1840): 166, 167, 193–94. For discussion of this bizarre notion, see Joseph Perles, "Ahron ben Gerson Aboulrabi," *REJ* 21 (1890): 247–49. Already a pained introductory footnote attached to Schorr's article by the editors of *Ṣiyyon* (p. 166) registered alarm at this "crooked" notion. In fact, Schorr misread comments in which Aboulrabi suggested that a few utterances in the Torah were originally made in another language. Along with others, Heinrich Graetz, *Geschichte der Juden*, vol. 8, 2nd ed. (Leipzig, 1890), 250 spotlighted Aboulrabi's idea on Schorr's say-so. Samuel David Luzatto (Shadal) reminded Schorr of a solemn duty to remove the "stumbling block" he had placed before readers, then became incensed when Schorr failed to do so. See Samuel David Luzatto, *'Igerot Shadal*, ed. Shealtiel Ayzik Gräber, 9 vols. (Cracow, [1882–94]), 6:1174 and Ezra Spicehandler, "Joshua Heschel Schorr: Maskil and Eastern European Reformist," *HUCA* 31 (1960): 214n 143.
2. Joseph Loeb Sossnitz and Kaufmann Kohler, "Aaron Ben Gershon Abulrabi of Catania," in *Jewish Encyclopedia*, 12 vols. (New York: Funk and Wagnalls, 1901–1906), 1:11. On Kohler, see Yaakov Ariel, "*Wissenschaft des Judentums* Comes to America: Kaufmann Kohler's Scholarly Projects and Jewish-Christian Relations," in *Die Entdeckung des Christentums in der Wissenschaft des Judentums*, ed. Görge K. Hasselhoff (Berlin: De Gruyter, 2010), 165–82.
3. Schorr, "Toledot," 167.
4. Schorr, "Toledot," 194–95.
5. Cecil Roth, "Jewish Intellectual Life in Medieval Sicily," *JQR* 47 (1956–57): 326–27; and Schorr, "Toledot," 166.

6. For more particulars on these scores, see Eric Lawee, "Aaron Aboulrabi: Maverick Exegete from Aragonese Sicily," *Hispania Judaica Bulletin* 9 (2013): 131–62.
7. See at note 236 in chapter 2, this volume. On *Perushim le-rashi*, see Abraham Yaari, *Ha-defus ha-'ivri be-qushta* (Jerusalem: Magnes, 1967), 86; Joseph Hacker, "Defusei qushta be-me'ah ha-shesh-'esrei," *'Areshet* 5 (1972): 480n101; and Marvin J. Heller, *The Sixteenth Century Hebrew Book: An Abridged Thesaurus*, 2 vols. (Leiden: Brill, 2003), 1:179. For its partially divergent printed forms, see Isaac Rivkind, "Diqduqei soferim," in *Sefer yovel likhevod Alexander Marx*, edited by Saul Lieberman, 2 vols. (New York: Jewish Theological Seminary of America, 1950), 2:409–10; Hacker, "Defusei," 480n101; and Yitzhak Yudlov, "Kamah she'arim le-sefer *perushim le-rashi* defus qushta?" *'Alei sefer* 17 (1992): 137–38.
8. This explains why Aboulrabi's work begins to appear only thirteen folios into the volume.
9. See his comment between the glosses on Gen 6:9 and 6:20 ([*Commentary on the Torah / Supercommentary on Rashi*] *in Perushim le-rashi* (Constantinople, 1525[?]), 18v. Hereinafter *Perushim le-rashi*.)
10. The only manuscript version (Bodleian Library, Oxford, MS Mich. 211/5, fols. 129–73) postdates the printed version and is very partial; see Ad. Neubauer, *Catalogue of the Hebrew Manuscripts in the Bodleian Library*, 2 vols. (Oxford: Clarendon, 1886–1906), 1:779 (no. 2245).
11. *Perushim le-rashi*, 12r.
12. Matteo Gaudioso, *La communità ebraica di Catania nei secoli XIV–XV* (Catania: Niccolò, 1974).
13. Without supplying evidence, Norman Roth's entry on Aboulrabi in *Medieval Jewish Civilization: An Encyclopedia*, ed. Norman Roth (New York: Routledge, 2003), 610, suggests his "very probable birth and education in Aragon." For the family's Spanish branch, see Fritz Baer, *Die Juden im christlichen Spanien*, 2 vols. (Berlin: Akademie, 1929–36), documents referenced in the indices s.v. "Abnarrabi" (vol. 1) and "Aburrabe" (vol. 2). For the early fourteenth-century reference to "los hermanos Abuarrabi" in Mayer Kayserling, "Review of *An Inquiry into the Sources of the History of the Jews in Spain* by Joseph Jacobs," *JQR* 8 (1896): 492; and Leopold Zunz, *Zur Geschichte und Literatur* (Berlin, 1845), 519.
14. Alan Ryder, *Alfonso the Magnamimous: King of Aragon, Naples and Sicily, 1396–1458* (Oxford: Clarendon, 1990), 195.
15. David Abulafia, "Le comunità di Sicilia dagli arabi all'espulsione," in *Storia d'Italia XI: Gli ebrei in Italia* (Rome: Giulio Einaudi, 1996), 47–82, is a fine overview. The fullest study is Angela Scandaliato, *Judaica minora sicula* (Florence: Giuntina, 2006). For late medieval Sicily generally, see Denis Mack Smith, *A History of Sicily: Medieval Sicily, 800–1713* (London: Chatto and Windus, 1968), 3–112. Prior to the Aragonese period were intervals of Angevin (1266–1282) and

Hohenstaufen domination (1194–1266), with the Normans preceding them, having wrested the island from the Muslims in the late eleventh century.

16. Robert Bonfil, *Jewish Life in Renaissance Italy*, trans. Anthony Oldcorn (Berkeley: University of California Press, 1994), 80; and E[liyahu] Ashtor, "Palermitan Jewry in the Fifteenth Century," *HUCA* 50 (1979): 225.
17. Nadia Zeldes, "Diffusion of Sicilian Exiles and Their Culture as Reflected in Hebrew Colophons," *Hispania Judaica Bulletin* 5 (2007): 307.
18. Israel M. Ta-Shma, "Gabbai, Moses Ben Shem-Tov," in *EJ*, 7:319, correcting a much earlier date given by previous biographers.
19. "Il 27 Settembre 1437 Aron Abulrabi si trova a Salemi (Trapani) per nominare come suo procuratore il neofita Guillermo de Ferrerio che avrebbe dovuto amministrare i suoi beni e curare i suoi interessi sia a Salemi che a Palermo, dove Abulrabi possedeva delle case da restaurare" (Not. de Guisardo Palmerino, vol. 8, 27 Settembre 1437, c. 7r, Biblioteca Comunale di Salemi). My thanks to Angela Scandaliato for sharing with me this unpublished document.
20. For his role as a physician, see Joseph Shatzmiller, "Jewish Physicians in Sicily," in *Gli ebrei in Sicilia sino all'espulsione del 1492, Atti del V Covegno internazionale Italia Judaica, Palermo 1992* (Rome: Ministerio per i beni culturali e ambientali, 1995), 345–54. For attendance at Padua, see Shatzmiller, *Jews, Medicine, and Medieval Society* (Berkeley: University of California Press, 1994). For his role as communal leader, see Salvatore Fodale, "Mosè Bonavoglia e il contestato *iudicatus generalis* sugli ebrei siciliani," in *Gli Ebrei in Sicilia dal tardoantico al medioevo*, ed. Nicolò Bucaria (Palermo: Flaccovio, 1998), 99–109. For the exegetical dispute with Bonavoglia involving a point of embryogenesis as it applied to purification laws, see Lawee, "Aaron Aboulrabi," 143–46.
21. *Perushim le-rashi*, 56r (on Gen 46:15) and 107v (on Lev 11:13). For dating, see Joseph Hacker, "Ha-negidut bi-ṣefon 'afriqah be-sof ha-me'ah ha-ḥamesh 'esrei," *Zion* 45 (1980–81): 127n34, which corrects the faulty date of 1420 in Perles, "Ahron Ben Gerson," 249. Hacker fixes 1447 as the date for the work on the basis of Aboulrabi's use of the blessing for the dead. As Bonavoglia's successor had taken office in 1446 after his death, however, this date may require slight revision; see Bartolomeo Lagumina and Giuseppe Lagumina, *Codice diplomatico dei Giudei di Sicilia*, 3 vols. (Palermo, 1884–1895), 1:464; and Perles, "Ahron Ben Gerson," 249.
22. Jean-Christophe Attias, *Ha-perush ke-di'alog: Mordekhai ben 'Eli'ezer Komṭino 'al ha-torah*, trans. Yisrael Meir (Jerusalem: Magnes, 2007), 31.
23. Three were apparently of a theological cast (*Sefer ha-nefesh, Nezer qodesh, Peraḥ 'elohut*), one an anti-Christian polemic (*Mateh 'aharon*), and one a grammatical treatise (*Sefer ha-meyasher*); see Lawee, "Aaron Aboulrabi," 154–56.
24. *Perushim le-rashi*, 13r.
25. Joseph Hacker, "Ziqatam ve-'aliyatam shel yehudei sefarad le-'ereṣ yisra'el, 1391–1492," *Qatedrah* 36 (1985): 16.

26. *Perushim le-rashi*, 37v.
27. For Aboulrabi in Rome, see Eric Lawee, "Graven Images, Astromagical Cherubs, Mosaic Miracles: A Fifteenth-Century Curial-Rabbinic Exchange," *Speculum* 81 (2006): 754–95 For other encounters while en route, see Lawee, "Aaron Aboulrabi," 159.
28. Regarding Judeo-Sicilian society, see his scathing aside on Rashi's gloss on the appointment by Moses of "wise and experienced men" to lead the Israelites in the wilderness (Deut 1:15). Noting the asymmetry between God's directive to promote "wise, discerning, and experienced" (Deut 1:13) men and the Torah's report that the appointees were "wise and experienced," Rashi cites the talmudic inference that Moses was unable to find leaders possessing the trait of discernment. Aboulrabi responds with mock astonishment "since in our own times on the island of Sicily many such people are [ostensibly] to be found, called 'discerning' while alive and [praised] with even greater exaggeration upon their demise"; see Rashi on Deut 1:15 and *Perushim le-rashi*, 149v (on Deut 1:15).
29. Ryder, *Alfonso*, 315. Prior to Aboulrabi's time, Sicilian Jews served an important function as translators, although usually only after leaving the island for southern Italy; see, e.g., David Abulafia, "The Jews of Sicily Under the Norman and Hohenstaufen Rulers," in *Ebrei e Sicilia*, ed. Nicolò Bucaria et al. (Palermo: Regione siciliana: Flaccovio Editore, 2002), 88; and Collette Sirat, "Les traducteurs juifs à la cour des rois de Sicile et de Naples," in *Traduction et traducteurs au Moyen Âge*, ed. Genivième Contamine (Paris: Éditions du Centre national de la recherche scientifique, 1989), 178–79.
30. *Perushim le-rashi*, 30v (on Gen 25:23). For Bashyatchi, see Daniel J. Lasker, "Maimonides and the Karaites: From Critic to Cultural Hero," in *Maimónides y su época*, ed. Carlos del Valle et al. (Madrid: Sociedad estatal de conmemoraciones culturales, 2007), 312.
31. *Perushim le-rashi*, 30r, 59r, 166r. For the Crimean melting pot, see Steven A. Epstein, *Purity Lost: Transgressing Boundaries in the Eastern Mediterranean, 1000–1400* (Baltimore, MD: Johns Hopkins University Press, 2007), 56–57.
32. *Perushim le-rashi*, 20v (on Gen 17:20).
33. *Perushim le-rashi*, 152r (on Deut 4.29).
34. Joseph Hacker, "''Im shakhaḥenu shem 'elohenu ve-nifros kapenu le-'el zar'—gilgulah shel parshanut 'al reqa' ha-meṣi'ut bi-sefarad bi-yemei ha-benayim," *Zion* 57 (1992): 247–74.
35. E.g., *Perushim le-rashi*, 25v (on Gen 21:33).
36. *Perushim le-rashi*, 99r (on Exod 40:35). On Lev 11:1 (105v), he states that "with God's help" he will "explain the Torah suitably" and "account for every anomalous matter."
37. See note 181 in chapter 3, this volume.
38. *Perushim le-rashi*, 13v.

39. *Perushim le-rashi,* 16v (on Gen 2:7). For Rashi's elision and compression of rabbinic sources, see *Ḥamishah ḥumshei torah: rashi ha-shalem,* 7 vols. to date (Jerusalem: Ariel, 1986–), *Bereshit,* 1:25n15.
40. *Perushim le-rashi,* 20v (on Gen 16:3).
41. *Perushim le-rashi,* 55v (on Gen 46:10).
42. *Perushim le-rashi,* 59r (on Gen 48:22).
43. *Perushim le-rashi,* 71r (on Exod 7:15).
44. *Perushim le-rashi,* 127v (on Num 12:1). In the fourteenth century, Joseph ibn Kaspi, *Maṣref la-kesef* in *Mishneh kessef,* ed. Isaac Last, 2 vols. (Cracow: Joseph Fischer, 1905), 2:254, exclaimed: "I am amazed at my predecessors. . . . [H]ow could they ever have imagined to explain something in the Torah as the antithesis of the text?"
45. For his enigmatic attitude toward Kabbalah, see Lawee, "Aaron Aboulrabi," 149–50. For a *remez* in the pericope on the one who tempts others to worship other gods, see *Perushim le-rashi,* 160v (on Deut 13:7), where, as with some earlier Jewish anti-Christian polemicists, Aboulrabi takes the phrase "your own mother's son" to "hint" at Jesus, who is alleged to have had a mother but no father, adding: "it suffices for the discerning one." For earlier sources, see Yehuda Liebes, *Studies in the Zohar,* trans. Arnold Schwartz, Stephanie Nakache, and Penina Peli (Albany: SUNY Press, 1993), 242n76. As Liebes observes, this understanding involves a surprising admission that Moses prophesied about Jesus and, moreover, "assumes that the Torah alludes to the Christian belief that Jesus had no father." Aboulrabi notes his invocation of this idea in his anti-Christian *Mateh 'aharon.*
46. *Perushim le-rashi,* 96r (on Exod 33:20).
47. *Perushim le-rashi,* 136v (on Num 21:30). Rashi, following Targum Onkelos, took *nir* as a nominal form, anticipating the findings of modern scholarship, for which see Paul D. Hanson, "Song of Heshbon and David's Nîr," *Harvard Theological Review* 61 (1968): 297–320.
48. See, e.g., the verdict on Rashi's insistence that גר is biliteral in *Perushim le-rashi,* 59r (on Gen 49:19): "*ve-ha-yashar he'erikh be-diqduqo . . . u-levasof yaṣa' mishpaṭo me'uqal.*" On Rashi's comment, see Henry Englander, "Rashi's View of the Weak, ע"ע, and פ"ן Roots (with Special Reference to the Views of Menahem b. Saruk and Dunash b. Labrat)," *HUCA* 7 (1930): 435–36.
49. Rashi on Gen 18:4.
50. *Perushim le-rashi,* 21v (on Gen 18:4–5).
51. Isaac Heinemann, *Darkhei ha-'aggadah,* 3rd. ed. (Jerusalem: Magnes, 1974), 29. By way of a rationale for this identification, Heinemann notes that it procures a temporal link between the generation of the flood and the generation of Abraham. For Melchizedek as a figure who "suddenly emerges from the shadows and as suddenly retreats into oblivion," see ,*The JPS Torah Commentary: Genesis,* commentary by Nahum M. Sarna (Philadelphia: Jewish Publication Society, 1989), 109.

52. See at note 116 in chapter 4, this volume.
53. *Perushim le-rashi*, 19v–20r (on Gen 12:6), reading for *derash rabbot* something like *midrashot rabbot*. For Nahmanides, who cites the same verse in Gen 10 as Aboulrabi, see *MGH: Sefer Bereshit*, ed. Menachem Cohen, 2 vols. (Ramat-Gan: Bar-Ilan University, 1993), 1:136–37.
54. Aboulrabi's successor, Elijah Mizrahi, put his finger on this issue, as well as yet another related contradictory gloss of Rashi; see Yeshayahu Maori, "'Aggadot ḥaluqot' be-ferush rashi la-miqra'," *Shenaton le-ḥeqer ha-miqra' ve-ha-mizraḥ ha-qadum* 19 (2009): 155–56; and in detail, Eitan Sandorfi, "Le-mi nitenah 'ereṣ yisra'el 'aḥar ha-mabbul," *Shema'tin* 136 (1999): 137–44. Mizrahi left it at noting, here as elsewhere, that the *Commentary* contained "dichotomous aggadot." Aboulrabi could also assert that such contradictions were to be found in the *Commentary*. For example, Rashi explained a textual feature regarding the concluding weekly lectionaries in Genesis as reflecting that "the eyes and hearts of Israel were closed" because of the onset of the bondage of the Israelites by the Egyptians around Jacob's death. Aboulrabi insists that "this interpretation is not possible" in Genesis, as Joseph was, during the period described, still a royal Egyptian ruler and Jacob a prophet venerated for his miraculous arrest of the plague (as Rashi elsewhere midrashically asserted). Indeed, no less than two midrashim later adduced by Rashi, including one that explicitly claimed that the Egyptian enslavement commenced only with Levi's death, stood at odds with the idea Rashi here set forth. Yet while Aboulrabi plays "stricturalist" when commenting on the gloss on Levi's death, he elsewhere chalks up the contradiction to dichotomous midrashim, adding that "one does not object from one to another." See *Perushim le-rashi*, 57r, 70r (on Gen 47:28 and Exod 6:16).
55. See at note 102 in chapter 2, this volume.
56. In this reading, Rashi depicted a point after Jacob rectified an interrupted awareness of God. See Eric Lawee, "The Supercommentator as Thinker: Three Examples from the Rashi Supercommentary Tradition," *Journal of Jewish Studies* 67 (2016): 357–61.
57. *Perushim le-rashi*, 56r (on Gen 46:29). In a comment on Gen 28:11 (35r), Aboulrabi clarifies that the midrash about how Jacob established the evening prayer must relate only to the timing of the prayer, as the prayer itself was established only later by Ezra and his court—as, Aboulrabi is keen to stress, another midrash teaches.
58. His halakhic proficiency is attested in technical comments on the laws beginning in Exod 21 (*Perushim le-rashi*, 87v–90r). His work's longest excursus, on Exod 12:15 (75r–v), relates to the verse "seven days you shall eat unleavened bread."
59. *Perushim le-rashi*, 113v (on Lev 21:1).
60. For this as a purport of איני מגלה פנים לתורה, see b. Sanhedrin 99a.

61. *Perushim le-rashi*, 164v (on Deut 19:19). For another invocation of this formula after disagreeing with a legal midrash, see *Perushim le-rashi*, 88r (on Exod 21:11), discussed at note 131, this chapter.
62. *Perushim le-rashi*, 88v (on Exod 21:6). The objection raised by Aboulrabi is addressed in *Pentateuch with Targum Onkelos, Haphtaroth and Rashi's Commentary*, ed. M. Rosenbaum and A. M. Silbermann, 5 vols. (Jerusalem: Silbermann Family, 1934), 2:108b, n2. The suggested textual emendation used to resolve it there does not, however, appear in Rashi's comment as recorded in *MGH: Sefer Shemot*, ed. Menachem Cohen, 2 vols. (Ramat-Gan: Bar-Ilan University, 2007–2012), 2:6.
63. Mordechai S. Goodman, "Hashqafat ra'ba' 'al perushei u-midrashei ḥazal," *Sinai* 133 (2004): 26–31; and Jay M. Harris, *How Do We Know This? Midrash and the Fragmentation of Modern Judaism* (Albany: SUNY Press, 1995), 89.
64. Isaac Hirsch Weiss, *Dor dor ve-dorshav*, 5 vols. (Vienna: 1871–91; repr. New York and Berlin: Plat u-Minkas, 1924), 75.
65. Perles, "Ahron Ben Gerson," 258.
66. Amos Frisch, "'Your Brother Came with Guile': Responses to an Explicit Moral Evaluation in Biblical Narrative," *Prooftexts* 23 (2003): 271–96.
67. Zevi Hirsch Hayot, *Mavo' ha-talmud*, in *Kol sifrei Maharaṣ Ḥayot*, 2 vols. (Jerusalem: Divrei Hakhamim, 1934), 1:322–23.
68. Heinemann, *Darkhei ha-'aggadah*, 50–51. For case studies in later perplexity, see Gilad Sasson, "Gishot 'apologeṭiyot le-sippur ha-miqra'i ha-murḥav 'al david ve-'avigayil bi-teshuvot r[abbi] David ben Zimra (ha-radbaz) ve-r[abbi] Levi ben Ḥabib (ha-ralbaḥ)," *Pe'amim* 130 (2012): 29–60.
69. Avraham Grossman, *Rashi*, trans. Joel Linsider (Oxford: Littman Library of Jewish Civilization, 2012), 104–106.
70. See Amos Frisch, "The Sins of the Patriarchs as Viewed by Traditional Jewish Exegesis," *Jewish Studies Quarterly* 10 (2003): 258–59.
71. David Berger, "On the Morality of the Patriarchs in Jewish Polemic and Exegesis," in *Understanding Scripture: Explorations of Jewish and Christian Traditions of Interpretation*, ed. Clemens Thoma and Michael Wyschogrod (New York: Paulist, 1987), 49–62; Avraham Grossman, *Ḥakhmei ṣorfat ha-rishonim: qorotehem, darkam be-hanhagat ha-ṣibbur, yeṣiratam ha-ruḥanit* (Jerusalem: Magnes, 1995), 488–93.
72. *Perushim le-rashi*, 38v (on Gen 30:38).
73. Sossnitz and Kohler, "Aaron Ben Gershon," 11.
74. *MGH: Sefer Bereshit*, 1:125 (on Gen 15:12); Frisch, "Sins," 259–60; and Reuven Firestone, "Prophethood, Marriageable Consanguinity, and Text: The Problem of Abraham and Sarah's Kinship Relationship and the Response of Jewish and Islamic Exegesis," *JQR* 83 (1993): 331–47.
75. Rashi on Gen 20:12.

76. *Perushim le-rashi*, 19v (on Gen 12:11). The example of *'eruv* is mentioned in the Rome printed edition (289, s.v. "*vayyishmor mishmarti*"). For Rashi on Abraham's observance of even rabbinic decrees, see Gen 26:5. For the highly complex and innovative nature of Rashi's blending together of midrashic sources in this series of glosses, see *Ḥamishah ḥumshei torah, Bereshit*, 2:21–23nn5–7. Aspects of the narrative require exceptions to this portrait of the biblical ancestors, even by Rashi; see Uriel Simon, *'Ozen milin tivḥan: meḥqarim be-darko ha-parshanit shel r[abbi] 'Avraham 'ibn 'Ezra* (Ramat-Gan: Bar-Ilan University Press, 2013), 320.
77. Ora Limor, *Ben yehudim le-noṣrim: yehudim ve-noṣrim be-ma'arav 'eropah 'ad reshit ha-'et ha-ḥadashah*, 5 vols. (Tel Aviv: Open University of Israel, 1993–98), 1:1–40; and Israel Jacob Yuval, *Two Nations in Your Womb: Perceptions of Jews and Christians in Late Antiquity and the Middle Ages*, trans. Barbara Harshav and Jonathan Chipman (Berkeley: University of California Press, 2006). The classic study of Edom's unexpected equation with Rome and Christendom is Gerson D. Cohen, "Esau as Symbol in Early Medieval Thought," in *Jewish Medieval and Renaissance Studies*, ed. Alexander Altmann (Cambridge, MA: Harvard University Press, 1967), 19–48.
78. Berger, "On the Morality," 50–51.
79. Avraham Grossman, *'Emunot ve-de'ot be-'olamo shel rashi* (Alon Shevut: Tevunot, 2008), 73–78, 156–58; Grossman, *Ḥakhmei ṣorfat*, 488–93.
80. Gwynn Kessler, *Conceiving Israel: The Fetus in Rabbinic Narratives* (Philadelphia: University of Pennsylvania Press, 2009), 47–64.
81. *Perushim le-rashi*, 30v (on Gen 25:22, reading "*perusho*" for "*pereshu*"). In the immediate continuation, Aboulrabi stresses the "considerable resemblance in temperament" between the fetuses "in contrast to all other twins" (*Perushim le-rashi*, 30v, 31v, on Gen. 25:23) Cf. Rashi on Gen 25:27: "As long as they were small, they were not recognizable through their deeds, and no one scrutinized them to determine their characters. As soon as they became thirteen years old, this one parted to the houses of study, and that one parted to idol worship." Aboulrabi's association of misbegotten midrash with menstruants, like his link between rabbinic reading techniques and "yarns of girls and their fantansies" (see note 124 in this chapter), requires additional contextualization
82. Nehama Leibowitz, *Limmud parshanei ha-torah u-derakhim lehora'atam: sefer bereshit* (Jerusalem: World Zionist Organization, 1975), 103. One of a very few recent scholars aware of Aboulrabi, she says that he "apparently did not . . . sense that the intention of the midrash was with respect to Israel and the idolatrous nations and the gulf separating them."
83. Rashi on Gen 27:19, 24. For Rashi's skewing of the rabbinic record in this case by studied exclusion, see Leora Hakohen, "Sugyot halakhiyot u-musariyot be-ma'aseh ha-'avot, be-'enei ha-parshanim ha-yehudim bi-yemei

ha-benayyim: rashi, ramban, ve-'ibn Kaspi" (MA thesis, Bar Ilan University, 1995), 14–18.

84. On Gen 27:19 and 35 (*MGH: Sefer Bereshit*, 2:18, 21). For discussion, see Aharon Mondschein, "'Hakhi qara' shemo ya'aqov, vayya'qeveni': la-metodologyah shel rashi ve-ra'ba' be-yaḥasam le-ma'aseh ha-'aqvah shel ya'aqov," *Talpiyot* 12 (2011): 50–61.
85. *Perushim le-rashi*, 33r–v (on Gen 27:19, 24).
86. *Perushim le-rashi*, 33r–v (on Gen 27:22).
87. *Perushim le-rashi*, 33r–34r.
88. b. Megillah 4:10.
89. Lev 18:7, 21:10; Deut 22:30, 27:20.
90. b. Shabbat 55b. For rabbinic views, see Bernard Grossfeld, "Reuben's Deed (Genesis 35:22) in Jewish Exegesis: What Happened There?" in *Biblical Interpretation in Judaism and Christianity*, ed. Isaac Kalimi and Peter J. Haas (New York: T & T Clark, 2006), 44–51.
91. James L. Kugel, *The Ladder of Jacob: Ancient Interpretations of the Biblical Story of Jacob and His Children* (Princeton, NJ: Princeton University Press, 2006), 97–99.
92. Rashi on Gen 35:22.
93. Rashi on Gen 35:22.
94. See the various commentaries to Gen 35:22 and Gen 49:3–4 in *MGH: Sefer Bereshit*, 2:84–85, 172. The true view is also found in Abraham ibn Ezra, *Yesod mora' ve-sod torah*, ed. Joseph Cohen and Uriel Simon, 2nd ed. (Ramat-Gan: Bar Ilan University Press, 2007), 151–52. Ibn Ezra surmised that Jacob refrained from conjugal relations with Bilhah (and, indeed, his remaining wives) after Reuben's defilement of her. By indicating that his sons "were twelve," the Torah hinted at this development, suggesting that after "Israel heard" of Reuben's turpitude he never again engaged in the activity that would have allowed him to have more children. This interpretation appears both in the *reportatio* of Joseph ben Jacob found in the "Alternative Commentary" (*Shitah 'aḥeret*) to Gen 35:22 (*MGH: Sefer Bereshit*, 2:84–85) and in *Yesod mora'*.
95. *Perushim le-rashi*, 33v.
96. Aboulrabi invokes Prov 12:16 again in his comment on Num 26:59 (*Perushim le-rashi*, 133v), now more in the manner of Ibn Ezra, when questioning the Torah's embarrassing reference to the fact that Amram, father of Moses, married his aunt.
97. Rashi on Num 16:6. The passage appears in *MGH: Sefer Bemidbar*, ed. Menachem Cohen (Ramat-Gan: Bar-Ilan University Press, 2011), 100, but is placed in square brackets, suggesting it is not authentic.
98. *Perushim le-rashi*, 133v (on Num 16:6). For Machiavelli on Moses, see William B. Parsons, *Machiavelli's Gospel: The Critique of Christianity in "The Prince"* (Rochester: University of Rochester Press, 2016), 99–100.

99. The term "Bible at eye-level" is shorthand for an intense debate conducted among Israeli rabbis of the Religious-Zionist camp involving, among other things, differing views on the degree to which it is permissible to impute to biblical heroes morally unbefitting acts as they are held to arise from biblical plain sense, often in defiance of well-known (and at times seemingly forced) midrashic counterreadings. For bibliography, see Amos Frisch, "He-ḥaṭe'u ha-'avot ha-'ahuvim? Le-darko shel ha-rav Meqlenburg be-sugyat ḥaṭa'ei ha-'avot ('al pi perusho le-sefer bereshit)," *'Iyyunei miqra' u-farshanut* 8 (2008): 635n42.
100. Several supercommentators thought that this comment applied only to the second view, a point disputed in Eleazar Touitou, "Darko shel rashi be-shimusho be-midreshei ḥazal: 'iyyun be-ferush rashi li-shemot 1:8–22," *Ṭalelei 'orot: shenaton mikhlelet 'orot yisrael* 9 (2000): 55.
101. Rashi on Exod 1:8; and *Perushim le-rashi*, 64v (on Exod 1:8).
102. See chapter 3, this volume. As adumbrations of the Canpantonian approach appear in the supercommentary of Aboulrabi's father-in-law Moses ibn Gabbai, it may be through him that incipient stages of Sefardic "speculation" came to Aboulrabi's notice. Aboulrabi does use the *'iyyun*-based lexicon when he describes the "ineluctability" (*hekhreaḥ*) of midrashic interpretations as they arise from some precise inference (*diyyuq*) (e.g., *Perushim le-rashi*, 35v, on Gen 28:11). Unlike Canpantonians, Aboulrabi also uses *diyyuq* to denigrate hyper-critical hair-splitting: *u-mah she-diyyeq bo ha-yashar kulo shibbush* (*Perushim le-rashi*, 48v, on Gen 40:20).
103. Rashi on Gen 43:8.
104. *Perushim le-rashi*, 53r (on Gen 43:8).
105. Rashi on Gen 11:29. For rabbinic sources, see Eliezer Segal, "Sarah and Iscah: Method and Message in Midrashic Tradition," *JQR* 82 (1992): 417–29.
106. On Gen 11:29 (*MGH: Sefer Bereshit*, 1:18).
107. *Perushim le-rashi*, 19r (on Gen 11:29).
108. Rashi on Gen 37:14.
109. Nehama Leibowitz, *Studies in Bereshit (Genesis)*, trans. Aryeh Newman, 4th rev. ed. (Jerusalem: World Zionist Organization, 1981), 395.
110. *Perushim le-rashi*, 45v (on Gen 37:14). For an example from the legal sphere where Aboulrabi endorses a midrash but shifts its interpretive rationale, see *Perushim le-rashi*, 165v (on Deut 22:12).
111. *Perushim le-rashi*, 19r (on Gen 12:1).
112. *Perushim le-rashi*, 157r (on Deut 8:1).
113. *Perushim le-rashi*, 35v (on Gen 28:10).
114. Rashi on Exod 14:7. Among the Hispano-Christian polemicists who decry the midrash are Raymond Martini, Joshua Halorki, and Alonso de Espina. See Jeremy Cohen, *A Historian in Exile: Solomon Ibn Verga, Shevet Yehudah, and the Jewish-Christian Encounter* (Philadelphia: University of Pennsylvania Press), 74.

115. *Perushim le-rashi*, 81r (on Exod 14:7).
116. *Perushim le-rashi*, 93v (on Exod 29:43).
117. *Perushim le-rashi*, 113v (on Lev 19:32).
118. *Perushim le-rashi*, 106r (on Lev 11:41).
119. *Perushim le-rashi*, 88v (on Exod 21:24).
120. Daniel J. Lasker, "The Interplay of Poetry and Exegesis in Judah Hadassi's *Eshkōl ha-kōfer*," in *Exegesis and Poetry in Medieval Karaite and Rabbanite Texts*, ed. Joachim Yeshaya and Elisabeth Hollender (Leiden: Brill, 2017), 198.
121. *Perushim le-rashi*, 166r (on Deut 25:4).
122. E.g., see *Perushim le-rashi*, 48r–v (on Gen 40:5) and 58r (on Gen 48:7).
123. Ephraim E. Urbach, "Hassagot ha-rabad 'al perush rashi la-torah?" *Qiryat sefer* 34 (1958): 101–108, gave examples of Aboulrabi's awareness of Pseudo-Rabad, but he focused only on similarities and thereby presented a distorted picture. All the examples he recorded are reproduced in the notes to *Sefer hassagot* in Eric Lawee and Doron Forte, "'Sefer hassagot' 'al perush rashi la-torah ha-meyuḥas le-rabad," *Kobez Al Yad* 26 (2018): 108–34, but we await a full study.
124. The phrase *ga'gu'ei banot ve-ḥamuqehem* may play off of Nahmanides's characterization of Rachel's address to Jacob (in her moment of deepest bitterness at her inability to achieve motherhood) as *ga'gu'ei nashim ha-'ahuvot*; see his comment on Gen 30:2 in *MGH: Sefer Bereshit*, 2:39.
125. For the first objection found elsewhere, see, e.g., Isaac Abarbanel, *Perush 'al ha-torah*, 3 vols. (Jerusalem: Benei Arabel, 1964), 1:293: "how could a girl of three go to the spring and draw water for all the camels and perform all the deeds related by scripture?"
126. *Perushim le-rashi*, 29v–30r (on Gen 25:19). I do not locate a source for Aboulrabi's premise, although midrashic legend tells of Rebecca losing her virginity at the time of her conferral to Isaac as a *result* of her fall; see Lieve M. Teugels, *Bible and Midrash: The Story of "The Wooing of Rebekah" (Gen. 24)* (Leuven: Peeters, 2004), 207–12. Aboulrabi posits a period of "many years" between Isaac's binding and his marriage, buttressing the point by pitting against Rashi a midrash mentioned earlier in the *Commentary*. As the sequel to the story of Isaac's binding begins, "[i]t came to pass after (*'aḥarei*) these things," it could be inferred on Rashi's own rabbinic premises that there was a considerable gap between the Akedah and Rebecca's birth, since this temporal formula is one the sages took to indicate an occurrence only "a long time" after the one previously related. For Rashi's articulation, following Genesis Rabbah (44:5), see on Gen 15:1: "Every place that [scripture] uses the word . . . *'aḥarei* it means that the [contiguous] texts should be [seen as temporally] separated (*muflag*)." Rounding out his reproach to Rashi's chronology, Aboulrabi stresses, like Eleazar Ashkenazi, that Isaac is called a "lad" (Gen 22:12). Aboulrabi thinks that the stage so designated falls between the ages of thirteen and twenty-one. By contrast, the near forty

years assigned to Isaac by Rashi stood at the outer limit of Aboulrabi's next stage, "maturity."

127. *Perushim le-rashi*, 20r (on Gen 16:3). For the rabbinic teaching as applied to Rebecca, and for this midrashic notion undergirding the chronology adopted by Rashi, see Teugels, *Bible and Midrash*, 213–20.
128. *Perushim le-rashi*, 70r (on Exod 6:20). For Pseudo-Rabad, see at note 167 in chapter 5, this volume.
129. *Perushim le-rashi*, 99r (Exod 40:17).
130. *Perushim le-rashi*, 124r (on Num 7:1).
131. *Perushim le-rashi*, 88r (on Exod 21:11). For the double entendre, see note 61, this chapter. For Pseudo-Rabad, see at note 196 in chapter 5, this volume.
132. See at note 68 in chapter 5, this volume.
133. *Perushim le-rashi*, 53v (on Gen 44:18).
134. *Perushim le-rashi*, 69v (on Exod 6:2). For Pseudo-Rabad, see at note 39 in chapter 5, this volume. For the Sefardic supercommentator, see at note 169 in chapter 3, this volume.
135. See note 43 in chapter 5, this volume.
136. *Perushim le-rashi*, 122r (on Num 3:16).
137. *Perushim le-rashi*, 35v (on Gen 28:11). In place of an elaborate geographic survey (on Gen 28:17) yielding Rashi's conclusion of a "shrinking of the earth" (*qefiṣat ha-'areṣ*), Aboulrabi locates the basis for the midrash in the use of an unusual word (*vayyifga'*).For Pseudo-Rabad, see at note 127 in chapter 5, this volume.
138. See at note 145 in chapter 5, this volume.
139. *Perushim le-rashi*, 95v (on Exod 32:4).
140. *Perushim le-rashi*, 64v (on Exod 2:14). For Pseudo-Rabad, see at note 142 in chapter 5, this volume.
141. *Perushim le-rashi*, 13r.
142. *Perushim le-rashi*, 65r (on Exod 3:15).
143. *Perushim le-rashi*, 70r (on Exod 6:3). For the theme of divine accommodation, see Stephen D. Benin, *The Footprints of God: Divine Accommodation in Jewish and Christian Thought* (Albany: SUNY Press, 1993).
144. Rashi on Gen 1:4.
145. *Perushim le-rashi*, 14r (on Gen 1:4). For Aboulrabi's cosmogony and its use of terminology drawn from different and even discordant traditions, see Dov Schwartz, "Divine Immanence in Medieval Jewish Philosophy," *Journal of Jewish Thought and Philosophy* 3 (1994): 275–77.
146. *Perushim le-rashi*, 14r (on Gen 1:4).
147. Rashi on Gen 1:5. For Rashi's insertion of angels into this comment, see Eleazar Touitou, "Rashi's Commentary on Genesis 1–6 in the Context of Judeo-Christian Controversy," *HUCA* 61 (1990): 174–75.

148. This reading takes the text as is rather than emending to read that God is always alone (*ve-tamid hu' yaḥid* or *ve-tamid heno yaḥid*). Aboulrabi could be saying that God is "always not alone" because God coexisted with primordial matter prior to its division into particulars, a view that comports with his understanding of creation; see Schwartz, "Divine Immanence," 275–77. On this view, the midrash cited by Rashi would be wrong in asserting that God was ever alone. This reading seems to fit best with the continuation, suitably emended (see next note).
149. *Perushim le-rashi*, 14v. I read "He was [never] alone in His world" (*lo' hayah yaḥid be-'olamo*) rather than "if so, He was alone in His world," to fit with what precedes and follows. In interpreting the opening verse of Genesis, Rashi says the verse does not impart *creatio ex nihilo* or even the teaching that heaven and earth preceded light, whence Aboulrabi's inference—although Rashi designates other elements (water, air, fire) that existed before the creation of heaven and earth. See Warren Zev Harvey, "Rashi on Creation: Beyond Plato and Derrida," *Aleph* 18 (2018): 34–35. In a long opening gloss on Gen 1:1, Aboulrabi speaks of the "primordial light" as a coinage of the kabbalists (*Perushim le-rashi*, 14v).
150. *Perushim le-rashi*, 14v.
151. Richard C. Steiner, "Saadia vs. Rashi: On the Shift from Meaning-Maximalism to Meaning-Minimalism in Medieval Biblical Lexicology," *JQR* 88 (1998): 236–45, esp. 239–41, for *yad*.
152. *Perushim le-rashi*, 70v (on Exod 7:4). Aboulrabi does not comment on Rashi's gloss on the first of the verses he cites or other places that suggest Rashi's explanations of "an actual hand" may have no bearing on the issue of divine corporeality. See Rashi on Exod 14:31, as translated in Steiner, "Saadia vs. Rashi," 240: "many meanings fit the word *yad*, but they are all the same as the meaning of an actual hand, which the interpreter adjusts according to the context." For an assessment of whether or not Rashi's "actual hand" is relevant to the issue of his corporealism, see Nathan Slifkin, "Was Rashi a Corporealist?" *Ḥakirah* 7 (2009): 85.
153. *Perushim le-rashi*, 127r (on Num 11:17).
154. Moses Maimonides, *The Guide of the Perplexed*, trans. Shlomo Pines, 2 vols. (Chicago: Chicago University Press, 1963), I:10 (1:37).
155. Moses ibn Gabbai, *'Eved shelomo*, ed. Moshe Filip (Petah Tikvah: Filip, 2006), 119, on Gen 25:23.
156. For background and brief discussion, see Yuval, *Two Nations*, 10–11.
157. *Perushim le-rashi*, 30r–v (on Gen 25:23).
158. *Perushim le-rashi*, 13v, 25v (on Gen 22:12). For further references, see Lawee, "Aaron Aboulrabi," 153n 86. In *Perushim le-rashi*, 147v–148r (on Num 35:14), Aboulrabi notes tutelage received from his father while a "fledging youth" in astrology without which, he believed, he would have been "banished" from life in the hereafter.

159. A preponderance of literary remains are in the areas of Bible, liturgy, and rabbinic writings; see Giuliano Tamani, "Manoscritti ebraici copiati in Sicilia nei secoli XIV–XV," *Henoch* 15 (1993): 107–12; Malachi Beit-Arié, "Additamenta to G. Tamani's Article on Hebrew Manuscripts Copied in Sicily," *Henoch* 15 (1993): 359–61; Henri Bresc, *Livre et société en Sicile (1299–1499)* (Palermo: [s.n.], 1971), 66; and Shlomo Simonsohn, *Between Scylla and Charybdis: The Jews in Sicily* (Leiden: Brill, 2011), 82–87.
160. Bresc, *Livre*, no. 221, item 2.
161. E.g., *Perushim le-rashi*, 35r (on Gen 28:10), 51v (on Gen 42:1), and 75v (on Exod 12:34).
162. Ibn Gabbai, *'Eved shelomo*, 42.
163. His responses to it as they frequently play out in Aboulrabi's pages remain to be studied. Some appear in footnotes in the Filip edition of Ibn Gabbai's work.
164. *Perushim le-rashi*, 76v (on Exod 12:40).
165. Aboulrabi notes that "there are those who interpret" the Akedah as an event seen prophetically by Abraham on the basis that God could not have desired child sacrifice. This is precisely the grounds on which Ashkenazi posits the prophetic character of the events described in the story. See Eleazar Ashkenazi, *Ṣafenat pa'neaḥ*, ed. Shlomo Rappaport (Johannesburg: Kayor, 1965), 71.
166. For more on this theme, see chapter 7, this volume.
167. Spicehandler, "Joshua Heschel Schorr," 213.
168. Moshe Peli, "Ha-biyografyah ke-janer ba-haskalah: demuto shel Yiṣḥaq 'Abarbanel ke-maskil ha-megasher ben shtei tarbuyot," *Meḥqerei yerushalayim be-sifrut 'ivrit* 16 (1997): 75–88. For *Ṣiyyon*, see Michael Reuven, *Y. M. Jost: 'avi ha-hisṭoriografyah ha-yehudit ha-modernit* (Jerusalem: Magnes, 1983), 139–41.
169. Shmuel Feiner, "Nineteenth-Century Jewish Historiography—The Second Track," in *Reshaping the Past: Jewish History and the Historians*, ed. Jonathan Frankel (New York: Oxford University Press, 1994), 29.

CHAPTER 7

1. Michael Ben Reuven (Pseudonym), ed., "Sefer 'alilot devarim," *Ozar Nechmad. Briefe und Abhandlungen jüdische Literatur betreffend* 4 (1863): 177–214. This article (hereinafter cited as "'Alilot devarim") comprises a brief introduction (177–78), the body of *'Alilot devarim* (179–95), and a commentary on it (196–214). For the work's title, based on a verse in Deuteronomy understood in a certain way, and its translation here, see note 90, this chapter. The main modern studies are Israel M. Ta-Shma, "Hekhan nithabber sefer ' 'Alilot devarim,'" *'Alei sefer* 3 (1977): 44–53; and Reuven (Robert) Bonfil, "Sefer ' 'Alilot devarim': pereq be-toledot ha-hagut ha-yehudit ba-me'ah ha-14," *Eshel Beer-Sheva* 2 (1980): 229–64. For the reason to believe that *'Alilot devarim* was written a fair time prior

to the earliest surviving exemplar of 1468, see Bonfil, "Sefer," 235–39. Even before writing his main article on *'Alilot devarim*, Ta-Shma, "Yedi'ot ḥadashot 'al 'tosafot gornish' ve-'inyanam," *'Alei Sefer* 2 (1976): 81n10, surmised that Raphael Kircheim was the work's pseudonymous editor. Bonfil, "Sefer," 230, concurred. For Kircheim's suggestion of Aboulrabi's authorship, which ultimately rests on very little, see " 'Alilot devarim," 178. For more on the author's mysterious pseudonym, Palmon ben Pelet, see at note 97, this chapter.

2. For *'Alilot devarim* as one of the most brilliant entries in the history of Hebrew satire, see Israel Zinberg, *The Struggle of Mysticism and Tradition Against Philosophical Rationalism*, vol. 3 of *A History of Jewish Literature*, ed. and trans. Bernard Martin, 12 vols. (Cleveland, OH: Case Western Reserve University Press, 1972–1978), 271.
3. " 'Alilot devarim," 207.
4. " 'Alilot devarim," 196. The commentary had long been recognized as an integral part of the work; see Ta-Shma, "Yedi'ot," 80n6. For other late medieval self-commenting texts, see Joseph M. Davis, "Philosophy, Dogma, and Exegesis in Medieval Ashkenazic Judaism: The Evidence of *Sefer Hadrat Qodesh*," *AJS Review* 18 (1993): 203n32.
5. " 'Alilot devarim," 183–84.
6. The attention that the author accords to Rashi's exegesis in general, and the *Commentary* in particular, has for some reason been almost entirely neglected in the main earlier studies. It goes unmentioned by Israel Ta-Shma despite his great discovery of *'Alilot devarim*'s anti-Ashkenazic animus and is referred to only very fleetingly by Bonfil, "Sefer," 246n75. The fullest discussion is in Avraham Gross, "Rashi u-masoret limmud ha-torah she-bi-khetav bi-sefarad," in *Rashi: 'Iyyunim bi-yeṣirato*, ed. Zevi Aryeh Steinfeld (Ramat-Gan: Bar-Ilan University Press, 1993), 36, although Gross unduly assumes *'Alilot devarim*'s Sefardic origins, as does Zinberg (*Struggle*, 272).
7. Bonfil, "Sefer," 254–55.
8. On such encomia, see Isadore Twersky, "Some Reflections on the Historical Image of Maimonides: An Essay on His Unique Place in Jewish History," in *The Legacy of Maimonides: Religion, Reason and Community*, ed. Yamin Levy and Shalom Carmy (Brooklyn, NY: Yashar, 2006), 1–48.
9. Uriel Simon, *'Ozen milin tivḥan: meḥqarim be-darko ha-parshanit shel r[abbi] 'Avraham 'ibn 'Ezra* (Ramat-Gan: Bar-Ilan University Press, 2013), 465–73. See further, Dov Schwartz, *Yashan be-qanqan ḥadash: mishnato ha-'iyyunit shel ha-ḥug ha-ne'oplaṭoni ba-filosofyah ha-yehudit ba-me'ah ha-14* (Jerusalem: Bialik / Mekhon Ben-Zvi, 1996); and the introductions and texts in *Ḥamishah qadmonei mefareshei r[abbi] 'Avraham 'ibn 'Ezra*, ed. Haim Kreisel (Beer-Sheva: Ben-Gurion University Press of the Negev, 2017).
10. "Haqdamat ba'al 'avvat nefesh," in *Ḥamishah qadmonei*, 6.

11. Moshe Halbertal, *Concealment and Revelation: Esotericism in Jewish Thought and Its Philosophical Implications*, trans. Jackie Feldman (Princeton, NJ: Princeton University Press, 2007), 35.
12. Schwartz, *Yashan*; and Dov Schwartz, *'Asṭrologyah u-magyah ba-hagut ha-yehudit bi-yemei ha-benayim* (Ramat-Gan: Bar-Ilan University Press, 1999), 62–91, 145–290.
13. Dov Schwartz, "Le-darkhei ha-parshanut ha-filosofit 'al perushei r[abbi] 'Avraham 'ibn 'Ezra," *'Alei sefer* 18 (1996): 93.
14. Arthur M. Melzer, *Philosophy between the Lines: The Lost History of Esoteric Writing* (Chicago: University of Chicago Press, 2014), 34.
15. Tzvi Langermann, "Abraham Ibn Ezra," in *Stanford Encyclopedia of Philosophy*, substantially revised on Oct 22, 2018, https://plato.stanford.edu/entries/ibn-ezra/.
16. He seems to have written after Moses ibn Tibbon, the son of the founder of the southern French Maimonidean school, whose Ibn Ezra supercommentary is known only from fragmentary citations; see Simon, *'Ozen*, 382–83, and Haim Kreisel, "Reshit ha-parshanut 'al perush ha-torah le-'ibn 'Ezra," in *Ḥamishah qadmonei mefareshei r[abbi] 'Avraham 'ibn 'Ezra*, ed. Haim Kreisel (Beer-Sheva: Ben-Gurion University of the Negev Press, 2017), 15–16. See in the same volume, Orly Shoshan, "Be'ur r[abbi] 'Eleazar ben Mattityah," 39–64.
17. Simon, *'Ozen*, 392.
18. Shoshan, "Be'ur," 56.
19. On Gen 18:1 (*Ḥamishah qadmonei*, 142).
20. Tamás Visi, "Ibn Ezra, A Maimonidean Authority: The Evidence of the Early Ibn Ezra Supercommentaries," in *The Cultures of Maimonideanism: New Approaches to the History of Jewish Thought*, ed. James T. Robinson (Leiden: Brill, 2009), 102–109, who also speaks of the role played by supercommentaries on Ibn Ezra in the latter-day "Maimonidean educational program."
21. On Exod 19:2 (*Ḥamishah qadmonei*, 414). For Eleazar as talmudist, see Simon, *'Ozen*, 393.
22. Shoshan, "Be'ur," 56.
23. See Judah ibn Moskoni, "Introduction to *'Even ha-'ezer*," ed. Abraham Berliner, *'Oṣar ṭov* 2 (1878): 6–9, Hebrew appendix to *Magazin für die Wissenschaft des Judenthums* 5. Note also the supercommentary with Greek glosses discussed in Nicholas de Lange, "Hebrew/Greek Manuscripts: Some Notes," *Journal of Jewish Studies* 46 (1995): 269.
24. Steven B. Bowman, *The Jews of Byzantium 1204–1453* (Tuscaloosa: University of Alabama Press, 1985), 138. For a Byzantine-originated copy of a Rashi supercommentary, see Malachi Beit-Arié, *QI*, 74n108.
25. Ibn Moskoni, "Introduction," 8.

26. For Ibn Ezra commentaries, see Mordechai Komtino, *Perush qadmon 'al sefer yesod mora': "be'ur yesod mora'" le-r[abbi] Mordekhai ben 'Eli'ezer Komṭino*, ed. Dov Schwartz (Ramat-Gan: Bar-Ilan University Press, 2010); and Jean-Christophe Attias, *Ha-perush ke-di'alog: Mordekhai ben 'Eli'ezer Komṭino 'al ha-torah*, trans. Yisrael Meir (Jerusalem: Magnes, 2007), 16. For the *Guide* commentary, see Mordechai Komtino, *Perush qadmon 'al sefer moreh nevukhim: be'uro shel rabbi Mordekhai ben 'Eli'ezer Komṭino 'al moreh ha-nevukhim la-rambam*, ed. Esti Eisenman and Dov Schwartz (Ramat-Gan: Bar-Ilan University Press, 2016).
27. Attias, *Ha-perush*, 121.
28. Attias, *Ha-perush*, 101.
29. Attias, *Ha-perush*, 128–30.
30. Attias, *Ha-perush*, 128–30.
31. Isadore Twersky, "Ha-hishpia' ra'ba' 'al ha-rambam?," in *Rabbi Abraham Ibn Ezra: Studies in the Writings of a Twelfth-Century Polymath*, ed. Isadore Twersky and Jay M. Harris (Cambridge, MA: Harvard University Center for Jewish Studies, 1993), 21–48 (Hebrew section).
32. Visi, "Ibn Ezra," 90–93. For Shabbetai's invocation of this text, see Attias, *Ha-perush*, 129.
33. Moshe Idel, *Absorbing Perfections: Kabbalah and Interpretation* (New Haven, CT: Yale University Press, 2002), 7.
34. Halbertal, *Concealment*, 5. For Nahmanides, see Oded Yisraeli, "Muqdam u-me'uḥar be-toledot ha'avarat ha-sod be-ferush ramban la-torah," *Zion* 79 (2014): 482–87.
35. Eric Lawee, "Sephardic Intellectuals: Challenges and Creativity (1391–1492)," in *The Jew in Medieval Iberia*, ed. Jonathan Ray (Boston: Academic Studies, 2012), 357–59.
36. See chapter 3, this volume.
37. See chapter 2, this volume.
38. See at note 158 in chapter 4, this volume.
39. On Gen 9:13, as in Eleazar Ashkenazi, *Safenat pa'neaḥ*, Moscow, Russian State Military Archive, MS 707/3/6, shelf-mark II, 8 (hereinafter RGVA), 34v; Askenazi, *Ṣafenat pa'neaḥ*, ed. Shlomo Rappaport (Johannesburg: Kayor, 1965), 40. For Ibn Ezra, see his comment on Gen 9:14 in *MGH: Sefer Bereshit*, ed. Menachem Cohen, 2 vols. (Ramat-Gan: Bar-Ilan University, 1993), 1:102.
40. Rashi on Gen 9:17.
41. Ashkenazi, *Ṣafenat pa'neaḥ*, on Gen 18:21, RGVA, 40r (Rappaport, 61). For the issue, see Howard Kreisel, "The Term Kol in Abraham Ibn Ezra: A Reappraisal," *REJ* 153 (1994): 29–66; and Elliot R. Wolfson, "God, the Demiurge and the Intellect: On the Usage of the Word KOL in Abraham Ibn Ezra," *REJ* 149 (1990): 77–111. For the encomium to Ibn Ezra, see RGVA, 21r-v; also in Abraham

Epstein, "Ma'amar 'al ḥibbur *Ṣafenat pa'neaḥ*," in *Kitvei R. 'Avraham 'Epshṭein*, ed. A. M. Haberman, 2 vols. (Jerusalem: Mosad Harav Kuk, 1949), 1:118–19.

42. For Maimonides, see *The Guide of the Perplexed*, trans. Shlomo Pines, 2 vols. (Chicago: University of Chicago Press, 1963), II:6 (2:265) and II: 42 (2:389). For discussion of Nahmanides's retort, see James A. Diamond, *Maimonides and the Shaping of the Jewish Canon* (New York: Cambridge University Press, 2014), 96–97.
43. Ashkenazi, *Ṣafenat pa'neaḥ*, on Gen 18:9, RGVA, 39v (Rappaport, 59). It is unclear what passage in Ibn Ezra Eleazar has in mind. A comment on Gen 18:1 (*MGH: Sefer Bereshit*, 1:158) cites "the commentators" in a way that may imply that the men appeared only in a vision.
44. Warren Zev Harvey, "Spinoza on Ibn Ezra's 'Secret of the Twelve,'" in *Spinoza's 'Theological-Political Treatise': A Critical Guide*, ed. Yitzhak Y. Melamed and Michael A. Rosenthal (New York: Cambridge University Press, 2010), 41–55; and T. M. Rudavsky, "The Science of Scripture: Abraham Ibn Ezra and Spinoza on Biblical Hermeneutics," in *Spinoza and Medieval Jewish Philosophy*, ed. Steven Nadler (Cambridge: Cambridge University Press, 2014), 74–77.
45. For supercommentarial approaches that variously affirm or evade this understanding, see Simon, *'Ozen*, 407–64; and Tamás Visi, "The Early Ibn Ezra Supercommentaries: A Chapter in Medieval Jewish Intellectual History" (PhD diss., Central European University, 2006), 276–93.
46. Ashkenazi, *Ṣafenat pa'neaḥ*, on Gen 12:6, RGVA 36r (Rappaport 46); Epstein, "Ma'amar," 1:127. Evidence of Canaan's previously more circumscribed limits appeared earlier, Eleazar suggested, in the verse indicating that the border of the Canaanites "extended from Zidon" (Gen 10:19), in which case it was possible that the Canaanites now expanded their holdings, "seizing [them] from another."
47. Ashkenazi, *Ṣafenat pa'neaḥ*, on Gen 12:6, RGVA 36r (Rappaport 46).
48. Ashkenazi, *Ṣafenat pa'neaḥ*, RGVA, 44r (Rappaport, 77).
49. Following a talmudic view, Rashi did (in his comment on Deut 34:5) allow for the possibility that the Torah's concluding section relating Moses's death was written by Joshua. For snippets of Rashi's ideas on the formation of the Torah, see Eran Viezel, "The Formation of Some Biblical Books, According to Rashi," *Journal of Theological Studies* 61 (2010): 32–37.
50. Ashkenazi, *Ṣafenat pa'neaḥ*, on Gen 12:5, 21:14, RGVA, 36r, 43r (Rappaport, 46, 68).
51. Ashkenazi, *Ṣafenat pa'neaḥ*, on Gen 22:1, RGVA, 43v (Rappaport, 69).
52. Ashkenazi, *Ṣafenat pa'neaḥ*, on Gen 3:5 RGVA, 24r (Rappaport, 17).
53. Rappaport (*Ṣafenat pa'neaḥ*, ix) found vehemence in the just-cited response to Ibn Ezra, but Eleazar's tone remains measured. His readers knew what true derision sounded like from his disapprobations of Rashi.

54. The issue of chronology is not alone among "literary-editorial" difficulties that the story raises. See Judah Goldin, "The Youngest Son or Where Does Genesis 38 Belong," *Journal of Biblical Literature* 96 (1977): 27–44.
55. Eric Lawee and Doron Forte, "'Sefer hassagot' 'al perush rashi la-torah ha-meyuḥas le-rabad," *Kobez Al Yad* 26 (2018): 117.
56. See chapter 5, this volume.
57. Lawee and Forte, "Sefer hassagot," 111–12 (2v).
58. Rashi on Num 7:19. Cf. Rashi on Num 7:23: "until this point [my comments were] in the name of Rabbi Moses Hadarshan." For Rashi's reliance on Moses in this case, see Hananel Mack, *Mi-sodo shel Moshe hadarshan* (Jerusalem: Bialik, 2010), 98.
59. Lawee and Forte, "Sefer hassagot," 127 (8v–9r).
60. Maimonides, *Guide,* III:26 (Pines, 2:509). For the complexities of Maimonides's argument, see Josef Stern, *Problems and Parables of Law* (Albany: SUNY Press, 1998), 15–48.
61. See at note 153 in chapter 4, this volume.
62. *MGH: Sefer Bereshit,* 1:25 (a condemnation tacitly directed at Christian allegorizing interpretation in this case).
63. See his commentary on Gen 2:11 regarding Saadia Gaon on the branches of the river issuing from Eden: "perhaps he saw them in a dream" (*MGH: Sefer Bereshit,* 1:40).
64. [*Commentary on the Torah / Supercommentary on Rashi*] in *Perushim le-rashi* (Constantinople, 1525[?]), 47v (on (Gen 38:1). The reconstruction of the argument here is somewhat conjectural, because the text may not be preserved immaculately.
65. Rashi on Deut 27:8. See Abraham J. Heschel, *Torah min ha-shamayim be-'aspaqlaryah shel ha-dorot,* 3 vols. (London: Soncino, 1965), 2:379; and Meir Bar-Ilan, "Ha-torah ha-ketuvah 'al ha-'avanim be-har 'eval," *Meḥqerei yehudah ve-shomron* 2 (1993): 29–42.
66. *MGH: Sefer Devarim,* ed. Menachem Cohen (Ramat-Gan: Bar-Ilan University Press, 2011), 185.
67. *Perushim le-rashi,* 167r (on Deut 27:8).
68. *MGH: Sefer Devarim,* 21. For sources on Og, see Natan Slifkin, *Sacred Monsters: Mysterious and Mythical Creatures of Scripture, Talmud and Midrash* (Brooklyn, NY: Zoo Torah / Yashar Books, 2007), 117–29.
69. Maimonides, *Guide,* II:47 (Pines, 2:407–408).
70. *Perushim le-rashi,* 149v (on Deut 3:11).
71. *Perushim le-rashi,* 151r (on Deut 3:11).
72. Rashi on Num 35:14.
73. *Perushim le-rashi,* 147v–148r (on Num 35:14). The passage contains testimony about his test of the efficacy of astral magic as imparted by "the scholars of the

aspects" (i.e., of the planets' angular relationships: conjunction, opposition, and so forth), as well as tutelage he received from his father in astrology while a "fledging youth." Aboulrabi even relates how astral magic helped him escape an unspecified brush with death.

74. Dov Schwartz, "'Ereṣ, maqom ve-kokhav: ma'amadah shel 'ereṣ yisra'el bi-tefisato shel ha-ḥug ha-ne'oplaṭoni ba-me'ah ha-14," in *'Ereṣ yisra'el ba-hagut ha-yehudit bi-yemei ha-benayin*, ed. Moshe Halamish and Aviezer Ravitzky (Jerusalem: Mekhon Ben-Zvi, 1991), 138–50.
75. *Perushim le-rashi*, 13v (on Gen 1:1).
76. Schwartz, *Yashan*, 28–29.
77. It is true that the author expresses no misgivings about the rabbinic sages or their legacy, but it does not necessarily follow that he had "great respect for the sages of the Talmud and their work" (Zinberg, *Struggle*, 272). Some critiques tacitly point to the roots of problems in ways that at least raise the prospect that *'Alilot devarim*'s valorization of the rabbinic heritage might, at least to some degree, be tactical.
78. "'Alilot devarim," 182: *gam hu lo' be'er mimmeno zulatei ha-ḥeleq ha-ma'asi ve-ha-domeh lo*. The word *zulatei* is lacking in London, MS Montifiore 266, 32v.
79. "'Alilot devarim," 198–99.
80. "'Alilot devarim," 182.
81. Reading *derashot* for *derushot* on the basis of MS Montifiore 266, 32v. For Ibn Ezra, see after note 72 in chapter 2, this volume.
82. "'Alilot devarim," 182.
83. "'Alilot devarim," 183, 190–91.
84. Reproduced in Bonfil, "Sefer," 231–32.
85. Ta-Shma, "Hekhan." Two scholars reinforced his finding in notes in later volumes: Yehoshua Mondschein, "He'erah," *'Alei sefer* 4 (1977): 180; and Yakov (Jacob) J. Schacter, "'Al sefer "Alilot devarim'," *'Alei sefer* 8 (1980): 148–50.
86. "'Alilot devarim," 187. For Ibn Ezra, see the commentary on Eccl 5:1 in *MGH: Ḥamesh megillot*, ed. Menachem Cohen (Ramat-Gan: Bar-Ilan University Press, 2012), 156–57, 159. For the attack's anti-Ashkenazic thrust, see Joseph Yahalom, "Aesthetic Models in Conflict: Classicist *versus* Ornamental in Jewish Poetics," in *Renewing the Past, Reconfiguring Jewish Culture*, ed. Ross Brann and Adam Sutcliffe (Philadelphia: University of Pennsylvania Press, 2004), 22–23. Maimonides's critique of *piyyuṭ* is not specifically anti-Ashkenazic, but is made on the grounds that much religious poetry contains philosophically problematic or even heretical elements. See Maimonides, *Guide*, I:59 (Pines, 1:137–403); and Gerald J. Blidstein, *Ha-tefilah be-mishnato ha-hilkhatit shel ha-rambam* (Jerusalem: Bialik, 1994), 129–31.
87. "'Alilot devarim," 199. As far as I know, no earlier study has made note of this comment.

88. The seminal study of this development, since amply discussed and debated, is Ephraim Kupfer "Li-demutah ha-tarbutit shel yahadut 'ashkenaz ve-ḥakhameha ba-me'ah ha-14–15," *Tarbiẓ* 42 (1972): 113–47. See further, e.g., David B. Ruderman, *Jewish Thought and Scientific Discovery in Early Modern Europe* (New Haven, CT: Yale University Press, 1995), 54–68; Davis, "Philosophy, Dogma," 195–222; and Tamás Visi, *On the Peripheries of Ashkenaz: Medieval Jewish Philosophers in Normandy and in the Czech Lands from the Twelfth to the Fifteenth Century* (Olomouc: Kurt and Ursula Schubert Center for Jewish Studies, 2011), 158–228.
89. "'Alilot devarim," 183. On the play *pilpul–bilbul,* not unique to this work, see Aviram Ravitsky, *Logiqah 'arisṭoṭelit u-metodologyah talmudit: yissumah shel ha-logiqah ha-'arisṭoṭelit ba-perushim la-midot she-ha-torah nidreshet bahen* (Jerusalem: Magnes, 2009), 225–26.
90. Here, as elsewhere, failure to consult the commentary can beget error. The title is based on a phrase in Deut 22:14, 17, which describes a man's charge that his wife lacked signs of virginity at the consummation of the marriage. The biblical context makes it easy to conclude that the title means something like "Made-up Charges" or "False Charges," and so it has been understood; see Ora Limor and Israel Jacob Yuval, "Skepticism and Conversion: Jews, Christians, and Doubters in *Sefer Ha-Nizzahon,*" in *Hebraica Veritas? Christian Hebraists and the Study of Judaism in Early Modern Europe,* ed. Allison P. Coudert and Jeffrey S. Shoulson (Philadelphia: University of Pennsylvania Press, 2004), 173; and Bill Rebiger, "The Early Opponents of the Kabbalah and the Role of Sceptical Argumentations: An Outline," in *Yearbook of the Maimonides Centre for Advanced Studies: 2016,* ed. Giuseppe Veltri (Berlin: De Gruyter, 2016), 44–45. It would be curious for an author to proclaim his work's slanderous content. In the case of *'Alilot devarim,* one could in theory chalk up this strange procedure to the work's "figurative-ironic" form, as does Benzion Netanyahu, *The Marranos of Spain from the Late 14th to the Early 16th Century According to Contemporary Hebrew Sources,* 3rd ed., updated and expanded (Ithaca, NY: Cornell University Press, 1999), 227n1. Still, Netanyahu translates *'Alilot devarim* as *The Book of Complaints,* which is closer to the mark. But the pseudonymous commentator "Joseph ben Meshulam," presumably identical with the author, clarifies that the *'alilot* refer to an "accusation" (*qeriyat tigar*) or "quarrel" (*riv*), hence my translation *Book of Accusations.* He also explains that the "words" (*devarim*) mentioned in the title refer to pilpulistic techniques. See "'Alilot devarim," 196. The biblical phrase containing *'alilah* in Deuteronomy is unique, making translation a challenge; see Heinz-Josef Fabry, "'ll," in *Theological Dictionary of the Old Testament,* ed. G. Johannes Botterweck, Helmer Ringgren, and Heinz-Josef Fabry, trans. David E. Green, 15 vols. (Grand Rapids, MI: Eerdmans, 1977–2012), 11:142. Bonfil, "Sefer," 254n111, notes the title's point of contact with the somewhat unusual exegesis given by Ibn Ezra in Deut 22: "*devarim*—either true or false."

91. "'Alilot devarim," 199.
92. For the passage, see Abraham ibn Ezra, *Yesod mora' ve-sod torah*, ed. Joseph Cohen and Uriel Simon, 2nd rev. ed. (Ramat-Gan: Bar-Ilan University Press, 2007), 91. For the assessment, see Langermann, "Abraham Ibn Ezra."
93. Though Herbert A. Davidson, *Moses Maimonides: The Man and His Works* (New York: Oxford University Press, 2005), 313–22, denies Maimonides's authorship of the *Treatise on Logic*, the scholarly consensus supports it. See Sarah Stroumsa, "On Maimonides and on Logic," *Aleph* 14 (2014): 259–63.
94. James T. Robinson, *Samuel Ibn Tibbon's Commentary on Ecclesiastes: The Book of the Soul of Man* (Tübingen: Mohr Siebeck, 2007), 112.
95. See at note 197 in chapter 2, this volume.
96. "'Alilot devarim," 184–85. The equation of Maimonides with the biblical Moses (*shemo ke-shem rabo*) appears again later in the work ("'Alilot devarim," 194).
97. "'Alilot devarim," 183.
98. On this aspect of the work, see Netanyahu, *Marranos*, 232–35, who offers an entirely unsustainable effort to shoehorn *'Alilot devarim* into the context of events in late medieval Spain.
99. "'Alilot devarim," 199.
100. "'Alilot devarim," 182.
101. For the equation of "strange" with "irrational," see note 172 in chapter 2, this volume.
102. See at note 160 in chapter 4, this volume.
103. Bonfil, "Sefer," 240.
104. Dov Schwartz, "Sefer 'Mesharet Moshe' be-'en ha-se'arah: tikhtovet ben r[abbi] Yedidyah Rakh le-r[abbi] Micha'el Balbo be-sugiyot ha-nevu'ah u-nevu'at moshe," *'Alei Sefer* 24–25 (2015): 82.
105. For the theory of Spanish origins and its refutation, see Ta-Shma, "Hekhan," 45–47.
106. Ta-Shma, "Hekhan."
107. Ashkenazi's work was completed around the time of Joseph's sojourn in Crete and was copied in Crete a couple of decades later.
108. See note 30 in chapter 6, this volume.
109. See at note 35 in chapter 4, this volume.
110. For Saul Hakohen, see Arthur M. Lesley, "The Place of the *Dialoghi d'Amore* in Contemporaneous Jewish Thought," in *Essential Papers on Jewish Culture in Renaissance and Baroque Italy*, ed. David Ruderman (New York: New York University Press, 1992), 184–85. For Delmedigo, see most recently Michael Engel, *Elijah del Medigo and Paduan Aristotelianism: Investigating the Human Intellect* (London: Bloomsbury, 2016).
111. Leah Naomi Goldfeld, "Perush la-torah shel Yehudah ben Shemaryah bi-khetav yad she-ba-genizah," *Kobez Al Yad* 10 (1982): 147.

112. For rationalist works of midrashic interpretation in more westerly seats of learning, see note 204 in chapter 5, this volume.
113. For Byzantine scholarly itinerancy, see Dov Schwartz, *Qame'ot segulot u-sekhaltanut ba-hagut ha-yehudit bi-yemei ha-benayim* (Ramat-Gan: Bar-Ilan University Press, 2004), 141–45. For Byzantine Jews' mobility generally, see David Jacoby, "The Jewish Communities of the Byzantine World from the Tenth to the Mid-Fifteenth Century: Some Aspects of Their Evolution," in *Jewish Reception of Greek Bible Versions: Studies in Their Use in Late Antiquity and the Middle Ages*, ed. Nicholas de Lange, Julia G. Krivoruchko, and Cameron Boyd-Taylor (Tübingen: Mohr Siebeck, 2009), 157–81.
114. Moshe Idel, "On Mobility, Individuals and Groups: Prolegomenon for a Sociological Approach to Sixteenth-Century Kabbalah," *Kabbalah* 3 (1998): 145–73.
115. Elijah Mizrahi, *She'elot u-teshuvot R. 'Eliyahu Mizraḥi* (Jerusalem: Hotsa'at sefarim "Darom," 1937), no. 80.
116. See the introduction to Elijah Mizrahi, *Perush rashi* (Venice, 1527).
117. Marvin J. Heller, *The Sixteenth Century Hebrew Book: An Abridged Thesaurus*, 2 vols. (Leiden: Brill, 2003), 1:189.
118. Pinchus Krieger, *Parshan-data': reshimat ha-perushim le-ferush rashi 'al ha-torah*, 2 vols. (Monsey, NY: Pinchus Krieger, 2005–2018), 1:128, 130.
119. Eric Lawee, "Biblical Scholarship in Late Medieval Ashkenaz: The Turn to Rashi Supercommentary," *HUCA* 86 (2015): 265–303.
120. Isserles's glosses are printed under the title "Qarnei re'em" in *Meged yeraḥim*, 2nd fascicle (1855): 59–65. For the characterization of Luria's enterprise cited, see the (unpaginated) introduction to Solomon Luria, *Yeri'ot shelomo* (Prague, 1609). For multiple versions of his work as recorded by different students, see Elchanan Reiner, "''En ṣarikh shum yehudi lilmod davar raq ha-talmud levado': 'al limmud ve-tokhanei limmud be-'ashkenaz bi-yemei ha-sefer ha-rishonim," in *Ta shema': meḥqarim be-madda'ei ha-yahadut le-zikhro shel Yisra'el M. Ta-Shma*, ed. Avraham (Rami) Reiner et al., 2 vols. (Alon Shvut: Tevunot, 2012), 2:727n33. On the Luria family's claim to a link with Rashi, see Yisrael Yaakov Yuval, *Ḥakhamim be-doram: ha-manhigut ha-ruḥanit shel yehudei germanyah be-shilhei yemei ha-benayim* (Jerusalem: Magnes, 1989), 249–52.
121. Mordechai Jaffe, *Levush 'orah* in *'Oṣar perushim 'al ha-torah*, 2 vols. (Jerusalem: Divrei Ḥakhamim, 1958), 1:124r.
122. Isaac Hakohen, *Mattenot 'ani* (Prague, 1604–1608), introduction. Cf. b. Sukkah 28a for *davar gadol* and *davar qatan* and b. Ḥullin 7a for *maqom lehitgadder bo*.
123. For a list, see Elijah Mizrahi, *Ḥumash ha-re'em*, ed. Moshe Filip, 6 vols. (Petah Tikvah: Filip, 1994), 1:16–23.
124. Three were printed, one by Mordechai Caravalio (Livorno, 1761), one by Elyakim Gitinio (Izmir, 1762), and one by Moses ben Shamayah (Livorno,

1825). A fourth work bearing this name (by Alon ben Maimon) remains in manuscript.

125. Judah Leib Eilenburg, *Minḥat yehudah* (Lublin, 1609).

126. Jacob ben Benjamin Slonik, *Naḥalat ya'aqov*, ed. Mordechai Cooperman, 3 vols. (Jerusalem: Michlalah College for Women, 1993), iii. For Spira's supercommentary *Sefer 'imrei shefer*, see Heller, *Sixteenth Century Hebrew Book*, 2:787.

127. Shabbetai Bass, *Siftei ḥakhamim*, in *'Oṣar perushim 'al ha-torah*, 2 vols. (Jerusalem: Divrei Ḥakhamim, 1958), ii.

128. For the description of Ibn Ezra, see Mizrahi, *Ḥumash ha-re'em*, 2:559. For the description of Nahmanides, see the responsum cited in note 115, this chapter.

129. Michael A. Shmidman, "On Maimonides' 'Conversion' to Kabbalah," in *Studies in Medieval Jewish History and Literature II*, ed. Isadore Twersky (Cambridge, MA: Harvard University Press, 1984), 375–86.

130. Moshe Rosman, "Innovative Tradition: Jewish Culture in the Polish-Lithuanian Commonwealth," in *Cultures of the Jews: A New History*, ed. David Biale (New York: Schocken, 2002), 519–70; Elchanan Reiner, "The Ashkenazi Élite at the Beginning of the Modern Era: Manuscript *versus* Printed Book," *Polin* 10 (1997): 85–98; and Reiner, "'En ṣarikh," 2:705–46.

131. Alfred L. Ivry, "Strategies of Interpretation in Maimonides' *Guide of the Perplexed*," in *The Frank Talmage Memorial Volume* (= *Jewish History* 6), 2 vols., ed. Barry Walfish (Haifa: Haifa University Press, 1993), 2:119.

132. Halbertal, *Concealment*, 68.

133. On which, see Moshe Idel, "On Angels and Biblical Exegesis in Thirteenth-Century Ashkenaz," in *Scriptural Exegesis: The Shapes of Culture and the Religious Imagination: Essays in Honour of Michael Fishbane*, ed. Deborah A. Green and Laura S. Lieber (Oxford: Oxford University Press, 2009), 211–44.

134. Adapting the formulation in Halbertal, *Concealment*, 36.

135. Raymond Aron, *Main Currents in Sociological Thought: Montesquieu, Comte, Marx, Toqueville, and the Sociologists and the Revolution of 1848*, trans. Richard Howard and Helen Weaver (Garden City, NY: Doubleday, 1968), 149.

136. Eran Viezel, "Le-mi mi'en rashi 'et perushav la-miqra'," *Beit Mikra* 52 (2007): 139–68.

AFTERWORD

1. Moshe Idel, "The Kabbalah's 'Window of Opportunities', 1270–1290," in *Me'ah She'arim: Studies in Medieval Jewish Spiritual Life in Memory of Isadore Twersky*, ed. Ezra Fleischer et al. (Jerusalem: Magnes, 2001), 171

2. Avivah Gottlieb Zornberg, *The Particulars of Rapture: Reflections on Exodus* (New York: Doubleday, 2001), 2.

3. Joseph Solomon Delmedigo, *Mikhtav 'aḥuz,* in *Melo ḥofnayyim,* ed. Abraham Geiger (Berlin, 1840), 20–21, reading *rabbanim* for *banim.*
4. Isaac Barzilay, *Yoseph Shlomo Delmedigo (Yashar of Candia): His Life, Works and Times* (Leiden: Brill, 1974), 72. Elsewhere, Delmedigo went so far as to assert, disingenuously by all indications, that Rashi was a master kabbalist acquainted with "many secrets and mysteries" despite omitting them from his *Commentary.* See ibid., 243.
5. Steven Nadler, *Spinoza: A Life* (Cambridge: Cambridge University Press, 1999), 93.
6. Benedict de Spinoza, *Theologico-Political Treatise,* in *Chief Works of Benedict de Spinoza,* trans. R. H. M. Elwes (New York: Dover, 1951), 269. Needless to say, Spinoza's relationship to Ibn Ezra is far more complex than this gibe suggests. See, most recently, T. M. Rudavsky, "The Science of Scripture: Abraham Ibn Ezra and Spinoza on Biblical Hermeneutics," in *Spinoza and Medieval Jewish Philosophy,* ed. Steven Nadler (Cambridge: Cambridge University Press, 2014), 59–78.
7. Rudavsky, "Science," 66.
8. Jay M. Harris, *How Do We Know This? Midrash and the Fragmentation of Modern Judaism* (Albany: SUNY Press, 1995), 126–31.
9. Warren Harvey, "Spinoza on Biblical Miracles," *Journal of the History of Ideas* 74 (2013): 663.
10. Contrast Daniel B. Schwartz, *The First Modern Jew: Spinoza and the History of an Image* (Princeton, NJ: Princeton University Press, 2012) with Alan Nadler, "Romancing Spinoza," *Commentary* 122 (December 2006): 25–30.
11. See Edward Breuer, *The Limits of Enlightenment: Jews, Germans, and the Eighteenth-Century Study of Scripture* (Cambridge, MA: Harvard University Center for Jewish Studies, 1996), esp. 177–222.
12. See Edward Breuer, trans., *Moses Mendelssohn's Hebrew Writings,* introduced and annotated by Edward Breuer and David Sorkin (New Haven, CT: Yale University Press, 2018), relevant references in the index s.vv. "Solomon b. Isaac (Rashi)."
13. Alan T. Levenson, *The Making of the Modern Jewish Bible: How Scholars in Germany, Israel, and America Transformed an Ancient Text* (Lanham, MD: Rowman & Littlefield, 2011), 33. See Abigail E. Gillman, "Between Religion and Culture: Mendelssohn, Buber, Rosenzweig, and the Enterprise of Biblical Translation," in *Biblical Translation in Context,* ed. Frederick Knobloch (Bethesda: University Press of Maryland, 2002), 101–105, who suggests (105) that Mendelssohn sought to "mitigate the innovative nature of his work through a variety of traditional strategies," hoping that "the reader's immediate visual experience of the Bible would contain no surprises."
14. The first edition to include the *Commentary* was produced in Fürth in 1802 (Breuer, *Moses Mendelssohn's Hebrew Writings,* 233). See also Abigail Gillman, *A History of German Jewish Bible Translation* (Chicago: University of Chicago Press, 2018), 84.

15. Steven M. Lowenstein, "The Readership of Mendelssohn's Bible Translation," *HUCA* 53 (1982): 187, 191–92.
16. Boaz Huss, "Admiration and Disgust: The Ambivalent Re-Canonization of the *Zohar* in the Modern Period," in *Study and Knowledge in Jewish Thought*, ed. Howard Kreisel (Beer-Sheva: Ben-Gurion University of the Negev Press, 2006), 203–37.
17. For an overview, see Marc Zvi Brettler and Edward Breuer, "Jewish Readings of the Bible," in *The New Cambridge History of the Bible*, vol. 4: *From 1750 to the Present*, ed. John Riches (Cambridge: Cambridge University Press, 2015), 297–312.
18. Jonathan Jacobs, "Rabbi Samson Raphael Hirsch as a *Peshat* Commentator: Literary Aspects of His Commentary on the Pentateuch," *RRJ* 15 (2012): 199.
19. Franz Rosenzweig, *On Jewish Learning*, ed. Nahum N. Glatzer (New York: Schocken, 1955), 36. Regarding the spiritual world to which Rashi was a conduit, Rosenzweig added that "even in our own times" it had "greater influence on Jewish character than we know or admit."
20. Levenson, *Making*, 155.
21. Edward L. Greenstein, "Sensitivity to Language in Rashi's Commentary on the Torah," *Solomon Goldman Lectures* 6 (1993): 51. For Hertz's enterprise, see Harvey W. Meirovich, *A Vindication of Judaism: The Polemics of the Hertz Pentateuch* (New York: Jewish Theological Seminary of America, 1998).
22. Levenson, *Making*, 182, 184.
23. Michael Avioz, "The Da'at Mikra Commentary Series: Between Tradition and Criticism," *Jewish Bible Quarterly* 34 (2006): 226–36. On popularized scholarship and Orthodox beliefs in the series, see S. David Sperling, "Modern Jewish Interpretation," in *The Jewish Study Bible*, ed. Adele Berlin and Marc Zvi Brettler (Oxford: Oxford University Press, 2004), 1918.
24. B. Barry Levy, "The State and Directions of Orthodox Bible Study," in *Modern Scholarship in the Study of Torah: Contributions and Limitations*, ed. Shalom Carmy (Northvale, NJ: Aronson, 1996), 50.
25. Levenson, *Making*, 182.
26. Original: *Vi der khumash mit di rashe / Vi der kugl mit der kashe.* For the poem and popular Yiddish song "Ale Brider" that it inspired, see Abigail Wood, *And We're All Brothers: Singing in Yiddish in Contemporary North America* (Farnham: Ashgate, 2013), 20. On Winchevsky, the pen name of Leo Benzion (Lipe Bentsien) Novotchovitch (Novakhovits), see Tanja Rubinstein, "An Alternative Version of Maimonides' Thirteen Principles of Faith," *Zutot* 13 (2016): 81–93.
27. Penny Schine Gold, *Making the Bible Modern: Children's Bibles and Jewish Education in Twentieth-Century America* (Ithaca, NY: Cornell University Press, 2004), 188.

28. "'Ashirah le-rashi," in Samson Meltzer, *Shirot u-baladot* (Tel Aviv: Dvir, 1959), 19–24, drawing in part on translations of John Hobbins, "That Was Your Stone, Dear Old Rashi, the Most Precious of Stones!" Ancient Hebrew Poetry (blog), http://ancienthebrewpoetry.typepad.com/ancient_hebrew_poetry/2009/05/that-was-your-stone-dear-old-rashi-the-most-precious-of-stones.html. See Avraham Grossman, *Rashi*, trans. Joel Linsider (Oxford: Littman Library of Jewish Civilization, 2012), 73.
29. S. Y. Agnon, *A City and Its Fullness* ed. Alan Mintz and Jeffrey Sacks (Jerusalem: Toby, 2016), 359–60.
30. *Pirqei Neḥamah: sefer zikaron le-Neḥamah Lebovits,* ed. Moshe Ahrend and Rut Ben-Meir ([Jerusalem]: Ha-Sokhnut ha-Yehudit le-Erets Yisra'el, 2001), 676. For the translation (slightly adjusted here) and further discussion, see Yael Unterman, *Nehama Leibowitz: Teacher and Bible Scholar* (Jerusalem: Urim, 2009), 375–79 (375–76 for the cited passage).
31. Mordechai Z. Cohen, "'Reproducing the Text': Nehama Leibowitz on Traditional Biblical Interpretation (*Parshanut Ha-Mikra*) in Light of Ludwig Strauss's Literary Theory," *Torah U-Madda Journal* 17 (2016–17): 1–34, esp. 5–15.
32. Emmanuel Levinas, "La lettre ouverte," *Rencontres. Chrétiens et Juifs* 51 (1977): 118. Even making allowances for the context, a lecture delivered upon the inauguration of a Rashi Center in Paris, the statement is remarkable. For the oral report, see *Moshe Idel: Representing God,* ed. Hava Tirosh-Samuelson and Aaron W. Hughes (Leiden: Brill, 2014), 171.
33. Shmuel Wygoda, "Une lecture philosophique de Rachi," in *Héritages de Rachi,* ed. René-Samuel Sirat (Paris: Éditions de l'éclat, 2006), 216.
34. Avivah Gottlieb Zornberg, *Genesis: The Beginning of Desire* (Philadelphia: Jewish Publication Society, 1995), xiv. Zornberg's conception of and rich use of the *Commentary* merits an in-depth study.
35. Sarah Levy and Steven Levy, *The JPS Rashi Discussion Torah Commentary* (Philadelphia: Jewish Publication Society, 2017).
36. "AlHaTorah.org Rashi Project" (ed. Aviva Novetsky) at http://alhatorah.org/Commentators:Rashi_Leipzig_1. For newsletters, see http://www.rashiyomi.com/.
37. Other essays are notable for their authors, if disappointing in content. Elie Wiesel devotes more than a third of his thin (in more ways than one) tome, *Rashi* (New York: Schocken, 2009), to a quasi-supercommentarial exposition of passages from the commentaries on Genesis (32–62), but this treatment provides little more than translations. To illustrate the paucity (36), consider his citation of the midrashic interpretation of Rashi, to which we have returned time and again, on "this time, bone of my bones." Wiesel calls the notion of Adam's serial bestiality "[a] surprising idea"—then moves on, adding nothing.
38. For the cited passages, see Chaim Rapoport, "The Lubavitcher Rebbe's Commentary on Rashi: Some Initial Reflections," 6 (with thanks to the author for

providing this unpublished manuscript) and Menachem M. Schneerson, *Studies in Rashi: From the Teachings of the Lubavitcher Rebbe, Menachem M. Schneerson,* trans. Y. Eliezer Danzinger (Brooklyn, NY: Kehot, 2011), ix, xii. See further Chaim Miller, *Turning Judaism Outward: A Biography of Rabbi Menachem Mendel Schneerson the Seventh Lubavitcher Rebbe* (Brooklyn, NY: Kol Menachem, 2014), 304–307.

39. For the implication of the *Commentary*'s revealed status like the Targum, see *Ḥamishah ḥumshei torah 'im perush rashi*, ed. Binyamin S. Moore (Jerusalem: Feldheim, 2002), xi. The topic of the *Commentary*'s quasi-prophetic status in modern times awaits systematic exploration. For translation according to Rashi, see *Ḥamishah ḥumshei Torah with Rashi's Commentary, Targum Onkelos, Haftaros and Commentary Anthologized from Classic Rabbinic Texts and the Works of the Lubavitcher Rebbe* (Brooklyn, NY: Kol Menachem, 2002), xii–xiii.
40. Yisrael Isser Zvi Herczeg, ed., *The Torah with Rashi's Commentary*, 5 vols. (Brooklyn, NY: Mesorah, 1999), 1. Note also the approbation of Rabbi Shmuel Kamenetsky, which appears at the front of the first volume (unpaginated). It states that disparate supercommentarial interpretations of Rashi are "indubitably true in the manner of [diverse interpretations of] the Torah about which [a rabbinic dictum has it that] 'these and those are the words of the living God.'" Such claims notwithstanding, the edition's producers are well aware of the phenomenon of textual variants and even refer to "researching" them (xiii).
41. The "Artscroll" producers of *The Torah with Rashi's Commentary* take their canonization of Rashi to new heights in their rendering of Song of Songs, where Rashi's allegorical reading is infiltrated into the translation of the scriptural love poems. This yields as the opening a translation that reads: "The song that excels all songs dedicated to God, the King to Whom peace belongs" and monstrosities like—for Song of Songs 1:12: "While the king sat at his table, my spikenard sent forth its fragrance"—"While the King was yet at Sinai my malodorous deed gave forth its scent as my Golden Calf defiled the covenant." See Nosson Scherman, ed., *The Complete ArtScroll Siddur* (New York: Mesorah, Publications, 1990) 298–99.
42. David Ben-Gurion, *'Iyyunim ba-tanakh* (Tel Aviv: Am Oved, 1969), 48–49. Ben-Gurion elaborated on such ideas elsewhere; see Anita Shapira, "Ben-Gurion and the Bible: The Forging of an Historical Narrative?" *Middle Eastern Studies* 33 (1997), 658.
43. Levenson, *Making*, 123.

Bibliography

PRIMARY SOURCES

Manuscripts

Anonymous. "Supercommentary on Rashi." In Leeuwarden, Provinciale Bibliotheek van Friesland, MS B.A. Fr. 19.

Anonymous. "Supercommentary on Rashi." In New York, Jewish Theological Seminary, MS Lutski 801.

Anonymous. "Supercommentary on Rashi." In New York, Jewish Theological Seminary, MS Lutski 802.

Anonymous. "Supercommentary on Rashi." In Warsaw, Jewish Historical Institute, MS 204.

Anonymous. "Supercommentary on Rashi." In Zurich, Zentralbibliothek, MS Heid. 26.

Anonymous. "Torah Commentary." In Moscow, Russian State Library, MS Guenzburg 265.

Ashkenazi, Eleazar. *Ṣafenat pa'neaḥ*. In Moscow, Russian State Military Archive, MS 707/3/6 (II:8).

Cambridge, University Library, MS Add. 377.3.

Ibn Gabbai, Moses. *'Eved shelomo*. Bodleian Library, MS Hunt. Don. 25.

Ibn Shoshan, Joseph. *Ḥazur ve-shoshan*. Oxford, Bodleian Library, MS Opp. Add. fol. 38.

Isserlein, Israel. *Be'urei maharai 'al ha-torah*. Parma, Biblioteca Palatina, MS 2382.

Kirimi, Abraham. *Sefat 'emet*. Bodleian Library, MS Opp. Add., fol. 45.

Leipzig, Universitätsbibliothek, MS B.H.1 (available at "AlHaTorah.org Rashi Project." Edited by Aviva Novetsky. http://alhatorah.org/Commentators:Rashi_Leipzig_1.)

Levi ben Avraham, *Livyat ḥen*. Munich, Bayerische Staatsbibliothek, MS Cod. hebr. 58.

Sefer 'alilot devarim. London, MS Montifiore 266.

Main Editions of Rashi's Commentary Used

Ḥamishah ḥumshei torah: rashi ha-shalem. 7 vols. to date. Jerusalem: Ariel, 1986.

Miqra'ot gedolot ha-keter: Sefer Bemidbar, edited by Menachem Cohen. 2 vols. Ramat-Gan: Bar-Ilan University Press, 2011.

Miqra'ot gedolot ha-keter: Sefer Bereshit, edited by Menachem Cohen. 2 vols. Ramat-Gan: Bar-Ilan University Press, 1993.

Miqra'ot gedolot ha-keter: Sefer Devarim, edited by Menachem Cohen. Ramat-Gan: Bar-Ilan University Press, 2011.

Miqra'ot gedolot ha-keter: Sefer Shemot, edited by Menachem Cohen. 2 vols. Ramat-Gan: Bar-Ilan University Press, 2007–2012.

Miqra'ot gedolot ha-keter: Sefer Vayyiqra, edited by Menachem Cohen. Ramat-Gan: Bar-Ilan University Press, 2013.

OTHER PRIMARY SOURCES

Aaron ben Elijah. *Sefer keter torah*. 5 vols. in 1. Gözleve (Eupatoria), 1867. Reprinted Ramleh, Israel, 1972.

Aaron ben Yosi. *Sefer ha-gan*. Edited by Yehiel M. Orlian. Jerusalem: Mosad Harav Kuk, 2009.

Abarbanel, Isaac. *Perush 'al ha-torah*. 3 vols. Jerusalem: Benei Arabel, 1964.

Abarbanel, Isaac. *Perush 'al nevi'im 'aḥaronim*. Jerusalem: Benei Arabel, 1979.

Abarbanel, Isaac. *Perush 'al nevi'im rishonim*. Jerusalem: Torah ve-Daat, 1955.

Abarbanel, Isaac. *Yeshu'ot meshiḥo*. Königsberg, 1861.

Aboulrabi, Aaron. [*Commentary on the Torah / Supercommentary on Rashi*]. In *Perushim le-rashi*. Constantinople, 1525[?].

Abraham ben David. *Sifra devei rav hu sefer torat kohanim . . . 'im perush . . . / rabenu 'Avraham ben David*. New York: Om, 1947.

Abraham ben ha-Rambam. *Perush rabbenu 'Avraham ben ha-rambam 'al bereshit u-shemot*. Edited by Ephraim Wiesenberg. Letchworth: Rabbi S. D. Sassoon, 1959.

Abrahams, Israel, ed. *Hebrew Ethical Wills*. 2 vols. 1926. Reprint 2 vols. in 1. Philadelphia: Jewish Publication Society, 1976.

Abulafia, Meir Halevi. *Ḥiddushei ha-ramah 'al masekhet sanhedrin*. New York: Hotsa'at H.Y.L, 1953.

Agnon, S. Y. *A City and Its Fullness*. Edited by Alan Mintz and Jeffrey Sacks. Jerusalem: Toby, 2016.

Almosnino, Samuel. *Perush le-perush rashi me-ha-rav ha-gadol rabbi Shemu'el 'Almosnino*. Edited by Moshe Filip. Petah Tikvah: Filip, 1998.

Anatoli, Jacob. *Malmad ha-talmidim*. Edited by L. Silbermann. Lyck, Prussia [now Ełk, Poland], 1866.

Ashkenazi, Eleazar. *Ṣafenat pa'neaḥ*. Edited by Shlomo Rappaport. Johannesburg: Kayor, 1965.

Ashkenazi, Saul Hakohen. *She'elot u-teshuvot Sha'ul Hakohen*. Venice, 1574. Photo offset, Jerusalem, 1966.

Astruc, Anselm. *Midreshei ha-torah*. Edited by Shimon Eppenstein. Berlin, 1899.

Bahya ben Asher. *Be'ur 'al ha-torah*. Edited by Hayyim D. Chavel. 3 vols. Jerusalem: Mosad Harav Kuk, 1966.

Bar Sheshet, Isaac. *She'elot u-teshuvot le-rabenu Yiṣḥaq bar Sheshet*. Edited by David Metzger. 2 vols. Jerusalem: Mekhon Yerushalayim, 1993.

Bass, Shabbetai. *Siftei ḥakhamim*. In *'Oṣar perushim 'al ha-torah*. 2 vols. Jerusalem: Divrei Ḥakhamim, 1958.

Ben Adret, Solomon. *Teshuvot ha-rashba' ha-meyuḥasot le-ha-ramban*. Tel Aviv: Eshel, 1959.

Ben-Gurion, David. *'Iyyunim ba-tanakh*. Tel Aviv: Am Oved, 1969.

Bokhrat, Abraham. *Sefer zikaron*. Edited by Moshe Filip. Corrected edition. Petah Tikvah: Filip, 1985.

Bonchek, Avigdor. *What's Bothering Rashi?: A Guide to In-Depth Analysis of His Torah Commentary*. 5 vols. Jerusalem: Feldheim, 1997–2002.

Botschko, Shaoul David. *Les lumières de Rachi*. 8 vols. Jerusalem–Paris: A.J. Press / Bibliophane–Daniel Radford / Lichma Diffusion / Etz Hayim, 2004–2012.

Canpanton, Isaac. *Darkhei ha-talmud*. Edited by Yitzhak Lange. Jerusalem: "Shalem" sokhnut le-hafaṣat sefarim, 1980.

Chaikin, Miriam. *Clouds of Glory: Legends and Stories about Bible Times*. New York: Clarion, 1998.

Da Fano, Menachem Azariah. *Gilgulei neshamot*. Jerusalem: Yerid Hasefarim, 1997.

David ben Samuel Halevi. *Divrei david*. Edited by Hayyim D. Chavel. Jerusalem: Mosad Harav Kuk, 1978.

Delmedigo, Joseph Solomon. *Mikhtav 'aḥuz*. In *Melo ḥofnayyim*. Edited by Abraham Geiger, 1–28. Berlin, 1840.

Duran, Profayt. *Ma'aseh 'efod*. Edited by John Friedländer and Jakob Kohn. Vienna, 1865.

Eilenburg, Judah Leib. *Minḥat yehudah*. Lublin, 1609.

Epstein, Barukh Halevi. *Torah temimah*. 5 vols. Vilna, 1902. Photo offset, Tel Aviv: M. & R. Grauer, 1981.

Hakohen, Isaac. *Mattenot 'ani*. Prague, 1604–1608.

Ḥamishah ḥumshei torah 'im perush rashi. Edited by Binyamin S. Moore. Jerusalem / New York: Feldheim, 2002.

Ḥamishah Ḥumshei Torah with Rashi's Commentary, Targum Onkelos, Haftaros and Commentary Anthologized from Classic Rabbinic Texts and the Works of the Lubavitcher Rebbe. Brooklyn, NY: Kol Menachem, 2002.

Ḥamishah qadmonei mefareshei r[abbi] 'Avraham 'ibn 'Ezra. Edited by Haim Kreisel. Beer-Sheva: Ben-Gurion University of the Negev Press, 2017.

Hayot, Zevi Hirsch. *Mavo' ha-talmud*. In *Kol sifrei Maharaṣ Ḥayot*. 2 vols. Jerusalem: Divrei Hakhamim, 1934.

Hayyim ben Bezalel. *Be'er mayyim ḥayyim*. Edited by S. F. Schneebalg. 3 vols. London: Honig, 1964–1971.

Herczeg, Yisrael Isser Zvi, ed. *The Torah with Rashi's Commentary*. 5 vols. Brooklyn, NY: Mesorah, 1999.

Hezekiah ben Manoah. *Ḥizzequni, perushei ha-torah le-rabbenu ḥizqiyah b"r manoaḥ*. Edited by Hayyim D. Chavel. Jerusalem: Mosad Harav Kuk, 1981.

Horowitz, Abraham ben Shabbetai Sheftel. *Yesh noḥalin*. Jerusalem: Chai Waldman, 1993.

Horowitz, Isaac. *Be'er yiṣḥaq*. Edited by Yehudah Cooperman. 2 vols. Jerusalem: Kiryah Ne'emanah, 1967.

Hyde, Thomas, ed., *Catalogus impressorum librorum Bibliothecae Bodlejanae in Academia Oxoniensi*. Oxford, 1674.

Ibn Daud, Abraham. *The Book of Tradition (Sefer Ha-Qabbalah)*. Edited by Gerson D. Cohen. Philadelphia: Jewish Publication Society, 1967.

Ibn Ezra, Abraham. *Perushei ha-torah le-rabbenu 'Avraham 'ibn 'Ezra*. Edited by Asher Weiser. 3 vols. Jerusalem: Mosad Harav Kuk, 1976.

Ibn Ezra, Abraham. *Safah berurah* (partial annotated edition). Edited by Michael Wilensky. In *Devir* 2 (1924): 274–302.

Ibn Ezra, Abraham. *Yesod mora' ve-sod torah*. Edited by Joseph Cohen and Uriel Simon. 2nd rev. and corrected ed. Ramat-Gan: Bar-Ilan University Press, 2007.

Ibn Gabbai, Moses. *'Eved shelomo*. Edited by Moshe Filip. Petah Tikvah: Filip, 2006.

Ibn Janach, Jonah. *Sefer ha-hassagah, hu' Kitāb al-mustalḥaq le-rabbi Yonah 'ibn Janaḥ be-targumo ha-'ivri shel 'Ovadyah ha-sefaradi*. Edited by David Téné, completed by Aharon Maman. Jerusalem: Bialik, 2006

Ibn Janach, Jonah. *Sefer ha-riqmah*. Hebrew translation by Judah Ibn Tibbon. Edited by Michael Wilensky. 2nd ed., 2 vols. Jerusalem: Akademyah la-Lashon ha-'Ivrit, 1964.

Ibn Kaspi, Joseph. *Maṣrefla-kesef*. In *Mishneh kesef*. Edited by Isaac Last. Cracow: Joseph Fischer, 1905.

Ibn Moskoni, Judah. "Introduction to *'Even ha-'ezer*." Edited by Abraham Berliner. In *'Oṣar ṭov* 2 (= Hebrew appendix to *Magazin für die Wissenschaft des Judenthums* 5) (1878): 1–10.

Ibn Tibbon, Moses. *Kitvei R. Moshe 'ibn Tibbon: Sefer pe'ah; Ma'amar ha-taninim; Perush ha-'azharot le-R. Shelomo 'ibn Gabirol*. Edited by Haim Kreisel, Colette Sirat, and Avraham Yisra'el. Beer-Sheva: Ben-Gurion University of the Negev Press, 2010.

Ibn Tibbon, Samuel. *Perush ha-millot ha-zarot*. In *Moreh nevukhim le-ha-rav Moshe ben Maimon ... be-ha'ataqat ha-rav Shemu'el 'ibn Tibbon 'im 'arba'ah perushim*. Warsaw, 1872. Photo offset, Jerusalem, 1961.

Ibn Verga, Solomon. *Shevet yehudah.* Edited by Azriel Shohat. Jerusalem: Bialik, 1946.

Ibn Yahya, Gedalyah. *Shalshelet ha-qabbalah.* Warsaw: Abraham Kahana, 1902.

Ibn Zarza, Samuel. *Meqor ḥayyim.* Mantua, 1559.

Isaiah di Trani. *Teshuvot ha-ri"d.* Edited by A. J. Wertheimer. Jerusalem: Mekhon ha-talmud ha-yisra'eli ha-shalem, 1967.

Isserlein, Israel. *Be'urei maharai 'al ha-torah.* Edited by Menachem Doitsh. Lakewood, NJ: Mekhon Be'er Ha-Torah, 1996.

Isserles, Moses. "Qarnei re'em." In *Meged yeraḥim,* 2nd fascicle (1855): 59–65.

Jacob ben Shabbetai. *Ḥizquni 'al perush rashi.* Edited by Moshe Filip. Petah Tikvah: Filip, 2009.

Jaffe, Mordechai. *Levush 'orah.* In *'Oṣar perushim 'al ha-torah.* 2 vols. Jerusalem: Divrei Ḥakhamim, 1958.

Joseph ben Moses. *Sefer leqeṭ yosher.* Edited by Jakob Freimann. Berlin: H. Itzkowski, 1902–1904. Photo offset, 2 vols. in 1. Jerusalem: Mekizei Nirdamim, 1964.

Judah ben Eleazar. *Minḥat yehudah: perush la-torah me-'et rabbi Yehudah ben 'Ele'azar mi-rabotenu ba'alei ha-tosafot. Bereshit* vol. 1. Edited by Hazoniel Touitou. Jerusalem: Mosad Harav Kuk, 2012.

Kanisal, Jacob. *Sefer rabbi Ya'aqov Qanisal 'al perush rashi.* Edited by Moshe Filip. Petah Tikvah: Filip, 1998.

Khalatz, Judah. *Mesiaḥ 'illemim.* Edited by Moshe Filip. Petah Tikvah: Filip, 2001.

Kimhi, Joseph. *Sefer ha-galui.* Edited by Henry J. Mathews, 1887. Photo offset, Jerusalem, 1966.

Kirimi, Abraham. "[Introduction to] *Sefat ha-'emet.*" Edited by Abraham Firkovich. *Ha-Karmel* 3 (1863): 53–54.

Komtino, Mordechai. *Perush qadmon 'al sefer moreh nevukhim: be'uro shel rabbi Mordekhai ben 'Eli'ezer Komṭino 'al moreh ha-nevukhim la-rambam.* Edited by Esti Eisenman and Dov Schwartz. Ramat-Gan: Bar-Ilan University Press, 2016.

Komtino, Mordechai. *Perush qadmon 'al sefer yesod mora': "be'ur yesod mora'" le-r[abbi] Mordekhai ben 'Eli'ezer Komṭino.* Edited by Dov Schwartz. Ramat-Gan: Bar-Ilan University Press, 2010.

Lehmann, Manfred R. *Perush rashi 'al ha-torah.* New York: Manfred and Anne Lehmann Foundation, 1981.

Levi ben Gershom. *Commentary on Song of Songs [by] Levi Ben Gershom (Gersonides).* Translated, with an introduction and annotations by Menachem Kellner. New Haven, CT: Yale University Press, 1998.

Levinas, Emmanuel. "La lettre ouverte." *Rencontres. Chrétiens et Juifs* 51 (1977): 118–20.

Little Midrash Says: A Digest of the Weekly Torah-Portion based on Rashi, Rishonim and Midrashim Adapted for Junior Readers and to Read Aloud. Brooklyn, NY: Benei Yakov, 1986.

Loew, Judah. *Gevurot 'adonai.* London: L. Honig, 1964.

Loew, Judah. *Ḥumash gur 'aryeh ha-shalem.* Edited by Joshua Hartman. 9 vols. Jerusalem: Mekhon Yerushalayim, 1989.

Luria, Solomon. *Yam shel shelomo.* Jerusalem: Mekhon Mishnat David, 1996.

Luria, Solomon. *Yeri'ot shelomo*. Prague, 1609.

Luzzatto, Samuel David. *'Igerot Shadal*. Edited by Shealtiel Ayzik Gräber, 9 vols. (Cracow, [1882–1894]).

Maarsen, Isaac. *Parshandata: the Commentary of Raschi on the Prophets and Hagiographs*. 3 vols. Amsterdam and Jerusalem, 1930–36.

Maimonides, Moses. *The Guide of the Perplexed*. Translated by Shlomo Pines. 2 vols. Chicago: Chicago University Press, 1963.

Maimonides, Moses. *Haqdamot ha-rambam la-mishnah*. Edited by Yitzhak Shailat. Jerusalem: Hoza'at Shailat, 1996.

Maimonides, Moses. *'Iggerot ha-rambam*. Edited by Yitzhaq Shailat. 2 vols. Jerusalem: Ma'aliyot, 1987–1988.

Maimonides, Moses. *Mishneh Torah: The Book of Knowledge by Maimonides*. Edited by Moses Hyamson. New York: Bloch, 1937.

Maimonides, Moses. *Moreh nevukhim le-ha-rav Moshe ben Maimon ... be-ha'ataqat ha-rav Shemu'el 'ibn Tibbon 'im 'arba'ah perushim*. Warsaw 1872. Reprint, Jerusalem, 1961.

Meltzer, Samson. *Shirot u-baladot*. Tel Aviv: Devir, 1959.

Menahem ben Zerah. *Ṣedah la-derekh*. Warsaw, 1880.

Michael ben Reuven (pseudonym), ed. "Sefer 'alilot devarim." *Ozar Nechmad. Briefe und Abhandlungen jüdische Literatur betreffend* 4 (1863): 177–214.

Miqra'ot gedolot ha-keter: Ḥamesh megillot. Edited by Menachem Cohen. Ramat-Gan: Bar-Ilan University Press, 2012.

Miqra'ot gedolot ha-keter. Sefer Tehilim. Edited by Menachem Cohen. 2 vols. Ramat-Gan: Bar-Ilan University Press, 2003.

Miqra'ot gedolot ha-keter: Sefer Yisha'yahu. Edited by Menachem Cohen. Ramat-Gan: Bar-Ilan University, 1996.

Mizrahi, Elijah. *Ḥumash ha-re'em*. Edited by Moshe Filip. 6 vols. Petah-Tikvah: Filip, 1994.

Mizrahi, Elijah. *Perush rashi*. Venice, 1527.

Mizrahi, Elijah. *She'elot u-teshuvot R. 'Eliyahu Mizraḥi*. Jerusalem: Hotsa'at sefarim "Darom," 1937.

Moses of Coucy. *Sefer miṣvot gadol*. Edited by Alter P. Farber. 2 vols. Jerusalem, 2001.

Nissim of Marseille. *Ma'aseh nissim: perush la-torah le-r[abbi] Nissim ben r[abbi] Mosheh mi-marseille*. Edited by Haim Kreisel. Jerusalem: Mekizei Nirdamim, 2000.

'Oṣar perushim 'al ha-torah. 2 vols. Jerusalem: Divrei Ḥakhamim, 1958.

Pentateuch with Targum Onkelos, Haphtaroth and Rashi's Commentary. Edited by M. Rosenbaum and A. M. Silbermann. 5 vols. Jerusalem: Silbermann Family, 1934.

Perushei rashi 'al ha-torah. Edited by Hayyim D. Chavel. Jerusalem: Mosad Harav Kuk, 1990.

Perushim le-rashi. Constantinople, 1525[?].

Rosenzweig, Franz. *On Jewish Learning.* Edited by Nahum N. Glatzer. New York: Schocken, 1955.

Samuel ben Abraham Saporta. "Katav 'asher shalaḥ ha-rav r[abbi] Shemu'el be-r[abbi] 'Avraham." In "Milḥemet ha-dat," edited by Shlomo Zalman Chaim Halberstam. *Yeshurun* 8 (1872–1875): 125–55.

Samuel ben Meir. *Perush ha-rashbam 'al ha-torah.* Edited by Meir (Martin) Lockshin. 2 vols. Jerusalem: Chorev, 2009.

Scherman, Nosson, ed. *The Complete ArtScroll Siddur.* New York: Mesorah Publications, 1990.

Schneerson, Menachem M. *Studies in Rashi: From the Teachings of the Lubavitcher Rebbe, Menachem M. Schneerson.* Translated by Y. Eliezer Danzinger. Brooklyn, NY: Kehot, 2011.

Shapira, Kalonymus Kalmish. *Sefer 'esh qodesh.* Jerusalem: Va'ad Hasidei Piaseznah, 1960.

Shaprut, Shem Tov ben. *Pardes rimmonim.* Sabbioneta, 1554.

Shemaryah ha-Ikriti. *'Elef ha-magen: perush 'al 'aggadot masekhet megillah le-R. Shemaryah ben 'Eliyahu ha-iqriṭi.* Edited by Aaron Ahrend. Jerusalem: Mekizei Nirdamim, 2003.

Slonik, Jacob ben Benjamin. *Naḥalat ya'aqov.* Edited by Mordechai Cooperman. 3 vols. Jerusalem: Michlalah College for Women, 1993.

Spinoza, Benedict de. *Theologico-Political Treatise.* In *Chief Works of Benedict de Spinoza,* translated by R.H.M Elwes. New York: Dover, 1951.

Taqanot qandi'ah ve-zikhronoteha. Edited by Elias S. Hartom and M.D.A Cassuto. Jerusalem: Mekize Nirdamim, 1943.

Theodor, J., and Ch. Albeck, eds. *Midrash Bereshit Rabbah.* 2nd ed. 3 vols. Jerusalem: Shalem, 1996.

Tosafot ha-shalem. Edited by Jacob Gellis. 9 vols. Jerusalem: Machon Harry Fischel, 1982.

Yedayah ben Avraham Ha-Penini (Bedersi). *Ketav ha-hitnaṣṣelut.* In Solomon ben Adret, *She'elot u-teshuvot r[abbi] Shlomo ben 'Adret.* Edited by Aaron Zaleznik. 7 vols. 1:118. Jerusalem: Mekhon Or ha-Mizrah, 1996.

Wiesel, Elie. *Rashi.* New York: Schocken, 2009.

Zornberg, Avivah Gottlieb. *Genesis: The Beginning of Desire.* Philadelphia: Jewish Publication Society, 1995.

Zornberg, Avivah Gottlieb. *The Particulars of Rapture: Reflections on Exodus.* New York: Doubleday, 2001.

SECONDARY SOURCES

Abecassis, Deborah. "Reconstructing Rashi's Commentary on Genesis from Citations in the Torah Commentaries of the Tosafot." PhD dissertation, McGill University, 1999.

Abrams, Daniel. *Kabbalistic Manuscripts and Textual Theory: Methodologies of Textual Scholarship and Editorial Practice in the Study of Jewish Mysticism*. Jerusalem: Magnes, 2010.

Abulafia, David. "Le comunità di Sicilia dagli arabi all'espulsione." In *Storia d'Italia, Annali 11/1: Gli ebrei in Italia*, edited by Corrado Vivanti, 47–82. Turin: Einaudi, 1996.

Abulafia, David. "The Jews of Sicily under the Norman and Hohenstaufen Rulers." In *Ebrei e Sicilia*, edited by Nicolò Bucaria et al., 69–92. Palermo: Flaccovio Editore, 2002.

Ahrend, Aaron. "'Al parshanut ha-'aḥaronim le-ferush rashi la-talmud." In *Rashi u-vet midrasho*, edited by Avinoam Cohen, 11–26. Ramat-Gan: Bar-Ilan University Press, 2013.

Ahrend, Aaron. "Perush megillat 'ester le-r[abbi] Shemaryah ben 'Eliyah ha-'iqriṭi." In *Meḥqarim be-miqra' uve-ḥinukh mugashim le-prof' Moshe 'Ahrend*, edited by Dov Rappel, 33–52. Jerusalem: Touro College, 1996.

Akhiezer, Golda. "Byzantine Karaism in the Eleventh to Fifteenth Centuries." In *Jews in Byzantium: Dialectics of Minority and Majority Cultures*, edited by Robert Bonfil et al., 723–61. Leiden: Brill, 2012.

Akinsha, Konstantin. *Manuscripts and Archival Documents of the Vienna Jewish Community held in Russian Collections: Catalogue*. Moscow: Rudomino, 2006.

Alfonso, Esperanza. "In Between Cultures: An Anonymous Commentary on the Book of Proverbs from Iberia." *Journal of Jewish Studies* 64 (2013): 119–56.

Allony, Nehemiah. *Ha-sifriyah ha-yehudit be-yemei ha-benayim: reshimot sefarim mi-genizat qahir*, edited by Miriam Frenkel and Haggai Ben-Shammai. Jerusalem: Mekhon Ben-Zvi, 2006.

Alter, Robert. *The Five Books of Moses: A Translation with Commentary*. New York: W.W. Norton, 2004.

Anderson, Gary A. *The Genesis of Perfection: Adam and Eve in Jewish and Christian Imagination*. Louisville, KY: Westminster John Knox Press, 2001.

Aptowitzer, V. "The Rewarding and Punishing of Animals and Inanimate Objects: On the Aggadic View of the World." *Hebrew Union College Annual* 3 (1926): 117–55.

Arbel, Benjamin. "Introduction [to special issue on "Minorities in Colonial Settings: The Jews in Venice's Hellenic Territories (15th-18th Centuries)]." *Mediterranean Historical Review* 27, no. 2 (2012): 117–28.

Arbel, Benjamin. "Notes on the Delmedigo of Candia." In *Non solo verso Oriente: Studi sull'ebraismo in onore di Piercesare Ioly Zorattini*, edited by Maddalena Del Bianco Cotrozzi, Riccardo Di Segni, and Marcello Massenzio. 2 vols., 2:119–30. Florence: Leo S. Olschki editore, 2014.

Ariel, Yaakov. "*Wissenschaft des Judentums* Comes to America: Kaufmann Kohler's Scholarly Projects and Jewish-Christian Relations." In *Die Entdeckung des*

Christentums in der Wissenschaft des Judentums, edited by Görge K. Hasselhoff, 165–82. Berlin: De Gruyter, 2010.

Arnold, Bill T., and John H. Choi. *A Guide to Biblical Hebrew Syntax*. New York: Cambridge University Press, 2003.

Aron, Raymond. *Main Currents in Sociological Thought*. Vol. 1: *Montesquieu, Comte, Marx, Toqueville, and the Sociologists and the Revolution of 1848*, translated by Richard Howard and Helen Weaver. Garden City, NY: Doubleday, Anchor Books, 1968.

Ashley, Kathleen, and Véronique Plesch. "The Cultural Processes of 'Appropriation'." *Journal of Medieval and Early Modern Studies* 32 (2002): 1–15.

Ashtor, E[liyahu]. "Palermitan Jewry in the Fifteenth Century." *Hebrew Union College Annual* 50 (1979): 219–51.

Assaf, Simha. *Meqorot le-toledot ha-ḥinukh be-yisra'el*. Edited by Shmuel Glick. 6 vols. New York and Jerusalem: Jewish Theological Seminary of America, 2002.

Attia, Élodie. "Targum's Layout in Ashkenazic Manuscripts: Preliminary Methodological Observations." In *A Jewish Targum in a Christian World*, edited by Alberdina Houtman, Eveline van Staalduine-Sulman, and Hans-Martin Kim, 99–122. Leiden: Brill, 2014.

Attias, Jean-Christophe. *Ha-perush ke-di'alog: Mordekhai ben 'Eli'ezer Komṭino 'al ha-torah*, translated by Yisrael Meir. Jerusalem: Magnes, 2007. (French original: *Le commentaire biblique: Mordekhai Komtino ou l'herméneutique du dialogue*. [Paris: Éditions du Cerf, 1991].)

Attias, Jean-Christophe. "Intellectual Leadership: Rabbanite-Karaite Relations in Constantinople as Seen Through the Works and Activity of Mordekhai Comtino in the Fifteenth-Century." In *Ottoman and Turkish Jewry: Community and Leadership*, edited by Aron Rodrigue, 67–86. Bloomington: Indiana University Press, 1992.

Attias, Jean-Christophe. "L'Âme et la Clef: De l'introduction comme genre littéraire dans la production exégètique du judaïsme médiéval." In *Entrer en matière: les prologues*, edited by Jean-Daniel Dubois and Bernard Roussel, 337–58. Paris: Cerf, 1998.

Auerbach, Erich. *Mimesis: The Representation of Reality in Western Literature*, translated by Willard R. Trask. Princeton, NJ: Princeton University Press, 1953.

Avioz, Michael. "The Da'at Mikra Commentary Series: Between Tradition and Criticism." *Jewish Bible Quarterly* 34 (2006): 226–36.

Bacher, Wilhelm. "L'exégèse biblique dans le Zohar." *Revue des études juives* 22 (1891), 33–46, 219–29.

Bacher, Wilhelm. "Raschi und Maimuni." *Monatsschrift für Geschichte und Wissenschaft des Judentums* 49 (1905): 1–11.

Baer, Yitzhak (Fritz). *Die Juden im christlichen Spanien: Urkunden und Regesten*. 2 vols. Berlin: Akademie-Verlag, 1929–1936.

Baer, Yitzhak. *A History of the Jews in Christian Spain*, translated by Louis Schoffman. 2 vols. Philadelphia: Jewish Publication Society, 1961–1966.

Banitt, Menahem. *Rashi: Interpreter of the Biblical Letter*. Tel Aviv: Chaim Rosenberg School of Jewish Studies, 1985.

Bar-Ilan, Meir. "Ha-torah ha-ketuvah 'al ha-'avanim be-har 'eval." *Meḥqerei yehudah ve-shomron* 2 (1993): 29–42.

Bar-Ilan, Meir. "Miflaṣot vi-yeṣurim dimyoniyim ba-'aggadah ha-yehudit ha-'atiqah." *Maḥanayim* 7 (1994): 104–13.

Bar-Levav, Avriel. "The Religious Order of Jewish Books: Structuring Hebrew Knowledge in Amsterdam." In *Mapping Jewish Amsterdam: The Early Modern Perspective (Dedicated to Yosef Kaplan on the Occasion of His Retirement) (= Studia Rosenthaliana* 44), edited by Shlomo Berger, Emile G. L. Schrijver, and Irene Zwiep, 1–27. Leuven: Peeters, 2012.

Bar-Levav, Avriel. " 'When I Was Alive': Jewish Ethical Wills as Egodocuments." In *Egodocuments and History: Autobiographical Writing in Its Social Context Since the Middle Ages*, edited by Rudolf Dekker, 45–60. Hilversum: Verloren, 2002.

Barr, James. " 'Determination' and the Definite Article in Biblical Hebrew." *Journal of Semitic Studies* 34 (1989): 307–35.

Barzilay, Isaac. *Yoseph Shlomo Delmedigo (Yashar of Candia): His Life, Works and Times*. Leiden: Brill, 1974.

Becker, Hans-Jürgen. "The Magic of the Name and Palestinian Rabbinic Literature." In *The Talmud Yerushalmi and Graeco-Roman Culture*, edited by Peter Schäfer, 391–407. Tübingen: J.C.B. Mohr, 2002.

Beit-Arié, Malachi. "Additamenta to G. Tamani's Article on Hebrew Manuscripts Copied in Sicily." *Henoch* 15 (1993): 359–61.

Beit-Arié, Malachi. *The Makings of the Medieval Hebrew Book: Studies in Palaeography and Codicology*. Jerusalem: Magnes, 1993.

Beit-Arié, Malachi. "Publication and Reproduction of Literary Texts in Medieval Jewish Civilization: Jewish Scribality and Its Impact on the Texts Transmitted." In *Transmitting Jewish Traditions: Orality, Textuality, and Cultural Diffusion*, edited by Yaakov Elman and Israel Gershoni, 225–47. New Haven, CT: Yale University Press, 2000.

Beit-Arié, Malachi. *Qodiqologyah 'ivrit*. Preprint internet version 9.0 (updated April 2018), edited by Zofia Lasman. http://web.nli.org.il/sites/NLI/Hebrew/collections/manuscripts/hebrewcodicology/Documents/Hebrew-Codicology-continuously-updated-online-version.pdf.

Beit-Arié, Malachi. "Transmission of Texts by Scribes and Copyists: Unconscious and Critical Interferences." *Bulletin of the John Rylands University Library of Manchester* 75 (1993): 33–51.

Bekins, Peter. "Non-Prototypical Uses of the Definite Article in Biblical Hebrew." *Journal of Semitic Studies* 58 (2013): 225–40.

Benbassa, Esther, and Aron Rodrigue. *Sephardi Jewry: A History of the Judeo-Spanish Community, 14th–20th Centuries.* Berkeley: University of California Press, 2000.

Benin, Stephen D. *The Footprints of God: Divine Accommodation in Jewish and Christian Thought.* Albany: SUNY Press, 1993.

Ben-Meir, Rut. "Kavim li-demuto shel moshe rabennu be-farshanuto shel ha-ramban." In *'Adam le-'adam: meḥqarim be-filosofyah yehudit bi-yemei ha-benayim u-va-'et ha-ḥadashah, mugashim le-prof' Ze'ev Harvi 'al yedei talmidav bi-melot lo shiv'im,* edited by Shemuel Vigodah et al., 162–83. Jerusalem: Magnes, 2016.

Ben-Menahem, Hanina. "Doubt, Choice and Conviction: A Comparison of the Kim Li Doctrine and Probabilism." *Jewish Law Annual* 14 (2003): 3–28.

Bensch, Stephen P. *Barcelona and Its Rulers, 1096–1291.* Cambridge: Cambridge University Press, 1995.

Ben-Shalom, Ram. *Yehudei provans: renesans be-ṣel ha-kenesiyah.* Raanana: Open University of Israel, 2017.

Ben-Simon, Yisrael. "Mishnato ha-filosofit ve-ha-'alegorit shel R. Ya'aqov 'Anatoli ve-hashpa'atah 'al ha-hagut ve-ha-'alegoryah ha-yehudit be-me'ot ha-13 ve-ha-14." PhD dissertation, Haifa University, 2010.

Berger, David. "Judaism and General Culture in Medieval and Early Modern Times." In *Judaism's Encounter With Other Cultures: Rejection or Integration,* edited by Jacob J. Schacter, 57–141. Northvale, NJ: J. Aronson, 1997.

Berger, David. "Miracles and the Natural Order in Naḥmanides." In *Rabbi Moses Naḥmanides (Ramban): Explorations in His Religious and Literary Virtuosity,* edited by Isadore Twersky, 107–28. Cambridge, MA: Harvard University Press, 1983.

Berger, David. "On the Morality of the Patriarchs in Jewish Polemic and Exegesis." In *Understanding Scripture: Explorations of Jewish and Christian Traditions of Interpretation,* edited by Clemens Thoma and Michael Wyschogrod, 49–62. New York: Paulist, 1987.

Berger, David. "Polemic, Exegesis, Philosophy, and Science: On the Tenacity of Ashkenazic Modes of Thought." *Simon Dubnow Institute Yearbook* 8 (2009): 27–39.

Berger, Isaiah. "Rashi be-'aggadat ha-'am." In *Rashi: torato ve-'ishiyuto,* edited by Simon Federbush, 147–79. New York: World Jewish Congress / Jewish Agency of New York, 1958.

Berger, Yitzhak. "*Peshat* and the Authority of *Ḥazal* in the Commentaries of Radak." *AJS Review* 31 (2007): 41–59.

Blenkinsopp, Joseph. "Genesis 12–50." In *The Pentateuch,* edited by Laurence Bright, 130–67. London: Sheed and Ward, 1971.

Blidstein, Gerald J. *Ha-tefilah be-mishnato ha-hilkhatit shel ha-rambam.* Jerusalem: Bialik, 1994.

Blidstein, Gerald J. "In the Shadow of the Mountain: Consent and Coercion at Sinai." *Jewish Political Studies Review* 4 (1992): 41–53.

Blidstein, Moshe. "How Many Pigs Were on Noah's Ark? An Exegetical Encounter on the Nature of Impurity." *Harvard Theological Review* 108 (2015): 448–70.

Bobichon, Philippe. "Quotations, Translations, and Uses of Jewish Texts in Ramon Martí's Pugio fidei." In *The Late Medieval Hebrew Book in the Western Mediterranean: Hebrew Manuscripts and Incunabula in Context*, edited by Javier del Barco, 266–96. Leiden: Brill, 2015.

Bonfil, Robert. *Jewish Life in Renaissance Italy*, translated by Anthony Oldcorn. Berkeley: University of California Press, 1994.

Bonfil, Robert. "Reading in the Jewish Communities of Western Europe in the Middle Ages." In *A History of Reading in the West*, edited by Guglielmo Cavallo and Roger Chartier, translated by Lydia G. Cochrane, 149–78. Amherst: University of Massachusetts Press, 1999.

Bonfil, Reuven (Robert). "Sefer "Alilot devarim': pereq be-toledot ha-hagut ha-yehudit ba-me'ah ha-14." *Eshel Beer-Sheva* 2 (1980): 229–64.

Borýsek, Martin. "The Jews of Venetian Candia: The Challenges of External Influences and Internal Diversity as Reflected in *Takkanot Kandiyah*." *Al-Masāq: Journal of the Medieval Mediterranean* 26 (2014): 241–66.

Bos, Gerrit. "R. Moshe Narboni: Philosopher and Physician, a Critical Analysis of *Sefer Oraḥ Ḥayyim*." *Medieval Encounters* 1 (1995): 219–51.

Bowman, Steven B. "The Jewish Experience in Byzantium." In *The Jewish-Greek Tradition in Antiquity and the Byzantine Empire*, edited by James K. Aitken and James Carleton Paget, 37–53. New York: Cambridge University Press, 2014.

Bowman, Steven B. *The Jews of Byzantium 1204–1453*. Tuscaloosa: University of Alabama Press, 1985.

Boyarin, Daniel. *Ha-'iyyun ha-sefaradi: le-farshanut ha-talmud shel megorashei sefarad.* Jerusalem: Mekhon Ben-Zvi, 1989.

Boyarin, Daniel. "Moslem, Christian, and Jewish Cultural Interaction in Sefardic Talmudic Interpretation." *Review of Rabbinic Judaism* 5 (2002): 1–33.

Boyarin, Daniel. *A Traveling Homeland: The Babylonian Talmud as Diaspora.* Philadelphia: University of Pennsylvania Press, 2015.

Brahami, Claude. "Le manuscrit hébreu 167 de la bibliothèque nationale de Paris contient-il une copie du Ḥīzqūnī?" *Revue des études juives* 127 (1968): 213–21.

Bresc, Henri. *Livre et société en Sicile (1299–1499)*. Palermo: [s.n.], 1971.

Brettler, Marc Zvi, and Edward Breuer. "Jewish Readings of the Bible." In *From 1750 to the Present*. Vol. 4 of *The New Cambridge History of the Bible*, edited by John Riches, 285–313. Cambridge: Cambridge University Press, 2015.

Breuer, Edward. *The Limits of Enlightenment: Jews, Germans, and the Eighteenth-Century Study of Scripture*. Cambridge, MA: Harvard University Center for Jewish Studies, 1996.

Breuer, Edward, trans. *Moses Mendelssohn's Hebrew Writings*. Introduced and annotated by Edward Breuer and David Sorkin. New Haven, CT: Yale University Press, 2018.

Breuer, Mordechai. *'Ohalei torah: ha-yeshivah, tavnitah ve-toledoteha.* Jerusalem: Zalman Shazar, 2003.

Breuer, Mordechai. "Min'u benekhem min ha-higayon." In *Mikhtam le-david: sefer zikaron ha-rav David 'Oqs*, edited by Yitzhak D. Gilat and Eliezer Stern, 242–61. Ramat-Gan: Bar-Ilan Univeristy Press, 1978.

Brin, Gershon. "Ben r[abbi] Yesha'yah mi-ṭrani la-parshanim ha-bizanṭiyim ha-qedumin." *Beit Mikra* 59 (2014): 60–75.

Brin, Gershon. *Re'u'el va-ḥaverav: parshanim yehudiyim mi-bizanṭyon mi-sevivot ha-me'ah ha-'asirit la-sefirah.* Tel-Aviv: Haim Rubin Tel Aviv University Press, 2012.

Brin, Gershon. "Shimushei r[abbi] Meyuḥas b[e]-r[abbi] 'Eliyahu bi-khelalei ha-parshanut she-nusḥu bi-leshon 'derekh ha-miqra'." *Beit Mikra* 58 (2013): 117–29.

Brody, Robert. "Ha-musag ha-ḥamaqmaq shel ha-qanon." In *Ha-qanon ha-samui min ha-'ayin: ḥiqrei qanon u-genizah*, edited by Menahem Ben-Sasson et al., 11–23. Jerusalem: Magnes, 2010.

Burnett, Charles. "The Coherence of the Arabic-Latin Translation Programme in Toledo in the Twelfth Century." *Science in Context* 14 (2001): 249–88.

Busi, Giulio. *Libri e scrittori nella roma ebraica del Medioevo.* Rimini: Luisè, 1990.

Buzzetti, Dino, and Peter Denley. "Maestri e scolari bolognesi nel tardo Medioevo: Per l'edizione elettronica delle fonti." In *La storia delle università italiane*, edited by L. Sitran Rea, 197–220. [Bologna]: LINT, 1996.

Camille, Michael. "Obscenity under Erasure: Censorship in Medieval Illuminated Manuscripts." In *Obscenity: Social Control and Artistic Creation in the European Middle Ages*, edited by Jan M. Ziolkowski, 139–54. Leiden: Brill, 1998.

Carruthers, Mary. *The Book of Memory: A Study of Memory in Medieval Culture.* 2nd ed. Cambridge: Cambridge University Press, 2008.

Catlos, Brian A. "Why the Mediterranean?" In *Can We Talk Mediterranean? Conversations on an Emerging Field in Medieval and Early Modern Studies*, edited by Brian A. Catlos and Sharon Kinoshita, 1–18. Cham, Switzerland: Palgrave Macmillan, 2017.

Celenza, Christopher S. "Creating Canons in Fifteenth-Century Ferrara: Angelo Decembrio's *De politia litterari*, 1.10." *Renaissance Quarterly* 57 (2004): 43–98.

Chartier, Roger. *Inscription and Erasure: Literature and Written Culture from the Eleventh to the Eighteenth Century*, translated by Arthur Goldhammer. Philadelphia: University of Pennsylvania Press, 2007.

Chazan, Robert. *The Jews of Medieval Western Christendom, 1000–1500.* Cambridge: Cambridge University Press, 2006.

Chernick, Michael. *A Great Voice That Did Not Cease: The Growth of the Rabbinic Canon and Its Interpretation.* Cincinatti, OH: Hebrew Union College Press, 2009.

Chiesa, Bruno, Meir Bar-Asher, and Sarah Stroumsa, eds. *Davar davur 'al 'ofa-nav: meḥqarim be-farshanut ha-miqra' ve-ha-qur'an bi-yemei ha-benayim mugashim le-Ḥaggai ben Shammai.* Jerusalem: Mekhon Ben-Zvi, 2007.

Coetzee, J. M. "What Is a Classic: A Lecture." In *Stranger Shores: Literary Essays, 1986–1999*, 1–16. New York: Viking, 2001.

Cohen, Barak Shlomo. "'May You Live to One Hundred and Twenty': The Extraordinary Life-Span of Several Babylonian Amoraim According to Rashi." *Review of Rabbinic Judaism* 10 (2007): 221–35.

Cohen, Gerson D. "Esau as Symbol in Early Medieval Thought." In *Jewish Medieval and Renaissance Studies*, edited by Alexander Altmann, 19–48. Cambridge, MA: Harvard University Press, 1967.

Cohen, Jeremy. *A Historian in Exile: Solomon Ibn Verga, Shevet Yehudah, and the Jewish-Christian Encounter*. Philadelphia: University of Pennsylvania Press, 2017.

Cohen, Mordechai Z. " 'The Best of Poetry...': Literary Approaches to the Bible in the Spanish *Peshat* Tradition." *Torah U-Madda Journal* 6 (1995–96): 15–57.

Cohen, Mordechai Z. "Emergence of the Rule of Peshat in Jewish Bible Exegesis." In *Interpreting Scriptures in Judaism, Christianity and Islam: Overlapping Inquiries*, edited by Mordechai Z. Cohen and Adele Berlin, 204–24. Cambridge: Cambridge University Press, 2016.

Cohen, Mordechai Z. "Gedolim ḥiqrei lev: regishut pesikhologit be-ferushei ramban la-torah u-le-'iyov." In *Teshurah le-'Amos: 'asupat meḥqarim be-farshanut ha-miqra' mugeshet le-'Amos Ḥakham*, edited by Moshe Bar-Asher, Noah Hakham, and Yosef Ofer, 213–33. Alon Shevut: Tevunot, 2007.

Cohen, Mordechai Z. "Hirhurim 'al ḥeqer ha-munaḥ 'peshuṭo shel miqra'' bi-teḥilat ha-me'ah ha-'esrim ve-'aḥat." In *'Leyashev peshuṭo shel miqra': 'asupat meḥqarim be-farshanut ha-miqra'*, edited by Eran Viezel and Sara Japhet, 5–58. Jerusalem: Bialik / Mandel Institute, 2011.

Cohen, Mordechai Z. "Nahmanides' Four Senses of Scriptural Signification: Jewish and Christian Contexts." In *Entangled Histories: Knowledge, Authority, and Jewish Culture in the Thirteenth Century*, edited by Elisheva Baumgarten, Ruth Mazo Karras, and Katelyn Mesler, 38–58. Philadelphia: University of Pennsylvania Press, 2017.

Cohen, Mordechai Z. "A New Perspective on Rashi of Troyes in Light of Bruno the Carthusian: Exploring Jewish and Christian Bible Interpretation in Eleventh-Century Northern France." *Viator* 48 (2017): 39–86.

Cohen, Mordechai Z. *Opening the Gates of Interpretation: Maimonides' Biblical Hermeneutics in Light of His Geonic-Andalusian Heritage and Muslim Milieu*. Leiden: Brill, 2011.

Cohen, Mordechai Z. " 'Reproducing the Text': Nehama Leibowitz on Traditional Biblical Interpretation (*Parshanut Ha-Mikra*) in Light of Ludwig Strauss's Literary Theory." *Torah U-Madda Journal* 17 (2016–17): 1–34.

Cohen, Mordechai Z. "The Qimhi Family." In *Hebrew Bible, Old Testament: The History of Its Interpretation*, edited by Magne Sæbø. Vol. I/2 of *From the Beginnings to the Middle Ages*. Part 2: *The Middle Ages*, 282–301. Göttingen: Vandenhoeck & Ruprecht, 1996.

Cohen, Mordechai Z. *Three Approaches to Biblical Metaphor: From Abraham Ibn Ezra and Maimonides to David Kimhi*. Leiden: Brill, 2003.

Cohen, Shaye J. D. "Does Rashi's Torah Commentary Respond to Christianity? A Comparison of Rashi with Rashbam and Bekhor Shor." In *The Idea of Biblical Interpretation: Essays in Honor of James L. Kugel*, edited by Hindy Najman and Judith H. Newman, 449–72. Leiden: Brill, 2004.

Cohen, Yonatan. "La-meyalledot ha-'ivriyot." *Lešonenu* 55 (1991): 295–97.

Colafemmina, Cesare. *The Jews in Calabria*. Leiden: Brill, 2012.

Cooper, Alan. "The Plain Sense of Exodus 23:5." *Hebrew Union College Annual* 59 (1988): 1–22.

Copeland, Rita. *Rhetoric, Hermeneutics, and Translation in the Middle Ages: Academic Traditions and Vernacular Texts*. Cambridge: Cambridge University Press, 1991.

Corazzol, Giacomo. "La vita culturale ebraica a Candia nei secoli XIV-XVI: l'impatto dell'immigrazione sulla cultura della comunità locale." PhD dissertation, University of Bologna, 2015.

Cranny-Francis, Anne, Wendy Waring, Pam Stavropoulos, and Pam Kirkby. *Gender Studies: Terms and Debates*. New York: Palgrave Macmillan, 2003.

Croatto, J. Severino. "'Abrek 'Intendant' dans Gén. XLI 41, 43." *Vetus Testamentum* 16 (1966): 113–15.

Cuffel, Alexandra. "Call and Response: European Jewish Emigration to Egypt and Palestine in the Middle Ages." *Jewish Quarterly Review* 90 (1999): 61–102.

D'Amico, John F. *Theory and Practice in Renaissance Textual Criticism: Beatus Rhenanus Between Conjecture and History*. Berkeley: University of California Press, 1988.

Dan, Joseph. "Ashkenazic Hasidism and the Maimonidean Controversy." *Maimonidean Studies* 3 (1992–93): 29–47.

Dan, Joseph. *The 'Unique Cherub' Circle: A School of Mystics and Esoterics in Medieval Germany*. Tübingen: Mohr Siebeck, 1999.

Davidovitch, Eliezer. "Be'ur r[abbi] Yish'ayah ben Meir." In *Ḥamishah qadmonei mefareshei r[abbi] 'Avraham 'ibn 'Ezra*, edited by Haim Kreisel, 65–86. Beer-Sheva: Ben-Gurion University of the Negev Press, 2017.

Davidson, Herbert A. *Moses Maimonides: The Man and His Works*. New York: Oxford University Press, 2005.

Davis, Joseph M. "Philosophy, Dogma, and Exegesis in Medieval Ashkenazic Judaism: The Evidence of *Sefer Hadrat Qodesh*." *AJS Review* 18 (1993): 195–222.

Davis, Joseph. "The Reception of the *Shulḥan 'Arukh* and the Formation of Ashkenazic Jewish Identity." *AJS Review* 26 (2002): 251–76.

De Lange, Nicholas. "Abraham Ibn Ezra and Byzantium." In *Abraham ibn Ezra y su tiempo*, edited by Fernando Díaz Esteban, 181–92. Madrid: Asociación Española de Orientalistas, 1990.

De Lange, Nicholas. *Greek Jewish Texts from the Cairo Geniza.* Tübingen: J.C.B. Mohr, 1996.

De Lange, Nicholas. "Hebrew/Greek Manuscripts: Some Notes." *Journal of Jewish Studies* 46 (1995): 262–79.

De Lange, Nicholas. "Hebrew Scholarship in Byzantium." In *Hebrew Scholarship and the Medieval World,* edited by Nicholas de Lange, 23–37. New York: Cambridge University Press, 2001.

De Lange, Nicholas. *Japheth in the Tents of Shem: Greek Bible Translations in Byzantine Judaism.* Tübingen: Mohr Siebeck, 2015.

De Visscher, Eva. *Reading the Rabbis: Christian Hebraism in the Works of Herbert of Bosham.* Leiden: Brill, 2014.

Del Punta, Francesco. "The Genre of Commentaries in the Middle Ages and Its Relation to the Nature and Originality of Medieval Thought." In *Was ist Philosophie Im Mittelalter? (= Miscellanea Mediaevalia 26),* edited by Jan A. Aertsen and Andreas Speer, 138–51. Berlin: De Gruyter, 1998.

Derrida, Jacques. "The Law of Genre," translated by Avita Ronell. *Critical Inquiry* 7 (1980): 51–81.

Diamond, James A. *Maimonides and the Shaping of the Jewish Canon.* New York: Cambridge University Press, 2014.

Diamond, James A. "Nahmanides and Rashi on the One Flesh of Conjugal Union: Lovemaking vs. Duty." *Harvard Theological Review* 102 (2009): 193–224.

Diggins, John Patrick. "The Oyster and the Pearl: The Problem of Contextualism in Intellectual History." *History and Theory* 23 (1984): 151–69.

Dinari, Yedidyah A. *Ḥakhmei 'ashkenaz be-shilhei yemei ha-benayim: darkhehem ve-khitvehem ba-halakhah.* Jerusalem: Bialik, 1984.

Dolgopolski, Sergey. *What Is Talmud?: The Art of Disagreement.* New York: Fordham University Press, 2009.

Dönitz, Saskia. "Shemarya ha-Ikriti and the Karaite Exegetical Challenge." In *Exegesis and Poetry in Medieval Karaite and Rabbanite Texts,* edited by Joachim Yeshaya and Elisabeth Hollender, 228–48. Leiden: Brill, 2017.

Dweck, Yaacob. "What Is a Jewish Book?" *AJS Review* 34 (2010): 367–75.

Efros, Israel. "Studies in Pre-Tibbonian Philosophical Terminology: I. Abraham Bar Hiyya, the Prince." *Jewish Quarterly Review* 17 (1927): 323–68.

Eidelberg, Shlomo. *Jewish Life in Austria in the XVth Century.* Philadelphia: Dropsie College, 1962.

Eidelberg, Shlomo. "Sefer 'be'ur 'al ha-torah'." *Horev* 14–15 (1960): 246–52.

Eisen, Robert. *The Book of Job in Medieval Jewish Philosophy.* New York: Oxford University Press, 2004.

Eisenstat, Yedida C. "Rashi's Midrashic Anthology: The Torah Commentary Re-Examined." PhD dissertation, Jewish Theological Seminary, 2014.

Elbaum, Jacob. *Petiḥut ve-histagrut: ha-yeṣirah ha-ruḥanit-ha-sifrutit be-folin uve-'arṣot 'ashkenaz be-shilhei ha-me'ah ha-shesh-'esrei.* Jerusalem: Magnes, 1990.

Elbaum, Jacob, and Chava Turniansky. "Tsene-Rene." *YIVO Encyclopedia of Jews in Eastern Europe.*http://www.yivoencyclopedia.org/article.aspx/Tsene-rene.

Elior, Ofer. "'Pri ha-gan' le-rabbi Shalom ben rabbi Yosef 'Anavi." *Kobez Al Yad* 21 (2012): 200–259.

Elior, Ofer. "Rabbi Yedidyah Rakh on Ezekiel's 'I Heard': A Case Study in Byzantine Jews' Reception of Spanish-Provençal Jewish Philosophical-Scientific Culture." In *Texts in Transit in the Medieval Mediterranean*, edited by Y. Tzvi Langermann and Robert G. Morrison, 29–46. University Park: Penn State University Press, 2016.

Elior, Ofer. *Ruaḥ ḥen yaḥalof 'al panai.* Jerusalem: Mekhon Ben-Zvi, 2017.

Elman, Yaakov. "Classical Rabbinic Interpretation." In *The Jewish Study Bible*, edited by Adele Berlin and Marc Zvi Brettler, 1844–1863. Oxford: Oxford University Press, 2004.

Elman, Yaakov. "'It Is No Empty Thing': Nahmanides and the Search for Omnisignificance." *Torah U-Madda Journal* 4 (1993): 1–83.

Elman, Yaakov. "Meiri and the Non-Jew: A Comparative Investigation." In *New Perspectives on Jewish-Christian Relations: In Honor of David Berger*, edited by Elisheva Carlebach and Jacob J. Schacter, 263–96. Leiden: Brill, 2012.

Elman, Yaakov. "Moses Ben Nahman / Nahmanides (Ramban)." In *Hebrew Bible / Old Testament: The History of Its Interpretation*, edited by Magne Sæbø. Vol. I/ 2 of *From the Beginnings to the Middle Ages.* Part 2: *The Middle Ages*, 416–32. Göttingen: Vanderhoeck & Ruprecht, 2000.

Elman, Yaakov. "The Suffering of the Righteous in Palestinian and Babylonian Sources." *Jewish Quarterly Review* 80 (1990): 315–39.

Elman, Yaakov, and Israel Gershoni, eds. *Transmitting Jewish Traditions: Orality, Textuality, and Cultural Diffusion.* New Haven, CT: Yale University Press, 2000.

Elqayam, Avraham. "Ha-zohar ha-qadosh shel Shabbetai Zvi." *Kabbalah* 3 (1998): 345–87.

Enenkel, Karel, and Henk Nellen. "Introduction." In *Neo-Latin Commentaries and the Management of Knowledge in the Late Middle Ages and the Early Modern Period (1400–1700)*, edited by Karel Enenkel and Henk Nellen, 1–78. Leuven: Leuven University Press, 2013.

Engel, Michael. *Elijah del Medigo and Paduan Aristotelianism: Investigating the Human Intellect.* London: Bloomsbury, 2016.

Englander, Henry. "Rashi's View of the Weak, ע"ע, and פ"ן Roots (With Special Reference to the Views of Menahem b. Saruk and Dunash b. Labrat)." *Hebrew Union College Annual* 7 (1930): 399–437.

Epstein, Abraham. "Ma'amar 'al ḥibbur *Ṣafenat pa'neaḥ.*" In *Kitvei R. 'Avraham 'Epshṭein*, edited by A. M. Haberman. 2 vols., 1:116–29. Jerusalem: Mosad Harav Kuk, 1949.

Epstein, Isidore. *The Responsa of Rabbi Simon B. Zemah Duran: As a Source of the History of the Jews in North Africa.* London: Oxford University Press, 1930.

Epstein, Marc M. "Another Flight into Egypt: Confluence, Coincidence, the Cross-cultural Dialectics of Messianism and Iconographic Appropriation in Medieval Jewish and Christian Culture." In *Imagining the Self, Imagining the Other: Visual Representation and Jewish-Christian Dynamics in the Middle Ages and Early Modern Period*, edited by Eva Frojmovic, 33–52. Leiden: Brill, 2002.

Epstein, Marc M. *The Medieval Haggadah: Art, Narrative, and Religious Imagination.* New Haven, CT: Yale University Press, 2010.

Epstein, Steven A. *Genoa and the Genoese, 958–1528.* Chapel Hill: University of North Carolina Press, 1996.

Epstein, Steven A. *Purity Lost: Transgressing Boundaries in the Eastern Mediterranean, 1000–1400.* Baltimore, MD: Johns Hopkins University Press, 2007.

Erel, Yossi. "Parshanut peshaṭ la-miqra' ve-halakhah pesuqah ba-'avodato shel ramban." *Jewish Studies Internet Journal* 8 (2009): 1–36.

Exceptional Printed Books, Sixty-Five Hebrew Incunabula. New York: Kestenbaum and Company, 2004.

Fabry, Heinz-Josef. "'ll." In *Theological Dictionary of the Old Testament*, edited by G. Johannes Botterweck, Helmer Ringgren, and Heinz-Josef Fabry, translated by David E. Green. 15 vols., 11:139–47. Grand Rapids, MI: Eerdmans, 1977–2012.

Fackenheim, Emil L. *Encounters Between Judaism and Modern Philosophy: A Preface to Future Jewish Thought.* New York: Basic Books, 1973.

Faierstein, Morris M. *Ze'enah U-Re'enah: A Critical Translation into English.* Berlin: De Gruyter, 2017.

Faur, José. *The Horizontal Society: Understanding the Covenant and Alphabetic Judaism.* 2 vols. Boston: Academic Studies, 2008.

Feiner, Shmuel. "Nineteenth-Century Jewish Historiography—The Second Track." In *Reshaping the Past: Jewish History and the Historians (= Studies in Contemporary Jewry X)*, edited by Jonathan Frankel, 17–44. New York: Oxford University Press, 1994.

Feldman, Aryeh Leib (Leon). "Teshuvot ha-ran le-hassagot ha-ramban 'al divrei rashi be-ferusho la-torah." *Sinai* 137 (2006): 208–17.

Fenton, Paul. "De quelques attitudes qaraïtes enver la Qabbale." *Revue des études juives* 142 (1983): 5–19.

Fenton, Paul. "Maïmonide et *L'Agriculture nabatéeanne.*" In *Maimonide: Philosophe et Savant (1138–1204)*, edited by Tony Lévy and Roshdi Rashed, 303–27. Leuven: Peeters, 2004.

Fenton, Paul B. "The Post-Maimonidean Schools of Exegesis in the East: Abraham Maimonides, the Pietists, Tanḥûm Ha-Yərušalmi and the Yemenite School." In *Hebrew Bible / Old Testament: The History of Its Interpretation*, edited by Magne

Sæbø. Vol. I/2 of *From the Beginnings to the Middle Ages*. Part 2: *The Middle Ages*, 433–55. Göttingen: Vanderhoeck & Ruprecht, 2000.

Fetterley, Judith. *The Resisting Reader: A Feminist Approach to American Fiction*. Bloomington: Indiana University Press, 1978.

Fine, Lawrence. *Physician of the Soul, Healer of the Cosmos: Isaac Luria and His Kabbalistic Fellowship*. Stanford, CA: Stanford University Press, 2003.

Finkelberg, Margalit. "Canon-Replacement Versus Canon-Appropriation: The Case of Homer." In *Cultural Repertoires: Structure, Function, and Dynamics*, edited by Gillis J. Dorleijn and Herman L.J. Vanstiphout, 145–60. Leuven: Peeters, 2003.

Finkelberg, Margalit, and Guy G. Stroumsa. "Introduction: Before the Western Canon." In *Homer, the Bible, and Beyond: Literary and Religious Canons in the Ancient World*, edited by Margalit Finkelberg and Guy G. Stroumsa, 1–8. Leiden: Brill, 2003.

Firestone, Reuven. "Prophethood, Marriageable Consanguinity, and Text: The Problem of Abraham and Sarah's Kinship Relationship and the Response of Jewish and Islamic Exegesis." *Jewish Quarterly Review* 83 (1993): 331–47.

Fishbane, Michael. *The Exegetical Imagination: On Jewish Thought and Theology*. Cambridge, MA: Harvard University Press, 1998.

Fishman, David E., Mark Kupovetsky, and Vladimir Kuzelenkov, eds. *Nazi-Looted Jewish Archives in Moscow: A Guide to Jewish Historical and Cultural Collections in the Russian State Military Archive*. Scranton, PA: University of Scranton Press, 2010.

Fishman, Talya. *Becoming the People of the Talmud: Oral Torah as Written Tradition in Medieval Jewish Cultures*. Philadelphia: University of Pennsylvania Press, 2011.

Fishman, Talya. *Shaking the Pillars of Exile: "Voice of a Fool," an Early Modern Critique of Rabbinic Culture*. Stanford, CA: Stanford University Press, 1997.

Fleischer, Ezra. *Piyyuṭei Shelomo ha-Bavli*. Jerusalem: Israel Academy of Sciences and Humanities, 1973.

Fodale, Salvatore. "Mosè Bonavoglia e il contestato *iudicatus generalis* sugli ebrei siciliani." In *Gli Ebrei in Sicilia dal tardoantico al medioevo*, edited by Nicolò Bucaria, 99–109. Palermo: Flaccovio, 1998.

Foka, Anna, and Jonas Liliequist. "General Introduction." In *Laughter, Humor, and the (un)Making of Gender: Historical and Cultural Perspectives*, edited by Anna Foka and Jonas Liliequist, 1–3. London: Palgrave, 2015.

Fox, Marvin. *Interpreting Maimonides: Studies in Methodology, Metaphysics, and Moral Philosophy*. Chicago: University of Chicago Press, 1990.

Fraenkel, Carlos. *Min ha-rambam li-Shemu'el 'ibn Tibbon: darko shel dalalah al-ha'irin le-moreh ha-nevukhim*. Jerusalem: Magnes, 2007.

Fraenkel, Miriam. "Qanon ve-ḥevrah: ha-qanon ha-sifruti ki-kheli le-gibbush ha-'ilit ha-ḥevratit be-ḥevrat ha-genizah." In *Ha-qanon ha-samui min ha-'ayin: ḥiqrei qanon u-genizah*, edited by Menahem Ben-Sasson et al., 88–110. Jerusalem: Magnes, 2010.

Frenkel, Miriam. "Book Lists from the Cairo Genizah: A Window on the Production of Texts in the Middle Ages." *Bulletin of the School of Oriental and African Studies* 80 (2017): 233–52.

Fraenkel, Yonah. "Ha-piyyuṭ ve-ha-perush: li-meqorot ha-'aggadah be-ferusho shel rashi la-torah." *'Iyyunei miqra' u-farshanut* 7 (2005): 475–90.

Frahm, Eckart. *Babylonian and Assyrian Text Commentaries: Origins of Interpretation.* Munich: Ugarit-Verlag, 2011.

Fram, Edward. "Some Preliminary Observations on the First Published Translation of Rashi's Commentary on the Pentateuch in Yiddish (Cremona, 1560)." *Hebrew Union College Annual* 86 (2016): 305–42.

Francesconi, Federica. "Jews under Surveillance: Censorship and Reading in Early Modern Italy." Early Modern Workshop: Jewish History Resources, vol. 6, at https://fordham.bepress.com/cgi/viewcontent.cgi?article=1082&context=emw.

Francesconi, Federica. "'The Passage Can Also Be Read Differently . . .:' How Jews And Christians Censored Hebrew Texts in Early Modern Modena." *Jewish History* 26 (2012): 139–60.

Frank, Daniel. "Elijah Yerushalmi and Karaite Ambivalence toward Rabbanite Literature," edited by Daniel Frank, and Matt Goldish. In *Rabbinic Culture and Its Critics: Jewish Authority, Dissent, and Heresy in Medieval and Early Modern Times*, 249–69. Detroit, MI: Wayne State University Press, 2008.

Frank, Daniel. "Ibn Ezra and the Karaite Exegetes Aaron Ben Joseph and Aaron Ben Elijah." In *Abraham ibn Ezra y su tiempo*, edited by Fernando Díaz Esteban, 99–107. Madrid: Asociación Española de Orientalistas, 1990.

Frank, Daniel. "Karaite Exegesis." In *Hebrew Bible / Old Testament: The History of Its Interpretation*, edited by Magne Sæbø. Vol. I/2 of *From the Beginnings to the Middle Ages.* Part 2: *The Middle Ages*, 110–28. Göttingen: Vanderhoeck & Ruprecht, 2000.

Frank, Daniel. "Karaite Exegetical and Halakhic Literature in Byzantium and Turkey." In *Karaite Judaism: A Guide to Its History and Literary Sources*, edited by Meira Polliack, 529–58. Leiden: Brill, 2003.

Freimann, Aron. "Manuscript Supercommentaries on Rashi's Commentary on the Pentateuch." In *Rashi Anniversary Volume*, 73–114. New York: American Academy for Jewish Research, 1941.

Freudenthal, Gad. "Abraham Ibn Daud, Avendauth, Dominicus Gundissalinus and Practical Mathematics in Mid-Twelfth Century Toledo." *Aleph* 16 (2016): 61–106.

Freudenthal, Gad. "Abraham Ibn Ezra and Judah Ibn Tibbon as Cultural Intermediaries. Early Stages in the Introduction of Non-Rabbinic Learning Into Provence in the Mid-Twelfth Century." In *Exchange and Transmission Across Cultural Boundaries: Philosophy, Mysticism and Science in the Mediterranean World,* edited by Sarah Stroumsa and Haggai Ben-Shammai, 52–81. Jerusalem: Israel Academy of Science and Humanities, 2013.

Friedman, Shamma. "Klum lo nisnes perush rashi be-vet midrasho shel ha-rambam?" In *Rashi: demuto vi-yeṣirato*, edited by Avraham Grossman and Sara Japhet. 2 vols., 2:403–64. Jerusalem: Zalman Shazar, 2008.

Friedman, Shamma. "Perushei rashi la-talmud: hagahot u-mahadurot." In *Rashi: 'iyyunim bi-yeṣirato*, edited by Zvi Aryeh Steinfeld, 147–75. Ramat-Gan: Bar-Ilan University Press, 1993.

Friedman, Shamma. "The Transmission of the Talmud and the Computer Age." In *Printing the Talmud: From Bomberg to Schottenstein*, edited by Sharon Liberman Mintz and Gabriel M. Goldstein, 143–54. New York: Yeshiva University Museum, 2005.

Frisch, Amos. "He-ḥaṭe'u ha-'avot ha-'ahuvim? Le-darko shel ha-rav Meqlenburg be-sugyat ḥaṭa'ei ha-'avot ('al pi perusho le-sefer bereshit)." *'Iyyunei miqra' u-farshanut* 8 (2008): 623–35.

Frisch, Amos. "The Sins of the Patriarchs as Viewed by Traditional Jewish Exegesis." *Jewish Studies Quarterly* 10 (2003): 258–73.

Frisch, Amos. "'Your Brother Came with Guile': Responses to an Explicit Moral Evaluation in Biblical Narrative." *Prooftexts* 23 (2003): 271–96.

Frojmovic, Eva. "Jewish Scribes and Christian Illuminators: Interstitial Encounters and Cultural Negotiation." In *Between Judaism and Christianity: Art Historical Essays in Honor of Elisheva (Elisabeth) Revel-Neher*, edited by Katrin Kogman-Appel and Mati Meyer, 281–305. Leiden: Brill, 2009.

Gabbay, Uri. "Specification as a Hermeneutical Technique in Babylonian and Assyrian Commentaries." *Hebrew Bible and Ancient Israel* 4 (2015): 344–68.

Galinsky, Judah. "An Ashkenazic Rabbi Encounters Sephardic Culture: R. Asher Ben Jehiel's Attitude towards Philosophy and Science." *Simon Dubnow Institute Yearbook* 8 (2009): 191–211.

Galinsky, Judah. "Ashkenazim in Sefarad: The Rosh and the Tur on the Codification of Jewish Law." *Jewish Law Annual* 16 (2006): 3–23.

Galinsky, Judah. "'Ve-zakhah zeh ha-ḥakham yoter mikulam she-ha-kol lamedu mi-sefarav': 'al tefuṣat ''Arba'ah ṭurim' le-rabbi Ya'aqov ben 'Asher mi-zeman ketivato ve'ad sof ha-me'ah ha-15." *Sidra* 19 (2004): 25–45.

Gamliel, Hanokh. *Rashi ke-farshan u-khe-valshan: tefisot taḥbiriyyot be-ferush rashi la-torah.* Jerusalem: Bialik, 2010.

Gaudioso, Matteo. *La communità ebraica di Catania nei secoli XIV–XV.* Catania: Niccolò, 1974.

Geiger, Abraham. "Shemaryah ha-'iqriṭi." *'Oṣar neḥmad* 2 (1856): 90–94.

Geiger, Ari. "A Student and an Opponent: Nicholas of Lyre and His Jewish Sources." In *Nicolas de Lyre: franciscain du XIVe siècle, exégète et théologien*, edited by Gilbert Dahan, 167–203. Paris: Institut d'Études Augustiniennes, 2011.

Gelbard, Shmuel. *Lifeshuṭo shel rashi: be'ur le-ferush rashi 'al ha-torah*. 5 vols. 2nd ed.. Tel Aviv: Mif'al Rashi, 1990.

Genette, Gérard. *Paratexts: Thresholds of Interpretation*, translated by Jane E. Lewin. Cambridge: Cambridge University Press, 1997.

Gershowitz, Uri. "Perush filosofi le-sefer ha-bahir me-ha-me'ah ha-14." *Judaica Petropolitana* 1 (2013): 20–40 (Hebrew section).

Gershowitz, Uri. "Perush sefer 'iyov le-r[abbi] 'Eliyahu ben 'Eli'ezer ha-yerushalmi be-heqsher ha-parshanut ha-filosofit ha-yehudit be-yemei ha-benayim." PhD disseration, Hebrew University of Jerusalem, 2008.

Gillman, Abigail E. "Between Religion and Culture: Mendelssohn, Buber, Rosenzweig, and the Enterprise of Biblical Translation." In *Biblical Translation in Context*, edited by Frederick Knobloch, 91–114. Bethesda: University Press of Maryland, 2002.

Gillman, Abigail E. *A History of German Jewish Bible Translation*. Chicago: University of Chicago Press, 2018.

Glasner, Ruth. "The Evolution of the Genre of Philosophical-Scientific Commentary: Hebrew Supercommentaries on Aristotle's Physics." In *Science in Medieval Jewish Cultures*, edited by Gad Freudenthal, 182–96. Cambridge: Cambridge University Press, 2011.

Glatt-Gilad, David A. "How Many Years Were the Israelites in Egypt?," TheTorah.com. http://thetorah.com/how-many-years-were-the-israelites-in-egypt/.

Goetschel, Roland. "L'exégèse de Rashi à la lumière du Maharal de Prague." In *Rashi 1040–1990: Hommage à Ephraïm E. Urbach*, edited by Gabrielle Sed-Rajna, 465–73. Paris: Cerf, 1993.

Goetschel, Roland. "Rashi et le Ḥizzeqûni sur la 'aqedah et les sacrifices." In *Rashi et la culture juive en France du Nord au moyen âge*, edited by Gilbert Dahan et al., 305–13. Paris-Leuven: Peeters, 1997.

Golb, Norman. *The Jews in Medieval Normandy*. Cambridge: Cambridge University Press, 1998.

Gold, Penny Schine. *Making the Bible Modern: Children's Bibles and Jewish Education in Twentieth-Century America*. Ithaca, NY: Cornell University Press, 2004.

Goldberg, Arnold. "The Rabbinic View of Scripture." In *A Tribute to Geza Vermes: Essays on Jewish and Christian Literature and History*, edited by Philip R. Davies and Richard T. White, 153–66. Sheffield: JSOT Press, 1990.

Goldfeld, Leah Naomi. "Perush la-torah shel Yehudah ben Shemaryah bi-khetav yad she-ba-genizah." *Kobez Al Yad* 10 (1982): 125–60.

Goldin, Judah. "The Youngest Son or Where Does Genesis 38 Belong." *Journal of Biblical Literature* 96 (1977): 27–44.

Goldreich, Amos. *Shem ha-kotev u-khetivah 'oṭomaṭit be-sifrut ha-zohar uve-modernizm*. Los Angeles: Cherub Press, 2010.

Goldstein, Miriam, and Itamar Kislev. "Abraham b. Ezra's 'Spirantized *peh* in the Arabic Language': The Rules of Grammar versus the Requirements of Exegesis and Polemic." *Journal of Jewish Studies* 67 (2016): 135–56.

Goodman, Mordechai S. "Hashqafat ra'ba' 'al perushei u-midreshei ḥazal." *Sinai* 133 (2004): 26–43.

Gordon, Cyrus H. "'This Time' (Genesis 2:23)." In *"Sha'arei Talmon": Studies in the Bible, Qumran, and the Ancient Near East Presented to Shemaryahu Talmon*, edited by Michael Fishbane and Emanuel Tov, 47–51. Winona Lake, IN: Eisenbrauns, 1992.

Gosselin, E. A. "A Listing of the Printed Editions of Nicolaus de Lyra." *Traditio* 26 (1970): 399–426.

Gottlieb, Isaac B. *Yesh seder la-miqra': ḥazal u-farshanei yemei ha-benayim 'al mukdam u-me'uhar ba-torah.* Jerusalem and Ramat-Gan: Magnes / Bar-Ilan University Press, 2009.

Graboïs, Arieh. *Les sources hébraïques médiévales.* Vol. II: *Les commentaires exégétiques.* Turnhout, Belgium: Brepols, 1993.

Graetz, Heinrich. *Geschichte der Juden.* Vol. 8, 2nd ed. Leipzig, 1890.

Graham, William A., and Navid Kermani. "Recitation and Aesthetic Reception." In *The Cambridge Companion to the Qur'an*, edited by Jane Dammen McAuliffe, 115–44. Cambridge: Cambridge University Press, 2006.

Greenspan, Nahman S. *Melekhet maḥashevet.* London: M.L. Tsaylingold, 1955.

Greenstein, Edward L. "Medieval Bible Commentaries." In *Back to the Sources: Reading the Classic Jewish Texts*, edited by Barry W. Holtz, 213–60. New York: Summit Books, 1984.

Greenstein, Edward L. "Sensitivity to Language in Rashi's Commentary on the Torah." *The Solomon Goldman Lectures* 6, edited by Mayer I. Gruber, 51–71. Chicago: Spertus College of Judaica Press, 1993.

Grendler, Paul F. "The Destruction of Hebrew Books in Venice, 1568." *Proceedings of the American Academy for Jewish Research* 45 (1978): 103–30.

Gries, Zeev. *The Book in the Jewish World: 1700–1900.* Oxford: Littman Library of Jewish Civilization, 2007.

Gross, Abraham. "Polmos 'al shiṭat ha-'shemirah': le-toledot limmud perush rashi 'al ha-torah be-dor gerush sefarad." *AJS Review* 18 (1993): 1–20 (Hebrew section).

Gross, Abraham. "Rashi u-masoret limmud ha-torah she-bi-khetav bi-sefarad." In *Rashi: 'iyyunim bi-yeṣirato*, edited by Zvi Aryeh Steinfeld, 27–55. Ramat-Gan: Bar-Ilan University Press, 1993.

Gross, Abraham. *Struggling with Tradition: Reservations about Active Martyrdom in the Middle Ages.* Leiden: Brill, 2004.

Grossfeld, Bernard. "Reuben's Deed (Genesis 35:22) in Jewish Exegesis: What Happened There?" In *Biblical Interpretation in Judaism and Christianity*, edited by Isaac Kalimi and Peter J. Haas, 44–51. New York: T&T Clark, 2006.

Grossman, Avraham. *'Emunot ve-de'ot be-'olamo shel rashi.* Alon Shevut: Tevunot, 2008.

Grossman, Avraham. "'Ereṣ yisra'el be-mishnato shel rashi." *Shalem* 7 (2002): 15–31.

Grossman, Avraham. "Hagahot r[abbi] Shema'yah ve-nosaḥ perush rashi la-torah." *Tarbiẓ* 60 (1990): 67–98.

Grossman, Avraham. *Ḥakhmei 'ashkenaz ha-rishonim: qorotehem, darkam be-hanhagat ha-ṣibbur, yeṣiratam ha-ruḥanit, me-reshit yishuvam ve-'ad li-gezerot 856 (1096)*. Jerusalem: Magnes, 1981.

Grossman, Avraham. *Ḥakhmei ṣorfat ha-rishonim: qorotehem, darkam be-hanhagat ha-ṣibbur, yeṣiratam ha-ruḥanit*. Jerusalem: Magnes, 1995.

Grossman, Avraham. "Ha-reqa' ha-hisṭori." In Nehama Leibowitz and Moshe Arend, *Perush rashi la-torah: 'iyyunim be-shiṭato*. 2 vols., 2:500–543. Jerusalem: Open University of Israel, 1990.

Grossman, Avraham. "Polmos dati u-megamah ḥinukhit be-ferush rashi la-torah." In *Pirqei Neḥamah: sefer zikaron le-Neḥamah Lebovits*, edited by Moshe Ahrend and Rut Ben-Meir, 187–205. Jerusalem: Ha-Sokhnut Ha-Yehudit, 2001.

Grossman, Avraham. *Rashi*, translated by Joel Linsider. Oxford: Littman Library of Jewish Civilization, 2012.

Grossman, Avraham. "Rashi's Rejection of Philosophy: Devine [sic] and Human Wisdoms Juxtaposed." *Simon Dubnow Institute Yearbook* 8 (2009): 95–118.

Grossman, Avraham. "Rishumam shel r[abbi] Shemu'el 'he-ḥasid' ha-sefaradi u-Re'u'el ha-bizanṭi be-vet midrasho shel rashi." *Tarbiẓ* 82 (2014): 447–67.

Grossman, Avraham. "The School of Literal Jewish Exegesis in Northern France." In *Hebrew Bible / Old Testament: The History of Its Interpretation*, edited by Magne Sæbø. Vol. I/2 of *From the Beginnings to the Middle Ages*. Part 2: *The Middle Ages*, 321–71. Göttingen: Vanderhoeck & Ruprecht, 2000.

Grossman, Avraham. *Ve-hu yimshol bakh?: ha-'ishah be-mishnatam shel ḥakhmei yisra'el bi-yemei ha-benayim*. Jerusalem: Zalman Shazar, 2011.

Gruber, Mayer I. "Light on Rashi's Diagrams from the Asher Library of Spertus College of Judaica." *The Solomon Goldman Lectures* 6, edited by Mayer I. Gruber, 73–85. Chicago: Spertus College of Judaica Press, 1993.

Gruber, Mayer I. *Rashi's Commentary on Psalms*. Atlanta, GA: Scholars Press, 1998.

Grunhaus, Naomi. *The Challenge of Received Tradition: Dilemmas of Interpretation in Radak's Biblical Commentaries*. Oxford: Oxford University Press, 2013.

Grunhaus, Naomi. "The Dependence of Rabbi David Kimhi (Radak) on Rashi in His Quotation of Midrashic Traditions." *Jewish Quarterly Review* 93 (2003): 415–30.

Gurfinkel, Eli. "Minḥat qena'ot le-r[abbi] Zekharyah ben Moshe ha-kohen mi-qandi'ah." *Kobez Al Yad* 20 (2011): 125–280.

Gutwirth, Eleazar. "Arragel on Ruth: Rashi in Fifteenth Century Castilian?" In *Rashi 1040–1990: Hommage à Ephraïm E. Urbach*, edited by Gabrielle Sed-Rajna, 657–62. Paris: Cerf, 1993.

Gutwirth, Eleazar, and Miguel Angel Motis Dolader. "Twenty-Six Jewish Libraries from Fifteenth-Century Spain." *The Library* 18 (1996): 27–53.

Haas, Jair. "Divine Perfection and Methodological Inconsistency: Towards an Understanding of Isaac Abarbanel's Exegetical Frame of Mind." *Jewish Studies Quarterly* 17 (2010): 302–57.

Hacker, Joseph. "Defusei qushta be-me'ah ha-shesh-'esrei." *'Areshet* 5 (1972): 457–93.

Hacker, Joseph. "Ha-'midrash' ha-sefaradi: sifriyah ṣiburit yehudit." In *Rishonim ve-'aḥaronim: meḥkarim be-toledot yisra'el mugashim le-'Avraham Grossman,* edited by Joseph R. Hacker, B. Z. Kedar, and Yosef Kaplan, 263–92. Jerusalem: Zalman Shazar, 2010.

Hacker, Joseph. "Ha-negidut bi-ṣefon 'afriqah be-sof ha-me'ah ha-ḥamesh 'esrei." *Zion* 45 (1980–81): 118–32.

Hacker, Joseph. "''Im shakhaḥenu shem 'elohenu ve-nifros kapenu le-'el zar': gilgulah shel parshanut 'al reqa' ha-meṣi'ut bi-sefarad be-yemei ha-benayim." *Zion* 57 (1992): 247–74.

Hacker, Joseph. "Jewish Book Owners and Their Libraries in the Iberian Peninsula, Fourteenth-Fifteenth Centuries." In *The Late Medieval Hebrew Book in the Western Mediterranean: Hebrew Manuscripts and Incunabula in Context,* edited by Javier del Barco, 70–104. Leiden: Brill, 2015.

Hacker, Joseph. "Ziqatam ve-'aliyatam shel yehudei sefarad le-'ereṣ yisra'el, 1391–1492." *Qatedrah* 36 (1985): 3–34.

Hailperin, Herman. *Rashi and the Christian Scholars.* Pittsburgh: University of Pittsburgh, 1963.

Hakohen, Leora. "Sugyot halakhiyot u-musariyot be-ma'aseh ha-'avot, be-'enei ha-parshanim ha-yehudim be-yemei ha-benayim: rashi, ramban, ve-'ibn Kaspi." Master's thesis, Bar-Ilan University,1995.

Halbertal, Moshe. *'Al derekh ha-'emet: ha-ramban vi-yeṣiratah shel masoret.* Jerusalem: Shalom Hartman Institute, 2006.

Halbertal, Moshe. *Concealment and Revelation: Esotericism in Jewish Thought and Its Philosophical Implications,* translated by Jackie Feldman. Princeton, NJ: Princeton University Press, 2007.

Halbertal, Moshe. *People of the Book: Canon, Meaning, and Authority.* Cambridge, MA: Harvard University Press, 1997.

Hamilton, Victor P. *Exodus: An Exegetical Commentary.* Grand Rapids, MI: Baker Academic, 2011.

Hanson, Paul D. "Song of Heshbon and David's Nîr." *Harvard Theological Review* 61 (1968): 297–320.

Ha-qanon ha-samui min ha-'ayin: ḥiqrei qanon u-genizah, edited by Menahem Ben-Sasson et al. Jerusalem: Magnes, 2010.

Harris, Jay M. *How Do We Know This? Midrash and the Fragmentation of Modern Judaism.* Albany: SUNY Press, 1995.

Harris, Robert A. "Concepts of Scripture in the School of Rashi." In *Jewish Concepts of Scripture: A Comparative Introduction,* edited by Benjamin D. Sommer, 102–22. New York: New York University Press, 2012.

Harris, Robert A. "Rashi's Introductions to His Biblical Commentaries." In *Shai le-Sarah Yafet: meḥqarim ba-miqra' be-farshanuto u-vi-leshono,* edited by Moshe Bar-Asher et al., 219–41 (English section). Jerusalem: Bialik, 2007.

Harris, Robert A. "What's In a Blessing? Rashi and the Priestly Benediction of Numbers 6:22–27." In *Birkat Kohanim: The Priestly Benediction in Jewish Tradition*, edited by Martin S. Cohen and David Birnbaum, 231–58. New York: New Paradigm Matrix, 2016.

Harvey, Warren Zev. "Maimonides' Critical Epistemology and *Guide* 2:24." *Aleph* 8 (2008): 213–35.

Harvey, Warren Zev. "Rashi on Creation: Beyond Plato and Derrida." *Aleph* 18 (2018): 27–49.

Harvey, Warren Zev. "Spinoza on Biblical Miracles." *Journal of the History of Ideas* 74 (2013): 659–75.

Harvey, Warren Zev. "Spinoza on Ibn Ezra's 'Secret of the Twelve'." In *Spinoza's 'Theological-Political Treatise': A Critical Guide*, edited by Yitzhak Y. Melamed and Michael A. Rosenthal, 41–55. New York: Cambridge University Press, 2010.

Hasselhoff, Görge K. "The Parisian Talmud Trials and the Translation of Rashi's Bible Commentaries." *Henoch* 37 (2015): 29–42.

Hasselhoff, Görge K. "Rashi's Glosses on Isaiah in Bibliothèque Nationale de France, Ms. Lat. 16558." In *Studies on the Latin Talmud*, edited by Ulisse Cecini and Eulàlia Vernet i Pons, 111–28. Barcelona: Publicacions de la Universitat Autònoma de Barcelona, 2017.

Havazelet, Avraham Yosef. "Be'ur 'amar neqe' 'al perush rashi la-torah." *Moriyah* 17 (1991): 117–22.

Haverkamp, Alfred. *Jews in the Medieval German Kingdom*, translated by Christoph Cluse. Trier University Library, 2015. www.ubt.opus.hbz-nrw.de/volltexte/2015/916/pdf/Jews_German_Kingdom.pdf].

Havlin, Shlomo Z. "'Al 'ha-ḥatimah ha-sifrutit' ki-yesod ha-ḥaluqah li-tequfot ha-halakhah." In *Meḥqarim be-sifrut ha-talmudit*, 148–92. Jerusalem: Israel Academy of the Sciences, 1983.

Havlin, Shlomo Z. "Haggahot." In *Encyclopaedia Judaica*, edited by Michael Berenbaum and Fred Skolnik. 22 vols., 8:217–21. Detroit, MI: Macmillan, 2007.

Heinemann, Isaac. *Darkhei ha-'aggadah*. 3rd. ed. Jerusalem: Magnes, 1974.

Heinemann, Joseph. "210 Years of Egyptian Exile." *Journal of Jewish Studies* 22 (1971): 19–30.

Heller, Marvin J. *The Sixteenth Century Hebrew Book: An Abridged Thesaurus*. 2 vols. Leiden: Brill, 2003.

Henderson, John B. *Scripture, Canon, and Commentary: A Comparison of Confucian and Western Exegesis*. Princeton, NJ: Princeton University Press, 1991.

Herman, Shael. "Rashi's Glosses *Belaaz*: Navigating Hebrew Scripture Under Feudal Lanterns." *Review of Rabbinic Judaism* 18 (2015): 102–34.

Heschel, Abraham J. *Torah min ha-shamayim be-'aspaqlaryah shel ha-dorot*. 3 vols. London: Soncino, 1962–1990.

Hettema, Th. L. "The Canon: Authority and Fascination." In *Canonization and Decanonization*, edited by A. Van Der Kooij and K. Van Der Toorn, 391–98. Leiden: Brill, 1998.

Hobbins, John. "That Was Your Stone, Dear Old Rashi, the Most Precious of Stones!" *Ancient Hebrew Poetry* (blog). http://ancienthebrewpoetry.typepad.com/ancient_hebrew_poetry/2009/05/that-was-your-stone-dear-old-rashi-the-most-precious-of-stones.html.

Hollender, Elisabeth. *Piyyut Commentary in Medieval Ashkenaz*. Berlin: De Gruyter, 2008.

Holo, Joshua. *Byzantine Jewry in the Mediterranean Economy*. Cambridge: Cambridge University Press, 2009.

Holton, David. "The Cretan Renaissance." In *Literature and Society in Renaissance Crete*, edited by David Holton, 1–16. Cambridge: Cambridge University Press, 1991.

Holub, Robert C. *Reception Theory: A Critical Introduction*. London: Methuen, 1984.

Holzman, Gitit. "Haqdamat sefer 'Mikhlol yofi' le-r[abbi] Shemu'el Ṣarṣah: hahadarah u-mavo'." *Sinai* 109 (1992): 16–46.

Horowitz, Carmi. "'Al perush ha-'aggadot shel ha-rashba: ben qabbalah le-filosofyah." *Daat* 18 (1987): 15–27.

Houtman, Alberdina. "The Role of the Targum in Jewish Education in Medieval Europe." In *A Jewish Targum in a Christian World*, edited by Alberdina Houtman, Eveline van Staalduine-Sulman, and Hans-Martin Kim, 81–98. Leiden: Brill, 2014.

Hughes, Aaron W. "Concepts of Scripture in Nahmanides." In *Jewish Concepts of Scripture: A Comparative Introduction*, edited by Benjamin D. Sommer, 139–56. New York: New York University Press, 2012.

Hughes, Aaron W. "Presenting the Past: The Genre of Commentary in Theoretical Perspective." *Method and Theory in the Study of Religion* 15 (2003): 148–68.

Huss, Boaz. "Admiration and Disgust: The Ambivalent Re-Canonization of the Zohar in the Modern Period." In *Study and Knowledge in Jewish Thought*, edited by Howard Kreisel, 203–37. Beer-Sheva: Ben-Gurion University of the Negev Press, 2006.

Huss, Boaz. "*Sefer Ha-Zohar* as a Canonical, Sacred and Holy Text: Changing Perspectives on the Book of Splendor Between the Thirteenth and Eighteenth Centuries." *Journal of Jewish Thought and Philosophy* 7 (1998): 257–307.

Huss, Boaz. *The Zohar: Reception and Impact*, translated by Yudith Nave. Oxford: Littman Library of Jewish Civilization, 2016.

Hyman, Arthur. "Maimonides as Biblical Exegete." In *Maimonides and His Heritage*, edited by Idit Dobbs-Weinstein, Lenn E. Goodman, and James A. Grady, 1–12. Albany: SUNY Press, 2009.

Iancu-Agou, Danièle. "L'importance des écrits de Rachi dans les bibliothèques juives médiévales de l'Europe du Sud." In *Héritages de Rachi*, edited by René-Samuel Sirat, 151–65. Paris: Éditions de l'éclat, 2006.

Idel, Moshe. *Absorbing Perfections: Kabbalah and Interpretation*. New Haven, CT: Yale University Press, 2002.

Idel, Moshe. "Ha-qabbalah ba-'ezor ha-bizanṭi: 'iyyunim rishonim." *Kabbalah* 18 (2008): 197–227.

Idel, Moshe. "Italy in Safed, Safed in Italy: Toward an Interactive History of Sixteenth-Century Kabbalah." In *Cultural Intermediaries: Jewish Intellectuals in Early Modern Italy*, edited by David B. Ruderman and Giuseppe Veltri, 239–69. Philadelphia: University of Pennsylvania Press, 2004.

Idel, Moshe. "'Iyyunim be-shiṭato shel ba'al 'sefer ha-meshiv': pereq be-toledot ha-qabbalah ha-sefaradit." *Sefunot* 17 (1983): 185–243.

Idel, Moshe. *Kabbalah and Eros*. New Haven, CT: Yale University Press, 2005.

Idel, Moshe. *Kabbalah: New Perspectives*. New Haven, CT: Yale University Press, 1988.

Idel, Moshe. "The Kabbalah's 'Window of Opportunities', 1270–1290." In *Me'ah She'arim: Studies in Medieval Jewish Spiritual Life in Memory of Isadore Twersky*, edited by Ezra Fleischer et al., 171–208. Jerusalem: Magnes, 2001.

Idel, Moshe. "Noctural Kabbalists." *ARCHÆVS: Études d'histoire des religions* 4 (2000): 49–74.

Idel, Moshe. "On Angels and Biblical Exegesis in Thirteenth-Century Ashkenaz." In *Scriptural Exegesis: The Shapes of Culture and the Religious Imagination: Essays in Honour of Michael Fishbane*, edited by Deborah A. Green and Laura S. Lieber, 211–44. Oxford: Oxford University Press, 2009.

Idel, Moshe. "On Maimonides in Nahmanides and His School." In *Between Rashi and Maimonides: Themes in Medieval Jewish Thought, Literature and Exegesis*, edited by Ephraim Kanarfogel and Moshe Sokolow, 131–66. Jersey City, NJ: Ktav, 2010.

Idel, Moshe. "On Mobility, Individuals and Groups: Prolegomenon for a Sociological Approach to Sixteenth-Century Kabbalah." *Kabbalah* 3 (1998): 145–73.

Idel, Moshe. "Preface." In Betty Rojtman, *Black Fire on White Fire: An Essay on Jewish Hermeneutics, from Midrash to Kabbalah*, translated by Steven Rendall, ix–xii. Berkeley: University of California Press, 1998.

Idel, Moshe. "Revelation and the 'Crisis of Tradition' in Kabbalah: 1475–1575." In *Constructing Tradition: Means and Myths of Transmission in Western Esotericism*, edited by Andreas B. Kilcher, 253–92. Leiden: Brill, 2010.

Irshai, Oded. "Dating the Eschaton: Jewish and Christian Apocalyptic Calculation in Late Antiquity." In *Apocalyptic Time*, edited by Albert Baumgarten, 113–53. Leiden: Brill, 2000.

Ivry, Alfred L. "Strategies of Interpretation in Maimonides' *Guide of the Perplexed*." In *The Frank Talmage Memorial Volume* (= *Jewish History* 6), edited by Barry Walfish. 2 vols., 2:113–30. Haifa: Haifa University Press, 1993.

Jackson, Bernard S. *Wisdom-Laws: A Study of the Mishpatim of Exodus 21:1–22:16*. Oxford: Oxford University Press, 2006.

Jacobs, Jonathan. *Bekhor shoro hadar lo: r[abbi] Yosef Bekhor Shor ben hemshekhiyut le-ḥiddush*. Jerusalem: Magnes, 2017.

Jacobs, Jonathan. "Ha-'im hikir ramban 'et perush rashbam la-torah?" *Madda'ei ha-yahadut* 46 (2009): 85–108.

Jacobs, Jonathan. "Rabbi Samson Raphael Hirsch as a *Peshat* Commentator: Literary Aspects of His Commentary on the Pentateuch." *Review of Rabbinic Judaism* 15 (2012): 190–200.

Jacobs, Jonathan. "Rashbam's Major Principles of Interpretation as Deduced from a Manuscript Fragment Discovered in 1984." *Revue des études juives* 170 (2011): 443–63.

Jacobs, Jonathan. "Tefuṣat perushei rashbam la-torah: mabaṭ meḥudash." *Beit Mikra* 62 (2017): 41–79.

Jacoby, David. "The Jewish Communities of the Byzantine World from the Tenth to the Mid-Fifteenth Century: Some Aspects of Their Evolution." In *Jewish Reception of Greek Bible Versions: Studies in Their Use in Late Antiquity and the Middle Ages*, edited by Nicholas de Lange, Julia G. Krivoruchko, and Cameron Boyd-Taylor, 157–81. Tübingen: Mohr Siebeck, 2009.

Jacoby, David. "Jews and Christians in Venetian Crete: Segregation, Interaction, and Conflict." In *"Interstizi": Culture ebraico-cristane a Venezia e nei suoi domini dal Medioevo all'Età moderna*, edited by Uwe Israel, Robert Jütte, and Reinhold C. Mueller, 239–75. Rome: Edizioni di Storia e Letteratura, 2010.

Jaffee, Martin S. "*Halakhah* in Early Rabbinic Judaism: Innovation beyond Exegesis: Tradition Before Oral Torah." In *Innovation in Religious Traditions: Essays in the Interpretation of Religious Change*, edited by Michael A. Williams, Collett Cox, and Martin S. Jaffee, 109–42. Berlin: De Gruyter, 1992.

Janssens, David. *Between Athens and Jerusalem: Philosophy, Prophecy, and Politics in Leo Strauss's Early Thought*. Albany: SUNY Press, 2008.

Japhet, Sara. *Dor dor u-farshanav: 'asupat meḥqarim be-farshanut ha-miqra'*. Jerusalem: Bialik, 2008.

Japhet, Sara. "The Tension between Rabbinic Legal Midrash and the 'Plain Meaning' (*Peshat*) of the Biblical Text—An Unresolved Problem?: In the Wake of Rashbam's Commentary on the Pentateuch." In *Sefer Moshe: The Moshe Weinfeld Jubilee Volume: Studies in the Bible and the Ancient Near East, Qumran, and Post-Biblical Judaism*, edited by Chaim Cohen, Avi Hurvitz, and Shalom M. Paul, 403–25. Winona Lake, IN: Eisenbrauns, 2004.

Jauss, Hans Robert. *Toward an Aesthetic of Reception*, translated by Timothy Bahti. Brighton: Harvester, 1982.

JPS Torah Commentary: Genesis. Commentary by Nahum M. Sarna. Philadelphia: Jewish Publication Society, 1989.

JPS Torah Commentary: Numbers. Commentary by Jacob Milgrom. Philadelphia: Jewish Publication Society, 1989.

Kamin, Sarah. *Rashi: peshuṭo shel miqra' u-midrasho shel miqra'*. Jerusalem: Magnes, 1986.

Kanarfogel, Ephraim. "The 'Aliyah of 'Three Hundred Rabbis' in 1211: Tosafist Attitudes Toward Settling in the Land of Israel." *JQR* 76 (1986): 191–215.

Kanarfogel, Ephraim. "Between Ashkenaz and Sefarad: Tosafist Teachings in the Talmudic Commentaries of Ritva." In *Between Rashi and Maimonides: Themes in Medieval Jewish Thought, Literature and Exegesis*, edited by Ephraim Kanarfogel and Moshe Sokolow, 237–74. Jersey City, NJ: Ktav, 2010.

Kanarfogel, Ephraim. "From Germany to Northern France and Back Again: A Tale of Two Tosafist Centres." In *Regional Identities and Cultures of Medieval Jews*, edited by Javier Castaño, Talya Fishman, and Ephraim Kanarfogel, 149–71. London: Littman Library of Jewish Civilization, 2018.

Kanarfogel, Ephraim. *The Intellectual History and Rabbinic Culture of Medieval Ashkenaz*. Detroit, MI: Wayne State University Press, 2013.

Kanarfogel, Ephraim. *Jewish Education and Society in the High Middle Ages*. Detroit, MI: Wayne State University Press, 1992.

Kanarfogel, Ephraim. "Medieval Rabbinic Conceptions of the Messianic Age: The View of the Tosafists." In *Me'ah She'arim: Studies in Medieval Jewish Spiritual Life in Memory of Isadore Twersky*, edited by Ezra Fleischer et al., 147–170 (English section). Jerusalem: Magnes, 2001.

Kanarfogel, Ephraim. "On the Role of Bible Study in Medieval Ashkenaz." In *The Frank Talmage Memorial Volume* (= *Jewish History* 6), edited by Barry Dov Walfish. 2 vols, 1:151–66. Haifa: Haifa University Press, 1993.

Kanarfogel, Ephraim. *"Peering Through the Lattices": Mystical, Magical, and Pietistic Dimensions in the Tosafist Period*. Detroit, MI: Wayne State University Press, 2000.

Kanarfogel, Ephraim. "Progress and Tradition in Medieval Ashkenaz." *Jewish History* 14 (2000): 387–315.

Kanarfogel, Ephraim. "Rashi's Awareness of Jewish Mystical Traditions and Literature." In *Raschi und sein Erbe*, edited by Daniel Krochmalnik, Hanna Liss, and Ronen Reichman, 23–34. Heidelberg: Universitätsverlag, 2007.

Kanarfogel, Ephraim. "Varieties of Belief in Medieval Ashkenaz: The Case of Anthropomorphism." In *Rabbinic Culture and Its Critics: Jewish Authority, Dissent, and Heresy in Medieval and Early Modern Times*, edited by Daniel Frank and Matt Goldish, 117–59. Detroit, MI: Wayne State University Press, 2008.

Kanarfogel, Ephraim, and Moshe Sokolow. "Rashi ve-rambam nifgashim be-genizah ha-qahirit: hafnayah 'el sefer 'mishneh torah' be-mikhtav me-'et 'ehad mi-ba'alei ha-tosafot." *Tarbiz* 67 (1998): 411–16.

Kaplan, Lawrence. "*Daas Torah*: A Modern Conception of Rabbinic Authority." In *Rabbinic Authority and Personal Autonomy*, edited by Moshe Sokol, 1–60. Northvale, NJ: J. Aronson, 1992.

Kasher, Menachem. *Sarei ha-'elef*. New York: Torah Shelemah, 1959.

Kayserling, Mayer. "Review of *An Inquiry into the Sources of the History of the Jews in Spain* by Joseph Jacobs." *Jewish Quarterly Review* (Original Series) 8 (1896): 486–99.

Kearney, Jonathan. *Rashi: Linguist Despite Himself: A Study of the Linguistic Dimension of Rabbi Solomon Yishaqi's Commentary on Deuteronomy*. New York: T&T Clark, 2010.

Keim, Katharina E. *Pirqei DeRabbi Eliezer: Structure, Coherence, Intertextuality*. Leiden: Brill, 2017.

Kellner, Menachem. *Maimonides on the "Decline of the Generations" and the Nature of Rabbinic Authority*. Albany: SUNY Press, 1996.

Kellner, Menachem. *Maimonides' Confrontation with Mysticism*. Oxford: Littman Library of Jewish Civilization, 2006.

Kellner, Menachem. "Overcoming Chosenness." In *Covenant and Chosenness in Judaism and Mormonism*, edited by Raphael Jospe et al., 147–72. Madison, NJ: Fairleigh Dickinson University Press, 2001.

Kellner, Menachem. "Rabbi Isaac Bar Sheshet's Responsum Concerning the Study of Greek Philosophy." *Tradition* 15 (1975): 110–18.

Kellner, Menachem. "Rashi and Maimonides on the Relationship Between Torah and the Cosmos." In *Between Rashi and Maimonides: Themes in Medieval Jewish Thought, Literature and Exegesis*, edited by Ephraim Kanarfogel and Moshe Sokolow, 23–58. Jersey City, NJ: Ktav, 2010.

Kessler, Gwynn. *Conceiving Israel: The Fetus in Rabbinic Narratives*. Philadelphia: University of Pennsylvania Press, 2009.

Kessler Mesguich, Sophie. "Early Christian Hebraists." In *Hebrew Bible / Old Testament: The History of Its Interpretation*, edited by Magne Sæbø. Vol. II: *From the Renaissance to the Enlightenment*, 254–75. Göttingen: Vanderhoeck & Ruprecht, 2008.

Klein, Elka. *Jews, Christian Society, and Royal Power in Medieval Barcelona*. Ann Arbor: University of Michigan Press, 2006.

Klein-Braslavy, Sara. "Gersonides as Commentator on Averroes." In *Without any Doubt: Gersonides on Method and Knowledge*, translated and edited by Lenn J. Schramm, 181–219. Leiden: Brill, 2011.

Klein-Braslavy, Sara. *Perush ha-rambam le-sippur beri'at ha-'olam*. 2nd ed., rev. and enl. Jerusalem: Reuven Mas, 1986.

Klein-Braslavy, Sara. *Perush ha-rambam le-sippurim 'al 'adam be-farashat bereshit: per-aqim be-toledot ha-'adam shel ha-rambam*. Jerusalem: Reuven Mas, 1986.

Klepper, Deeana Copeland. *The Insight of Unbelievers: Nicholas of Lyra and Christian Reading of Jewish Text in the Later Middle Ages*. Philadelphia: University of Pennsylvania Press, 2007.

Kneller, Rivka. "Haznaḥat limmud ha-miqra' bi-yemei ha-benayim u-ve-shilhei ha-'et ha-ḥadashah." In *Mas'at moshe*, edited by Shaul Miezlisch, 188–225. Tel Aviv: Kneller Family, 1989.

Kneller, Rivka. "Ma'amar yiqqavu ha-mayyim: ḥibbur parshani filosofi li-Shemu'el 'ibn Tibbon." PhD dissertation, 2 vols., Tel Aviv University, 2011.

Kolatch, Yonatan. *Masters of the Word: Traditional Jewish Bible Commentary from the First through Tenth Centuries*. Jersey City, NJ: Ktav, 2006.

Kozodoy, Maud. *The Secret Faith of Maestre Honoratus: Profayt Duran and Jewish Identity in Late Medieval Iberia*. Philadelphia: University of Pennsylvania Press, 2015.

Kraemer, Joel L. "Maimonides on the Philosophic Sciences in His Treatise on the Art of Logic." In *Perspectives on Maimonides: Philosophical and Historical Studies*, edited by Joel L. Kraemer, 77–104. Oxford: Oxford University Press, 1991.

Kreisel, Howard (Haim). *Judaism as Philosophy: Studies in Maimonides and the Medieval Jewish Philosophers of Provence*. Boston: Academic Studies, 2015.

Kreisel, Howard. *Maimonides' Political Thought: Studies in Ethics, Law, and the Human Ideal*. Albany: SUNY Press, 1999.

Kreisel, Howard. "Philosophical Interpretations of the Bible." In *The Cambridge History of Jewish Philosophy: From Antiquity Through the Seventeenth Century*, edited by Steven Nadler and T. M. Rudavsky, 88–120. Cambridge: Cambridge University Press, 2009.

Kreisel, Haim. "Reshit ha-parshanut 'al perush ha-torah le-'ibn 'Ezra." In *Ḥamishah qadmonei mefareshei r[abbi] 'Avraham 'ibn 'Ezra*, edited by Haim Kreisel, 11–38. Beer-Sheva: Ben-Gurion University of the Negev Press, 2017.

Kreisel, Howard. "The Term Kol in Abraham Ibn Ezra: A Reappraisal." *Revue des études juives* 153 (1994): 29–66.

Krieger, Pinchus. *Parshan-data': reshimat ha-perushim le-ferush rashi 'al ha-torah*. 2 vols. Monsey, NY: P. Krieger, 2005–2018.

Kugel, James L. "The 'Bible as Literature' in Late Antiquity and the Middle Ages." *Hebrew University Studies in Literature and the Arts* 11 (1983): 20–70.

Kugel, James L. *The Idea of Biblical Poetry: Parallelism and Its History*. New Haven, CT and London: Yale University Press, 1981.

Kugel, James L. *In Potiphar's House*. San Francisco: HarperCollins, 1990.

Kugel, James L. *The Ladder of Jacob: Ancient Interpretations of the Biblical Story of Jacob and His Children*. Princeton, NJ: Princeton University Press, 2006.

Kugel, James L. *Traditions of the Bible: A Guide to the Bible As It Was at the Start of the Common Era*. Cambridge, MA: Harvard University Press, 1998.

Kugel, James L. "Two Introductions to Midrash." *Prooftexts* 3 (1983): 131–55.

Kupfer, Ephraim. "Li-demutah ha-tarbutit shel yahadut 'ashkenaz ve-ḥakhameha ba-me'ah ha-14–15." *Tarbiẓ* 42 (1972): 113–47.

Lagumina, Bartolomeo, and Giuseppe Lagumina. *Codice diplomatico dei Giudei di Sicilia*. 3 vols. Palermo, 1884–1895.

Lampert, Laurence. *The Enduring Importance of Leo Strauss*. Chicago: University of Chicago Press, 2013.

Langermann, Y. Tzvi. "Abraham Ibn Ezra." In *The Stanford Encyclopedia of Philosophy*. Substantially revised on Oct 22, 2018. https://plato.stanford.edu/entries/ibn-ezra/.

Langermann, Y. Tzvi. "Review of R. Abraham Ibn Ezra, *Yesod Mora ve-Sod Torah*." *AJS Review* 30 (2006):460–62.

Langermann, Tzvi. "Science in the Jewish Communities of the Byzantine Cultural Orbit: New Perspectives." In *Science in Medieval Jewish Cultures*, edited by Gad Freudenthal, 438–53. Cambridge: Cambridge University Press, 2011.

Lasker, Daniel J. "'Arikhut ha-yamim shel ha-qadmonim: dat u-madda' ba-hagut yehudit bi-yemei ha-benayim." *Dine Israel* 26–27 (2010): 49–65.

Lasker, Daniel J. *From Judah Hadassi to Elijah Bashyatchi: Studies in Late Medieval Karaite Philosophy*. Leiden: Brill, 2008.

Lasker, Daniel J. "The Interplay of Poetry and Exegesis in Judah Hadassi's *Eshkōl ha-kōfer*." In *Exegesis and Poetry in Medieval Karaite and Rabbanite Texts*, edited by Joachim Yeshaya and Elisabeth Hollender, 187–206. Leiden: Brill, 2017.

Lasker, Daniel J. "Jewish Knowledge of Christianity in the Twelfth and Thirteenth Centuries." In *Studies in Medieval Jewish Intellectual and Social History Festschrift in Honor of Robert Chazan*, edited by David Engel, Lawrence H. Schiffman, and Elliot R. Wolfson, 97–109. Leiden: Brill, 2012.

Lasker, Daniel J. "Maimonides and the Karaites: From Critic to Cultural Hero." In *Maimónides y su época*, edited by Carlos del Valle et al., 311–25. Madrid: Sociedad estatal de conmemoraciones culturales, 2007.

Lasker, Daniel J. "Rashi and Maimonides on Christianity." In *Between Rashi and Maimonides: Themes in Medieval Jewish Thought, Literature and Exegesis*, edited by Ephraim Kanarfogel and Moshe Sokolow, 3–21. Jersey City, NJ: Ktav, 2010.

Lauer, Rena. "Cretan Jews and the First Sephardic Encounter in the Fifteenth Century." *Mediterranean Historical Review* 27 (2012): 129–40.

Lawee, Eric. "Aaron Aboulrabi: Maverick Exegete from Aragonese Sicily." *Hispania Judaica Bulletin* 9 (2013): 131–62.

Lawee, Eric. "Biblical Scholarship in Late Medieval Ashkenaz: The Turn to Rashi Supercommentary." *Hebrew Union College Annual* 86 (2015): 265–303.

Lawee, Eric. "Embarrassment and Re-Embracement of a Midrash on Genesis 2." In *Vixens Disturbing Vineyards: The Embarrassment and Embracement of Scriptures (A Festschrift Honoring Harry Fox Le'Veit Yoreh)*, edited by Aubrey Glazer et al., 192–207. Boston: Academic Studies, 2010.

Lawee, Eric. "'Epigon no'az: R. 'Ele'azar 'Ashkenazi ben R. Natan ha-bavli u-ferusho la-torah 'ṣafenat pa'neaḥ'." In *'Asupah le-yosef: qoveṣ meḥqarim shai le-Yosef Haqer*, edited by Yaron Ben Naeh et al., 170–86. Jerusalem: Zalman Shazar, 2014.

Lawee, Eric. "Exegesis and Appropriation: Reading Rashi in Late Medieval Spain." *Harvard Theological Review* 110 (2017): 494–519.

Lawee, Eric. "From Sefarad to Ashkenaz: A Case Study in the Rashi Supercommentary Tradition." *AJS Review* 30 (2006): 393–425.

Lawee, Eric. "A Genre is Born: The Genesis, Dynamics, and Role of Hebrew Exegetical Supercommentaries." *Revue des études juives* 176 (2017): 295–332.

Lawee, Eric. "Graven Images, Astromagical Cherubs, Mosaic Miracles: A Fifteenth-Century Curial-Rabbinic Exchange." *Speculum* 81 (2006): 754–95.

Lawee, Eric. "Isaac Abarbanel: From Medieval to Renaissance Jewish Biblical Scholarship." In *Hebrew Bible / Old Testament: The History of Its Interpretation*, edited by Magne Sæbø.. Vol. II: *From the Renaissance to the Enlightenment*, 190–214. Göttingen: Vanderhoeck & Ruprecht, 2008.

Lawee, Eric. *Isaac Abarbanel's Stance Toward Tradition: Defense, Dissent, and Dialogue*. Albany: SUNY Press, 2001.

Lawee, Eric. "Maimonides in the Eastern Mediterranean: The Case of Rashi's Resisting Readers." In *Maimonides After 800 Years: Essays on Maimonides and His Influence*, edited by Jay M. Harris, 183–206. Cambridge, MA: Harvard University Center for Jewish Studies, 2007.

Lawee, Eric. "The Path to Felicity: Teachings and Tensions in *'Even Shetiyyah* of Abraham Ben Judah, Disciple of Hasdai Crescas." *Mediaeval Studies* 59 (1997): 183–223.

Lawee, Eric. "The Reception of Rashi's *Commentary on the Torah* in Spain: The Case of Adam's Mating with the Animals." *Jewish Quarterly Review* 97 (2007): 33–66.

Lawee, Eric. "Sephardic Intellectuals: Challenges and Creativity (1391–1492)." In *The Jew in Medieval Iberia*, edited by Jonathan Ray, 350–91. Boston: Academic Studies, 2012.

Lawee, Eric. "'Servant of Solomon': Sensitivity to Language and Context in Moses Ibn Gabbai's Supercommentary on Rashi's Commentary on the Torah." *Ve-'Ed Ya'aleh (Gen 2:6): Essays in Biblical and Ancient Near Eastern Studies Presented to Edward L. Greenstein*. Forthcoming.

Lawee, Eric. "The Sins of the Fauna in Midrash, Rashi, and Their Medieval Interlocutors." *Jewish Studies Quarterly* 17 (2010): 56–98.

Lawee, Eric. "The Supercommentator as Thinker: Three Examples from the Rashi Supercommentary Tradition." *Journal of Jewish Studies* 67 (2016): 340–62.

Lawee, Eric, and Doron Forte. "'Sefer hassagot' 'al perush rashi la-torah ha-meyuḥas le-rabad." *Kobez Al Yad* 26 (2018): 77–134.

Lazarus-Yafeh, Hava. *Intertwined Worlds: Medieval Islam and Bible Criticism*. Princeton, NJ: Princeton University Press, 1992.

Leibowitz, Nehama. "Darko shel rashi be-hava'at midrashim be-ferusho la-torah." In *'Iyunim be-sefer shemot*. 2nd ed., 495–524. Jerusalem: World Zionist Organization, 1970.

Leibowitz, Nehama. *Limmud parshanei ha-torah u-derakhim lehora'atam: sefer bereshit*. Jerusalem: World Zionist Organization, 1975.

Leibowitz, Nehama. *Studies in Bereshit (Genesis)*, trans. Aryeh Newman, 4th rev. ed. Jerusalem: World Zionist Organization, 1981.

Leiman, Shnayer Z. "Ve-'et kol 'asher 'aṣavveh 'otekha: Was Rashi's Torah Scroll Flawed?" *Judaic Studies* 2 (2003): 3–21.

Lerner, Ralph. *Playing the Fool: Subversive Laughter in Troubled Times*. Chicago: University of Chicago Press, 2009.

Lesley, Arthur M. "The Place of the *Dialoghi d'Amore* in Contemporaneous Jewish Thought." In *Essential Papers on Jewish Culture in Renaissance and Baroque Italy*, edited by David Ruderman, 170–88. New York: New York University Press, 1992.

Levenson, Alan T. *The Making of the Modern Jewish Bible: How Scholars in Germany, Israel, and America Transformed an Ancient Text*. Lanham, MD: Rowman & Littlefield, 2011.

Levine, Michelle J. *Nahmanides on Genesis: The Art of Biblical Portraiture*. Providence, RI: Brown University, 2009.

Levinson, Bernard M. "The Human Voice in Divine Revelation: The Problem of Authority in Biblical Law." In *Innovation in Religious Traditions: Essays in the Interpretation of Religious Change*, edited by Michael A. Williams, Collett Cox, and Martin S. Jaffee, 35–71. Berlin: De Gruyter, 1992.

Levinson, Bernard M. "*You Must Not Add Anything to What I Command You*: Paradoxes of Canon and Authorship in Ancient Israel." *Numen* 50 (2003): 1–51.

Levy, B. Barry. "The State and Directions of Orthodox Bible Study." In *Modern Scholarship in the Study of Torah: Contributions and Limitations*, edited by Shalom Carmy. Northvale, NJ: Aronson, 1996.

Levy, Sarah, and Steven Levy. *The JPS Rashi Discussion Torah Commentary*. Philadelphia: Jewish Publication Society, 2017.

Licht, Yaakov. "Le-darko shel ha-ramban." In *Teudah* 3: *Meḥqarim be-sifrut ha-talmud bi-leshon ḥazal u-ve-farshanut ha-miqra'*, edited by Mordechai A. Friedman et al., 227–33. Tel Aviv: University Publishing Projects, 1983.

Liebes, Yehuda. *Studies in the Zohar*, translated by Arnold Schwartz, Stephanie Nakache, and Penina Peli. Albany: SUNY Press, 1993.

Limor, Ora. *Ben yehudim le-noṣrim: yehudim ve-noṣrim be-ma'arav 'eropah 'ad reshit ha-'et ha-ḥadashah*. 5 vols. Tel Aviv: Open University of Israel, 1993–98.

Limor, Ora, and Israel Jacob Yuval. "Skepticism and Conversion: Jews, Christians, and Doubters in *Sefer Ha-Nizzahon*." In *Hebraica Veritas? Christian Hebraists and the Study of Judaism in Early Modern Europe*, edited by Allison P. Coudert and Jeffrey S. Shoulson, 159–80. Philadelphia: University of Pennsylvania Press, 2004.

Lipshitz, Avraham. "Ha-ra'ba' be-ferushei ba'alei ha-tosafot 'al ha-torah." *Ha-Darom* 28 (1969): 202–21.

Liss, Hanna. *Creating Fictional Worlds: Peshat-Exegesis and Narrativity in Rashbam's Commentary on the Torah*. Leiden: Brill, 2011.

Liss, Hanna. "Scepticism, Critique, and the Art of Writing: Preliminary Considerations on the Question of Textual Authority in Medieval Peshaṭ Exegesis." In *Yearbook of the Maimonides Centre for Advanced Studies*, edited by Bill Rebiger, 15–46. Berlin/Boston: De Gruyter, 2018.

Lockshin, Martin I. *Rabbi Samuel Ben Meir's Commentary on Genesis*. Lewiston, NY: Edwin Mellen, 1989.

Lockshin, Martin I. "Tradition or Context: Two Exegetes Struggle with Peshat." In *From Ancient Israel to Modern Judaism: Essays in Honor of Marvin Fox*, edited by Jacob Neusner, Ernest S. Frerichs, and Nahum M. Sarna. 4 vols., 2:173–86. Atlanta, GA: Scholars, 1989.

Lorberbaum, Yair. "'Haṭ'oznekhah u-shema' le-divrei ḥakhamim': biqoret ha-'aggadah ba-'moreh nevukhim'." *Tarbiẓ* 78 (2009): 203–30.

Lorberbaum, Yair. "Temurot be-yaḥaso shel ha-rambam le-midrashot ḥazal." *Tarbiẓ* 78 (2009): 81–122.

Lowenstein, Steven M. "The Readership of Mendelssohn's Bible Translation." *Hebrew Union College Annual* 53 (1982): 179–213.

Mack, Hananel. "The Bifurcated Legacy of Rabbi Moses Hadarshan and the Rise of *Peshat* Exegesis in Medieval France." In *Regional Identities and Cultures of Medieval Jews*, edited by Javier Castaño, Talya Fishman, and Ephraim Kanarfogel, 73–92. London: Littman Library of Jewish Civilization, 2018.

Mack, Hananel. "''Im lavan garti ve-taryag miṣvot shamarti'—darkah shel ha-derashah mi-sifro shel r[abbi] Moshe hadarshan 'el perush rashi la-torah." *Tarbiẓ* 65 (1996): 251–61.

Mack, Hananel. "'Maṣati bi-yesodo shel rabbi Moshe ha-darshan': mah hevi' u-mah lo hevi' rashi be-ferushav mi-torato shel r[abbi] Moshe ha-darshan." In *Rashi: demuto vi-yeṣirato*, edited by Avraham Grossman and Sara Japhet. 2 vols., 2:327–51. Jerusalem: Zalman Shazar, 2008.

Mack, Hananel. *Mi-sodo shel Moshe hadarshan*. Jerusalem: Bialik, 2010.

Maharal: 'aqdamot – pirqei ḥayyim, mishnah, hashpa'ah, edited by Elchanan Reiner. Jerusalem: Zalman Shazar, 2015.

Mak, Bonnie. *How the Page Matters*. Toronto: University of Toronto Press, 2011.

Malachi, Zvi. *Be-no'am siaḥ: peraqim mi-toledot sifrutenu*. Lod: Habermann Institute for Literary Research, 1983.

Mandelbrote, Scott, and Joanna Weinberg, eds. *Jewish Books and Their Readers: Aspects of the Intellectual Life of Christians and Jews in Early Modern Europe*. Leiden: Brill, 2016.

Mann, Jacob. "A Commentary to the Pentateuch à la Rashi's." *Hebrew Union College Annual* 15 (1940): 497–527.

Maori, Yeshayahu. "''Aggadot ḥaluqot' be-ferush rashi la-miqra'." *Shenaton le-ḥeqer ha-miqra' ve-ha-mizraḥ ha-qadum* 19 (2009): 155–207.

Maori, Yeshayahu. "'Al nusaḥ perush rashi la-torah she-hayah lifnei ramban." In *Sha'arei lashon: meḥqarim bi-leshon ha-'ivrit, ba-'aramit u-vi-leshonot ha-yehudim mugashim le-Moshe bar 'Asher*, edited by Aharon Maman, Steven E. Fassberg, and Yohanan Breuer. 3 vols., 1:188–219. Jerusalem: Bialik, 2007.

Maori, Yeshayahu. "'Ha-yerushalmi ha-katuv be-ferushei rashi' (ramban la-bemidbar 4:16) ve-nosaḥ divrei rashi." *'Iyyunei miqra' u-farshanut* 7 (2005): 385–97.

Maori, Yeshayahu. "Nosaḥ perush rashi la-torah: maṣav ha-meḥqar." In *Rashi: demuto vi-yeṣirato*, edited by Avraham Grossman and Sara Japhet. 2 vols., 1:63–98. Jerusalem: Zalman Shazar, 2008.

Maori, Yeshayahu. "'Tiqqun soferim' ve-'kinnah ha-katuv' be-ferush rashi la-miqra'." In *Neṭi'ot le-david: sefer yovel le-David Halivni*, edited by Yaakov

Elman, Ephraim B. Halivni, and Zvi A. Steinfeld. 99–108. Jerusalem: Orhot Press, 2004.

Marciano, Yoel. "Ḥakhamim bi-sefarad ba-me'ah ha-ḥamesh-'esrei: ḥinukham, limmudam, yeṣiratam, ma'amadam, u-demutam." PhD dissertation, Hebrew University of Jerusalem, 2012.

Marciano, Yoel. "Me-'aragon le-qasṭilyah: le-toledot shiṭat limmudam shel ḥakhmei sefarad ba-me'ah ha-ḥamesh 'esreh." *Tarbiẓ* 77 (2008): 573–99.

Marcus, Ivan G. "Exegesis for the Few and for the Many: Judah He-Hasid's Biblical Commentaries." *Meḥqerei yerushalayim be-maḥashevet yisra'el* 8 (1988): 1–24 (English section).

Marcus, Ivan G. "A Jewish-Christian Symbiosis: The Culture of Early Ashkenaz." In *Cultures of the Jews: A New History*, edited by David Biale, 449–516. New York: Schocken, 2002.

Marcus, Ivan G. "Rashi's Choice: The Humash Commentary as Rewritten Midrash." In *Studies in Medieval Jewish Intellectual and Social History: Festschrift in Honor of Robert Chazan*, edited by David Engel, Lawrence H. Schiffman, and Elliot R. Wolfson, 29–45. Leiden: Brill, 2012.

Marcus, Ivan G. Sefer Hasidim *and the Ashkenazic Book in Medieval Europe.* Philadelphia: University of Pennsylvania Press, 2018.

Marcus, Ivan G. "Why Did Medieval Northern French Jewry (Ṣarfat) Disappear?" In *Jews, Christians and Muslims in Medieval and Early Modern Times: A Festschrift in Honor of Mark R. Cohen*, edited by Arnold E. Franklin et al., 99–117. Leiden: Brill, 2014.

Marx, Moses. "On the Date of Appearance of the First Printed Hebrew Books." In *Alexander Marx Jubilee Volume*, edited by Saul Lieberman, 2 vols. 1:481–502). New York: Jewish Theological Seminary of America, 1950.

Marx, Tzvi. "Judaic Doctrine of Scripture." In *Holy Scriptures in Judaism, Christianity and Islam: Hermeneutics, Values and Society*, edited by Hendrik M. Vroom and Jerald D. Gort, 43–56. Amsterdam: Rodopi, 1997.

McKee, Sally. *Uncommon Dominion: Venetian Crete and the Myth of Ethnic Purity.* Philadelphia: University of Pennsylvania Press, 2000.

Medieval Jewish Civilization: An Encyclopedia. Edited by Norman Roth. New York: Routledge, 2003.

Meirovich, Harvey W. *A Vindication of Judaism: The Polemics of the Hertz Pentateuch.* New York: Jewish Theological Seminary of America, 1998.

Melamed, Abraham. *'Al kitfei 'anaqim: toledot ha-polmos ben 'aḥaronim le-rishonim ba-hagut ha-yehudit be-yemei ha-benayim u-ve-reshit ha-'et ha-ḥadashah.* Ramat-Gan: Bar-Ilan University, 2003.

Melamed, Ezra Zion. *Mefareshei ha-miqra': darkhehem ve-shiṭotehem.* 2nd ed., 2 vols. Jerusalem: Magnes, 1979.

Melzer, Arthur M. *Philosophy Between the Lines: The Lost History of Esoteric Writing.* Chicago: University of Chicago Press, 2014.

Merchavia, Ch. *Ha-talmud bi-re'i ha-naṣrut*. Jerusalem: Bialik, 1970.

Merchavia, Ch. "Quntres neged ha-talmud mimei serefat ha-talmud be-'iṭalyah." *Tarbiẓ* 37 (1967): 78–96, 191–207.

Michael, Reuven. *Y. M. Jost: 'avi ha-hisṭoriografyah ha-yehudit ha-modernit*. Jerusalem: Magnes, 1983.

Miller, Chaim. *Turning Judaism Outward: A Biography of Rabbi Menachem Mendel Schneerson the Seventh Lubavitcher Rebbe*. Brooklyn, NY: Kol Menachem, 2014.

Mincer, Rachel Zohn. "The Increasing Reliance on Ritual Handbooks in Pre–Print Era Ashkenaz." *Jewish History* 31 (2017): 103–28.

Minnis, A. J. *Medieval Theory of Authorship: Scholastic Literary Attitudes in the Later Middle Ages*. 2nd ed. Aldershot: Scolar, 1988.

Minnis, A. J., and A. B. Scott, eds. *Medieval Literary Theory and Criticism, c. 1100–c. 1375: The Commentary Tradition*. Oxford: Clarendon Press, 1988.

Modigliani, Anna. "Tipografi a Roma (1467–1477)." In *Gutenberg e Roma: le origini della stampa nella Città dei Papi (1467–1477)*, edited by Massimo Miglio and Orietta Rossini, 41–48. Naples: Electa Napoli, 1997.

Mondschein, Aharon. "'Hakhi qara' shemo ya'aqov, vayya'qeveni': la-metodologyah shel rashi ve-ra'ba' be-yaḥasam le-ma'aseh ha-'aqvah shel ya'aqov." *Talpiyot* 12 (2011): 50–61.

Mondschein, Aharon. "'Ḥakhmei ha-masoret bade'u mi-libam ṭe'amim li-mele'im u-le-ḥaserim': 'al ma'avaqo shel r[abbi] 'Avraham 'ibn 'Ezra be-niṣṣul ha-ketiv ha-miqra'i ke-kheli parshani." *Shenaton le-ḥeqer ha-miqra' ve-ha-mizraḥ ha-qadum* 19 (2009): 245–321.

Mondschein, Aharon. "Le-yaḥaso shel ra'ba' 'el ha-shimmush ha-parshani be-middat ha-gemaṭriyah." *Teudah* 8 (1982): 137–61.

Mondschein, Aharon. "R[abbi] 'Avraham 'ibn 'Ezra – ha-'ish neged ha-zerem." *Beit Mikra* 49 (2004): 140–55.

Mondschein, Aharon. "Rashi, rashbam ve-'ibn 'Ezra shonim mishnatam be-sugiyat 'tiqqun soferim'." *'Iyyunei miqra' u-farshanut* 8 (2008): 409–50.

Mondschein, Aharon. "'Ve-'en bi-sefarav peshaṭ raq 'ehad mini 'elef': le-derekh ha-hityaḥasut shel ra'ba' le-ferush rashi la-torah." *'Iyyunei miqra' u-farshanut* 5 (2000): 221–48.

Mondschein, Yehoshua. "He'erah." *'Alei sefer* 4 (1977): 180.

Moshe Idel: Representing God. Edited by Hava Tirosh-Samuelson and Aaron W. Hughes. Leiden: Brill, 2014.

Müller, Jörg R. "'*Ereẓ gezerah*: 'Land of Persecution': Pogroms against the Jews in the *regnum Teutonicum* from c. 1280 to 1350." In *The Jews of Europe in the Middle Ages (Tenth to Fifteenth Centuries)*, edited by Christoph Cluse, 245–58. Turnhout, Belgium: Brepols, 2004.

Muter Goldberg, Silke. "Language and Gender in Early Modern and 19th Century Jewish Devotional Literature." In *Gender, Tradition, and Renewal*, edited by Robert L. Platzner. Oxford: Peter Lang, 2005.

Nadler, Alan. "Romancing Spinoza." *Commentary Magazine* 122 (December 2006): 25–30.

Nadler, Steven. *Spinoza: A Life*. Cambridge: Cambridge University Press, 1999.

Netanyahu, B. *The Marranos of Spain from the Late 14th to the Early 16th Century According to Contemporary Hebrew Sources*. 3rd ed., updated and expanded. Ithaca, NY: Cornell University Press, 1999.

Neubauer, Ad. *Catalogue of the Hebrew Manuscripts in the Bodleian Library*. 2 vols. Oxford: Clarendon, 1886–1906.

Neubauer, Ad. "Commentar zu Rashi's Pentateuch-Commentar von Dossa aus Widdin." *Israelietische Letterbode* 8 (1882–83): 37–54.

Neubauer, Ad. "Ergänzungen und Verbesserungen zu Abba Mari's מנחת קנאות aus Hanschriften." *Israelietische Letterbode* 4/ 5 (1878– 79): 4:122– 32, 160– 73; 5:53–58, 71–83.

Novak, David. *The Image of the Non-Jew in Judaism: An Historical and Constructive Study of the Noahide Laws*. New York: E. Mellen, 1983.

Nuriel, Avraham. "Ha-shimmush ba-milah 'gharib' be-'moreh nevukhim'." In *Galui ve-samui ba-filosofyah ha-yehudit be-yemei ha-benayim*, 158–64. Jerusalem: Magnes, 2000.

Oakley, Francis. *The Western Church in the Later Middle Ages*. Ithaca, NY: Cornell University Press, 1979.

Ofer, Yosef. "Histaigut semuyah mi-midrashim be-ferushei rashi la-torah." *'Iyyunei miqra' u-farshanut* 8 (2008): 279–92.

Ofer, Yosef. "Mapot 'ereṣ yisra'el be-ferush rashi la-torah – u-ma'amado shel k[etav] y[ad] leipzig 1." *Tarbiẓ* 76 (2007): 435–44.

Ofer, Yosef, and Jonathan Jacobs. *Tosafot ramban le-ferusho la-torah she-nikhtevo be-'ereṣ yisra'el*. Jerusalem: Herzog Academic College and World Union of Jewish Studies, 2013.

Offenberg, Adri K. *A Choice of Corals: Facets of Fifteenth-Century Hebrew Printing*. Nieuwkoop: De Graaf, 1992.

Offenberg, Adri K., ed. *Catalogue of Books Printed in the XVth Century Now in the British Library; BMC Part XIII: Hebraica*. The Netherlands: Hes & De Graaf, 2004.

Offenberg, Adri K. "What Do We Know about Hebrew Printing in Guadalajara, Híjar, and Zamora?" In *The Late Medieval Hebrew Book in the Western Mediterranean: Hebrew Manuscripts and Incunabula in Context*, edited by Javier del Barco, 313–37. Leiden: Brill, 2015.

Ogren, Brian. *Renaissance and Rebirth: Reincarnation in Early Modern Italian Kabbalah*. Leiden: Brill, 2009.

Orfali, Moisés. "Alusiones polémicas a la exégesis de Rasi en la controversia de Tortosa." *Helmantica* 36 (1985): 107–17.

Ovadyah, Avraham. "Perush r[abbi] 'E[liyahu] Mizraḥi 'al rashi." In *Ketavim nivḥarim*. 2 vols., 1:140–98. Jerusalem: Mosad Harav Kuk, 1942.

Pacios Lopez, Antonio. *La Disputa de Tortosa*. 2 vols. Madrid: Consejo superior de investigaciones cientificas, 1957.

Parsons, William B. *Machiavelli's Gospel: The Critique of Christianity in "The Prince."* Rochester, NY: University of Rochester Press, 2016.

Pasternak, Nurit. "Marchion in Hebrew Manuscripts: State Censorship in Florence, 1472." In *The Hebrew Book in Early Modern Italy*, edited by Joseph R. Hacker and Adam Shear, 26–55. Philadelphia: University of Pennsylvania Press, 2011.

Pawley, Christine. "Seeking 'Significance': Actual Readers, Specific Reading Communities." *Book History* 5 (2002): 143–60.

Pedaya, Haviva. *Ha-ramban – hit'alut: zeman maḥzori ve-teqst qadosh*. Tel Aviv: Am Oved, 2003.

Pearce, S. J. *The Andalusi Literary & Intellectual Tradition: The Role of Arabic in Judah Ibn Tibbon's Ethical Will*. Bloomington: Indiana University Press, 2017.

Peli, Moshe. "Ha-biyografyah ke-janer ba-haskalah: demuto shel Yiṣḥaq 'Abarbanel ke-maskil ha-megasher ben shtei tarbuyot." *Meḥqerei yerushalayim be-sifrut 'ivrit* 16 (1997): 75–88.

Penkower, Yitshak S. "Hagahot nosafot shel rashi le-ferusho 'al ha-torah." In *'Or le-me'ir: meḥqarim be-miqra', ba-leshonot ha-shemiyot, be-sifrut ḥazal u-ve-tarbuyot 'atiqot mugashim le-Mayer Gruber*, edited by Shamir Yona, 363–409. Beer-Sheva: Ben-Gurion University of the Negev Press, 2010.

Penkower, Yitshak S. "Hagahot rashi le-ferusho la-torah." *Jewish Studies Internet Journal* 6 (2007): 1–48.

Penkower, Yitshak S. "Nosaḥ ha-miqra' she-'amad lifnei rashi ke-fi she-hu mishtaqqef be-ferushav la-miqra'." In *Rashi: demuto vi-yeṣirato*, edited by Avraham Grossman and Sara Japhet. 2 vols., 1:99–122. Jerusalem: Zalman Shazar, 2008.

Penkower, Yitshak S. "Shnei ḥakhamim ha-nizkarim be-khitvei ha-yad shel perushei rashi la-miqra' – r[abbi] Yehudah ve-r[abbi] Yehudah ha-darshan." In *Shai le-Sarah Yafet: meḥqarim ba-miqra', be-farshanuto, uvi-leshono*, edited by Moshe Bar-Asher et al., 233–47. Jerusalem: Bialik, 2007.

Penkower, Yitshak S. "Tahalikh ha-qanonizaṣiyah shel perush rashi la-torah." In *Limmud ve-da'at be-maḥashavah yehudit*, edited by Haim Kreisel. 2 vols., 2:123–46. Beer-Sheva: Ben-Gurion University of the Negev Press, 2006.

Perarnau i Espelt, Josep. "Notícia de més de setanta inventaris de llibres de jueus gironins." In *Per a una història de la Girona jueva*, edited by David Romano. 2 vols., 1:283–334. Gerona: Ajuntament de Girona, 1988.

Peretz, Yosi. "Shnayim miqra' ve-'eḥad targum: le-'or ha-mimṣa be-khitvei ha-yad ha-'ashkenaziyim shel ha-torah bi-yemei ha-benayim." *Ṭalelei 'Orot* 14 (2008): 53–61.

Perles, Joseph. "Ahron ben Gerson Aboulrabi." *Revue des études juives* 21 (1890): 246–69.

Perry, Micha. "Byzantium's Role in the Transmission of Jewish Knowledge in the Middle Ages: The Attitude toward Circumcision." In *Jews in Byzantium: Dialectics of Minority and Majority Cultures,* edited by Robert Bonfil et al., 643–58. Leiden: Brill, 2012.

Perry, Micha. *Masoret ve-shinui: mesirat yeda' be-qerev yehudei ma'arav 'eropah bi-yemei ha-benayim.* Tel-Aviv: Hakibbutz Hameuhad, 2010.

Pessin, Sarah. "Matter, Metaphor, and Privative Pointing: Maimonides on the Complexity of Human Being." *American Catholic Philosophical Quarterly* 76 (2002): 75–88.

Pirqei Neḥamah: sefer zikaron le-Neḥamah Lebovits, edited by Moshe Ahrend and Rut Ben-Meir. Jerusalem: Ha-Sokhnut ha-Yehudit, 2001.

Polliack, Meira. "The Spanish Legacy in the Hebrew Bible Commentaries of Abraham Ibn Ezra and Profayt Duran." In *"Encuentros" and "Desencuentros": Spanish Jewish Cultural Interaction Throughout History,* edited by Carlos Carrete Parrondo et al., 83–103. Tel Aviv: University Publishing Projects, 2000.

Pormann, Peter E., ed. *A Descriptive Catalogue of the Hebrew Manuscripts of Corpus Christi College, Oxford.* Cambridge: D.S. Brewer, 2015.

Posen, Rafael B. "Yaḥaso shel rashi le-targum 'onkelos." In *Rashi: demuto vi-yeṣirato,* edited by Avraham Grossman and Sara Japhet. 2 vols., 2:275–93. Jerusalem: Zalman Shazar, 2008.

Posnanski, Adolf. *Schiloh, ein beitrag zur geschichte der messiaslehre.* Leipzig: J.C. Hinrichs, 1904.

Prebor, Gila. "Darko ha-parshanit shel rashi be-shimusho be-midreshei ḥazal be-ferusho le-qohelet." *Shenaton le-ḥeqer ha-miqra' ve-ha-mizraḥ ha-qadum* 19 (2009): 209–29.

Prebor, Gila. "'Sepher ha-ziqquq' shel Domenico yerushalmi." *Italia* 18 (2008): 7–296.

Preschel, Tovia. "Supercommentaries on the Pentateuch." In *Encyclopaedia Judaica,* edited by Michael Berenbaum and Fred Skolnik. 22 vols., 19:315–16. Detroit, MI: Macmillan, 2007.

Priel, Yosef. "Darko ha-parshanit shel rabbi Ḥizqiyah ben Manoaḥ (Ḥizzequni) be-ferusho la-torah." PhD dissertation, Bar-Ilan University, 2010.

Rabinowitz, Louis I. "The Study of a Midrash." *Jewish Quarterly Review* 58 (1967): 143–61.

Rachaman, Yosefah. "'Ibbud midrashim be-ferusho shel rashi la-torah." *Teudah* 3 (1983): 261–68.

Rapel, Dov. "Ha-ramban 'al ha-galut ve-'al ha-ge'ulah." In *Ge'ulah u-medinah,* 79–109. Jerusalem: Misrad ha-hinukh veha-tarbut, 1979.

Rapel, Dov. *Rashi: temunat 'olamo ha-yehudit.* Jerusalem: Misrad ha-ḥinukh ha-tarbut ve-ha-sporṭ, 1995.

Rapoport, Chaim. "The Lubavitcher Rebbe's Commentary on Rashi: Some Initial Reflections." Unpublished manuscript.

Ravitsky, Aviram. "Aristotelian Logic and Talmudic Methodology: The Commentaries on the 13 Hermeneutic Principles and Their Application to Logic." In *Judaic Logic*, edited by Andrew Schumann, 117–42. Piscataway, NJ: Gorgias, 2010.

Ravitsky, Aviram. *Logiqah 'arisṭoṭelit u-metodologyah talmudit: yissumah shel ha-logiqah ha-'arisṭoṭelit ba-perushim la-midot she-ha-torah nidreshet bahen*. Jerusalem: Magnes, 2009.

Ravitzky, Aviezer. "Aristotle's *Meteorology* and the Maimonidean Modes of Interpreting the Account of Creation." *Aleph* 8 (2008): 361–400.

Ravitzky, Aviezer. "'Haṣivi lakh ṣiyyunim' le-ṣiyyon: gilgulo shel ra'ayon." In Aviezer Ravitzky, *'Al da'at ha-maqom: meḥqarim ba-hagut ha-yehudit u-ve-toldoteha*, 34–73. Jerusalem: Keter, 1991.

Ravitzky, Aviezer. "'Ma'amad raglei ha-mequbbalim be-rashei ha-filosofim?' 'Al vikkuaḥ qandi'ah ba-me'ah ha-ḥamesh-'esrei." In Aviezer Ravitzky, *'Al da'at ha-maqom: meḥqarim ba-hagut ha-yehudit u-ve-toldoteha*, 182–211. Jerusalem: Keter, 1991.

Ravitzky, Aviezer. "'The Ravings of Amulet Writers': Maimonides and Disciples on Language, Nature and Magic." In *Between Rashi and Maimonides: Themes in Medieval Jewish Thought, Literature and Exegesis*, edited by Ephraim Kanarfogel and Moshe Sokolow, 93–130. Jersey City, NJ: Ktav, 2010.

Ray, Jonathan. *The Sephardic Frontier: The Reconquista and the Jewish Community in Medieval Iberia*. Ithaca, NY: Cornell University Press, 2006.

Raz-Krakotzkin, Amnon. *The Censor, the Editor, and the Text: The Catholic Church and the Shaping of the Jewish Canon in the Sixteenth Century*, translated by Jackie Feldman. Philadelphia: University of Pennsylvania Press, 2007.

Rebiger, Bill. "The Early Opponents of the Kabbalah and the Role of Sceptical Argumentations: An Outline." In *Yearbook of the Maimonides Centre for Advanced Studies: 2016*, edited by Giuseppe Veltri, 39–58. Berlin: De Gruyter, 2016.

Reiner, Avraham (Rami). "Bible and Politics: A Correspondence Between Rabbenu Tam and the Authorities of Champagne." In *Entangled Histories: Knowledge, Authority, and Jewish Culture in the Thirteenth Century*, edited by Elisheva Baumgarten, Ruth Mazo Karras, and Katelyn Mesler, 59–72. Philadelphia: University of Pennsylvania Press, 2017.

Reiner, Avraham (Rami). "Mumar 'okhel nevelot le-te'avon—pasul? mashehu 'al nosaḥ u-ferusho bi-yedei rashi." In *Lo yasur shevet mi-yehudah: hanhagah, rabanut, u-qehilah be-toledot yisra'el—meḥqarim mugashim le-prof' Shim'on Schwarzfuchs*, edited by Joseph R. Hacker and Yaron Harel, 219–28. Jerusalem: Bialik, 2011.

Reiner, Elchanan. "The Ashkenazi Élite at the Beginning of the Modern Era: Manuscript versus Printed Book." *Polin* 10 (1997): 85–98.

Reiner, Elchanan. "Ben 'ashkenaz li-rushalayim: ḥakhamim 'ashkenazim be-'ereṣ yisra'el le-'aḥar ha-mavet ha-shaḥor." *Shalem* 4 (1984): 27–62.

Reiner, Elchanan. "''En ṣarikh shum yehudi lilmod davar raq ha-talmud levado': 'al limmud ve-tokhanei limmud be-'ashkenaz be-yemei ha-sefer ha-rishonim." In *Ta shema': meḥqarim be-madda'ei ha-yahadut le-zikhro shel Yisra'el M. Ta-Shma*, edited by Avraham (Rami) Reiner et al. 2 vols, 2:705–46. Alon Shvut: Tevunot, 2012.

Reiner, Elchanan. "Temurot bi-yeshivot polin ve-'ashkenaz ba-me'ot ha-tet-zayin - ha-yod-zayin ve-ha-vikkuaḥ 'al ha-pilpul." In *Ke-minhag 'ashkenaz u-folin: sefer yovel le-Chone Shmeruk: qovets meḥkarim be-tarbut yehudit*, edited by Israel Bartal, Ezra Mendelsohn, and Chava Turniansky, 9–80. Jerusalem: Zalman Shazar, 1993.

Rendsburg, Gary A. "The Joseph Story: Ancient Literary Art at Its Best." http://thetorah.com/the-joseph-story-ancient-literary-art-at-its-best/.

Revel, Bernard. "Inquiry into the Sources of Karaite Halakah." *Jewish Quarterly Review* 3 (1913): 337–96.

Richler, Benjamin, ed. *Hebrew Manuscripts in the Vatican Library: Catalogue*. Vatican City: Biblioteca apostolica Vaticana, 2008.

Rigler, Michael. "Ha-yehudim be-'iyei 'agan ha-yam ha-tikhon ha-mizraḥi ke-sappaqei sefarim." *'Alei sefer* 21 (2010): 75–90.

Rivkind, Isaac. "Diqduqei soferim." In *Sefer yovel likhevod Alexander Marx*, edited by Saul Lieberman, 2 vols., 2:401–32. New York: Jewish Theological Seminary of America, 1950.

Robinson, James T. "The Ibn Tibbon Family: A Dynasty of Translators in Medieval 'Provence'." In *Be'erot Yitzhak: Studies in Memory of Isadore Twersky*, edited by Jay M. Harris, 193–224. Cambridge, MA: Harvard University Center for Jewish Studies, 2005.

Robinson, James T. "Samuel ibn Tibbon," in *Stanford Encyclopedia of Philosophy*, http://plato.stanford.edu/entries/tibbon/.

Robinson, James T. *Samuel Ibn Tibbon's Commentary on Ecclesiastes: The Book of the Soul of Man*. Tübingen: Mohr Siebeck, 2007.

Robinson, James T. "Samuel Ibn Tibbon's Commentary on Ecclesiastes and the Philosopher's Prooemium." In *Studies in Medieval Jewish History and Literature III*, edited by Isadore Twersky and Jay M. Harris, 83–146. Cambridge, MA: Harvard University Press, 2000.

Robinson, James T. "We Drink Only from the Master's Water: Maimonides and Maimonideanism in Southern France, 1200–1306." In *Epigonism and the Dynamics of Jewish Culture*, edited by Shlomo Berger and Irene E. Zwiep, 27–60. Leuven: Peeters, 2008.

Roness, Yitzhak, and Aviad Y. Hollander. "Keṣad yihiyu ha-yeladim na'im: rabbi 'Eli'ezer ve-ha-'ugeniqah be-'enei ḥazal." *Jewish Studies Internet Journal* 10 (2012): 25–44.

Rosemann, Philipp W. *The Story of a Great Medieval Book: Peter Lombard's Sentences.* Peterborough: Broadview, 2007.

Rosenberg, Shalom. "''Arba'ah ṭurim' le-r[abbi] 'Avraham be-r[abbi] Yehudah talmido shel don Ḥasdai Qresqes." *Meḥqerei yerushalayim be-maḥashevet yisra'el* 3 (1984): 525–621.

Rosenberg, Shalom. "Higayon, safah u-parshanut ha-miqra' bi-khetavav shel r[abbi] Yosef 'ibn Kaspi." In *Dat ve-safah,* edited by Moshe Hallamish and Asa Kasher, 105–14. Tel Aviv: University Publishing Projects, 1981.

Rosenblum, Jordan D. *The Jewish Dietary Laws in the Ancient World.* New York: Cambridge University Press, 2016.

Rosman, Moshe. "Innovative Tradition: Jewish Culture in the Polish-Lithuanian Commonwealth." In *Cultures of the Jews: A New History*, edited by David Biale, 519–70. New York: Schocken, 2002.

Roth, Cecil. "Jewish Intellectual Life in Medieval Sicily." *Jewish Quarterly Review* 47 (1956–57): 317–35.

Roth, Pinchas. "Rabbinic Politics, Royal Conquest, and the Creation of a Halakhic Tradition in Medieval Provence." In *Regional Identities and Cultures of Medieval Jews,* edited Javier Castaño, Talya Fishman, and Ephraim Kanarfogel, 173–91. London: Littman Library of Jewish Civilization, 2018.

Roth, Pinchas. "Regional Boundaries and Medieval Halakhah: Rabbinic Responsa from Catalonia to Southern France in the Thirteenth and Fourteenth Centuries." *Jewish Quarterly Review* 105 (2015): 72–98.

Rothschild, Jean-Pierre. "*Scientia bifrons*: Les ambivalences de la *'hokhmâh* (*sapientia/scientia*) dans la pensée juive du moyen âge occidental après Maïmonide." In *"Scientia" und "Ars" Im Hoch- und Spätmittelalter* (= *Miscellanea Mediaevalia* 22), edited by Ingrid Craemer-Ruegenberg and Andreas Speer. 2 vols., 2:667–84. Berlin: De Gruyter, 1994.

Rozenthal, Judah. "Rashi ve-ha-rambam be-ha'arakhat ha-dorot." In *Meḥqarim u-meqorot*. 2 vols., 1:117–25. Jerusalem: Reuven Mas, 1967.

Rubin, Rehav. *Portraying the Land: Hebrew Maps of the Land of Israel from Rashi to the Early 20th Century.* Berlin: De Gruyter, 2018.

Rubinstein, Tanja. "An Alternative Version of Maimonides' Thirteen Principles of Faith." *Zutot* 13 (2016): 81–93.

Rudavsky, Tamar M. "The Science of Scripture: Abraham Ibn Ezra and Spinoza on Biblical Hermeneutics." In *Spinoza and Medieval Jewish Philosophy*, edited by Steven Nadler, 59–78. Cambridge: Cambridge University Press, 2014.

Ruderman, David B. *Early Modern Jewry: A New Cultural History.* Princeton, NJ: Princeton University Press, 2010.

Ruderman, David B. *Jewish Thought and Scientific Discovery in Early Modern Europe.* New Haven, CA: Yale University Press, 1995.

Russ-Fishbane, Elisha. "Between Politics and Piety: Abraham Maimonides and His Times." PhD dissertation, Harvard University, 2009.

Russ-Fishbane, Elisha. "Maimonidean Controversies After Maimonides: The Egyptian Context." *Hebrew Union College Annual* 88 (2017): 159–202.

Ryder, Alan. *Alfonso the Magnamimous: King of Aragon, Naples and Sicily, 1396–1458.* Oxford: Oxford University Press, Clarendon, 1990.

Sackson, Adrian. *Joseph Ibn Kaspi: Portrait of a Hebrew Philosopher in Medieval Provence.* Leiden: Brill, 2017.

Sáenz-Badillos, Ángel. "Jewish and Christian Interpretations in Arragel's Biblical Glosses." In *Medieval Exegesis and Religious Difference: Commentary, Conflict, and Community in the Premodern Mediterranean*, edited by Ryan Szpiech, 142–54. New York: Fordham University Press, 2015.

Sagi, Avi. "'He Slew the Egyptian and Hid Him in the Sand': Jewish Tradition and the Moral Element." *Hebrew Union College Annual* 67 (1996): 55–76.

Sagi, Avi. *The Open Canon: On the Meaning of Halakhic Discourse*, translated by Batya Stein. London: Continuum, 2007.

Sainte-Beuve, Charles Augustin. "What Is a Classic?" In *Literary and Philosophical Essays: French, German and Italian (= The Harvard Classics 32)*, edited by Charles W. Eliot, 126–39. New York: P.F. Collier, 1910.

Saleh, Walid A. "Preliminary Remarks on the Historiography of *Tafsīr* in Arabic: A History of the Book Approach." *Journal of Qur'anic Studies* 12 (2010): 6–40.

Sand, Efraim. "'Aqevot shel parshanut yehudit-bizanṭit be-ferushei rashi u-vet midrasho." *Madda'ei ha-yahadut* 50 (2015): 1–47.

Sandman, Israel Moshe. "The MeSOBEB NeTIBOT of Samuel Ibn Matut ('Motot'): Introductory Excursus, Critical Edition, and Annotated Translation." 2 vols. PhD dissertation, University of Chicago, 2006.

Sandorfi, Eitan. "Le-mi nitenah 'ereṣ yisra'el 'aḥar ha-mabbul." *Shema'tin* 136 (1999): 137–44.

Sanneh, Lamin. *Beyond Jihad: The Pacifist Tradition in West African Islam.* Oxford: Oxford University Press, 2016.

Saperstein, Marc. *Decoding the Rabbis: A Thirteenth-Century Commentary on the Aggadah.* Cambridge, MA: Harvard University Press, 1980.

Sarna, Nahum. "Abraham Ibn Ezra as an Exegete." In *Rabbi Abraham Ibn Ezra: Studies in the Writings of a Twelfth-Century Polymath*, edited by Isadore Twersky and Jay M. Harris, 1–21. Cambridge, MA: Harvard University Center for Jewish Studies, 1993.

Sarna, Nahum. "Rashi the Commentator." In *Studies in Biblical Interpretation*, 127–37. Philadelphia: Jewish Publication Society, 2000.

Sasson, Gilad. "Gishot 'apologeṭiyot le-sippur ha-miqra'i ha-murḥav 'al david ve-'avigayil bi-teshuvot r[abbi] David ben Zimra (ha-radbaz) ve-r[abbi] Levi ben Ḥabib (ha-ralbaḥ)." *Pe'amim* 130 (2012): 29–60.

Scandaliato, Angela. *Judaica minora sicula*. Florence: Giuntina, 2006.

Schabel, Chris. "Religion." In *Cyprus: Society and Culture 1191–1374*, edited by Angel Nicolaou-Konnari and Chris Schabel, 157–218. Leiden: Brill, 2005.

Schacter, Jacob J. "'Al sefer "Alilot devarim'." *'Alei sefer 8* (1980): 148–50.

Scheindlin, Raymond. "Merchants and Intellectuals, Rabbis and Poets: Judeo-Arabic Culture in the Golden Age of Islam." In *Cultures of the Jews: A New History*, edited by David Biale, 313–86. New York: Schocken, 2002.

Schiller-Szinessy, S. M. *Catalogue of the Hebrew Manuscripts Preserved in the University Library, Cambridge*. Cambridge: University Library, 1876.

Schlossberg, Eliezer. "'Iyyunim be-darkhei parshanuto shel R. Meyuḥas ben 'Eliyahu." *Megadim* 23 (1995): 83–96.

Schmelzer, Menahem H. "Hebrew Incunabula: An Agenda for Research." In Menahem H. Schmelzer, *Studies in Jewish Bibliography and Medieval Hebrew Poetry*, 30–37 (English section). New York: Jewish Theological Seminary of America, 2006.

Schoenfeld, Devorah. *Isaac on Jewish and Christian Altars: Polemic and Exegesis in Rashi and the Glossa Ordinaria*. New York: Fordham University Press, 2013.

Schorr, Joshua Heschel. "Toledot ḥakhmei yisra'el: r[abbi] 'Aharon 'Al Rabi." *Ṣiyyon* 1 (1840): 166–68, 193–96.

Schwartz, Baruch J. "Perusho shel rashi li-shemot 6:1–9: beḥinah meḥudeshet." In *'Leyashev peshuṭo shel miqra': 'asupat meḥqarim be-farshanut ha-miqra'*, edited by Eran Viezel and Sara Japhet, 100–111. Jerusalem: Bialik / Mandel Institute, 2011.

Schwartz, Daniel B. *The First Modern Jew: Spinoza and the History of an Image*. Princeton, NJ: Princeton University Press, 2012.

Schwartz, Dov. *'Asṭrologyah u-magyah ba-hagut ha-yehudit bi-yemei ha-benayim*. Ramat-Gan: Bar-Ilan University Press, 1999.

Schwartz, Dov. "Divine Immanence in Medieval Jewish Philosophy." *Journal of Jewish Thought and Philosophy* 3 (1994): 249–78.

Schwartz, Dov. "'Ereṣ, maqom ve-kokhav: ma'amadah shel 'ereṣ yisra'el bi-tefisato shel ha-ḥug ha-ne'oplaṭoni ba-me'ah ha-14." In *'Ereṣ yisra'el ba-hagut ha-yehudit be-yemei ha-benayim*, edited by Moshe Halamish and Aviezer Ravitzky, 138–50. Jerusalem: Mekhon Ben-Zvi, 1991.

Schwartz, Dov. "Filosofyah ki-kheli tiqshoret be-bizanṭyon be-shilhei yemei ha-benayim: r[abbi] Mikha'el ben Shabbetai Balbo ve-r[abbi] Shalom ben Yosef 'Anavi." *Sefunot* (new series) 10 (2017): 317–93.

Schwartz, Dov. "From Theurgy to Magic: The Evolution of the Magical-Talismanic Justification of Sacrifice in the Circle of Nahmanides and His Interpreters." *Aleph* 1 (2001): 165–213.

Schwartz, Dov. *Ha-ra'ayon ha-meshiḥi ba-hagut ha-yehudit bi-yemei ha-benayim*. Ramat-Gan: Bar-Ilan University Press, 1997.

Schwartz, Dov. "He'arot 'al perushei shir ha-shirim le-R. Shemaryah ha-'iqriṭi." In *Sefer zikaron le-rav Yosef ben David Qapaḥ*, edited by Zohar Omer and Hananel Sari, 319–33. Ramat-Gan: Lishkat rav ha-qampus shel 'universiṭat Bar-Ilan, 2001.

Schwartz, Dov. "Le-darkhei ha-parshanut ha-filosofit 'al perushei r[abbi] 'Avraham 'ibn 'Ezra." *'Alei sefer* 18 (1996): 71–114.

Schwartz, Dov. *Ma'avaq ha-paradigmot: ben te'ologyah le-filosofyah ba-hagut ha-yehudit bi-yemei ha-benayim*. Jerusalem: Magnes, 2018.

Schwartz, Dov. "'Meharsim,' 'talmudiyim' ve-'anshei ha-ḥokhmah: 'emdato ve-darshanuto shel r[abbi] Yehudah ben Shemu'el 'ibn 'Abbas." *Tarbiẓ* 62 (1993): 585–615.

Schwartz, Dov. "Perush filosofi ve-qabali shel r[abbi] Micha'el ben Shabbetai Balbo le-mizmor 29 be-tehilim." *Kobez Al Yad* 24 (2016): 205–58.

Schwartz, Dov. *Qame'ot segulot u-sekhaltanut ba-hagut ha-yehudit bi-yemei ha-benayim*. Ramat-Gan: Bar-Ilan University Press, 2004.

Schwartz, Dov. *Raḥaq ve-qeruv: hagut yehudit be-bizanṭyon be-shilhei yemei ha-benayim*. Jerusalem: Magnes, 2016.

Schwartz, Dov. "Sefer 'Mesharet Moshe' be-'en ha-se'arah: tikhtovet ben r[abbi] Yedidyah Rakh le-r[abbi] Micha'el Balbo be-sugiyot ha-nevu'ah u-nevu'at moshe." *'Alei Sefer* 24–25 (2015): 81–187.

Schwartz, Dov. "Seridim mi-perusho shel r[abbi] Shemaryah ha-'iqriṭi la-torah." In *'Alei sefer* 26–27 (2017): 95–148.

Schwartz, Dov. *Yashan be-qanqan ḥadash: mishnato ha-'iyyunit shel ha-ḥug ha-ne'oplaṭoni ba-filosofyah ha-yehudit ba-me'ah ha-14*. Jerusalem: Bialik / Mekhon Ben-Zvi, 1996.

Schwarz, A. Z. *Die hebräischen Handschriften in Österreich*. Leipzig: K. W. Hiersemann, 1931.

Sed-Rajna, Gabrielle. "Some Further Data on Rashi's Diagrams to His Commentary on the Bible." *Jewish Studies Quarterly* 1 (1993/94): 149–57.

Segal, Eliezer. "The Exegetical Craft of the *Zohar*: Toward an Appreciation." *AJS Review* 17 (1992): 31–49.

Segal, Eliezer. "Midrash and Literature: Some Medieval Views." *Prooftexts* 11 (1991): 57–65.

Segal, Eliezer. *Reading Jewish Religious Texts*. Abingdon: Routledge, 2012.

Segal, Eliezer. "Sarah and Iscah: Method and Message in Midrashic Tradition." *Jewish Quarterly Review* 82 (1992): 417–29.

Segal, Lester A. "Late-Fourteenth Century Perception of Classical Jewish Lore: Shem Tob Ben Isaac Shaprut's Aggadic Exegesis." In *From Ancient Israel to Modern Judaism: Intellect in Quest of Understanding: Essays in Honor of Marvin Fox*, edited by Jacob Neusner, Ernest S. Frerichs, and Nahum M. Sarna. 4 vols., 2:206–28. Atlanta, Ga.: Scholars Press, 1989.

Sela, Shlomo. *Abraham ibn Ezra and the Rise of Medieval Hebrew Science.* Leiden: Brill, 2003.

Sela, Shlomo, and Gad Freudenthal. "Abraham Ibn Ezra's Scholarly Writings: A Chronological Listing." *Aleph* 6 (2006): 13–55.

Septimus, Bernard. *Hispano-Jewish Culture in Transition: The Career and Controversies of Ramah.* Cambridge, MA: Harvard University Press, 1982.

Septimus, Bernard. "'Ide'ologyah leshonit ve-hegmonyah tarbutit: teshuvah le-r[abbi] Shemu'el de Medina, meqoroteha ve-hashlakhoteha." In *Rishonim ve-'aḥaronim: meḥkarim be-toledot yisra'el mugashim le-'Avraham Grossman,* edited by Joseph R. Hacker, B. Z. Kedar, and Yosef Kaplan, 293–308. Jerusalem: Zalman Shazar, 2010.

Septimus, Bernard. "A Medieval Judeo-Spanish Poem on the Complementarity of Faith and Works and Its Intellectual Roots." In *New Perspectives on Jewish-Christian Relations: In Honor of David Berger,* edited by Elisheva Carlebach and Jacob J. Schacter, 227–39. Leiden: Brill, 2012.

Septimus, Bernard. "'Open Rebuke and Concealed Love': Naḥmanides and the Andalusian Tradition." In *Rabbi Moses Naḥmanides (Ramban): Explorations in His Religious and Literary Virtuosity,* edited by Isadore Twersky, 11–34. Cambridge, MA: Harvard University Press, 1983.

Septimus, Bernard. "Piety and Power in Thirteenth-Century Catalonia." In *Studies in Medieval Jewish History and Literature,* vol. I, edited by Isadore Twersky. Cambridge, MA: Harvard University Press, 1979.

Septimus, Bernard. "What Did Maimonides Mean by *Madda*'?" In *Me'ah She'arim: Studies in Medieval Jewish Spiritual Life in Memory of Isadore Twersky,* edited by Ezra Fleischer et al., 83–110 (English section). Jerusalem: Magnes, 2001.

Shapira, Anita. "Ben-Gurion and the Bible: The Forging of an Historical Narrative?" *Middle Eastern Studies* 33 (1997): 645–74.

Shapira, Israel. "Parshanei rashi 'al ha-torah." *Bizaron* 2 (1940): 426–37.

Shapiro, Marc B. *The Limits of Orthodox Theology: Maimonides' Thirteen Principles Reappraised.* Oxford: Littman Library of Jewish Civilization, 2004.

Sharpe, Kevin. *Reading Revolutions: The Politics of Reading in Early Modern England.* New Haven, CT: Yale University Press, 2000.

Shatzmiller, Joseph. "Jewish Physicians in Sicily." In *Gli ebrei in Sicilia sino all'espulsione del 1492, Atti del V Covegno internazionale Italia Judaica, Palermo 1992,* 345–54. Rome: Ministerio per i beni culturali e ambientali, 1995.

Shatzmiller, Joseph. *Jews, Medicine, and Medieval Society.* Berkeley: University of California Press, 1994.

Shatzmiller, Joseph. "Les tossafistes et la première controverse maïmonidienne." In *Rashi et la culture juive en France du Nord au moyen âge,* edited by Gilbert Dahan et al., 55–82. Paris-Leuven: Peeters, 1997.

Shatzmiller, Joseph. "Li-temunat ha-maḥaloqet ha-rishonah 'al kitvei ha-rambam." *Zion* 34 (1969): 126–44.

Shaveh, Ariel. "Ha-'ivrit shel rashi: 'al-pi kitvei yad nivḥarim shel ha-perush la-torah." PhD dissertation, Hebrew University of Jerusalem, 2017.

Shavit, Yaacov. "Introduction [to special issue on 'Canon and Holy Scriptures']." *Teudah* 23 (2009): xi–xvi.

Shear, Adam. *The Kuzari and the Shaping of Jewish Identity, 1167–1900*. Cambridge: Cambridge University Press, 2008.

Shear, Adam, and Joseph R. Hacker. "Introduction." In *The Hebrew Book in Early Modern Italy*, edited by Joseph R. Hacker and Adam Shear, 1–16. Philadelphia: University of Pennsylvania Press, 2011.

Shmidman, Michael A. "On Maimonides' 'Conversion' to Kabbalah." In *Studies in Medieval Jewish History and Literature*, vol. II, edited by Isadore Twersky, 375–86. Cambridge, MA: Harvard University Press, 1984.

Shneor, David. "Sugyat mapot rashi le-miqra': meḥqeran ve-he'edran mi-mahadurot ha-defus shel perusho." *Shenaton le-ḥeqer ha-miqra' ve-ha-mizraḥ ha-qadum* 24 (2016): 255–66.

Shoshan, Orly. "Be'ur r[abbi] 'Eleazar ben Mattityah." In *Ḥamishah qadmonei mefareshei r[abbi] 'Avraham 'ibn 'Ezra*, edited by Haim Kreisel, 39–64. Beer-Sheva: Ben-Gurion University of the Negev Press, 2017.

Signer, Michael A. "Rashi's Reading of the Akedah." In *Memoria–Wege jüdischen Erinnerns: Festschrift für Michael Brocke zum 65. Geburtstag*, edited by Birgit E. Klein and Christiane E. Müller, 613–25. Berlin: Metropol, 2005.

Simon, Uriel. *'Ozen milin tivḥan: meḥqarim be-darko ha-parshanit shel r[abbi] 'Avraham 'ibn 'Ezra*. Ramat-Gan: Bar-Ilan University Press, 2013.

Simon, Uriel. "Ibn Ezra's Harsh Language and Biting Humor: Real Denunciation or Hispanic Mannerism." In *Abraham ibn Ezra y su tiempo*, edited by Fernando Díaz Esteban, 325–34. Madrid: Asociación Española de Orientalistas, 1990.

Simon, Uriel. "Interpreting the Interpreter: Supercommentaries on Ibn Ezra's Commentaries." In *Rabbi Abraham Ibn Ezra: Studies in the Writings of a Twelfth-Century Polymath*, edited by Isadore Twersky and Jay M. Harris, 86–128. Cambridge, MA: Harvard University Center for Jewish Studies, 1993.

Simon, Uriel. "Madua' 'azav r[abbi] 'Avraham 'ibn 'Ezra' 'et sefarad 'be-nefesh nivhelet'?" In *Zer rimonim: meḥqarim ba-miḳra' u-ve-farshanuto muqdashim le-prof[esor] Rimon Kasher*, edited by Michael Avioz, Elie Assis, and Yael Shemesh, 489–502. Atlanta, GA: Society of Biblical Literature, 2013.

Simon, Uriel. "Transplanting the Wisdom of Spain to Christian Lands: The Failed Efforts of R. Abraham Ibn Ezra." *Simon Dubnow Institute Yearbook* 8 (2009): 139–89.

Simonsohn, Shlomo. *Between Scylla and Charybdis: The Jews in Sicily*. Leiden: Brill, 2011.

Sirat, Colette. *Hebrew Manuscripts of the Middle Ages*, edited and translated by Nicholas de Lange. Cambridge: Cambridge University Press, 2002.

Sirat, Collette. *A History of Jewish Philosophy in the Middle Ages*. Rev. ed. Cambridge: Cambridge University Press, 1985.

Sirat, Colette. "Les traducteurs juifs à la cour des rois de Sicile et de Naples." In *Traduction et traducteurs au Moyen Âge*, edited by Genivièνe Contamine, 169–91. Paris: Éditions du Centre national de la recherche scientifique, 1989.

Sivan, Hagith. "Canonizing Law in Late Antiquity: Legal Constructions of Judaism in the Theodosian Code." In *Homer, the Bible, and Beyond: Literary and Religious Canons in the Ancient World*, edited by Margalit Finkelberg and Guy G. Stroumsa, 213–25. Leiden: Brill, 2003.

Sklarz, Miriam (Hoffman). "Ha-leshonot 'shibbesh' u-'fittah' be-tokhaḥto shel ramban le-ra'ba'." *'Iyyunei miqra' u-farshanut* 8 (2008): 553–71.

Sklarz, Miriam. "Darko shel ramban be-'immuṣ divrei ra'ba' ve-hava'atam shelo be-shem 'omram." *Shenaton le-ḥeqer ha-miqra' ve-ha-mizraḥ ha-qadum* 24 (2016): 285–302.

Sklarz, Miriam. "Hashlakhat 'avram le-khivshan ha-'esh be-khitvehem shel ra'ba' ve-ramban: ben parshanut, shirah u-derashah." *'Areshet* 3 (2012): 23–33.

Sklarz, Miriam. "''O she-hayah mi-ma'aseh nisim' – meqom ha-nes be-hakhra'otav ha-parshaniyot shel ramban." *Bet miqra'* 58 (2013): 100–116.

Sklarz, Miriam. "Sodotav shel ra'ba' be-ferush ramban la-torah—ziqato shel minuaḥ ve-heqsher parshani." In *Zer rimonim: meḥqarim ba-miḳra' u-ve-farshanuto muqdashim le-prof[esor] Rimon Kasher*, edited by Michael Avioz, Elie Assis, and Yael Shemesh, 503–23. Atlanta, GA: Society of Biblical Literature, 2013.

Sládek, Pavel. "The Printed Book in 15th- and 16th-Century Jewish Culture." In *Hebrew Printing in Bohemia and Moravia*, edited by Olga Sixtová, 9–30. Prague: Jewish Museum–Academia, 2012.

Sławiński, Janusz. "Reading and Reader in the Literary Historical Process." *New Literary History* 19 (1988): 521–39.

Slifkin, Natan. *Sacred Monsters: Mysterious and Mythical Creatures of Scripture, Talmud and Midrash*. Brooklyn, NY: Zoo Torah / Yashar Books, 2007.

Slifkin, Natan. "Was Rashi a Corporealist?" *Ḥakirah* 7 (2009): 81–105.

Sluiter, Ineke. "The Dialectics of Genre: Some Aspects of Secondary Literature and Genre in Antiquity." In *Matrices of Genre: Authors, Canons, and Society*, edited by Mary Depew and Dirk Obbink, 183–203. Cambridge, MA: Harvard University Press, 2000.

Sluiter, Ineke. "The Violent Scholiast: Power Issues in Ancient Commentaries." In *Writing Science: Medical and Mathematical Authorship in Ancient Greece*, edited by Markus Asper, 191–213. Berlin: De Gruyter, 2013.

Smith, Barry. "Textual Deference." *American Philosophical Quarterly* 28 (1991): 1–12.

Smith, Denis Mack. *A History of Sicily: Medieval Sicily, 800–1713*. London: Chatto and Windus, 1968.

Smith, Jonathan Z. "Sacred Persistence: Toward a Redescription of Canon." In *Imagining Religion: From Babylon to Jonestown*, 36–52. Chicago: University of Chicago Press, 1982.

Smith, Lesley. "Nicholas of Lyra and Old Testament Interpretation." In *Hebrew Bible / Old Testament: The History of Its Interpretation*, edited by Magne Sæbø. Vol. II: *From the Renaissance to the Enlightenment*, 49–63. Göttingen: Vanderhoeck & Ruprecht, 2008.

Sokolow, Moshe. "T'rumah: Wood in the Wilderness." Posted February 4, 2011. http://www.jewishideasdaily.com/4248/weekly-portion/trumah-wood-in-the-wilderness/?

Solotorevsky, Myrna. "The Model of Midrash and Borges's Interpretative Tales and Essays." In *Midrash and Literature*, edited by Geoffrey H. Hartman and Sanford Budick, 253–64. New Haven, CT: Yale University Press, 1986.

Soloveitchik, Haym. "Catastrophe and Halakhic Creativity: Ashkenaz – 1096, 1242, 1306 and 1298." *Jewish History* 12 (1998): 71–85.

Soloveitchik, Haym. "The Halakhic Isolation of the Ashkenazic Community." In *Collected Essays I*, 31–38. Oxford: Littman Library of Jewish Civilization, 2013.

Soloveitchik, Haym. "History of Halakhah – Methodological Issues: A Review Essay of I. Twersky's *Rabad of Posquières*." *Jewish History* 5 (1991): 75–124.

Soloveitchik, Haym. "Three Themes in the *Sefer Ḥasidim*." *AJS Review* 1 (1976): 311–57.

Sonne, Isaiah. "Le-reshito shel ha-defus ha-'ivri bi-sefarad." *Kiryat sefer* 14 (1937–38): 368–78.

Sonne, Isaiah. "Le-viqoret ha-ṭeqsṭ shel perush rashi 'al ha-torah." *Hebrew Union College Annual* 15 (1940): 37–56 (Hebrew section).

Sossnitz, Joseph Loeb, and Kaufmann Kohler. "Aaron Ben Gershon Abulrabi of Catania." In *The Jewish Encyclopedia*. 12 vols., 1:11. New York: Funk and Wagnalls, 1901–1906.

Sperling, S. David. "Modern Jewish Interpretation." In *The Jewish Study Bible*, edited by Adele Berlin and Marc Zvi Brettler, 1908–19. Oxford: Oxford University Press, 2004.

Spicehandler, Ezra. "Joshua Heschel Schorr: Maskil and Eastern European Reformist." *Hebrew Union College Annual* 31 (1960): 181–222; vol. 40/41 (1970): 503–28.

Spicehandler, Ezra. "Mikhtevei Yehoshua' Heschel Schorr le-Barukh Felsental." *Hebrew Union College Annual* 28 (1957): 1–26 (Hebrew Section).

Spiegel, Yaakov Shmuel. *'Amudim be-toledot ha-sefer ha-'ivri: hagahot u-megihim*. 2nd ed. Ramat-Gan: Bar-Ilan University Press, 1996.

Spitzer, Shlomo. *Bne chet: die österreichischen Juden im Mittelalter. Eine Sozial- und Kulturgeschichte*. Vienna: Böhlau, 1997.

Spitzer, Shlomo. "Ha-'ashkenazim ba-ḥaṣi ha-'i ha-balqani be-me'ot ha-15 ve-ha-16." *Mi-mizraḥ u-ma'arav* 1 (1974): 59–79.

Spitzer, Shlomo. *Halakhot u-minhagei rabbi Shalom mi-neustadt*. Jerusalem: Mekhon Yerushalayim, 1977.

Spitzer, Shlomo. "Yedi'ot 'al rabbi Dosa ha-yevani me-ḥibburo 'al ha-torah." In *Sefer zikaron le-ha-rav Yiṣḥaq Nissim*, edited by Meir Benayahu. 4 vols., 4:177–84. Jerusalem: Yad ha-rav Nissim, 1985.

Steiner, Richard C. "Meaninglessness, Meaningfulness, and Super-Meaningfulness in Scripture: An Analysis of the Controversy Surrounding Dan 2:12 in the Middle Ages." *Jewish Quarterly Review* 82 (1992): 431–49.

Steiner, Richard C. "Saadia vs. Rashi: On the Shift from Meaning-Maximalism to Meaning-Minimalism in Medieval Biblical Lexicology." *Jewish Quarterly Review* 88 (1998): 213–58.

Steinmetz, Devorah. "A Portrait of Miriam in Rabbinic Midrash." *Prooftexts* 8 (1988): 35–65.

Steinschneider, Moritz. *Catalogus Librorum Hebraeorum in Bibliotheca Bodleiana*. Berlin, 1852–60.

Stern, David. "The First Jewish Books and the Early History of Jewish Reading." *Jewish Quarterly Review* 98 (2008): 171.

Stern, David. "The Hebrew Bible in Europe in the Middle Ages: A Preliminary Typology." *Jewish Studies Internet Journal* 11 (2012): 1–88.

Stern, David. *The Jewish Bible: A Material History*. Seattle: University of Washington Press, 2017.

Stern, David. "On Canonization in Rabbinic Judaism." In *Homer, the Bible, and Beyond: Literary and Religious Canons in the Ancient World*, edited by Margalit Finkelberg and Guy G. Stroumsa, 227–52. Leiden: Brill, 2003.

Stern, David. "The Rabbinic Bible and Its Sixteenth-Century Context." In *The Hebrew Book in Early Modern Italy*, edited by Joseph R. Hacker and Adam Shear, 76–108. Philadelphia: University of Pennsylvania Press, 2011.

Stern, Gregg. *Philosophy and Rabbinic Culture: Jewish Interpretation and Controversy in Medieval Languedoc*. Abingdon: Routledge, 2009.

Stern, Josef. *The Matter and Form of Maimonides' Guide*. Cambridge, MA: Harvard University Press, 2013.

Stern, Josef. *Problems and Parables of Law*. Albany: SUNY Press, 1998.

Stock, Brian. *Listening for the Text: On the Uses of the Past*. Baltimore, MD: Johns Hopkins University Press, 1990.

Stow, Kenneth R. "The Burning of the Talmud in 1553, in Light of Sixteenth-Century Catholic Attitudes Toward the Talmud." In *Essential Papers on Judaism and Christianity in Conflict: From Late Antiquity to the Reformation*, edited by Jeremy Cohen, 401–28. New York: New York University Press, 1991.

Stow, Kenneth R. Review of *The Censor, the Editor, and the Text* by Amnon Raz-Krakotzkin. *AJS Review* 33 (2009): 181–85.

Strauss, Leo. *Natural Right and History*. Chicago: Chicago University Press, 1950.

Strauss, Leo. *Spinoza's Critique of Religion*, translated by E. M. Sinclair. 2nd. ed. New York: Schocken, 1962.

Stroumsa, Sarah. "Between 'Canon' and Library in Medieval Jewish Philosophical Thought." *Intellectual History of the Islamicate World* 5 (2017): 28–54.

Stroumsa, Sarah. "On Maimonides and on Logic." *Aleph* 14 (2014): 259–63.

Sturges, Robert S. "Medieval Authorship and the Polyphonic Text: From Manuscript Commentary to the Modern Novel." In *Bakhtin and Medieval Voices*, edited by Thomas J. Farrell, 122–38. Gainesville: University Press of Florida, 1995.

Szilágyi, Krisztina. "A Fragment of a Book of Physics from the David Kaufmann *Genizah* Collection (Budapest) and the Identity of Ibn Daud with Avendauth." *Aleph* 16 (2016): 11–31.

Tabori, Yosef. "Perush rashi le-'ester u-meqorotav." In *Rashi: demuto vi-yeṣirato*, edited by Avraham Grossman and Sara Japhet. 2 vols., 2:295–309. Jerusalem: Zalman Shazar, 2008.

Talbi, Chayim. "Le-hishtalshelutah shel qeri'at shnayim miqra' ve-'eḥad targum." *Kenishta* 4 (2010): 155–90.

Talmage, Frank Ephraim. *Apples of Gold in Settings of Silver: Studies in Medieval Jewish Exegesis and Polemics*, edited by Barry Dov Walfish. Toronto: Pontifical Institute of Mediaeval Studies, 1999.

Talmage, Frank Ephraim. *David Kimhi: The Man and the Commentaries*. Cambridge, MA: Harvard University Press, 1975.

Talmage, Frank. "Keep Your Sons from Scripture: The Bible in Medieval Jewish Scholarship and Spirituality." In *Understanding Scripture: Explorations of Jewish and Christian Traditions of Interpretation*, edited by Clemens Thoma and Michael Wyschogrod, 81–101. New York: Paulist, 1987.

Tamani, Giuliano. "Manoscritti ebraici copiati in Sicilia nei secoli XIV–XV." *Henoch* 15 (1993): 107–12.

Tamar, David. "Demuto ha-ruḥanit shel r[abbi] [Yisra'el 'Isserlein." *Sinai* 32 (1953): 175–85.

Ta-Shma, Israel M. "The Acceptance of Maimonides' *Mishneh Torah* in Italy." *Italia* 13–15 (2001): 79–90.

Ta-Shma, Israel M. "Gabbai, Moses Ben Shem-Tov." In *Encyclopaedia Judaica*, edited by Michael Berenbaum and Fred Skolnik. 22 vols., 7:319. Detroit, MI: Macmillan, 2007.

Ta-Shma, Israel M. "Halakhah, qabbalah u-filosofyah bi-sefarad ha-noṣerit (le-biqoret ha-sefer 'Toledot ha-yehudim bi-sefarad ha-noṣerit)." In *Keneset meḥqarim: 'iyyunim ba-sifrut ha-rabbanit be-yemei ha-benayim*. 4 vols., vol. 2: *Sefarad*, 279–98. Jerusalem: Bialik, 2004–2010.

Ta-Shma, Israel M. *Ha-sifrut ha-parshanit la-talmud be-'eropah uvi-ṣefon 'afriqah: qorot, 'ishim, ve-shiṭot*. 2 vols. Jerusalem: Magnes, 2004.

Ta-Shma, Israel M. "Hassagot." In *Encyclopaedia Judaica*, edited by Michael Berenbaum and Fred Skolnik. 22 vols., 8:453–54. Detroit, MI: Macmillan, 2007.

Ta-Shma, Israel M. "Hekhan nitḥabber sefer "Alilot devarim'." *'Alei sefer* 3 (1977): 44–53.

Ta-Shma, Israel M. "Le-toledot ha-qesharim ha-tarbutiyim ben yehudei bizanṭyon ve-'ashkenaz." In *Me'ah She'arim: Studies in Medieval Jewish Spiritual Life in Memory of Isadore Twersky*, edited by Ezra Fleischer et al., 61–70 (Hebew section). Jerusalem: Magnes, 2001.

Ta-Shma, Israel M. "Le-toledot ha-sifrut ha-rabbanit be-yavan ba-me'ah ha-14." *Tarbiẓ* 62 (1993): 101–14.

Ta-Shma, Israel M. "Li-yedi'at maṣṣav limmud ha-torah bi-sefarad ba-me'ah ha-15." In *Dor gerush sefarad*, edited by Yom Tov Assis and Yosef Kaplan, 47–62 (Hebrew Section). Jerusalem: Zalman Shazar, 1999.

Ta-Shma, Israel M. "Midrash 'leqaḥ ṭov' – riq'o ve-'ofyo." In *Keneset meḥqarim: 'iyyunim ba-sifrut ha-rabbanit be-yemei ha-benayim*. 4 vols., vol. 3:*' Iṭalyah u-vizanṭyon*, 259–94. Jerusalem: Bialik, 2004–2010.

Ta-Shma, Israel M. "The 'Open' Book in Medieval Hebrew Literature: The Problem of Authorized Editions." In *Creativity and Tradition: Studies in Medieval Rabbinic Scholarship, Literature and Thought*, 193–200. Cambridge, MA: Harvard University Center for Jewish Studies, 2006.

Ta-Shma, Israel M. "Parshanut miqra' 'ivrit-bizanṭit qedumah, seviv shenat 1000, min ha-genizah." *Tarbiẓ* 69 (2000): 247–56.

Ta-Shma, Israel M. "Qunṭres 'Sodot ha-tefilah' le-rabbi Yehudah He-Ḥasid." In *Keneset meḥqarim: 'iyyunim ba-sifrut ha-rabbanit be-yemei ha-benayim*. 4 vols., vol. 1: *'Ashkenaz*, 208–301. Jerusalem: Bialik, 2004–2010.

Ta-Shma, Israel M. "Rabbenu 'Asher u-veno r[abbi] Ya'aqov ba'al ha-ṭurim: ben 'ashkenaz li-sefarad." *Pe'amim* 46–47 (1991): 75–91.

Ta-Shma, Israel M. "Rabbi Yosef Qaro ben 'ashkenaz li-sefarad: le-ḥeqer hitpashṭut sefer ha-zohar." *Tarbiẓ* 59 (1990): 153–70.

Ta-Shma, Israel M. *Rabbi Zeraḥyah ha-levi ba'al ha-ma'or u-venei ḥugo: le-toledot ha-sifrut ha-rabbanit be-provans*. Jerusalem: Mosad Harav Kuk, 1992.

Ta-Shma, Israel M. "Rabbinic Literature in the Late Byzantine and Early Ottoman Periods." In *Jews, Turks, Ottomans: A Shared History, Fifteenth Through the Twentieth Century*, edited by Avigdor Levy, 52–60. Syracuse, NY: Syracuse University Press, 2002.

Ta-Shma, Israel M. "Rabbinic Literature in the Middle Ages." In *The Oxford Handbook of Jewish Studies*, edited by Martin Goodman, 219–40. Oxford: Oxford University Press, 2002.

Ta-Shma, Israel M. "Rishonim." In *Encyclopaedia Judaica*, edited by Michael Berenbaum and Fred Skolnik. 22 vols., 17:339–43. Detroit, MI: Macmillan, 2007.

Ta-Shma, Israel M. "Sefer 'nimmuqei ḥumash' le-rabbi Yisha'yah di-ṭrani." In *Keneset meḥqarim: 'iyyunim ba-sifrut ha-rabbanit be-yemei ha-benayim*. 4 vols., vol. 3: *'Iṭalyah u-vizanṭyon*, 259–94. Jerusalem: Bialik, 2004–2010.

Ta-Shma, Israel M. " 'Sefer rossina': parshanut miqra' derom 'iṭalqit mi-sof ha-me'ah ha-'aḥat 'esrei." *Tarbiẓ* 72 (2003): 567–80.

Ta-Shma, Israel M. "The Study of Aggadah and Its Interpretation in Early Rabbinic Literature." In *Creativity and Tradition: Studies in Medieval Rabbinic Scholarship, Literature and Thought*, 201–11. Cambridge, MA: Harvard University Center for Jewish Studies, 2006.

Ta-Shma, Israel M. "Tosafot gornish: mahutan ve-yaḥasan 'el shitot ha-'pilpul' ve-ha-'ḥiluqim'." In *Keneset meḥqarim: 'iyyunim ba-sifrut ha-rabbanit be-yemei ha-benayim*. 4 vols., vol. 1: *'Ashkenaz*, 345–55. Jerusalem: Bialik, 2004–10.

Ta-Shma, Israel M. "Yedi'ot ḥadashot 'al 'tosafot gornish' ve-'inyanam." *'Alei Sefer* 2 (1976): 79–90.

Tate, R. B. "The Medieval Kingdoms of the Iberian Peninsula (to 1474)." In *Spain: A Companion to Spanish Studies*, edited by P. E. Russell, 65–103. London: Methuen, 1973.

Teugels, Lieve M. *Bible and Midrash: The Story of "The Wooing of Rebekah" (Gen. 24)*. Leuven: Peeters, 2004.

Teugels, Lieve M. "The Creation of the Human in Rabbinic Interpretation." In *The Creation of Man and Woman: Interpretations of the Biblical Narratives in Jewish and Christian Traditions*, edited by Gerard P. Luttikhuizen, 107–27. Leiden: Brill, 2000.

Thiriet, Freddy. *La Romanie vénitienne au Moyen Age: le développement et l'exploitation du domaine colonial vénitien, XIIe–XVe siècles*. Paris: E. de Boccard, 1975.

Tirosh-Samuelson, Hava. "Jewish Philosophy on the Eve of Modernity." In *History of Jewish Philosophy*, edited by Daniel H. Frank and Oliver Leaman, 499–573. London: Routledge, 1997.

Tishbi, Peretz. "Defusei-'eres ('inqunabulim) 'ivriyim: sefarad u-fortugal." *Kiryat Sefer* 61 (1986–87): 521–46.

Touitou, Eleazar. " 'Al gilgulei ha-nosaḥ shel perush rashi la-torah." *Tarbiẓ* 56 (1986): 211–42.

Touitou, Eleazar. "Darko shel rashi be-shimusho be-midreshei ḥazal: 'iyyun be-ferush rashi li-shemot 1:8–22." *Ṭalelei 'orot: shenaton mikhlelet 'orot yisrael* 9 (2000): 51–78.

Touitou, Eleazar. *"Ha-peshaṭot ha-mitḥaddeshim be-khol yom": 'iyyunim be-ferusho shel rashbam la-torah*. Ramat-Gan: Bar-Ilan University Press, 2003.

Touitou, Eleazar. "Rashi and His School: The Exegesis on the Halakhic Part of the Pentateuch in the Context of the Judeo-Christian Controversy." In *Medieval Studies in Honour of Avrom Saltman*, edited by Bat-Sheva Albert, Yvonne Friedman, and Simon Schwarzfuchs, 231–51. Ramat-Gan: Bar-Ilan University Press, 1995.

Touitou, Eleazar. "Rashi's Commentary on Genesis 1–6 in the Context of Judeo-Christian Controversy." *Hebrew Union College Annual* 61 (1990): 159–83.

Tribble, Evelyn B. *Margins and Marginality: The Printed Page in Early Modern England.* Charlottesville: University Press of Virginia, 1993.

Twersky, Isadore. "Aspects of the Social and Cultural History of Provençal Jewry." In *Studies in Jewish Law and Philosophy*, 180–202. New York: Ktav, 1982.

Twersky, Isadore. "The Beginnings of Mishneh Torah Criticism." In *Studies in Jewish Law and Philosophy*, 30–51. New York: Ktav, 1982.

Twersky, Isadore. "The Contribution of Italian Sages to Rabbinic Literature." In *Italia Judaica: Atti del I Convegno Internazionale Bari*, 383–400. Rome: Multigrafica, 1983.

Twersky, Isadore. "Ha-hishpia' ra'ba' 'al ha-rambam?" In *Rabbi Abraham Ibn Ezra: Studies in the Writings of a Twelfth-Century Polymath*, edited by Isadore Twersky and Jay M. Harris, 21–48 (Hebrew section). Cambridge, MA: Harvard University Center for Jewish Studies, 1993.

Twersky, Isadore. *Introduction to the Code of Maimonides (*Mishneh Torah). New Haven, CT: Yale University Press, 1980.

Twersky, Isadore. "Introduction." In *Rabbi Moses Naḥmanides (Ramban): Explorations in His Religious and Literary Virtuosity*, edited by Isadore Twersky, 1–9. Cambridge, MA: Harvard University Press, 1983.

Twersky, Isadore. *Rabad of Posquieres: A Twelfth-Century Talmudist.* Cambridge, MA: Harvard University Press, 1962.

Twersky, Isadore. "Some Non-Halakhic Aspects of the Mishneh Torah." In *Jewish Medieval and Renaissance Studies*, edited by Alexander Altmann, 95–118. Cambridge, MA: Harvard University Press, 1967.

Twersky, Isadore. "Some Reflections on the Historical Image of Maimonides: An Essay on His Unique Place in Jewish History." In *The Legacy of Maimonides: Religion, Reason and Community*, edited by Yamin Levy and Shalom Carmy, 1–48. Brooklyn, NY: Yashar, 2006.

Tzeitkin, Yehiel. "Me'afyenei parshanut ha-miqra' bi-yeṣirotehem shel parshanei ha-peshaṭ benei ha-'askolah ha-maimonit shel provans ba-me'ot ha-13 – ha-14," PhD dissertation, Bar-Ilan University, 2011.

Ulmer, Rivka. *Egyptian Cultural Icons in Midrash*. Berlin: De Gruyter, 2009.

Unterman, Yael. *Nehama Leibowitz: Teacher and Bible Scholar*. Jerusalem: Urim Publications, 2009.

Urbach, Ephraim. "Ba-meh zakhah rashi la-to'ar 'parshandata'?" In Ephraim Urbach, *Meḥqarim be-madda'ei ha-yahadut*, edited by Moshe David Herr and Yonah Fraenkel. 2 vols., 1:15–22. Jerusalem: Magnes, 1998.

Urbach, Ephraim E. "Hassagot ha-rabad 'al perush rashi la-torah?" *Qiryat sefer* 34 (1958): 101–108.

Van Boxel, Piet. "Robert Bellarmine Reads Rashi: Rabbinic Bible Commentaries and the Burning of the Talmud." In *The Hebrew Book in Early Modern Italy*, edited by Joseph R. Hacker and Adam Shear, 121–32. Philadelphia: University of Pennsylvania Press, 2011.

Van der Toorn, K., and P. W. van der Horst. "Nimrod Before and After the Bible." *Harvard Theological Review* 83 (1990): 1–29.

Verman, Mark, and Shulamit Adler. "Path Jumping in the Jewish Magical Tradition." *Jewish Studies Quarterly* 1 (1993–94): 131–48.

Vidal, Pierre. *Les juifs des anciens comtés de Rousillon et de Cerdagne.* Perpignan: Mare Nostrum, 1992.

Viezel, Eran. "The Formation of Some Biblical Books, According to Rashi." *Journal of Theological Studies* 61 (2010): 16–42.

Viezel, Eran. "Ha-perush ha-meyuḥas le-rashi le-sefer 'ezra-neḥemyah." *Jewish Studies Internet Journal* 9 (2010): 1–58.

Viezel, Eran. "Le-mi mi'en rashi 'et perushav la-miqra'." *Beit Mikra* 52 (2007): 139–68.

Viezel, Eran. "' 'Osim 'oznayim le-toratam shel parshanim, ke-'oznei kli she-'ohazin 'oto bam'." *Shenaton le-ḥeqer ha-miqra' ve-ha-mizraḥ ha-qadum* 20 (2010): 261–81.

Viezel, Eran. "R. Judah He-Hasid or R. Moshe Zaltman: Who Proposed That Torah Verses Were Written After the Time of Moses?" *Journal of Jewish Studies* 66 (2015): 97–115.

Viezel, Eran. "The Secret of the Popularity of Rashi's Commentary on the Torah." *Review of Rabbinic Judaism* 17 (2014): 207–17.

Viezel, Eran. "Targum Onkelos in Rashi's Exegetical Consciousness." *Review of Rabbinic Judaism* 15 (2012): 1–19.

Visi, Tamás. "The Early Ibn Ezra Supercommentaries: A Chapter in Medieval Jewish Intellectual History." PhD dissertation, Central European University, 2006.

Visi, Tamás. "Ibn Ezra, A Maimonidean Authority: The Evidence of the Early Ibn Ezra Supercommentaries." In *The Cultures of Maimonideanism: New Approaches to the History of Jewish Thought*, edited by James T. Robinson, 89–131. Leiden: Brill, 2009.

Visi, Tamás. *On the Peripheries of Ashkenaz: Medieval Jewish Philosophers in Normandy and in the Czech Lands from the Twelfth to the Fifteenth Century.* Olomouc: Kurt and Ursula Schubert Center for Jewish Studies, 2011.

Visotzky, Burton L. *Reading the Book: Making the Bible a Timeless Text.* New York: Anchor Books, 1991.

Walfish, Barry D. "Medieval Judaism." In *Commentaries (Genre)*. In *Encyclopedia of the Bible Online 2012*. https://www.degruyter.com/view/EBR/MainLemma_34537.

Walton, Michael T., and Phyllis J. Walton. "In Defense of the Church Militant: The Censorship of the Rashi Commentary in the *Magna Biblia Rabbinica*." *Sixteenth Century Journal* 21 (1990): 385–400.

Weil, Gérard E. *La bibliothèque de Gersonide d'après son catalogue autographe*. Leuven: Peeters, 1991.

Weiss, Isaac H. *Dor dor ve-dorshav*. 5 vols.. Vienna, 1871–91. Reprint New York and Berlin: Plat u-Minkas, 1924.

Williams, Benjamin. "*Glossa Ordinaria* and *Glossa Hebraica*: Midrash in Rashi and the *Gloss*." *Traditio* 71 (2016): 179–201.

Wolfson, Elliot R. "Anonymity and the Kabbalistic Ethos: A Fourteenth-Century Supercommentary on the Commentary on the Sefirot." *Kabbalah* 35 (2016): 55–112.

Wolfson, Elliot R. "By Way of Truth: Aspects of Nahmanides' Kabbalistic Hermeneutic." *AJS Review* 14 (1989): 103–78.

Wolfson, Elliot R. "God, the Demiurge and the Intellect: On the Usage of the Word KOL in Abraham Ibn Ezra." *Revue des études juives* 149 (1990): 77–111.

Wolfson, Elliot R. "The Secret of the Garment in Naḥmanides." *Daat* 24 (1990): xxv–xlix.

Wood, Abigail. *And We're All Brothers: Singing in Yiddish in Contemporary North America*. Farnham: Ashgate, 2013.

Woolf, Jeffrey R. "Admiration and Apathy: Maimonides' *Mishneh Torah* in High and Late Medieval Ashkenaz." In *Be'erot Yitzhak: Studies in Memory of Isadore Twersky*, edited by Jay Harris, 427–53. Cambridge, MA: Harvard University Center for Jewish Studies, 2005.

Woolf, Jeffrey R. "Between Diffidence and Initiative: Ashkenazic Legal Decision-Making in the Late Middle Ages (1350–1500)." *Journal of Jewish Studies* 52 (2001): 85–97.

Woolf, Jeffrey R. *The Fabric of Religious Life in Medieval Ashkenaz (1000–1300): Creating Sacred Communities*. Leiden: Brill, 2015.

Woolf, Jeffrey R. "The Life and Responsa of Rabbi Joseph Colon b. Solomon Trabotto." PhD dissertation, Harvard University, 1991.

Wygoda, Shmuel. "Une lecture philosophique de Rachi." In *Héritages de Rachi*, edited by René-Samuel Sirat, 215–25. Paris: Éditions de l'éclat, 2006.

Yaari, Abraham. *Ha-defus ha-'ivri be-qushta*. Jerusalem: Magnes, 1967.

Yahalom, Joseph. "Aesthetic Models in Conflict: Classicist versus Ornamental in Jewish Poetics." In *Renewing the Past, Reconfiguring Jewish Culture*, edited by Ross Brann and Adam Sutcliffe, 21–30. Philadelphia: University of Pennsylvania Press, 2004.

Yardeni, Ada. *The Book of Hebrew Script: History, Palaeography, Script Styles, Calligraphy and Design*. London: Oak Knoll, 2002.

Yassif, Eli. "Rashi Legends and Medieval Popular Culture." In *Rashi 1040–1990: Hommage à Ephraïm E. Urbach*, edited by Gabrielle Sed-Rajna, 483–92. Paris: Éditions du Cerf, 1993.

Yisraeli, Oded. "Midrashic Disputations in the *Zohar*." *Hebrew Union College Annual* 84–85 (2013–14): 127–46.

Yisraeli, Oded. "Muqdam u-me'uḥar be-toledot ha'avarat ha-sod be-ferush ramban la-torah." *Zion* 79 (2014): 477–506.

Yisraeli, Yosi. "A Christianized Sephardic Critique of Rashi's *Peshaṭ* in Pablo de Santa María's *Additiones ad Postillam Nicolai de Lyra*." In *Medieval Exegesis and Religious Difference: Commentary, Conflict, and Community in the Premodern Mediterranean*, edited by Ryan Szpiech, 128–41. New York: Fordham University Press, 2015.

Yudlov, Yitzhak. "Kamah she'arim le-sefer *perushim le-rashi* defus qushta?" *'Alei sefer* 17 (1992): 137–38.

Yuval, Israel Jacob. *Two Nations in Your Womb: Perceptions of Jews and Christians in Late Antiquity and the Middle Ages*, translated by Barbara Harshav and Jonathan Chipman. Berkeley: University of California Press, 2006.

Yuval, Yisrael Y. *Ḥakhamim be-doram: ha-manhigut ha-ruḥanit shel yehudei germanyah be-shilhei yemei ha-benayim*. Jerusalem: Magnes, 1989.

Yuval, Yisrael Y. "Rishonim ve-'aḥaronim, antiqui et moderni." *Zion* 57 (1992): 369–94.

Zaborowski, Jason R. "From Coptic to Arabic in Medieval Egypt." *Medieval Encounters* 14 (2008): 15–40.

Zeldes, Nadia. "Diffusion of Sicilian Exiles and their Culture as Reflected in Hebrew Colophons." *Hispania Judaica Bulletin* 5 (2007): 303–32.

Zellentin, Holger M. *Rabbinic Parodies of Jewish and Christian Literature*. Tübingen: Mohr Siebeck, 2011.

Zevulun, Rivka. "Ha-nosaḥ shel perush rashi la-torah ba-defusim ha-rishonim: yaḥasam zeh le-zeh ve-hishtalshalut nosḥam 'ad le-mahadurot yamenu." 2 vols. Master's thesis, Hebrew University of Jerusalem, 1997.

Zimmer, Yitzhak (Eric). *Gaḥalatan shel ḥakhamim: peraqim be-toledot ha-rabanut be-germanyah ba-me'ah ha-shesh-'esreh u-va-me'ah ha-sheva'-'esreh*. Beer-Sheva: Ben-Gurion University of the Negev Press, 1999.

Zinberg, Israel. *The Struggle of Mysticism and Tradition against Philosophical Rationalism*. Vol. 3 of *A History of Jewish Literature*, edited by Bernard Martin. 12 vols. Cleveland, OH: Case Western Reserve University, 1972–1978.

Zinberg, Israel. *Toledot sifrut yisra'el*. 2nd ed., 7 vols. Rehavia and Tel Aviv: Kibbutz Ha-Artzi / Yosef Sherberk, 1959–71.

Zunz, Leopold. *Zur Geschichte und Literatur*. Berlin, 1845.

Subject Index

Aaron ben Elijah the Younger, 129
Aaron ben Joseph the Elder, 126–27, 129, 156
Abarbanel, Isaac, 52–54, 99–100, 326n121, 371n125
Aboab, Isaac, 61–62
Aboulrabi, Aaron ben Gershon, 7, 196–231
  Abraham ibn Ezra and, 206–7, 212–13, 247–50, 369n98
  acceptance and defense of midrash, 214–21
  'Alilot devarim and, 235, 251
  on astrology and astral magic, 249–50, 379–80n73
  criticism of Rashi's *Commentary* by, 200–7
  Eleazar Ashkenazi and, 203, 226, 230
  father of (Gershon), 229–30
  kabbalah and, 202, 365n45
  Karaites and, 198, 206–7, 220
  on legal midrash *(midrash halakhah)*, 204–7, 219–20, 366n58
  life and work of, 197–200, 229–30, 257, 362n13, 373n158
  lost writings of, 198, 363n23
  Maimonidean orientation of, 224–26, 228, 229, 248–49
  Moses ibn Gabbai (father-in-law) and, 60, 197, 198, 228–29, 230
  Nahmanides and, 203, 204, 208, 220–21, 366n53, 371n124
  Nezer ha-qodesh (lost work), 225
  in *Perushim le-rashi* (1525), 77, 197
  plain sense / *peshaṭ* approach, 202–4
  Pseudo-Rabad and, 151, 191, 196–97, 200–1, 214–15, 221–24, 226, 230, 371n123
  reason for focus on Rashi, 200
  reception of, 196–97, 231
  rhetoric of resistance used by, 226–29, 230–31
  Sicily, on leadership of, 364n28
  on sins of biblical patriarchs and matriarchs, 207–14
  "the Straight One" *(Ha-yashar)*, as cognomen for Rashi, 200
  supercommentator, viewed as, 200, 217, 218
Aboulrabi, Shalom, 213–14
Abraham (biblical figure)
  Akedah, 47–48, 136–37, 139–40, 371–72n126, 374n165
  angelic encounter of, 129, 192, 202–3, 243–44
  donkey used by Abraham, Moses, and Messiah (midrash), 98–102, 158–59, 326n117, 327n126
  Lot, separation from, 190

use of "dwarfs on the shoulders of giants" image, 93
Ishmael (biblical figure)
divine blessing of, 199
role in instigating Akedah (midrash), 137
Islam
Aboulrabi's despair over flourishing of, 199
Almohad rule in Spain, 39, 40, 44, 63–64
Constantinople's fall to (1453), 120, 198
Genesis 17:20, Muslim controversialists seeing allusion to Muhammad in, 358n173
Quran, commentaries on, 84, 114
Israel of Krems, 322n78
Isserlein, Israel ben Petahiah
Be'urim le-rashi (Explications of Rashi), 90–91, 92–93
on Jacob's instruction "go down" (Gen 42:2), 28–29
use of the *Commentary* in connection with "twice scripture," 38, 92
Isserles, Moses
glosses on Mizrahi, 260
Shulḥan 'arukh (with Joseph Karo), 5, 37
Italy. *See also* Sicily
Aboulrabi in, 199, 257
'Alilot devarim and, 256–57
distinctive version of Rashi's *Commentary* in, 18
early print editions of Rashi's *Commentary* in, 72–73
Ibn Ezra in, 44
influence of Sefardic scripts in, 73, 312n208
Pseudo-Rabad's *Sefer hassagot*, claimed origin in, 193
Ivry, Alfred, 263
'iyyun (Sefardic "speculation"), 110–15, 215.–16 *See also* Canpanton, Isaac
Jacob (biblical figure)
acacia trees used in tabernacle brought to Egypt by (midrash), 162–63
in academy of Shem and Eber (midrash), 161
blessed by Isaac, 164, 209–12
dream-revelation at Bethel, 103, 129
in Egypt and meeting with Pharaoh, 141–43, 345n128
Esau and, 209–12
Joseph, meeting with, 50
observing commandments (midrash), 18, 74
sex determination of Dinah and (midrash), 161
stones fusing around head of (midrash), 70–71
supernatural journey of (midrash), 173–74
wrestling with angel, 189–90
Jacob ben Asher, *'Arba'ah ṭurim*, 37, 51–52, 55, 74
Jacob ben Isaac Ashkenazi of Janów, *Ṣe'enah u-re'enah* (Yiddish: *Tzenerene*), 90–91, 165
Jacob ben Shabbetai (*Sefer Ḥizzequni*), 68, 72
Jacob Tam (Jacob ben Meir; grandson of Rashi), 17, 35, 39–40, 42, 64, 84–85
Jaffe, Mordechai, *Levush 'orah*, 260
Japhet, Sara, 86
Jerònim de Santa Fe (formerly Joshua Lorki or Ha-Lorki), 56, 370n114
Jesus, polemical references to, 189, 365n45
The Jewish Encyclopedia (1901), 196
Jochebed (mother of Moses), 183–85, 207–8, 222, 247–48
Jonathan ben David Ha-Kohen, 62
Jonathan ben Uzziel, 61
Joseph ben Eliezer
copying Ibn Ezra supercommentary in Crete, 122–23

Index of Manuscripts

Index of References to Biblical Verses

This index covers references to verses cited/interpreted by Rashi as well as by Eleazar Ashkenazi, "Pseudo-Rabad," and Aaron Aboulrabi